Human Sexuality

Human Sexuality

RAYMOND ROSEN
College of Medicine and Dentistry of New Jersey/
Rutgers Medical School

LINDA REICH ROSEN
Douglass College

 ALFRED A. KNOPF   *New York*

To Joshua

First Edition
987654321
Copyright © 1981 by Alfred A. Knopf, Inc.

Manufactured in the United States of America Composed by Ruttle, Shaw & Wetherill, Inc., Philadelphia, Pa. Printed and bound by R. R. Donnelley & Sons, Co., Crawfordsville, Ind.
Cover art: *Joy of Life.* Painting by Henri Matisse. Photograph by J. R. Eyerman/Life Picture Service.

Library of Congress Cataloging in Publication Data

Rosen, Raymond, 1946–
  Human sexuality.

  Bibliography: p.
  Includes index.
  1. Sex customs. 2. Hygiene, Sexual. 3.
Sex (Psychology) 4. Sexual ethics. 5. Sexual deviation.
I. Rosen, Linda, 1948–   joint author. II. Title.
HQ21.R83   613.9'5   80-26029
ISBN 0-394-32028-X

Cover design: BETTY BINNS GRAPHICS
Text design: BETTY BINNS GRAPHICS
Picture research: LYNN GOLDBERG
Biological drawing: CECILE DURAY-BITO
Other drawings: ISADORE SELZER

Foreword

Our educational system is organized in a fashion that focuses almost exclusively on the transmission of knowledge from one generation to the next. The underlying goals of this system, however, are more than the teaching of facts; indeed, the essence of higher education involves developing habits of thought, attitudes towards inquiry, standards of evidence, and values. The enterprise is successful when the student can analyze data and ask questions, within the broader context of human values and concerns.

Because psychology deals with the human condition, it contains not only the possibility but the *inevitability* of confronting students with problems of values. Unlike animals and plants, humankind makes choices based not only on dispassionate analysis but on a set of values that informs us of how we *ought to* live.

I believe that the Rosens have created a textbook on human sexuality that addresses these overriding concerns of college education. This book engages the reader in a search for answers, a testing of hypotheses, a respect for data as well as theory. And it does so through prose that is uncommonly lucid and at a level that both respects the intellectual capacities of students, and yet appreciates the need for gradualness and patience in the presentation of material that is sometimes complex and even puzzling.

There are several features of this book that, to my mind, make it outstanding and unique. While requiring that the reader have no special background in psychology, biology, or sociology, the Rosens have succeeded in discussing the material in a highly sophisticated way. Data and hypotheses are introduced clearly so that the reader can achieve a deep understanding of human sexuality without, on the one hand, getting lost in overly technical details, or, on the other hand, coming to believe that sexuality is simply an intricate plumbing system or the heat generated by two bodily surfaces rubbing against each other.

In addition, special coverage is given to issues of concern to women (and, presumably, of concern to men who are concerned about women). For example, reproduction and contraception are dealt with in an unusually complete and empathic fashion. Further, the authors attend with care and sensitivity to relationship factors in human sexuality, even devoting an entire section of Chapter 3 to love, a topic that has preoccupied humankind (and songwriters) for thousands of years, and one that will certainly be of interest to students of human sexuality as well. There are also many case examples, drawn from the first author's extensive clinical experience as a sex therapist; these illustrate vividly some of the abstractions inherent in any general discussion of human behavior. Finally, the authors present issues in research design and methodology to help readers evaluate things for themselves, a skill that is important not only for reading this textbook but also in making informed decisions later on in their lives. The development of such a critical capacity would seem especially useful, given the plethora of self-proclaimed experts and hucksters and the heavy media exposure of topics relating to the sexual facet of human experience.

But the book does much more. It conveys a sensitivity about the human condition that will, I believe, be beneficial to the student long after specific facts are forgotten. Readers will be moved to examine their basic attitudes about sex without being challenged, or coerced, to adopt a *particular* set of values. Readers will also be invited to confront their perhaps unverbalized prejudices, fears, and

attitudes about their own sexuality, and will acquire an appreciation for the exquisiteness of this central part of life that may have eluded them in previous college courses or life experiences. In addition, readers will be provided with material that may help them make some choices, form some judgments, become more of what they are capable of being.

Specific examples. In Chapter 13 there is a scholarly discussion of sex and physical disability. The reader learns not only what kinds of incapacities can be caused by various physical illnesses and injuries, but also acquires a gut appreciation of what it is like to have no sensation below the waist in a culture that sometimes appears obsessed with genital sensations. The Rosens present facts and raise questions in such a way as to invite the reader to deal with social problems that might have escaped his or her awareness until now, and which transcend the scope of a textbook on human sexuality. For instance, readers may find themselves considering those problems in medical education that tend to support a conspiracy of silence between physician and patient about the sexuality of a physically handicapped person. The reader learns that cardiac patients are often worried about returning to a customary sex life and that there are data on heart rate during orgasm that relate to the risks such patients actually face by enjoying sex. The conclusion is that physicians should deal openly with these oft-unspoken concerns or else refer the patient to someone who can and will do so.

It is my belief that students *want* to confront moral issues, and that instructors can, without imposing their own values, help them do so. Few readers of this book will go on to make original contributions to the study of human sexuality, but all of them will enter the world of the fully adult (if they have not already done so) and be challenged constantly to make value judgments of major consequence to their own lives and the lives of others. This book can help them with these challenges.

I was told some twenty years ago at my Commencement from college that I was being welcomed into the company of educated men and women. I was reminded that while my liberal arts education might not have equipped me immediately to earn a living, the ideas to which I had been exposed and the methods of inquiry I had been given an opportunity to acquire might enable me to make sound moral judgments and to take responsi-

bility for them. This book, which I am pleased to commend for your critical attention, is that rare text which is up-to-date, literate, accurate, lucid, and perhaps most importantly, capable of exerting those influences that are, for many of us, the essence of our educational enterprise.

Gerald C. Davison, Ph.D.
Professor of Psychology and
Director of Clinical Training
University of Southern California

Preface

Human Sexuality has grown out of our experiences in sex education, sex research, and sex therapy during the 1970's. For us, and indeed for the academic community at large, this was the decade during which human sexuality became an accepted part of the university curriculum. In the research laboratory, innovative scientific methods were applied in an effort to answer age-old sexual questions. And in therapists' offices and clinics, the treatment of sexual problems became a recognized specialty, with its own counseling techniques. Perhaps most importantly, sexuality became a daily topic in the media of the 1970's, a subject worthy of discussion, education, and understanding. Of course, such changes were not abrupt. The sexual revolution—as these developments are often termed—might be dated as far back as the turn of the century. But in the

1970s it appeared that many of the revolutionaries and visionaries of the past had finally joined the respectable mainstream of society.

The goals of this text are ambitious, in keeping with the scope and complexity of the subject of human sexuality. Through our years of teaching experience, we have come to appreciate the need for both breadth and depth in sex education. Thus, we have attempted to integrate biological and social perspectives on sexuality and to balance scientific fact with a consideration of how sexual values and issues affect our lives. The text's coverage is as broad as we could make it, including reproductive issues, developmental theories, and a diversity of health and social topics. At the same time, we have aimed for depth of discussion by pointing out the theoretical controversies and methodological problems that confront sexologists today. Above all, we have tried to encourage an attitude of informed awareness, critical judgment, and sensitive understanding in our readers.

Two common problems often arise for both teachers and students of human sexuality. First, there is the popular notion that the adult in our society should not need to be taught about sexual matters because such knowledge comes naturally and spontaneously as one matures. Thus, many men feel that it is unmasculine to ask questions about sex, while women often feel inhibited and embarrassed about certain sexual topics. Within this framework, the posing of a sexual question is tantamount to admitting one's own immaturity or inadequacy. Second, there is a common fear that the acquisition of sexual knowledge will have an immediate and profound effect on our sexual behavior. This fear takes many forms, ranging from the image of unbridled sexual promiscuity among the sexually educated to the image of students permanently shell-shocked by too much sexual information too early in life. At the root of this fear is the notion that sexual information, unlike other topics of study, is simply too powerful for us to control and use in a moral and healthy way.

In writing our book, we have obviously rejected these beliefs that sex education is either unnecessary or dangerous. Certainly, students who enroll in a human sexuality course have expressed their desire to learn more about themselves and others. And while many students will indeed be influenced by what they learn, we prefer to think that the influence of such learning is always preferable to the influence of uncertainty or ignorance. Our primary goal in writing this book, then, is to encourage our readers to make informed choices about sexuality.

Those of us who write about "scientific"

sexuality are sometimes accused of replacing the poetry, romance, and mystery of sex with a dry collection of charts, graphs, and statistics. This is certainly not our intention, nor do we believe that it is even a possibility. As we note repeatedly in the pages that follow, sexuality is a complex emotional experience intimately tied to our feelings about ourselves and our loved ones. Scientific facts are presented not to deny these feelings, but rather, in the hope that our understanding of our sexual selves will be broadened and deepened.

Human Sexuality reflects the influence and contributions of a great many colleagues, students, therapy clients, friends, and acquaintances.

Among our colleagues, we are especially indebted to Richard Cross and Sandra Leiblum, with whom we have worked closely and productively over eight full years and who have contributed to the concepts and content of the book in so many ways; to G. Terence Wilson, who now, as always, is an extraordinary friend providing invaluable guidance and support; and to John Gagnon and Cathy Stein Greenblat, who have helped and advised us in innumerable instances.

Several academic colleagues have generously provided us with their help at important times. We particularly appreciate the contributions of June Reinisch, Lonnie Barbach, Julia Heiman, Elaine Hatfield, and Jeffrey Fracher. Gordon MacDonald, of the department of anatomy at Rutgers, provided many valuable suggestions about the manuscript, and Ed Brecher has been a source of inspiration throughout. We are also indebted to John Money, of the Johns Hopkins University, and Frank Beach of the University of California for providing valuable insights.

Our friend and colleague, Gerald Davison, of the University of Southern California, provided us with both a meticulous critique of the manuscript and a great deal of intellectual stimulation.

Leonard Krasner, by permitting us to use his home and extensive library, gave us a spurt of energy just when we needed it most. And Betty Dodson has contributed to the spirit of the book in ways too numerous to mention.

At Random House, we owe our gratitude to an editorial staff that just would not quit, long after we were ready to turn in the typewriters. We wish to specifically thank our acquiring editor Virginia Hoitsma, and Marilyn Miller, who was our project editor. Also, we are indebted to Stephanie Wald, who first introduced us to Random House.

We would also like to thank the following reviewers who provided their comments, criticisms, and suggestions:

Gene G. Abel, The University of Tennessee;

Henry R. Angelino, The Ohio State University;
Alen Berkey, Miami Dade Community College;
Sue Carter-Porges, University of Illinois at Urbana-Champaign;
David A. Edwards, Emory University;
Randy D. Fisher, Florida Technological University;
James H. Geer, State University of New York at Stony Brook;
Arnold Gerall, Tulane University;
Elaine Hatfield, University of Wisconsin;
Gerhard Neubeck, University of Minnesota;
Beverly B. Palmer, California State University;
Valerie Pinhas, Nassau Community College;
Robert H. Pollack, University of Georgia;
Marvin Rytting, Indiana University/Purdue University at Indianapolis;
Sergio Yulis, McGill University.

Finally, to our secretaries, Agnes Bertelson and Janice Fusco; to our students, Steven Josephson, Etienne Perold, and Beverly Brysk; and to our dear sister, Merle, our heartfelt thanks.

Piscataway
1981

Contents

PART TWO

HUMAN SEXUAL RESPONSE

Contents

Contents

PART FIVE
CURRENT ISSUES AND CONCERNS

1

THE CONTEXT OF
HUMAN SEXUALITY

ONE

Perspectives on Sexuality

Overview

In an old Indian parable, four blind men are trying to describe an elephant. The first man, feeling the elephant's leg, decides it is a tree trunk. The second, touching its tail, believes that he is holding a rope. The third feels the elephant's ear and believes it is a fan, and the fourth man, touching the elephant's body, says that "This is something without beginning or end."

Trying to describe human sexuality presents much the same problem. Depending on the approach we take, our descriptions about the subject will vary greatly. Thus, the biologist studies anatomy and hormones, the psychologist describes the role of learning and motivation, and the anthropologist makes cross-cultural comparisons. Each has an accurate, but only partial, view of a subject that truly seems "without beginning or end." The closest we can come to a total picture of human sexuality is by combining and comparing many different approaches.

In this introductory chapter, we will consider four widely used perspectives in the study of human sexuality today. A cross-cultural perspective allows us to compare our own sexual customs with those of other societies. A life-cycle perspective considers the sexual changes that are part of each individual's development. Scientific studies of sexual behavior add yet another perspective. Finally, we will consider the role that *attitudes* and *values* generally play in the shaping of our sexual choices.

[3]

A Cross-Cultural Perspective

It is well to know something of the manners of various people, in order more sanely to judge our own, and that we do not think that everything against our modes is ridiculous and against reason, as those who have seen nothing are accustomed to think. (René Descartes, Discourse on Method)

MANGAIAN SEXUAL CUSTOMS*

Mangaia is a small, mountainous Polynesian island located in the South Pacific. Its name means peace. Although the people of Mangaia have been exposed to Western religion and customs for several hundred years, many of their sexual attitudes and behaviors continue to reflect traditional cultural patterns.

The Mangaian child is welcomed into an extended and close family system. Typically, the birth is attended by a grandmother, the husband or father, and a midwife. Sexual intercourse continues until the time of birth, as Mangaians believe that frequent intercourse will ease the child's path. After birth, young boys and girls are permitted to play together until the age of about 4; then, males and females separate into same-sex groups, which characterize Mangaian social interactions for the remainder of the life cycle. Brothers and sisters, husbands and wives, fathers and daughters, are never supposed to appear in public with one another—to do so would be a serious breach of social decorum. Furthermore, family members do not discuss sex with

*Most of the material in this section is from D. S. Marshall, Sexual Behavior in Mangaia. In D. S. Marshall and E. G. Suggs (Eds.) *Human Sexual Behavior.* New York: Basic Books, 1971, pp. 103–162.

one another. Despite these restrictions, Mangaian children are fully aware of the "facts of life" before they are 8 or 9 years old.

The Mangaians draw a sharp dividing line between what is permissible in public and what is acknowledged to be private. Thus although the family will never talk about sex, the child is free to watch the "private" sexual activities of parents and siblings within the one-room Mangaian home. And while public social contact between men and women is frowned upon, the Mangaians are sensitive to, and joke about, the sexual implications of all aspects of behavior. Their interest in the genitals is evidenced by the large vocabulary they have to describe various parts of genital anatomy; for instance, they have many words to describe the size and shape of the clitoris.

Masturbation and sex play are accepted among children when conducted "in private," and nudity is tolerated among males as long as they are uncircumcised. Circumcision as practiced by the Mangaians is far more than surgery—it is a rite of passage during which the male is given detailed instruction in sexual technique by a specially selected male expert. After two weeks of instruction, the expert arranges for the boy to have intercourse with a mature and experienced female, who continues to teach him about the timing and positions that will bring a woman to orgasm. In terms of sexual technique, the Mangaians are most concerned with frequent and long-lasting intercourse, and relatively unconcerned with foreplay, coital position, or demonstrations of affection. The "good man" is one who gets on with the "work" of intercourse, and precoital activities are seen as "fooling around." Also, the "good man" is expected to bring his partner to orgasm at least two or three times before the final, simultaneous orgasm. Orgasmic dysfunction among women is practically unknown, so a man who does not provide his partner with several orgasms gets a reputation as a poor lover.

Affection or intimacy is not a prerequisite for sexual intercourse. In fact, the reverse is true—affection grows as a result of successful sexual contact, and the woman expects a satisfactory sexual experience as proof that the man desires her. Young men and women have many sexual partners before deciding to marry; such sexual experimentation is not disapproved of as long as it follows established guidelines for "privacy." For example, while the courting couple may not be seen together in public, they are relatively free to have sex in secluded places or even in the woman's home. The custom of "mōtoro" or "sleep crawling" permits the young man to slip into the woman's family hut and have intercourse so long as he is discreet and leaves before morning. As a result of these contacts, many Mangaian women become pregnant or bear children before marriage. These children are not stigmatized as illegitimate, and pregnancy does not necessarily lead to marriage.

The Mangaians believe that frequent sexual intercourse is necessary for good health. So when a husband is away from home for any length of time, it is accepted that he will seek sexual partners and that his wife will do the same. As long as these affairs are conducted with discretion, they cause no disharmony within the marriage. Among the unmarried, it is expected that males will seek a variety of partners, and there is no disapproval of this behavior—in fact, it adds to the male's status and reputation. As a result, the rate of intercourse in Mangaian society is far higher than in most Western cultures, as is the incidence of female orgasm. However, love as we know it—

that is, warm and affectionate feelings between sexual partners—does not seem to play a major role in Mangaia. Mangaians select their sexual partners on the basis of physical attractiveness or prowess in using certain sexual techniques, but with little regard for long-term emotional attachment or love (Marshall, 1971).

CULTURAL VARIATION

From our perspective, the sexual customs of Mangaia may seem exotic, difficult to understand, and even immoral. Certainly the Mangaians would find very puzzling our Western sexual attitudes and behaviors—such as our traditional emphasis on premarital chastity and marital fidelity, our insistence on love as a prerequisite for sex, and the relatively high percentage of women who do not experience orgasm during intercourse. Similarly, we might be puzzled by the sexual customs of a variety of other cultures. Like the members of any society, we have a natural tendency to think that the way we do things is the best and only way to do them, and this cultural ethnocentrism is particularly evident in regard to sexuality. As we shall see in this book, however, human beings arrange their sexuality in a wide array of patterns. To understand ourselves and others, we must approach each pattern with an open and nonjudgmental mind.

When we look at sexuality in other societies, we may find ourselves asking certain questions: Is this custom "better" or "worse" than our own? Is it "normal" or "abnormal"? Is it "moral" or "immoral"? Such comparisons come almost automatically, but they are not always productive or relevant. We cannot expect the Mangaians, with their vastly different history and environment, to follow our sexual

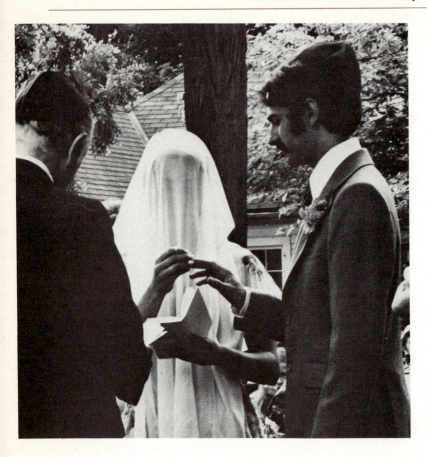

Orthodox Jewish wedding ceremony. The bride is veiled so that only the groom will be able to see her until after the ceremony is completed. (© *Joel Gordon, 1980*)

rules; nor should we follow their rules or judge ourselves according to their sexual customs. There is little about human sexuality that cannot be developed, shaped, and altered by the social context in which it takes place.

We have little difficulty accepting the fact that people from different parts of the world have, say, differing styles of home building; homes must be suited to environmental and social conditions, so we see nothing "bad" or "wrong" about igloos, tepees, or thatch huts. In general, however, this tolerance for diversity does not extend to human sexuality. Unlike home building, styles of dress, or methods of transportation, sexuality tends to be viewed as something that comes naturally and has a

single "best" or "correct" form of expression. But it is a mistake to assume that just because we are born with sexual equipment, we are also born with the knowledge of when, where, and how to use this equipment. As anthropologist Ashley Montagu notes:

Contrary to popular belief, sex is neither an instinct nor a basic need. It is a very strong drive, but it is not one that has to be satisfied if the organism is to survive, such as the needs for oxygen, liquid, food, sleep, activity, bowel and bladder elimination, and the like. Nor does sex constitute a fixed action pattern which upon the appropriate stimulus unfolds in a stereotyped reaction. Sex is something one must, for the most part, learn. The anatomical and physiological equipment is all there, but how to behave about it is something that one must acquire from experience, through learning. Unfortunately, most people . . . remain terribly confused about sex all their lives. (Montagu and Matson, 1979, pp. 127–128)

If we accept this notion that sexuality is essentially a learned human activity, then questions of normality and morality become answerable only within a specific cultural context. Clearly, what is normal for us holds little appeal to the Mangaians, nor are our standards applicable to the rest of the world. Indeed, even within our own culture there is an enormous range of sexual standards and practices. For instance, our ancestors believed that masturbation was dangerous to body and soul, that women never enjoyed sex, and that too many orgasms depleted a man's strength. Nowadays, these views are much less commonly held. Obviously, what was "normal" sexual expression for the married couple in 1900 would, at the least, be considered unusual in 1980.

INDIVIDUAL VARIATION

In addition to sexual variance among different *cultures*, among different *segments* of a culture, and within a culture at different *times* in its history, there is perhaps the greatest single source of diversity—the sexual differences among *individuals*. Each of us is born with unique physical and mental capabilities, and each of us interacts with the environment in a unique way. We are all subject to slightly different social pressures and learning experiences, so it is not surprising that no two people express their sexuality in exactly the same manner. Further, even the same person is likely to alter his or her sexual attitudes and behaviors at different times in the life cycle in order to adapt to changing life experiences and pressures.

Given these many sources of variability in human sexuality, it would probably be most comfortable and least worrisome if each of us could accept our sexual selves as we are, without reference to what others do or believe. But it seems to be part of human nature to wonder if we are "normal," and to measure ourselves against the behavior of others. Such comparisons might be productive if we had a good definition of what "normal sexuality" means; but as we shall see in this book, every attempt to define normal sexuality has some drawbacks and every sexual rule has some exceptions.

The term "abnormal" is applied in medical pathology to conditions which interfere with the physical well-being of a living body. In a social sense, the term might apply to sexual activities which cause social maladjustment. Such an application, however, involves subjective determinations of what is good personal living, or good social adjustment; and these things are not as readily determined as physiologic well-being in an organic body. It is not possible to insist that any departure from the sexual mores, or any participation in socially taboo activities, always, or even usually, involves a neurosis or psychosis. (Kinsey *et al.*, 1948, p. 201)

In other words, Kinsey does not believe that there is anything inherently normal or abnormal about an individual's sexual activity. Instead, "the way in which each group reacts to a particular sort of history determines the 'normality' or 'abnormality' of the individual's behavior—in that particular group" (p. 202). For instance, in the Victorian era it was considered normal for a woman to be anorgasmic during intercourse, whereas today the same behavior is taken as a sign of sexual dysfunction. In the same way, the ancient Greeks saw homosexual love as the highest form of interpersonal relationship, whereas most people

Love and Sex in China Today

In contrast to the burgeoning science of sexology in the Western world, there is almost no scientific attention paid to sexuality in Communist China today. In large part, the sexual attitudes and behaviors of the Chinese are a reflection of their country's political needs; since society's requirements are considered to be of far greater importance than those of any individual, love and sex are akin to counterrevolutionary activities. Personal gratification is supposed to come from work and participation in the Communist system, and not from fulfilling "selfish" desires for romance and sexual pleasure. Thus the Chinese receive little sex education, prefer not to talk about sex, and have virtually no access to sources of help for sexual problems.

This seemingly Victorian approach toward sexuality is a fairly recent phenomenon. In pre-Communist times, the Chinese had a relatively matter-of-fact attitude toward sex; it was considered a natural urge that, like eating or sleeping, should be satisfied at the right time and in the appropriate place. Ancient Chinese writings often contained explicit descriptions of sexual activity, and prostitution was tolerated rather than condemned. Love and romance, however, was a rare and unimportant theme. Marriages were based on economic and social considerations, not on the Western ideal of romantic love.

In today's China, romantic love continues to play a very small role in the formation of marriages. Since China is a sexually-segregated society, the "go-between" often is involved in introducing eligible men and women. Courtship and dating are not common because of a lack of privacy, nor are they socially approved activities. Generally, women are not allowed to marry until they reach their mid-twenties, and the age for males is even later. Further, couples are not permitted to marry without the approval of the Communist party secretary at their place of work. After marriage, there are strong incentives for having only one child, and birth control is easily available to achieve this goal.

Within this somewhat ascetic system, sexual satisfaction is rarely a goal of any importance. Sex-

today see such relationships as a symptom of emotional disturbance.

Clearly, the prevailing values of a particular culture have a great deal to do with what is sexually acceptable and what is frowned upon or unacceptable (see the boxed insert). But to further complicate matters, it is not always easy to define a sexual value system. For example, on the one hand we are supposed to be in the midst of a "sexual revolution"; on the other hand, most of our sex laws and customs can be traced back to a Judeo-Christian tradition that is thousands of years old. As we shall see, this tradition continues to have a powerful effect on contemporary sexual attitudes even though its influence on our sexual behavior is much less clear-cut.

This American woman scholar was married in China to a man she met there. His relatives were astonished, when during the ceremony, the couple kissed. Such open displays of affection are rare in modern China. *(Fox Butterfield/ NYT Pictures)*

ual information has no place in the classroom, bookstore, or cinema, or even in private conversation. Styles of dress tend to minimize sexuality, and little attention is paid to being sexually attractive. For many women, there is no expectation that sex might be pleasurable—indeed, it is often considered an unpleasant marital duty or an embarrassment. Thus the relatively minor

sexual activity of kissing, so taken for granted in our culture, is often seen as a promise of marriage in China.

While the sexual puritanism of China seems difficult to understand for Americans in the midst of a sexual revolution, we should keep in mind that sexual standards are constantly shifting in response to changing social and political needs. At this time, China is best served by a system that inhibits population growth while focusing the attention of her people on work rather than on personal pleasure. Within this context, China's new puritanism makes a great deal of sense.

A Life-Cycle Perspective

To everything there is a season, and a time for every purpose under heaven: a time to be born and a time to die; a time to plant and a time to uproot. (Ecclesiastes 3:1–2)

A cross-cultural perspective enables us to see that the time and place in which we live

have a major influence on our sexuality. What is normal and natural among the Mangaians, for example, is far from the sexual standard in the United States today; indeed, not only our sexual behavior but also the meanings we give to sexuality will vary depending on our culture's sexual values. But this perspective—the comparison of one culture's values with those of another—reveals only one facet of our sexual lives. An entirely different facet is illuminated when we examine sexuality from a life-cycle perspective.

What is the life cycle? According to psychologist Daniel Levinson (1978), the term "life cycle" suggests that the course of life has a particular character and follows a certain basic sequence. Inherent in the concept of the life cycle is the notion that we all follow a common path from birth to death. Certainly this path will vary depending on our culture, but it also has certain universal characteristics and follows the same basic sequence of events. For instance, we must all undergo the physical changes associated with puberty. In some cultures these changes are celebrated with elaborate ritual, in others they are virtually ignored; but the fact of puberty is universal. A second concept inherent in the notion of the life cycle is that our lives are made up of periods or stages (see Figure 1.1). The stages of childhood have been fairly well researched, but the stages of adulthood have only recently begun to receive attention—in such books as *The Seasons of a Man's Life* (Levinson, 1978) and *Passages* (Sheehy, 1974). According to these authors, the process of development does not stop at some arbitrarily selected age; rather, development and change proceed throughout the entire span of our lives. Such development

is not a smooth and continuous flow; it proceeds in fits and starts, stimulated by the universal events that are part of life: birth, puberty, marriage, pregnancy and child rearing, menopause, aging, and so on. Each such event brings with it the need to make new adjustments, to learn, and to grow.

Levinson compares the stages of the life cycle with the seasons of the year; each season has its own distinctive character and importance to the whole, and in the same way, each stage of the life cycle has different needs and meanings. The passage from one season to another may be relatively smooth, or as is often the case, it may precipitate some type of life crisis. The way in which we experience these changes depends on both the nature of the ex-

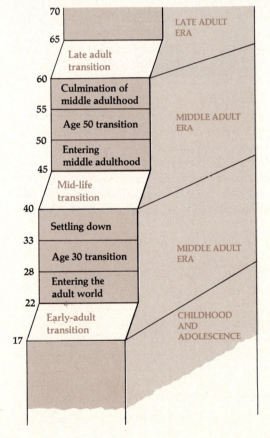

FIGURE 1.1

Developmental periods over the life course. This chart illustrates the approximate ages at which the key stages of adult development usually take place. Development does not cease after adolescence but continues throughout our lives. (*Levinson, 1978, p. 57*)

[10]

ternal event—say, childbearing—and our internal perception of the event. Thus, the woman who has always expected and wanted to bear children may have a vastly different response to birth than the woman whose goals and life style are severely disrupted by the same event. Both women will have to make adjustments, but the nature of these adjustments may be vastly different.

The life-cycle perspective clearly has a valuable application in the study of human sexuality. First, it focuses attention on the individual while simultaneously drawing attention to the universality of certain life changes. Also, it emphasizes the internal, or subjective, aspects of sexuality; we ask not only *what* is happening but also how it is perceived and what it *means* to the individual involved. Dealing with these personal issues is not easy—they are usually more elusive and subtle than the observable aspects of sexual behavior. Being more difficult to talk about, however, does not mean that such issues are less important. The subjective aspects of sexuality include a very broad range of human experience. Consider for a moment the fact that most people spend far more time thinking about sexuality than actually engaging in sexual behavior. Purely objective studies of sexuality, such as Kinsey's work, overlook the important role of subjective experience; the life-cycle perspective actively encourages such discussion.

Another value of the life-cycle perspective is that it recognizes the interaction between biology and personal experience. At each of the "seasons" in our lives, our bodies have different sexual capacities—for example, vaginal lubrication in women and penile erection in men tend to occur more slowly with increased age. In turn, these biological changes influence the nature of the sexual experience, although not necessarily in a single direction. On the one hand, a slowed sexual response might be distressing to the older man or woman who feels they are losing their sexual "potency"; on the other hand, this same slowing down might lead to a more relaxed and caring sexual interaction.

Although a life-cycle perspective implies that we will move through a predictable sequence of developmental stages, it does not tell us what the nature of the transition from one stage to another will be. Thus for some, the transition from childhood to adult sexuality will be relatively easy; for others, it will involve some emotional strain. Certainly our culture has a powerful influence on the relative ease of these transitions. In describing the sexual behavior of children in other societies, Clellan Ford and Frank Beach (1951) found the majority of "primitive" cultures to be tolerant and permissive about childhood sexual activity; children are allowed or even encouraged to masturbate, to observe adult sexual behavior, and to engage in sex play with one another. In such cultures, the transition to adult sexuality does not present a major break with the past. In contrast, most Western societies, including the United States today, are restrictive regarding childhood sexuality; children are punished for sex play and guarded from any exposure to sexual information. Thus the achievement of adult status brings with it a new set of sexual responsibilities for which the young person has little or no preparation. So it is not surprising that in our own and many other cultures, the onset of adult sexuality brings with it a major set of crises and upheavals.

Crises in sexual development might also be expected when we enter a particular stage too quickly or too slowly. We are supposed to make our life-cycle transitions at the "right" time according to the standards set by our society. We expect puberty to take place in the early teens—both the "early maturer" and the "late maturer" may suffer considerable personal discomfort at being out of step with their age-mates. Similarly, we may feel out of step if we miss the "due dates" at which we are expected to pass through a number of other sexual milestones: loss of virginity, marriage, childbirth, and so on. Indeed, those of us who completely miss one of these milestones—the man or woman who decides to remain celibate or the married couple who decide not to have children—may often feel the need to justify being different from the norm in order to live comfortably with these differences.

In addition to its emphasis on change, growth, and development, the life-cycle perspective is centered on the experience of the *individual*. While there are certainly many universals in our experience as sexual beings, there is also room for the unique differences in how we feel, think, and act. We know, for example, that each snowflake in a snowstorm has a unique shape although all snowflakes follow the same physical laws. In the same way, the physical and social laws that govern our sexuality interact with but do not seem to obscure in any way our unique identity as individuals.

Sexology: The Emerging Science of Sexuality

We live in an age that turns to science for the answers to our problems, just as our forefathers might have turned to religion or witchcraft. The staggering scientific achievements of this century have inalterably changed the course of human history—we have split the atom, sent a man to the moon, developed satellite communications, eliminated most infectious diseases, broken the genetic code, and so on. However, looking back on the history of science we observe that the physical sciences—such as astronomy, physics, and chemistry—got off to a much earlier start than the social and behavioral sciences. For example, our modern theories of astronomy date back to 1543, when Copernicus proposed the rotation of the planets around the sun. The sciences of psychiatry, psychology, and sociology, as we know them today, date back only to the latter part of the nineteenth century. As relative newcomers to the domain of science, these disciplines have not yet achieved the degree of public acceptance or respectability of the natural sciences. But the birth of modern psychiatry was all-important in paving the way for the development of *sexology*—the science of sexual behavior.

Like any new scientific discipline, sexology in the nineteenth century had its share of superstitious beliefs and fanciful theories. If we consider that many of the myths about masturbation originated in the writings of the early sexologists and the unfair treatment of such topics as female sexuality and homosexuality by most experts in the field, we might question whether more harm than good has been done in the name of science. And perhaps our grandchildren will look back a hundred years from now with similar skepticism about today's scientific views of sex. While there is much to be learned from scientific studies of sexuality, it is also important to recognize their biases and limitations.

It is difficult for us to imagine the social climate at the time the first scientific studies of sexual behavior were conducted.

That time was the reign of Queen Victoria in England and Kaiser Wilhelm in Germany. The moral code had banished the topic of sex, and even in medical circles the subject was treated

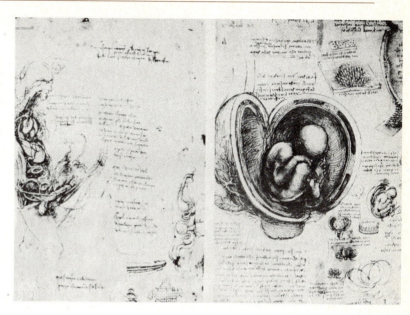

Illustrations of reproductive anatomy from the notebooks of Leonardo da Vinci. The illustration on the left shows the anatomy of intercourse, the one on the right, the development of the fetus. It was not until 1677 — when the inventor of the microscope, Anton van Leeuwenhoek, observed the existence of sperm — that insemination was understood; and it was not until the twentieth century that the notion of the sperm cell fusing with the egg was finally appreciated.

with nothing but disdain, or ignored altogether. Those who took it up, did so often at their personal peril. They were threatened with prosecution in court on charges of lewdness or pornography. (Musaph, 1977, pp. 8–9)

Who were the first sexologists, and what was the nature of their contributions? With the benefit of historical hindsight, we can now identify some of the major and minor actors in the drama. Among the significant but less important figures were Albert Moll (1862–1939), a German scientist who organized the first international conference on sexology after World War I; Auguste Forel (1848–1931), a French physician and social reformer whose writings covered various aspects of sexuality and women's rights; Magnus Hirschfeld (1868–1935), who founded the first institute for sex research in Germany; and Iwan Bloch (1872–1922), a German dermatologist who coined the term "sexology" and emphasized the effects of culture on sexual behavior.

Having introduced the "supporting cast," we can now turn our attention to the "leading actors" — the men who opened the way for sexology in the twentieth century. Four names stand out in bold relief: Richard von Krafft-Ebing, Henry Havelock Ellis, Sigmund Freud, and Theodore Hendrik Van de Velde. All were born in Europe in the middle part of the nineteenth century, were formally educated as physicians, and made the study of human sexuality a central part of their life's work. A brief review of their individual contributions will show the profound impact that their ideas have had.

RICHARD VON KRAFFT-EBING (1840–1902)

Born in Mannheim, Germany, of a very distinguished family, Richard von Krafft-Ebing studied medicine in Germany, Austria, and Switzerland. He specialized in neurology and psychiatry and, through his prolific publications in both fields, became one of the most highly respected European physicians of his time. As a medical scientist, his trademark was the case study method, a technique of in-depth analysis of individual patients. Krafft-Ebing made extensive use of his great skill in clinical observation—both in his work for the courts as an expert in insanity trials and in his famous textbooks of psychiatry.

The contribution that ensured for him a permanent place in the history of science was his textbook on the sexual disorders, *Psychopathia Sexualis*. Krafft-Ebing elected to write his major work in Latin, intending it to be accessible only to the highly educated specialists in his field. After its first publication in 1886, he revised the book twelve times, adding in the process more than 200 detailed case histories covering all the known forms of "sexual aberration." Since his death, the book has been translated into many languages, and it can still be found in most bookstores today.

As a psychiatrist, Krafft-Ebing was primarily concerned with the abnormalities of sexual behavior, which in the nineteenth century were commonly termed "perversions." Sexual perversions were believed to be due to disease or "degeneration" of the nervous system, which could be caused by either hereditary factors or some form of traumatic experience. Based on his observation of the frequency of masturbation among his patients, Krafft-Ebing drew the erroneous conclusion that masturbation was also an important contributing factor. He was clearly not aware of the prevalence of masturbation in the general population and mistakenly assumed that it was practiced only by sexual deviants. This points to a more general problem inherent in the case-study method of investigation—the scientist should always compare his "abnormal" sample with a suitably matched "normal" control group, to determine in which ways the abnormal subjects differ from the normal. Had Krafft-Ebing taken such a precaution, he may have reached a completely different conclusion about the role of masturbation as a cause of sexual disorders.

The following case study from *Psychopathia Sexualis* illustrates Krafft-Ebing's approach to his subject matter. Although it is typical in some respects, it is also one of the more innocuous cases presented by the author. In the book there are many lurid descriptions of violent lust-murders and acts of extreme sadism.

Case 225. P., laborer, aged twenty-nine. Family heavily tainted. Emotional, irritable, masturbated since childhood. When ten years old he saw a boy masturbate into a woman's handkerchief. This gave the direction to P.'s sexual life. He stole handkerchiefs from pretty girls and masturbated into them. His mother tried every means to break him of this habit; she admonished him, took the stolen handkerchiefs away and bought him new ones, all in vain. He was caught by the police and punished for theft. He then went to Africa and served in the army with an excellent record. On his return to France he resumed his old practices. He was only potent if the prostitute held a white handkerchief in her hand during the act. He married in 1894 and sustained his virility by grasping a handkerchief during coitus. (1965, pp. 561–562)

Krafft-Ebing may have succeeded in bringing sexual disorders into the study of psychiatry, but his work was unduly biased by his moralistic and puritanical outlook. As one writer notes:

For many centuries in our culture, sex has been denounced from the pulpits as a sin and punished in the courts as a crime. Richard von Krafft-Ebing added a third ground for the repression and the suppression of human sexuality. He portrayed sex in almost all of its manifestations as a collection of loathsome diseases. (Brecher, 1969, p. 50)

HENRY HAVELOCK ELLIS (1858–1939)

The Englishman Henry Havelock Ellis did as much as anyone to set the direction for the science of sexology in the twentieth century. One writer (Hoenig, 1977) has compared the influence of Havelock Ellis on the cultural and

Havelock Ellis with his wife, Edith Lees Ellis. Although Ellis was a great pioneer explorer of the psychology of sexuality (for example, he was one of the first advocates of the right of women to a full sexual existence), in his private life, he was sexually inhibited and frustrated. *(Courtesy, Lafitte Collection)*

social climate of our age to that of Marx or Freud. Another (Bullough, 1976) claims it was Ellis, probably more than anyone else, who popularized the concept of individual and cultural relativism in sex. And Yale University philosopher Paul Robinson (1976) credits Ellis' work in sexology for "the emergence of the modern sexual ethos."

Havelock Ellis was born in Croydon, a suburb of London, and grew up in the company of his mother and four sisters, as his father was a sailor who spent most of his time at sea. Ellis' early life was not happy, and he has been described as a nervous and high-strung young man who suffered from major sexual inhibitions. Perhaps due to his mother's dominating influence, Ellis led a very sheltered life during his early years. When he married Edith Lees at the age of 32, both Ellis and his wife were virgins, and the marriage was reportedly never consummated because of his extreme premature ejaculation. Later in life, however, Ellis entered into a relationship with a young French woman, Françoise Delisle, with whom he seems to have enjoyed a more satisfactory sexual relationship.

Like Krafft-Ebing, Ellis made extensive use of the case-history method. But unlike his predecessor, he was less interested in the diseases and pathology of sexual "perversion" and more concerned with documenting the wide range of individual variations that can be found in all societies. "Ellis was a naturalist, observing and collecting information about human sexuality instead of judging it, and as such can be considered the forerunner of the sex researchers of today" (Bullough, 1976, p. 643). On the basis of innumerable case histories, Ellis drafted his monumental work *Studies in the Psychology of Sex*, which was published in six volumes between 1897 and 1910. His ideas were not well received in the repressive and puritanical climate of Victorian England, and much of his work was initially published abroad.

Although Ellis covered a wide range of subjects in his writing, his opinions on masturbation, homosexuality, and female sexuality were particularly influential. He presented arguments that masturbation was an essentially harmless activity and a legitimate form of sexual release for men and women of all ages. With respect to homosexuality, Ellis believed that it was a genetically determined but nonpathological sexual variation. He presented many case studies of highly respected and productive members of society who were homosexuals. Finally, unlike many of his contemporaries, Ellis recognized fully the sexual capacity of women and placed the female sexual response on a par with that of the male.

SIGMUND FREUD (1856–1939)

Born in Moravia, in Central Europe, Sigmund Freud lived and worked for most of his life in Vienna and died in London. During the course of his long and productive life, Freud became the founder of the psychoanalytic movement and the most influential figure in modern psychiatry and psychology. Like his English contemporary Havelock Ellis, Freud challenged many of the prevailing Victorian concepts of sexuality, and through his voluminous writings on the subject, he made sex a central issue in the study of human behavior.

As the oldest son of a middle-class Jewish family, Freud was apparently his mother's favorite throughout his childhood. In 1873 he entered medical school and became a keen student of physiology, studying under the physiologist Brücke, who introduced him to the idea of energy forces in the human body. The concept of conservation of energy was very important in physiology at the time and greatly influenced Freud's subsequent theories of the mind and the sexual instinct (libido).

After his graduation from medical school, Freud entered the field of neurology and spent some years doing brain research. He married

at this time, and during the course of his marriage, he had three sons and three daughters. During his early years in medical practice, Freud was subject to depressed moods and anxiety attacks, for relief of which he quite often used the drug cocaine.

Freud's interest in the mind and the unconscious seems to have been sparked by his association with the French psychiatrist Jean Charcot in 1886. Charcot introduced Freud to the use of hypnosis in the treatment of emotional disorders, and Freud used this technique for some time before abandoning it in favor of his own free-association method. In 1900 he published *The Interpretation of Dreams*, his first major work, in which he began to develop his theories of the mind. In 1905 he published *Three Essays on the Theory of Sexuality*, which shocked the scientific community by proposing an elaborate theory of infantile sexuality. Freud attempted to trace back the origins of adult neuroses to disturbances in childhood sexuality and to show the significance of childhood sexuality for all aspects of personality development. These ideas are discussed in detail in Chapter 2.

Although his theories went through numerous changes and revisions, sexuality remained a central theme of Freud's writing throughout his lifetime. For example, in *Civilization and Its Discontents*, published in 1930, he attempted to prove that suppression and redirection of the sexual instinct leads to the development of culture in advanced societies. In addition to the sexual drive, Freud also placed great importance on the instinct for *aggression*; he viewed the two drives as the source of all human conflict.

Sigmund Freud was clearly one of the most controversial figures in the history of science. While his critics have been as numerous and outspoken as his followers, no one can deny the enormous impact of his ideas. In his biography of Freud, Sulloway (1979) argues that

Freud's achievements on the subject of sexology are of two types: first, he synthesized the theories and works of earlier sex researchers, and second, he provided a unique psychoanalytic framework for understanding these theories.

THEODORE HENDRIK VAN DE VELDE (1873–1937)

The fourth important figure in the emergence of modern sexology was the Dutch gynecologist Theodore Hendrik Van de Velde. Unlike his predecessors, Van de Velde was directly concerned with the education and sexual satisfaction of "normal" married couples—the sexual majority, so to speak. Although he did make certain original observations of sexual physiology, it is not as a researcher or theorist that he is important. Rather, we owe to him the concept, still popular today, that every man and woman has the right to sexual satisfaction. With his emphasis on positions of intercourse, methods of foreplay (including oral-genital stimulation), and suggestions for afterplay, Van de Velde was responsible for the practical aspects of the sex education of the first generation of post-Victorians.

Van de Velde's major contribution was his highly popular marriage manual, *Ideal Marriage*, first published in 1926 and subsequently translated and reprinted in almost every country of the world. We owe to him our appreciation of the devastating effects of sexual ignorance on male and female sexual performance. On the basis of his extensive clinical experience as a gynecologist, Van de Velde came to the conclusion that both sexes can and should be taught how to give and receive sexual pleasure, and this was the major goal of his book. As Edward Brecher has observed:

The [Victorian] delusion still survived that where love and affection reign, sex will take care of itself. Van de Velde's patients illustrated the disastrous consequences of this delusion. He learned from them that no matter how loving a couple may be, sexual response is *not* automatic. He therefore prescribed in detail the specific bodily techniques—the kisses, the caresses, the thrusts—by means of which his patients and his readers could translate their emotional commitments into physiological responses and orgasms. (1969, p. 84)

Some of Van de Velde's ideas have become outdated. For example, his emphasis on simultaneous orgasm as the goal of intercourse has been seriously challenged by most of the present generation of sex therapists. Also, much of his writing reveals a sexist bias, with the husband portrayed in the role of teacher and initiator and the wife encouraged to show modesty and "proper femininity" in her approach to sexual relations. Despite these limitations, we are greatly indebted to Van de Velde for his steadfast belief in the practical aspects of sexology and his attempts to make them accessible to all segments of society.

Sexology Today

We each have complete access to only one sexual history—our own. To satisfy our curiosity about how we compare with the rest of the world, we are usually forced to rely on information that is limited and often unreliable. For example, we may question our friends, but we have no assurance that the information they provide will be accurate. Whereas people are relatively honest in reporting their age, height, or occupation, they are generally reluctant to describe their favorite type of foreplay or the best coital position for reaching orgasm.

A second source of sexual information is the media—books, movies, magazines, and so on—but here again there are limitations. The media have a natural tendency to report on what is new and different, rather than on what is average and ordinary. A flood of articles on such activities as "swinging" makes for interesting reading but is not necessarily an accurate reflection of the current sexual scene.

A third source of sexual information is research on the sexual behavior of animals. Animal research has the advantage of being "scientific" and relatively free of reporting bias. Further, animal researchers are able to manipulate the behavior of their subjects in ways that would be unethical for human subjects—for instance, by administering hormones or performing surgery. Animal research is valuable in giving us a perspective on our own sexual behavior, but it does have one major drawback: the tremendous importance of culture and language in guiding human sexual behavior is not duplicated in any other branch of the animal kingdom, so it is relatively difficult to generalize from the fairly rigid sexual behavior of animals to the complex varieties and meanings of human sexuality.

SURVEY LIMITATIONS

Overall, our best source of sexual information is that provided by researchers who have interviewed or surveyed large numbers of people. Several such studies have appeared in the past 30 years (see Table 1.1), each with its own strengths and weaknesses. The primary strength of survey research is that it gives us access to many more sexual histories than we could reach on our own. Counterbalancing this strength are a number of potential weaknesses that should be kept in mind when reading survey data.

Volunteer bias and sampling limitations. Do people who answer sex surveys differ from those who refuse to respond? Carol Tavris and Susan Sadd, authors of *The Redbook Report on Female Sexuality*, (1977) discuss the possibility that there are two groups of people who will not answer sex surveys—"those who are perfectly happy and those who are perfectly miserable." The happy group, having no sexual problems, cannot see the value of sex research; the miserable group finds the entire subject of sex distasteful and embarrassing. Often, sex surveys are criticized for overrepresenting the sexually liberal and underrepresenting those with more conservative attitudes, because liberals may be more likely to respond to such surveys.

Research on "volunteer bias" has yielded mixed results. Abraham Maslow and J. M. Sakoda (1952) compared students who had volunteered for the 1948 Kinsey studies with

"Strange to say the habits of birds and flowers have done as little to clarify the human scene as almost any other two manifestations in nature." (*From* Is Sex Necessary? *by James Thurber and E. B. White*)

those who did not volunteer. They found that volunteers scored higher on a test that measured self-esteem, and also were more sexually active than those who did not volunteer. In contrast, a more recent study showed that there were almost no differences between a group of men and women who volunteered to fill out a sex survey and a random group that required personal persuasion before they would agree to participate; although the two groups differed in their willingness to provide sexual information, they did not differ in sexual attitudes or experience (Bauman, 1973).

Related to the problem of volunteer bias is that of sampling limitations. Under ideal circumstances, a researcher would know the general characteristics of the entire population being studied—such as age, income, educational level, religious and racial background, urban or rural region, area of the country, and so on. Then a small sample would be selected that accurately represented all these variables. Unfortunately, sex research is usually performed in circumstances that are less than ideal, and almost any study can be criticized as overrepresenting some groups and underrepresenting others.

Alfred Kinsey's research is generally acknowledged as being the most extensive in terms of sampling, but even Kinsey has been criticized for underrepresenting blacks, the poor, and the uneducated in his sample, as well as for problems of volunteer bias. In an attempt to overcome volunteer bias, Kinsey used many "100 percent samples"—that is, he would select a particular group (such as a college class, fraternity, or sorority) and be sure to interview *every* member of that group. While 100 percent samples do eliminate the problem of volunteer bias, they also require enormous persistence and persuasiveness on the part of the researcher.

Perhaps the most widely criticized sex survey of recent years is *The Hite Report* (Hite, 1976), which is described as "a nationwide study" but is actually based on a very biased

TABLE 1.1
The Major Sex Surveys

Author	Date	Title	Number	Source	Sample
Kinsey *et al.*	1948	*Sexual Behavior in the Human Male*	6,300 males	Interviews	"100% samples" + partial samples
Kinsey *et al.*	1953	*Sexual Behavior in the Human Female*	5,940 females	Interviews	"100% samples" + partial samples
Ford & Beach	1951	*Patterns of Sexual Behavior*	190 cultures	Anthropological research	
Athanasiou *et al.*	1970	"Sex" (article in *Psychology Today*)	20,000 males & females	Questionnaire	*Psychology Today* readers
Sorenson	1973	*Adolescent Sexuality in Contemporary America*	411 males & females	Questionnaire	Random samples of adolescents aged 13 to 19 years
Hunt	1974	*Sexual Behavior in the 1970's*	982 males, 1,044 females	Questionnaire	Random sample
Hite	1976	*The Hite Report*	3,019 females	Questionnaire	Various magazine readers & mailout respondents
Tavris & Sadd	1977	*The Redbook Report on Female Sexuality*	100,000 females	Questionnaire	Married female readers of *Redbook* magazine
Bell & Weinberg	1978	*Homosexualities*	686 males, 293 females	Interviews	Homosexuals in the San Francisco area

sample of women. Many of Shere Hite's respondents were members of the women's movement, through which she distributed her questionnaire; and her remaining subjects were drawn from the readership of such publications as *Oui, The Village Voice, Mademoiselle,* and *Ms.* Her respondents were more likely to be urban, unmarried, well-educated, and of a "feminist" orientation than would be expected in a random sample of women. To point out these sampling limitations is not to imply that Hite's research is invalid — certainly her report has made a powerful statement about the ways that some women view sex and is valuable as a collection of sexual autobiographies. But it is important to remember that Hite is reporting on a special group of women, and her statistics must be interpreted as such.

Hite acknowledges that the purpose of her report is "to share how we have experienced our sexuality" and to "stimulate a public discussion and reevaluation of sexuality," but many other sex surveys that purport to portray "average" sexual behavior also suffer from sampling limitations. For instance, the *Redbook* report (Tavris and Sadd, 1977) sampled only married readers of *Redbook* magazine, and the *Psychology Today* report (Athanasiou et al., 1970) sampled only the readers of *Psychology Today* magazine. These sampling limitations are likely to be found, in some form, in almost any study of sexuality; but even in the absence of a "perfect sample" we can still learn a great deal from surveys, as long as we recognize their deficiencies.

Research techniques. Yet another problem of sex surveys is the method by which information is obtained. Those most used are the direct interview and questionnaires of the closed- or open-ended type (see Table 1.1). Each of these techniques has advantages and disadvantages. For instance, Kinsey's research is based almost exclusively on person-to-person interviews, in which subjects were questioned, often for several hours, about their sexual histories. This intensive questioning enabled the interviewer to inquire in depth about a variety of sexual topics and also to test the accuracy and honesty of the subject's reporting. Aside from the time and expense of performing such interviews, Kinsey noted that developing the interviewers for his survey was a long and arduous process that took a full year of training. According to Kinsey (1948), a good interviewer must be sexually knowledgeable, nonjudgmental, unbiased, sensitive, and able to establish rapport with the subject.

The *Redbook* survey provides a good example of the closed-ended questionnaire. Subjects were asked to reply to seventy-five specific questions; each question was followed by a set of specific answers, and the subject had simply to check the response that best answered the question in her case. The advantage of this method is that it is a relatively efficient and easy way for the subject to provide sexual information. The disadvantage is that subjects were forced to respond in a predetermined way, leaving little room for detail or variation. In contrast, Hite used an open-ended questionnaire that allowed subjects to respond at length and in detail on a variety of topics. However, participants in the Hite survey had to be willing to devote several hours to completing the questionnaire. Further, since the questions were open-ended, the responses were so varied as to make comparison among the responses of different women very difficult.

The nature of the research technique that is selected can have a major influence on the type of people who are willing to respond. The type of women who were willing to respond to the lengthy and difficult Hite survey were probably different from the type of women who answered the short and simple *Redbook* survey. In addition, the research method can influence the type of information that is reported. Hite asked about masturbation as follows: "Do you enjoy masturbation? Physically? Psychologically? Is it more intense with or without a partner?" (1976, p. 402). Hite also asked her subjects to reveal their masturbatory method with a drawing or detailed description. In contrast, the *Redbook* survey asked: "Have you ever masturbated since your marriage?" and "Would you describe this as a sexually satisfying experience?" and provided specific answers such as "Often" or "Occasionally" where the answer was not a simple yes or no (Tavris & Sadd, p. 163). The Kinsey interviewer, on the other hand, was trained to ask direct questions and place the burden of denial on the subject; for instance, the subject would be asked "How often do you masturbate?" rather than "Do you masturbate?" Each survey was attempting to elicit information about masturbation, but it is likely that in each case the form of the question influenced the answer given.

THE KINSEY REPORTS

Although Kinsey and his associates were certainly not the first to survey human sexual behavior, their work remains the standard against which all other sex research is measured. It is not uncommon for present day researchers to use Kinsey's data as a yardstick for measuring change, and in many minds, Kinsey's volumes remain the most reliable source of information about American sexual behavior (Robinson, 1976).

Alfred Charles Kinsey (1894–1956) was born in Hoboken, New Jersey, and grew up in a very religious, middle-class home. He began his career in zoology studying gall wasps and was appointed to the faculty of Indiana University in 1920. However, it was not until 1937, that he began to teach a course in sex education and to develop a research interest in human sexuality. He is possibly this country's most significant contributor to the field.

In addition to its effect on the scientific community, Kinsey's research brought human sexuality into the public consciousness. The two volumes sold about half a million copies. At a time when sexual topics were rarely discussed openly, Kinsey adopted a scientific approach that "allowed public discussion of premarital sexuality, oral-genital sex, homosexuality, penises, vaginas, and orgasms. Putting a percentage in front of the topic made it speakable" (Gagnon, 1978, p. 93). While people remained hesitant to discuss their own sexual behavior, they were less hesitant to criticize and evaluate Kinsey's work. The media played a major role in this public discussion of sexuality: an obscure Midwestern zoologist and his colleagues became front-page news, and a sexual message was carried into every home in the nation (Gagnon, 1978).

Kinsey's taxonomic approach is well-known; he is thought to have studied human sexuality in much the same way that a biologist might study the sex lives of any other animal—categorizing behavior in an objective fashion and making no value judgments about this behavior. Indeed, Kinsey may have cultivated the impression that his work was purely empirical, assuming that the public would be more likely to accept statistics than a sexual value system. However, a closer examination of Kinsey's work indicates that very often he did not play the role of a neutral observer. Kinsey had strong opinions about human sexuality, and these opinions are expressed in his assumptions and conclusions.

One writer (Robinson, 1976) describes several facets of what he calls "Kinsey's sexual ideology." Perhaps the major facet was Kinsey's insistence on sexual tolerance—that is, that sexual behavior should be accepted and not judged. Kinsey recognized the enormous variability of human sexual behavior—with so many people behaving in so many different ways, he believed it was impossible to establish standards for "normality." Better simply to accept with tolerance the enormous range of human sexual activity.

Another factor in Kinsey's sexual ideology was his naturalism. As a zoologist, Kinsey was prone to draw comparisons between the sexual behavior of humans and that of the lower animals: "Natural designated for him continuity between human behavior and that of the lower species, while unnatural implied the absence of such continuity" (Robinson, 1976, p. 55). Thus Kinsey suggested that many socially unacceptable behaviors were natural because they were present among animals. Indeed, he believed that human sexual problems often resulted from social training that went against the natural sexual tendencies of other mammals.

Although we tend to think of *Sexual Behavior in the Human Male* (1948) and *Sexual Behavior in the Human Female* (1953) as a single extended piece of work, there are some major differences between the two volumes. In the male volume Kinsey devoted a great deal of time to elaborating the influence of social class on sexual behavior. While upper- and lower-class males reported the same overall *amount* of sexual activity, Kinsey found numerous differences in the *types* of activity. For example, the incidence of premarital intercourse was far higher among lower-class males than among upper-class males. In contrast, upper-class males masturbated with greater frequency than those in the lower classes. Similarly, lower-class males tended to favor intercourse in the "missionary position" and included little sexual foreplay. In contrast, upper-class males were more likely to participate in a variety of noncoital activities such as petting, oral and manual stimulation, and to use several intercourse positions. Generally, Kinsey

One of Kinsey's findings was that the social class one belonged to affected one's sexual behavior. This finding was, however, later disputed. (*Culver Pictures*)

regarded lower-class behavior as more "natural"—that is, closer to the behavior of animals—and upper-class behavior as more contaminated by the effects of social learning.

In addition to the factor of class, Kinsey described male sexuality in a variety of other dimensions: age, marital status, religion, rural/urban background, and so on. These same dimensions appeared in the volume on female sexuality, but their importance in explaining behavior had diminished considerably. In fact, the only social variable found to be related to female sexuality in a major way was religion: religious women were less sexually active and less orgasmic than women without strong religious convictions.

In the male volume, Kinsey often suggested that female sexuality develops more slowly and is less responsive than male sexuality. But analysis of the data collected for the female volume did not always support this belief. Thus Kinsey reversed his earlier opinions and wrote instead about the great similarities in male and female sexuality. Although he recognized that there were also differences, he did not attribute such differences to anatomy. For instance, Kinsey did not believe that possession of a penis conveyed special sexual benefits on the male, nor did he think that the ab-

sence of a penis limited female sexuality. He predated the work of Masters and Johnson by noting that the processes of sexual arousal and orgasm are physically identical in men and women.

However, data in the female volume did show that women made less use of such sexual outlets as masturbation and nocturnal sex dreams. From this evidence, Kinsey concluded that females were not as sensitive to psychological influences. For instance, females reported less fantasy and less arousal by visual stimulation than did males. Kinsey even suggested that differential sensitivity to psychological influences was related to differences between the male and female brain. This point of view is given less credence today, when sex differences in arousal are more likely to be attributed to social learning.

According to Robinson (1976) Kinsey appears as "this century's foremost sexual demystifier." Instead of viewing sex as magical, romantic, dangerous, or frightening, Kinsey made it simply a fact of life. No matter how taboo an activity, Kinsey described it as merely one more variation within the enormous range of human sexual behavior. In so doing, he helped to make sexuality a less painful and more accepted part of our lives.

Masters and Johnson

If the current tentative approach to sex education is to achieve the widespread popular support it deserves, there must be physiologic fact rather than phallic fallacy to teach. (Masters and Johnson, 1966, p. v)

The publication of *Human Sexual Response* in 1966, the first book by Masters and Johnson, in which they described the results of their extensive laboratory studies of male and female

sexual response, was a landmark event in the history of scientific sexology. The impact of their work has been enormous, and they are generally regarded as among the foremost sexologists of our time. In 1970, their second book, *Human Sexual Inadequacy*, was published and has since become a major textbook on the causes and treatment of sexual problems. In addition, they have written about sexual relationships in *The Pleasure Bond* (1970) and about homosexuality in *Homosexuality in Perspective* (1979). Their research continues today at the Masters and Johnson Institute located in St. Louis, Missouri.

William Howell Masters was born in Cleveland, Ohio, in 1915. With a developing interest in laboratory research, he entered the University of Rochester Medical School, where he embarked on the first stage of his lifelong interest in reproductive behavior. His first research study, on the estrus cycle of the rabbit, was performed in the laboratory of George Washington Corner, Rochester's famous professor of anatomy. Masters was granted his M.D. degree in 1943. He then went on to a residency in obstetrics and gynecology at Washington University School of Medicine, where he has remained a member of the faculty ever since.

His first experiments in the field of human sexuality were on the effects of hormone replacement therapy on postmenopausal women. These experiments served to establish his reputation as a serious researcher and enabled Masters to set up his famous laboratory studies of sexual response. In 1957 he began to interview prospective subjects for the laboratory study; at that time, Masters decided to bring in a woman, Virginia Johnson, in order to establish a dual-sex interviewing team for working with both clinical patients and experimental subjects.

Virginia Johnson was born in the Missouri Ozarks in 1925 and was raised in a rural environment. At Missouri University she studied psychology and sociology. She married a musician in 1950, with whom she had two children. After separating from her husband in 1956, Johnson decided to seek broader work experience and was selected by Masters to become a member of his interviewing team. Johnson has often been described as a warm, sensitive, and empathic interviewer, who complements the firm and authoritative style of Masters. After working together for more than 15 years, Masters and Johnson were married in 1971.

Although Masters and Johnson have performed the most extensive psychophysiological research on sexual arousal and orgasm, they were not the first to undertake this type of experimentation. For instance, a laboratory study was carried out by a New York gynecologist, Robert Latou Dickinson, and the results were published in his classic textbook *Human Sex Anatomy* in 1933 (see Chapter 2). In this text, Dickinson presented illustrations of the female vagina based on direct observations; to make these drawings, he constructed a glass tube in the shape of a penis that was inserted into the vagina; Dickinson then observed and recorded the basic elements of female sexual response during masturbation.

Although Kinsey is best known for his work as an interviewer and surveyer of human sexuality, he too conducted physiological research on arousal and orgasm. Because of public opposition to such work, Kinsey played down this aspect of his research. However, in *Sexual Behavior in the Human Female* (1953) he did include a chapter, "Physiology of Sexual Response and Orgasm," in which he presented the results of his original research on cardiovascular changes during arousal and orgasm.

These earlier studies by Dickinson and Kinsey paved the way for the intensive, large-scale investigations conducted by Masters and Johnson. Their first study of male and female sexual response took more than 10 years to complete, involved the participation of 694 volunteer subjects ranging in age from 18 to 89, and resulted in the laboratory observation of more than 14,000 sexual acts. Most subjects were paid volunteers who readily agreed to masturbate or perform intercourse with their partners while being filmed or recorded by physiological measurement devices.

During the early stages of their research program, Masters and Johnson were criticized severely for two specific aspects of their study. First was their use of prostitutes as subjects in the study of female sexuality. Aside from moral or legal issues, Masters and Johnson did acknowledge several problems with this population—prostitutes tend to change their place of residence often and are therefore difficult to locate for follow-up research. In addition, prostitutes often have genital problems due to the nature of their occupation, which makes them inappropriate in the study of "normal" female sexual response.

The second aspect of their early work that attracted criticism was their use of the "artificial coition machine"—a penis-shaped device that was mechanically driven into the female subject's vagina and through which intravaginal responses to sexual stimulation could be observed. Masters and Johnson describe this device as follows:

The artificial coital equipment was created by radiophysicists. The penises are plastic and were developed with the same optics as plate glass. Cold-light illumination allows observation and recording without distortion. The equipment can be adjusted for physical variations in size, weight, and vaginal development. The rate and depth of penile thrust is initiated and controlled completely by the responding individual. . . . The equipment is powered electrically. (1966, p. 21)

The major objection was not that the device was unscientific—it had been proved useful and accurate—but that it presented an overly mechanistic approach to the study of human sexuality. Not wishing to reinforce this image of their work, Masters and Johnson hastily withdrew the device from their laboratory procedures. According to one reporter (McGrady, 1972), the machine has not been used since and is kept hidden from public view in a room to which only Masters and Johnson have access.

We are greatly indebted to Masters and Johnson for dispelling many sexual myths and fallacies. Three examples serve to illustrate their importance in this regard. First, they demonstrated that the size of a man's penis is

Among the most significant contributions of Masters and Johnson to our understanding of sexuality have been the laboratory study of sexual anatomy and physiology, the development of short-term treatments for sexual dysfunctions, and, most recently, their study of homosexual behavior. One of their specific findings that has changed our view of sexuality is that orgasms during masturbation produce the same physiological responses as orgasms during intercourse. (© *Dirck Halstead/Liaison Agency)*

generally unrelated to any aspect of his sexual performance. Second, they found no evidence to support the idea that there are physiological differences between "vaginal" and "clitoral" orgasms in women. Third, they presented physiological proof that women are able to have multiple orgasms. The full details of their research on sexual response are presented in Chapter 5. In Chapter 9 we consider their approach to the causes and treatment of sexual problems, and in Chapter 3 we look at their more recent work on homosexuality.

Perhaps even more important than the specific findings of their research is the change that has taken place in public attitudes toward sex research. Laboratory studies of sexuality are now being conducted in almost every major university in the United States, and research in this field has finally achieved respectability. Because Masters and Johnson were able to demonstrate the practical value of their work in dealing with a variety of sexual problems, research on human sexuality is now seen as a valuable contribution to the health and behavioral sciences.

Certainly there have been enormous changes in the science of sexology in the past century. Krafft-Ebing would probably be shocked and surprised that his work on sexual psychopathology was the "ancestor" to Masters and Johnson's laboratory measurement of human sexual response. And in much the same way, we cannot know what directions sexology will take in the century to come. It is possible that scientists will take an increasingly nonmoralistic and nonjudgmental view of human sexual behavior, but it is also possible that we will return to the more stringent sexual standards of the past. Science, like other aspects of our social structure, often acts like a pendulum, swinging from one extreme position to another. We do know that science interacts with culture; on the one hand, the scientist may be an innovator whose work changes the way a culture looks at sexuality. But on the other hand, the scientist may produce results that simply confirm the prevailing sexual standards of the time. When we look at scientific research, then, it is important to retain a certain distance and skepticism. In the light of today's sexual standards, Krafft-Ebing's work seems biased and even misinformed; it seems equally possible that sexologists of the next century will look back at current research with the same misgivings.

Sexual Values and the Judeo-Christian Tradition

The most blessed thing in life and the only thing worth living for is to put one's lips to a woman's lips, one's body on her body, and one's genitals in her genitals. (Poem of Ibn Saud, an Islamic king)

It is better to marry than to burn. (St. Paul, 1 Corinthians 7:9)

Like sexuality, the topic of religion can provoke strong personal and public responses; some people use religious tradition to develop a private standard of behavior, others believe that their religion provides a code applicable to all groups. Certainly, the teachings of all major religions include standards of behavior regarding human sexuality—standards that may be as varied and complex as those provided by differing cultures. In examining these standards, we should keep in mind that the sexual values proposed by any religion are subject to change and interpretation. For example, many of the Judeo-Christian sexual values that we take for granted do not come directly from the Bible—they are interpretations developed by later religious authorities. Even today, religious standards of sexual conduct continue to evolve in response to the changing needs of modern society.

Despite these changes, we can make certain generalizations about the influence of the Judeo-Christian tradition on current sexual practices. Overall, this tradition can be described as the most sexually restrictive and puritanical of all major religions (Bullough, 1976). While the Old Testament encouraged sexual relations for procreative purposes—"Be fruitful and multiply"—there is strong condemnation of all nonprocreative sexual expression. Thus masturbation, homosexuality, extramarital sex, and premarital sex have all been considered sinful and in some cases have

Jan Van Eyck, *Marriage of Giovanni Arnofini and Giovanna Cennami*, 1434. This great painting portrays the religious sanctity of the Christian marriage. Each of the everyday objects has a religious significance. For example, the dog symbolizes the virtue of faithfulness; the fruit symbolizes the fruit from the Garden of Eden, and the mirror on the wall symbolizes purity. *(National Gallery)*

Sex and Sin

During the course of history there have been many attempts to explain why some forms of sexual expression are considered "good" and others "evil" or "sinful." As we have seen, the writings of St. Paul and St. Augustine did more to shape Christian sexual values than did any direct statements by Jesus himself. References to sexual conduct in the Bible are often vague and inconsistent, and are subject to a variety of interpretations. Basically, however, the impression we are left with is that sex is an activity fraught with the perils of sin.

In his "Essay on Human Sexuality," Isaac Asimov (1979) writes that from an early age he was struck by people's obsession with the sinfulness of sex, which appeared to bother the pious much more than such worldly sins as unethical business practices, political trickery, or social injustice. In course of time, he came to see this obsession as a possible legacy of the population needs in biblical times. When infant mortality rates were high and life expectancy short, human survival depended on people having as many children as possible. All sexuality had thus to be directed toward conception; sex for pure pleasure was wasteful and therefore sinful—and this was especially true of such sexual activities as masturbation and homosexuality, which could never result in procreation.

But as Asimov points out, the needs of our own time are very different. In today's conditions of low infant mortality and long life expectancy, when the real danger to human survival is no longer a dwindling population but a population explosion, sex as sin no longer makes sense.

Perhaps, as a matter of necessity, society should stop trying to legislate morality and instead permit those sexual activities that give satisfaction and don't involve any chance of unwanted conception. Maybe what is "unnatural" in today's world is for people to become parents when all they actually want is pleasure (Asimov, 1979, p. 379).

Psychologist Albert Ellis also makes a strong case against viewing sex as sin, basing his arguments on rationality and humanism. Why, he asks, should the rules of sexual conduct be any different from the rules governing any other form of human interaction? A sexual act should not be regarded as wrong simply because it is sexual. It is wrong only if it in some way violates general ethics and morality. Thus even rape is not wrong simply because it involves intercourse "but because it consists of forceful, freedom-depriving, injurious intercourse; and it is its breach of human consent rather than its sexuality which constitutes its wrongness" (Ellis, 1969, p. 85).

---

even incurred punishment as severe as the death penalty.

We also find in the Old Testament the origins of the sexual "double standard" and the subordinate status of women. For instance, the family structure of the ancient Hebrews was strongly patriarchal and male-dominated; women were usually portrayed as lacking spiritual and intellectual abilities and as capable of using "feminine wiles" to lead men astray. Thus Eve persuaded Adam to taste the serpent's apple, and the daughters of Lot were supposed to have given him so much wine that he lost his senses and committed incest with them. In the book of Leviticus, adultery by a married woman warranted the death penalty, but the extramarital relations of married men were not regarded as adultery.

Within the context of marriage, however, the Old Testament encouraged active sexual expression: "Enjoy life with the wife you love" (Ecclesiastes 9:9). In addition to its primary purpose of procreation, marital sex was seen as a positive means of cementing the marital relationship. A wife whose husband was unable or unwilling to have intercourse with her was entitled to a divorce, and abstinence or celibacy had no place in Judaism for either priests or lay persons. In general, then, the cardinal rule of sexual conduct in the Old Testament was that sexual activity was approved only within the confines of a legal heterosexual marriage.

The early Christians adopted this basic code of sexual behavior, with one addition. Primarily as a result of the writings of St. Paul, a prohibition was introduced against all forms of sensual pleasure, even when such pleasure took place within marriage. St. Paul also believed that the most profound spiritual enlightenment could be achieved only through complete sexual abstinence. Consequently, celibacy became the prescribed practice for all clergy in the Roman Catholic church. St. Paul wrote that for those who were unable to maintain this highest state, it was better to marry than to risk the sin of nonmarital sexual expression. Interestingly, Jesus was almost completely silent on the subject of sex except for his admonitions against divorce.

The New Testament continued the Old Testament's tradition of male dominance and sexism: "Wives, submit yourselves unto your husbands, as is fit in the Lord" (Colossians 3:18). Women continued to be seen as a source of temptation and spiritual danger, and all religions following in the Judeo-Christian tradition have been male-dominated throughout history.

The position of the church on sexual matters continued to evolve under the influence of certain key figures. In particular, the writings of St. Augustine (354–430) had a great impact on the increasingly sex-negative position of the Roman Catholic church. Before converting to Christianity, St. Augustine led a sexually active life and even had a son outside of marriage. With his conversion, however, he opted for a life of celibacy and renounced all forms of physical and sexual pleasure. Indeed, so zealous was St. Augustine that he even expressed regret that human reproduction could not be achieved in a way that did not involve the degradation of sexual intercourse, and he deplored such sexual "vices" as masturbation and homosexuality. Due largely to his influence, Christianity in the Middle Ages developed into a religion of sexual asceticism.

Although the reformed churches of Luther and Calvin subscribed to the same basic tradition of sexual puritanism, they did not accept the Roman Catholic position on celibacy. Both men married; Martin Luther, who had been a monk, married a nun named Katharina von Bora in 1525. The Protestant commitment to religious freedom did not, however, involve a recognition of the sexual rights of individuals: sexual intercourse between married partners remained the only approved form of sexual conduct. Luther also placed great emphasis on the sanctity of the family, an institution that he cast in a strongly patriarchal framework. According to one author, "He saw the role of husband and father in terms of the role of monarch of the realm. He ascribed to it sovereign powers" (Gennep, 1977, p. 1333).

The overall effect of Western religious tradition has been to place large categories of sexual conduct under the rubric of sin (see the boxed extract). But it might be said that this set of sexual standards has been honored more in the breach than in the observance. Certainly, there is a personal cost for those many individuals who have tried but failed to live up to the sexual demands of their religious beliefs. We know that some of these demands — for instance, the ban on masturbation — have had little effect in deterring our actual behavior; masturbation is near universal for males and is also practiced by the majority of females. Instead of reducing the incidence of masturbatory behavior, the religious prohibition often seems to induce guilt and anxiety in a large number of people. Furthermore, religious values have been used by some to justify the oppression of sexual minorities and women. For example, the issue of contraception continues to be a major issue within the Roman Catholic church, as does the ordination of female clergy as well as the status of homosexuals.

In recent years, there have been some signs of change within the churches in response to public opinion favoring more tolerant sexual value systems. Certain groups, such as the Unitarians and the United Methodists, have publicly acknowledged their commitment to sex education for young people and have taken steps to institute large-scale programs of sex education across the country. Recognizing the importance of sexual adjustment within marriage, the clergy have also been taking a more active role in counseling adults with sexual problems. Changing sexual values have caused changes within the Roman Catholic church, as an increasing number of clergy in the United States have followed their consciences on such matters as homosexuality, divorce, and contraception. These are signs that the traditional response of the churches regarding sexual conduct may be giving way to a different stance.

Summary

Human sexuality can be viewed from many different perspectives. In this chapter we have considered culture, the life cycle, science, and religion as four major influences on our sexuality. However, there is much to be learned about the relatively new science of sexology; the ideas and beliefs of today may well give way to new and perhaps radically different views in the years to come.

1. Culture is a major factor in determining people's view of sexual "normality," as is evident from a cross-cultural examination of sexual customs.

2. In addition to differences among cultures, sexual practices vary widely within a culture. Tremendous changes have taken place in our own society over the past hundred years, as we have gradually emerged from the sexually repressive climate of the nineteenth century.

3. A life-cycle perspective focuses on the successive stages of human development and on the unique experiences of the individual along life's course. Each stage may require new sexual and emotional adjustments on the part of the individual, and our culture does not always prepare us adequately for those adjustments.

4. Sexology has made substantial advances over the past century. Among the early pioneers, Havelock Ellis and Freud were particularly influential; and more recently, Kinsey and the team of Masters and Johnson have had an enormous impact.

5. Surveys of sexual behavior have provided useful data, but they have suffered from various serious methodological problems.

6. The influence of religion has been considerable, reflecting in particular the traditional bias of our Judeo-Christian heritage against all types of nonprocreational sex, as well as against sex as a pleasurable activity. In recent years a more tolerant attitude has developed among some church groups regarding both of these traditional biases.

TWO

Sexual Development

Overview

In a well-known psychological method for starting group discussions, persons are asked to complete the sentence "I am _____" with words that describe themselves. What are the first words that come to your mind? Almost invariably, the list includes at least one gender-related term—"female," "male," "husband," "wife," "son," "daughter," or the like. The most enduring and consistent aspect of our personal identities is that of being male or female. We use this fundamental dichotomy to identify ourselves, our friends, and every individual we meet, hear, or read about.

In recent years, our society has seen the line between male and female blur at points. There are unisex clothes and unisex hairstyles; yet most of us would find it difficult to imagine life without any male/female distinctions. Think about the problems of conversing with someone whose sex you are unable to determine or whose sex has been altered by surgery. How would you announce the birth of a child whose sex is ambiguous? Can you picture yourself as a member of the opposite sex? These examples emphasize how much we rely on a male/female view of the world, and how we view this distinction as something that is permanent, unchangeable, and completely dichotomous. It is virtually impossible to imagine a real person who is neither male nor female.

We live in a world that separates men and women on many levels. In her book *Sexual Politics*, Kate Millet (1970) goes so far as to say that "male" and "female" are two completely different cultures, with men and women leading totally different lives. In response to the women's movement, however, traditional sex roles have been redefined to some extent; we now find women studying at West Point or working in steel mills, while men teach in nursery schools and take courses in needlepoint. Given this growing complexity and diversity of sex roles, it is almost surprising that the vast majority of us do develop an identity that is clearly male or female. We are not born with this knowledge, but we do learn, in stages, to locate ourselves in the maze of sexual styles and behaviors. While this process of defining our sex roles continues throughout the life cycle, the core of our gender identity — "I am female" or "I am male" — is usually firmly set very early in childhood.

In this chapter, our sexual beginnings as male and female are described. We consider the factors that affect sexual differentiation, from the moment of conception until the start of adulthood. We explore the relative contributions of nature and nurture — that is, biology and environment — to developing gender identity and sex roles. And we discuss the ways in which infants, children, and adolescents learn about and express their sexuality.

Defining the Terms

We are not always consistent and clear about what we mean by the terms "sex," "gender," "gender identity," "gender role," "masculinity," "femininity," and "sexual orientation." In this section we will provide some of the definitions offered by researchers concerned with sexual development and discuss some of the issues and concepts underlying these definitions.

SEX AND GENDER

Sex and gender are not the same thing, although their influences may be interactive. Robert Stoller (1968) defines *sex* as that which is biological, the clear anatomical and physiological differences between males and females; *gender*, on the other hand, is viewed as a psychological phenomenon and refers to behavior. John Money and Anke Ehrhardt (1972) distinguish two elements of gender: *imperative* and *optional*. The imperative elements correspond to what Stoller calls "sex" — those physi-

ical differences that are necessary if we are to carry out our reproductive functions. These differences are universal, not subject to environmental influences, and are firmly rooted in our biological unfolding as males and females. They include the female's ability to menstruate, gestate (carry a fetus until delivery), and lactate (provide milk for the baby), and the male's ability to impregnate.

All other differences between men and women are in some sense optional; that is, they are influenced, shaped, and encouraged by the culture in which we live, rather than dictated by our biological natures. These optionals include both gender identity and gender (or sex) roles. *Gender identity* is commonly defined as our private sense of being male or female (Money & Ehrhardt, 1972), whereas the way we express our private sense of identity is our *gender role*.

Sex is often seen as *dichotomous*, while gender is placed on a continuum. Simply stated this is because it is improbable to have the biological equipment of both a male and a female. In the vast majority of cases, our sexual architecture is either male or female and cannot be both. Gender, however, is a more flexible dimension. The shape of our genitals does not automatically lead us to act in "masculine" or "feminine" ways. Further, because gender roles are influenced to a great degree by cultural norms and standards, we find that individuals define masculine and feminine behaviors in many ways.

In most traditional Western societies, it has been considered masculine to be aggressive, independent, and logical, whereas femininity has been generally characterized by submissiveness, dependency, and emotionality. However, anthropology teaches us that expressions of masculinity and femininity vary considerably from one culture to another. Many cultures survive and reproduce with gender role stereotypes that are in direct opposition to our own. For instance, Margaret Mead (1939) has described vastly different patterns of temperament and gender role in three primitive societies of New Guinea. One tribe produced men and women who were emotional, gentle, and nurturant. In a neighboring tribe, the women were practical and aggressive, the men sensitive, submissive, and vain. The third tribe was characterized by extreme aggressiveness on the part of both men and women. Each of these tribes had its own arrangements for child rearing and care.

According to Mead, the creation of gender roles is but remotely connected to the biological differences between women and men. Clearly, only a male can impregnate and only a female can carry a child to delivery. However, it is quite a leap to assume that only a female can sew and only a male can repair automobiles. These elements of our gender role are exaggerated consequences of the physical differences between the sexes.

Thus while most cultures give the role of child caretaker to the female, it seems likely that under the pressure of necessity, most men could also fill this role. Similarly, while men are commonly assigned the role of breadwinner, most women can adequately fill this role and may consciously choose to do so rather than have children and take on the nurturant role. In this sense, the gender roles prescribed by our culture are optional. While the imperatives set the stage for reproduction, the optionals provide a social structure in which females and males cooperate to raise their children.

One final point is that gender and sex are not always bound together. For most of us, there is a good fit between the two. That is, we tend to act in ways that are expected of us on the basis of our sexual anatomy. Boys, having the physical characteristics of males, generally behave in ways their culture labels "masculine." Similarly, girls learn a "feminine" role that is prescribed for them because they have female sexual characteristics. However, there are exceptional individuals whose sexual physiology does not match their gender. The most striking example of this mismatch is the *transsexual*, whose physical characteristics are at odds with gender identity and gender role. For example, a male transsexual may have the normal male reproductive architecture but the personal preference and desire for living as a female.

MASCULINITY AND FEMININITY

In the past, masculinity and femininity were often conceptualized as opposite ends of a continuum. Thus as an individual became more masculine, he or she necessarily became less feminine. Within this framework, it was impossible to be *both* masculine and feminine. Many of the tests that measure this trait (for example, the masculinity/femininity scale of the Minnesota Multiphasic Personality Inven-

Louise Nevelson. *Atmosphere and Environment* 1 1966. As you can see by the caption, this piece of art was made by a woman. From the way that it looks, would you have guessed the artist to be a male or a female? Why? *(Collection, The Museum of Modern Art, New York, Mrs. Simon Guggenheim Fund)*

tory, the MMPI) use this single-dimension model. However, a single continuum, in which more of one trait equals less of another, does not always fit our experience of female and male behavior.

A more recent approach to evaluating masculinity and femininity, developed by Sandra Bem (1974), is the measurement of *androgyny*. According to Bem, conceptualizations of masculinity and femininity as bipolar ends of a single continuum have served to obscure the possibility that many individuals might be androgynous — that is, *both* masculine and feminine, depending on the particular situation — and that strongly sex-typed individuals might be seriously limited in the range of behaviors available to them. For instance, the male who attempts to live within a narrowly masculine self-concept may be restricted in his ability to express the human traits that are stereotyped as female (emotionality, dependency, nurturance, and so on). Similarly, the woman who has rigid beliefs about what it means to be a female may be unable to express the range of behaviors normally stereotyped as masculine

(assertiveness, logicality, independence). Bem suggests that an androgynous self-concept allows men and women to engage in cross-gender behaviors, thus enlarging their flexibility to respond in different ways as new situations arise.

The Bem Sex-Role Inventory was designed as a measure of androgyny (see Table 2.1). The items included in this instrument were selected by judges who rated them as strongly desirable for males (e.g., aggressive, ambitious, self-reliant, dominant), strongly desirable for females (e.g., affectionate, cheerful, compassionate, warm), or neutral in value (e.g., friendly, sincere, happy, likable). When the test is administered, subjects are asked to rate themselves on each of the items. Three scores may be derived, reflecting the extent to which subjects view themselves as masculine, feminine, or androgynous. The androgyny score is calculated from the ratio of masculine to feminine self-ratings. Thus an individual who rates himself or herself as equally masculine and feminine would be completely androgynous, that is, totally flexible in the demonstration of masculine and feminine attributes.

SEXUAL ORIENTATION

For most of us, part of the expression of our gender role includes erotic interest in members of the "opposite" sex. *Sexual orienta-* *tion,* which refers to our choice of erotic object, may be heterosexual, homosexual, or bisexual. In the past, these categories were viewed as completely distinct from one another. However, we now recognize that an individual's sexual orientation may change over the life span. Further, we recognize that sexual orientation is not necessarily an all-or-none phenomenon. Kinsey and his colleagues rated

TABLE 2.1
The Bem Sex-Role Inventory

Masculine items	Feminine items	Neutral items
Acts as a leader	Affectionate	Adaptable
Aggressive	Cheerful	Conceited
Ambitious	Childlike	Conscientious
Analytical	Compassionate	Conventional
Assertive	Does not use harsh language	Friendly
Athletic	Eager to soothe hurt feelings	Happy
Competitive	Feminine	Helpful
Defends own beliefs	Flatterable	Inefficient
Dominant	Gentle	Jealous
Forceful	Gullible	Likable
Has leadership abilities	Loves children	Moody
Independent	Loyal	Reliable
Individualistic	Sensitive to the needs of others	Secretive
Makes decisions easily	Shy	Sincere
Masculine	Soft spoken	Solemn
Self-reliant	Sympathetic	Tactful
Self-sufficient	Tender	Theatrical
Strong personality	Understanding	Truthful
Willing to take a stand	Warm	Unpredictable
Willing to take risks	Yielding	Unsystematic

Source: S. Bem, "The Measurement of Psychological Androgyny," *Journal of Consulting and Clinical Psychology,* Vol. 42, No. 2 (1974), p. 157.

Male and female subjects were given a list of traits and asked to rate them in terms of their desirability for a man or a woman in American society today. The items in column 1 are those characteristics generally deemed by men and women to be desirable for males, the items in column 2 the characteristics deemed to be desirable for females. The items in column 3 are characteristics deemed no more desirable for one sex than for the other. The items were then formed into a sex role inventory, that is, the subjects were asked to rate, on a 7-point scale, how well each item described themselves. The inventory yields three scores: masculinity, femininity, and androgyny. It should be noted that within this model, masculinity and femininity are not mutually exclusive dimensions. That is, more masculinity does not necessarily imply less femininity, and vice versa. An individual scores high on the androgyny scale if he or she reports an approximately equal number of masculine and feminine traits.

sexual orientation on a 7-point scale, indicating that it was a continuum rather than divisible into discrete categories (Kinsey, Pomeroy, and Martin, 1948).

According to some researchers (e.g., Money and Ehrhardt, 1972), the preference for a same-sex erotic partner is generally indicative of a gender identity that is partly masculine and partly feminine. The logic of this viewpoint might be as follows: "I am a male, but I am attracted to males rather than females, and this sexual orientation is not part of the male gender role." That is, the male's attraction to males may stem from a partly female gender identity.

A different view of homosexual sexual orientation is provided by the work of Evelyn Hooker, who conducted in-depth and extensive interviews with thirty male homosexuals. She defines the problem of the male homosexual in this way:

In our society, irrespective of the degree to which the male homosexual fulfills the male gender role expectations in all other respects, he fails, according to societal judgment, in at least one: he is inappropriately erotically focused on males, not females (Hooker, 1965, p. 35).

Among her sample, Hooker found several possible solutions to this problem. A few of her subjects accepted the notion that there are both masculine and feminine male homosexuals—that is, in regard to sexual orientation some male homosexuals act in ways that are comparable to heterosexual males whereas others play the role commonly assigned to heterosexual females. Thus, some of these men were stereotypically masculine in situations involving work, friendship, or recreation but saw themselves as feminine in a sexual situation. Another solution, adopted by only one man in her sample, is to characterize oneself as belonging to an intermediate, or "third," sex. A third solution, the one most commonly adopted by Hooker's subjects, is to define oneself as both masculine and homosexual. Such men see themselves as on the masculine end of a masculine/feminine continuum and do not view their preference for a same-sex partner as inconsistent with this judgment. Hooker concluded that psychological gender identity as perceived by her subjects seemed to bear little relation to sexual practice. (The nature of homosexual relationships is discussed more fully in Chapter 3.)

Sexual Differentiation: Becoming Male or Female

How do we become male or female? Because we classify people so automatically into female and male, we tend to take for granted the chain of events leading to the formation of gender identity, that is, our private sense of being male or female. In fact, explanations of this process are complex and controversial. Most researchers in this area accept an interactive model, in which biology sets certain broad limitations on our behavior and society can work either to emphasize or to deemphasize these limitations.

WHAT IS A MALE? WHAT IS A FEMALE?

These two questions are deceptively simple. For example, an individual is not a male simply because he has a penis; a man might lose his penis, through accident or surgery, and still be convinced of his maleness. Further, a transsexual with a normal penis might be convinced that his true gender identity is female. Similarly, the presence of female genitals does not always guarantee a female gender identity.

Actually, our maleness or femaleness is a product of many different aspects of our growth. *Sexual differentiation,* the process of becoming male or female, is accomplished in a series of stages. At each stage, we can develop in either a male or a female direction. The vast majority of us consistently follow one of these directions. However, there are some individuals whose development is inconsistent and takes turns in both male and female directions. By studying these individuals, we can gain insight into the factors that contribute to gender identity.

Richard Green (1974) has listed seven steps of development that establish adult gender identity as clearly female or male: genetic sex, gonadal sex, hormonal secretions, internal sex organs, external genitals, sex label given at birth, and gender identity formed within the first few years of life. The normal female will have an XX chromosome pattern, ovaries that secrete feminizing hormones, and the internal and external organs of a female. At birth she will be labeled as female, and she will soon develop a female gender identity. Similarly, a normal male will have an XY chromosome pattern, testes that secrete masculinizing hormones, and the internal and external sexual organs of a male. He will be labeled as male on his birth certificate and will develop a male gender identity.

At each of these stages, development could proceed in either a male or a female direction. When the program unfolds smoothly, there will be a steady progression toward an adult sexuality that is consistently male or consistently female in genital appearance, genital

(© Shelly Rusten 1980)

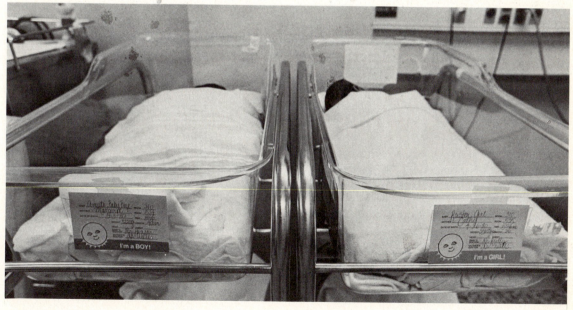

function, and gender identity. However, this program may be disrupted in any of several ways. For instance, a genetic defect may alter the biological components of development so that the child's reproductive system is ambiguous—neither completely male nor completely female. An expectant mother who is given hormones to maintain a precarious pregnancy may have a child whose external genitals are sexually ambiguous.

Even if the biological aspects of the program unfold smoothly, environmental factors, such as rearing conditions, may disrupt the formation of gender identity. Green (1974) has suggested that when parents are emotionally ambivalent about their child's sex, this confusion can lead to a gender identity problem. However, the adaptiveness of the human being is such that a clear gender identity can develop even when the program has been disrupted.

A well-known case study that illustrates the importance of rearing as a contributor to gender identity is presented by Money and Ehrhardt (1972). Normal male identical twins were born and initially reared as males by their parents. During circumcisions performed at seven months of age, the penis of one of the twins was completely destroyed through surgical accident, and there was no hope of reconstructing it. A consulting physician recommended that this twin be reared as a female and that surgery be used to reconstruct his genitals into those of a female. After almost a year of indecision, the parents consented to this procedure. The baby's birth certificate was changed, its clothing and hairstyle were altered, and surgical reconstruction began. In other words, this male baby was changed to a female. The parents learned to treat the child as a girl, and she began to act in feminine ways. After many years of follow-up, the child had developed a completely female

gender identity; she looked different from her twin brother and acted differently from him. At puberty, she did not develop male secondary sexual characteristics because her testes had been removed. Female secondary sexual characteristics, such as breast growth, were stimulated by the administration of feminizing hormones. Although she does not menstruate and will not be able to bear children, her physical appearance is that of a normal female.

This case illustrates the point that our gender identity is a function of more than being born with male or female genitals. Our sense of ourselves as male or female develops from many sources, with environmental factors playing a major role in the process. While individuals may have ambiguous sexual organs, they are almost never ambiguous about whether they think of themselves as male or female.

CHROMOSOMAL DIFFERENTIATION

Throughout history, men and women have wondered what determines a child's sex, and many theories have been proposed. For instance, at one time it was believed that semen from the right testicle would produce a male child, semen from the left a female. Another theory suggested that the direction the penis faced at the time of insemination was the critical factor: a right-facing penis produced males, a left-facing one females. Which ovary, right or left, released that particular month's egg has also been implicated in sex determination.

Modern research has provided us with a definitive answer about the beginnings of male and female development. Every cell in our bodies has 23 pairs of chromosomes, and each chromosome has hundreds of genes. Only one pair of chromosomes, the *sex chro-*

mosomes, are directly related to sexual development. The remaining 22 pairs are called *autosomes* and carry nonsexual messages. Each egg produced by a female has half this number — 22 single autosomes and a single sex chromosome, commonly labeled the X chromosome. Each sperm cell produced by a male contains 22 single autosomes and either an X or a Y sex chromosome. When X meets X, a female develops; when X meets Y, a male develops.

Scientists have developed several laboratory techniques enabling us to determine the type and number of sex chromosomes present in our body cells. For instance, the *Barr technique,* used in identifying genetic defects, is based on the fact that the cells of human females contain a tiny clump at the edge of the cell nucleus. This clump, called the Barr body, can be detected with chemical stains. Usually the number of Barr bodies is one less than the number of X chromosomes. Thus the normal female cell will have one Barr body and the normal male cell will have none. The cells of females who are born with more than two X chromosomes will have more than one Barr body. In addition to its use in identifying genetic defects, this technique has become popular as a means of verifying the sex of athletes in such sporting events as the Olympics.

On the basis of birth and miscarriage data it is estimated that there are about 140 XY conceptions for every 100 XX conceptions. However, more of the XY conceptions fail to develop, so at birth the ratio is about 105 males to every 100 females. This ratio helps to counterbalance the fact that male infants have a higher mortality rate than female infants.

There are several exceptions to the standard XX or XY pattern, which usually involve either the loss or addition of a chromosome. For example, in *Turner's syndrome* only one X chromosome is present, making the genetic pattern XO. The resulting infant will have a female body type but will be sterile. She will generally have external genitals that appear female but will have no ovaries. At puberty she must take supplemental hormones if female secondary sexual characteristics are to develop. No parallel condition (that is, a YO pattern) exists for the male. Apparently the embryo cannot survive without at least one X chromosome.

The presence of an additional chromosome to form an XXY pattern is seen in individuals with *Klinefelter's syndrome.* Children with this syndrome develop a male body type but generally have small external genitals and are sterile. They are vulnerable to a number of psychological disorders, particularly mental retardation. Another pattern is the XYY, or "supermale." These men are usually taller than average but look like normal males. This genetic irregularity has been associated with behavioral problems such as excessive impulsiveness and aggressiveness. At present it is unclear why this relationship exists, and not all men with the XYY pattern are subject to behavioral problems (Hook, 1973).

Another chromosomal abnormality is that of females who develop an XXX pattern, resulting in a normal female appearance but diminished fertility. Finally, a rare exception to the normal pattern of sex chromosome distribution is *mosaicism,* in which different cells of the body have different sex chromosome patterns.

In each of these examples it may be noted that *if a Y chromosome is present, a male will develop,* even in the presence of two Xs. *If no Y chromosome is present, the embryo will develop as female,* regardless of whether there are one, two, three, or more Xs.

The sex chromosome pattern influences the development of the reproductive organs in the sense that it determines whether the *gonads*, or sex glands, will differentiate as ovaries or as testes. However, it also influences other nonsexual aspects of development. The female X chromosome is considerably larger than the male Y chromosome and carries many genes in addition to those responsible for sexual differentiation. Some of the genes on the X chromosome provide the female with greater protection from a variety of noninfectious disorders: for example, color blindness, such blood-clotting disorders as hemophilia, and vitamin D–resistant rickets (Hamburg and Lunde, 1966). Also, females seem to be more resistant to infectious diseases and to the effects of physical deprivation, whereas males tend to have higher mortality rates at all stages of life. These differences in health may be related to the disparity in size between the X and Y chromosomes. Although normal females have a double dose of the larger X chromosome, normal males have only one X chromosome paired with the smaller Y chromosome. If one of the female's X chromosomes is defective in some way, the second X may compensate for or mask this defect. However, if the male's single X chromosome is deficient, the smaller Y cannot protect him against potential defects.

DIFFERENTIATION OF SEXUAL ORGANS

The Bible tells us that Eve was created from Adam's rib. When Adam was presented with his mate, he said:

Now this, at last—bones from my bones, flesh from my flesh! This shall be called woman, for from man was this taken. (Genesis 2:23)

From this statement came the conventional wisdom of the ages: man is the primary and natural sex, woman a derivation or alteration of this basic unit. Contemporary research does not support this view. In fact, if such a thing as the "primary" sex exists, research tells us that it is the female. This will become clear as we describe the process by which the sexual organs differentiate and develop.

At conception, the primitive structures that will develop into the sexual organ systems have *bipotentiality*, that is, they have the potential to become either male or female. Although the chromosomes make a fixed contribution to development in either the male or female direction, the rudiments of male and female internal sexual organs exist in both sexes. Furthermore, the external genitals develop from a common structural base.

For the first 6 weeks of life, male and female embryos appear identical and proceed along a common path. The original XX or XY cell multiplies millions of times, with each new cell carrying the same genetic messages. The embryo forms growth buds that have the potential to develop in either the male or female direction. Each embryo has an undifferentiated pair of gonads that will become either ovaries or testes. There are also two sets of internal sexual structures that can develop into either male or female internal organs (see Figure 2.1). One set, the *Wolffian ducts*—named after Kaspar Wolff, the anatomist who identified them—has the potential to become the male internal organs. The other set, the *Mullerian ducts*—named after Johannes Müller—can develop into the female reproductive organs. Finally, there is a common *genital tubercle*, a small swelling of external tissue that may become either a clitoris or a penis.

About 6 weeks after conception, the male and female embryos begin to take separate paths in their development. From this point on, maleness will develop only if something is added to the embryo. This crucial ingredient is the *androgens*, or masculinizing hormones.

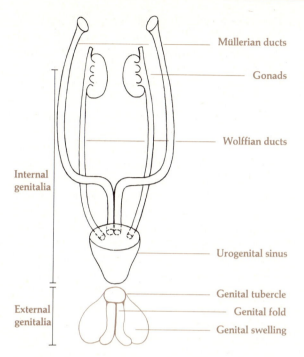

tion of androgens and will therefore have a masculinizing effect.

The testes also secrete a substance known as the *Mullerian inhibitor*. All that we know about this substance is that it inhibits the development of the Mullerian ducts. Under its influence, the Mullerian ducts begin to disintegrate, although their remnants remain, even in the adult male. At the same time, the hormone mixture secreted by the testes causes the Wolffian ducts to develop as the male internal sexual system (see Figure 2.2). It is interesting to note that the level of androgens circulating in the bloodstream of the 10-week-old male embryo is comparable to levels found in adult males. These high androgen levels begin to fall

FIGURE 2.2
Pathways for differentiation of the male genital system. *(Goldstein, 1976, p. 68)*

FIGURE 2.1
Schematic representation of the undifferentiated genital system. Differentiation of the Müllerian and Wolffian ducts typically begins about 7 weeks after conception and continues until about the 12th week, by which time, the external genitalia have taken form.

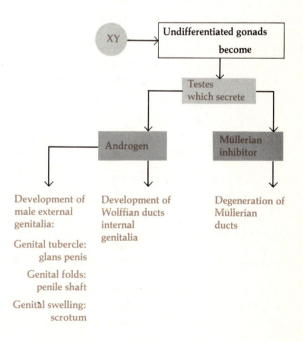

The Y chromosome in the male embryo sends a message to the as yet undifferentiated gonads. While we do not know precisely how this message is transmitted, we do know that it causes the gonads to develop as male testes and begin to secrete a mixture of hormones. Both male and female hormones are present, but the hormone mixture has a greater propor-

at about 20 weeks, and such levels will next be found only after the boy reaches puberty.

In the absence of a Y chromosome, the embryo takes a female path of development. It continues in an undifferentiated state until about 12 weeks, when the gonads begin to develop into ovaries (see Figure 2.3). The ovaries do not secrete a female hormone mixture until puberty, but they do develop a supply of immature egg cells that are more than sufficient to last a lifetime.

Ovarian production of female hormones, the *estrogens*, does not appear to be necessary for development to proceed in the female direction. Female differentiation occurs in the *absence* of male hormones. Thus the natural baseline of sexual tissues in the embryo is female. Unless male hormones are added, pushing the embryo toward male development, it will continue along the female path. In the absence of male hormones, the Wolffian system will atrophy and disappear.

The final stage of sexual differentiation is the molding of male or female external genitals. We have already noted that both sets of structures develop from a common base. Before differentiation begins, the embryo has a genital tubercle, a pair of genital folds, and a genital swelling (see Figure 2.1). If no male hormones are added, the external genitals take on a female appearance. The genital tubercle shrinks and becomes the *clitoris*, or female erectile organ. The genital folds become the *labia minora*, or "inner lips," and the clitoral hood. The genital swelling turns into the *labia majora*, or "outer lips," and the single opening is divided in two, separating the vaginal entrance from the urethral entrance.

When male hormones are present, the primitive genital structures are diverted from this female path and develop in the male direction. The genital tubercle grows to become the *penis*, or male erectile organ. The two folds of skin fuse around the penis, and the two swellings also fuse together to form the *scrotal sac*, a pouch behind the penis. When the fetus is about 7 months old, the *testes* will usually descend into this sac. The single opening, which is now enclosed in the penis, will become the *urethral tube*. It is connected with both the bladder and the internal sexual organs.

FIGURE 2.3
Pathways for differentiation of the female genital system. *(Goldstein, 1976, p. 69)*

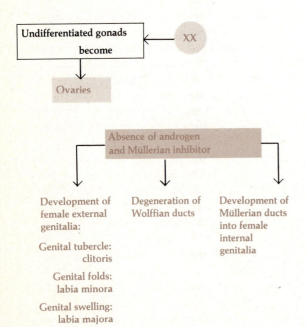

PRENATAL DISORDERS

At birth, an infant is identified as a boy or a girl by the shape of the external genitals. Usually this judgment will be correct; however, a small number of children are born as *hermaphrodites*. (The word "hermaphrodite" comes from the names of the Greek gods Hermes and Aphrodite, whose mating was believed to have resulted in a two-sexed child.) While it is impossible to be both completely male and completely female, the development of some individuals is ambiguous, having elements of both the male and the female reproductive systems. In these cases, the entry of a child's sex on its birth certificate may be largely a matter of the attending physician's judgment.

In general, it seems that the male path of development is more vulnerable to some form of disruption. While female differentiation is almost automatic in the absence of androgens, male differentiation can proceed only if the push toward femaleness is suppressed. For instance, if the Mullerian inhibitor is missing, a genetic male's Mullerian ducts may develop into a uterus and uterine tubes. In addition, he will have a complete set of internal male organs.

Another possibility is that a genetic male may secrete adequate amounts of the correct male hormone mixture but his tissues may be unable to use these hormones. This is called the *androgen insensitivity syndrome*. The genetic male with this condition appears to be a normal female at birth. The external genitals develop as if there were no androgens present, forming a clitoris, labia minora, and labia majora. However, the tissues have responded to the Mullerian inhibiting substance secreted by the undescended testes, so that there are no internal female organs. At birth, the fully functioning testes do not descend, and the child is labeled a female. In fact, the condition may not be discovered until puberty. At that time, the absence of menstruation will generally lead to a physical examination in which the undescended testes are discovered. Generally, the child with androgen insensitivity can lead a normal life as a woman, although she will never menstruate or bear children.

What happens if large amounts of androgens are present in the body of a genetic female? In this condition, the *adrenogenital syndrome,* the source of excess androgen is the adrenal cortex, a hormone-producing gland located just above the kidney. The adrenal cortex is supposed to secrete a hormone called cortisol. When it does not function correctly, it secretes a defective form of cortisol that acts like an androgen in the body. Another source of excess androgen in the female may be contributed by the mother. In past years many women were given synthetic hormones to minimize the possibility of miscarriage. These hormones tend to have a masculinizing effect on the fetus.

In both these conditions, the effect of the excess male hormones is to masculinize the genetic female. The extent of the masculinization depends on the amount of androgen present and the stage of fetal development at which it occurred. Usually, the internal organs will remain female but the external genitalia take on a masculine appearance. In some cases, there is a fully developed penis and scrotal sac, although no testes exist. In other cases, there may be an enlarged clitoris. Finally, some infants are born with external genitals that are so ambiguous that sex assignment becomes a question of judgment rather than of physical appearance. Surgery can generally be used to construct more normal appearing female genitals but is unsuccessful at constructing a larger penis. Hormonal supplements are often necessary at puberty to ensure that sexual development proceeds in a clear direction. Children with adrenogenital syndrome have been successfully raised as either males or females, the most important factor being that they are consistently treated as a member of the selected gender.

Thus it is clear that *anatomy is not necessarily destiny.* While chromosomes, hormones, and gonads all contribute to our development as male or female, none of them is sufficient to explain this development completely.

PRENATAL HORMONES AND THE BRAIN

In nineteenth-century America, in general, young women were thought too frail to withstand the strain of college life; that they had neither the physical strength nor the intellectual capacity for the discipline of study. Young men's minds, on the other hand, were considered ripe for rigorous training in reason and logic. The assumption underlying this view is that basic differences are manifested not only in the bodily structures of men and women but in their nervous systems (including the brain) as well. The notion that male and female brains are different in structure and function is called *brain dimorphism* and is highly controversial.

One area in which the brain is clearly dimorphic is in the pattern of hormone release after puberty. Female physiology is *cyclic* — that is, the types and proportions of hormones circulating in the female's body vary in a regular monthly, or menstrual, cycle. In contrast, male physiology is considered to be *acyclic*; although male hormones do appear to rise and fall at certain intervals, there is no clear monthly pattern. The presence or absence of cyclicity is determined by the hypothalamus, which regulates the release of gonadotropic hormones (hormones that regulate the activity of the ovaries or testes) from the pituitary gland. (The role of hormones in sexual and reproductive behavior is discussed in detail in Chapter 6.)

In this respect, there are indeed differences between the male and female brain. However, some researchers have suggested that brain dimorphism goes far beyond this basic effect on adult hormone levels. For instance, Milton Diamond (1976) believes that separate brain circuits in males and females are responsible for sex differences in our behavior. According to Diamond, the display of "masculine" or "feminine" behaviors may be influenced by the environment in some ways but is largely the result of biological or neural programs established in the brain before birth. Researchers have also suggested that prenatal hormones are responsible for male/female differences in sexual behavior, personality, and even intelligence. However, much of the research that supports these notions has been performed on animals, and its application to humans is certainly open to question. With animals, it is possible to experiment by removing or adding specific hormones and then observing subsequent effects on behavior. It is obviously impossible to perform such research with humans; experimenters can study only the behavioral outcomes of abnormal hormone levels in the developing fetus. But again, it is very questionable how much we can extrapolate from research with abnormal subjects to explain the normal course of development.

Research on brain dimorphism in shaping personality or intelligence is particularly controversial and complex. We know, for instance, that when female monkeys are exposed to prenatal androgens, they tend to show more "masculine" patterns of play activity than do untreated females. In human females, this type of behavior is usually labeled tomboyism — that is, play patterns characterized by traditionally male interest in rough outdoor play and high levels of physical energy. Indeed, some evidence suggests that when human females are prenatally exposed to masculinizing hormones, they show more tomboy behavior than a control group of normal girls (Money and Ehrhardt, 1972). However, we also know that many females without prenatal androgen exposure also behave like tomboys; in fact, the very notion that children's play activity can be

(© *Lawrence Frank 1978*)

categorized as male or female is open to some criticism as we reevaluate our sex role stereotypes. The findings of research on sex differences in intelligence are even less clear. To date, there is no conclusive evidence that prenatal hormone exposure can alter intelligence levels (Reinisch, 1976). Finally, we should keep in mind that even if abnormal prenatal hormone levels are related to certain male/female differences in behavior or personality, this would tell us little about the sex differences we might find in normal boys and girls.

Psychosexual Development

In a sense, sexual development begins when sperm meets egg and the chromosomal blueprint of XX or XY establishes a biological predisposition for maleness or femaleness. In addition, the intrauterine environment, and especially prenatal hormones, contribute to subsequent development. At the moment of birth there are already present in the human baby what can best be described as "potentials" or "tendencies" or "predispositions" for development. However, if we think of a baby as a lump of dough with the potential to become bread, the influence of the environment in kneading, molding, and baking the unformed dough will ultimately determine its shape, texture, and taste. To carry this simple analogy one step further, there are certainly limits to what the baker can produce once the dough has been mixed—we cannot get rye bread from white flour, and similarly, the environment is limited to the extent in which it can shape our sexuality; the "mixing of the dough" from conception to birth clearly places certain constraints on subsequent development. For example, a biological male will never be able to experience lactation and breast feeding, no matter what environmental pressure may be brought to bear on him.

The scientific term *interactionism* is often used to describe this general approach to development. One researcher describes interactionism as "a point of view that sees all development as a product of *both* individual predispositions *and* forces in the environment. All growth results from a rich and perpetual interplay between these two necessary and equally potent forces" (Gardner, 1978, p. 253). There is surely no area of human development to which this approach is more applicable than the development of sexuality. The dough from which we are formed and the way in which we are baked interact continuously throughout the life cycle in determining who and what we are as sexual beings.

With this important concept in mind, we will now consider the specific events and stages in sexual development from birth through childhood, puberty, and adolescence, and into adult sexuality. Like the course of true love, which seldom runs smooth, the course of sexual development is characterized by several important transitions and stages and by numerous "bumps in the road" from infancy to old age. Yet it can be viewed as a *continuous* process, in the sense that important sexual events and experiences take place from the moment of birth (and perhaps before) and

continue throughout the life cycle. For this understanding we are greatly indebted to the work of Sigmund Freud, who debunked the popular nineteenth-century Victorian myth of the sexual "innocence" of children. Prior to the acceptance of Freud's ideas about the sexual development of children, it was widely believed by both experts and the public that sexuality first manifested itself during adolescence, and that children could be effectively reared as asexual innocents until that time. Although serious disagreement still exists today about the specific events and psychological significance of childhood sexuality, the general notion of *continuity* of sexual development has been widely accepted.

Before proceeding with our description of psychosexual development, some further words of caution and clarification are called for. First, generalizations about human behavior suffer from the serious flaw that they tend to obscure all-important *individual differences.* When we consider, for example, the differences in sexual development between little boys and little girls, we risk losing sight of the enormous variations that are found within each gender. Another, related problem is the determination of norms for sexual development; at this time we have no absolute standards for judging normality, and the word "normal" is used in a statistical sense, if at all. Further, as the work of Mead (1939) and other anthropologists has shown, the process of "normal" sexual development varies greatly from one culture to another. Finally, the sexual development of children is always studied and recorded by adults, who naturally assign adult meanings and values to sexual acts.

FROM BIRTH TO PRESCHOOL

At birth the human infant is a tiny, vulnerable, and totally dependent organism. Cutting the umbilical cord is only the first small step

For the infant, the first emotional bond is that of attachment toward the mother. *(Edith and Issac, Newtown, Pennsylvania 1974. Photo by Emmet Gowin, Courtesy Light Gallery, New York)*

on the path toward an independent existence, and for the first few months the newborn baby may still take his or her nourishment directly from the mother's breast. There is a second and perhaps equally important basic need the newborn infant has in the first months of life, and that is the need to be touched and held (Montagu, 1979). Because it is the natural mother, in almost all instances, who meets these vital needs, it follows that the first and strongest bond of attachment is to the mother.

At the time of birth, the nervous system of the infant is only partially developed. In fact, the only coordinated responses that all babies are capable of are the sucking and swallowing reflexes, perhaps because the sensory nerves in the lips, tongue, and mouth are much more highly developed than in any other part of the body (Gadpaille, 1975). As the mouth of the infant seems to play such a major role in the first 12 or 18 months of development, this period is often referred to as the *oral stage*.

With respect to male/female differences, we have already noted that males have a higher mortality rate than females at birth. Girls also show less variability on a variety of physical dimensions. In other words, they are less likely to fall at the extremes on such measures as height, weight, and intelligence. Female development is more stable over time, so that it is easier to predict the adult female's height on the basis of measurements taken during childhood than to make comparable predictions for the male.

Male and female infants show a variety of behavioral differences in the first few years of life. For example, one researcher (Korner, 1969) examined the behavior of thirty-two male and female infants 2 to 3 days after birth. She found that the girls were more likely to show reflexive smiling and also engaged in more rhythmical mouthing, whereas the boys showed more startle responses. Howard Moss (1974) studied the behavior of infants at 3 weeks and 3 months of age. He found that males were more likely to show irritable behavior, were fussier, and were more difficult to calm. Males seemed to function at a less organized and efficient level, and appeared to be less responsive to social stimuli and learning contingencies. Mothers were more likely to interact with their male infants, perhaps in an attempt to monitor and calm their irritable behaviors. However, mothers were more likely to reinforce vocalizations in their infant daughters. Moss suggests that the greater irritability of males may reflect their greater vulnerability to environmental stress. Females appear to be better physically equipped to withstand adverse conditions, and they mature at more rapid rates.

Some investigators (e.g., Kagan, 1975) have reported a slight tendency for infant females to display fear and anxiety more frequently and more intensely than infant males. Kagan (1971) found that the female infant under 6 months of age is more likely than the male to cry in a strange setting. Further, females under one year of age are more likely than males of similar age to inhibit motoric responses in a laboratory setting, preferring to stay close to their mothers. Male infants maintained less contact with their mothers and were more likely to move toward a toy.

Kagan (1975; 1976) suggests that these early sex differences may have some biological basis. The female infant seems to be more physically mature at birth. For instance, the central nervous system, bones, and muscles of the newborn female are generally more ad-

vanced than those of the newborn male. Female developmental precociousness may also include the brain and cognitive functioning, which may explain why female infants generally learn to speak earlier than male infants, and why their mothers are more likely to attend to and reinforce their early attempts at vocalization. Female precocity might also explain early differences in susceptibility to fear. If the female shows advanced cognitive development, she is likely to be more aware of the elements in her familiar home environment than the male infant. Thus she will be more alert to a change in environment, such as a trip to the laboratory, and is more likely to respond to that change, perhaps by showing fear.

In a thorough review of the available research on sex differences, Eleanor Maccoby and Carol Jacklin (1974) conclude that only four types of male/female differences have been fairly well established: girls have greater verbal ability; boys excel in visual-spatial and mathematical ability and are more aggressive. Maccoby and Jacklin believe that there is little, or at best ambiguous, evidence supporting sex differences in fear, anxiety, activity level, competitiveness, dominance, compliance, nurturance, or tactile sensitivity. They suggest that whereas biological factors may be implicated in sex differences in aggression, sex differences in other areas of behavior seem to be more influenced by social pressure. Parents do tend to treat their male and female offspring in different ways — for instance, boys are handled and played with more roughly and are more likely to receive physical punishment. However, Maccoby and Jacklin also note a surprising degree of similarity in the rearing of boys and girls.

While a biological basis for some sex differences may exist, we are still left with the question of how society should treat these differences. Rearing and socialization processes in most cultures tend to emphasize and exaggerate the extent to which the sexes differ in, say, aggressiveness. Maccoby and Jacklin suggest that another option is for society to minimize sex differences, for example, by moderating male aggression rather than preparing women to submit to male aggression and by encouraging rather than discouraging nurturant behavior in males. Even where biology does provide different input toward male/female behavior, its influence is by no means inevitable.

Genital responses in infancy. It may come as a surprise to many to learn that male infants can be observed to have erections from the time of birth on. Moreover, it appears that stimulation of the penis has a special effect on the baby boy.

It can easily be observed that, however young, stimulation of a baby's penis results in erection and a sense of pleasure. It might be thought that the erection is simply a poorly developed spinal reflex and conveys no special sensation to the infant, but common experience teaches better. In many cultures, including our own, fussy infants may be quieted by genital stroking and tickling. In his earliest weeks, the infant boy probably cannot localize the sensation that pleases him, but the pleasure and the relaxing effect are evident. (Gadpaille, 1975, p. 49)

In addition to direct tactile stimulation, erections can be caused by almost any intense emotion in the infant boy. Sleep research has also shown that erections occur regularly during the sleep cycle, just as they do in adult males. Although female infants obviously lack the external manifestations of genital arousal, they do begin to touch and explore their genitals as soon as they have the necessary coordination.

Even more surprising than the occurrence of genital responses is the evidence of orgasm in both male and female infants. The Kinsey study reported observations of orgasm in boys

as early as 5 months, and in the case of one baby girl, as early as 4 months (Kinsey, Pomeroy, and Martin, 1948). Infant orgasms seem to have many of the same characteristics as their adult counterparts, including rapid pelvic thrusting, erection (in the male), and a build-up of body tension to the point of climax, followed by a period of calm and relaxation.

Although infants do appear to have the physiological capacity for erection and orgasm, we should emphasize again the point made by Gagnon (1977), that such behavior should not be equated with its adult counterpart. Sexual responses in infants demonstrate the very early development of the reflex pathways that mediate sexual arousal and orgasm, but until the higher brain centers that control thoughts and perceptions have also developed, we cannot compare in the subjective experiences or feelings associated with the behavior.

Masturbation by infants leads to a variety of responses in parents. At one extreme are parents who are shocked or dismayed to see overt sexual behavior in their baby and are likely to remove the child's hand or distract the child every time it occurs. At the other extreme are parents who have learned—as more and more parents are learning—that infant masturbation is a normal and healthy part of development, and are prepared to accept it without interference. In between are those parents who have intellectually accepted the infant's masturbation but whose feelings of disapproval are nevertheless communicated to the child (Gadpaille, 1975).

Personality development in the infant. Erik Erikson, a renowned expert on child development, believes that the quality of the relationship between infant and mother makes a permanent impression on subsequent personality development. Specifically, Erikson (1963) pro-

The Effects of Early Social Deprivation on Psychosexual Development:

Harry Harlow, a highly respected psychologist at the University of Wisconsin, began a series of experiments in the 1950s to determine the role of early social experience on emotional and sexual development. These studies are regarded today as classics in the field of developmental psychology and are still referred to by most experts in the field. Although Harlow chose rhesus monkeys as the subjects for his studies, the findings and conclusions of his research have been very influential in explaining important aspects of human development.

As an *experimental psychologist,* Harlow was openly critical of the Freudian approach, which relied exclusively on the retrospective reports of adults concerning the importance of childhood events. He was determined to study the problem directly through the use of controlled experiments in which subjects could be systematically deprived of certain early experiences to determine the effects on subsequent development. For ethical reasons Harlow was unable to conduct these experiments on human infants, so he chose an animal species closely related to *Homo sapiens*—the rhesus monkey.

In the first series of experiments (Harlow, 1959), infant monkeys were separated from their mothers a few hours after birth. Because infant monkeys are able to nurse from bottles immediately after birth, their physical survival was not at risk. Harlow was interested in studying what qualities of the mother would be missed most by the maternally deprived infants. He therefore constructed a number of different "surrogate mothers" out of materials such as wire and cloth, and observed the effects of these models on the behavior of the infant monkeys. Even though they received equal quantities of milk from both models, the monkeys greatly preferred the cloth-covered surrogates and spent a

posed that a basic sense of trust and self-acceptance is the first important psychological goal, but that mistrust and self-doubt are all too often the consequences of this stage of development. The total dependency of the infant on the caretaking of the mother makes him or her vulnerable both physically and emotionally. According to Erikson, those infants who are unable to master their feelings of mistrust go on to develop very serious emotional disorders as adults.

Whether or not we accept Erikson's proposition at face value, evidence from various sources suggests that the effects of *maternal deprivation* during infancy can be serious and long-lasting (Bowlby, 1969; see the boxed extract). Infants reared in institutions, for example, who have brief and sporadic contact with a variety of adult caretakers, may develop serious interpersonal difficulties including an inability to develop meaningful relationships as adults. Attachment to the mother seems to reach a peak at about 12 months, after which it remains strong during the second year and begins to diminish when the child is about 3 years old. The weakening of maternal attachment in the latter part of infancy allows the child the opportunity to explore the environment and seek out new relationships—the second essential stage of development.

great deal of time clinging to them. According to Harlow (1959), the results demonstrated the importance of bodily contact — both the immediate comfort it supplies and its role in forming the infant's attachment for the mother.

Subsequent studies (Harlow and Harlow, 1962) compared the relative effects of maternal deprivation with the effects of depriving the monkeys of contact with other infants. In an elaborate series of experiments, the Harlows raised one group of monkeys in total isolation, another group with maternal contact but no peer play, and a third group with peer contact but no mothers or only mother surrogates. The period of deprivation ranged from a few months to several years. As one would expect, the effects of total isolation were the most drastic; the monkeys raised in this condition were incapable of any social, sexual, or defensive behavior in later life. However, a somewhat surprising finding was that maternal deprivation was less damaging to subsequent social and sexual behavior than deprivation of peer contact; play with

peers was apparently even more necessary than mothering for the development of effective social relations. Concerning the duration of deprivation, the Harlows found that somewhere between 3 and 6 months of deprivation caused irreversible damage. The monkeys appeared able to recover if the deprivation period was terminated in less than 3 months.

What implications for human development can be drawn from these studies? If we assume that human infants have the same or similar basic emotional needs to those of the rhesus monkeys, then the Harlow studies can be taken as strong scientific evidence of the crippling effects of early social deprivation. More specifically, these studies point to the great significance of physical contact in the development of the mother-infant attachment bond, and the necessity of play with other infants in the development of the capacity for adult sexual relationships.

Toddlers and Preschoolers
I watch my daughter. From morning to night her body is her home. She lives in it and with it. When she runs around the kitchen she uses all of herself. Every muscle in her body moves when she laughs, when she cries. When she rubs her vulva, there is no awkwardness, no feeling that what she is doing is wrong. She feels pleasure and expresses it without hesitation. She knows when she wants to be touched and when she wants to be left alone. She doesn't have to think about it — it's a very direct physical asking or responding to someone else. It's beautiful to be with her. I sometimes

feel she is more a model for me than I am for her! Occasionally I feel jealous of the ease with which she lives inside her skin. I want to be a child again! It's so hard to get back that sense of body as home. (Quoted in Boston Women's Health Collective, *1976, p. 40)*

The remarkable physical growth and maturation of the nervous system during the second year of life produces two of the major milestones of early development — walking and talking. Healthy toddlers tend to be intensely curious, with enormous energy for independent exploration of the surrounding environment. We usually date toddlerhood from about 18 months, at which time most infants are able to walk independently, if rather unsteadily. The increasing maturation of the nervous system has another important effect — the ability to learn voluntary control of elimination — and the process of *toilet training* typically begins about this time.

Freud was so impressed with the influence of toilet training on subsequent personality development that he referred to this period as the *anal stage*. Children who experience overly strict or demanding toilet training, according to Freud, are predisposed to develop "anal" personalities in later life, meaning a tendency to be compulsive about cleanliness and neatness. Such a person may also associate the "dirtiness' of the anus or urethra with the adjacent genitals, and develop chronic sexual inhibitions. These Freudian speculations have made a considerable impact on psychoanalytic theories of development, but they are generally unsubstantiated by scientific research.

In a classic study of the methods and consequences of toilet training (Sears, Maccoby, and Levin, 1965), a wide age range was found — from about 6 months to over 3 years — at which children successfully acquired bowel control. In general, however, the later training was begun, the easier it appeared for the child to learn control. The researchers also discovered a wide variety of training methods used, ranging from very permissive to very strict and punitive. It seemed that although strict training procedures were no more effective in accomplishing the task, they tended to produce a somewhat greater degree of emotional upset in the children. The degree of emotional disturbance produced by strict toilet training also varied according to how warm or cold the mother's interactions were in other respects. In other words, a warm mother could use relatively strict toilet training methods without producing much distress. This suggests an im-

portant qualification of the Freudian hypothesis — that it is not toilet training in and of itself that affects personality, but rather how the toilet training fits in with the overall parent-child relationship. Toilet training practices also vary widely from one culture to another.

The discipline of toilet training is only one of several important areas in which the child's socialization takes place. Parents are called upon with increasing frequency to restrain or limit the toddler's activities, both for the child's own protection and for the well-being of the family as a whole. In their attempts to promote socially acceptable behavior, many parents place increasing restrictions on masturbation, nudity, and other expressions of the toddler's natural curiosity in the body and bodily functions. Parents also begin to pay increasing attention to the sex role behavior of the child, communicating such messages as "Dolls are for girls, and guns are for boys."

Another natural consequence of the inquisitive explorations of the toddler is the observation of parents in the act of sexual intercourse. This experience of "the primal scene," as psychoanalysts call it, was once thought to be a traumatic experience for a young child. Although no scientific evidence exists on the subject, experts nowadays believe that it is unlikely that the child suffers any direct harm from the experience itself, unless the parents make the experience traumatic through their reactions.

Copulatory privacy is so embedded in our society's sexual taboo that the idea of learning about sexual intercourse by seeing it in real life shocks most people. The fact is, however, that millions of the world's children grow up to be quite normal sexually in families whose members all sleep together in the same living space, with sexual intercourse an open secret if it is a secret at all. Sexual intercourse can safely be explained to our children as a game grown-ups play. (Money and Tucker, 1975, pp. 134–135)

In societies where it is permitted, children of both sexes express a natural curiosity toward each other's bodies. *(Susan Shapiro)*

The toddler's natural interest in the human body typically leads him or her to early *sex play* with other children. This usually begins sometime during the third year, depending upon the opportunity to interact with other children and the level of developmental maturity of the child. We learn from cross-cultural studies that sex play, which usually involves looking and touching and sometimes mutual masturbation, is extremely common in all societies that do not place strong restrictions on such behavior. Clelland Ford and Frank Beach (1951) found such sex play so common both among human children and among the young of other primates such as monkeys and apes that they were led to conclude that the underlying drive toward such play is a hereditary feature of the species.

Ford and Beach also found that acceptance of sex play varies greatly from one society to another, and that cultures that are more tolerant in this respect are also more likely to allow children to observe adult sexual behavior and to give young children frank and honest information about sexual matters. Children in these societies generally grow up with fewer sexual inhibitions and problems than children who are deprived of such early sexual learning.

Another important aspect of sexual development at this age is the acquisition of *sexual labels*, or words to describe genital anatomy and the reproductive process. Here again, we find that many parents become uncomfortable when asked such questions as "Where do babies come from?" or "Where did mommy's penis go to?" One study (Sears, Maccoby, and Levin, 1957) found that two of the most common responses of American mothers were mislabeling and nonlabeling—both of which can lead to erroneous or magical ideas in the mind of the child. These distortions are likely to create conflicts and anxieties for children when they are subsequently presented with more accurate information.

According to Dr. Benjamin Spock (1976), one of our society's most respected authorities on child care, these questions are first likely to be asked when the child is between 2½ and 3½ years of age. He offers the following advice to concerned parents:

Don't think of it as an unwholesome interest in sex. To them (children) it's just like any other important question at first. You can see why it would work the wrong way to shush them, or scold them, or blush and refuse to answer. That would give them the idea they are on dangerous ground, which is what you want to avoid. On the other hand, you don't need to be solemn as if you were giving a lecture. . . . To the question of how babies get out, a good answer is something to the effect that when they are big enough they come out through a special opening that's just for that purpose. It's just as well to make it clear that it is not the opening for bowel movements or for urine. (Spock, 1976, pp. 409, 415)

Sexual interest and curiosity seem to reach a peak when the child is about 4 or 5 years old. For this reason, Freud referred to this period as the *phallic stage*. He used the term "phallic" in describing this stage for both girls and boys, as he believed that the little girl who discovers that boys have something she does not will invariably develop "penis envy" at this time. The notion of penis envy has not been widely accepted outside of traditional psychoanalysis and is often seen nowadays as an erroneous basis for justifying male superiority.

This peak of childhood sexuality could be due, in part, to the development at about this time of the child's capacity to perceive sexual odors (Gadpaille, 1975). Other factors, such as

increasing experience with masturbation and sex play with other children, are also probably of some significance. Although there may be a general increase in sexual interest at about 4 or 5 years of age, we should bear in mind the importance of *individual differences* in sexual development. Kinsey notes that many children show no overt sexual activity or interest until adolescence (Kinsey *et al.*, 1953), even though most individuals are born with the necessary anatomical equipment and the capacity to respond to tactile stimulation. Also, children begin to become aware at about this age that overt masturbation or sex play is socially unacceptable behavior; they may continue their sexual explorations but in a more private way.

According to anthropologist Ashley Montagu (1979), there are important differences in the body contact of the average parent with a 5-year-old boy and with a girl of the same age. He proposes that girls receive more touching (e.g., hugging and holding) from both parents, for different reasons: mothers do not wish to be overly seductive with their growing sons, and fathers may begin to experience "homophobia"—a fear that too much display of affection with men may lead their sons to subsequent homosexuality. Following this line of reasoning, Montagu believes that the withdrawal from physical contact with boys from this age onward leads to the development of a society in which men are much less physically expressive in general. He thus explains an important aspect of adult sex role differences as due to preschool differences in physical contact.

Sex role acquisition via identification: opposing viewpoints. Identification with the same-sex parent was for Freud the logical and healthy outcome of the Oedipus complex. (See the boxed extract.) While other Freudian concepts, such as "castration anxiety" and "penis

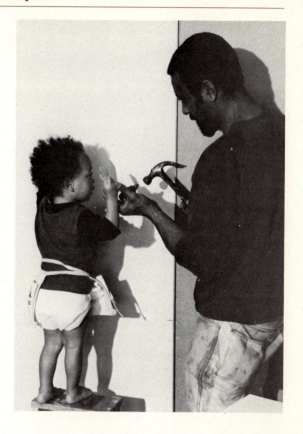

envy," have not been well substantiated, the concept of identification has been very widely accepted as an explanation of how boys come to associate themselves with their fathers, and girls with their mothers. Little boys do often express the desire to be "just like daddy," and little girls to be "just like mommy." In the course of identification, children acquire not only the specific behaviors of the same-sex parent (e.g., cooking, throwing a ball) but also attitudes, values, and a variety of other subtle sex role characteristics. Much of this learning appears to take place in the years preceding puberty.

Psychologists who have been dissatisfied with the Freudian explanation of why children learn to identify with the same-sex parent have proposed some interesting alternative theories. One of the first major departures from the Freudian approach (Miller and Dollard, 1941) used the concept of *imitation*, which is a simpler form of identification, and showed that children can be taught to imitate by means of conventional reward-and-punishment training. The reason children learn to imitate the behavior of the same-sex parent, according to these researchers, is that they are reinforced (rewarded) for doing so. For example, if little boys are praised for acting like daddy, they will continue to imitate his behavior to gain further rewards. Without the process of reinforcement, however, imitation will not take place, according to this point of view.

This early conditioning approach to imitation was subsequently modified and expanded by researchers who demonstrated that children are able to acquire new behavior through a process called *observational learning*, which does not necessarily involve direct reinforcement of the child's behavior (Bandura and Walters, 1963). Children learn to model their behavior after adults (not necessarily parents) who are perceived to have control over important rewards. Thus if a little boy imitates his father, it is because he perceives his father as a source of potential rewards, even if these rewards are not directly provided for imitation. According to this approach, the *social-learning theory*, we would predict that cross-sex imitation would be more likely to occur if the parent of the opposite sex was perceived by the child as the more powerful

(continued on page 60)

How Sigmund Freud Resolved the Dilemmas of Childhood Sexuality: The Oedipus Complex

In the year 1900, Freud presented to the scientific world what he and many others regarded as his most important contribution, *The Interpretation of Dreams.* This book contained a lengthy discussion of childhood sexuality and the major role of the Oedipus complex in the development of personality. Although Freud qualified and modified his original theories in subsequent papers, such as "The Passing of the Oedipus Complex" in 1924 and "Some Psychological Consequences of the Anatomical Distinction Between the Sexes" in 1925, the role of the Oedipus complex remained central to his explanation of psychosexual development. It is fair to state that the Oedipus complex has been one of the most controversial as well as one of the most influential scientific theories of the twentieth century. The theory was based to a large extent on Freud's self-analysis (Jones, 1953) and formed the foundation of much of his analytic work with patients. Let us briefly consider the essential elements of the theory.

The infant's dependence on the mother's nurturance during the early years of childhood (the oral stage) makes the mother into the first important "love object" for both boys and girls. Then, as the boy discovers the pleasure of his penis—and the girl her lack of it—(the phallic stage), the love for the mother develops into a sexual urge. Freud proposed that a boy at about age 3 experiences a strong incestuous wish to take his father's place in becoming his mother's lover. Sexual jealousy of the father as rival for the mother's affections is the basis for the Oedipus complex in boys. For girls, the story unfolds somewhat differently, as we shall presently see.

The legend of Oedipus was taken by Freud from the ancient Greek tragedy *Oedipus Rex* by Sophocles. According to the Greek legend, Oedipus was the son of Laius, king of Thebes. Prior to Oedipus' birth, an oracle warned that he would one day murder his father, and this led Laius to abandon the baby Oedipus outside the city. However, Oedipus was rescued and raised by foreigners. As a young man, he returned to Thebes, unwittingly having killed his father along the road. He then went on, also unwittingly, to marry his mother Jocasta and have children by her. When it was finally revealed that Oedipus had killed his father and married his mother, he blinded himself and left the city for good.

Freud commented thus on the plight of Oedipus:

His fate moves us only because it might have been our own, because the oracle laid upon us before our birth the very curse which rested upon him. It may be that we were all destined to direct our first sexual impulses toward our mothers, and our first impulse of hatred and violence toward our fathers. (1938, p. 308)

But unlike the young man Oedipus, the boy of 3 knows that his father is infinitely bigger and stronger than himself, and the boy naturally fears his father's retaliation. This fear of reprisal takes a specific form, according to Freud, namely the fear of castration. Every little boy is thus faced with the inevitable conflict between a sexual desire for his mother and a fear of castration by his father. A healthy resolution of the conflict occurs only when the boy opts for *identification* with his father, as a necessary and inevitable compromise solution. Identification allows him to share (vicariously) in his father's sexual relationship with his mother without provoking retaliation or castration by the father. This critical phase in psychosexual development leads, according to Freud, to the establishment of a permanent male sex role and heterosexual orientation, and additionally to the development of a superego (conscience).

For girls, a parallel but slightly different sequence of events is supposed to occur. The Oedipus complex—or Electra complex, as it is sometimes called in girls— is preceded by the little girl's discovery that she does *not* have a penis, and the feeling that she has already been castrated. She naturally blames her mother for this fact.

The result of this phase of "penis envy" is a weakening of the bond with the mother and a growing preference for the father, who has the organ she is missing. For her, the Oedipus complex results in a sexual desire for the father and a jealousy of the mother. Castration anxiety is not an effective motivator for girls, as it is for boys, because the little girl believes that castration has already taken place.

 In girls the motive for the destruction of the Oedipus complex is lacking. Castration has already had its effect, which was to force the child into the situation of the Oedipus complex. Thus the Oedipus complex escapes the fate which it meets within boys: it may either be slowly abandoned or got rid of by repression, or its effects may persist far into women's mental life. (Freud, 1925, p. 196)

Freud proposed that this difference in outcome of the Oedipus complex was the basis of some of the major male/female differences in adulthood. Because she is less threatened by castration anxiety, the girl is supposed to develop a

weaker superego (conscience), which leads her as a woman to be more intuitive and less principled than a man. For girls, the resolution of the Oedipus complex also results in their wishing for a baby, which is seen by Freud as a symbolic compensation for the loss of the penis. Through identification with her mother she strives, unconsciously, to have her father's baby.

The fact that most people have no awareness or recollection of such events in their own childhood was explained by Freud as due to the mechanism of "repression," which causes the experiences of the Oedipus complex to be buried in the unconscious. The final proof of his theories, he argued, was that it was only through years of intensive psychoanalysis that one could expect to uncover the truth of childhood sexuality and the Oedipus complex. That the conscious mind resists these memories so vigorously was, he believed, proof of their great force and power.

How do we evaluate this theory by today's sexual values, attitudes, and information? One clear limitation of Freud's oedipal theory is that it was developed largely from introspection and the study of Freud's patients. When the theory is submitted to scientific research, however, there is little evidence to support it. In addition to being unscientific, the theory has been justly criticized as sexist in its attempt to explain psychosexual development in terms of the presence or absence of a penis. Further, the Oedipus and Electra complexes have little value in explaining development in the many families where either the mother or the father is absent. However, Freud's highly speculative theory did make a major contribution to our understanding of sexuality; it highlighted the fact that children can have sexual feelings, and that childhood sexuality can have an important influence on later sexual expression.

source of rewards. However, this seems to be more true for girls than for boys.

Compared to boys, the girls showed a greater readiness to imitate the behavior exhibited by an opposite-sex model. This difference probably reflects both the differential cultural tolerance for cross-sex behavior displayed by males and females and the relatively greater positive reinforcement of masculine-role behavior in our society. (Bandura and Walters, 1963, p. 98)

Yet another theoretical explanation of identification has been proposed by Lawrence Kohlberg and Edward Zigler (1967), who follow what is called the *cognitive-developmental* approach to sex role acquisition. According to these authors, identification with the same-sex parent follows naturally from the child's early gender identity formation (usually by age 3) and the perceived similarity in gender of the same-sex parent. Thus a little boy will begin to imitate his father when he makes the following cognitive step: "I am a male, and daddy is also a male." According to Kohlberg, we acquire our sex roles and the identification with the same-sex parent through a process of *mental deduction* — rather than one of emotional conflict, as in the Freudian theory, or reward and punishment, as in the social-learning approach. In both the Freudian and the social-learning approach, identification is the end result of the developmental process; in the cognitive-developmental approach, the process is believed to begin with the perception of sexual identity and the knowledge that "boys are like daddy, and girls are like mommy."

What overall conclusions can be drawn from these different theoretical positions? Judging by the amount of attention and controversy generated in this field, it appears that the general issue of sex role acquisition, and the more specific question of the role of identification in the process, are of central importance to our understanding of psychosexual development.

Despite the widespread disagreements among psychologists concerning the hows and whys of the process, we can conclude that much of our learning of sex roles takes place through identification, imitation, or modeling (the terms are used interchangeably nowadays). Furthermore, it appears that this process begins very early and is well developed, perhaps irreversibly so, before the onset of puberty.

John Money agrees that identification is a major source of sex role learning but argues that it is not the only important source. He adds a second principle, *complementation*, to the process: "Identification, a long-familiar principle, refers to learning that takes place by direct copying or imitation of a model. Complementation, not so familiar, refers to learning the behavior of another, so that one's own behavior complements or reciprocates it in response" (Money, 1977, p. 66). Money believes that we all develop "schemas," or mental sets, for both identification and complementation. Thus when a little boy observes his father opening a door for his mother, he is learning two complementary sex role schemas — males are expected to open doors for females, and females are expected to walk through the open doorway ahead of the male. The following is an explanation of how these two schemas coexist:

The emphasis on identification and the neglect of complementation in most theories of child development and in the studies based on them has obscured the significance of your other-sex . . . structures. Your other-sex schema serves as your guide to behavior that is not appropriate for you, but *is* appropriate for the other sex. It not only tells you negatives — how not to think, feel, and behave — but also what to expect of the other sex, and so frames your perception of, and influences your reaction to, members of the other sex. You might say that the positive coding of your same-sex schema puts green lights in some behavior lanes while the negative coding of your other-

sex schema puts red lights in other lanes both to warn you off and to tell you where the other traffic is going. (Money and Tucker, 1975, pp. 142–143)

Early gender disturbances. Although most children have a sense of personal gender identity by the age of 3, there are some exceptions to this general pattern. One study (Rosen, Rekers, and Friar, 1977) suggests that there are two aspects to child gender disturbances: the extent to which a child identifies with his sex and the extent to which the child performs behaviors appropriate to the opposite sex. The boy with a *cross-gender identification* not only behaves in socially defined feminine ways— such as wearing female clothing and cosmetics and preferring female friends and roles—but

also wishes to be or believes he is a girl. The boy showing *gender behavior disturbances* may display some feminine behaviors but is sure that he is male. The best way to distinguish between these two problems is to question the child about his gender identity and preferences.

One researcher (Green, 1976) has reviewed a large number of cases of "feminized" boys, that is, biological males who identify as females by the time they are 3 years old. Green's study was an attempt to determine whether this gender identity disturbance could be traced to a particular kind of family constellation. He found very few noticeable differences between the families of normal and feminized boys: no differences were found in age or educational level of the parents, ethnic or religious background, number of siblings, or birth order. Although 83 percent of the feminized boys expressed the desire to be girls, there was no difference in how close their mothers felt toward them. However, the feminized boys were more likely to have been separated from their fathers before they were 5 years old.

The feminized boys were less inclined to participate in sports or rough play, were more often loners or rejected by others, and related best to little girls of the same age. Many of them preferred to dress in female clothing, to play with dolls, and to role-play the mother. Cross-gender behavior was most obvious when these children played alone, indicating

Modification of Deviant Sex Role Behaviors

In recent years, the use of behavioral techniques to modify "deviant" behaviors has expanded to include sexual dysfunctions and problems. Along with this expansion has come a good deal of controversy over the types of problems that are appropriate for behavioral intervention. For instance, suppose the so-called deviant behavior is not defined as a problem by the person who commits it but is viewed as a problem according to cultural norms? Should the therapist attempt to modify this behavior simply because it goes against prevailing societal standards of what is normal? The issue becomes still more complex when we consider the "deviant" behavior of children. The decision to initiate therapy is usually made by concerned adults, generally the parents, who believe they have the child's interests at heart. By initiating therapy, they try to steer their child's behavior into the cultural mainstream.

A specific example of this issue is provided by a study performed by George Rekers and Oscar Lovaas (1974). They describe the effective use of behavioral treatment to modify the deviant sex role behaviors of a male child, Kraig—a physically normal child of about 5 years of age who was referred for treatment of a severe case of cross-gender identification. The authors describe his behavior as follows:

He had a history of cross-dressing since he was 2 years old; at that time, he also began to play with cosmetic items of his mother and grandmother. When the mother's clothing was unavailable, Kraig very frequently improvised in cross-dressing—e.g., mop or towel over head for long hair, or long shirt for a dress. Kraig continually displayed pronounced feminine mannerisms, gestures, and gait, as well as exaggerated feminine inflection and feminine content of speech. He had a remarkable ability to mimic all the subtle feminine behaviors of an adult woman. At the same time, he seemed void of masculine behaviors, being both unable and unwilling to play the "rough-and-tumble" games of boys his age in his immediate neighborhood. He regularly avoided playing with his brother, he declined to defend himself among peers, and he was very fearful of getting hurt. (Rekers and Lovaas, 1974, p. 174)

that they probably had some awareness of parental disapproval of this type of behavior.

According to Green (1974), the mother of a feminized son often perceives her child as unusually attractive and responsive to her. She invests a great deal of time and emotion in her baby boy. He, in turn, develops a strong identification with his mother and uses her belongings as objects of play. She rewards these early behaviors by calling them cute. The father is usually much less available, and

the boy develops little attraction to the father's belongings. As the boy grows older, the cycle of alienation continues when the father feels neglected by his "mama's boy" son. At school, the boy often encounters difficulties in relating to his peers, whose teasing adds to his growing sense of alienation from maleness. While mother may continue to support his feminine interests, father will typically deny the evidence of femininity because of anxiety about being an inadequate role model for his

Rekers and Lovaas list four reasons why a boy such as Kraig should be treated. First, they note that his behavior was leading to social isolation and ridicule. Although society could afford to be more tolerant of Kraig's behaviors, the authors point out that the reality of present cultural norms is intolerance. Second, the early onset of such a problem often leads to even more severe problems in adulthood, including an increased risk of suicide, depression, self-mutilation, or arrest. Third, it seemed advisable to intervene while Kraig was still a child, as adult transsexuals usually do not respond to therapy other than sex-change surgery. Finally, Kraig's parents were alarmed and distressed by Kraig's behavior and were eager to obtain professional help.

In designing the treatment program, Rekers and Lovaas believed that two types of training would be necessary, one to eliminate female behaviors, the other to teach Kraig the appropriate male substitute behaviors and skills. They found that the second type of training was largely unnecessary. Kraig already had some skill in performing gender-appropriate responses, although he chose not to display these responses when female activities were available. With behavior modification techniques, however, Kraig learned to enhance his masculine behaviors and suppress or devalue his feminine behaviors.

The outcome of this treatment program was clearly successful in terms of the goals originally formulated by Kraig's parents and therapists. As a more typical male, Kraig may well avoid the isolation and ridicule he would have received for continued feminine preferences. Nevertheless, many people might disagree with the necessity for therapy (Winkler, 1977). They might argue that Kraig was forced to conform to a social stereotype of what little boys should do, that this stereotype is restrictive and outdated, and that little consideration was given to Kraig's preferences as an individual. In a sense, the treatment of boys such as Kraig serves to perpetuate restrictive sex role definitions. On the other hand, it is easy to empathize with the concerns of Kraig's parents.

son. After repeated difficulties with school and friends, such a family may seek professional help. Treatment usually includes all family members. The father will be encouraged to interact more directly with his son, while the mother will be encouraged to reward her son for more masculine behaviors (as seen in the boxed extract). While this approach centers on family interactions, Green also acknowledges the possibility that prenatal hormone levels may predispose some boys toward a feminized identity and behavior.

Feminized males have received much more attention than masculinized females, for several reasons. First, young girls seem less susceptible to serious gender disturbances. For example, the ratio of males to females among those applying for transsexual surgery is about four to one, and males are far more likely to be treated for such deviant behaviors as fetishism, transvestism, and voyeurism. As we saw earlier, something must be added to differentiate a male from the female path of embryonic development, and it has been suggested that this additive principle for male development applies to psychosexual as well as physical growth. It is conceivable that feminized boys started on the wrong foot by receiving too little androgen before birth.

Second, we should keep in mind that our culture is usually far more lenient with cross-gender behavior if it is exhibited by a female. The tomboy is an accepted role in our culture and may bring the little girl many rewards, whereas the sissy or sensitive boy is the object of concern and derision. Females are often permitted to dress in "masculine" clothing, but males who cross-dress are labeled *transvestites* and may be subject to severe legal penalties. Similarly, female bisexuality seems to be more socially acceptable and less threatening than male bisexuality. Perhaps it is a reflection of our cultural chauvinism that male behaviors are rewarded in both girls and boys, whereas female behaviors are approved of only for girls. In this sense, the young girl's gender role has considerably more flexibility than the young boy's, as she can vary her behavior without losing her sense of identity and without incurring parental disapproval or punishment. Thus it may be that some of the "psychosexual frailty" of the male (Money and Ehrhardt, 1972) is, in fact, due to the greater tolerance for cross-gender behaviors in the female.

FROM KINDERGARTEN TO PUBERTY

The period from kindergarten to puberty is one in which a great deal of social and intellectual development takes place. As the child spends increasingly longer periods of time outside the home, either at school or in the company of peers, he or she becomes more independent of the family and more concerned with approval and acceptance by teachers and classmates. Achievement motivation is an important determinant of success in these new activities.

With respect to psychosexual development during this period, Freud called the middle years the *latency stage* because he believed that successful resolution of the Oedipus complex results in repression of the sex drive until puberty. Although the Freudian concept of latency has been very influential and is sometimes used as a rationalization against sex education in elementary school, it is not substantiated by objective studies of childhood sexuality.

Children pursue the course of their psychosexual development in blithe disregard of an expected sexual latency. Their only nod in the direction of the theoretical expectations is that they have learned to play according to adult rules. They learn to fulfill the letter of the law, even as they proceed secretly in their own ways. (Gadpaille, 1975, p. 189)

Kinsey found that the number of girls and boys who have experienced orgasm shows a gradual but steady increase in the years prior to puberty (Kinsey *et al.*, 1953). Similarly, exploratory sex play with peers appears to increase steadily during these years. The experience of girls begins to differ markedly from boys, however, as puberty draws near. Parents tend to be more protective of little girls than of little boys and insist that they show more "modesty." Kinsey and his colleagues argued strongly that preadolescent sexual inactivity does not reflect the effects of a latency period but is imposed by the culture, especially if the child is female.

Considerable support for this point of view can be found in the cross-cultural studies of Ford and Beach. These authors found that the

The years before puberty are a time for experimenting with sexual play. *(Michelle Vignes/Icon)*

amount of sexual activity in prepubertal children depends entirely on the degree of sexual permissiveness in the society. Where they are permitted to do so, children gradually increase their sexual activities both as they approach puberty and during adolescence. For example:

Sexual life begins in earnest among the Trobrianders at six to eight years for girls, ten to twelve for boys. Both sexes receive explicit instruction from older companions whom they imitate in sex activities. Sex play includes masturbation, oral stimulation of the genitals of the same and opposite sex, and heterosexual copulation. At any time a couple may retire to the bush, the bachelor's hut, an isolated yam house, or any other convenient place and there engage in prolonged sexual play with full approval of their parents. (Ford and Beach, 1951, p. 191)

Sex play with peers is also an important source of sexual information in our society, although we are obviously much less permissive in this regard than the Trobriand Islanders. In fact, it seems that during the middle childhood years we acquire in our society the basic notions of sexual privacy and secrecy that characterize much of our adult sex lives as well. It is not surprising, therefore, that we find during this period a marked increase in sexual fantasies, the most private aspect of our sexual experience. The availability of explicit sexual materials, or pornography, in our society also contributes to some extent to sexual fantasies in prepubescent boys and girls.

Sex play with peers occurs about equally with the same sex and the opposite sex (Kinsey *et al.*, 1953). The effects of early sex role training are apparent in the fact that boys tend to initiate this behavior more often than girls. As already noted, parents tend to be more restrictive toward girls. The motives for sex play during this period may be very different from the motives that guide similar behavior between adults.

Many boys participate in some form of the "circle jerk," in which they get together for the purpose of exhibiting themselves, comparing their sex organs, proving their sexual prowess by getting an erection, and engaging in either self-induced or mutual masturbation. Sometimes, such homosexual play with their male peers may actually help young boys to feel more potent as men. Because of their conditioning in the cultural emphasis that equates masculinity with sexual performance and virility, boys may gain self-assurance from such exhibitionism. By showing off their penises, exploring their ability to attain and sustain an erection, and handling each other's genitals, boys may get to accept and to feel more confidence in their maleness. (Sarnoff and Sarnoff, 1979, p. 149)

Another important aspect of the socialization process during this period is the increased interest in role playing, in which children rehearse with each other the occupational and social roles available in our society. Such role playing also has the important effect of reinforcing gender identity, as boys generally rehearse masculine roles and girls feminine roles. Exposure to television, movies, and books greatly stimulates these role-playing activities by providing children with an endless source of role models from which to choose. The role playing of interpersonal relationships allows children the opportunity to express their feelings about what it is like to fall in love, and this kind of role playing may lead to the development of "crushes" on schoolteachers, high status peers (e.g., the smartest or most attractive child in the class), or pop music idols. Such feelings in a boy or girl of 10 may be very intense, although they are typically not explicitly sexual in character.

Sexual interactions between adults and children. According to Kinsey

There is a growing concern in our culture over the sexual contacts that pre-adolescent children sometimes have with adults. . . . Press reports might lead one to conclude that an appreciable percentage of all children are subjected, and frequently subjected, to sexual approaches by adult males, and that physical injury is a frequent consequence of such contacts. (Kinsey et al., 1953, p. 116)

How commonly does contact between adults and preadolescent children occur? Kinsey reported that 24 percent of the females in his sample recalled at least one instance prior to puberty of being approached sexually by an adult male (Kinsey *et al.*, 1953). However, the definition of "adult male" used by Kinsey was any male at least 5 years older than the girl and no less than 15 years of age. This means that Kinsey could have included in his statistics contacts between boys of 15 and girls of 10 — not exactly what most of us would regard as adult-child encounters. Clearly, the question of definition substantially affects the incidence reported. Of those females in the Kinsey sample who had been sexually approached by an adult, 80 percent reported that this had occurred only once, and in most cases the approach had involved nothing more than exposure of the man's genitals or only verbal approaches.

Cross-cultural studies have demonstrated that there are some societies, although few, in which it is an accepted social custom for adults to initiate children into sexual intercourse. The Lepcha of Indian, for example, "believe that girls will not mature without benefit of sexual intercourse. . . . Older men occasionally copulate with girls as young as eight years of age. Instead of being regarded as a criminal offense, such behavior is considered amusing by the Lepcha" (Ford and Beach, 1951, p. 191). In many primitive societies, children share the same sleeping quarters as their parents and frequently observe all forms of sexual activity.

Although most people in our society would regard sexual contact between an adult and a child as a form of exploitation or child abuse, there is no clear consensus concerning the overall effects of such an experience on the child. There are currently studies in progress to determine the relationship between sexual dysfunction in adult women and early sexual abuse. According to sociologists Gagnon and Simon (1970), the child is more likely to be harmed by the effects of discovery than by the sexual experience itself.

Whatever the reasons, it is apparent that in our society it is not acceptable for children to be introduced to sexuality through physical contact with adults. Even if the act goes undiscovered, the memory of a childhood sexual experience with an adult can be a major source of subsequent guilt or anxiety. In addition, adults who engage in sexual relations with children are likely to be less than adequately adjusted individuals, as we shall see in Chapter 12.

PUBERTY AND ADOLESCENCE

The bodily changes that mark the onset of puberty also signal the end of childhood and the start of a new phase of psychosexual development—adolescence. The term "puberty"—which is derived from the Latin word for growing up—has traditionally been applied to girls who reach *menarche*, the time of the first menstrual period, and boys who experience their first ejaculation (Gadpaille, 1975). However, menarche and first ejaculation actually occur some time after the appearance of the first important signs of puberty, such as the development of breasts and pubic hair (Tanner, 1971). Most experts today regard puberty

as a sequence of physiological events that extends over a 3- to 4-year period in females and an even longer period in males (see Figure 2.4).

The term "adolescence" generally refers to the cultural and psychosocial adaptations that

FIGURE 2.4
Physical changes during puberty. The height spurt reaches a peak at about age 12 in girls and about age 14 in boys. The bars represent the duration (average ages for beginning and end) of the events of puberty. *(Tanner, 1973, p. 40)*

Puberty growth rates in girls

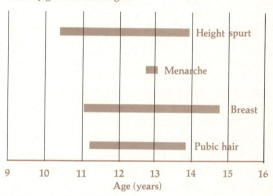

Puberty growth rates in boys

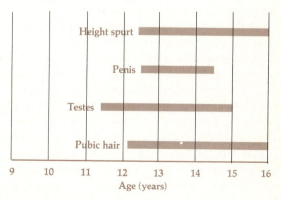

characterize the individual's response to puberty. It is also a critical period of transition between childhood and the adult world. In primitive societies, where highly structured "rites of passage" are used to facilitate the transition, the period of adolescence may last for only a year or two. In our society, however, with its complex social and technological demands on adulthood, adolescence has become a protracted and difficult process, often lasting into the late teens or even the early twenties. According to Erik Erikson (1963), adolescence is above all a period of identity formation, which involves considerable emotional conflict and role confusion.

The biological changes of puberty are precipitated by hormone release—principally estrogen in females and testosterone in males. Although the biochemistry of puberty is a complex and intricate process that is discussed fully in Chapter 6, we will summarize here some of the most important facts:

1. Puberty in both males and females appears to be triggered by a kind of "biological clock" located in the hypothalamus, an important part of the limbic system of the brain (Money and Tucker, 1975). Signals from the hypothalamus to the pituitary—the "master gland" of the hormone system—result in production of gonadotropic hormones, which in turn stimulate the activity of the gonads—the testicles in males and the ovaries in females. This stimulation of the gonads results in a huge upsurge of sex hormone release, which creates both the physical and the emotional changes associated with puberty.

2. The biological changes of puberty typically take place from one to two years earlier in females than in males. Some noticeable budding of the breasts typically begins in girls around the age of 11, and the first menstrual period usually occurs between the ages of 12 and 13. For boys, the change in size of the scrotum and testes is usually observable from about age 12, and the first ejaculation is likely to occur between 13 and 14. As yet, no generally accepted explanation exists for the earlier onset of puberty in girls, but it is consistent with the general trend toward earlier maturation of females from the time of birth on.

3. There is a wide range of individual differences in both the age of onset and the duration of puberty. Physical disease or emotional stress, for example, can precipitate, delay, or prolong puberty for months or even years. Of interest is the trend described by an English scientist, J. M. Tanner (1968), toward the earlier age of puberty, which has dropped steadily by about 4 months in every 10 years in most Western countries in which statistics are available. Tanner found that girls now begin menstruation an average of 2.5 to 3.3 years earlier than they did a century ago, and the earlier onset of puberty is also associated with a progressive increase in average height and weight during childhood—suggesting earlier maturation on a number of dimensions. How do we account for this earlier maturation phenomenon? Tanner believes that is is mostly due to environmental factors, particularly the effects of better nutrition.

4. The increase in hormones during puberty affects both genital and nongenital aspects of physical development. Pubic hair changes from a downy to a wiry texture, and axillary hair begins to grow in the armpits. In girls, the most marked changes are the budding of the breasts and the spreading of the pelvic bones—to provide room for a baby to pass through. At the same time, subcutaneous fat starts collecting in ways that round the body. In boys, the larynx is enlarged, which causes the voice to deepen—erratically at first. The muscles and bones grow heavier, and facial hair eventually becomes a beard.

5. Associated with these major bodily changes during puberty are a variety of psy-

Precocious Puberty

We have noted that although most girls enter puberty from the age of 11 on, and boys from 12 or 13 on, there is a wide range of individual differences, especially among males. When puberty occurs years earlier than expected, however, it may reflect the effects of some medical (endocrinological) abnormality, which should be diagnosed and treated by a physician specialist.

According to some researchers (Ehrhardt and Meyer-Bahlburg, 1975), precocious puberty can begin shortly after birth but is more frequent at the age of 6 to 8 years. The condition may be secondary to some more general medical abnormality, including a lesion in the brain or in the glands, or it may be "spontaneous" or "ideopathic"—meaning that it is simply a characteristic of that particular individual (or that diagnosis of the underlying medical cause is impossible). Precocious puberty sometimes runs in families, or it may affect only one of several siblings.

Precocious puberty presents special problems for both child and parents. Sex education and frank communication about pubertal development is very important for the early developing child, who is often totally deprived of the usual peer exchange on these matters. In addition to menstruation and the development of secondary sexual characteristics, the child experiencing precocious puberty also tends to be much larger than his or her peers, making for additional adjustment problems. Can drugs be used to treat the condition? If certain progesterone compounds are administered to girls undergoing precocious puberty, breast enlargement and menstruation may be inhibited, but the girl will continue to grow in size at an abnormal rate. The drug may also impair fertility at a later age. When precocious puberty is due to the adreno-genital syndrome (as in cases of genetic females who are masculinized by an excess of androgen), use of the drug cortisone has proved very helpful in delaying the maturation process. For most cases of precocious puberty, however, whether in males or females, there is no simple medical treatment and specialists recommend extensive psychological counseling for the child and parents involved.

chological body-image problems that must be dealt with by adolescents of both sexes. Although infants also go through enormous physical changes during the first two years of life, they do not have to deal with the self-consciousness that accompanies the physical changes of puberty. "Unlike infants in the earlier period, adolescents have the pain and pleasure of observing the whole process: they watch themselves with alternating feelings of fascination, charm, and horror as the bodily changes occur. Surprised, embarrassed, and uncertain, adolescents constantly judge themselves in comparison with others and continually revise their self-images" (Craig, 1979, p. 425).

The difference in age of onset of puberty between boys and girls results in certain additional psychosocial difficulties. Among a group of typical 12-year-old boys and girls, we would expect to find that the girls are taller and bigger, and both physically and emotionally more mature. It is not uncommon for girls of this age to adopt an attitude of dominance or superiority toward their male peers, who seem to be acting like "silly little boys" at a time that girls are experiencing the first signs of womanhood. Boys typically deal with the anxiety this situation creates by defensively joining together in all-male groups or gangs, which stay as far removed from the girls and their activities as possible (Gadpaille, 1975). Sports and games are another important source of refuge for boys of this age.

Adolescent sexuality. As girls begin to menstruate and boys to ejaculate, the time of reproductive capacity—the ability to conceive and bear children—is at hand. It should be noted, however, that an adolescent girl's first few menstrual cycles do not always include ovulation, and it may be several months or even years until she reaches the peak of fertility. Similarly, the onset of ejaculation in males may occur before the sperm are sufficiently developed for impregnation to take place. Again, we must remember the importance of individual differences, as there are many reported instances of pregnancy and childbirth in girls as young as 11 or 12 years of age. In view of the developing reproductive capacity of the individual following puberty, the subject of birth control and contraception is strongly emphasized in modern sex education for adolescents (Pomeroy, 1968; Gordon, 1973). According to one writer (Sorenson, 1973), most adolescents begin sexual intercourse without contraceptives.

The strong taboos against incest in our society may lead to additional stresses being experienced by adolescents in some cases and the parents of adolescents in others. A gradual withdrawal from physical contact may occur as the adolescent instinctively senses this to be a potential conflict area. That this reaction

may have primitive and instinctive origins is illustrated by the account of a psychologist (Temerlin, 1975) who raised a female chimpanzee. When Lucy, the chimpanzee, was a baby, she developed a great deal of affection toward her human "father" and would frequently touch him, embrace him, and even initiate mouth kissing as an expression of affection. Starting with her first showing of menstrual blood, however, she immediately withdrew from such physical intimacy and began to avoid him throughout her fertile period. At the same time, she began to act very seductively to any and all other adult males (human) who entered the household.

Masturbation, or self-stimulation, is an important aspect of adolescent sexuality. For most males, the first ejaculation seems to occur during masturbation. In a few instances, the first ejaculation occurs during sleep, in the form of a *nocturnal emission*, or "wet dream." Kinsey reported a very wide range of frequencies of nocturnal emissions, ranging from only once or twice a year to more than 10 times a week (Kinsey, Pomeroy, and Martin, 1948). About 50 percent of the men in the Kinsey sample recalled nocturnal emissions at some time during adolescence. Can a woman have a "wet dream"? Some women experience sexual orgasms during sleep that appear to be similar to the nocturnal emissions of males. For example, one of the girls in the Sorenson (1973) study recalled having had orgasms in her sleep from the time she was 6 or 7 years of age.

Concerning the incidence of masturbation during adolescence, there are two important facts to be considered. First, masturbation to orgasm is much more common among adolescent males than among adolescent females. For example, Kinsey reported that 82 percent of the male sample had masturbated to orgasm by age 15, compared to 20 percent of the female sample (Kinsey *et al.*, 1953). Second, adolescents of both sexes are today masturbating at an earlier age than they did a generation ago. Hunt compared the incidence of adolescent masturbation in his study with that found by Kinsey 25 years ago:

In Kinsey's sample, 45 percent of all males had masturbated by the time they were 13; in our own sample, fully 63 percent have done so by that age. Among the females the shift is, as we might have anticipated, still more striking, since they have traditionally been subject to far greater psychosocial inhibiting forces than males. In Kinsey's sample only 15 percent [of females] had masturbated to orgasm by the time they were 13, while in our own sample the figure is 33 percent, or more than twice as large. In every age grouping, our males and females seem to have begun somewhat earlier, on the average, than Kinsey's people in comparable age groupings a generation ago. (Hunt, 1974, p. 77)

Even thought adolescents seem to be masturbating in higher numbers and at earlier ages, evidence from recent surveys suggests that the activity remains a major source of guilt and embarrassment (Sorenson, 1973; Hunt, 1974). Adolescents still find masturbation more difficult to discuss than any other sexual topic (Gadpaille, 1975). Many adolescents regard masturbation as an immature and socially unacceptable sexual outlet, even if they are sufficiently educated to understand that it is essentially normal behavior. Kinsey found this to be especially true in lower-class or less-educated males, who tended to regard masturbation as incompatible with true "masculinity"; they were therefore more likely to seek heterosexual outlets via petting or intercourse at an earlier age than males from a higher socioeconomic background. Hunt's data, however, suggest that the effects of social class on adolescent masturbation have diminished considerably since Kinsey's time.

In two important respects masturbation changes more for males than for females after puberty. First, while both males and females are capable of masturbation to orgasm prior to puberty, the additional capacity to ejaculate significantly affects the subjective experience of masturbation for males after puberty. In fact, many adult men can still recall their first experience of ejaculation, which is experienced as a powerfully rewarding event for some and a frightening or disturbing occurrence for others. Ejaculation typically becomes the goal or end point of male adolescent masturbation, and the release of tension associated with orgasm and ejaculation becomes a major source of satisfaction. Second, the use of sexual fantasies during masturbation is almost universal among adolescent males, considerably less common among adolescent females (Kinsey *et al.*, 1953; Hunt, 1974). Kinsey believed that males could be more easily conditioned to a variety of sexual stimuli than females, and that sexual fantasies are a major source of sexual conditioning for adolescent males. An alternative explanation is that boys in our culture are given more permission or tacit encouragement for sexual experimentation, and that most erotic stimuli (books and magazines) are primarily oriented toward a male audience.

Several survey studies conducted in the past decade shed additional light on the subject of adolescent sexuality today (Kantner and Zelnik, 1972; Sorenson, 1973; Vener and Stewart, 1974). The underlying question addressed in these survey studies is: "Is a sexual revolution taking place in adolescence today?" The increasing rates of teen-age pregnancy and venereal disease have focused public concern on important issues of adolescent sexuality. Although differences in sampling and interviewing techniques make it difficult to compare the results of different studies directly, we can draw certain tentative conclusions about emerging trends.

First, it is clear that adolescents today are experiencing intercourse more frequently and at

an earlier age than a generation ago. Kinsey reported that only 3 percent of females and 40 percent of males had experienced intercourse by the age of 15 (Kinsey *et al.*, 1953). The highest incidence of adolescent intercourse experience was found by Sorenson (1973) — 30 percent of girls and 44 percent of boys between the ages of 13 and 15. (An additional 17 percent of boys and 7 percent of girls had their first intercourse experience by age 12.) On the other hand, two researchers (Vener and Stewart, 1974) did not find rates as high as those of Sorenson; only 17 percent of their 13- to 15-year-old females were engaging in intercourse, and 33 percent of the 13- to 15-year-old males. Vener and Stewart explain this difference as due to the possible biases in Soren-

son's study produced by requiring parental consent for participation in the study (about one-third of the parents refused). The percentages found by Vener and Stewart are probably a more accurate guide, as they conform closely to those found by two other researchers (Kantner and Zelnik, 1972), who used a very large sample of over 4,000 young women in their study. The overall conclusion to be drawn is that the age of first intercourse appears to have decreased dramatically for girls since Kinsey's time. For boys, however, the study results are equivocal.

Adolescents today also appear to be more involved than earlier generations in a wide range of heterosexual petting activities. Petting usually progresses from tentative hand holding to kissing to manual or oral stimulation of the breasts and genitals. Vener and Stewart point out that studies of adolescent sexuality frequently fail to obtain accurate information about petting because the questions asked are either too vague or too ambiguous. In their study on adolescent sexuality they used the questionnaire shown in Table 2.2.

That petting serves an important function in helping to coordinate the patterns of male and female sexual response has been emphasized by a number of authorities (Kinsey *et al.*, 1953; Gagnon and Simon, 1973). Heavy petting—petting that includes direct stimulation of the genitals of either sex—may also serve as an alternative to intercourse for those adolescents who wish to experience sexual intimacy while preserving their virginity. While younger adolescents are notoriously clumsy and inept, by the time they reach college most adolescents have achieved a reasonable degree of proficiency in managing "the petting script."

Perhaps the most significant change in adolescent sexuality has been the development of more tolerant and positive attitudes toward sexuality in general, and particularly a loosening of the double standard so prevalent in previous generations. For example, more than two-thirds of the adolescents in the Sorenson

TABLE 2.2

Adolescent Sexuality

How often have you:	Never (1)	Seldom (2)	Sometimes (3)	Frequently (4)	Very Frequently (5)
Held hands with someone of the opposite sex (not including relatives)?	1	2	3	4	5
Held your arm around or been held by someone of the opposite sex (not including relatives)?	1	2	3	4	5
Kissed or been kissed by someone of the opposite sex (not including relatives)?	1	2	3	4	5
Necked (prolonged kissing and hugging) with someone of the opposite sex?	1	2	3	4	5
Been involved in light petting (feeling above the waist) with someone of the opposite sex?	1	2	3	4	5
Been involved in heavy petting (feeling below the waist) with someone of the opposite sex?	1	2	3	4	5

Have you gone all the way with someone of the opposite sex?

1. Never
2. Once
3. 2 to 5 times
4. 6 to 12 times
5. 13 or more times

With how many people of the opposite sex have you gone all the way?

1. I have not gone all the way.
2. One person
3. 2 to 3 people
4. 4 to 6 people
5. 7 or more people

Source: A. M. Vener and C. S. Stewart, "Adolescent Sexual Behavior in Middle America Revisited: 1970–1973," *Journal of Marriage and the Family*, November 1974, p. 730.

(1973) study endorsed the statement that any form of sexual behavior is acceptable, provided that it is not coercive or harmful to the participants. A majority of the respondents refused to believe that a sexual act could be immoral simply because it contravened the rules of society. In addition, 69 percent of the males and 55 percent of the females in the study agreed with the statement: "So far as sex is concerned, I do what I want to do, regardless of what society thinks." Vener and Stewart (1974) conclude that ample evidence exists that a revolution in adolescent attitudes toward premarital sexual permissiveness has occurred. They assert that these attitudinal changes have, in fact been far greater than the changes in actual behavior.

Homosexual behavior among adolescents. We have already noted that sex play with members of the same sex is an important aspect of sexual learning prior to puberty. For some adolescents, more commonly males, homosexual activity during early adolescence is a natural continuation of prepubertal sex play. Others experience homosexual activity for the first time after puberty. Kinsey and his colleagues found that 27 percent of their male sample had had some homosexual experience between puberty and age 15 (Kinsey, Pomeroy, and Martin, 1948). It is important to remember that the maturational gap between boys and girls reaches a peak during puberty, and many boys may feel threatened by sex play with girls of the same age. Curiously, Sorenson (1973) found that only 11 percent of the adolescent males in his sample had experienced one or more homosexual experiences. Perhaps the increased availability of teen-age girls to sexual advances has reduced the incentive for same-sex experiences since Kinsey's time. Or Sorenson's sample may have been less than honest on this subject.

What happens to the homosexual relationships of adolescence? It is clear that in most cases they represent nothing more than a passing phase, after which the individual adopts a heterosexual life style.

During their late teens many males experience considerable personal conflict over their homosexual activities, because they have become more conscious of social reactions to such contacts. Particularly in that period, many individuals attempt to stop their homosexual relations, and try to make the heterosexual adjustments which society demands. (Kinsey, Pomeroy, and Martin, 1948, p. 629)

Kinsey and his colleagues believed that while most of these young men are able to make a successful transition from homosexual to predominantly heterosexual relationships, there are some (less than 5 percent of the total male sample) who go on to develop an exclusive homosexual orientation. The Kinsey study also found that adolescent homosexual activity was most frequent among males who matured earlier, who masturbated more often prior to puberty, and who were less religiously devout.

For many adolescent boys, the experience of a sexual contact with another male is not viewed as "homosexuality" in the sense that adults use the word. Such acts are not usually integrated into the mainstream of development (Gagnon and Simon, 1973). In the view of another author, "Homosexual experiences in adolescence are not infrequent, yet they are not the norm. These experiences are not 'abnormal' (sic). They may provoke crises in cases where adolescents worry that they will become homosexuals, but for the vast majority of adolescents the crisis as well as the homosexuality passes" (Manaster, 1977, p. 165). Even adolescent males who prostitute themselves to older homosexual "clients" usually view themselves as heterosexuals who are only using sex for money (Reiss, 1961). We have little information to indicate why a small but significant minority of adolescents do not "outgrow" their homosexual phase, why they go on to become exclusive homosexuals as adults. Many experts believe that an *exclusively* homosexual orientation is established in the period of psychosexual development prior to puberty and may be related to the conditions of early sex role learning (Money and Tucker, 1975).

Homosexual experiences are much less common among adolescent girls. For example, only about 3 percent of the women in Kinsey's sample had had homosexual relations to the point of orgasm during adolescence. This statistic was somewhat qualified by Kinsey, who pointed out that a much larger percentage of adolescent girls have homosexual feelings that they usually do not act upon (Kinsey *et al.*, 1953). Sorenson (1973) reported that 6 percent of female adolescents in his sample had had one or more homosexual experiences. Gagnon and Simon (1973) make the point that all

women, whether heterosexually or homosexually inclined, are socialized into a more passive sexual role and are less likely to initiate overt sexual behavior outside the context of a long-term or committed emotional relationship. An exception to this would be the girls in a reformatory or penal institution, where adolescent girls do frequently enter into homosexual relationships. By and large, however, it seems that overt homosexual behavior is much less common among adolescent females than among adolescent males.

Finally, it is interesting to note that in some primitive cultures it is customary for all adolescent boys to engage in a period of socially approved homosexuality as part of the initiation process into manhood. For example, among the Batak people of Sumatra and the Amins of New Guinea, adolescent males seem to pass easily from the homosexual to the heterosexual stage and what appear to be very stable and long-lasting marriages (Money and Tucker, 1975).

Conclusion

There is no clear line demarcating the end of adolescence and the beginning of adulthood in our society. For us, adolescence represents both a culmination of childhood development and a period of preparation for adulthood. We can define the end of adolescence in psychological terms following Erik Erikson's notion that this is the stage of identity formation — by saying that adolescence ends when the individual develops a firm and stable adult identity. Or we can define the end of adolescence in terms of external changes, such as marriage or graduation from high school or college. Neither definition is completely satisfactory,

however, as it is obvious that while many adults are still struggling with their sense of identity, a few individuals still in high school are clearly adults from a psychological point of view. What is important is not exactly how adolescence is defined, but that we recognize it as a period of transition from childhood into the occupational and interpersonal roles of adulthood.

We continue to develop and grow throughout the life cycle, even if later development is not as obvious or dramatic as that in the early years. Gadpaille (1975) proposes that we can divide sexual development into three major cycles, which he calls "the cycles of sex." The first is childhood, the second adolescence, the third psychosexual development throughout adult life. Thus as we emerge from adolescence, we enter the third cycle of psychosexual development—adulthood.

The first important task facing the young adult is the development of intimate relationships and the integration of the developing capacity for sexual response within the context of adequate interpersonal functioning. The major emotional task of the young adult, according to Erik Erikson (1963), is to risk his or her newly found identity in the "fusion" process of intimate relationships. In the next chapter we will explore in depth the nature of intimacy and pair bonding, the next important phase of psychosexual development. Much of the earlier development of the individual bears on this process and influences the direction and outcome of the "third cycle." However, a number of significant new elements enter the picture, as the young man or woman enters the diverse and complex social structure of adulthood in our society today.

Summary

Our sense of ourselves as male or female, and the ways in which we express our masculinity or femininity, are basic to our development as sexual beings. This developmental process begins early in the life cycle, and continues through adolescence and adulthood. In this chapter, sexual differentiation and development have been discussed from both the biological and the social perspectives. To summarize:

1. Sexual differentiation begins in the months following conception, and at birth the genitals are clearly male or female. As a consequence of the sexual labelling of the newborn, there will be differences in the ways that adults behave toward the child as well as differences in the ways that the child learns to think about himself or herself. Sexual identity —the subjective sense of being male or female —is firmly established in the preschool years.

2. An interaction of nature and nurture, biology and the environment, contribute to psychosexual development. Genital responses and sex play are a part of this developmental process in children, although the meanings of these behaviors are not sexual in the sense that adults define sexuality. In some cultures children learn about sexuality through observation or explicit instruction, but in our own culture, sexual messages are usually transmitted in an indirect fashion.

3. Sex roles—that is, the ways in which sexual identity is expressed and experienced—are acquired in a number of ways. Some authorities stress identification with the same-sex parent, while others emphasize the importance of imitation, observational learning, complementation, and reward and punishment.

4. At the time of puberty, increased hormone levels cause a variety of physical changes in the developing adolescent. These changes in bodily function and appearance are accompanied by psychosocial changes; for instance, the adolescent male or female must cope with a changing body image and the self-

consciousness that is often part of pubertal growth. In addition, at puberty the adolescent achieves the beginnings of reproductive maturity, although his or her emotions and sexual experiences are far from mature. Masturbation is a common part of the process of learning about one's sexuality, as are sexual fantasies and heterosexual dating. Homosexual feelings are not uncommon during this phase, although they may entail some personal conflict and confusion.

Overview

Love Relationships

DEFINING LOVE / THE ORIGINS OF LOVE / LOVE
PROBLEMS / LOVE AND SEXUALITY

Heterosexual Patterns and Relationships

PAIR-BONDING / DATING AND COURTSHIP /
MARRIAGE

Homosexual Patterns and Relationships

HISTORICAL BACKGROUND / CROSS-CULTURAL
PERSPECTIVES / RECENT DEVELOPMENTS /
HOMOSEXUAL BEHAVIORS AND IDENTITIES /
ROLES AND LIFE STYLES

Bisexuality

Nonsexual Life Styles: Celibacy and Abstinence

Summary

THREE

Sexual Relationships and Life Styles

Overview

This chapter introduces an important and major theme of this book: that sexuality is a way of relating to our fellow human beings, and that many of the greatest rewards—and disappointments—of human sexuality arise from the nature of our sexual relationships and life styles. The issue of sexual relationships encompasses much more than the question of whom we choose to go to bed with. It touches on some of the deepest questions of personal identity, social roles, and interpersonal values. If we were to ask the question, "What is especially *human* about human sexuality?" we would certainly have to answer in terms of our sexual relationships and life styles. It is also in these areas that we find, predictably, the greatest degree of cultural variation.

The range of life styles existing even within our own society is a distinctive characteristic of modern life, leading some people to mourn the loss of "traditional family values" while others celebrate their newly found freedom.

Personal choices about relationships and life styles carry enormous consequences for the individual, yet they are perhaps the choices for which we are least prepared. "Sometimes I feel our education has as one of its major goals the bringing up of individuals to live in isolation cages," observed Carl Rogers (1972, pp. 214–215). The decision to marry, for example, will shape the future course of our lives in a most profound way; yet a marriage license is far easier to obtain than a driver's license, for which we insist on highly

[79]

structured and compulsory educational programs.

Sexual relationships and life styles are greatly influenced by the culture in which we live. Some cultures insist on monogamy, others favor polygamy; some cultures demand a strict standard of marital fidelity, others support and encourage a variety of extramarital relationships; homosexuality is forbidden in some societies, openly practiced in others. By considering these various patterns, we may develop a broader and more meaningful perspective on how our own society influences and structures our sexual relationships.

Can you remember the first time you fell in love? This experience, which can take us to the heights of human happiness or cause the deepest despair, often sets the stage for our relationships and choice of life style. We live in a culture that endorses sexual relationships based on love, one in which more people marry for love than for any other reason. Who we love, and how we express this love, are crucial in determining the sexual life style with which we identify. Therefore, this chapter begins by describing the many forms of love and the various ways it can influence our lives.

Love Relationships

DEFINING LOVE

Love, we agree, is a most important and powerful human experience. We might also agree that love is a complex and diverse emotion that takes many different forms through the life cycle. But when we try to explain the meaning and implications of love, we are likely to run into some confusion; probably, there are as many definitions of love as there are people in the world, and love is a uniquely personal experience. Consider the following definitions.

St. Paul:

Love is patient; love is kind and envies no one. Love is never boastful, nor conceited, nor rude; never selfish, not quick to take offense. Love keeps no score of wrongs; does not gloat over other men's sins, but delights in the truth. There is nothing love cannot face; there is not limit to its faith, its hopes, and its endurance. (I Corinthians 13: 4-7)

Rollo May:

We define love as a delight in the presence of the other person and an affirming of his value and development as much as one's own. (1975, p. 116)

William Shakespeare:

Let me not to the marriage of true minds
Admit impediments. Love is not love
Which alters when it alteration finds,
Or bends with the remover to remove:
O, no! it is an ever-fixed mark,
That looks on tempests and is never shaken;
It is the star to every wandering bark,
Whose worth's unknown, although his height be
    taken.
Love's not Time's fool, though rosy lips and
    cheeks
Within his bending sickle's compass come;
Love alters not with his brief hours and weeks,
But bears it out even to the edge of doom.
    If this be error, and upon me prov'd,
    I never writ, nor no man ever lov'd.
(From *Sonnet* CXVI)

The Velveteen Rabbit Learns About Love

The Velveteen Rabbit is a beautiful children's story, written by Margery Williams (Doubleday, 1958), in which stuffed animals and nursery toys talk to one another about life, love, and most important of all, how toys become "real."

Nursery magic is very strange and wonderful, and only those playthings that are old and wise and experienced like the Skin Horse understand all about it.

"What is REAL?" asked the Rabbit one day. "Does it mean having things that buzz inside you and a stick-out handle?"

"Real isn't how you are made," said the Skin Horse. "It's a thing that happens to you. When a child loves you for a long, long time, not just to play with, but REALLY loves you, then you become Real. It doesn't happen all at once. You become. It takes a long time. Generally, by the time you are Real, most of your hair has been loved off, and your eyes drop out and you get loose in the joints and very shabby. But these things don't matter at all, because once you are Real you can't be ugly, except to people who don't understand."

These definitions have in common an ideal vision of love, a picture of what love at its highest level should be. They describe an emotion that is gentle and unselfish, timeless and enduring. We can contrast this notion of ideal love with the more down-to-earth love of our daily lives. For instance, while love may be unselfish, it can also be the basis of such selfish feelings as possessiveness and jealousy; while love may be intensely pleasurable, it can also be very painful; while love may last a lifetime, it can also be a fickle and short-lived experience. Some people find that love expands their life options, others are inhibited or stifled by love. We might suggest that the opposites of love are hate, loneliness, or selfishness, but we know that for some people these opposites are a part of the love relationship.

Not only are there great individual differences in the feeling and expression of love, but we may also experience different kinds of love for the same individual. The following are some ways in which love might be categorized: maternal or paternal love, platonic love, romantic love, sexual love, companionate love, religious love, love of humanity, and so on. Philosophers and psychologists have attempted their own categorizations, often resorting to the Greek terms as a basis for distinguishing one kind of love from another. For example:

Eros is often considered to be synonymous with need and desire. Erotic love is also defined by sensual or sexual intimacy—or at least the urge or craving for it. Eros may also express a love of beauty.

Agape is love in its most altruistic form. When we unselfishly devote our attentions to another, we express our agape. The Latin word *caritas* also expresses this kind of love or caring for another.

Philia is the friendship component of love, sometimes referred to as brotherly or sisterly love.

Perhaps there is an even more fundamental or pure wellspring for all three of these types of love. It has been suggested, for example, that the capacity for love is an instinctive response to our awareness of life. When the influential psychotherapist Abraham Maslow was recovering from a severe heart attack, he wrote to his friend Rollo May:

The confrontation with death—and the reprieve from it—makes everything look so precious, so sacred, so beautiful that I feel more strongly than ever the impulse to love it, to embrace it, and to let myself be overwhelmed with it. My river has never looked so beautiful. . . . Death, and its ever present possibility makes love, passionate love, more possible. I wonder if we could love passionately, if ecstasy would be possible at all, if we knew we'd never die. (May, 1969, p. 98)

In this letter, Maslow reveals a love of life that is erotic and sensual but also profound and intellectual. He also expresses very eloquently the joy to be found in such feelings of pure love.

Perhaps, like Voltaire, we should conclude that "there are so many sorts of love that one does not know where to seek a definition of it." To St. Paul, love was an expression of our basic humanity and goodness; to others, love may mean sex or security or possession or even "never having to say you're sorry." Each definition has validity for a certain person at a specific time and place. But even without a universal definition, we have no difficulty in identifying the love relationships in our lives.

THE ORIGINS OF LOVE

There are two major schools of thought on the development of the love relationship. The first approach, the "imperative" or "instinctive," sees love as a force or drive that shapes human behavior from within. According to Freud, the origin of this force was the psyche, and he viewed love as a transformation, a sublimation, of this more basic sexual instinct, or libido. In contrast, Plato placed the source of the love force outside of the individual; he believed that we are pulled toward someone who will make us feel whole. Although Freud and Plato differ as to the source of love, they agree that it is a manifestation of instinctive urges that must be expressed in one form or another.

Also in the Freudian tradition is the view of Karl Menninger (1970), that love is the expression of the basic life instinct. In keeping with classic psychoanalytic thought, Menninger believed that love will always find some outlet, even if it has to be transformed, or sublimated, in the process. For the soldiers in Napoleon's army, their weapons of destruction became the objects of love:

Roy Lichtenstein. *"I love you you, but . . ."* (Courtesy, Leo Castelli Gallery. Collection of Alberto Urlich. Photo by Rudolph Burckhardt.)

It was now the great glory of these men to take care of their guns. They loved tenderly the merciless monsters. They lavished caresses and terms of endearment upon the glittering, death-dealing brass. The heart of man is a strange enigma. Even when most degraded it needs something to love. These blood-stained soldiers, brutalized by vice, amid all the horrors of battle, lovingly fondled the murderous machines of war. . . . The unrelenting gun was the stern cannoneer's lady-love. He kissed it with unwashed, mustached lips. . . . Affectionately he named it Mary, Emma, Lizzie. (Menninger, 1970, p. 264)

According to Freud, all forms of love originate from the sexual instinct (libido) — thus even the mother-child caretaking relationship is based on a sort of sublimated sexuality.

Other "instinct" theories of love, however, follow completely different lines. For example, the German ethologist Irenäus Eibl-Eibesfeldt (1974) has suggested that Freud was "hitching the cart before the horse" by proposing that mother-child love was an expression of sexual instincts. Instead, Eibl-Eibesfeldt theorized that mother-child love is the *basic* instinct, and that sexual behavior in the adult is derived from this instinct. In other words, our adult expressions of sexuality are a sublimation of the instinctive love between mother and child. The views of Freud and Eibl-Eibesfeldt are similar, however, in that they both see love as an imperative part of human development, an instinct that must be expressed in one form or another.

In the second major school of thought regarding the origins of love, the "optional" or "learning" approach, culture and personal experience are seen as the factors that shape the development of feelings of love. We, for example, live in a love-oriented culture — love between parent and child and between mature adults is highly valued; we cannot conceive of a "normal" life style that does not contain love relationships. Our novels, movies, and popular music are filled with love themes, and children grow up viewing love and marriage as a necessary part of the adult experience. Our culture reinforces us for being in love, and we feel deprived and incomplete without it. But this strong emphasis on love has not existed in all cultures at all times. In some cultures marriage is far more likely to be based on financial or familial considerations than on feelings of love. Moreover, in the Europe of several hundred years ago, when infant mortality rates were extremely high, parental love tended to be expressed only after a child had passed a critical age and seemed likely to survive.

In the learning approach detailed by Elaine Walster and William Walster (1978), passionate love has two important components: a physiological state of arousal and a cognitive labeling process. Suppose a physiological state involving sweaty palms, a flushed face, and a pounding heart. Before the emotion can be labeled, one needs to take account of the external environment. If one is standing at the edge of a precipice, the emotion might be labeled fear; if one is arguing with an enemy, the emotion might be labeled anger; if one is in the presence of an attractive and appropriate sexual partner, one might think that one is "in love." Of course, this is a simplification of the labeling process, but the important point is that the label is optional. Even in the presence of an attractive partner, one could identify the emotion slightly differently ("It's only infatuation") or totally differently ("I'm very annoyed"). This optional, social-learning explanation emphasizes the highly subjective and personal manner in which love is experienced, but it does not deny the importance of the experience to the individual.

The notion of "love scripts," which comes from transactional analysis (Berne, 1971; Steiner, 1974), also conveys the idea of a learned, optional way of expressing love. For example, according to Berne some of us are programmed at an early stage to play the role of losers or winners ("frogs versus princes"). To a large extent, these love scripts influence whether or not we define ourselves as successful in love relationships. A person who is a "frog" in script terms will always reject an appropriate love partner in favor of someone who is likely to be rejecting, whereas a "prince" will look for accepting and appropriate love partners. The way our love relationships turn out, according to transactional analysis, depends on the particular script we are playing out.

LOVE PROBLEMS

If we accept the notion of "love scripts" it follows that one major source of frustration and depression is the inability to follow a desired script, that is, a failure to satisfy this socially acquired need. One investigator calls depression the "no love script" and observes that "large numbers of people in this country are in a constant unsuccessful quest for a successful, loving relationship" (Steiner, 1974, p. 92). So, having celebrated the joys of love, we must now attend to some of love's hazards and problems. For many of us, the most painful experiences in life arise from our love relationships. Indeed, the losses and disappointments of love can be even more unforgettable than its joys. Psychologists find that the greater the individual's need for or dependency upon love, the more vulnerable he or she will be to its problems.

Love addiction. According to social psychologist Stanton Peele, dependency on love can be as crippling and destructive as dependency on an addictive drug.

When a person goes to another with the aim of filling a void in himself, the relationship quickly

becomes the center of his or her life. It offers him a solace that contrasts sharply with what he finds everywhere else, so he returns to it more and more, until he needs it to get through each day of his otherwise stressful and unpleasant existence. When a constant exposure to something is necessary in order to make life bearable, an addiction has been brought about, however romantic the trappings. The ever-present danger of withdrawal creates an ever-present craving. (Peele, 1976, p. 70)

For the love addict, the symptoms of withdrawal may be as severe as those of the drug addict—or even more traumatic—and may include physical discomfort, depression, anxiety, hopelessness, and other symptoms of emotional distress. Even if we disagree with Peele that dependency on love can be an addiction, it is certainly true that some people develop an unhealthy or even crippling investment in a love relationship. Erich Fromm (1956) cautioned against such *symbiotic* love feelings, in which the identity of the participants is diminished or submerged in a couple identity. He recommended instead that lovers strive to develop a relationship in which their integrity and individuality are reinforced.

Love and dominance. For some people, being in love is equated with an unhealthy desire to either dominate or be dominated. A couple may form a tacit agreement that one partner will lead and the other follow, or the two may constantly struggle for control of the love relationship. Another option is to share control, with each partner taking turns at being leader and follower. When lovers also relate to one another as companions, there is much less likelihood that either one will be abused or taken advantage of. Passionate or romantic love in which there is little companionship, however, can easily lead to a situation of psychological (and even physical) dominance (Walster and Walster, 1978). An extreme example of this sort of relationship is the wife who is physically abused by her husband and

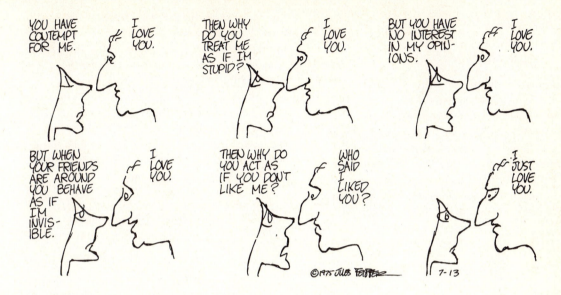

This cartoon by Jules Feiffer illustrates the notion that loving and liking may be quite separate for some individuals. (© *Jules Feiffer*)

reports that this abuse is proof of his love for her. Similarly, being mistreated may actually intensify feelings of love, as in the words of a one-time popular song:

I don't like you, but I love you
Seems that I'm always thinking of you
Though you treat me badly
I love you madly
You really got a hold on me.
(Smokey Robinson, "You've Really Got a Hold on Me," 1962)

Unrequited love. At some time in our lives, most of us will experience a one-sided love affair. Adolescents frequently develop crushes on unattainable partners—a teacher, actor, or rock music star—and although these experiences may be painful while they last, they are usually quickly forgotten. Unfortunately, the tendency to fall in love with someone out of reach does not end with adolescence, and many adults know the frustration and disap-

pointment of unrequited love. This experience has been glamorized by poets and songwriters—for example, the courtly love of the European Middle Ages, in which the love of a knight for a married noblewoman was, by definition, a love with no sexual or companionship possibilities. But the truth is that unrequited love is usually unrewarding and quite painful. Eric Berne takes some of the glamor out of unrequited love by remarking, "Some say one-sided love is better than none, but like half a loaf of bread, it is likely to grow hard and moldy sooner" (1976, p. 119).

Love and jealousy. In our society, jealousy and possessiveness have often been considered part and parcel of the love experience. Indeed, the most jealous lover may be viewed as the one who cares the most, and the romantic love script usually includes a strong possessiveness component. A lover who is not troubled by a partner's interest in another may be

Loving and Liking

Psychologists Elaine and William Walster (Walster and Walster, 1978) believe that loving and liking are two separate aspects of a relationship and that these aspects can be independently assessed. According to them, some relationships are high on passionate love but low on companionate love (liking); others are high on companionate love but have little spark, or passion. It is a rare relationship that is high on both factors.

Figure 3.1 reproduces the Walsters' set of 9-point scales for rating a relationship according to these two dimensions. First, select the partner (spouse, lover, or friend) who is to be the object of the rating. Then, for each item, choose the number from 1 ("disagree completely") through 9 ("agree completely") that best represents your feelings about that partner. The totals for the two scales may then be compared to determine which dimension of the relationship is stronger, the romantic or the companionate.

Source: E. Walster and G. W. Walster, *A New Look at Love* (New York: Addison-Wesley, 1978), p. 17–18.

PASSIONATE LOVE SCALE

1. I feel that I can confide in _____ about virtually everything.

1	2	3	4	5	6	7	8	9

Disagree   Agree to some extent   Agree completely

2. I would do almost anything for _____.

1	2	3	4	5	6	7	8	9

3. If I could never be with _____, I would feel miserable.

1	2	3	4	5	6	7	8	9

LIKING/COMPANIONATE LOVE SCALE

1. I think that _____ is unusually well-adjusted.

1	2	3	4	5	6	7	8	9

Disagree   Agree to some extent   Agree completely

2. I have great confidence in _____'s good judgment.

1	2	3	4	5	6	7	8	9

3. _____ is one of the most likable people I know.

1	2	3	4	5	6	7	8	9

ANSWER SHEET

LOVING SCALE

Your feelings

1 _____

2 _____

3 _____

LIKING SCALE

Your feelings

1 _____

2 _____

3 _____

Now add them all up.

TOTAL: _____

TOTAL: _____

FIGURE 3.1

seen as uncaring, and lovers may attempt to provoke a jealous reaction to assure themselves that their love relationship is still strong. Yet as Margaret Mead has noted, "jealousy is not a barometer by which the depth of love can be read. It merely records the degree of the lover's insecurity. It is a negative, miserable state of feeling having its origin in the sense of insecurity and inferiority" (1960, p. 94).

It is not uncommon for some people to show very extreme reactions of jealousy—husbands may shoot their wives, or wives divorce their husbands, at the faintest suspicion that there is a third person intruding on the pair-bond. Although such reactions may be socially disapproved of if they are violent or extreme, they tend to be glorified and reinforced by popular culture.

Walster and Walster (1978) describe two basic components in the jealousy reaction: first, the jealous partner may feel that his or her pride has been injured; second, there may be a sense that "property rights," or the right of ownership, have been violated. According to these researchers, the predominant male response to jealousy is either outward denial ("I don't give a damn") or anger directed toward the partner. For females, the predominant responses are self-blame ("What did I do wrong?") and attempts to win the partner back.

LOVE AND SEXUALITY

Within certain religious and cultural traditions, the only moral justification for sexual activity has been the desire to bear children. The majority of our society, however, no longer holds this view. Instead, we have accepted love as a valid reason for entering a sexual relationship; love serves to legitimize sexual relationships in which there is no re-

productive intention. Morton Hunt (1974) notes, for instance, that while adolescents are more sexually active now than they were in the 1940s, it is largely within the framework of our culture's long-cherished values of intimacy and love that this new sexual freedom operates. Casual, recreational, or unemotional sex make up a very small proportion of the sexual activity reported in Hunt's survey. Indeed, our culture tells us that sex is meaningful only when it occurs as an expression of love for another.

If love has become an acceptable reason for sexual intimacy, it is not surprising that many people convince themselves that they are in love in order to justify sexual experimentation. But by convincing ourselves that we are in love each time we enter a sexual relationship, we may create a new set of difficulties. One researcher argues, for example, that "while more sex is taking place, it seems that relationships are often more staid and confining than ever. Since sex is still usually rationalized by assuring oneself that one's lover is someone special, the pressures toward closing oneself off prematurely are actually increasing" (Peele, 1976, p. 145). As sexual experimentation starts earlier and earlier in the life cycle, young people also tend to "fall in love" at an earlier age.

A great deal of popular support exists for the notion that sex with love is healthy and worthwhile whereas casual, or uninvolved, sex is a sign of emotional problems and is bound to be unsatisfying. Thus Fromm (1956) observed that although physical attraction may create a momentary illusion of union, sex without love results in a feeling of estrangement that is even more marked than before. In the same way, those who look for "cool sex," or sex without love, are suffering, according to Rollo May (1975), from certain basic fears or inadequacies. Love, suggests May, can easily create anxieties, and one way of avoiding these love fears is to "play it cool" and seek sex without love.

For certain individuals, sex and love are completely antithetical. In some cases, a strong religious indoctrination causes a man to develop a "madonna/prostitute" syndrome, in which women are viewed as either very good or very bad. While in this script the "madonna," or good woman, is the ideal love object, it is the "prostitute," or bad woman, toward whom sexual desire is directed. Sexual performance problems arise for these men when they attempt to combine sex with love. A similar difficulty exists for men who develop sexual fetishes—that is, attraction to inanimate objects—but cannot become aroused in the presence of a loved one.

Ultimately, the value of sex with or without a love component is a personal decision. Obviously some people in our society find casual sex a positive and satisfying experience whereas others firmly reject such experiences. This difference of opinion cannot be reconciled other than by accepting the diversity of human sexual behavior. As one writer notes:

Under ideal circumstances, sex can be a healthy, healing influence, bringing people together and enriching their lives. Some insist that this powerful agent should be held back until other interactions have occurred, such as a wedding ceremony or "falling in love." Others argue that sexual activity helps promote friendship and that it should be used early in a relationship. Each individual must decide such questions for himself and should respect those whose decisions are different. (Cross, 1979, p. 20)

Heterosexual Patterns and Relationships

There is no single pattern in the formation of heterosexual relationships. Even those among us who follow the culturally approved pattern of dating, engagement, marriage, parenting, and lifelong fidelity may show a great deal of diversity in the specifics of the pattern; some of us prolong the dating phase into our twenties or thirties, others virtually omit dating and marry while in our teens; some of us delay parenting, others have children in the early years of marriage. Many of us, perhaps even the majority, do not follow the culturally approved pattern: we may choose not to marry, or we may choose to marry several times. We may decide that although marriage fits our needs, parenting or fidelity does not.

Regardless of the choices we make, we are all subject to social pressures that encourage us to see as normal the predominant heterosexual life styles of our culture. By looking at other cultures, however, we can see that our ideas of what is normal are not shared around the world. For example, we see our early twenties as a good time to marry. In contrast, teenage marriage is the rule in many countries, while the Chinese believe that marriage should be delayed until the late twenties or even early thirties. Similarly, some cultures see dating or engagement as a time for sexual experimentation, whereas other cultures insist on virginity until marriage. As is the case for most aspects of human sexuality, a diversity of patterns in heterosexual relationships is the rule rather than the exception.

PAIR-BONDING

Perhaps the closest we can come to making a generalization about heterosexual patterns is that human beings seek to form *pair-bonds*. By a pair-bond, we mean an intense emotional relationship between two individuals. Two critical aspects of this relationship are *trust* and *self-disclosure*: trust grows as we disclose more about ourselves, and conversely, self-disclosure is greatly facilitated by an atmosphere of trust. For most people, a third aspect of the pair-bond is *long-term commitment*—a promise that the intimacy of the pair-bond will be permanent. A fourth feature common to many pair-bonds is *exclusivity*, based on a belief that intimacy can exist only when it is not shared outside of the primary relationship.

It has been suggested that the nature of adult sexual relationships is based, to some extent, on patterns of child rearing. According to one researcher,

Pair-bonding, which may involve a high degree of monogamy or sexual exclusivity, is often found in species in which the male participates in care and rearing of the young. If the parental role is solely the female's responsibility and "fatherhood" does not exist, mating between males and females does not necessitate protracted precopulatory courtship or formation of a close and enduring heterosexual relationship. (Beach, 1976, pp. 305–306)

For example, among certain animal species, such as the northern wolf, where child-care is shared by both parents, the adult pair-bond is so strong that the partners will remain completely faithful until one or the other dies. In contrast, the male deer or antelope contributes nothing to the child-rearing process and does not form a pair-bond with his mate. Advocates of *sociobiology*—a discipline that attempts to explain social behavior by looking at biological processes—believe that this same pattern can be extended to describe human pair-bonding (see the boxed extract). In most human societies, the child is most likely to prosper when it receives the attention of both parents, so pair-bonding is strong, exclusive, and relatively permanent. Thus, we would expect that where a father is not crucial to the raising of his children, the pair-bond will be weakened.

Of course, we could suggest numerous nonbiological bases for the formation of pair-bonds: to avoid alienation and loneliness, to enhance emotional security, to express and receive love, to share physical intimacy. In the words of the English poet John Donne, "No man is an island"; we all seek other human beings with whom to establish bonds of intimacy. In the following sections, we will look at how this search takes place, and the patterns that result as heterosexual relationships are formed.

DATING AND COURTSHIP

We can assume that for all cultures, the goal of courtship or dating is the formation of heterosexual pair-bonds. However, as John Money (1977) notes, there are many ways of integrating human pair-bonding into the totality of a society's customs. One of the most well-known variations of courtship is the Scandinavian tradition of night courtship.

Night-courting traditionally was a warm-weather institution, for the rigors of a northern winter dictated that all members of the household keep warm at night around the great log fireplace of the communal kitchen and living room. When winter ended, and people segregated into their separate sleeping quarters, the single girls of the household took to their special sleeping quarters in the girls' house. Typically they occupied the loft, accessible by anterior ladder, of a small storage barn. Once inside the building, the girls could fasten the door. Their guests would join them by climbing a rope ladder thrown down from the upper window.

As guests to join them, they might invite up a

(continued on p. 92)

The Sociobiology of Courtship and Mating Behavior

What can we learn by studying the courtship and mate selection behavior of other, nonhuman species? Sociobiologist David Barash (1977) argues that the courtship and mate selection patterns of all species that reproduce sexually are extremely important in determining reproduction and the ultimate evolutionary success of the species. Natural selection, according to the sociobiologists, accounts for the mating patterns unique to each species. If a particular mating strategy leads to fewer or weaker offspring in a given species, then that strategy is less likely to be favored by the individual species members. The underlying principles of courtship and mate selection emerge when we compare the patterns that are observable in a wide diversity of species.

First, there is the question of choice of a specific partner for mating. "This is the major function of *courtship,* a characteristic set of behaviors occurring between male and female directly concerned with mating and reproduction" (Barash, 1977, p. 144). Generally, courtship rituals increase the chance of mating with a member of the same species, of the appropriate gender, and with certain desired traits. In certain species it also serves to reduce aggression and increase cooperation, which may be essential to future child rearing. Courtship can also be called a kind of "sexual advertising," in which the male usually plays the role of "salesman" and the female the role of "discriminating customer" (Barash, 1977). The sociobiological explanation of this basic gender difference is that the female (of most species) makes a much greater commitment of time, resources, and future mating ability when she accepts the reproductive burdens and responsibilities of mating. Once the male has performed the function of insemination, his biological role in reproduction is usually complete and he is left free to copulate with other females. From the point of view of the female, courtship may play an important role in selecting a mate who is more likely to assist in raising her offspring. In this respect, offspring survival is a secondary, but perhaps very important, function of both courtship and mate selection.

Sociobiologists have also studied the types of social bonding that accompany the mate selection process in a great many species. Table 3.1 summarizes each of the significant mating systems observed in birds and animals. Each system (e.g., monogamy, polygyny, polyandry) has certain costs and benefits that determine the choice of system for each species. A basic rule is that in those species in which the male contributes little to the nourishment or raising of offspring (e.g., mammalian herbivores) polygyny is far more common than monogamy. On the other hand, among carnivores and most bird species, a female alone may not be able to provide sufficient food for her young, and these species will therefore be more likely to favor monogamous mating systems. A natural example of polyandry (one female with several males) occurs in those species of birds in which the male has the role of incubating the eggs and the female is free to find another mate, who may then take on the role of incubating a second batch of eggs.

TABLE 3.1
Classification of Animal Mating Systems

System	Definition	Example
MONOGAMY	Reproductive unit of one male and one female; pair-bond formed	
Annual monogamy	Bonds formed anew each year	Small passerine birds: sparrows, warblers, etc.
Perennial monogamy	Bond retained for life	Swans, geese, eagles, gibbons
POLYGAMY	Reproductive unit of one individual of one sex and several of another; pair-bond formed	
Polygyny	One male bonded with several females	
Serial	One male bonded with several females during a breeding season, but only one at a time	Pied flycatchers
Simultaneous	One male bonded with several females simultaneously during the breeding season	Red-winged blackbirds, fur seals, elk, etc.
Polyandry	One female bonded with several males	
Serial	One female bonded with several males during a breeding season, but only one at a time	Rheas
Simultaneous	One female bonded with several males simultaneously during the breeding season	Jacanas
PROMISCUITY	No bonds formed	Grouse, bears, wildebeests

Source: D. P. Barash, *Sociobiology and Behavior* (New York: Elsevier Press, 1977), p. 161.

The mating systems that are promiscuous are usually those in which there is considerable competition or sexual advertising among the males, and the female will choose the most desirable male for each successive mating.

How does sociobiology account for pair-bonding in humans? Again, the necessities of child rearing are proposed as the fundamental principle:

Human infants are totally helpless and require the committed attention of one parent, invariably the woman, since she is also adapted to nourish her newborn. It would certainly help if there was a daddy around to hunt, scavenge, defend the female and her child, and so forth. Given that, during our evolutionary development, offspring were more likely to be successful if they received the committed assistance of at least two adults, selection would favor any mechanism that kept the adults together. Sex may be such a device, selected to be pleasurable for its own sake, in addition to its procreative function. (Barash, 1977, p. 297)

roving band of youths who, of a summer evening, went about the countryside to serenade the girls whom they wanted to meet. The girls would recognize the boys by their voices, and so would decide whether or not to welcome them—or rather, whether one particular girl wanted to meet one particular boy. After a period of general sociability, if it became obvious that a couple wanted to be left alone, then on subsequent occasions it would be arranged for the boy to stay alone with the girl overnight.

Staying overnight did not imply that sexual intercourse would automatically take place. He who was allowed to stay had to comply with a traditional set of rules. At first he must sleep with all his clothes on, and above the covers; then clothed, but under the covers, until finally he and his girlfriend agreed to copulation.

It was at this point that the couple announced to their families and the community their intention of betrothal, and the appropriate festivities were celebrated. If no pregnancy ensued, then marriage was not obligatory. In fact, without a pregnancy, marriage might be discouraged. (Hertoft, 1977, p. 507)

The night courtship tradition, which worked well in the rural communities of Scandinavia up to the beginning of this century, is certainly alien to modern-day Americans. Probably, the courtship customs we take for granted would seem equally alien in other parts of the world. Indeed, dating as we know it is a relatively recent phenomenon, one that first appeared on the American college scene about 50 years ago and steadily increased in popularity. Before the advent of dating, contact between courting couples was mostly limited to general social occasions or to the front parlor of the girl's home and was usually under the watchful eye of a chaperon. Also, parents of that time were more actively involved in the selection of an appropriate mate for their child, a decision that was considered too important to be left to the whims of courting couples.

To a perceptive observer, much of the su-

perficiality and competitiveness of dating was already apparent in 1940s:

The game is described as dating; boys take out girls, girls have to be asked, boys have to ask, both must dress correctly according to the adolescent styles of the moment, the date must be conducted in some way so that it can be known to the rest of the group—otherwise it doesn't count. . . . The boy who longs for a date is not longing for a girl. He is longing to be in a situation, mainly public, where he will be seen by others to have a girl, and the right kind of girl, who dresses well and pays attention. . . . He takes her out as he takes out his new car, but more impersonally, because the car is his for good but the girl is his only for the evening. (Mead, 1949, pp. 285–287)

Although the "dating game" of today may have lost some of these highly ritualized and inflexible characteristics, it is not without its trials and tribulations. Moreover, as the average age at first marriage increases, men and women are spending more years overall in this phase. One observer (McCary, 1975) estimates that women now date an average of a little more than 6 years, men an average of more than 8 years. Unlike the courting in most animal species, in which the sole purpose of courtship is the selection of a mate, dating in contemporary society serves a variety of important functions: it acts as an affirmation of masculinity and femininity, as young men and women demonstrate through dating their attractiveness to the opposite sex; it provides a semistructured social situation for the learning and rehearsal of basic social and sexual skills; and it allows for shared entertainment and recreation away from home and parental constraints. Nevertheless, mate selection and pair-bonding are still the primary function of the courtship mode that we know as dating.

Dating relationships pass through a number of important stages. In the first stage, casual dating, the partners are either too young or in-

Dating practices are strongly influenced by the teenager's peer group. Surveys indicate that young people today begin dating at an earlier age, and dating relationships are more sexually permissive than at any time in the past. *(Susan Shapiro)*

sufficiently interested to pursue the relationship beyond a short-term, limited involvement. For the older "single," such dating may serve the purpose of providing partners for relatively impersonal sexual encounters. At a later stage, couples who have been dating for some time may move toward establishing an exclusive, or steady, relationship. Although there is no generally accepted definition of "going steady," this phase is important because it signifies a level of commitment and the formation of a pair-bond. The last important stage before marriage is engagement,

which signifies that marriage is anticipated and planned for. The older term, "betrothal," meant a legally binding promise to marry, whereas our term, "engagement," signifies an intention that does not constitute a legal contract.

The sexual side of dating. Perhaps the most striking change in American dating practices over the past 50 years has been in attitudes toward sexual activity. Certainly, the official religious and moral position, both in the past and in the present, has been to require abstinence for both males and females. But for most of our dating history we have actually practiced a double standard, in which men are expected to push for sexual contact and women are expected to resist such pressure. Only very recently have we seen the emergence of a permissive standard that is supposed to apply equally to males and females. In discussing these changing standards, it should be noted that we are not talking only about sexual intercourse; in the 1930s and 1940s, behaviors such as necking and petting were usually condemned by parents as severely as premarital intercourse is today. Indeed, the older reader may recall when kissing on the first date was a hotly debated issue, whereas nowadays, kissing is almost taken for granted.

On the basis of his questionnaire studies, sociologist Ira Reiss has drawn several conclusions about current attitudes. His overall assessment is that an enormous change has taken place in the premarital sex scene, most important being the felt legitimacy of the sexual choice. Although many parents today do not accept this legitimacy and still believe that abstinence is the only proper path, "the majority of young people believe the choice is legitimately theirs in sex as it is in politics, religion, and other personal areas of their existence" (Reiss, 1977, pp. 315–316).

Although he characterizes the current premarital scene as "permissive," Reiss finds that for most young people the presence of a relatively stable and affectionate relationship is still a necessary condition for full sexual expression. Only a small minority of Reiss' respondents subscribed to "permissiveness without affection." Thus it seems that love has replaced marriage as the major justification for sexual experimentation. This trend appears to be true even in predominantly Catholic societies such as Quebec (Crepault, 1976).

Reiss also investigated the factors that in-

crease or decrease sexual permissiveness during dating. Parental attitudes and the closeness of family ties seem to have a limiting effect, as does the strength of religious commitment. On the other hand, the attitudes of peers and friends tend to facilitate sexual permissiveness. A study of 421 undergraduates at Washington State University, however, found some interesting differences between men and women. For example, female permissiveness was most strongly related to parental attitudes and the frequency of church attendance, whereas male permissiveness was most directly affected by the perceived sexual standards of peers and friends. In general, influences outside the family had a weaker effect on females than on males (Libby, Gray, and White, 1978).

What are the pros and cons of sexual permissiveness during dating? On the positive side are several studies, starting with the Kinsey report (Kinsey et al., 1953), showing that premarital sexual experience is correlated with a woman's subsequent sexual satisfaction during marriage. Given this correlation, many young couples are unwilling to marry before testing their sexual compatibility. There is the additional argument that premarital sex increases intimacy and strengthens a relationship, whereas abstinence can build tension and frustration. Finally, it is recognized that while young people are starting to date earlier, they are getting married later, and it may be unrealistic to expect abstinence to be maintained over such a long period.

On the negative side is the ever-present possibility of premarital pregnancy. Even though effective contraception is available to the adolescent, statistics show that many dating couples do not use birth control techniques. Premarital sex is often competitive, exploitative, and impersonal. Boys may feel increasing pressure to "score," and girls may feel mature only if they are coitally active. Ad-

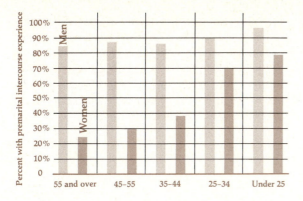

FIGURE 3.2

The incidence of premarital intercourse. Although there has been a dramatic increase in the number of women who have sex before marriage, there has been a much smaller increase in the number of men with premarital intercourse experience. (Hunt, 1973, p. 74)

olescence is normally a difficult period of transition in which young people strive to attain adult status; pressures toward sexual performance may add to the strains of growing up. Young people may feel caught between the conflicting values of parents and peers; by pleasing one group, they risk rejection by the other. As Kinsey observed, "For a person who believes that premarital intercourse is morally wrong (and yet engages in it) there may be conflicts which can do damage not only to marital adjustment, but to the entire personality of the individual" (Kinsey et al., 1953, p. 561).

Despite these conflicts, the numbers of men and women having premarital intercourse has steadily increased. As shown in Figure 3.2, the change for men has been quite small, whereas female sexual experience before marriage has increased dramatically. Hunt (1973) suggests

that this reflects a decline in the sexual double standard.

MARRIAGE

Customs of marriage, like those of courtship and dating, show great variation at different times and in different places. There are three basic types of marriage: *monogamy* (or marriage between one man and one woman), *polygyny* (in which a man may have two or more wives), and *polyandry* (in which a woman may have two or more husbands). Although most modern societies permit only monogamy and have legal prohibitions against marriage with more than one partner, which is termed "bigamy," we seem to have developed a new marriage form that might be called *serial monogamy*, that is, a series of consecutive monogamous relationships.

The notion that marriage should be based on romantic love is far from universal, although it is a powerful belief in our own culture. According to Ashley Montagu,

When one surveys marital relations in nonliterate societies, it is found that while the notion of marriage for love is not unknown, it is seldom possible to practice it. Marriages are usually arranged by the elders, and the spouses have to adjust to each other as well as they are able. In many nonliterate societies, as for example, the Australian aborigines and in innumerable African societies, the female may be married at puberty to a male who is old enough to be her grandfather. . . . Such marriages are frequently notably successful. . . . The fact that such marriages do occur between spouses of extremely different age groups who have been brought together in an arranged union indicates that adjustment in marriage under quite unpromising conditions is possible. (1962, p. 179)

In the United States, we live in a culture that strongly reinforces the importance of marriage. Indeed, "Americans believe in marriage above all. They marry earlier, remain un-married less often, and remarry after divorce more frequently and more rapidly than people of any other industrialized nation. They look to their marital relationship for their greatest satisfaction in life'' (Udry, 1971, p. 2). Along with our belief in marriage, though, some-times doubts arise about whether marriage as it now stands can survive the stresses of mod-ern life. Opinion polls tend to underscore this ambivalence: people typically report that the institution of marriage has weakened in the past decade but at the same time indicate that they believe it to be necessary and important (see the boxed extract).

What are the alternatives to the traditional marriage contract? Throughout history, we can find numerous examples of groups that tried to develop alternative styles of marriage. The Oneida Community, set up by John Humphrey Noyes in Oneida, New York, prac-ticed group marriage for about 30 years, until the pressures of public disapproval forced its disbandment. By contrast, the community of the Shakers, a group founded by Ann Lee, was based on the principle of celibacy. Although the Shaker community lasted for more than 50 years, it was unable to recruit enough members to carry on its beliefs. Literally thou-sands of communes, practicing various forms of group marriage, mushroomed and died out in the 1960s and the early 1970s.

Less radical alternatives involve main-taining the basic pair-bonding aspect of mar-riage but modifying some of the assumptions implicit in the marriage contract. For instance, the concept of *open marriage*, in which hus-band and wife are free to form sexual liaisons outside the marriage, was developed as an al-ternative to lifelong sexual fidelity. In addi-tion, our culture has come to question whether the husband is solely responsible for the fami-ly's economic support and the wife solely responsible for the domestic chores. Finally,

we have come to question the myth that mo-nogamy can meet all of our social, sexual, and personal needs. Indeed, given the weight of our expectations—that marriage will provide lifelong intimacy, security, excitement, and stability—it is not at all surprising that many marriages buckle under the weight.

Sex in marriage. To judge by the number of books, magazine articles, and television pro-grams dealing with sexual dysfunction, and by the recent spread of sex therapy clinics across the country, we might conclude that marital sexuality is in serious trouble in the United States. This conclusion is reinforced by such authorities as William Masters and Virginia Johnson, who have estimated that some form of sexual dysfunction exists in as many as half of all contemporary marriages. But we should see this conclusion in the con-text of two recent developments in our per-spectives on sexuality: first, we are far more willing to discuss our sexual problems openly and seek help for them, and second, we have very high expectations for the experience of marital sexuality. As one researcher notes

The progress our society has made toward fuller and freer sexuality has revolutionized our expec-tations and made many of us so intolerant of our dissatisfactions that we forget the improvement that has taken place in our lives; like all partially liberated people, we are more discontented now than we were before our lot began to improve. (Hunt, 1974, p. 179)

What did our ancestors expect from marital sexuality? Throughout most of Western his-tory, reproduction and not pleasure was the goal of sexual activity. Thus even within the confines of marriage, couples were expected to limit the frequency of ''sexual indulgence.'' In Victorian England, married women were ex-pected to tolerate sex only for the sake of ma-ternal goals, and many married men sought sexual gratification within a thriving prostitu-

A Statistical Look at Marriage, Divorce, and the Family

MARRIAGE

☐ About 90 percent of Americans will be married at some time in their lives.

☐ In about one of every six American marriages, at least one spouse has been married previously.

☐ The average age at first marriage has been increasing since about 1950. For example, according to the U.S. Census Bureau, the median age in 1960 was 22.8 for men and 20.3 for women; in 1978, the median age was 24.2 for men and 21.8 for women.

☐ In 1978, there were 48 million married households in the United States.

☐ In 1978, 2.2 million marriages were contracted in the United States.

DIVORCE

☐ U.S. Census Bureau data show that the divorce rate

— In 1940 was about 2 per 1,000 persons
— Following World War II rose to 4.3 per 1,000 persons
— In 1960 dropped to 2.2 per 1,000 persons
— In 1978 soared to 5.1 per 1,000 persons

☐ In 1978, there were 1.1 million divorces in the United States.

☐ It has been estimated that if present trends continue, nearly 4 of every 10 American marriages will end in divorce.

CHILDREN

☐ The number of American children involved in divorce was 361,000 in 1956; it had increased to 1,117,000 by 1976.

☐ The number of one-parent families headed by women was 5.6 million in 1970; by 1978, it was 8 million—an increase of 43 percent.

☐ In 1960, 9 percent of all children lived with one parent; by 1978, the number had increased to 19 percent of all children.

SINGLES

☐ By 1978, one of every five American households contained only one person—an increase of 42 percent over the 1970 figures.

☐ In 1960, the proportion of never-married women between the ages of 25 and 29 was 10.5 percent; by 1978, it had increased to 18 percent. For men, the figures were 21 percent in 1960 and 28 percent in 1978.

COHABITATION

☐ The number of unmarried couples who live together more than doubled between 1970 and 1978.

☐ For couples under the age of 25, the number of unmarried couples living together increased by a factor of 8—from 29,000 such couples in 1970 to 236,000 in 1978.

☐ In 1978, there were a total of 1.1 million unmarried couple households in the United States.

---

tion industry, rather than at home. Indeed, prominent theologians and physicians of the nineteenth century proposed that a couple should have sexual intercourse only as often as they desired to become parents. Physician William Alcott, who wrote a popular marriage manual in 1866, advised that "the pleasures of love, no less than the strength of the orgasm, are enhanced by their infrequency." In keeping with this view, Alcott advocated intercourse no more than once per month and called on "divine law" as supporting his argument. Our ancestors not only accepted these limits on coital frequency but also had limited expectations about female pleasure during intercourse. The notion that women were capable of orgasm was considered somewhat improper.

In the twentieth century, however, many of our ideas about marital sexuality began to change. Female orgasm came to be recognized and to be seen as important to marital satisfaction. *Simultaneous orgasm* — in which husband and wife reach orgasm at the same moment — came to be accepted as the standard measure of healthy sexuality. Then women started to feel pressured to have not just one but mul-

tiple orgasms, and couples were told that sex should be varied, creative, and frequent throughout marriage. Facing these rising expectations, it is not at all surprising that many couples became disappointed with a sex life that did not meet society's high standards. Thus as Hunt suggests, unrealistic expectations may be clouding the true picture of marital sexuality. The evidence from recent sex surveys — such as the *Redbook* survey (Tavris and Sadd, 1977) and the *Playboy* survey (Hunt, 1974) — indicate that American couples are having sex more often, more effectively, and with a greater variety of foreplay and intercourse techniques than the generation surveyed by Kinsey. Even though these newer samples may be biased toward more sexually liberal or open-minded respondents, the size and consistency of the survey results do indicate a meaningful and positive set of changes in marital sexuality. (These changes are presented in greater detail in Chapters 7 and 8.)

Perhaps the greatest problem that most couples face is how to avoid having marital sex become a matter of routine and habit. In particular, as sociologist Jessie Bernard points out, "For the man or woman to whom the excitement of sex is really the excitement of the chase and conquest there is, almost by definition, no way to keep marital sex from becoming boring" (1975, p. 17). If we consider that most married couples have intercourse about twice a week, then the average frequency in a year of marriage is about 100; after a decade of marriage, this means 1,000 intercourse experi-

Among the things that have changed about marital sexuality is the encouraging of sexual fantasy as a way to be creative sexually.
(© *Joel Gordon 1976*)

ences with the same partner. Although these figures are just rough averages, they are representative enough to illustrate the essential problem: How is it possible to maintain interest and excitement in an activity that is repeated 1,000 times or more? Added to this boredom or habituation problem are a variety of other complications associated with marriage. For example, sexual activity may become a relatively low priority when it must compete with the demands of pregnancy, child rearing, home care, career concerns, and financial pressures. Finally, in our youth-oriented culture, the physical attractiveness of one's spouse, and the care taken with one's own appearance, may decline with age.

In coping with these problems, we find that married couples change and adjust their sexual relationship in a number of important ways over time:

1. In the early years of marriage, sexual activity is typically initiated by the male; with time, responsibility may be more equally divided or the female may take greater responsibility for initiation.

2. As sexual interactions become less passionate and romantic, couples may refocus their sexual activity toward such goals as intimacy and relaxation.

3. One of the major advantages of having the same sexual partner over a long period of time is the opportunity to practice specific skills or sexual techniques, and to adjust to one another's sexual needs and rhythms. Thus the lack of novelty may be compensated for by increasing proficiency in, for instance, sexual stimulation and orgasmic ability.

4. As the sexual relationship becomes more comfortable and relaxed, married couples may be more willing to experiment with sharing each other's fantasies. Modern marriage manuals such as *The Joy of Sex* by Alex Comfort (1972) encourage sharing and even acting out sexual fantasies as a way of enhancing the sexual script.

5. Finally, an extramarital sexual experience on the part of either husband or wife may, in some instances, facilitate the marital sexual relationship. As we shall see in the next section, however, this strategy may involve considerable risk or danger to the marriage.

Extramarital relationships.
According to some observers: A curious paradox of adult American society is that the overwhelming majority disapprove of extramarital sex; yet large numbers, including many who disapprove, practice it. (Sprenkle and Weiss, 1978, p. 279)

Regarding extramarital sex, there is certainly an enormous conflict between our attitudes and beliefs on the one hand and our practices on the other. Adultery is explicitly prohibited by the seventh commandment, and it is regarded as a primary legal justification for divorce. Opposition comes not only from the Judeo-Christian religious tradition but also from our heritage of viewing marriage as a form of property rights—sexual infidelity is often seen as a violation of ownership. Indeed, the words we use to describe extramarital sex —"cheating," "unfaithfulness," "adultery"— are pejorative terms that convey a strong negative value judgment. When the theme of extramarital sex is taken up by movies, television, and books, it is usually portrayed as risky, divisive, and destructive behavior that leads to unhappiness and punishment.

These attitudes are not shared by all other cultures. Clellan Ford and Frank Beach (1951) found that of the 139 societies they studied, 61 percent placed strong restrictions on the extramarital liaisons of married women but were much more accepting of male infidelity. Among the eighty-five societies that officially disapproved of extramarital sex, were seventeen in which the practice was extremely common and punished only when the participants were very indiscreet. And in some societies, the custom of "wife lending" was socially regulated and approved:

The Chukchee of Siberia furnish an interesting example of this sort of permissiveness with respect to extra-mateship liaisons. Chukchee men often travel to distant communities and each married man generally makes special arrangements with some man in each of the communities he has occasion to visit. These arrangements are such that wherever he goes he may engage in a sexual liaison with his host's mate in return for permitting these men the same privileges when they visit his community. (Ford and Beach, 1951, pp. 114–115)

Less common are arrangements in which a woman is permitted several lovers as well as several husbands. One such society, the Toda of India, has no word for adultery. Among the Bena of Africa, both married men and married women frequently have extramarital affairs that, if discovered, generally result in no more than a brief outburst of temper.

Within the historical background of our own society, the Victorian era of the late nineteenth century was characterized by a strong double standard with respect to extramarital relationships. This comes as no surprise when we recall that while Victorian society elevated chastity in women, it openly acknowledged the "animal passions" of men. Although marriage and the family were held in very high regard, a man with money or power would often keep a mistress or resort to prostitutes to satisfy his desire for extramarital sex. Infidelity by a married woman, however, occurred much less frequently and was viewed as a major and reprehensible indiscretion.

The legacy of this Victorian double standard is apparent in Kinsey's (1953) data on the extent of extramarital sex in the United States: by age 40, about 50 percent of men but only 26 percent of women had experienced some form of extramarital relationship. Differences were also recorded in the ways that men and women responded to discovering a spouse's infidelity. Men were twice as likely as women

to cite the spouse's extramarital activities as a prime factor in divorce.

How much change has taken place since Kinsey's time? We might expect that with the shift toward more tolerant sexual attitudes, and with the increased attention being paid to extramarital sex, an enormous growth in the incidence and frequency of extramarital sex over the past 25 years would have occurred. Not so, according to Morton Hunt:

Our data in this area suggest that in the past generation there has been almost no measurable increase in the number of American husbands who ever have extramarital experience, and only a limited increase in the number of American wives who do so. . . . Only among men under 25 do we find any significant increase, but even that increase is of moderate proportions. As for our sample of married women, there is no evidence of any overall increase in incidence compared to a generation ago. Among wives under 25, however, there is a very large increase, but even this has only brought the incidence of extramarital behavior for these young women close to—but not yet on a par with—the incidence of extramarital behavior among under-25 husbands. (1974, p. 254)

Thus it appears that while the double standard is breaking down for the younger age group, the overall rates of extramarital activity have hardly changed. Hunt contends that it is one thing for people to be willing to have frank and open discussions on this topic, quite another for couples to risk endangering their marriage. In fact, when Hunt asked why people were *not* engaging in extramarital relationships, he found that legal and religious reasons were seen as far less important than the perception that such behavior would pose a threat to the security of the marriage.

This threat aspect of extramarital sex is almost taken for granted in our society. As portrayed in novels and movies, the "affair" is typically a highly secretive activity involving elaborate deception and certain to lead to divorce. To what extent is this stereotype based on reality? Two sociologists (Sprenkle and Weiss, 1978) analyzed existing information on extramarital "scripts." The following is a summary of their conclusions:

1. There is a very wide range of alternative extramarital scripts, depending on such factors as whether the spouse has knowledge of the relationship, the quality of the marriage relationship, and the degree to which one or both spouses have extramarital relationships.

2. Considering the large numbers of men and women who have engaged in extramarital sex, this behavior should be regarded as a normal part of the contemporary marriage experience—at least in the statistical sense.

3. Extramarital sex is sometimes, but not always, motivated by marital dissatisfaction. Nor is it always the cause of marital problems. About half the studies reviewed by these authors did show evidence of a correlation between extramarital sex and degree of marital unhappiness; but in the remaining studies, it appeared that extramarital sex was a neutral factor or even, in a few cases, a positive factor. For instance, one study—of 437 upper-middle-class marriages—found that the marriage relationship remained at least as good qualitatively as that existing between the average nonadulterous pair. This was true both for cases in which the spouse knew about the affair and for those in which the affair was secret (Cuber, 1969). This finding should be interpreted with caution, however, because of the biased nature of the sample.

4. There is an almost endless list of possible motives for engaging in extramarital sex. Among the more common motives found by Kinsey were an interest in more varied sexual experiences, pressure from a friend or spouse, status seeking, a need for greater autonomy or independence, and a desire to punish the

Extramarital affairs, which have become more common in our society, may have either positive or negative consequences, depending on the nature of the marital relationship. Alex Katz. *Cocktail Party.* (Courtesy, Harry N. Abrams, Inc. Photo by Rudolph Burckhardt.)

spouse for a previous infidelity. For those individuals motivated by a desire for greater sexual satisfaction, the indications are that the extramarital relationship may prove something of a disappointment. Hunt reported that 35 percent of women with extramarital experience failed to have orgasm with their extramarital partner, as compared with only 7 percent who failed most of the time with their husbands. However, orgasm is only one aspect of sexual satisfaction.

For many men and women the physical delights of the act are much outweighed by its various psychic rewards, in particular the renewed sense of personal desirability, the illusion of recaptured youth, the intensity of awareness and the rediscovery of poetry and passion. At the same time, along with these positive satisfactions many men and women continue to feel severe tensions, the nagging fear of discovery and the torment of inner conflict and guilt. (Hunt, 1974, p. 277)

While acknowledging that extramarital relationships can prove disruptive to marriage, many experts have recently taken the position that such relationships can also be beneficial to the individual and to the marriage. For example, one study based on interviews (Knapp and Whitehurst, 1977) showed that among couples actively involved in extramarital relationships and defining their marriages as "sexually open," only a minority of the marriages could be viewed as distressed. In the majority of cases, the marriages were relatively satisfactory and contained little conflict; the benefits reported for these marriages included freedom from fear of secret affairs, greater equality in the relationship, and a sense of relief at not being responsible for meeting all of the spouse's emotional and sexual needs.

Roger Libby (1977) also argues that comarital, or consensual, sexual relationships—which involve the consent or negotiated cooperation of the spouse, as distinct from the traditional

Group Marriage and Swinging

In exploring new sexual options, a number of people—both married and single—have experimented with unconventional forms of sexual activity, such as "swinging," group sex, and group marriage. For some people, these activities are one-time or occasional sexual adventures that are outside of the mainstream of their daily lives; for others, the appeal is so great that a new life style may develop around the sexual adventure.

SWINGING

In recent years, alternate sexual life styles have received a great deal of publicity in the media: newspapers carry advertisements for "like-minded couples," and clubs and hotels cater to "swingers" or those interested in group sex parties, or "orgies." It is virtually impossible, however, to state with any accuracy how many people are actually involved in such activities. On the basis of the data available to him, Hunt (1974) estimated that 2 percent, at most, of married couples had experienced mate swapping of one sort or another. For many of these couples, the experience had occurred only once. Although this seems a very small percentage, we should keep in mind that, if accurate, it represents close to 1 million married couples. Other estimates have been as high as 8 million (Denfield and Gordon, 1970). Most researchers report that the majority of swingers belong to a conventional, middle-class, and often professional segment of society.

One of the most complete research studies of swingers was conducted by Gilmartin (1977), who compared 200 actively swinging California couples with a control group of nonswinging couples matched for age, level of education and income, and presence or absence of children. The following is a summary of Gilmartin's findings on the differences between these two groups:

1. Swingers reported an unhappier childhood, more distant relationships with parents, and a greater incidence of separated or divorced parents than did controls. As adults, swingers interacted much less with close family and relatives.

2. On the other hand, swingers appeared to be more social in other respects—they spent a significantly greater amount of time with friends and acquaintances, including those not involved in swinging.

3. Although no overall differences were found between the religious or political affiliations of the two groups, the swingers participated much less actively in organized religion and politics.

4. In general, the swingers had begun dating at an earlier age, had "gone steady" with more partners prior to marriage, and tended to have married earlier than controls. Also, they had had their first intercourse experience at an earlier age and had had more premarital experience than the controls. Gilmartin suggests that for the swingers, social and sexual relationships were more important and rewarding at all stages of development.

5. The availability of literature about swinging was an important factor in determining the first swinging experience for 75 percent of the swinging couples. In almost all cases, it was the husband who first acquired the literature and then took the initiative in persuading his wife to become involved. In some cases, the wife's resistance to swinging was not diminished by the actual experience; in many other cases, the wives became more enthusiastic than their husbands, after a number of successful experiences.

6. When swinging and nonswinging couples were asked to rate their overall satisfaction with their marriages, the swingers reported slightly higher ratings. They also reported more frequent sexual relations with their spouses, and less boredom in their marriages.

Gilmartin concludes that for the couples in this study, the key element in making swinging a successful experience was value congruence between the spouses: "Of vital importance is how the partners view their behavior. If both partners can be mentally and emotionally satisfied in a swinging situation, then this type of sexual expression will not do any harm to their relationship" (1977, p. 185). Needless to say, if the sexual value system of either husband or wife does not include the possibility of swinging, then this behavior will cause conflict in the marriage and will not be incorporated into the couple's sexual life style.

GROUP MARRIAGE

Perhaps the most radical expression of sexual liberation is the group marriage. Like other experiments in group living, such as the commune, group marriages are usually founded on an idealistic attempt to replace the nuclear family. On the basis of an extensive study of group marriages, Larry and Joan Constantine (1977) concluded that although sex was an important determinant in the formation or dissolution of a group marriage, it was certainly not the crucial factor. They also reported that group marriages are confronted with a variety of practical problems in managing the sexual relationships of the participants:

Along the way, many strategies for pairing were tried, with even an occasional resort to a deck of cards. One group created a scheme whereby women controlled the sleeping arrangements one month and men controlled them the next. Bedroom arrangements varied, from each person having a bed and personal room to all participants in a single bed. (1977, p. 190)

These researchers concluded that faced with these and other problems, most group marriages break up relatively quickly.

and more deceptive adulterous relationship—may be beneficial to marriage. Yet another expert, Gerhard Neubeck (1969), a former president of the American Association of Marriage Counselors, feels that it is natural for married people to be attracted to outside relationships, and that it is possible to negotiate acceptable ground rules for extramarital affairs. Finally, Robert and Anna Francoeur, in an article entitled "Hot and Cool Sex," describe the potential advantages of open extramarital relationships:

Comarital or as we call them, *satellite relations*, are based on the premise that given the complexities of today's life, the varieties of educational backgrounds and personal expectations, we can no longer expect a spouse to totally and completely satisfy all one's needs. The comarital or satellite relationship becomes possible only when one is secure in one's own self-identity and in one's pair-bonded relation, when one does not consider his or her partner property that cannot be shared without being lost. (1977, pp. 308–309)

To balance these relatively positive views of extramarital relationships, we should point out that an affair can and sometimes does have strongly negative effects. For couples who view sexual infidelity as the ultimate transgression—and this view is extremely common in our culture—the discovery of a "cheating" spouse may completely end marital trust and intimacy. While consensual extramarital arrangements can aid in ending guilt and fear of discovery, few couples are emotionally attuned to frank discussions of this topic; discussions of extramarital liaisons are more likely to stimulate jealousy and possessiveness than cooperation and openness. Our religious, moral, and legal traditions strongly support the ideal of sexual monogamy—an ideal that has a major influence on our *attitudes* towards extramarital sex but a relatively weak impact on our extramarital *behavior*. Not surprisingly, this gap between what we think and what we do can cause severe marital distress.

Homosexual Patterns and Relationships

In general, discussions of heterosexuality tend to be relatively uncomplicated by questions of morality, legal sanctions, social deviance, psychological health, or etiology. Because our culture views heterosexuality as the normal course of development, we see little need to explain why it occurs. Thus even the most unusual forms of expressing heterosexuality—swinging, for instance—seem to require less explanation than the choice of a same-sex partner.

It is possible, of course, to describe various homosexual life styles without asking how and why they occur. To some extent this is how Kinsey researched homosexual activity—by

asking how often and with whom it occurred, not whether it was right or normal. The latter questions are part of our public consciousness, however, and they are also part of the reality of being homosexual within our culture. Homosexuality takes place within a social context; it would be difficult to understand the experience of being homosexual without at least a brief discussion of how our cultural tradition has viewed this form of sexual expression.

HISTORICAL BACKGROUND

Our religious traditions are strongly antihomosexual. For example, the Old Testament states: "If a man also lie with mankind as he lieth with a woman, both of them have committed an abomination: they shall surely be put to death; their blood shall be upon them" (Leviticus 20:13). This negative view continues in the writings of later religious authorities and, with a few exceptions, remains part of the Judeo-Christian ethic to this day. The notion that homosexuality is sinful or immoral has also been incorporated into our legal system. In medieval England, church laws against *sodomy*, or anal intercourse, became part of English civil law, and these "crimes against nature" were punishable by death. English immigrants to the United States brought these laws with them. Thus the Pilgrims of Massachusetts declared homosexual activity to be a capital offense with severe penalties. Although the legal penalties for homosexual behavior have become less severe with time, most states continue to maintain statutes that outlaw the performance of certain sexual acts even by consenting adults. (We should note that these laws could equally be applied to certain heterosexual acts.) Of course, laws against homosexuality are not enforced in most localities, just as arrests for "unnatural" heterosexual behavior are relatively unusual; but the police and the legal system do retain the option of applying these laws when they see fit to do so.

CROSS-CULTURAL PERSPECTIVES

A look at other cultures, and at other historical periods, reveals a great variety of attitudes and customs regarding homosexual activity, ranging from acceptance and encouragement to severe disapproval and punishment. The Ford and Beach (1951) survey, for example, shows that among seventy-six societies providing information about homosexual practices, 64 percent accepted or approved of such behavior under certain circumstances. In examining these and other cross-cultural data, however, we must remember certain distinctions. In particular, we must distinguish between homosexual behavior that conforms with certain social norms and customs in a culture and homosexual behavior that reflects a strong individual preference. For example, among the Big Nambas of the New Hebrides, homosexuality was part of the rites of circumcision; an older man acted as guardian and lover of the young boy before circumcision, and again after a thirty-day interval. This custom was regarded as necessary to strengthen the boy's penis (Bullough, 1976).

Another important distinction is between exclusive homosexuality and bisexuality (Davenport, 1976). A culture that advocated exclusive homosexuality would soon die out. So while some cultures make a place for the exclusive homosexual, they are unlikely to make homosexuality the norm. On the other hand, many cultures accept bisexual behavior if it follows prescribed rules and customs. In the Siwan tribe of Africa, for example, all males are expected to engage in anal intercourse with other males; but they are also expected to marry and to engage in heterosexual affairs. A man who does not participate in all of these types of sexual activity is considered strange. In contrast, the only form of homosexual activity condoned by the Dahomean tribe of Africa is mutual masturbation.

From their survey, Ford and Beach (1951) draw several general conclusions. First, among those societies where homosexual activity appears to be relatively rare, usually strong and specific sanctions are exacted against such behavior. Second, in a society that condones homosexual behavior, such behavior is most common among adolescents and is less likely to be approved for adults. Finally, reports of female homosexual activity are far more unusual than reports of male activity; this may reflect a true contrast in sexual behavior, or it may simply indicate that female homosexuality receives less attention in the culture than does male homosexuality.

Western societies have displayed a bewildering variety of attitudes toward homosexuality over the ages. We seem to be the heirs of two widely differing cultural and sexual traditions—that of the ancient Greeks and that of Judeo-Christian religious thought. The ancient Greeks are described by one writer (Bullough, 1976) as a "sex-positive" culture—that is, a culture in which few aspects of sexual expression were ritually prohibited and the experience of sexual pleasure was seen as a valuable and worthwhile goal. Physical health and beauty were an important part of the Greek ideal, and the naked male body symbolized for the Greeks the epitome of both physical and emotional love. Within this system of beliefs, the Greeks institutionalized and approved an *erastes-eromenos* relationship—the Greek citizen acted as teacher and role model (*erastes*) to his student-lover (*eromenos*). Also in ancient Athens, Sparta, and other Greek city-states, each adult male was expected to act as mentor to a boy, prior arrangements having been made with the boy's parents. A strong emotional component was attached to such relationships, which might be described as "homoerotic"—that is, a love between two males, a form of love that the Greeks considered the highest expression of human existence. The sexual component, however, is less clear; the Greeks did not endorse homosexual activity in general, and some authors have suggested that there was no sexual contact between erastes and eromenos. Other researchers find evidence that sexual contact between males was condoned, but only within prescribed limits. For example, male prostitution was disapproved of, as was sexual contact between adult males, but sexual love between an adult and an adolescent boy was permitted.

How did homoeroticism fit into the overall pattern of Greek life? While we tend to view the Greeks as the founders of democracy, the status of women within their political system was extremely low. Women were not included in most aspects of political and social life; a married woman spent most of her time confined to the home and had little contact with the outside world. Love or friendship between husband and wife was not considered desirable, nor was it common. The family unit, however, was highly esteemed; its primary function was the production of children. Thus exclusive homosexuality was frowned upon because every Greek male was expected to marry and have children. Homosexual love was acceptable for a young man from the time he had his hair cut (at about age 16) through his military training and for a short time thereafter until he was fully accepted as a citizen. He was then expected to assume a heterosexual life style. Finally, as a mature adult, he was encouraged to take under his custody a young man, who would then repeat the cycle.

From the Judeo-Christian tradition we get a completely different perspective on homosexuality and, indeed, on sexuality in general. Early Christianity has been sometimes characterized as a "sex-negative" religion, in that all physical pleasure was seen as interfering with spiritual growth. Within this framework, complete sexual abstinence was the highest form of existence, but marital sex for procreative purposes was also approved. All other forms of sexual contact, including homosexuality, were seen as sinful. Interestingly, relatively few direct references to homosexuality occur in either the Old or the New Testament. Most of the religious hostility to homosexuality came later, in the form of commentaries by Jewish and Christian scholars.

The legacy of this tradition is still evident in the sexual laws of the contemporary United States. Most states do not have specific laws against homosexual activity, but almost all states prohibit what they call "crimes against nature" or "unnatural acts," terms that are interpreted to include homosexual behavior. It is only in very recent years that a few states have granted legal protection to homosexual activity between consenting adults. Attempts to legislate "gay rights" bills granting the homosexual protection from job or housing discrimination have met with great resistance in many communities, and it is likely that this battle will continue in the years to come.

RECENT DEVELOPMENTS

In recent years, a shift has occurred in the way that homosexuality tends to be viewed. "Ever since the Freudian revolution, and especially since the Second World War," writes Szasz, "it has become intellectually fashionable to hold that homosexuality is neither a sin nor a crime but a disease" (1965, p. 129). This does not mean, however, that we have accepted homosexual behavior as normal, only that we have come to portray the homosexual as someone in need of treatment rather than punishment. In response to this view, numerous forms of therapy, most of which have little success, have been developed. According to Szasz, this classification of homosexuality as a disease does not represent progress for the homosexual, nor does it remove moral judgments of the homosexual's life style. Being labeled sick rather than criminal simply substitutes one set

Homosexuals—both male and female—are today becoming increasingly vocal in their efforts to promote understanding and respect for gay rights. (© *Joel Gordon 1979*)

of sanctions—such as hospitalization and compulsory treatment—for another.

In response to their low status within America's social, legal, and psychiatric establishments, homosexuals began to organize the gay liberation movement. Generally, the turning point in the movement is dated as June 1969, when a group of homosexual men rioted outside a gay bar in New York City against police harassment. Although homosexual organizations had existed before this time, the so-called "Stonewall riots" brought a large amount of attention and publicity to the new movement's goals. Seeing themselves as members of a repressed minority, homosexuals have sought to assert their right to pursue their own life style without legal or social interference.

As part of this movement, there have been attempts to change traditional psychiatric views on homosexuality. One of the first professional organizations to recognize the legitimate rights of homosexuals was the Association for the Advancement of Behavior Therapy, whose president in 1973, Dr. Gerald Davison, issued a strong positive statement about homosexuality. Also in 1973, the American Psychiatric Association voted to drop the category "homosexuality" from their classification of mental illnesses. However, they substituted a new subcategory, "sexual orientation disturbance," which applies to those individuals troubled by their homosexuality. Other organizations concerned with mental health issues, such as the American Psychological Association, have made public statements that homosexuality per se does not constitute evidence of pathology or of adjustment problems. These new perspectives do not, however, reflect the views of all mental health workers, many of whom continue to see homosexuality as a mental health problem.

In the same way, there has been some liberalization of the general public's views on homosexuality. Yet a considerable number of people retain a traditional moral or religious stance on this issue. George Weinberg (1973) characterizes the prevailing attitude as "homophobia"—that is, an irrational fear of homosexuality that is present in heterosexuals and homosexuals alike. This fear has negative consequences for homosexuals, who may internalize society's negative views, so that they come to dislike themselves and must hide or deny their sexual preferences. Homophobia also limits the behavior of the heterosexual population; for example, Weinberg points out that heterosexual males typically inhibit expressions of closeness, both physical and emotional, because they fear being labeled homosexual. Indeed, one research study showed that heterosexual male medical students were unable to look at films of nude males without having their own penises shrink in size (McConaghy, 1967). Such clear evidence of fear, suggests Weinberg, means that homophobia limits our interpersonal behavior in much the same way that claustrophobia limits our use of elevators.

HOMOSEXUAL BEHAVIORS AND IDENTITIES

When do we label an individual as homosexual? This is perhaps the most complicated and troubling question that researchers have confronted in recent years. Certainly it is important that we agree on what we mean when we use the term "homosexual"; at the same time, we should be aware that there are a multitude of possible definitions for this term. Consider the following brief case studies:

1. John is married and has three children. All of his sexual intercourse experiences have been with his wife. When he masturbates, however, John fantasizes only about males; and although he does not intend to act out his fantasies, he does find that he is sexually attracted to several of his male friends.

2. Sally is a college student who had a 2-year sexual relationship with her female roommate. When the relationship broke up, she began dating and subsequently married a male student, with whom she has a pleasurable sex life.

3. After an adolescence that included dating and sex with girls, Donald joined the army and was stationed in an isolated research base. While there, he developed a close and loving relationship with another man that included sexual contact. When he was transferred nearer to his home, he resumed his heterosexual dating pattern.

4. Michael is a young man who earns money as a homosexual prostitute; he accepts money from older males who want to perform oral sex on him. When he goes home to the woman with whom he lives, Michael speaks derisively about these men.

5. After twenty years of marriage and two children, Ginny divorces her husband under bitter and hostile circumstances. She moves in with another divorced woman and, after several months, the two of them begin a sexual and love relationship that continues for several years. Before this experience, Ginny had never fantasized about or considered the possibility of sex with another woman.

6. Mark says that he knew he was different from other boys at the age of 7 or 8 years. Now middle-aged, he has never had sex with a woman, although he has many female friends. He has been involved in a series of sexual relationships with other men since adolescence.

Although we might agree that the last case is clearly one of homosexuality, we would have more difficulty in categorizing the previous cases. If we were to define homosexuality simply in terms of participation in any sexual activity with a same-sex partner, then all but John would be labeled homosexual. Such a definition would, according to Kinsey

and his colleagues (1953), include a large percentage of men and a sizable group of women; he found that about 37 percent of males and 13 percent of females had at least one sexual experience leading to orgasm with a same-sex partner sometime between adolescence and old age. Among those individuals who remained unmarried, these proportions were even higher: about one-half of all males and one-quarter of all females.

Most of the men and women who reported some homosexual activity in Kinsey's surveys were not, however, exclusively homosexual throughout the life cycle. Like Donald or Ginny, a great many were homosexually active only over a short time span; others reported only one homosexual experience in their entire lives. In fact, only 4 percent of males, and an even smaller percentage of females, were exclusively homosexual. Clearly, then, it would be an oversimplification to label as homosexual anyone who had ever experienced a homosexual contact; the vast majority of such people have also experienced satisfactory heterosexual interactions. Looking at these data, Kinsey concluded that the term "homosexual" had little or no value in describing a particular type of personality or sexual identity. For Kinsey, the word "homosexual" was useful only in characterizing *behavior*; thus he might speak of homosexual acts, but he would not talk about homosexual people or homosexual personality.

This same viewpoint was argued by C. A. Tripp, in his book *The Homosexual Matrix:*

Part of the difficulty in viewing homosexuality is that it is largely amorphous—a behavioral category of individuals who are about as diffusely allied with each other as the world's smokers or coffee drinkers, and who are defined more by social opinion than by any fundamental consistency among themselves. And since homosexuals differ as much from each other as they do from heterosexuals, it is not feasible to divide them into "types." . . . The enormous social variation between people who engage in homosexuality tends to gain what little uniformity it has from the kinds of pressures they may or may not have to contend with. (1975, pp. 127–128)

In other words, both Kinsey and Tripp reject the notion that people who engage in homosexual behaviors can be grouped into specific personality categories. Just as we cannot describe the heterosexual personality, we cannot assume that we know anything about a man or woman's personality simply because that individual has experienced some form of homosexual contact.

In response to the dilemma of how to describe homosexual activity, Kinsey developed his famous 7-point scale of sexual orientation. At the zero end of the scale are those individuals who are exclusively heterosexual in both fantasy and behavior; at the other end (point 6 on the scale) are those whose behavior and fantasies are exclusively homosexual. In the middle are those men and women who show equal amounts of heterosexual and homosexual activity. Figure 3.3 shows the percentages of men and women who fall into the various points along the continuum. At the time of its publication, this continuum represented a radical departure from conventional thinking; indeed, popular stereotypes continue to view homosexuality as an all-or-nothing phenomenon, in spite of the fact that a great many people fall somewhere between the extremes of exclusive heterosexual or homosexual orientation.

While Kinsey's contribution continues to be recognized, some researchers have pointed out that there are problems with his conceptualization. For example, Kinsey's finding that 37 percent of males had at least one homosexual experience to the point of orgasm has often been used to support the notion that homosexual activity is a "normal" or at least norma-

tive part of sexual experience. In fact, when sociologists reanalyzed these data (Gagnon and Simon, 1973), they found that more than half of these men were exclusively heterosexual from their late teens on; they caution that we cannot draw any clear conclusions from limited homosexual experience in the context of adolescent sexual experimentation. According to these researchers, only 6 percent of the male sample had really extensive experiences with homosexual activity.

A more serious problem with Kinsey's scale is that it fails to take into account how people view their own behavior. This is a theme that runs throughout Kinsey's work; he focused on what people did, not on what they thought or felt. In rejecting the notion of a "homosexual personality," Kinsey also chose to ignore the fact that people do indeed attach labels to their own behavior. And while the extent of heterosexual or homosexual behavior may fall along a continuum, the self-labeling process is more likely to be either-or in nature. For example, Michael, the homosexual prostitute, engaged in homosexual behavior without viewing himself as homosexual in orientation. In contrast, John, who did not engage in overt homosexual acts, may well have seen himself as homosexually oriented because of his fantasies and his sexual attraction to other males. To complicate matters further, people such as Sally or Ginny may view themselves as heterosexual at some times in their lives and as homosexual at other times. Current relationships and life styles may often have a more immediate influence on self-labeling than past experiences.

Thus far we have described two dimensions in the definition of homosexuality — participation in homosexual activities and the identification or labeling of oneself as homosexual. Yet another dimension is labeling by the outside world. Being considered a member of a "deviant" or at least "variant" group is bound

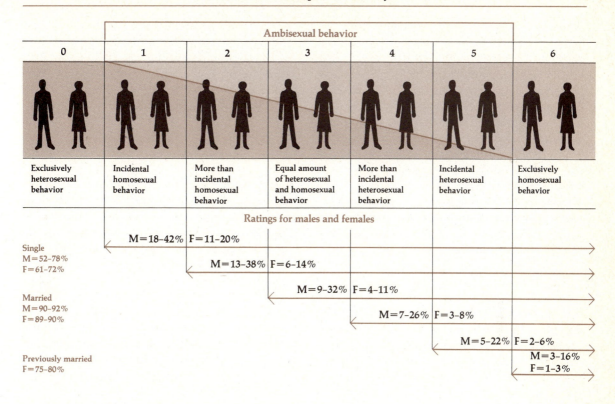

FIGURE 3.3

The Kinsey Sexual Orientation Rating Scale. The percentages in each category for males(M) and females(F) are approximations based on Kinsey's 1948 and 1953 studies and the number of subjects reporting varying degrees of homosexual experience. Despite Kinsey's notion of a continuum of sexual orientation, most people view themselves as falling clearly into one category or the other. *(After Kinsey, 1948 and 1953)*

to affect an individual's behavior and identity. In fact, as Tripp noted, the pressures exerted on homosexually oriented people by society may be the main experience such people have in common. For example, decisions about whether to "come out" or remain "in the closet" are a common part of the homosexual experience. In addition, many homosexually oriented people internalize society's negative value judgments about their behavior and life style. An individual who is labeled as homosexual is expected to look, act, and respond in certain ways, and these cultural expectations may well have real effects on behavior.

Given these differing perspectives on what it means to be homosexual, it is not surprising that some researchers have opted for a definition stressing variety. For example, Alan Bell and Martin Weinberg titled their research *Homosexualities: A Study of Diversity Among*

Men and Women (1978). In the same vein, Gagnon writes that "there is not one homosexuality, but a multiplicity of ways of organizing a homosexual preference into other ongoing life styles and commitments" (1977, p. 237). Gagnon notes that although "being homosexual" is sometimes very important to one's decisions, thoughts, and behavior; at other times, sexual orientation of whatever kind is irrelevant to our lives. And just as we would have difficulty in defining a single type of heterosexuality—for instance, are religious celibates or the severely handicapped to be considered heterosexual even if they do not engage in any sexual activity?—we have a problem describing a single type of homosexuality.

Finally, most questions about the causes or origins of homosexuality are based on assumptions that are common to the heterosexual world. For instance, we assume that if nothing "goes wrong" in the process of development, then all human beings will become heterosexual. Within this framework, the development of a homosexual orientation sets us looking for some problem or "abnormality" to explain why an individual deviates from heterosexuality. However, aside from our strong cultural prejudice against homosexuality, we have no reason to assume that all individuals are naturally heterosexual, or that all homosexuals are the result of unnatural or troubled development. Another assumption is that heterosexuality and homosexuality are discrete and opposite categories; but as Kinsey and others have pointed out, people's sexual orientations cannot be so neatly pigeonholed, and we will not find clear, one-dimensional explanations for the vast range of human sexual preferences. Finally, we have assumed that by knowing a person "is homosexual," we also know a great deal about his or her personality, family structure, gender identity, life style, and so on. In fact, we expect there to be

some common thread in the lives of all men and women labeled homosexual. But in the same way that diversity is the hallmark of heterosexuality, there is no reason to assume that homosexuals have anything more in common than their sexual orientation.

ROLES AND LIFE STYLES

Our culture is filled with popular stereotypes about the homosexual life style and homosexual roles. In terms of life style, for example, the media tend to focus on those homosexuals who live in predominantly gay communities in such large cities as New York and San Francisco; emphasis is placed on homosexual "promiscuity" and "cruising," as well as on the militancy and flamboyance of these groups. Yet this image reflects only a small proportion of the homosexually oriented population. Persons who choose to hide or disguise their homosexuality are likely to lead a very different style of life. Thus we must keep in mind that the research to be reviewed in this section can be applied only to a restricted sample of homosexuals, within particular geographic locations, and at a specific time in history. Because they do not participate in such research, we have no way of knowing how the "silent majority" of homosexuals conduct their lives.

In the most recent Kinsey Institute study (Bell and Weinberg, 1978), a sample of approximately 1,500 male and female homosexuals were interviewed about their sexual roles, relationships, and life styles. Although the study was limited to residents of San Francisco, it was reasonably representative in terms of race, religion, and age. A major conclusion of this research was that homosexual life styles can be classified into five categories:

1. Close-coupleds: Individuals in this group tend to see themselves as "happily married." They maintain a close relationship with one partner

According to recent research (Bell and Weinberg, 1978), for both male and female homosexuals, there are five types of lifestyles, including close-coupled, that is, having an intimate relationship with one partner. *(Cynthia Copple)*

and appear to be the most well-adjusted sub-group.

2. Open-coupleds: These particular individuals maintain a stable relationship with one particular partner but also engage in numerous sexual relationships outside of the primary relationship. This life style was found to be the most prevalent among the male homosexuals but was relatively uncommon among the lesbians, who tended to prefer the close-coupled relationship.

3. Functionals: The authors compare this group to the swinging singles of the heterosexual world. Functionals are usually very active in meeting new sexual partners and show little interest in settling down.

4. Dysfunctionals: This category includes individuals who are intrinsically dissatisfied with their life styles or who are experiencing major problems with sexual performance. Not surprisingly,

the men and women in this group were found to be more susceptible to deep emotional conflicts and serious social adjustment difficulties.

5. Asexuals: The individuals in this group are essentially loners—either through choice or through the inability to find a partner. Many of the males in this group were "closet" homosexuals who seldom interacted with other homosexual men.

This list does not, according to Bell and Weinberg, exhaust the possibilities of life style variations ". . . while the present study has taken a step forward in its delineation of types of homosexuals, it too fails to capture the full diversity that must be understood if society is ever fully to respect, and ever to appreciate, the way in which individual homosexual men and women live their lives" (1978, p. 231). The authors do suggest, however, that the individual adjustment and emotional well-being of the homosexual depends to a large extent on the kind of life style that is engaged in.

Although Bell and Weinberg reported that a substantial number of homosexuals live in coupled relationships, they also addressed the issue of homosexual promiscuity. Specifically, there is a common cultural belief that homosexual men are far more likely than either lesbians or heterosexual men and women to engage in impersonal sexual activity with a large number of partners. To some extent, this view is accurate. For example, Kinsey found that whereas 51 percent of males who engaged in some homosexual activity reported having only one or two partners, 22 percent reported having ten or more partners. In contrast, among females engaging in some homosexual activity, 71 percent had one or two partners and only 4 percent reported having ten or more partners. In Bell and Weinberg's study, this difference is even more apparent: large numbers of sexual partners—ranging into the hundreds—were common in at least one-half of the sample of homosexual men. Many of these men also reported, however, that they usually spent some time with their partners and exchanged a certain amount of personal information, suggesting that these relationships were not entirely impersonal. The majority of lesbians, in contrast, had experienced sexual relationships with fewer than ten partners; moreover, most of these women reported that they had never had "impersonal sex," in the sense of sexual contact with a stranger. About 75 percent reported that they were currently involved in a stable, long-term relationship with another woman.

How do we explain these large numbers of partners among homosexual men as compared with lesbians or heterosexual men and women? The most common explanation, suggested by Gagnon and Simon (1973), is that promiscuity has less to do with sexual ori-entation as such than with our socialization as males or females. Women, whether heterosexually or homosexually oriented, are brought up in ways that stress the formation of long-term emotional commitments; thus although the lesbian chooses as her partner another female, she is just as interested in love and affection as is the heterosexual woman. Males, on the other hand, are often socialized in ways that permit them to separate sexual expression from emotion and long-term commitment. Whereas heterosexual men are limited in their ability to have casual sexual relationships by the relative scarcity of like-minded female partners, there is no such limitation for homosexual men, since casual male sexual partners are freely available within certain settings. An alternative explanation, proposed by Martin Hoffman (1968), is that male homosexual promiscuity is caused, in part, by social pressures. The heterosexual world tends to strongly oppose male homosexuality. This opposition may cause the male homosexual to feel considerable anxiety about his sexual identity, and this anxiety may lead, in turn, to difficulty in maintaining emotional involvements. Because lesbianism is less visible, less common, and perhaps less threatening to the larger society, lesbians may be less affected by antihomosexual attitudes and therefore better able to maintain affectional relationships.

Regardless of the reason, it is true that homosexual men have access to a variety of meeting places where they can make contacts with other males. For example, in the United States today there are a significant number of "gay bars," which are known to members of the homosexual community. Although a few of these bars cater to lesbians, the overwhelming majority are designed for a male homosexual clientele. A survey of such bars included the following observations:

Gay men, true to the male role, venture out when and where they choose; and wherever there is a large concentration of males to support them, gay bars sprout and thrive. They can be found near every large military base and major university. . . . Contrary to popular misconception, gay bars vary tremendously in character, atmosphere and clientele and usually reflect the character of their local surroundings far more than that of a distinctive subculture. There are gay bars in the South where farm hands listen to country-western music, gay bars in the Midwest where truck drivers stop over on long hauls across the country, just as there are gay bars in the East dominated by a social elite. (Sage, 1979, pp. 150–151)

In addition to the gay bar, some male homosexuals use public baths and toilets ("tearooms") as places to make sexual contacts. The main characteristic that such places have in common is the opportunity for impersonal sexual activity. In other respects, however, the gay baths script is quite different from the public toilets script. The physical environment of the bath is designed to facilitate comfortable, relaxed, and sensuous sexual contact. In contrast, contact in public toilets is usually hasty and fearful and is often experienced as sordid by one or both participants.

A fairly new addition to the homosexual meeting scene are the dances and social gatherings sponsored by such homosexual organizations as the Student Homophile Association. These events tend to provide a more personal and less stigmatized atmosphere for male and female homosexuals to meet new people without the need for sexual contact. An even newer trend is the attempt of some homosexuals to bring their partners to traditionally heterosexual social events such as the senior prom. In some cases, institutions and legal authorities have forbidden this practice, but in other cases, homosexual couples have been accepted as regular social participants.

Within the homosexual life styles and relationships described above, there are certain specific roles that homosexual men and women may adopt for various reasons. Homo-

sexual slang, for example, makes use of such terms as "butch" or "fem," "dyke" or "queen" to describe roles that express masculinity or femininity in a homosexual context. Although a small proportion of lesbians always play the stereotyped masculine ("bull-dyke") role, and a small proportion of male homosexuals act effeminately at all times, the majority of homosexual men and women cannot be categorized in this way. Some male homosexuals appear to go through a temporary phase of experimentation with effeminate roles, sometimes including the use of a female name, and this phase might occur at the time of "coming out" (Gagnon and Simon, 1973). However, such exaggerated roles are usually frowned upon both by the larger heterosexual community and by many individuals within the homosexual community, so that these roles are typically reserved for certain settings or specific sexual relationships. Many homosexuals never experiment with cross-sex role playing. In the same way, while some homosexuals may consistently play a passive or active role within the homosexual relationship, the majority, like most heterosexuals, vary their roles from one sexual experience to another.

The stereotype of the aging homosexual as someone who is unable to find sexual partners without resorting to prostitutes does not appear to be accurate. For example, a study of male homosexuals in the Los Angeles area (Kelly, 1977) found that while older homosexuals tended to have fewer partners, many of them maintained an active relationship with someone in the same general age bracket and did not appear to be sexually dissatisfied. Indeed, these men seemed to experience many problems that were common to older heterosexuals—for instance, they were particularly concerned with health issues and institutionalization. These results were also noted by Martin Weinberg and Colin Williams (1974) in their research comparing homosexual men from different age groups. While the problems of the older homosexual were those commonly associated with the aging process in general in this society, these men did not appear significantly more unhappy than a comparable group of young homosexual males. In fact, the study found that the older men appeared to have fewer conflicts about their sexual orientation and had reached a higher level of self-acceptance than had the younger men.

Bisexuality

Although we have chosen to describe bisexuality (also known as ambisexuality) in a separate section, it is difficult to know whether it really constitutes a distinct sexual life style. If we adopt Kinsey's definition, that a *bisexual* is any individual rated 1 through 5 on the sexual orientation continuum—that is, anyone who is not exclusively heterosexual or exclusively homosexual—then we are indeed including a large group of men and women. Some of these people will be predominantly heterosexual with occasional homosexual experience, others will be predominantly homosexual with occasional heterosexual experience. Relatively few will be those rated 3 on the Kinsey scale—that is, those who engage in equal amounts of heterosexual and homosexual activity. Thus the life style of the bisexual might range from conventional heterosexual marriage to homosexual activism, the criterion of bisexuality being merely sexual contact with one or more members of both sexes at some time.

Another, more restricted, definition is provided by Masters and Johnson. They describe the ambisexual as "a man or woman who unreservedly enjoys, solicits, or responds to overt sexual opportunity with equal ease and interest regardless of the sex of the partners, and who, as a sexually mature individual, has never evidenced interest in a continuing relationship" (1979, pp. 145–146). In this definition, ambisexuality implies the inability to form lasting emotional commitments, and therefore involves more than just a person's sexual preferences. Masters and Johnson based this definition, in part, on the findings of their research with twelve ambisexual subjects (six men and six women). Although these subjects showed essentially identical patterns of physiological response as heterosexual and as homosexual subjects, their psychosexual and emotional responses were not typical. For instance, ambisexuals made their sexual choices not on the basis of the gender of the partner but simply on the basis of the opportunity to engage in sexual activity with someone perceived as attractive in some way. According to Masters and Johnson, the main determinant of choice for this group is the opportunity itself, with little consideration given to other characteristics of the potential partner. Finally, these subjects were described as lonely people, since they did not seem to be directly involved in close love or family relationships.

Of course, this portrait of bisexuals as confused or conflicted individuals who have difficulty in making emotional commitments is simply one of many views of the "bisexual personality." Another perspective sees bisexuals as people in the vanguard of sexual liberation—men and women who can express their sexuality without regard to gender preference and other conventional restrictions. Still another view is that bisexuals are really uncommitted homosexuals—for example, some homosexual organizations see bisexuals as

Differences in definition as to what constitutes bisexuality, make it difficult to determine whether or not it is a distinct life style. (© *Leonard Speier 1980*)

"fence-sitters," who do not have the courage to admit their true sexual orientation. Finally, some people view bisexuality as a sort of political statement; such people may have little actual experience with same-gender sex, but they believe in the innate bisexuality of all people and would like to be able to maintain sexual and emotional relationships with same-gender partners. Probably, there is some validity to each of these views. As is true of heterosexuality and homosexuality, there may well be many varieties of bisexuality and many bisexual life styles.

A study in which 127 bisexuals volunteered to complete a survey questionnaire about their sexual experiences and current life style (Klein, 1978) revealed three categories of bisexuals:

1. *Transitional bisexuals:* Those in the process of changing their orientation—from heterosexual to homosexual or from homosexual to heterosexual. For such men and women, bisexuality may serve as an intermediate or transitional stage in the development of a new sexual preference.

2. *Historical bisexuals:* Those whose activities may have been predominantly heterosexual or homo-

sexual in the past, but who also have a significant amount of bisexual experience or fantasy.

3. *Sequential bisexuals:* Those who alternate between having male and female lovers but are involved in only one sexual relationship at a time.

Klein concludes that to define a person as bisexual simply because he or she has had sex with members of both sexes is an oversimplification, because there are numerous dimensions to a person's sexual life style and orientation. Many people have sexual contact with members of both sexes, but relatively few would clearly label and identify themselves as being committed to a bisexual life style. Indeed, Klein found that the self-described bisexuals in his study tended to adopt this label relatively late in their development. For example, whereas most exclusive heterosexuals and homosexuals identify their sexual preference during the adolescent years, the average age of the males and females in Klein's sample when they first adopted the bisexual label was 24 years. Before this time, most had considered themselves to be predominantly heterosexual. Male bisexuals had had their first homosexual experience at about 18 years of age, while for females, this experience had occurred at about 23 years of age. Because Klein's sample was small and highly selective, however, we should be cautious about generalizing these findings to the total bisexual population.

The bisexual faces a particular set of problems that do not confront either heterosexuals or homosexuals. Unlike the heterosexual, the bisexual gets little support from social conventions and traditional moral standards. And unlike the homosexual, the bisexual does not have the support of an organized community of like-minded men and women. In fact, the bisexual may feel considerable pressure to make a choice and identify with a more well-established sexual preference and life style.

Nonsexual Life Styles: Celibacy and Abstinence

Celibacy and abstinence are very broad terms that might be applied to a number of different situations. First, abstinence may be lifelong. Lifelong *celibacy* would include that of the Catholic priest or nun who takes a vow of chastity and is committed to single-minded service of the church. It would also include the celibacy of those men and women who for reasons beyond their control cannot find sexual partners although they would like to, or who are limited by physical or mental disability. Second, abstinence may be restricted to a particular segment of one's life. Temporary abstinence may be voluntary, as in the case of a person going through a difficult or complicated period of life who finds it easier to give up sexuality than to cope with sexual relationships, or involuntary, as in the case of a woman whose pregnancy might be threatened by sexual activity. Furthermore, abstinence may be total, as in the case of the individual who forgoes all forms of sexual activity including masturbation and fantasy, or it may be partial, as in the case of a man or woman who believes in maintaining premarital virginity but does not object to masturbation.

The path of lifelong celibacy is typically chosen on the basis of strong moral or re-ligious conviction. Membership in the Roman Catholic priesthood, for instance, entails a necessary commitment to celibacy, following the preachings of St. Paul, who viewed marriage as a potential distraction to those leading a spiritual life. Similarly, other religious groups, such as the Bahá'i, consider physical purity to be a necessary prerequisite of spiritual purity. The following statement, by a practicing nun, expresses the point of view of the religious celibate:

As a member of a religious order, I find that celibacy or virginity is a positive quality indicative of a consecrated way of life. It is a grace enabling me more easily to devote my entire being to God with an undivided heart, viewing life from a sacred perspective, as a means of growing in love and perceiving truth. What might seem to some an unnatural way of life has become second nature to me over the years, a life that spiritualizes the natural by means of intention. (DeLora and Warren, 1977, pp. 300–301)

Temporary abstinence may be chosen for any of several reasons and for varying periods of time. One study (Laws and Schwartz, 1977) found three common motivations for temporary abstinence:

1. *Hygiene and health:* Individuals who have

suffered from the effects of sexually transmitted diseases, or who have strong fears of contracting some form of venereal disease, may opt for sexual abstinence—either for a brief period or for several years.

2. *Political consciousness—feminism:* Among the more radical and politically committed feminists are those who believe that all male-female relationships are intrinsically oppressive and demeaning to women. Some of these women are able to adopt a lesbian life style as congruent with their beliefs; but for those unable to accept same-sex relationships, abstinence may be preferred: "While the women who make this decision as part of a political philosophy are relatively few in number, it might be hypothesized that many individuals do this on a temporary basis after a disappointing relationship or a series of bad relationships" (p. 162).

3. *Situational necessity:* There may be temporary periods in one's life when the demands and pressures of work or family, or poor physical health, require sexual abstinence. Further-more, during periods of intense emotional or career stress, many people lose interest in sexual relations and enter into a period of either partial or total abstinence. (Chronic loss of sexual interest, however, can become a serious problem, as will be discussed in detail in Chapter 9.)

Can sexual abstinence be harmful? Sexual appetite is very different from other appetites such as hunger or thirst, in that human beings may choose to do without sex for most or all of their lives without endangering their physical survival in any way. While we may question whether celibacy might cause or result from psychological or emotional problems, there is no question that it presents little physical risk to the individual. On the other hand, there is no scientific evidence to support the contention of yogis and other Eastern spiritual authorities that sexual abstinence enhances physical health and vitality. The decision to abstain from sexual interaction is fundamentally a question of personal values and should not be confused with issues of physical health.

Summary

1. In our own culture, love tends to play a major role in the selection of a sexual partner, but this emphasis on romantic love is not shared by all other societies.

2. Definitions of love vary and may include both sexual and nonsexual feelings.

3. There are a number of types of problems that are often associated with a love relationship: jealousy, unrequited love, and love addiction.

4. While for most people sex and love belong together, there is a great deal of variety in the relationships that we form to express our loving and sexual needs.

5. The most acceptable relationship in our culture is the heterosexual pair-bond. The formation of such pair-bonds typically starts with courtship and dating, and each culture has its own set of rules and expectations guiding this behavior. Courtship in the United States has become increasingly permissive regarding sexuality in the past few decades, particularly for females.

6. Just as sexual standards during courtship have changed, there have also been some changes in the role of sex in marriage. For instance, although sexual fidelity is our cultural norm, there has been an increase in the incidence of extramarital relationships. Maintaining a satisfying sexual relationship in mar-

riage presents a challenge to some couples.

7. One of the most controversial issues in human sexuality is the homosexual relationship. Kinsey and his colleagues showed that a variety of homosexual experiences exist, and this view is confirmed by evidence from cross-cultural research. For example, there is an important distinction between occasional homosexual experiences and a long-standing homosexual identity.

8. Bisexuality and celibacy are less common sexual life styles about which we have relatively little scientific information. Like other sexual life styles, they may be temporary or permanent, total or partial, and may serve many different needs.

Sex and Aging

To the many harmful "isms" which exist in our society—racism, sexism, and so on—we must add a form of prejudice that will affect all of us in later life: ageism. In our youth-oriented culture, older men and women are subject to a number of stresses which may have little or nothing to do with the actual process of physical aging. For example, old people are typically faced with mandatory retirement, declining financial resources, and the feeling that they have become a burden rather than a resource to their families. Although some cultures revere the aged as sources of wisdom and maturity, we have tended to remove them from the mainstream of American life. Our stereotypes about what the elderly want and need from life, however, are often very far from the truth. This may be especially true in regard to the role of sexuality in the lives of older men and women.

According to Margaret Kuhn, head of the activist Gray Panther group, the sexuality of the aged is subject to several extremely harmful myths (1976). These myths, which are part of the general folklore of aging, cause us to see old people as asexual and unattractive and at the same time, they make the aged feel embarrassed and self-conscious about their real sexual needs. Among the most destructive myths, Kuhn includes the notions that:

1. Sex doesn't matter in old age.

Older men and women are not expected to care about sexuality, and we tend to think that they should gracefully give up sexual activity with increasing age. In part, this myth may be rooted in a religious tradition that condones sex only when procreation is a possible outcome. Thus,

until quite recently, we have ignored the sexual needs of women who have passed menopause because their sexuality no longer has a valid justification. Similarly, we little consider the sexuality of older men whose responsiveness may have slowed or changed in nature.

2. Interest in sex is abnormal for old people.

Since sex is not supposed to be important for old people, it is not surprising that we give negative labels to individuals whose sexual interest continues throughout their life span. The sexually interested older male is often viewed as a "dirty old man" or "lecher," while the sexually interested female may be called "vain" or "silly."

3. Remarriage after loss of spouse should be discouraged.

The approved script in our culture involves marriage in our twenties, child-bearing and rearing, and then, with increasing age, a relatively asexual companionship with our spouse. Should a husband or wife lose their marital partner, particularly in the older years, it is generally not expected that there will be a remarriage. In part, this is because we do not expect that older people will have a continued need for sexual contact. Adult children may often discourage their parents from remarriage because of personal insecurities. Even when a remarriage is accepted, we tend to see it as "cute," as if the people involved were children, rather than as a serious commitment to continued intimacy and sexual contact.

4. "It is all right for old men to seek younger women as sex partners, but it is ridiculous for old women to be sexually involved with younger men."

In a culture in which sexuality is often equated with the image of a young female, the older woman is sometimes seen as asexual and unattractive. Not only do we deny her sexuality, but we tend to believe something is "wrong" when a younger man finds her attractive. It is a well known fact that males tend to die at earlier ages than females; so, at a time when a woman may have difficulty locating a partner of her own age, she is also criticized for finding a younger male partner.

5. "Old people should be separated by sex in institutions to avoid problems for the staff and criticism by families and the community."

One result of our stereotypes about aging and sexuality is the enforced segregation of men and women in nursing homes and other institutions. Even married couples may be separated in such institutions. Alex Comfort notes that:

Nursing homes appear to be run by people with sexual problems—otherwise it would be difficult to explain the attempt to run them as mixed-sex nunneries. . . . It has been shown that residential homes which follow the sexual mores of the outside world, instead of those of a boarding school, have happier and less deteriorated customers, and a vastly lower consumption of tranquilizers, than the conventional 'home' (p. 197, 1976)

Nevertheless, nursing home residents are often treated as children who cannot be trusted to make their own sexual decisions. Further, the right to privacy, which we accord to most adults as a matter of course, is often denied to the elderly. Thus, at a time when older men and women may have an increased need for the intimacy of close physical contact, we tend to place them in institutions which do not recognize these needs.

In keeping with our general view that sexuality is inappropriate for the elderly, there has been relatively little research on their sexual interest or responsiveness. The aged are, however, becoming an increasingly larger segment of our society. In 1900, only 4 percent of the United States population consisted of individuals over the age of 65. In contrast, the 1970 United States census found that about 10 percent—or 20 million people—of the population was over the age of 65, and 10 million people were over the age of 75. Clearly, the needs of such a large segment of the population cannot be ignored. It seems likely that in the future, the activism of groups such as the Gray Panthers, and our increasingly open attitudes towards sexuality, will ease some of our stereotypes about sexuality and aging.

PHYSIOLOGICAL CHANGES WITH AGING

Without question, the process of aging leads to changes in sexual physiology. For women, there may be certain abrupt changes—for instance, decreased hormone levels—at the time of menopause. For men, these changes tend to occur more gradually. Sexual function does not, however, suddenly deteriorate or disappear when we retire from work, receive our first social security check, or spot our gray hairs. Rather, sexual physiology changes continuously throughout the life cycle as a part of the general process of aging. For example, the male refractory period is usually shortest for the young teenager and increases with each decade; the changes may be greater between the ages of 15 and 30 than they are between the ages of 45 and 60. Since we do not believe that sexual aging incapacitates the 30 year old man, it makes little sense to suggest that men over 65 cannot also adjust their sexual scripts to incorporate the process of physiological aging. In fact, available research indicates that physiology plays a relatively small role in determining the sexual satisfaction of the older man or woman when compared with such factors as sexual interest and a lifetime of particular sexual patterns and habits.

To date, the most complete study of sexual response in older men and women was reported by Masters and Johnson in 1966. A total of 61 older women provided psychophysiological data, and interview data was obtained from 152 women. Because Masters and Johnson were interested in examining menopausal and post-menopausal women, about half of the women were between the ages of 41 and 50. The remainder ranged in age from 51 to a high of 78 years. Psychophysiological data was also obtained for 39 men: about half of these males were between the ages of 51 and 60, with the remainder ranging from 61 to 89 years of age. In addition, interview data was provided by 212 males. It should be noted that this was certainly not a random sample of aging men and women. Masters and Johnson found that most aging males and females were quite reluctant to become involved in their research, and it seems likely that those who consented to participate were more sexually active and less inhibited than the people who refused participation.

Before presenting their results, Masters and Johnson explain that while they compared the responses of aging subjects with those of younger participants, this does not suggest that the responses of aging subjects are in any way "abnormal"; subjects from different age groups are compared only to show the progression of age-related changes in sexuality. In other words, what is "normal" for a 20 year old is not "normal" for a 60 year old; each age group has its own particular norms of sexual responsiveness.

In describing the sexual response cycle of aging females, Masters and Johnson found that while certain responses were comparable to younger women—for instance, nipple erection—other responses showed a slowing or lessening in intensity. The "sex flush" which is common in younger women, for example, was less prevalent among the aged. Although clitoral response to stimulation followed the same basic patterns as in younger years, there were several differences in vaginal response. In post-menopausal women, lowered levels of sex hormones cause the vagina to become shorter and narrower, and the tissues of the vaginal walls are usually thinner and less expansive. For some aging women, these changes may cause discomfort during and after intercourse, as the vagina becomes irritated from penile friction. In addition, the most reliable indicator of female sexual arousal—vaginal lubrication—tends to be slower and less intense than in younger women. Interestingly, three women in this sample (one of whom was 73 years of age) showed lubrication responses similar to those of young women. Interview data indicated that these three women had maintained active sex lives—including intercourse one to two times per week—throughout their adult lives.

The vaginal contractions of orgasm were of the same type observed in younger women; however, while younger women tend to show between five and 10 contractions, the older women averaged three to five contractions. Once again, the three sexually active women described above were exceptions to the general rule—that is, they showed about the same number of contractions as in the younger group. Finally, resolution tended to occur more quickly in the older women. Masters and Johnson summarize as follows:

Generally, the intensity of physiologic reaction and duration of anatomic response to effective sexual stimulation are reduced through all four phases of the sexual cycle with the advancing years . . . . Regardless of involutional changes in the reproductive organs, the aging human female is fully capable of sexual performance at orgasmic response levels, particularly if she is exposed to regularity of effective sexual stimulation. (p. 238)

Indeed, Masters and Johnson repeatedly stress the importance of a regular sex life to the sexual functioning of the aging woman. Although menopause has definite effects on hormone levels in all females, it appears that hormonal decreases tell only part of the story of aging female sexuality. For women who have always led an active and satisfying sexual life style, hormonal decreases may be little more than an inconvenience which requires adjustments in the sexual script. For other women whose sexual lives have been infrequent or unsatisfying, menopause may present insurmountable obstacles to further sexual behavior. Thus, hormone replacement therapy may ease some of the physical discomforts of intercourse for the aging woman, but they will not directly increase her sexual interest.

According to Masters and Johnson, the predominant affect of aging on male sexuality is that each stage of the sexual response cycle lasts a longer span of time. For instance, in the young man penile erection normally occurs in less than five seconds; for older men, it may take considerably longer, even when the sexual stimulation is experienced as extremely arousing. Further, the older man can maintain an erection for long periods of time without ejaculating. It is not clear, however, whether this is because the older male has a less intense sexual response or simply due to his increased experience at controlling his ejaculation.

Like the aging female, the aging male experiences orgasmic contractions which are essentially the same in pattern as his younger counterpart. Also like the female, there tend to be fewer contractions. Typically, the seminal fluid is expelled with less force than in the younger man. In addition, the feeling of "ejaculatory inevitability" commonly reported by young males tends to be much shorter, or absent, in older men. Further, resolution—that is, the return to an unstimulated state—usually occurs much more rapidly with increasing age, sometimes within a few seconds. The refractory period, when the male cannot have another erection, becomes much longer, especially in men past the age of 60. Finally, Masters and Johnson report that most aging males are completely satisfied with one or two ejaculations per week. Even when the refractory period is relatively short, and a man's sexual partner prefers to have intercourse more than twice per week, the man is not likely to ejaculate, or to be interested in ejaculating, more than once or twice per week. However, the absence of an "ejaculatory urge" does not mean that the older man cannot enjoy sexual activity or provide pleasure to his partner.

SEXUAL BEHAVIOR AND AGING

We have seen that biological aging does place some limits on our sexual functioning. Our sexual "decline" does not appear suddenly when we reach any particular age—rather, according to Kinsey, there is a steady decline in sexual activity beginning in our teens. Kinsey found that this was especially true for males:

There are no calculations in all of the material on human sexuality which give straighter slopes than the data showing the decline with age in the total outlet of single males, or the similar curve showing the decline in outlet for the married males. (1948, p. 227)

For instance, married males show a mean of 4.8 sexual outlets (that is, sexual activity leading to orgasm) in their teens, dropping to 1.8 per week at the age of 50 and 0.9 per week at the age of

70. In addition to this overall decrease in sexual activity, Kinsey reported a number of more specific changes with age: a decrease in morning erections, slowing of the erectile response, a decrease in the ability to have several orgasms within a short period of time, and even a change in the angle at which the erect penis is held.

Kinsey does point out, however, that great individual differences exist in the ways we respond to the aging process. In his sample of 87 white males over the age of 60, the mean frequency of sexual activity was 1.0 per week for 65 year olds, 0.3 for 75 year olds, and less than 0.1 for 80 year olds. However, there were several exceptions to this decline — for instance, one 70 year old man reported averaging more than seven ejaculations per week, and an 88 year old man was having intercourse as often as once per week. Thus, although group averages of sexual activity always show a general decline with age, it seems likely that averages may distort the activity of particular individuals within the group. For instance, one possibility is that with increasing age, more and more men become sexually inactive, but at the same time, men who remain sexually active do not decrease their levels of activity. In a study reported by Martin (1977), it was found that men tended to develop patterns of sexual activity which continued throughout the lifecycle. Thus, men who reported high levels of sexual activity in their early years of marriage tended to maintain this pattern into old age. In contrast, men who were comfortable with lower levels of activity during their 20's and 30's — say, once or twice per month — were likely to be content with even lower activity levels during old age.

Up to this point we have discussed the effects of biological aging and previous sexual patterns on the sexual behavior of the aging male. A final set of factors is also important: the immediate physical, psychological and social status of the older man. For example, the man who is physically healthy in his later years is likely to be more sexually interested than the man who is suffering from the effects of various diseases. In addition, the availability of a compatible sexual partner will play an important role in maintaining sexual interest. Further, the attitude that sexual activity is normal and appropriate for older men will aid in continuing sexual interest.

Masters and Johnson suggest a number of psychological variables which contribute to the lessening of sexual activity and interest with increasing age (1966). For instance, monotony with a single sexual partner over 30 or 40 years of marriage may cause loss of sexual interest. This factor may be particularly important if the female partner has lost interest in continuing sexual intercourse, or if the couple is unwilling or unable to vary their sexual script. The man may also lose interest if he has become deeply involved in vocational and economic pursuits. Someone who is preoccupied with his work, may simply be too fatigued, both physically and mentally, to devote much energy to sexuality. Fatigue and lack of energy may also be caused by bad health habits such as overindulgence in alcohol or overeating. Finally, aging males may be especially susceptible to the "fear of failure" which plays such an important role in causing erectile dysfunction. For instance, the factors already mentioned — monotony, fatigue, alcohol use — may contribute to a single instance of erectile failure; and after one occasion of failure, a man may be reluctant to risk additional failures, preferring instead to withdraw completely from sexual activity. In addition, the cultural expectation that older men cannot and should not be sexually active may lead a man to become discouraged and give up on his sex life. Fortunately, many of these problems can be reversed with sex therapy and sex education. Several studies have shown that when the marital relationship is good, and when the problem has been of relatively short duration, older couples can respond successfully to conventional sex therapy techniques (Berman and Lief, 1976).

In some ways, the sexuality of the aging female parallels that of the aging male. For example, female intercourse rates decrease gradually over time in much the same way as do male rates. This is not surprising, since intercourse depends upon the availability of a cooperative partner; in Kinsey's time (and perhaps in our own as well), intercourse rates were largely determined by male interest and not by female desire. Thus, declining intercourse rates do not necessarily reflect the level of a woman's sexual interest. A better measure, according to Kinsey (1953), is a solo sexual activity, such as masturbation. In fact, Kinsey found that female masturbation rates gradually rise to a maximum point that is maintained until about 60 years of age. Indeed, many older women in Kinsey's survey expressed the desire for higher intercourse rates and blamed any decline on their husband's lack of interest. This problem may be further exacerbated by the fact that in our culture, women are encouraged to marry men who are older than themselves.

Unlike the aging male, the aging female experiences a clear event—menopause—which causes a variety of physical changes. Some women may choose to use this event to discontinue a dissatisfying sex life. Others, who were satisfied with their sexual experiences, may learn to compensate for menopausal changes. As noted earlier, menopause does not create any insurmountable barriers to sexuality, and for some women, re-

moval of the fear of pregnancy may actually have a stimulating affect on their sexuality.

While there seem to be few physiologic limits on female sexuality, a number of other factors tend to contribute to an overall decline with age. The presence of a partner will certainly play a role, and this may be particularly important in a culture where older women far outnumber older men. Also, women are subject to the same factors—monotony, fatigue, ill health—which limit the sexuality of the aging male. Finally, older women may feel that they are victims of a double dosage of sexual discrimination—first, because they are old, and second, because they are female: traditionally, our culture has been relatively unconcerned with the sexual needs of both these groups.

Before concluding this discussion, we should mention the results of a study that takes exception to the notion that sexuality declines gradually with age. According to George and Weiler (1979), the "straight slope" described by Kinsey and others may be produced by methodological artifacts. For instance, most studies rely on cross-sectional samples—that is, a group of 50 year olds is compared with a group of 60 year olds and/or 70 year olds. The problem with this design, say George and Weiler, is that each of these age groups reached sexual maturity at a different time in our history. If we assume that sexual standards have become more open and liberal with the passage of time, then we would expect that individuals growing up in the 1920's would have different intercourse rates than those who learned about sexuality in 1910. The best solution to this problem is to use a longitudinal design in which people growing up in, say, 1920, are questioned about their sexuality when they reach 50, 60, or 70 years of age. Another problem with previous research is that it groups together adults who are sexually inactive with adults who maintain sexual activity. Naturally, as more and more people become sexually inactive, the average rates for those who maintain sexual activity will show a gradual decline.

George and Weiler present the results of a study that corrected for these methodological problems. They studied 278 male and female subjects, all of whom were married. Each subject was interviewed four times, with two-year intervals between each interview session. Results indicated that sexual activity remained remarkably stable over time for those subjects who reported that they did engage in sexual intercourse. For instance, a subject who reported engaging in intercourse once per week at the first interview was likely to provide the same estimate at the fourth interview. However, with the passage of time, an increasing number of subjects reported that sexual relations had stopped completely. The overall pattern differed from the "gradual decline" described by Kinsey and others. The authors conclude that for the majority of middle-aged and older couples, sexual activity rates remain stable. With time, however, more and more couples completely stop all sexual activity. The reasons most often given for stopping intercourse were the attitudes or physical condition of the male partner.

2

HUMAN SEXUAL RESPONSE

FOUR

Sexual Anatomy

Overview

At first glance, a chapter about sexual anatomy would seem to have little relevance to our day-to-day lives as sexual beings. After all, we are capable of moving gracefully without any knowledge about our muscular and skeletal anatomy, and we can think perfectly well without understanding the anatomy of the brain. In the same way, most people can go through all phases of the sexual life cycle with little or no information about genital structure and function. Until very recently, such information was available only to scientists and physicians, and it was even considered somewhat improper for the average person to know too much about the genital organs and how they work.

In the 1980s, however, most sex educators and therapists see a great deal of value in teaching about sexual anatomy. Without such knowledge, sex remains a mystery instead of an accepted part of life. While some people can have sexually adequate lives without much anatomical knowledge, a great many others can derive major benefits from the study of anatomy. For example, many of us have questions about our own anatomical normality, and these doubts can seriously interfere with a positive sexual self-image. Since the genitals, or genitalia, are almost always kept hidden from sight, we have little direct information about how our own genitals compare with those of others. The study of sexual anatomy plays an important role in filling this informational gap. Furthermore, learning about sexual anatomy helps to dispel the negative attitudes toward the genitalia that most of us have grown up with. By developing our sense of the intricate and wonderful ways in which these organs function, our discomfort and disgust may be replaced with appreciation, even awe.

Learning about sexual anatomy also helps us toward a better understanding of reproductive function. The design of our sexual architecture is primarily related to reproductive capacity: the sexual anatomy of the male can be viewed as a sperm delivery system, that of the female as a system for conception, pregnancy, and childbirth. To carry out these reproductive roles, it is almost always necessary to engage in sexual behavior, so the study of anatomy is also valuable in understanding our sexual function. (The few exceptions would include artificial insemination and the recent efforts to create "test-tube" babies.) While some organs—for instance, the female clitoris—play no direct part in reproduction, and others—for instance, the male prostate gland—play no direct role in sexual activity, the overall genital system is designed to accomplish both of these overlapping and interactive functions.

Themes that are stressed in other sections of this book also appear in this chapter. For example, there are many *individual differences* in sexual anatomy that are well within the bounds of normality. Although the basic structure of the genitals is the same for all females and for all males, there are also many minor variations that make each of us unique. Another theme is that of the balance of *similarities* and *differences* between males and females. Because they play such different roles in the reproductive process, the male and female genital systems show major differences in design and appearance. However, if we remember that both sexes develop genital systems from the same primitive structures

(continued on page 134)

Illustrating Sexual Anatomy: The Work of Robert Latou Dickinson

There is an old saying that a picture is worth a thousand words, and this saying is certainly appropriate to the study of sexual and reproductive anatomy. Words alone cannot convey the intricacy, complexity, and unique characteristics of human anatomy. Prior to this century, however, scientists and physicians were extremely reluctant to approach the subject of sexual anatomy directly. In the puritanical climate of the Victorian era, it was considered obscene to produce drawings or photographs of the human genitalia, and even publishers of medical textbooks exercised the greatest restraint in this regard. The first individual in this century to question these values, and devote a major part of his life's work to studying human sexual anatomy, was Robert Latou Dickinson (1861–1950).

Dickinson's contribution is remarkable for several reasons. He was a gynecologist who began his practice in 1882—the height of the Victorian period. During the course of his long career, Dickinson examined and treated many thousands of women in his New York offices. In his sensitivity and open-mindedness about sexual matters, Dickinson was well ahead of his time. He was a good listener, and through his many years of gynecological practice he was able to record the enormous sexual anxiety and frustration experienced by women raised in Victorian times. Two of his books, *A Thousand Marriages* (1932) and *The Single Woman* (1934), contain a great many case histories of this type.

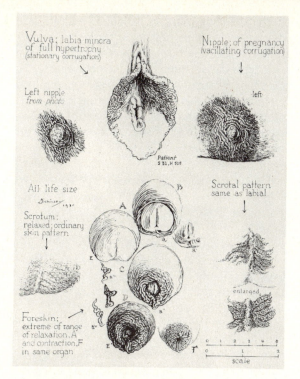

Perhaps even more impressive than his contribution as a practicing physician was Dickinson's life-long study of sexual anatomy. As part of this study, he produced a series of wonderfully artistic illustrations that were sketched from real life. In order to observe female internal anatomy directly, Dickinson pioneered the use of a glass observation tube that could be inserted into the vagina; when a light was passed through the tube, it was possible to record the changes in the cervix and in the vaginal lining during sexual response. This same technique was used 30 years later in the laboratory studies of Masters and Johnson.

Dickinson was also responsible for the development of the electric vibrator as a therapeutic tool for nonorgasmic women. He prescribed the use of the electric vibrator during masturbation as a first step in learning to reach orgasm. Again, in this regard he was almost 50 years ahead of his time.

FIGURE 4.1

Illustration from *Human Sex Anatomy* by Robert Latou Dickinson. These hand-drawn sketches show the patterns of skin corrugation in the female nipple (upper left), inner lips of the vulva (upper middle), nipple during pregnancy (upper right), foreskin of the uncircumcised penis (lower middle), and scrotal surface (lower left and right). Notice the similarity in skin surface puckering of these various parts of the male and female anatomy.

Dickinson's findings were published in *Human Sex Anatomy* (1933), which is now regarded as a classic work in this field. Dickinson was extremely skilled as an illustrator and was a meticulous scientific observer.

Finally, in the course of his many years of observing and sketching the countless variations in sexual anatomy, Dickinson made some unusual discoveries. For instance, he noticed that the pattern of skin corrugations on the foreskin of the penis, the inner lips of the vulva, and the areolae of the nipples is almost identical (see Figure 4.1). Although he offered no explanation of this curious phenomenon, we cannot fail to be impressed by the perceptiveness of his observation.

present in the first few months after conception, it is easy to see why the male and female genitals also have some basic similarities. A third theme is the *changing* structure and function of the genitals through the life cycle. Like our sexual behaviors, attitudes, relationships, and concerns, our sexual anatomy continues to change and develop as we pass through all the phases of the sexual life cycle.

In the first major section of this chapter, these life-cycle changes in sexual anatomy are discussed, with emphasis on the primitive origins of our anatomical development. In the subsequent sections, the structure of the pelvis is described, and then the female and male genitals. While anatomy is basically a biological discipline, we also discuss the sexual, psychological, and social consequences of genital structure.

Sexual Anatomy Through the Life Cycle

Human sexual anatomy is designed to accomplish its reproductive functions; that is, female sexual architecture reflects the female reproductive functions of menstruation, gestation, and lactation, and male sexual architecture is designed to accomplish impregnation. Because males and females play such different roles in the reproductive process, we would expect male and female sexual anatomy to differ in many important ways. We should be aware, however, that there are also many similarities in the genital architecture of the two sexes.

These physical similarities stem from the first few months of embryonic life. As noted in Chapter 2, the fetus initially has neither male nor female genitalia; it has a set of primitive structures that can differentiate into either male or female genital anatomy. For instance, if the fetus is female, the Mullerian system, which is present in all fetuses, will develop into the Fallopian, or uterine, tubes and a uterus; if the fetus is male, the Mullerian system will degenerate, leaving several apparently useless remnants—the appendix testis and the prostatic utricle. Similarly, the Wolffian system will develop into male internal reproductive organs if the fetus is male but will degenerate if the fetus is female. The path that is taken will depend on the amount and type of steroids, or sex hormones, that are present during the early weeks of life. However, remnants of the "opposite path"—that is, the path that is not followed—will remain throughout life.

Since male anatomy and female anatomy develop from a common set of primitive structures, there are many *homologues* in adult sexual anatomy. Homologues are organs or structures that correspond in origin to other organs or structures. For example, the female clitoris and the male penis are homologous organs—they develop from the same primitive structure (see Figure 4.2). They do not, however, play the same role in adult sexual function; the penis is involved in reproduction, urination, and sexual response, while the clitoris is involved only in sexual response. Some homologous structures do, however, play similar roles in male and female adults. For instance, the testes and the ovaries develop from the same primitive tissue, and both are involved in synthesizing and secreting sex hormones.

While the male and female sexual systems show many areas of overlap—such as the clitoris and the penis both developing from the same type of primitive tissue—there are also many instances of complementarity between the two systems. For instance, the acidity of the vagina is normally too high for sperm to

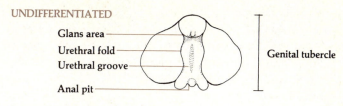

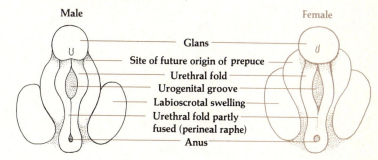

FIGURE 4.2

Three stages in the differentiation of male and female external genitalia. (1) Undifferentiated stage—appears during the second month of pregnancy. (2) Differentiated stage—about the third month of pregnancy. (3) Fully developed stage—at the time of birth.

survive long enough for impregnation. To neutralize this acidity, the male has highly specialized "accessory glands of reproduction" that secrete fluids to mix with the sperm, enabling them to survive longer within the vagina.

Human sexual anatomy undergoes dramatic changes during adolescence, when a sudden increase in hormone levels causes a variety of

physical changes. (These physical changes are fully described in Chapter 6). Less dramatic changes take place throughout the entire life cycle. For example, during the menstrual cycle the female genitals show a series of changes in the amount and type of their secretions, their coloring, and even their position. Further, during pregnancy a great many physical changes occur that are not reversed even after childbirth; for instance, the uterus remains somewhat larger than in the woman who has never given birth, the areolar tissue of the nipple darkens in color, and the external genitals often take on a darker color due to increased blood supply.

Older women experience a sudden drop in hormone levels at the time of menopause; for males, this decrease in hormone levels occurs more gradually. Just as the rest of the body shows signs of aging—such as wrinkled skin

and decreased muscle tone—the genitals are also affected by the aging process. In the female, the genitals may become paler in color, due to decreased blood supply and low hormone levels. In the male, the same age-related changes may cause a less vigorous sexual response. However, the physical changes that accompany aging do not necessarily mean that sexual interest and pleasure are lessened, for men and women are capable of leading a full and active sex life throughout the life cycle.

Pelvic Structure in Males and Females

In humans, the pelvic bone structure is designed to serve two basic functions: first, it enables us to stand and move in an upright positiion, by supporting and balancing the weight of the upper torso; second, it contains and protects many of the sexual organs, and in the female, it is constructed in such a way as to facilitate pregnancy and childbirth.

The word "pelvis" means basin. While the pelvic bones do form the shape of a basin, there are openings at both the top end—called the *pelvic inlet*—and the bottom end—called the *pelvic outlet*. The pelvic girdle includes the two hipbones, which are connected to the lower part of the spinal column at the back of the body. The pelvis forms a complete circular basin.

Pelvic structure is designed to accomplish somewhat different functions in males and females, so there are a number of anatomical differences in pelvic size, shape, and tilt. Some of these differences are apparent from the moment of birth—for example, the female infant tends to have a larger pelvic outlet than the male infant. But the biggest differences between males and females do not develop until the time of puberty, when the influence of rising hormone levels contributes to the charac-

teristic male or female body shape. The rising estrogen levels in females at puberty stimulate the growth of the pelvis so that it assumes its adult form. The female pelvis is lighter, more rounded, more shallow, and wider than the male pelvis, to accommodate pregnancy and delivery. If the pelvic outlet is too small to allow passage of the head of the baby, a Caesarean section (an operation in which the child is removed through an abdominal incision) is required to deliver the baby.

The adult male pelvis is constructed to serve different functions. At puberty, male hormones stimulate the growth of muscles that are usually heavier and larger than in the female. Because the male pelvis must support more weight, it is heavier, deeper, and narrower than the female pelvis. At its widest point, the male pelvic inlet averages about 125 mm. (5.20 in.), and the outlet averages about 85 mm. (3.54 in.). In contrast, the female pelvic inlet averages 131 mm. (5.46 in.), and the outlet averages 125 mm. (5.20 in.). These size differences become even more dramatic when we consider that the average male is considerably taller and heavier than the average female is.

The sexual organs located within the pelvic

basin are supported, at the pelvic outlet, by the muscles of the *pelvic diaphragm*. The pelvic diaphragm includes the *coccygeus muscles* and the *levator ani*; together, these muscles form a hammock that holds the pelvic organs in place. In females, the pelvic diaphragm helps to maintain the position of the uterus—thus, it is important that the stress caused by pregnancy be counteracted with appropriate exercises. Weakness in the pelvic diaphragm can lead to incontinence as well as to sexual and reproductive problems. William Hartman and Marilyn Fithian (1972) have noted that a simple set of exercises for the pelvic muscles may enhance orgasmic capacity in some women.

The levator ani, which is the major muscle system of the pelvic diaphragm, is made up of paired muscles that interlock and work together. Between the two sides of the levator ani are openings for the passage of the urethra and the anal canal to the outside of the body. In the female, the vaginal opening also passes through the levator ani.

The pelvic region is supplied by a complex network of blood vessels and nerves. The organs within the pelvis are supported and separated by ligaments and fibrous tissue. The perineum is the area between the legs of a standing person. It contains the termini of the alimentary tract (anus) and the genito urinary tract. The anal region is the same for males and females, but the genito urinary tract is quite different. In the female, the urinary and reproductive-sexual systems are completely separate, although they are located in close proximity to each other. In the male, the penis is involved in both urinary and sexual function.

Female Sexual Anatomy

Discussions of the female reproductive and sexual system are usually divided into two parts: *interal anatomy*, including the ovaries, Fallopian tubes, uterus, and vagina; and *external anatomy*, including the labia majora, labia minora, and clitoris. Until quite recently, scientists knew far more about internal anatomy, probably because the internal sexual system is more directly involved in reproduction. The external genitals, linked more closely with sexual response, received little scientific attention until the twentieth century. Perhaps the first major study of female external anatomy was carried out by Dickinson (1933), who measured and diagrammed the variety and structure of the external genitals (see the boxed extract). In introducing his work, Dickinson compared the variability in genital features with the variability in facial features and illustrated the extraordinary variety he observed with hundreds of drawings and sketches.

As is the case with most aspects of human sexuality, variability is the rule rather than the exception. Within certain broad anatomical limits, every woman will show distinct and individual characteristics in the size, shape, coloring, skin texture, hair distribution, and positioning of the sexual organs.

THE INTERNAL ORGANS

The ovaries. The female gonads, or *ovaries*, serve two functions: they secrete sex hormones, or steroids, and during the childbearing years, they mature and release an egg cell at each menstrual cycle.

Ovarian development begins when the fetus is about 6 weeks old, and by 3 months, the ovaries have descended toward the pelvic area. At birth, the ovaries contain about 400,000 *primary oocytes*, the immature cells that will develop into mature ova. Since the average woman releases a total of only about 400 mature ova during her menstrual years, the vast majority of oocytes degenerate without reaching maturity.

In the infant, the ovary is a pale, sausage-shaped structure with a smooth surface. Gradually, the ovary increases in size and weight, with most of this growth occurring after the first menstrual cycle. In the adult woman, the ovary is about the size and shape of an un-shelled almond. During the menstrual years, the ovary turns a grayish color and the surface becomes increasingly pitted and irregular. The reason for this change in appearance is that lacking a direct connection to the uterine tube, each egg cell released during ovulation must break through, or rupture, the ovarian wall. Usually this rupture is rapidly repaired, but a small amount of bleeding may occur at this time. Finally, in the woman who has passed the menopause, the ovary becomes smaller and more puckered as it ceases to release ova or secrete hormones.

The two ovaries are located on either side of the uterus (see Figure 4.3). They are held in place by *ovarian ligaments*, which run between

FIGURE 4.3

Sagittal section of female internal anatomy. Note the position of the ovary, uterus, vagina, rectum, and bladder.

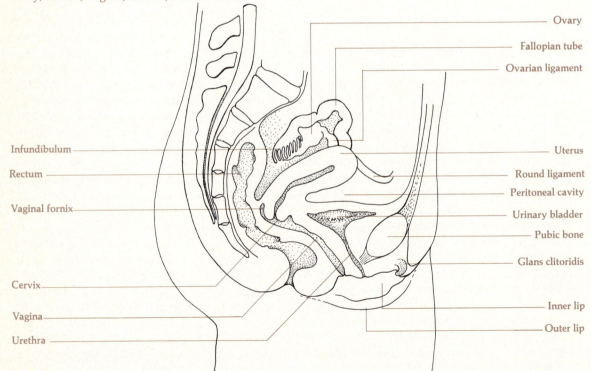

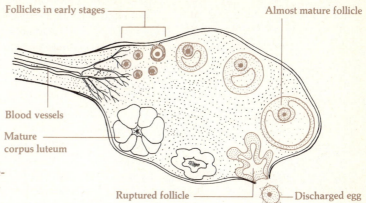

Follicles in early stages

Almost mature follicle

Blood vessels

Mature
corpus luteum

Ruptured follicle

Discharged egg

FIGURE 4.4

Schematic representation of ovum development, ovulation, and corpus luteum formation.

the pelvic walls, the ovaries, and the uterus, but the exact position of the ovaries may vary from one woman to another. Further, childbirth may alter the position of the ovaries to some extent.

Each ovary contains a number of compartments, called *follicles*, at various stages of development (see Figure 4.4). Each follicle contains an ovum. As a follicle begins to develop, it sinks toward the center of the ovary, which has a rich blood supply. This development of the follicle is stimulated by changing hormone levels and continues for about 12 days, until the follicle moves back toward the outer surfaces of the ovary. Then, in a process we do not yet understand, one of the follicles becomes dominant, continuing to grow in size while the other follicles begin to degenerate. Generally, only one follicle becomes completely mature during each menstrual cycle.

As this dominant follicle matures, it locates itself next to the ovarian wall. (Chromosomal numbers in the egg cells have been halved since before birth. Thus each ovum contains only 23 individual chromosomes, instead of the 23 *pairs* contained in all other cells.) Ovulation occurs when the expanding follicle wall

opens and the egg and some surrounding cells are released through the wall of the ovary and into the peritoneal cavity. The follicle, now without the egg, remains within the ovary and becomes the *corpus luteum*, or "yellow body." This structure will secrete hormones that will help to maintain a possible pregnancy. If pregnancy does not occur, the corpus luteum will shrink and degenerate within 2 weeks. The absence of its hormone leads to the next menstrual period. If pregnancy does occur, the corpus luteum will expand and continue to secrete hormones for about the first 2 months of the pregnancy.

Usually, the two ovaries alternate in their maturation and release of the egg cell, with each ovary releasing an egg every second month. However, it is possible to ovulate and become pregnant with only one functioning ovary. Further, the ovaries may at times release more than one egg during a single menstrual cycle, resulting in the possibility of fraternal, or nonidentical, twins.

The uterine (fallopian) tubes. The two uterine tubes, also called the *oviducts* (literally, "egg tubes") or Fallopian tubes (after a six-

Female Genital Aesthetics

If you were shown a thousand photographs of human faces, you would have no difficulty in selecting your own face from among the others; we are so familiar with our facial features — their unique shapes, coloring, size — that we recognize ourselves instantly. If you are like the vast majority of people, however, you would not be able to recognize a photograph of your genitals, even if you had to select it from among only two or three pictures.

Most cultures encourage genital modesty at the expense of self-knowledge. We are taught to hide our genitals from others, and even from ourselves. Women are far more likely than men to be unaware of the appearance of their own genitals, and for obvious reasons: the male sees his own genitals several times a day because of their external location. He is also likely to have seen other males' genitals — in locker rooms, bathrooms, and other all-male groupings. Thus he has some idea of what the "ideal" male genitals look like and has some notion of how his own compare with this ideal. Not so with females. Women are unlikely to see their own or other women's genitals unless they make a deliberate decision to look — and most women have been taught not to do so.

As a result, women usually learn about genital anatomy by studying diagrams and charts. Unfortunately, most charts and diagrams focus on genital "plumbing" — which tube is connected to which — ignoring the appearance of the external genitals. When the external genitals are portrayed, it is usually in the form of a standardized diagram that conveys little of the enormous variability among different women. A woman who examines anatomical diagrams and then compares these diagrams with her own appearance will often find differences that may lead her to question her own normality.

Betty Dodson, an erotic artist, relates the following story of genital self-discovery and confusion:

Somewhere around the age of 10 or 12 I wanted to see what I looked like "DOWN THERE." . . . When the house was empty I got my mother's big ivory hand mirror from her dresser and went into my bedroom, closed the door, and went over by the window with sunlight pouring in. I looked . . . and was instantly horrified! I was obviously deformed. I happen to have the style of genitals that has the inner lips extended and when I saw them hanging out the only association I could make visually was that they looked like those things that hang down from a chicken's neck, a wattle. I thought I had

teenth-century Italian anatomist named Fallopius), function mainly as a transport system. They move the egg cell toward the uterus and, at the same time, permit and facilitate the movement of sperm toward the egg. They also provide a hospitable environment and nutrition for survival.

Each uterine tube extends from the top of the uterus to one of the ovaries. Each tube is about 4 inches (10.16 cm.) long. The wall of the tube has three layers: an outer layer, a double layer of muscle, and a mucous lining. Within the tube are cells with tiny hairlike appendages, called *cilia*, that cause the egg to be swept toward the uterus. There are also cells that secrete nutrients for the egg cell.

The uterine tubes are not directly connected to the ovaries. When the follicle ruptures the

stretched them like that from masturbating . . . I swore off masturbation on the spot, asking God to get rid of those things that hung down, in exchange for my promise to be a good girl, stop swearing, love my little brothers, and to keep my room clean. (Dodson, 1974, p. 23)

After agonizing over this secret "deformity" for 20 years, Dodson organized workshops for women interested in learning more about their own sexuality. Not surprisingly, she found many other women expressing concern about their normality. By showing women photographic slides of female genitals, Dodson demonstrated that variations in women's genital features are as normal as variations in their facial features.

Increasingly, women's self-help groups and manuals such as *Our Bodies, Ourselves* have stressed the importance of women being familiar with and accepting of their own genitals. Since absence of such acceptance can lead to embarrassment and self-consciousness, many sex therapists advise women with sexual difficulties to begin therapy by learning about and examining their own genitals. Lonnie Barbach, for example, maintains that for women who are having difficulties in experiencing orgasm, genital self-examination is a necessary step in learning about sexual response.

type of chemical attraction exists between the egg cell and the uterine tube.

The uterine tubes become increasingly narrow toward the uterus, and at the place where the tube enters directly into the uterine wall, the opening in the tube is only about 1 mm. — smaller than the head of a pin.

The ovum is moved toward the uterus in two ways: the cilia in the uterine tube produce a sweeping motion toward the uterus, and the muscular layer of the tube causes a peristaltic, or wavelike, motion in the same direction.

The ovum usually takes about 3 days to make the journey from ovary to uterus. However, it is capable of being fertilized for only between 6 and 24 hours, that is, at the beginning of its journey along the uterine tube. Thus, fertilization usually takes place in the third of the tube closest to the ovary. By the time the egg has passed through this section of the tube, it has become "overripe," that is, it is beginning to degenerate and can no longer be fertilized. If fertilization does occur, the fertilized egg will continue to travel along the tube toward the uterus, where it will implant itself within the uterine wall. (In rare instances, the egg may implant itself in an area other than the uterus; this is called an *ectopic* pregnancy because implantation is not in the uterus. The fetus will not be able to survive if implanted within the uterine tube, but if it grows too large before it degenerates, it may rupture the uterine tube.)

wall of the ovary, it must travel a short distance to enter the fringed end of the tube, called the *infundibulum*. It is not yet clear exactly how this transfer of the egg from the ovary to the tube is accomplished. Some researchers have suggested that the egg is swept into the tube by the action of the *fimbriae*, the fingerlike projections that surround the top of the ovary. Other scientists believe that some

The uterus. The *uterus,* or womb, is involved in both reproductive and sexual functioning. During pregnancy, it provides a hospitable and nourishing environment for fetal implantation and growth, and during childbirth, contractions of the uterine muscles propel the fetus through the birth canal. In addition, the uterus shows muscular contractions during orgasm.

The uterus shows two patterns of changes.

First, there is a lifelong pattern of growth and development that extends from birth to old age. At the seventh month of fetal life, the uterus shows an accelerated growth in size that lasts until a few days after birth. This growth spurt is a response to high levels of estrogen found in the mother during the 2 months that precede delivery. The newborn, cut off from the maternal estrogen, experiences reduction of its uterine size, which then remains small until about 2 years before the menstrual cycle begins. Then, in response to increasing hormone levels, the uterus grows to its adult size; in women who have not had children, it is about 3 inches (7.62 cm.) long, approximately the size and shape of an inverted pear (see Figure 4.5). After childbirth, the uterus tends to be larger in size, although the shape remains the same. Finally, after the menopause, the uterus again shrinks in size and may become as small as in the prepubertal female.

Although the uterus is held in place by a series of ligaments, its position is not fixed. For instance, when the bladder or rectum is full, the uterus shifts position. Moreover, childbirth often causes a change in uterine position. When a woman is standing upright and her bladder and rectum are empty, the uterus tends to lie in a horizontal position, with the top, or *fundus*, toward the front of the body.

The bottom, or neck, of the uterus is called the *cervix* and extends into the vagina. The *cervical os* is the small opening at the center of the cervix. Normally, this passageway between the vagina and the uterus is very small, and at certain times during the menstrual cycle, it may be blocked entirely. The cervix contains glands that secrete different types of mucus at varying stages of the menstrual cycle. The consistency changes from stage to stage. During ovulation, the cervical glands secrete a mucus that is easily penetrable by sperm; at other times, the cervical mucus forms a "plug" that cannot be penetrated by sperm. These cervical mucus changes have been used as a means of predicting ovulation, and therefore may be useful as a contraceptive technique (see Chapter 11).

The uterus has three layers: an outer covering, a layer of muscle, and a mucous layer, or *endometrium*. The bulk of the uterus is muscular tissue; these muscles are dense, firm, and interlaced in all directions. During pregnancy, the muscle fibers expand greatly in size, and new fibers are added. When childbirth is triggered by changing hormone levels, the uterine muscles contract in powerful spasms that move the fetus toward the cervix. At this time, the cervical os expands greatly, permitting the fetus to pass through to the vagina.

FIGURE 4.5

Cross-sectional representation of the uterus of a mature woman. The shape of the mature uterus has been compared to that of a ripe pear. Note that the *cervical os* (opening between the cervix and the larger part of the uterus) extends up into the uterus.

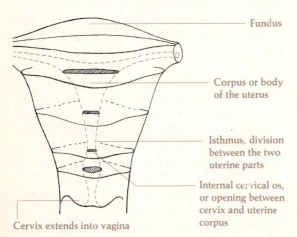

Fundus

Corpus or body of the uterus

Isthmus, division between the two uterine parts

Internal cervical os, or opening between cervix and uterine corpus

Cervix extends into vagina

The second pattern of uterine development and change occurs during each menstrual cycle. The purpose of these changes is to provide a nourishing environment in the uterus if pregnancy should occur; if pregnancy does not occur, this environment is shed during menstruation. The major uterine changes take place in the endometrium, although the outer layer and muscles of the uterus may also change in appearance and shape.

Sexual function of the uterus. Masters and Johnson (1966) have demonstrated that the uterus shows several changes during sexual arousal and orgasm. The uterus becomes increasingly elevated in position during sexual arousal, thus changing the position of the cervix as well. After orgasm, the uterus returns to its unstimulated position. Contrary to previous thought, the cervix does not secrete mucus during sexual response. Masters and Johnson also observed that after orgasm, some women showed a widening of the cervical os, a response that may aid sperm transport to the uterus. They also report that at orgasm, the muscles of the uterus show a pattern of contractions that are suggestive of the contractions occurring at the early stages of childbirth — that is, the contractions move in waves from top to bottom. From this observation, Masters and Johnson concluded that there is no truth to the belief that the uterus "sucks up" seminal fluid, since the pattern of contractions moves in the opposite direction to that necessary for uterine suction to occur. In fact, these contractions may be the reason many women in the menstrual phase report increased bleeding immediately after orgasm; the powerful contractions of the uterine muscles during orgasm cause the menstrual fluid to be expelled into the vagina.

The vagina. The vagina plays an important role in both sexual arousal and reproductive function, and often these roles overlap. For instance, the vaginal lubricant secreted when a woman is sexually aroused facilitates penile penetration and may also enhance the ability of sperm to survive in the vagina. Similarly, the muscular contractions that take place during sexual orgasm may aid the movement of sperm through the cervix.

Like the uterus, the vagina is normally a small organ, with little internal space. In the resting state, the walls of the vagina touch one another. However, the muscles in the vagina are capable of considerable expansion. During childbirth, the vaginal walls can expand enough to accommodate the passage of a baby's head, which is usually about 10 cm. (4 in.) in diameter.

The vagina is usually placed at about a 45-degree angle, with the outer end — called the *introitus* — closer to the front of the body and the inner end slanting back toward the spinal column. In shape, it resembles an elongated S, changing direction three times, although the angles are slight. Typically, the vagina is between 8 and 10 cm. (3.2 and 4 in.) in length; it is shorter in the prepubertal female and also tends to shrink in women who have passed the menopause.

The connective tissue of the vagina contains a rich network of blood vessels. During the early stages of sexual arousal, blood fills these vessels, and the pressure of the pooled blood causes the internal mucous layer to "sweat" drops of fluid on the vaginal walls. Masters and Johnson (1966) reported that this lubrication response may be seen within 20 seconds after the start of effective sexual stimulation.

The inner two-thirds of the vagina has relatively few sensory nerve endings and is usually insensitive to all sensations except pressure. The outer third of the vagina, however, is more richly supplied with nerve endings and thus is more sensitive to physical sensation in general.

Before puberty, the vaginal membranes are thin and fragile. After the menarche (first menstrual period), these membranes thicken in response to rising hormone levels. Unlike the uterus, the vagina shows only minor changes during different phases of the menstrual cycle. After the menopause, lowered hormone levels cause the vaginal walls to become thinner and less richly supplied with blood. Also, lubrication in response to sexual stimulation may be insufficient for penile penetration, and an artificial lubricant may be necessary to facilitate intercourse.

THE EXTERNAL ORGANS (VULVA)

The labia majora. The *mons pubis* is a layer of soft, fatty tissue that is covered with pubic hair and lies over the joint of the pelvic bones (see Figure 4.6). Extending from the bottom of the mons are two skin folds called the *labia majora,* or "outer lips." The outer lips are also covered with pubic hair on their outer surfaces; the inner surfaces are smooth and tend to be thicker toward the front of the body.

They contain numerous sebaceous (oil-producing) glands, sweat glands, and fat cells, and have a rich blood supply. In the sexually unstimulated female, they normally meet to enclose and protect the organs located between them. During sexual arousal, however, the blood flowing into the pelvic area causes them to swell in size and separate to some degree.

The labia minora. The *labia minora,* or "inner lips," are a smaller, thinner set of skin folds enclosed within the outer lips. They are more deeply pigmented than the vagina and show a variety of color changes during sexual arousal. The inner lips have no sweat glands, fat cells, or hair, but there are many small sebaceous glands close to the skin surface. In addition, the labia minora have a rich network of blood vessels and nerve cells, making them very sensitive to touch. During sexual arousal, the inner lips may show a two- to three-fold increase in diameter, and color changes may vary from deep pink to purplish-red. There is also a great deal of variety in the size of the unstimulated labia minora. In some women,

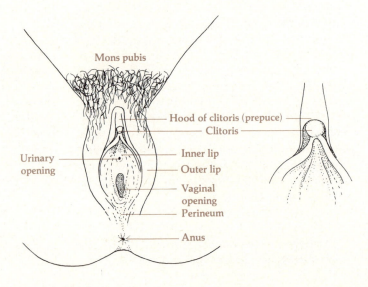

FIGURE 4.6

Front view of the vulva (external genitalia) of a mature woman. Right: enlarged view of the clitoris showing the clitoral hood (prepuce) adjoining the inner lips (labia minora). Stimulation of the inner lips is generally transmitted to the nerve endings in the clitoris.

Mons pubis

Hood of clitoris (prepuce)
Clitoris
Urinary opening
Inner lip
Outer lip
Vaginal opening
Perineum
Anus

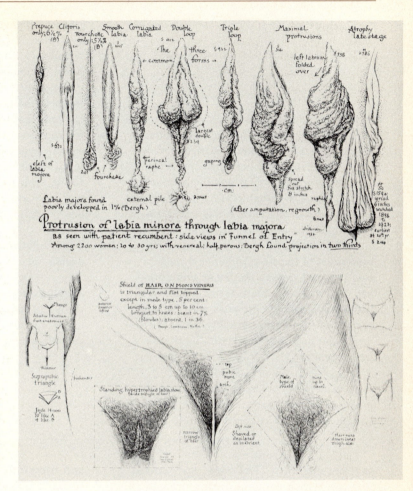

FIGURE 4.7

Variations in the appearance of the inner lips (labia minora) observed by Robert Latou Dickinson. Individual differences in sexual anatomy are the rule rather than the exception.

they remain tucked between the labia majora, in others, they extend below the outer lips. Often, one side will be somewhat longer than the other. Each labium can be divided into two parts: the lower division surrounds the vestibule, while the upper division passes above the clitoris, meets the other labium, and forms a skin fold called the *clitoral prepuce* — that is, the clitoral hood.

Vestibular area. The *vestibule* is the area located between the two labia minora, or inner lips: it contains a number of small mucous glands, which secrete fluids into the vestibular area. Both the urethra (urinary tract) and the vagina have their external openings in the vestibule, the vaginal orifice being located below the urethral orifice (see Figure 4.6).

On either side of the vaginal orifice, beneath the labia minora, are the *vestibular bulbs*, two masses of erectile tissue that are analogous to the erectile tissue in the penis. Each of these bulbs is about 3 cm. (1.2 in.) long. During sexual arousal, these bulbs fill with blood

Female Ejaculation — Fact or Fantasy?

Do females ejaculate? Victorian pornography is filled with references to female ejaculation, or "spending," and for many centuries there was a widespread belief that both men and women emitted a reproductive fluid at the moment of orgasm. In the twentieth century, however, the notion of female ejaculation was firmly discarded by such authorities as Kinsey and Masters and Johnson. Sexologists reasoned that the concept of female ejaculation was simply a male fantasy based on the faulty assumption that since males ejaculate during orgasm, females should react in the same way. Nowadays, research on the female sexual response cycle almost never mentions the possibility that females ejaculate.

If ejaculate is defined as emitting a fluid *containing sperm,* then females cannot ejaculate. If ejaculate is defined as emitting a fluid during orgasm, however, then there may be a possibility of female ejaculation. Many sex researchers —Havelock Ellis, for example—have noted that some women report emitting a jet of fluid during orgasm. Typically, this emission of fluid is assumed to result from orgasmic muscle contractions that squeeze out drops of vaginal lubricant. According to this explanation, the woman who secretes a large amount of vaginal lubricant during sexual arousal and then has strong muscular contractions during orgasm may appear to ejaculate. Another explanation is that the fluid ejaculated at orgasm is urine.

The belief that only vaginal fluids are emitted during orgasm has recently been challenged. In their research, Sevely and Bennett (1978) examined historical and anatomical data on the possibility of female ejaculation and rediscovered a long-forgotten and neglected aspect of female genital anatomy—the "female prostate."

and become firm. They are surrounded by muscles, which contract during orgasm.

Bartholin's glands, also called the vestibular glands, are also located on either side of the vaginal orifice, behind the vestibular bulbs. They are homologous to the bulbourethral glands in the male and consist of two small, rounded bodies. Each gland secretes fluid into the vestibule via a small duct that emerges just lateral to the hymen.

Before the research of Masters and Johnson, Bartholin's glands were thought to be the source of the vaginal lubricant secreted during sexual arousal. Masters and Johnson showed that in fact these glands secrete only about one to three drops of mucoid material, and then only late in the excitement phase of sexual arousal. The greatest amount of secretion from these glands was found after long bouts of sexual intercourse, and often there was no secretion at all following masturbation. Masters and Johnson concluded that while Bartholin's glands did secrete some fluid during sexual activity, their contribution was very small compared to the secretions coming from the vaginal walls.

The hymen. The hymen is located at the entrance to the vagina and has no known physical function among women. For centuries, however, it has been assigned a cultural function: to determine whether a female has had

In males, the prostate gland supplies a large part of the volume of the seminal fluid, or ejaculate. Females do have a homologous structure to the male prostate: the primitive tissue that becomes the prostate in males develops into the *para-urethral ducts of Skene* (named after the scientist who described them) in females. While the male prostate is a discrete, firm body located just below the bladder, the female prostate is a system of very small glands located around the urethra. Most of these glands drain through a pair of small ducts just below the urethral opening. According to Netter (1974), the female prostatic system is a vestigial remnant of the male prostate and is of interest only because it is susceptible to infection and disease. Sevely and Bennett disagree; they suggest that the female prostate may play a role in female sexual function and pleasure.

Since there is a female prostatic system, it is possible that women who emit a fluid during orgasm are having an ejaculation of prostatic, and not vaginal, fluids. Not all women have this experience. Anatomists have reported a great deal of variability in the amount and location of prostatic tissue in different women. Possibly, women with greater amounts of prostatic tissue are more likely to ejaculate, as are women whose prostatic ducts are anatomically exposed near the urethral orifice. For instance, some women report that they began experiencing ejaculation only after childbirth, an event that may serve to expose the para-urethral ducts.

To date, there is almost no research documenting the extent of female ejaculation. While it seems likely that the vast majority of women do not experience an ejaculation, this does not mean that it is impossible. It is important to recognize the possibility of female ejaculation, if only to reassure those women who experience it that it is a normal event.

sexual intercourse or is still "virgin." Although examination of the hymen does not provide clear evidence about a woman's sexual activity, the intact hymen remains a symbol of virginity in many cultures.

The hymen is formed during the early stages of embryological development and is typically a thin membrane that separates the vagina from the external genitals. Both the inner and outer surfaces of the hymen are covered by a layer of mucous membrane. Hymens come in many sizes, shapes, and thicknesses. Most, however, have an opening large enough to allow the passage of menstrual fluid when a girl reaches the menarche, and also allow the use of a tampon, even if a female is not yet sexually active. Only rarely does the hymen form a complete barrier to the vagina, a condition known as an *imperforate hymen*.

During the maturational process, the hymen may stretch in a variety of ways, sexual intercourse being only one means of widening the opening to the vagina. It may be stretched by finger pressure or by masturbation within the vagina. For some women, the hymen has a large enough opening to cause little discomfort at first intercourse; for others, gradual stretching may be necessary to avoid pain during intercourse. Even among sexually active women, however, remnants of the hymen still may remain quite visible around the vaginal opening.

The clitoris. The clitoris has only recently become a subject of scientific research. Once again, Robert Latou Dickinson must be given credit for the first major English-language publication describing the structure and function of the clitoris. His work has been followed by a number of other important research studies, most notably those of Masters and Johnson.

Why has the clitoris been ignored by the scientific community for so many centuries? In part, the explanation may lie in the fact that the clitoris is not necessary for reproduction — while the penis is both a reproductive and a sexual organ, the clitoris has no function other than the sexual. Since the clitoris seems to have no other purpose than enhancing female sexual pleasure, and since many cultures have been unconcerned with (or even doubted the existence of) female sexual pleasure, it is not surprising that only in recent years has clitoral structure and function been considered a suitable topic for study.

This is not to say that all cultural groups have ignored the existence of the clitoris. One article (Huelsman, 1976) describes two very different approaches to the clitoris by various "primitive" cultural groups. Among certain Arab and African groups, for instance, removal of the clitoris is part of the rites of passage common to all females. There is evidence that clitoral removal was performed in ancient Egypt; it has also been found among people as diverse in geographic location as the aborigines of Australia and certain Indian tribes of South America. Among certain Muslim groups, a procedure analogous to male circumcision — that is, removal of the clitoral prepuce — is performed to this day. It is difficult for us to understand exactly why these genital mutilations are approved in these cultures. Huelsman notes that the most drastic forms of surgery have been performed in areas where males and females are socially isolated from

each other, where the male role is extremely dominant, and where female sexual pleasure is ignored while female modesty is stressed. According to Mary Jane Sherfey (1972), female sexual drive is so strong that cultural order can be established only if males impose drastic measures to curb this powerful drive. Genital surgery would certainly accomplish this purpose.

Not all primitive peoples have had this negative approach to the clitoris, however. Many Polynesian and Micronesian cultures — groups that tend to accept and even encourage female sexual pleasure — believe that a large clitoris is a sign of sexual power, in much the same way that a large penis is thought to indicate male potency. In some of these cultures, attempts are made to enlarge the clitoris and the labia through manual and oral stimulation.

How has Western medical science dealt with the clitoris? In the eighteenth century, surgical removal of the clitoris was a not uncommon treatment for a variety of medical and pseudomedical conditions, examples being epilepsy, "nymphomania," "excessive masturbation," and a clitoris considered to be larger than normal. In addition, female circumcision — removal of the prepuce — was thought by many Victorian medical practitioners to be an effective treatment against the "dangers" of masturbation.

The clitoris is not unique to the human female. Its existence has been described in various species of reptiles and birds, and it is found consistently among all female mammals (McFarland, 1976). In many mammalian species, the anatomy of the clitoris is quite similar to that in the human species. However, it is not at all clear that the nonhuman females in these species experience orgasm, although the clitoris may serve several other functions: for instance, in some species manipulation of the clitoris is necessary to induce ovulation; in others, clitoral stimulation is required to induce the female to accept male sexual advances.

Clitoral anatomy. The *clitoris* consists of three connected structures: a pair of *crura* (legs), which join to form the *clitoral body* and end in a small, rounded *clitoral glans*. Only the glans is visible on the surface of the body, although it is usually covered by the clitoral hood, or prepuce. The crura lie below the surface of the skin. The clitoral crura are attached to the pelvic bone structure and are covered with two small muscles; the clitoral body is attached to the pubic bones by a suspensory ligament. Like the penis, the clitoris consists of erectile tissue—the clitoral body is made up of two *corpora cavernosa*. In addition to a rich network of blood vessels, the clitoris has a large number of nerve endings that make it very sensitive to touch.

According to Masters and Johnson, the average size of the clitoral glans is about 4 to 5 mm. (.18 in.) in diameter. In their research, however, they have seen clitoral glands measuring from 2 mm. (.08 in.) up to 1 cm. (.39 in.), and they consider this range of variation to be within normal anatomic limits. There is also a great deal of variation in the length of the clitoral body and the crura, which may be long and thin or short and thick; their size bears little relationship to the size of the clitoral glans.

Clitoral anatomy and sexual responsiveness. In attempting to understand female sexual function and dysfunction, many people have looked for explanations in clitoral anatomy. For instance, it has been suggested that the intensity of the female's sexual response is related to the size of the clitoris. (Note the similarity with our "phallic fallacy" that male sexual performance is related to the size of the penis.) However, Masters and Johnson (1966) have found no relationship at all between clitoral size and either the speed or the intensity of female sexual response. Also, among

women reporting orgasmic difficulties there is a great deal of variability in clitoral size.

Another myth to be dispelled is that female sexual response is related to the distance between the clitoral glans and the vaginal orifice. According to this theory, the further the glans is from the vaginal orifice, the more difficulty there will be in reaching orgasm; with closer placement, the clitoris will get more direct stimulation during intercourse and thus orgasm will be quicker. However, both Dickinson and Masters and Johnson report this theory to be untrue. Dickinson found that women with a close placement between clitoris and vaginal orifice were no more likely to be orgasmic than those with far placement. Further, Masters and Johnson reported that even when close placement is present, the penis does not come into direct contact with the clitoris—penile stimulation of the clitoris during intercourse is almost always indirect.

THE BREASTS

Although the breasts are not part of the genital system, they are certainly considered to be "sex organs" in our culture. Just as a large penis is symbolic of male potency, large breasts have symbolized female eroticism, for both men and women. The ideal woman as portrayed by such magazines as *Playboy* is often large-breasted. In contrast, the ideal woman of such fashion-oriented magazines as *Vogue* is usually small-breasted so that the clothes she is modeling will hang better. A variety of surgical procedures have been developed so that breasts that are "too large" can be reduced and breasts that are "too small" can be augmented.

In addition to their symbolic function, the female breasts play a very real role in two aspects of female sexuality. First, some women respond sexually to breast stimulation and show a variety of breast changes during the sexual response cycle. In fact, some women are able to experience orgasm through breast stimulation alone. Second, they function as a source of nourishment for the young; all mammals have *mammary*, or milk-producing, *glands*. Even though most women in our culture do not choose to breast feed their young, the anatomy of the breasts is designed to serve this function.

The breasts undergo a variety of changes during the life cycle. In the newborn, both male and female, small but distinct mammary glands are present. In fact, some infants secrete a small amount of milklike fluid in the first few weeks after birth. This secretion is stimulated as a result of the mother's extremely high hormone levels crossing the placenta while the fetus is still in the uterus. Several weeks after birth, these hormones disappear from the infant's body; the breasts then go through a period of quiescence that continues through childhood. At the onset of puberty, rising hormone levels stimulate breast development in the female. At this time, a small number of males also experience some breast development, a condition called *gynecomastia* that usually results from some type of hormone imbalance. Male breast development also occurs if a man is given female hormones; male-to-female transsexuals, for example, are routinely given female hormones so that they will develop breasts.

Anatomy. The female breast consists of fat cells, glandular tissue, and fibrous tissue. The number of fat cells, which seems to be determined in part by heredity, is the main factor in breast size — the more fat cells, the larger the breast. However, the size of the breast has almost no effect on a woman's ability to breast feed or on the sexual sensitivity of her breasts.

Each breast contains about fifteen to twenty milk glands, or mammary lobes, which are

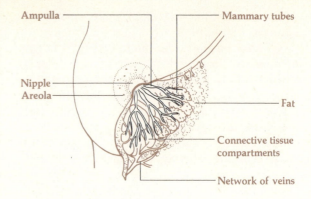

FIGURE 4.8
Internal anatomy of the breast in a mature woman.

held in place by connective tissue. Each of these milk-producing lobes is connected, via a series of ducts, to the nipple. Before each duct reaches the nipple, there is a small storage area, called an *ampulla*, which can hold a small amount of milk. The size of the mammary glands varies with a woman's age and childbearing status. As noted, the breasts show increasing development during the years following puberty; they reach their fullest stage of development only after childbirth. During the entire course of a normal, 9-month pregnancy, high levels of estrogen and progesterone cause a series of breast changes that permit breast feeding after birth. (A fuller discussion of these breast changes is included in Chapter 10.) Finally, after the menopause, lowered hormone levels alter the size and structure of the breasts. In addition to these long-term changes, the breasts show changes in size and structure in response to the changing hormone levels found during each menstrual cycle. In spite of these long- and short-term changes in the breast, about the same number of mammary lobes are found in the breasts of women of about the same age and childbearing status.

On the external surface of the breast is the *nipple*, which is surrounded by the areola. Each of the fifteen or twenty ducts from the mammary lobes terminates in a very small hole on the surface of the nipple. The nipple also contains erectile tissue. When it fills with blood, the nipple usually becomes firm and erect. Nipple erection is also caused by contraction of a number of small involuntary muscle fibers in the surrounding areola. When the breast is exposed to sexual stimulation, cold temperatures, or tactile stimulation from tight clothing, these muscle fibers contract and the nipple appears to become erect. The areola is of a darker pigment than the surrounding skin of the breast; although the exact color varies from one woman to another, both the areola and the nipple tend to darken with age and pregnancy. The surface of the areola has a slightly bumpy appearance, caused by the presence of a series of sebaceous (oil-producing) glands near its surface. The function of these glands is to create a lubricant that protects the nipple

from the irritant effect of the infant's saliva during nursing. Finally, the external surface of the breast often contains a certain amount of hair growth around the outside of the areola; this hair growth tends to increase with age and is related to hormonal changes.

Breast problems. Since the breasts are functioning glands that respond to a variety of hormonal changes, they are prone to several types of physical problems. We will not, of course, describe the full range of breast diseases in our text; but certain types of breast problems are so common as to involve a very large number of women. For example, many women experience breast tenderness and swelling just before menstruation, a condition called *mastodynia.* This is due to the build-up of fluids and tissue throughout the body during this phase of the menstrual cycle. Usually, the swelling and tenderness disappear as menstruation begins. With increasing age, however, this lumpiness and swelling may become more chronic—that is, the lumps may increase in size or not disappear completely during menstruation. Usually, these lumps are round and movable, and often they are tender. Al-

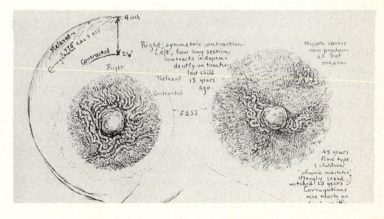

FIGURE 4.9
Hand-drawn illustrations of the nipple and areola by Robert Latou Dickinson. Note that Dickinson paid particular attention to the patterns of skin corrugation in the areola.

though they cause women a great deal of concern, they are rarely related to any form of breast cancer. Often, they disappear or decrease in size after pregnancy. However, the danger of cancer makes it very important that women learn to examine themselves and become familiar with breast changes.

Male Sexual Anatomy

The male reproductive and sexual system is made up of external organs—the penis, scrotum, and testes—and internal organs and ducts—such as the vas deferens, prostate, and Cowper's gland. From a reproductive standpoint, the system is designed to produce sperm cells and transport them through the internal structures and then out through the urethra in the penis. Both ejaculation and urination are accomplished via this duct that runs through the length of the penis.

The penis is the primary organ of sexual response, and penile erection is the main physiological sign of arousal in the male. The rest of the male sexual system is also involved in sexual responsiveness, however. For instance, Masters and Johnson (1966) have observed changes in the scrotum during sexual arousal. The hormones secreted by the testes also play a role in keeping the male sexual system "tuned up."

The male's sexual and reproductive functions can be completely separated with modern scientific techniques. For example, the man who has undergone vasectomy—an operation involving the cutting of the vas deferens—is incapable of playing his reproductive role but has no resultant problems with sexual performance. In contrast, the recent discovery that fertilization can occur in a test tube means that men with sexual problems may still be able to fulfill their reproductive function. Overall, however, the male sexual system is best understood as designed to fulfill both sexual and reproductive roles.

THE TESTES

The male *testes* are homologous to the female ovaries: they both develop from the same primitive structures, and they both perform the same basic functions. While the ovaries mature egg cells and release primarily female hormones, the testes produce sperm cells and release primarily male hormones, or *androgens*.

The testes differ from the ovaries, however, in their location in the body. When the male fetus is about 8 weeks old, the testes are little more than a spindle-shaped mass contained within the abdominal cavity (Netter, 1974). By the seventh month of development, the testes have usually descended into a pouch beneath the inguinal canal. A small number of male babies—between 1 and 7 percent—are born with undescended testes, a condition called *cryptorchidism*. Usually, this condition corrects itself during the first few months after birth. Little is known about the factors that trigger the descent of the testes, but it has been suggested that the mother's hormones play a role in this important developmental process.

The minute tubes inside the testes of a prepubescent boy gradually expand into *seminiferous tubules*. The development of

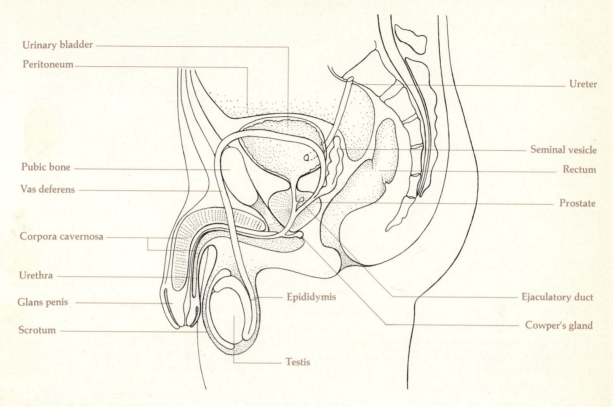

FIGURE 4.10

Sagittal section of male internal anatomy. Note the location of the bladder, prostate gland, vas deferens, seminal vesicle, and rectum.

sperm cells inside these tightly coiled little tubes—a process called *spermatogenesis*—begins before puberty and is fully functioning by about the age of 16 years. Spermatogenesis continues throughout the male life cycle, although there is a marked slowing of the process in the later years.

In the adult male, the testes are oval-shaped organs carried in a pouch of skin called the *scrotum*. Each testis is about 38 mm. (1.5 in.) in length and contains about 500 seminiferous tubules (see Figure 4.11). The testes are sus-

pended in the scrotal pouch by the spermatic cord. Usually, the left testis hangs a little lower in the pouch than the right testis. The skin on the outside of the scrotum has a distinctive, wrinkled appearance, is sparsely covered with hair, and contains many sweat glands, which assist in the heat control process.

Inside the scrotal pouch, each testis is covered by a thick capsule, the *tunica albuginea*, which serves as additional protection for the seminiferous tubules. These testicular ducts are tightly coiled into about 250 small

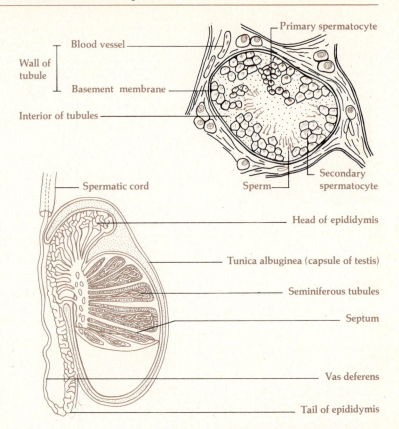

Wall of tubule

Blood vessel

Basement membrane

Interior of tubules

Primary spermatocyte

Secondary spermatocyte

Sperm

Spermatic cord

Head of epididymis

Tunica albuginea (capsule of testis)

Seminiferous tubules

Septum

Vas deferens

Tail of epididymis

FIGURE 4.11
(Left) Cross section of an adult male testis. (Right) The inside of a seminiferous tubule, with the sperm cells in various stages of spermatogenesis.

chambers—if uncoiled, the ducts would stretch to almost a mile in length. In between these ducts, the testis contains a number of large cells—called the *Leydig*, or *interstitial, cells* —which produce and secrete male hormones.

From the seminiferous tubules, the sperm cells move to the rete testis*, where they drain into another convoluted duct system called the *epididymis*. Although the epididymis measures only about 3.8 cm (1.5 in.), it is so convoluted that if unrolled, it would measure about 20 feet in length. Within this structure the sperm cells continue to mature for about 2 weeks, then pass into the long transportation duct called the *vas deferens*. Finally, the sperm

* A network of ducts in the testis.

cells move through the vas deferens into the *urethra*, through which they leave the body during ejaculation. The word "vasectomy" is derived from the vas deferens, which is cut in the male sterilization procedure.

Cooling of the testes. To provide the optimal environment for sperm generation and growth, it appears that the testes must be maintained at a temperature about 3 degrees Celsius (37.4°F) cooler than the rest of the body. If scrotal temperature rises much more above 34 degrees Celsius (93.2°F), less sperm are produced, sperm motility (movement and activity) is reduced, and a greater number of spontaneous mutations take place. Sperm cells are so sensitive to heat that even tight underwear or an extended hot bath can temporarily affect male fertility.

Through evolution, a number of specific mechanisms have developed that help to maintain scrotal temperature within the optimal range. For example, the surface of the scrotal sac contains a large number of sweat glands that help to maintain heat loss through evaporation. A network of tiny blood vessels also assist in the cooling process, by conduction. In addition, the testes may move toward or away from the body's heat through the action of the *cremaster muscle*. When environmental temperature is too high, this muscle relaxes, and the testes move further from the groin so that they may cool. The cremaster muscle responds also to emotional stress or sexual excitement by contracting, thus elevating the testes closer to the body. It seems possible, then, that chronic emotional stress could affect male fertility by interfering with the normal processes that regulate the temperature of the testes.

Masters and Johnson (1966) have noted the similarity between the male scrotal sac and the labia majora in the female. In the same way that the labia majora respond to sexual arousal by filling with blood, the scrotal sac and testes also show increased blood flow and muscle tension in response to sexual stimulation. This increased muscle tension causes the testes to be pulled in closer to the groin, a change that may occur suddenly just before or during ejaculation. After orgasm, the muscle relaxes and the scrotal sac returns to its normal position. If sexual arousal is extended over a long period of time, the cremaster muscle will go through cycles of tension and relaxation, leading to an up-and-down movement of the testes. As the cremaster muscle contracts, it pulls on the spermatic cord and draws the testes toward the groin; as the muscle relaxes, the cord is released and the testes move away from the groin. Since the cremaster muscle is part of the involuntary (autonomic) nervous system, men

are usually unaware of this testicular movement. However, the movement may be related to reproductive function; Masters and Johnson have observed that ejaculation occurs less forcibly in men who do not show testicular elevation during orgasm.

THE INTERNAL ORGANS

The internal sexual organs of the male can be seen as a sperm delivery system. On its way from the testes to the penile urethra, the sperm mixes with fluids from three accessory glands of reproduction (Netter, 1974): the prostate, the seminal vesicles, and Cowper's glands (see Figure 4.12). These internal organs play an important role in balancing the chemical com-

FIGURE 4.12
Schematic cross-sectional representation of the prostate, seminal vesicles, and urethra. Note how the ejaculatory duct passes through the prostate and where the ejaculatory duct and Cowper's gland openings join the urethra.

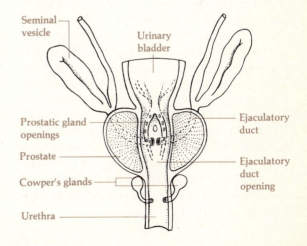

position of the seminal fluid. Although the fluids produced by these glands are not directly responsible or absolutely necessary for impregnation, properly balanced seminal fluid does help the sperm cells to live longer within the acid environment of the vagina. In addition, the prostate supplies the semen with *prostaglandins*, a hormonal substance that causes contractions of the uterus and is thought to aid in fertilization. Thus the internal organs contribute a number of important chemicals that enhance male fertility.

The prostate. The prostate, located below the bladder, is usually smaller than a golf ball and weighs about 28.3 grams, or one ounce (see Figure 4.9). Within the prostate is a complex and intricate series of ducts, which continually secrete *prostatic fluid.* In addition to the prostaglandins, the prostatic fluid contains a number of important biochemical substances. For example, a substance called *fibrinogenase* causes temporary coagulation of the semen inside the vagina, preventing the semen from dripping out before fertilization can occur. The alkaline quality of prostatic fluid also assists in fertilization, by buffering the acidity of the vagina, thus allowing sperm to survive longer.

Before puberty, the prostate is inactive. In response to rising hormone levels at puberty, the prostate increases in size and begins to secrete fluid. In the sexually mature male, the gland is more or less continually active, secreting a milky solution that is either discharged during ejaculation or mixed with urine from the bladder. Since the prostate is stimulated by hormones from the testes, it is not surprising that removal of the testes (castration) or the use of female hormones will interfere with prostatic function. In addition, the prostate can become inflamed—a condition called *prostatitis* that may cause considerable discomfort or pain.

It is possible for the prostate to be felt or stimulated directly through the rectum. In fact, the gland may be quite sensitive to stimulation, especially during anal intercourse. Homosexual males frequently report that ejaculation is triggered by prostatic stimulation from anal intercourse. During a medical examination, a physician will assess the size of the prostrate through the rectum.

The seminal vesicles. Each *seminal vesicle* is a single coiled and bulging tube located between the bladder and the rectum. The tube joins the *ductus deferens* (duct of the vas deferens) and enters the prostate through the *ejaculatory ducts.* After sperm from the vas deferens mix with secretions from the seminal vesicles, they pass through the prostate via the ejaculatory duct. Secretions from the seminal vesicles contain a high proportion of fructose, a natural sugar that aids sperm motility.

Cowper's glands. Each of the two Cowper's glands is about the size of a pea and is located between the prostate and the penile urethra. Due to their position alongside the urethra, Cowper's glands are also called the *bulbourethral glands.*

It appears that the function of these glands is to produce an alkaline secretion that neutralizes the acidity of the urethra. Since the urethra is the male outlet for urine, and urine is an acid fluid, it is important to neutralize this acidity before passage of the alkaline ejaculatory fluid. The amount of fluid produced by Cowper's glands is usually no more than a drop or two and is released before the actual ejaculation. However, there may be considerable variation, from one man to another and from one sexual encounter to another, in the amount of fluid produced.

Since the Cowper's glands' secretions appear as preejaculate, it may be possible for a man to impregnate a woman even if he withdraws before he ejaculates. Although sperm is neither produced nor stored in the Cowper's glands themselves, it is possible for sperm secreted into the urethra from the ejaculatory duct to be carried along with the alkaline fluid secreted by Cowper's glands. If this were the case, the preejaculate could contain enough sperm to cause conception. This is one reason why withdrawal is considered an unreliable birth control technique (see Chapter 11).

THE PENIS

There is surely no other part of the male anatomy that carries the emotional significance of the penis. The phallus has been viewed as a primary symbol of power in almost all cultures (see the boxed extract). Even in the present age of apparent sexual enlightenment, men continue to be preoccupied with the size, appearance, and function of the penis (Zilbergeld, 1978). Men whose penises are quite within the normal range may express the desire for a larger or more effective organ. Unfortunately, the large penis is still regarded by many men and women as a sign of virility and manliness.

From a reproductive point of view, the simple but important function of the penis is to convey semen containing sperm cells into the female's vagina. In this respect, the size and appearance of the penis are rather unimportant; although the penis responds to sexual stimulation by becoming erect, full erection is not essential for either ejaculation or impregnation to take place. From the point of view of sensory pleasure, however, the penis is the primary sexual organ of the male.

The anatomy of the penis can be described in two parts: the tip and the shaft (see Figure 4.12). The tip is also called the *glans* (from the Latin word for acorn). The urethra passes through both the shaft and the glans, terminating in a slit-shaped opening called the

meatus. Dickinson (1933) observed that the tissue of the glans is especially soft and yielding, perhaps adapted through evolution to avoid injury to the internal organs of the female during sexual intercourse. The surface of the glans is generally smooth or slightly wrinkled in appearance. Although the area of greatest sensitivity varies from one man to another, it is generally the shaft of the penis or the *corona* — a ridge of tissue separating tip from shaft — that is most responsive to tactile stimulation. The ventral (underneath) surface of both the glans and the shaft is usually more sensitive than the dorsal (topside) surface.

The shaft of the penis contains arteries, veins, small blood vessels, and erectile tissue. Unlike the organ in some other mammals, the human penis does not contain any bones. Inside the shaft are three hollow, spongelike cylinders that run through the length of the penis. The two upper cylinders are called the *corpora cavernosa*, and the lower cylinder is called the *corpus spongiosum*. The urethra runs through the corpus spongiosum.

At the base of the penis, the cylinders, or cavernous bodies, form *crura* (legs) that anchor the penis to the pubic bone. The lower, spongy body does not attach directly to the pubic bone but enlarges into the *bulb* of the penis, located within the groin. Two sets of muscles enclose the root of the penis: the *ischiocavernosus* muscles, which fasten around the crura of the cavernous bodies, and the *bulbocavernosus* muscles, which are wrapped around the bulb. Contractions of these muscles aid in the expulsion of semen or urine through the urethra. However, they are relatively unimportant in producing penile erection.

The mechanism of erection. Penile *erection* is caused by increased blood flow into the three penile bodies. When the penis is in a flaccid, or nonerect, state, the penile bodies are similar to

(continued on page 160)

Phallic Facts and Fallacies: Cross-Cultural Images of the Penis

No organ of the body has been assigned as many symbolic meanings as the penis. Aside from its obvious physical functions, the penis plays an important role in many cultural beliefs, rituals, and practices. Among both ancient and modern civilizations, the penis has been used to symbolize fertility, power, male domination, aggression, even life itself. While these symbolic meanings may have little to do with a man's personal experiences, they are bound to have some influence on how he views his own sexuality.

The writings and art of most ancient cultures include some description, usually in very respectful tones, of the significance of the penis. The ancient Romans, for instance, worshiped a god of fertility called Priapus. According to legend, Priapus was the offspring of Aphrodite and Dionysus and was an exceedingly ugly child with enormous genitals. His symbol was, of course, a giant phallus, and many Romans kept statues of Priapus in their gardens. Both the Greeks and the Romans ascribed magical powers to the penis, and phallic symbols were worn to ward off the evil eye and bring good luck.

In the East, the ancient peoples of India and Japan often embellished their erotic art with images of men with enormous penises. This concern with penile size is also evident in the *Kama Sutra.* A man was classified as being in one of three groups—Hare, Bull, or Horse—depending on the size of his penis. (A woman was classified as Deer, Mare, or Elephant, according to the depth of her vagina.) Vatsayana, author of the *Kama Sutra,* advises that the men from each group select a female partner of corresponding size. Should a man be unfortunate enough to have the wrong-sized mate, Vatsayana includes a variety of sexual positions to make the pair more compatible.

In more recent times, the penis has continued to play a central role in the work of many prominent authors. D. H. Lawrence gives the penis a life of its own in several of his novels. In *Lady Chatterley's Lover,* for instance, the hero's penis is described as proud, lordly, terrifying, and lovely; it even has a name of its own—John Thomas.

The frequent result of this enormous focus on the power of the penis is concern on the part of the individual male that he will not "measure up." Zilbergeld (1978) describes the fantasyland penis as coming in only three sizes: large, gigantic, and too big to get through the door. This fantasy penis is described as a weapon, a rod, a battering ram, and so on. Bearing little relationship to the real world, the fantasy penis is always ready for more, never tires, and is always "hard as steel." In actuality, "penises come in a variety of shapes and sizes (as do testicles), and about the only thing most penises have in common is that they are the wrong size and shape as far as their owners are concerned" (Zilbergeld, 1978, p. 94).

Opposing the fantasy model are certain well-documented facts about the size of the real penis. Among the first researchers to measure and record penile size was Robert Latou Dickinson (1933), whose conclusions were supported by the work of Masters and Johnson (1966).

Dickinson reported that the average size of the erect penis was 15.5 cm. (6.2 in.).

Masters and Johnson reported their findings on penis size in a section entitled "Penile Fallacies," to highlight the many misconceptions about the penis. One such fallacy is that a large flaccid penis will also show a larger increase during erection. In fact, their results showed that smaller flaccid penises tended to show a slightly greater increase during erection than larger flaccid penises. They reported that among their subjects, the normal size range for the flaccid penis was between 8.5 cm. (3.4 in.) and 10.5 cm. (4.2 in.), with an average of about 9.5 cm. (3.8 in.). Next, they compared forty men who measured between 7.5 and 9 cm. (3 in. and 3.5 in.) when flaccid with forty men who measured 10 to 11.5 cm. (3.9 in. to 4.5 in.) in the flaccid state. They found that the smaller penises increased in length by an average of 7.5 to 8 cm. (3 in. to 3.2 in.) during full erection, while the larger penises increased by an average of 7 to 7.5 cm. (2.8 in. to 3 in.). One subject, whose penile length when flaccid was 7.5 cm. (3 in.), measured 16.5 cm. (6.6 in.) when erect; another subject, who measured 11 cm. (4.4 in.) when flaccid, also measured 16.5 cm. when fully erect. Thus, Masters and Johnson have concluded that there is no evidence for the notion that a large flaccid penis shows greater size increases during erection than a small flaccid penis.

Another common penile fallacy is that there is a relationship between a man's skeletal size and the length of his penis. Again, there is no support for this belief—large men are no more likely to have large penises than small men. In fact, the largest penis measured by Masters and Johnson, which was 14 cm. (5.6 in.) when flac-

cid, belonged to a man who was only 5 feet 7 inches tall and weighed 152 pounds. The smallest flaccid penis they observed measured 6 cm. (2.4 in.) and belonged to a man who was 5 feet 11 inches tall and weighed 178 pounds.

How important is penis size to sexual satisfaction? Sexual advice columns repeatedly stress that penile size is far less important than sexual technique, and Zilbergeld found that among 400 women responding to his survey about sexuality, not one mentioned penis size as an important factor in sexual satisfaction. This does not mean, however, that women are completely unaware of differences in penis size; like men, women are susceptible to the fantasy penis described in books, magazines, and movies, and some women do have personal preferences as to the "perfect penis." However, very few women, according to Zilbergeld, are prepared to let this preference determine their choice of sexual partner. In the same way that a man may forgo his fantasies about large-breasted women if he finds love with a compatible partner who has small breasts, most women will accept less than a "perfect penis" if its owner meets their needs in other ways.

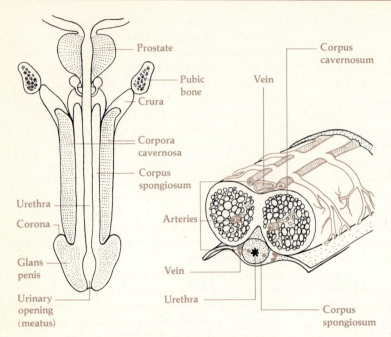

Prostate
Pubic bone
Crura
Corpora cavernosa
Corpus spongiosum
Urethra
Corona
Glans penis
Urinary opening (meatus)

Corpus cavernosum
Vein
Arteries
Vein
Urethra
Corpus spongiosum

FIGURE 4.13

Two schematic cross sections of the penis. (Left) longitudinal section: Note how the corpora cavernosa (upper bodies) form the crura, which attach to the pubic bone. (Right) cross section through the shaft indicating the major blood vessels of the penis. Erection is caused when the spongy bodies (corpora), which are composed of erecticle tissue, fill with blood.

a compressed sponge. During sexual arousal, the *sinuses*, or spaces, of the sponge become filled with blood, causing a thickening and lengthening of the penis. At one time, it was believed that erection was due to constriction of the veins of the penis, but now it appears that it is the active opening of the arteries and small blood vessels that is most important to erection (Masters and Johnson, 1966).

The arteries that supply blood to the penis are controlled by nerves from the sacral (bottom) part of the spinal cord. When these nerves are stimulated, nerve impulses cause the blood vessels of the penis to dilate, or expand, permitting blood to fill the three penile bodies. As the spongy erectile tissue is encapsulated within a tough, fibrous membrane, increasing pressure causes the erect penis to become firm, making penetration of the vagina easier to accomplish. Dickinson (1933)

noted the paradoxical fact that the firmness of an erection is related to the relaxation of the penile blood vessels. Should emotional or physical stress interfere with this relaxation response, a man may experience difficulty in getting or maintaining a full erection.

The mechanisms of *detumescence*, or loss of erection, are less well understood. Detumescence seems to result from the narrowing, or constriction, of the small arteries and blood vessels, causing less blood to flow into the penis. In addition, there may be a slight increase in the blood flow out of the penis through the veins during detumescence, but this has not been clearly proven. When detumescence fails, a condition known as *priapism* results; in this medically dangerous condition, the erection may persist for a long period of time, and surgical intervention may be necessary to correct any vascular damage.

MALE CIRCUMCISION

At birth, the penis of the male infant is covered with a layer of thin, loose skin. Part of this skin folds over upon itself and covers the penile glans; this fold of skin is called the *prepuce* or *foreskin*. It begins to develop in about the third month after conception and is homologous to the clitoral hood, the fold of skin that covers the clitoral glans. *Circumcision* is a surgical procedure in which the prepuce is pulled forward over the penile glans and then cut, leaving the penile glans completely exposed. This procedure, which is nearly universal in the United States and in many other national and religious groups, is typically performed soon after birth.

The practice of circumcision seems to have originated in ancient times and is often associated with certain religions, most notably Judaism and Mohammedanism. But the Greek historian Herodotus believed that the ancient Egyptians were the first culture to practice widespread circumcision of both males and females. Pictures of circumcised males appear on some of the early Egyptian tombs, and writings indicate that it was a religious rite, performed by priests rather than physicians. Among the ancient Jews, the practice of circumcision was an act of religious faith: Abraham was instructed: "You shall circumcise the flesh of your foreskin, and it shall be the sign of the covenant between us" (Genesis 17:11). Among the Muslins, also, circumcision is a necessary act of religious faith and is often performed as a public ceremony. Since the practice of circumcision is not mentioned in the Koran, Bullough (1976) suggests it was a common Arab custom that Muhammad adopted without comment.

Circumcision is also a rite of faith or a rite of passage in a wide variety of "primitive" cultures. In many such tribes, circumcision is part of an initiation rite that is performed when a young boy reaches puberty, and it signifies his passage into adult status and privileges. Ford and Beach (1951) point out that most African societies in their sample did not permit young males to have sexual intercourse until they had gone through initiation rites that included circumcision.

Among developed nations, circumcision is far more likely to be performed for "hygienic" reasons than as a religious or social act of faith. Generally, the procedure takes place within a week of birth. The medical arguments for circumcision include cleanliness—the uncircumcised penis may accumulate dirt and smegma (collected secretions), which can lead to infection—and the possibility of a lowered rate of penile cancer for the male and lowered chances of cervical cancer for his female partner. However, the relationship between circumcision and cancer is not at all clear. Furthermore, people who argue against routine circumcision suggest that an uncircumcised male can easily be taught to clean beneath the foreskin, eliminating the chance of infection. Recently, many physicians and parents are reexamining the necessity for the routine circumcision of newborn males.

The effects of circumcision on sexual functioning has been a topic of concern and controversy for some time. On the one hand, it was believed that the circumcised male, whose penile glans is completely exposed during sexual intercourse, would be more likely to develop a problem with premature or rapid ejaculation. On the other hand, it was argued that the uncircumcised male, whose penis is generally covered except during intercourse, would be less sensitive to erotic stimulation. Research by Masters and Johnson (1966), demonstrated that there was very little difference in the ejaculatory control of circumcised and uncircumcised men. Further, they found no differences in sensitivity to light tactile stimulation. Among the thirty-five uncircumcised males in their sample, twenty-nine showed a significant amount of foreskin retraction during sexual intercourse—that is, the foreskin moved back over the body of the penis, leaving the penile glans as exposed to stimulation as it would be in a circumcised male.

Summary

In this chapter, we have tried to balance a focus on the many detailed anatomical differences between the two genders on the one hand with discussion of the general overlap and complementarity of their functions on the other. Overemphasis of the differences can obscure important underlying similarities. From the notion of embryological homologues developing in the male or female fetus to the complementarity of reproductive function in the adult sexual organs, we see similarities and differences between the genders in delicate evolutionary balance.

As we have seen, the genitals play an important role on a number of levels—they are our reproductive system, and they are also the means for expressing our sexuality. In addition, genital anatomy often plays a part in our psychological self-image—our feelings of "normality" or "deviance," sexual potency, attractiveness, and pride or shame in our sexuality. On the broader social level, we compare and evaluate our sexuality with current social standards of what is desirable and attractive. The genitals have played a symbolic role in almost all cultures, and from our own culture we learn that unlike many other parts of the body, the genitals have profound meaning and significance in our lives.

To summarize:

1. First and foremost, the design of our sexual architecture is related to reproductive function. The male genital system is designed to fill its reproductive role—the production and maturation of sperm and their mixture with fluids that permit survival and impregnation within the female. In turn, the female genital system is designed to fill its reproductive role—the maturation and release of an ovum that can be fertilized and the furnishing of an environment that can protect and nourish the fetus until birth.

2. At the same time, genital anatomy has important effects on sexual functioning. For example, even though the clitoris plays no direct role in conception and pregnancy, it contains many nerve endings that are especially sensitive to sexual stimulation. The primary male organ, the penis, serves both sexual and reproductive functions.

3. Adult male and female sexual anatomy develops from the same primitive physical structures. Therefore, there is a great deal of overlap between the male and female genitals—for instance, despite differences in appearance, the clitoris and the penis develop from the same primitive tissues and play some of the same roles in the adult. Both genders receive maximal sexual stimulation through the glans. In addition, there are many remnants, or vestiges, of the anatomy of the "opposite" sex in each of us.

4. The genitals change in structure, function, and appearance through the life cycle.

From a few weeks after birth (at which time maternal hormones are still present in the baby's body) until the time of puberty, the genitals show few changes. Then, under the influence of rising hormone levels, the genitals take on an adult appearance and are capable of reproductive function. During this phase, menstruation, pregnancy, and childbirth may cause additional changes in female genital structure and appearance. Later, the aging process and decreasing hormone levels cause a final series of changes in both males and females.

5. Individual differences in anatomical appearance are the rule rather than the exception. Just as no two people have identical faces, no two people have identical sexual anatomy. These normal individual differences have no direct effect on our sexual functioning, although they may influence our feelings of sexual attractiveness and competency.

FIVE

Sexual Psychophysiology

Overview

Sexual arousal and orgasm are, of course, profound emotional responses, and human emotions involve both psychological and physiological processes. When we are afraid, for example, we show measurable physiological changes (our heart beats faster and we perspire more) as well as experiencing the subjective feeling of fear. The same is true of sexual arousal and orgasm—they involve both changes in bodily function and the perceptions and emotions that accompany these changes. Thus while most textbooks on human sexuality present the psychological and physiological aspects in separate chapters, we have chosen instead to present an integrated account of the psychophysiology of sexual response.

Psychophysiology refers to interaction between the higher mental processes and the responses of the muscles and organs of the body. It is a fundamental psychophysiological principle that physiological response to a stimulus will be influenced by past experiences. For instance, a woman who has learned to anticipate the intense pleasure of orgasm may respond rapidly to sexual stimulation, whereas a woman who has learned not to expect to reach orgasm may show little response to the same type of stimulation. In addition, experiences and emotions in the current situation influence the way the body responds. Thus sexual feeling is heightened by awareness of the body's physiological responses to stimulation (penile erection and vaginal lubrication, for example).

To understand what it means to be sexually

aroused, then, we must look at all parts of the nervous system, from the highest centers of the cerebral cortex to the most minute nerve fibers in the genital organs. In the first section of this chapter we try to answer the question What causes sexual arousal? by examining the factors, both physical and psychological, that make one type of stimulus a sexual "turn-on," whereas another type of stimulus produces little or no sexual response.

The physiological responses identified with sexual arousal can be organized into a *sexual response cycle*. As we shall see in the second section, there are several possible ways of describing this sexual response cycle, including the use of two-, three-, and four-stage models. In the final sections of this chapter, we discuss the various physiological changes associated with sexual excitement and orgasm, and note the role of subjective perceptions as well. While some aspects of male and female sexual response are different, such as the ejaculation response, this chapter emphasizes the broad similarities that exist between the sexes.

Sexual Psychophysiology

Would you consider taking part in a laboratory experiment on human sexuality? Although the results of such studies are fairly well-known in our society, few people are aware of what it means to participate in this work. Since many of these research projects take place on college campuses, we have chosen to describe the experience of a typical male undergraduate—call him Ken—who has volunteered to become part of a psychophysiological investigation of sexuality.

On the day that Ken is scheduled to appear at the lab, he feels somewhat nervous and apprehensive: Will he be asked to undress? Will they measure his "virility"? How well will he do? Walking to the lab, Ken imagines the experiment with a mixture of feelings—excitement, anticipation, and a considerable amount of anxiety.

At the assigned room, Ken is met by a male graduate student attired in a white lab coat. On the far side of the room, Ken sees a large and complicated-looking piece of equipment. This, Ken is told, is a polygraph—a device that will transform the electrical signals produced by his body into a pen-and-ink record. The polygraph has numerous dials for adjusting the signals, and also a set of pens to record the signals across a moving sheet of paper. Ken is somewhat intimidated by the equipment and wonders if he might get an electrical shock from it. The researcher reassures him that the equipment is all perfectly safe and, therefore, cannot hurt him.

The researcher explains to Ken that the purpose of the experiment is to investigate how much voluntary control a subject can exert over his sexual response. Ken will be asked to increase and decrease his sexual arousal using only mental imagery. In the course of the experiment he will also be shown an erotic movie. Before the experiment can begin, however, Ken must fill out a short questionnaire in which he describes the state of his physical health, whether he uses any legal or illegal drugs, and the extent of his sexual experience. He must also sign a notice of "informed consent" in which he verifies that he understands the purpose of the experiment and agrees to participate.

After completing the paperwork, Ken and the researcher walk to a small adjoining room. Ken sees that the room has been sound-proofed and notices the projector and screen.

In the center of the room is a comfortable reclining chair, and next to the chair is a table with bottles, cotton swabs, and various types of equipment on it. Ken can also see that the wires from the equipment are connected, through a small hole in the wall, to the polygraph in the next room.

Ken is asked to sit in the reclining chair while the researcher begins the "hook-up"; this involves connecting Ken to a number of measurement devices. First, a belt is strapped around his chest to measure his breathing. Next, several small flat metal disks, called electrodes, are taped to his chest to measure his heart rate. A second set of electrodes is taped to his arm to measure muscle tension. Ken jokes with the researcher about all the equipment and wires: How will he be able to become sexually aroused in the midst of so much technology? The researcher reassures Ken that there is usually no problem, but cautions him against moving around and displacing some of the equipment.

Finally, Ken is asked to unzip his pants and place the "penile plethysmograph" around his penis. The plethysmograph looks something like a thin rubber band with an attached wire (see Figure 5.1), and Ken asks the researcher how this device will measure his sexual arousal. The researcher explains that the plethysmograph is actually a thin rubber tube that is filled with a strand of mercury. Coming through the attached wire is a tiny amount of electrical current, which flows through the mercury. As Ken's erection appears, the rubber tube will stretch; in turn, the strand of mercury will become thinner, and this will change the flow of electrical current. These changes in electrical flow will be recorded by the polygraph. With this technique, even very small changes in the diameter of the penis can be measured. In fact, the device is so sensitive that every pulse of blood into the penis can be recorded.

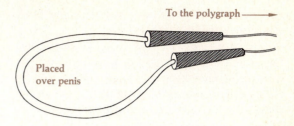

To the polygraph ⟶

Placed over penis

FIGURE 5.1

The penile plethysmograph consists of a fine strand of mercury inside a thin rubber tube that is connected to a recording device (polygraph). This mercury gauge, one of several different types of penile plethysmograph, is the most commonly used apparatus for studying male erections in the laboratory. (*Rosen and Keefe, 1978*)

After all the measuring devices are in place, the researcher turns down the lights and leaves the room. Ken is instructed, through a voice over an intercom, to relax for the next few minutes. Although he tries to do so, he finds that the hook-up and the situation have made him quite tense. He tries breathing deeply and feels himself calm down. After what seems like a long while, Ken hears the voice telling him to try, using only mental imagery, to produce an erection. Ken concentrates on his last sexual experience with his girlfriend, but in the darkness he finds it difficult to know whether he actually has an erection. He tells himself to relax, and in a short time he feels that he has succeeded in becoming aroused. Just as he is beginning to enjoy himself, he hears the voice instructing him to try to return to the unaroused state. This time, Ken concentrates on unpleasant imagery—he imagines his last exam, and when that does not work, he thinks about a film he has seen about venereal disease.

Next, Ken hears the sound of a projector and the movie screen in front of him lights up. As he watches the erotic movie, he knows that he is becoming aroused again. But, just as his sexual response is becoming very intense, he hears the voice instructing him to remain unaroused while he watches the film. This time the task is even more difficult, and Ken finds that he is tensing his body as he tries to think about unpleasant things. Finally, the movie screen goes dark and the researcher returns to remove the recording equipment.

When Ken is asked if he would like to see his polygraph record, he consents eagerly. At first, the record looks like a confusing squiggle of lines; then the researcher explains what each of the lines means. Ken can see that the line that recorded his sexual arousal shows a clear rise and fall as he produced and then lost his erection. He also notices that both his breathing and his heart rate had increased when he was excited. Ken leaves the lab feeling pleased with his performance and fascinated by the technology that had made it possible to transform his physical and emotional responses into a clear and measurable record.

From this experiment and others like it, scientists have learned a great deal about the mediation of human sexual response. By *mediation*, we mean the ways in which the nervous system processes sexual signals. In the previous chapter, on sexual anatomy, we explained the structure and function of the sexual organs—for instance, how the spongy tissue of the penis can fill with blood to cause an erection, and how the pressure of blood in the vaginal walls causes lubrication. It is a big step, however, from understanding the physiology of sexual response to knowing when and why this response will take place. In the remainder of this section, we discuss the deli-

cate interaction between physiology and psychology that seems to determine human sexual response.

REFLEXOGENIC AND PSYCHOGENIC STIMULI

Why is a certain look, type of caress, or physical setting very stimulating to one person but not to another? Why do some people require physical stimulation in order to become aroused, whereas others respond more quickly to mental imagery and fantasy? Clearly, sexual arousal is more than a push-button response that is universally triggered by a particular stimulus. In order to understand why one situation, time, or place, but not another causes sexual arousal, it is necessary to explore the interplay between the brain and the sexual organs.

One such approach, suggested by Weiss (1972), is that sexual stimuli can be divided into two categories: *reflexogenic* and *psychogenic*. Direct tactile stimulation of the "erogenous zones" causes sexual arousal in a *reflexive*, or automatic, manner. For instance, when the penis is stroked, a signal is sent to a relay in the lower part of the spinal cord; in turn, a signal is sent back to the penis for erection. This type of response is reflexogenic in the same way that the knee-jerk response is a reflex. The higher centers of the brain are not directly involved in this chain of events. It is for this reason that some men with spinal cord injuries are able to have reflexive erections even though they have no sensation in the pelvic area.

The second type of sexual stimulation is *psychogenic*—that is, the stimuli are processed by the higher brain centers. Included in this category are sights, sounds, tastes, smells, and touches. Also included are thoughts, images, fantasies, and memories. Through any one of

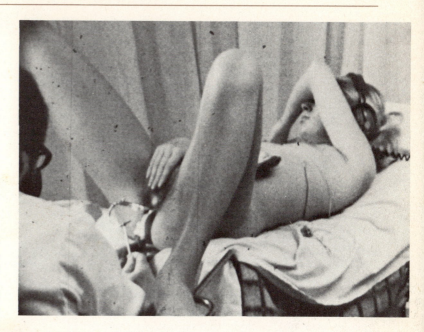

Recording of sexual response in
the laboratory. From the film,
*Physiological Response of the
Sexually Stimulated Female.*
(Courtesy, Gorm Wagner, M.D., and
Focus International, Inc.)

these types of psychogenic stimuli, it is possible to become sexually aroused with no direct tactile stimulation of the genitals. Recall Ken's experiences in the laboratory—the memory of a sexual interaction with his girlfriend and the sight of an erotic movie were each sufficient in themselves to cause penile erection.

In many instances, however, we become sexually aroused by some *combination* of reflexogenic and psychogenic stimulation. During masturbation, for example, people commonly use both direct tactile stimulation and some form of psychogenic stimulation such as fantasy or erotic literature. Similarly, during sexual intercourse most couples are aroused by both the physical stimulus of bodily contact and the psychological stimulus provided by the sight and sound of the partner. The scientific term for this interaction between the physical and the psychological is *synergism.* Weiss provides several examples of how reflexive and psychic stimulation act in a synergistic fashion. For instance, a man who sees an erotic picture will probably require less tac-

tile stimulation to produce an erection than a man who is not in the presence of such psychic stimulation. In the same way, such emotions as anxiety or guilt may inhibit a man or woman's sexual response to any kind of tactile stimulation.

Reflexogenic stimulation follows a fairly simple pathway through the nervous system; it is therefore easier to explain than psychogenic stimulation, which involves the complex processes of learning, memory, emotion, and other mental functions. An individual's past experiences play a very important role in determining which types of psychogenic stimulation will be perceived as arousing and which will have little erotic value. The process of learning about sexual stimulation often begins in childhood when the young boy or girl feels pleasure from touching the genitals. In turn, the pleasurable sensations lead to more touching. If the touching occurs in an environment with particular sights, smells, or sounds, it is possible that these psychic stimuli will also become associated with pleasure.

For instance, a girl who is taking a bath may discover that when she cleans her genitals she feels pleasure; she repeats this behavior during subsequent baths, and after a while, the sound of the water or the smell of the soap may become associated with pleasure. At this point, simply running the bath water may be sufficient to evoke some feelings of sexual pleasure.

During adulthood this process continues, as the individual's sexual experience widens and as he or she enters successive phases of the life cycle. The learning process also involves associating certain stimuli with negative or unpleasant sexual consequences. Suppose, for instance, that a man experiences problems in attaining an erection while in the presence of a woman who wears a certain type of perfume; after several such experiences, it is possible that he will not be able to respond to any woman who wears that same perfume. In much the same fashion, suppose a woman and her sexual partner are interrupted by her parents; it is possible that the anxiety or guilt generated by this episode will become associated with the woman's sexual interactions in the future.

In order to understand which psychogenic stimuli will be sexually arousing for a particular individual, then, it is necessary to look into that individual's past experiences and learning history.

Learning and conditioning in connection with human sexual behavior involve the same sorts of processes as learning and conditioning in other types of behavior. . . . The variations which exist in adult sexual behavior probably depend more upon conditioning than upon variations in the gross anatomy or physiology of the sexual mechanisms. (Kinsey, 1953, p. 644)

Although each person's experiences will be unique, we may also expect some commonali-
(continued on page 173)

Sexual Response and the Nervous System

The nervous system is the communications network of the body and can be compared to the telephone communications system of a modern city. The nerve fibers, which transmit electrical signals to all parts of the body, function like telephone cables. The relays and switchboard of the nervous system are found in the brain and

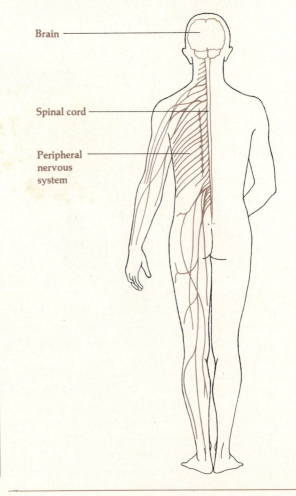

Brain

Spinal cord

Peripheral nervous system

spinal cord. The nervous system both receives and transmits the messages that determine our thoughts, feelings, and behavior. For example, when a man sees a nude woman, the nerve cells of his eyes code the stimulus and then the message is transmitted to the brain; if the brain processes the stimulus as "sexy," the nervous system will send a message out, triggering responses of the glands, muscles, and sexual organs.

Anatomically, the nervous system is divided into the *central nervous system,* or *CNS* (the brain and spinal cord), and the *peripheral nervous system* or *PNS,* which consists of the nerve fibers linking the muscles, glands, and sense organs with the CNS (see Figure 5.2)

In our analogy of the telephone system, the CNS handles both incoming and outgoing calls. Messages traveling from the sense organs and other parts of the body to the CNS provide input; messages traveling from the brain or spinal cord through the peripheral nervous system to the muscles and glands are the output.

This output travels through either the *somatic* or the *autonomic* branch of the peripheral nervous system (see Figure 5.3). In broad terms, the somatic nerve fibers connect the CNS with the striped (striated) muscles of the body—those that are necessary for motor activity, such as walking or talking. Muscle tension during sexual arousal is caused by stimulation of the so-

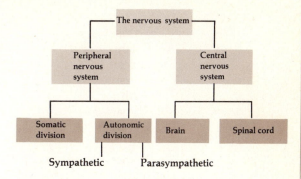

FIGURE 5.3
Diagram of the various parts of the nervous system. Notice that all parts of the nervous system are involved in sexual response.

matic nervous system. But other signs of sexual arousal, such as vaginal lubrication or penile erection, are stimulated by the autonomic nervous system. In general, the autonomic nervous system controls the smooth muscles lining the internal organs, the heart, and the glands, both sexual and nonsexual. The functions of these muscles and glands are considered to be largely *involuntary*—that is, not under our conscious control. Thus, it is much harder to exercise deliberate control over the rate of heartbeat, for example, than it is to raise an arm or a leg.

The autonomic nervous system can be further subdivided into the *sympathetic* and *parasympathetic* branches (see Figure 5.4). These two systems have different anatomical pathways and use different chemical substances to activate the smooth muscles and glands. For instance, the nerve endings of the parasympathetic system are referred to as *cholinergic* because they release acetylcholine to transmit their messages; the sympathetic nervous system is referred to as *adrenergic* because it releases adrenaline and noradrenaline. The two systems also serve dif-

FIGURE 5.2
Schematic representation of the nervous system. The central nervous system (CNS) includes the brain and the spinal cord. All other nerve fibers are included in the peripheral nervous system.

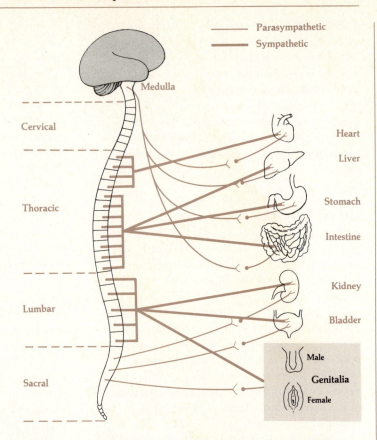

Parasympathetic
Sympathetic

Medulla

Cervical

Thoracic

Lumbar

Sacral

Heart

Liver

Stomach

Intestine

Kidney

Bladder

Male
Genitalia
Female

FIGURE 5.4

Schematic representation of the sympathetic and parasympathetic branches of the autonomic nervous system. The autonomic nervous system plays a critical part in the physiological aspects of male and female sexual response.

ferent functions. Under most circumstances, the sympathetic nervous system responds during periods of stress, that is, when there is a need for vigorous activity; the parasympathetic system is dominant during periods of relaxation. Their functions are sometimes described as *antagonistic,* since more of one tends to mean less of the other.

Most organs of the body, including the sexual organs, receive messages from both the sympathetic and the parasympathetic nervous systems. For example, when a man's penis becomes erect or a woman's vagina is lubricated, we are witnessing the effects of the parasympathetic nervous system causing *vasodilation* (or expansion

of the arterial blood vessels). As the person becomes more aroused, the sympathetic nervous system plays a greater role, causing increases in blood pressure and heart rate. At the time of orgasm, the sympathetic nervous system may take over completely; ejaculation is set off by a sudden discharge in the sympathetic nervous system. The release of adrenaline caused by this sudden discharge creates an autonomic imbalance, which is quickly compensated for by a release of acetylcholine from the parasympathetic nervous system. This phenomenon, sometimes referred to as *parasympathetic rebound,* contributes to the subjective feeling of warmth and relaxation that often occurs after orgasm.

ties in what is sexually arousing. The repeated pairing of certain sights, sounds, thoughts, and so on with particular sexual consequences will serve to "condition" a man or woman to a special set of psychogenic stimuli.

PSYCHOLOGICAL DETERMINANTS OF SEXUAL RESPONSE

Thus far, we have discussed the relatively simple process of conditioning by association in establishing the sexual value of a particular stimulus. However, a stimulus can also acquire sexual meaning through a variety of more complex psychological processes. We often use the phrase "in the mood," for instance, to refer to a certain mental state in which we are likely to initiate or respond to a partner's sexual advances. Defining what it

means to be "in the mood" is not a simple matter; it requires taking into account our thoughts, feelings, beliefs, attitudes, and fantasies. At times, we are aware of the reasons why we are or are not "in the mood"; at other times, we are unaware of the sources of our reaction to a sexual stimulus. At times our feelings are spontaneous and uncomplicated; in other instances, we experience conflicts and hesitation. Given the complexity of human emotions and thoughts, it is not at all surprising that the sexual experience can vary greatly from one person to another, and from one occasion to another for the same person.

Researchers (Byrne and Byrne, 1977) have described three major components that influence our response to sexual stimulation: an *informational* component, an *affective* response system, and an *imaginative* capacity (see Figure 5.5):

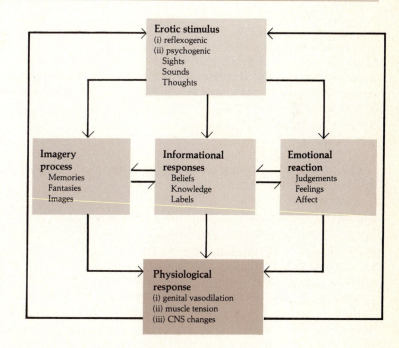

FIGURE 5.5

How erotic stimuli are processed: diagram showing the major psychological components that mediate a sexual response.
(Adapted from D. Bryne and Bryne, 1977, p. 502)

1. The *informational component* consists of our beliefs, labels, and expectations concerning sexuality. For example, a person who believes that fellatio is a perversion or a sign of mental illness is unlikely to engage in such behavior, and the idea of performing fellatio would probably be a sexual "turn-off." On the other hand, for the person who thinks that fellatio is a healthy and desirable activity, the idea of fellatio would be a kind of sexual "turn-on."

2. The *affective,* or *emotional, component* consists of our subjective perceptions and feelings about a sexual stimulus and can vary from very positive to very negative. Included in this category are the associated feelings, such as joy, guilt, or anxiety, that can accompany a sexual experience. For example, we would expect that in most cases, a loved partner would be a more effective sexual stimulus than someone whom we dislike.

3. The *imaginative component* refers to those mental images and fantasies evoked by a sexual stimulus. Researchers since Kinsey have emphasized the importance of these mental images in determining sexual response. Moreover, "part of imaginative activity seems to involve the evocation of memories of one's own past sexual acts, and arousal tends to be greatest in response to reminders of what the individual has personally experienced" (Byrne and Byrne, 1977, p. 505). Indeed, psychophysiological studies indicate that people can quickly learn to turn themselves on and off with the use of appropriate fantasies and images (Rosen, 1973; Rosen *et al.*, 1975).

From Figure 5.5, we can see that these three cognitive components interact with one another. For instance, if we believe that fellatio is unhealthy, this belief will influence our feelings about and imagery of the act. Or if there is a disagreement between our fantasies about a sexual act and our beliefs about it, we may experience conflict in our responses to that stimulus. This type of conflict is often present regarding extramarital sexual activity; we may fantasize that the activity would be pleasurable but at the same time be put off by the belief that such behavior is wrong or destruc-

tive. Finally, there is a feedback loop between our physiological response and the erotic stimulus—as is indicated by the arrows around the outside of the diagram. In other words, as we become more aware of our physical arousal to a particular stimulus, that stimulus will be perceived as increasingly arousing.

One additional factor crucial in determining our sexual response is not included in this model—that is, whether or not we are paying attention to the sexual stimulus. If the sexual stimulus is not attended to, or if there is a distraction from it, then a sexual response may not occur. This point was demonstrated in a laboratory experiment (Geer and Fuhr, 1976). Subjects listened to erotic tape recordings through one side of an earphone headset while simple mental arithmetic problems were played through the other earphone. At the same time, a plethysmograph was used to measure the subjects' erectile responses. The researchers found that distraction definitely reduced the amount of erection produced in response to the erotic tape. This finding can be extended to many real-life situations in which we are distracted from a sexual stimulus by the sound of a television in the next room, by the smells of freshly cooked food, or by thoughts of tomorrow's final exam.

COMPARING MALE AND FEMALE
SEXUAL RESPONSE

The old French saying *vive la difference* expresses the notion that there are important differences in the ways that men and women respond, and that these differences can be a source of pleasure to both. Other cultural views, however, emphasize more negative aspects of the differences between the sexes.

The myth goes [that] men are very simple creatures when it comes to sex. They have no special requirements, they are almost always ready and willing, and their only problem is how to get enough of it. According to this myth . . . there is quite a lot to be learned . . . about why women think and act as they do sexually and how their many, mysterious problems in this area can be dealt with—but little or nothing to be learned or said about men and sex. (Zilbergeld, 1978, p. 2)

Needless to say, there are times when the sexual response of *both* men and women is mysterious and complex, and there are times when it is direct and simple for both.

In the same vein, there is a common stereotype that women need affection and intimacy in order to respond sexually whereas men can perform regardless of their relationship with the partner. While there may be some truth to this stereotype—young men, for example, may be very easily aroused in almost any situation, whereas women are subject to more sources of social inhibition—there are also many exceptions; many women are able to perform adequately without a strong emotional relationship; and many men are unwilling or unable to become sexually aroused in an impersonal situation. Further, as our culture accepts a greater amount of flexibility in sex role behaviors in nonsexual situations, we find that men and women show more overlap in their behavior in sexual situations as well. For instance, a woman who has learned to be assertive in her work and social relationships may well find it easier to initiate, and be more dominant in, a sexual relationship.

Another common stereotype is that men and women have differing *sex drives*. Men are usually characterized as being more driven by their sexual needs than women are, and also as having less control over their physiological responses. This issue is clouded by the fact that we do not really have an adequate, standardized definition of "sex drive." The stereotype of men having a stronger sex drive may be derived, in part, from the initiatory role that men often assume in sexual situations. But the fact that males are more likely to initiate sex

does not necessarily mean that they have more desire than their female partners, nor does it mean that they will be more physiologically aroused by the experience. Also, we know that approximately equal numbers of men and women have sought help in recent years for the problem of lack of sexual desire (see Chapter 9).

Experts tend to disagree on the extent to which male and female sexual response patterns are fundamentally similar or different. Although Kinsey believed that men tend to be more easily conditioned by their sexual experiences than women are, he also stressed the basic similarities in how men and women react physiologically. Masters and Johnson also focused on these similarities:

Parallels between the anatomic responses of the human male and female to effective sexual stimulation have been established. . . . The parallels in reaction to effective sexual stimulation emphasize the physiologic similarities in male and female responses rather than the differences. Aside from obvious anatomic variants, men and women are homogeneous in their physiologic responses to sexual stimuli. (1966, pp. 284–285)

They noted that vaginal lubrication in the woman parallels penile erection in the man; both responses occur as a result of vascular (blood flow) changes. Increased muscle tension, and changes in heart rate, blood pressure, and respiration (breathing), are common to men and women during sexual excitement. Finally, the physiological changes of orgasm, as well as the subjective experience of orgasm, tend to show a great deal of overlap in men and women.

Now that Masters and Johnson's conclusions regarding the similarities between male and female sexual response have been widely accepted, there is a trend toward studying these similarities in the psychophysiological laboratory. Initially, psychophysiological experiments focused on the male—partly because male sexual arousal was fairly easy to measure with the use of the penile plethys-mograph. For scientists to be able to measure female sexual arousal, it was necessary first to find a response analogous to penile erection and then to develop the technology for measuring this response. Masters and Johnson solved the first problem by establishing that vaginal lubrication was analogous to penile erection; the problem of measurement was solved by the development of the *vaginal photocell plethysmograph* (see Figure 5.6). This instrument, shaped something like a tampon, measures the amount of light reflected from the walls of the vagina. When a woman is sexually aroused, the vaginal walls fill with blood (which results in lubrication), and less light is reflected to the photocell; thus the polygraph effectively records increases in blood flow (Sintchak and Geer, 1975). Because both penile erection and vaginal lubrication are caused by the same basic physiological process—vasocongestion (pooling of blood) in the pelvic area—the results of research with the vaginal plethysmograph are basically comparable to results obtained with the penile plethysmograph.

One application of this technology is a study in which psychologist Julia Heiman compared male and female arousal responses to tape-recorded scenes that were either erotic, romantic, or neutral. She found that

explicit sex, not romance, is what turns people on —women as well as men. The great majority of both sexes responded physiologically and subjectively to the erotic and erotic-romantic tapes, and not to the romantic or control contents. Women, in fact, rated the erotic tapes as more arousing than men did. (1975, p. 67)

Heiman also asked her male and female subjects to fantasize about a sexual scene; again, she found that both groups were comparable in their ability to produce a significant physiological response on the basis of fantasy alone.

In earlier sections, we discussed the role of psychogenic stimuli in producing a sexual arousal response. The relatively simple process of conditioning, and the more complex processes of cognitive, emotional, and informational mediation, are all involved in making a particular stimulus seem "sexy" to us. Of course, all of these mediators will come

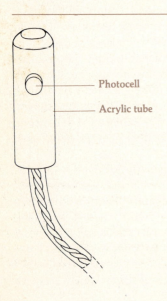

Photocell

Acrylic tube

FIGURE 5.6

The vaginal plethysmograph is a device used to measure vaginal blood flow in the sexually stimulated female. The device, about the size and shape of a tampon, is inserted into the vagina. It contains a light that is reflected against the vaginal walls, and a photocell that is sensitive to this reflected light. When a female is sexually aroused, the blood flowing into the vaginal walls will change the intensity of the reflected light, providing a measure of sexual arousal that is roughly analogous to the penile plethysmograph.

into play for both men and women. And while men and women may have different types of experiences in learning about sexual stimuli, there is no strong reason to assume that the differences between the sexes will always be greater than the differences within either one of the sexes.

Overall, then, we must conclude that there is a greater degree of similarity than difference in the response patterns of males and females. Both sexes experience the same basic physiological responses during sexual arousal, and sexual arousal tends to peak for both sexes in the physiological event of orgasm. In the next section, we continue to discuss these similarities as they appear during the various stages of sexual arousal.

Stages of Sexual Response

In the previous section, we discussed why men and women will become aroused in some situations but not in others; the answer to this question involved a complex mixture of physical, cognitive, and emotional factors. In this section, we turn our attention to the question of the stages of human sexual response in the course of a single sexual experience. Think of human sexual response as being like a train journey; we have already described some of the factors that determine whether or not we will board the train. Now we will talk about what actually happens during the journey.

For many years, this journey was seen as a single event, with much the same character from the start to the end of the ride. More recent conceptualizations, however, have begun to reflect the notion that human sexual response is cyclical in nature—that is, that there are a number of stages between the beginning and ending of a sexual experience.

Scientific models of the stages of the sexual response cycle have been constructed by researchers who have studied sexual behavior. Although each of these models contains the idea that there are stages, some disagreement exists as to precisely how many stages there are. Thus, there are two-stage, three-stage, and four-stage models. As we shall see, there is some overlap between the models and also

some interesting differences. A common theme underlying all models of sexual response is that there is an *orderly time sequence* of events. There are differences, however, in where each researcher chooses to place the line dividing one stage from the next. To understand how these differences can occur, let us return to the metaphor of the train journey. Suppose that the train always starts slowly, then builds up speed, and finally slows down as it approaches its destination. One view of the journey might be that it has two phases: an increase in speed followed by a decrease in speed. An equally valid view is that the journey has three phases: slow, fast, and then slow again. Both views are accurate and simply reflect different ways of looking at the same journey.

A TWO-STAGE MODEL

Prior to the work of Masters and Johnson, most writers described two important stages in the sexual response cycle. Prominent among these writers was Havelock Ellis, who used the terms *tumescence* and *detumescence* to describe sexual response (see Figure 5.7). These words can be defined as the flow of

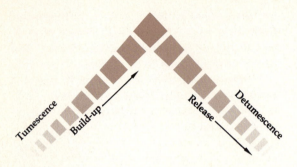

FIGURE 5.7
A two-stage model of the sexual response cycle. *(Derived from Ellis, 1906)*

blood into and out of the pelvic area during arousal and orgasm. But Ellis also used the terms to signify the entire process of building up and discharging sexual energy:

Tumescence is the piling on of the fuel; detumescence is the leaping out of the devouring flame whence is lighted the torch of life to be handed from generation to generation. The whole process is . . . exactly analogous to that by which a pile is driven into the earth by the raising and then the letting go of a heavy weight which falls on the head of the pile. In tumescence the organism is slowly wound up and force accumulated; in the act of detumescence the accumulated force is let go and by its liberation the sperm-bearing instrument is driven home. (1906, p. 142)

For Ellis, sexual energy was a fundamental part of human life, but it was not a totally automatic process. He believed that the act of becoming sexually aroused involved a conscious and voluntary form of behavior called "courtship," in which a man or woman found a sexual partner and then began the process of accumulating sexual energy. Although the quotation cited above seems to refer to male sexuality, Ellis believed that courtship, tumescence, and detumescence were equally important for men and women.

A THREE-STAGE MODEL

The model of the sexual response cycle developed by Helen Kaplan (1979) contains three stages: desire, excitement, and orgasm (see Figure 5.8). Kaplan proposes this model in light of her experiences as a sex therapist; she notes that sexual dysfunction tends to fall into these three categories, and that it is possible to be "inhibited" in one of these areas while functioning normally in the other two.

The three phases are physiologically related but discrete. They are interconnected but governed by separate neurophysiological systems. Metaphorically, orgasm, excitement, and desire may be thought of as having a "common generator" but each has its own "circuitry." (1979, p. 6)

This model is most significant in its inclusion of "desire" as a separate stage of the sexual response cycle. Unlike excitement or orgasm, desire does not involve the genital organs; instead, according to Kaplan, it involves sensations that motivate a person to seek out or become available to sexual experience. In some ways, then, desire is analogous to the person who is standing on the railway plat-

FIGURE 5.8
A three-stage model of the sexual response cycle. *(Kaplan, 1979)*

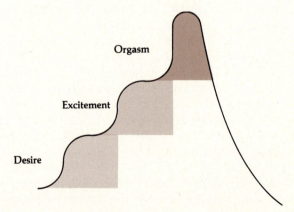

form and having to decide whether he or she wants to make the journey. A person who is highly interested in travel will probably board the waiting train, whereas the homebody may decide to let it pass without boarding. However, if the homebody should for some reason be forced to board, this does not mean that he or she cannot cope with the train ride; indeed, it is possible that the trip will be enjoyed as much as by a seasoned traveler. In much the same way, a person who has little desire for sex may, when pressured to participate, be as aroused and orgasmic as the person who is highly sexually motivated.

A FOUR-STAGE MODEL

For many members of the scientific community, and for the public as well, Masters and Johnson's four-stage model (1966) is synonymous with the sexual response cycle. The four-stage model has had a profound effect on how

we think about human sexual response, although as we have shown, it is only one of several possible ways in which to describe the "train journey."

Whereas Kaplan's three-stage model arose out of her experiences in treating sexual dysfunction, the four-stage model developed by Masters and Johnson was born in the psychophysiological laboratory. That is, their model was derived from experiments much like the one that Ken participated in. The data upon which they based their model were supplied by hundreds of men and women who volunteered to be "hooked up" while engaging in masturbation or intercourse. Not surprisingly, there is no "desire" stage in their model; desire, which is basically a subjective experience, does not fit well in Masters and Johnson's objective, physiological approach to sexual response.

The four stages of their model are excitement, plateau, orgasm, and resolution (see Figure 5.9). Briefly, *excitement* involves gradu-

FIGURE 5.9

A four-stage model of the sexual response cycle. (Above) the typical male pattern, with the refractory period immediately after orgasm. The dotted line suggests that after the refractory period, additional arousal and orgasm may be possible. (Below) three variations of the typical female pattern. In (a) the pattern most closely resembling the male cycle, the woman is shown as able to have additional orgasms; there is no refractory period. In (b) the response pattern shown is that of a woman who rises rapidly to orgasm, without a plateau phase, and then returns quickly to the unaroused state. According to Masters and Johnson, there is more variability in the female response cycle than in that of the male. (*Masters and Johnson*)

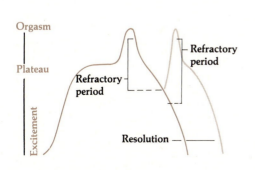
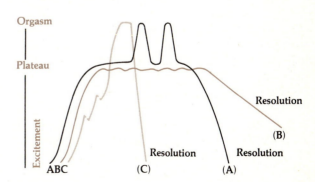

ally increasing levels of sexual arousal—in males, the most common sign of excitement is erection; in females, it is vaginal lubrication. During the *plateau* phase, a maximum level of arousal is reached. The term "plateau" may be somewhat misleading, however, since it implies that there is a continuous level of high arousal; in fact, most individuals increase and decrease in arousal level before they reach orgasm. During the *orgasm* phase, muscle tension and genital blood flow are at a maximum. Rhythmic muscle contractions occur in both the male and female genitals; in males, ejaculation usually accompanies these muscle contractions. After the male ejaculates, he experiences a *refractory period* during which time the penis will not respond to further stimulation. For women, however, there is no necessary refractory period, and some women are capable of having several orgasms during the same period of stimulation. In the final stage, *resolution*, the body returns to its prestimulation state.

Despite the widespread use that has been made of this model, it has been argued that there is little justification, either subjective or physiological, for distinguishing between the excitement and plateau phases. For instance, excitement and plateau do not tend to be experienced as qualitatively different states. Further, with only one exception, the physiological changes that begin during excitement continue into the plateau phase. (The single exception is the female orgasmic platform, which is discussed in greater detail in a later section.) As one researcher points out,

> As far as the male is concerned, . . . the scheme of four phases proves altogether irrelevant. It merely creates the impression of scientific precision where none exists. Ironically, Havelock Ellis's doctrine of tumescence and detumescence, though more general, turns out to be a more appropriate and far less pretentious abstraction, since it allows for both those phenomena that are cumulative and those that are sudden and evanescent rather than imposing boxlike categories that correspond to neither. (Robinson, 1976, p. 130)

Masters and Johnson point out that their model is an abstraction of human sexual response. But in fact, all the models are essentially abstractions—helpful in organizing the response cycle into a series of stages over an orderly time sequence but not to be taken as absolute standards. Being derived from studies of large groups of people, they tend to represent averages, but they do not necessarily show how any one individual will behave during a sexual experience.

Physiological Aspects of Sexual Excitement

Up to this point, we have emphasized the psychogenic factors that determine our response to sexual stimulation. But as Kinsey noted:

> Whatever the poetry and romance of sex, and whatever the moral and social significance of human sexual behavior, sexual responses involve real and material changes in the physiologic functioning of the . . . [person]. (1953, p. 594)

It is these physiological changes that were of primary interest to Masters and Johnson in their laboratory research.

Before reviewing these changes, however, it is important to recognize that human sexual response has both universal and idiosyncratic elements. That is, some of the physical changes occurring during arousal and orgasm take place in almost all men and women—for example, the muscular contractions accompanying orgasm. Other changes occur in some men and women but not in others—for example, the "skin flush." We should also bear in mind that even when two people show the same physiological changes during arousal, their perception of these changes is likely to differ.

Two basic physiological processes play a major role in the way that the body responds during arousal and orgasm; these are vasocongestion and myotonia. *Vasocongestion* refers to the opening up or dilation of the small blood vessels in the pelvic area. When the flow of blood into the area temporarily exceeds the amount of blood being drained out by the veins, the tissues become *engorged* with blood. This vascular engorgement is controlled by the autonomic nervous system (see the boxed extract).

The pooling of blood in the tissues and small blood vessels gives rise to some of the characteristic sensations associated with sexual arousal. For example, some people experience vascular engorgement as a feeling of warmth and heaviness. For others, the sensation may be a tingling or itching of the genitals. In fact, the word "prurient," which the dictionary defines as "obsessively interested in sexual matters," is derived from the Latin word *prurire,* meaning to itch. With full engorgement of the blood vessels, a man or woman might also experience a pulsing or throbbing sensation.

Myotonia refers to increases in muscle tension. During sexual arousal, there is an increase in the tension of both the smooth (involuntary) and the striated (voluntary) muscles (see the boxed extract). Some individuals deliberately increase muscle tension by

contracting the muscles of the thighs, abdomen, or buttocks. By increasing the level of muscle tension in this way, a more powerful orgasmic reaction may be produced. At orgasm, the muscle tissue of the penile urethra contracts, as do the muscles of the vagina. Although there are wide variations in individual patterns of myotonia, some degree of muscle tension is a necessary component in the sexual response cycle.

THE SEXUALLY STIMULATED FEMALE

The first and most obvious physiological sign of sexual arousal in women is *vaginal lubrication.* As discussed in Chapter 4, the lubricant is exuded directly from the vaginal walls; that is, the pressure of blood filling the small blood vessels of the vagina causes small drops of liquid to form on the vaginal walls.

Although the amount of lubricant will vary greatly from one woman to another, vaginal lubrication appears to be a universal sign of sexual arousal. Some women are aware of a moist, sometimes sticky, feeling in the vagina soon after sexual stimulation begins. The quantity of liquid produced may be so great as to be mistaken for a "female ejaculation," or there may be only a thin film of lubricant. Women who have passed the menopause are likely to produce smaller amounts of lubricant; if this condition leads to discomfort, it can usually be remedied by the use of artificial lubricants or an estrogen supplement (see Chapter 6).

Lubrication is thought to aid conception in two ways: first, it makes penile penetration of the vagina easier; second, it seems to have an "antacid" effect that helps the sperm to stay alive longer.

Vaginal lubrication is also associated with a special odor. This odor may differ depending on the phase of the menstrual cycle or how sexually aroused the woman is. At the psychological level, vaginal odors may cause varying reactions: for some people such odors are offensive, for others they are a powerful sexual stimulus.

Vasocongestion also causes changes in the color and shape of the vagina and surrounding sexual tissue. Increased blood flow causes the vaginal walls to turn a deeper red or purple. As excitement builds, increased muscle tone raises the uterus and causes the inner two-thirds of the vagina to lengthen and expand. During the later stage of arousal that Masters and Johnson refer to as the plateau phase, there is also marked vasocongestion of the outer third of the vagina, which narrows the diameter of the canal—a response labeled by Masters and Johnson as the *orgasmic platform*. In addition to vaginal distention, the *labia minora*, or inner lips, become larger and thicker with increased vasocongestion. They may also show striking color changes to dark shades of red or purple. In women who have

given birth, the *labia majora*, or outer lips, also fill with blood and show color and size changes. Before a woman has given birth, the outer lips tend to separate and are somewhat flattened during sexual arousal.

The organ of maximum sexual sensitivity in the female, the *clitoris*, also changes during excitement. Both the length and width of the clitoris increase, although these changes are not usually noticeable without laboratory measurement. The clitoral hood that covers most of the clitoral glans also thickens and expands as its tissues are filled with blood.

Vasocongestion also causes changes in other parts of the body. For example, the skin flush is produced when blood fills the small vessels close to the skin surface. Masters and Johnson refer to this reaction as the *maculopapular sex flush*. Most women show some degree of this flush response, although there are wide individual differences in the extent to which the chest, throat, neck, and stomach are affected. In addition, the breasts show an overall en-

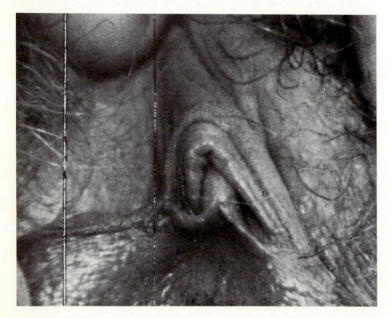

The engorgement of the clitoral glans during sexual arousal is caused by increased blood flow to the area, in much the same way that erection in the male is caused by engorgement of the penis. From the film, *Physiological Response of the Sexually Stimulated Female. (Courtesy, Gorm Wagner, M.D., and Focus International, Inc.)*

largement due to vasocongestion. The actual increase in size will vary from woman to woman, with an increase of as much as one-quarter over the unstimulated state being possible. In addition, vasocongestion often causes size and color changes in the areolae.

As sexual excitement builds, muscle tension increases in both the voluntary and involuntary muscle groups. For example, one of the earliest signs of sexual arousal in the female is nipple erection, a response caused by contraction of the involuntary muscles. With the approach of orgasm some women also begin to show involuntary, spasmodic contractions of muscles in the abdomen, buttocks, and thighs. Facial tension is also one part of the normal myotonia reaction.

Along with increases in muscle tension, there are also changes in the cardiovascular and respiratory systems. For example, blood pressure and heart rate increase as sexual excitement builds, and breathing may become faster and deeper as orgasm approaches.

THE SEXUALLY STIMULATED MALE

Sexual arousal in the male is usually identified with penile erection. The mechanism of erection was described in Chapter 4; briefly, vasodilation of the arteries of the penis causes the three spongy bodies, or corpora, to fill with blood and become firm. At the same time, the outflow of blood through the veins is decreased by the closing of tiny valves in the veins. If the process continues, the end result is a build-up of pressure until the expansion limit of the penile sheath is reached. At this point, the penis appears firm and fully erect.

Penile erection, like vaginal lubrication, is controlled by the autonomic nervous system. It is important to understand this aspect of sexual physiology because it explains why men are unable to "will" an erection in the same way that a finger may be moved at will. Further, it is the parasympathetic branch of the autonomic nervous system that plays the major role in causing erection; therefore, high levels of sympathetic nervous system activity, as might exist if a man were very anxious or fearful, would interfere with the erection response (see the boxed extract).

Once erection is present, it will usually be maintained until either the male ejaculates or the stimulation causing vasodilation is lost. For instance, a man who is temporarily distracted during sexual intercourse may lose some of his erection. If stimulation is resumed, he will probably recover the erection in a short period of time. Older men frequently experience partial erections, or a temporary loss of erection during intercourse, probably due to the loss of elasticity in the blood vessels supplying blood to the penis.

Apart from erection, men show many of the same physiological signs of arousal as women. About 30 percent of men show the flushing response on some part of their body. Most men also show some amount of nipple erection. As sexual excitement builds, the pulse rate is likely to quicken, and breathing becomes faster and deeper. At this point, signs of increasing muscle tension become noticeable, and blood pressure may be greatly elevated.

Masters and Johnson have also described observable changes in the scrotal sac and testes. During the early stages of sexual arousal, there is a thickening and elevation of the scrotal sac. The cremasteric muscles shorten, causing the testes to move upward toward the body. With further sexual arousal, the testes may show a size increase as great as 50 percent. Just before ejaculation, the testes will be drawn up close to the inguinal canal. According to Masters and Johnson, this testicular elevation is a reliable sign that ejaculation is about to occur.

Sexual Responses During Sleep

Almost all men have had the experience of waking up in the morning with a firm erection. Many men attribute these erections to the pressure of urine in the bladder, but in fact urine pressure usually has little or no direct effect on erection. Instead, it appears that erections occur at regular intervals throughout the night and are associated with a particular stage of sleep known as REM sleep.

From EEG (electroencephalographic) studies of the brain during sleep, we have learned that all adults show a dramatic change in brain waves about once every 90 minutes throughout the night. During the subsequent 10 or 15 minutes, almost all muscles relax, breathing and heart rate become irregular, and rapid eye movements are observed—hence the term "REM sleep." This stage of sleep is also known as "paradoxical sleep" because although the brain waves and eye movements indicate a state of alertness, the person is in fact most deeply asleep and is least likely to be awakened by external stimuli. Most dreaming also takes place during this stage. Penile erections are a normal part of the REM stage of sleep.

The association between erection and REM sleep has been clearly demonstrated in a number of experiments. In one study (Fisher *et al.*, 1965), several different measures of penile tumescence showed a clear and consistent correlation with EEG signs of REM sleep. In recent years, these "sleep erections" have been used to diagnose cases of organically caused impotence. Suppose a man is experiencing erectile dysfunction with his sexual partner. If a sleep erection test reveals that there are no nighttime erections, the dysfunction might well have a physical or organic cause; on the other hand, if the

The Sexual Orgasm

Sexual orgasm has been a subject of myth and misunderstanding for centuries. But in the past few decades, physiological research has done much to clear up this confusion. For instance, scientists have investigated such things as Freud's distinction between the "immature" clitoral orgasm and the "mature" vaginal orgasm, the notion that there is a difference between orgasms achieved during intercourse and those reached through masturbation, and the common belief that male and female orgasms are vastly different phenomena. Briefly, we can sum up the results of this research as follows: In a physical sense, an orgasm is an orgasm is an orgasm, regardless of the type and source of stimulation, or whether or not it is experienced by a male or a female.

What is orgasm? The essence of orgasm is a feeling. We cannot describe it without discussing both the psychological and the physiological, the brain and the body. The physiological responses during intercourse and masturbation may look identical on a polygraph record yet be experienced in vastly different ways. Masters and Johnson found no measurable difference between vaginal and clitoral orgasms in their laboratory, but some

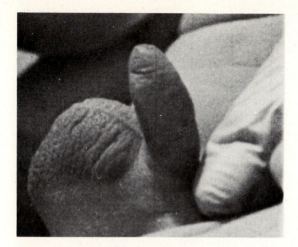

Penile erections occur frequently during both the sleeping and waking periods of male infants. This photograph shows the erection response of a newborn baby. From the film, *Physiological Response of the Sexually Stimulated Male. (Courtesy, Gorm Wagner, M.D., and Focus International, Inc.)*

sleep erection test shows that he is having nocturnal erections, then it would seem more likely that his problem is psychogenic.

Is there a corresponding phenomenon in women? Although less research has been performed on the sexual responses of women during sleep, one study (Abel *et al.,* 1979) found some interesting parallels between the patterns of men and women. When they measured and recorded blood flow in the walls of the vagina during sleep, these researchers found that the pulse pressure increased markedly during REM periods—that is, during the same periods that males normally experience erections. While this technique has not yet been tested on women with sexual problems, there is a good possibility that it will come to be used as extensively as the sleep erection test is used in the diagnosis of impotence.

women insist that they experience two distinct types of orgasm. Thus to understand orgasm, we must consider the total configuration of mind and body responses.

In general, the similarities between male and female orgasm seem to outweigh the differences. The build-up and discharge of sexual tension are physiologically the same in men and women. There are also very clear similarities in the subjective experience of orgasm—a point dramatically illustrated in a study by Ellen Vance and Nathaniel Wagner in which twenty-four male and twenty-four female subjects described their feelings during orgasm. Seventy judges (including male and female gynecologists, psychologists, and medical stu-

dents) were asked to identify the writer of each description as male or female. The following are some examples of the descriptions given:

A sudden feeling of lightheadedness followed by an intense feeling of relief and elation. A rush. Intense muscular spasms of the whole body. Sense of euphoria followed by deep peace and relaxation.

Basically, it's an enormous buildup of tension, anxiety, strain followed by a period of total oblivion to sensation, then a tremendous explosion of the buildup with a feeling of wonderfulness and relief.

Intense excitement of entire body. Vibrations in stomach—mind can consider only your own desires at the moment of climax. After, you feel like you're floating—a sense of joyful tiredness.

I really think it defies description by words. Combination of waves of very pleasurable sensations and mounting of tensions culminating in a fantastic sensation and release of tension. (Vance and Wagner, 1976, pp. 93–94)

Judges were not able to differentiate male and female descriptions.

It is possible that, as one subject stated, orgasm "defies description by words." Our vocabulary for describing orgasm is fairly limited. Note the frequency with which such words as "tension," "build-up," and "release" appear in the descriptions. Males and females share equally in this word shortage but still produce descriptions of orgasm that are remarkably similar. As the authors conclude, "these findings suggest that the experience of orgasm for males and females is essentially the same."

ORGASM: SINGLE, SEQUENTIAL, OR MULTIPLE?

In 1953, Kinsey reported that about 15 percent of the women interviewed in his sample were able to have several orgasms during the same sexual encounter. This finding was greeted with some skepticism. After all, it was only 50 years since Havelock Ellis had struggled to convince his contemporaries that women do experience sexual arousal and orgasm—and in much the same ways as men do.

Masters and Johnson went one step further than Kinsey by demonstrating, with physiological measures, that multiple orgasm is a very real phenomenon. They showed that after she has had her first orgasm, a woman can return to the plateau phase and after further stimulation may experience a second, third, or even subsequent orgasm. In some women, the succession of orgasms can be so close in time that they appear to experience one long and continuous orgasm.

Shere Hite, in her survey of female sexuality, argues that there is a difference between *sequential* and *multiple* orgasm. According to Hite:

Multiple orgasm is not the same thing as restimulating yourself every few minutes to have another orgasm—which we will call sequential orgasms. Multiple orgasms, which are much rarer, are several orgasms with no break in between (with the stimulation continuing, of course). Sequential orgasms can be continued indefinitely by many women. (1976, p. 89)

In addition, Hite found that some women preferred to have only one orgasm at a time because they felt that the clitoris had become too sensitive for further stimulation. Other women stated that multiple orgasms were more intense and more satisfying.

The number of orgasms that women prefer to have is largely a function of individual history, learning experiences, and the cooperativeness of the partner. For instance, some women are satisfied with one orgasm during intercourse but prefer to have more than one when masturbating. Other women may be emotionally satisfied by intercourse even without orgasm. A woman may find that she is multiply orgasmic with one sexual partner and unable to reach orgasm with another.

Kinsey also reported that some men were capable of several orgasms, each with ejaculation, during a single sexual encounter (1948). This capacity declines with age. Among men in their teens and twenties, 15 to 20 percent are able to have more than one orgasm; but only about 3 percent of men past the age of 60 retain this capacity.

Most males seem to be limited in their capacity for multiple orgasm because of what Masters and Johnson term the *refractory period*. During this time period, which follows ejaculation, further sexual stimulation is ineffective and may even be experienced as un-pleasant. In young men the refractory period may last only a few minutes, in older men it may extend for hours.

One study (Robbins and Jensen, 1978) explored the male capacity for multiple orgasm. The thirteen men in this study showed a series of "preejaculatory" orgasms culminating in a final orgasm with ejaculation. Physiological measures of one subject's heart rate, respiration, and muscle tension indicated that these preejaculatory orgasms were indeed "real" orgasms. These findings suggest that men who are able to learn to reach orgasm without ejaculating may experience multiple orgasm in much the same way as women do. The study also highlights the fact that the orgasm and ejaculation responses in males can be sep-arated—at least for a certain number of men.

It seems, then, that both multiple orgasm and sequential orgasm are a physiological reality. Most men in our culture have learned to expect only one orgasm, but this does not nec-essarily reflect the limits of their capacity. Similarly, some women are content with one orgasm, although they may be able to have considerably more than one. The limit on the number of orgasms a man or woman experiences seems more a reflection of cultural con-ditioning than of physiological potential. Again, we must stress the importance of indi-vidual differences in orgasm preference, and the fact that there is no one "ideal" pattern of sexual orgasm.

PHYSIOLOGICAL RESPONSES DURING ORGASM

Sexual orgasm in both men and women is a physiological *reflex* that must be elicited by a specific stimulus.

Sexual orgasm constitutes one of the most amaz-ing aspects of human behavior. There is only one other phenomenon, namely sneezing, which is physiologically close in its summation and explo-sive discharge of tension. Sneezing is, however, a localized event, while sexual orgasm involves the whole of the reacting body. (Kinsey, 1953, p. 631)

What triggers orgasm? Stimulation of the nerve endings in the genitals is the most typi-cal stimulus for orgasm, but there are a num-ber of exceptions to this general rule. Several of the women and a few of the men whom Kinsey interviewed claimed to be able to reach orgasm purely through fantasy. Some women have also reported reaching orgasm through breast or anal stimulation. Among male homo-sexuals it is not uncommon for orgasm to be induced through stimulation of the prostate gland during anal intercourse. Despite these exceptions, however, it is genital stimulation that most often triggers the orgasm reflex.

As noted earlier in the chapter, there is a marked build-up of vasocongestion and myo-tonia just prior to orgasm. As muscle tension reaches a peak, there may be involuntary spasms and jerking of various muscle groups. Although the pattern of myotonia before orgasm varies from one individual to another, muscle tension is a critical component of the orgasmic experience. In fact, it is the build-up of muscle tension during sexual arousal that is a major factor in stimulating the orgasmic response.

Along with myotonia, there are cardio-vascular and respiratory changes occurring just prior to and during orgasm. For example, the normal resting heart rate is about 70 beats per minute. During sexual orgasm, it is not uncommon for the heart rate to exceed 150 beats per minute. In addition, blood pressure shows maximum increases just before and during orgasm. Similarly, whereas the average respiration rate in the resting state is about 12 breaths per minute, rates as high as 41 breaths per minute have been found to be associated with orgasm (Fox and Fox, 1969). However, some men and women will stop breathing just prior to orgasm. The physiological effects of these different breathing patterns are not yet understood.

During the orgasm itself, men and women show regular, rhythmic contractions of the muscles surrounding the genital organs. These contractions usually occur at .8-second intervals and involve the vagina, uterus, and anal sphincter in women. In men, similar contractions occur in the muscles located at the base of the penis, the seminal vesicles, the prostate, and the anal sphincter.

The physiology of ejaculation. The most striking and obvious disparity between male and female responses during orgasm is the male *ejaculation.* Ejaculation seems to take place in two stages: during the first, the *emission* phase, sperm and seminal fluids are moved through the genital ducts to the urethra. A sphincter muscle located between the urethra and the urinary bladder contracts to prevent these fluids from traveling into the bladder. During the second, the *expulsion* phase, semen is ejaculated from the urethra. The primary cause of this expulsion is the strong contraction of the bulbocavernosus muscle located at the base of the penis. The force of the expulsion will be affected by such factors as age, the degree of sexual arousal, and the duration of time since the last ejaculation.

According to Masters and Johnson (1966), ejaculation represents "the physiological expression of male orgasmic experience." In other words, they regard ejaculation as an integral part of the orgasmic response in men. For most men it is true that orgasm and ejaculation take place at the same time. However, under some circumstances a man might have ejaculation without orgasm, or orgasm without ejaculation. For example, men who have suffered spinal cord injuries sometimes reach orgasm without ejaculating. And as was described earlier, some men report having several preejaculatory orgasms before a final orgasm with ejaculation.

Brain changes during orgasm. Since orgasm is both a mental and a physical experience, it is not surprising that the changes seen throughout the body are paralleled by some striking changes in brain function. A study conducted at Rutgers Medical School (Cohen *et al.,* 1976) has demonstrated that orgasm is indeed accompanied by a unique pattern of brain waves, and that this pattern is found in both men and women.

We have learned from experiments using the electroencephalogram (EEG), which measures the electrical activity of the brain, that different states of consciousness will affect both the frequency (speed) and amplitude (size) of brain waves. Differences have also been found between the activity in the left and right halves of the brain. The left hemisphere (dominant for right-handed people) has been linked to verbal or logical thought process. The right (nondominant) hemisphere plays a greater part in spatial or intuitive thinking. One study (Galin and Ornstein, 1972) found that the two sides of the brain reacted differently when subjects switched from a verbal to a visual task. Another study (Goldstein *et al.,* 1973) also found dramatic changes in the relationship between the two hemispheres of the brain when subjects experienced drug hallucinations.

It seems reasonable to expect that during orgasm, too, there will be a change in electrical activity on the two sides of the brain. One of the few earlier studies on brain activity during orgasm was reported by Kinsey in 1953. He presented the work of Abraham Mosovich, showing that there are extra large and extra slow brain waves at orgasm. Kinsey compared this pattern with that seen during petit mal epileptic seizures. Although of interest, this research does not tell us much about specific changes in consciousness.

The study conducted at Rutgers Medical School (Cohen *et al.,* 1976) examined the physiological responses of four male and three female subjects. Each subject volunteered to masturbate to orgasm while physiological recordings, including an EEG, were taken. All subjects were in good health and ranged in age from 21 to 32 years.

After recording electrodes had been attached, subjects first fantasized about erotic material and then began to masturbate. Masturbation was done either with the hand or with an electric vibrator. The four male subjects were able to produce one orgasm at each experimental session, whereas the three females climaxed between one and three times per session.

Figure 5.10 shows the typical pattern of brain waves recorded before, during, and after orgasm. There is a clear difference between the right and left hemispheres just prior to and at the moment of orgasm. In the right hemisphere the frequency decreases to about 4 cycles per second, whereas in the left hemisphere it remains at about 10 cycles per second. Also, the amplitude of the response is much higher in the right than in the left hemisphere.

The changes shown in Figure 5.10 were typical for all right-handed subjects. For the one left-handed subject, the relationship was reversed, with decreased frequency and greater amplitude in the left hemisphere. It made no difference which hand the subject used for masturbating; when one of the right-handed males masturbated with his left hand, the right side of the brain still showed the unusual high-amplitude, slow-frequency effect.

These EEG findings provide us with an objective demonstration of the unique brain processes involved in orgasm. The patterns of brain waves observed in the study are quite unlike those observed under any other laboratory circumstances. Perhaps this is why subjects find it so difficult to describe, in words, the orgasmic experience—the orgasmic state simply cannot be compared to any other state of consciousness.

AFTER ORGASM

During the *resolution phase,* the physiological processes involved in sexual arousal are re-

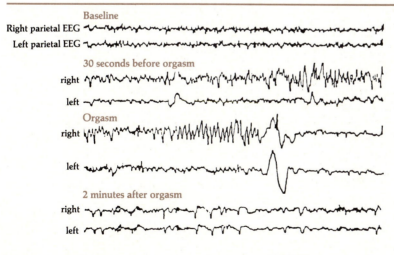

FIGURE 5.10
Graph of EEG changes before, during, and after orgasm.

versed. Blood begins to flow out of the tissues and muscles in the pelvic area. Detumescence takes place, and genital swelling decreases. Some men and women also show a marked perspiration response that results in a thin film of sweat over much of the body. With the relaxation of muscle tension there is often a feeling of calm and relaxation. Laughing or crying are also common responses.

As with the arousal and orgasm phases, there are wide individual differences in the way people feel after orgasm. Some individuals experience a sense of exhaustion often followed by sleep. Others feel refreshed and invigorated after orgasm. A questionnaire study (Leiblum and Miller, 1980) evaluated subjective responses to the postorgasmic period and found a wide range of reactions. For example, some subjects reported a sense of letdown or even of mild depression. For other subjects, the time after orgasm was experienced as a period of elation or even euphoria. There were no consistent differences in the reports of men and women; both groups showed wide variations in their subjective responses.

RESOLUTION WITHOUT ORGASM

Not every sexual encounter ends in orgasm. Although estimates vary, there are clearly a large number of sexual interactions in which one or both partners do not reach orgasm.

Resolution without orgasm includes the same physiological processes that take place with orgasm. However, it may take considerably more time for blood to leave the genital area. Similarly, muscle tension and other signs of sexual arousal will recede more gradually.

The pelvic area may remain congested (filled with blood) for several hours.

An individual's subjective response to sexual experiences without orgasm will vary. If it happens only occasionally, it may not be considered a problem. However, a consistent absence of orgasm may lead to frustration and unhappiness.

Sometimes I feel psychologically inadequate because the feeling in the air is that modern liberated women have orgasms most or all of the time, whereas I do not seem to have the need to have orgasms. Probably I have a low sex drive. Nevertheless, I resent the pressure placed on me and other women to have orgasms. Every time I read a survey that says Masters and Johnson or other researchers have found that x percent of women almost always have orgasms, I feel psychologically inadequate. But except when I read about the expectations for women's sexual performances, I feel quite satisfied regarding my sex life. (Quoted from Hite, 1976, p. 117)

Helen Kaplan (1974) has reviewed the reactions that a woman may have when she fails to reach orgasm. Some women seem able to adapt to the situation and they report satisfaction even without orgasm. However, other women find that their steady disappointment gradually leads to less interest in sex.

In our culture there appears to be a difference in expectations regarding orgasm for men and women. Unless the man is able to ejaculate every time he has sexual relations, he is not likely to feel sexually satisfied. On the other hand, Masters and Johnson encourage couples to accept female orgasm during 50 percent or more of sexual encounters as "normal." It is worth considering how many men would be prepared to settle for orgasm only half the time.

Summary

1. Sexual response consists of certain near universal physiological changes, namely vasocongestion and myotonia. In turn, these changes produce the signs of arousal: penile erection, vaginal lubrication, skin flush, nipple erection, and so on.

2. The response to particular types of sexual stimuli depends on many factors that are personal and unique, such as place in the life cycle, sexual history, attitudes, information, emotions regarding sexuality, and so on.

3. A variety of sexual stimuli can provoke a sexual response. Examples of psychogenic stimulation would be the visual stimulus of an erotic movie and self-generated erotic fantasy. An example of reflexogenic stimulation would be the touching of the genitals.

4. There is a close interaction between physical and psychological response to sexual stimulation. If a person is extremely anxious while experiencing sexual stimulation, for instance, we might expect this emotion to interfere with his or her sexual response. In turn, awareness of physical response leads to increased sexual arousal.

5. The changes of the sexual response cycle can be described (a) by Havelock Ellis' two-stage model involving tumescence and detumescence; (b) by Kaplan's three-stage model involving desire, excitement, and orgasm; or (c) by Masters and Johnson's four-stage model involving excitement, plateau, orgasm, and resolution.

6. Many of the responses to sexual stimulation, such as vasocongestion and myotonia, are identical in males and females, and each sex responds to both reflexogenic and psychogenic forms of stimulation. A great deal of research, and particularly the work of Masters and Johnson, has shown that although men and women have different genital architecture, the total body response to sexual arousal and the experience of desire and orgasm are basically the same for men and women.

SIX

Hormones and Sexuality

Overview

In this chapter, we examine the fluctuations, functions, and effects of the natural body hormones during the stages of the adult life cycle. While hormones have a direct influence on reproductive capacity and on male or female physical appearance, their relationship to sexual behavior is complex and far from clearly understood. For instance, changing hormonal levels are directly related to the female menstrual cycle, the maintenance of pregnancy, and the menopause. The male ability to produce sperm is also directly influenced by hormone levels. However, such variables as the frequency of sexual contact, the choice of sexual object, and the level of sexual performance simply cannot be explained solely by hormonal factors.

Our information about hormones and their effects comes from a wide variety of sources. Research with animals provides us with a comparative perspective on the importance of hormones. In general, the sexual behavior of lower animals such as the rat is more rigidly tied to hormone levels than is the sexual behavior of nonhuman primates such as the chimpanzee. Following this trend, the sexual behavior of humans seems even less tied to hormonal influence. Thus while the information provided by the comparative psychologist is of interest, we must be wary of broad generalizations from animal to human sexual behavior.

Another source of information is the work of biochemists, who have studied the structure of hormones, and their synthesis and action in the body. While we will not describe this work in detail, it is crucial to a great deal of the psychologist's research on hormones and sexuality. Most important, it permits the psychologist to measure hormone levels and to relate these measurements to sexual behavior. In addition, biochemical research has enabled the scientist to synthesize hormones in the laboratory and use these synthetic hormones for both experimental and therapeutic purposes.

Psychological research provides us with information about the relationship between an individual's hormone levels and his or her behavior. The psychologist may focus on endogenous (naturally occurring) hormones or study the effects of exogenous (externally administered or synthetic) hormones. Hormone levels may be related to a wide variety of behavioral variables—sexual desire, sexual performance, orgasmic capacity, sexual orientation, and so on. In summarizing this research, we find that sexual responses to hormonal events are characterized by the individuality, diversity, and flexibility that are the hallmarks of all human behavior.

The diversity of responses to hormonal events is explained, in part, by the variables studied by sociologists and anthropologists. These disciplines have shown us that sexuality is shaped by the beliefs, attitudes, myths, and stereotypes of our culture. We believe that it is worthwhile to recognize and understand sexual mythology, because while it may be inaccurate, it continues to exert some influence on expressions of human sexuality.

With our increasing knowledge about the biochemistry of life processes, it is often tempting to explain a variety of sexual phenomena in terms of hormone levels. However, most attempts to do this have yielded mixed and contradictory results; there is rarely a one-to-one relationship between hormones and sexual behavior, and there seems to be an exception to every hormonal "rule." The individual—his or her personality, developmental history, sexual experiences, beliefs, attitudes, and cultural environment—is a major factor in the response to hormonal events.

Hormones and the Endocrine System

The word "hormone" comes from the Greek *hormon* which means "to arouse or set in motion." Hormones do set in motion the processes necessary for sexual and reproductive function. The sources of these hormones are the *endocrine glands*, often called the ductless glands because they release their products directly into the bloodstream. The endocrine glands synthesize hormones from substances in the bloodstream, and then release these hormones into the bloodstream for distribution throughout the body.

The activities of the endocrine glands are "supervised" by the *hypothalamus*, a brain structure that is responsible for regulating the internal environment of the body. In the previous chapter, we noted that the hypothalamus sends messages to the autonomic nervous system, triggering either sympathetic or parasympathetic activity. These messages are crucial to the experience of arousal and orgasm. The hypothalamus also regulates hormone levels by secreting chemicals called *releasing factors*. These releasing factors travel through a group of blood vessels, called the *portal system*, to the pituitary gland (also called the hypophysis) located at the base of the brain (see Figure 6.1). This link between the

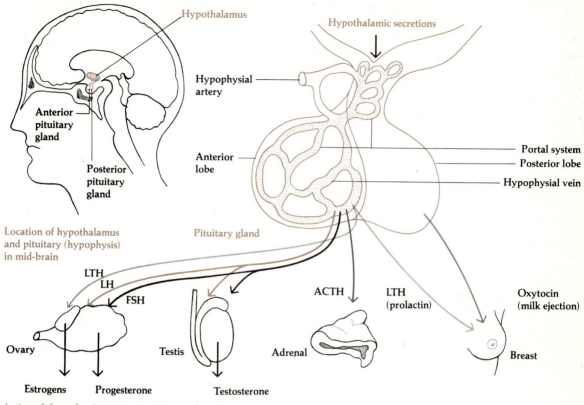

Location of hypothalamus and pituitary (hypophysis) in mid-brain

Action of the endocrine system on target end-organs

FIGURE 6.1

Schematic representation of the endocrine system showing the position of the hypothalamus, pituitary, and gonads in the male and female.

hypothalamus and the endocrine glands enables our hormone levels to respond to input from the external environment. For instance, the hypothalamus might receive the environmental information, via the higher cortical centers, that a sexually stimulating object is present. In turn, the hypothalamus relays this information to the pituitary gland via releasing factors. These releasing factors cause the pituitary to alter its output of hormones, resulting in a change in the level of hormones released by the gonads. These same pathways are involved when our hormone levels change

in response to anxiety, fear, stress, anger, and a variety of other interactions, with the environment.

The endocrine glands most directly involved in sexual functioning are the *anterior pituitary*, the *adrenal glands*, and the *gonads*—either testes or ovaries. The pituitary, a pea-sized structure at the base of the brain, plays a major role in regulating the functioning of the gonads. The sexual hormones secreted by the anterior pituitary are follicle-stimulating hormone (FSH), luteinizing hormone (LH), and prolactin, also called the pregnancy hormone.

These are called *gonadotropins* because they stimulate the gonads to produce hormones. In the adult female, FSH and LH act synergistically (that is, they combine to produce an effect that neither could accomplish alone) to mature the ovum-containing follicles in the ovaries and to stimulate release of the egg. They also stimulate the ovaries to produce and secrete the major feminizing hormones, *estrogen* and *progesterone*. In the adult male, FSH is necessary for the maturation of sperm cells. LH is called the *interstitial-cell-stimulating hormone* (ICSH) in the male (although it is chemically identical to LH in the female) because it stimulates the production of the masculinizing hormone, *testosterone*, in the interstitial cells of the testes. *Prolactin* regulates progesterone production and is involved in the production of milk by the mammary glands after childbirth.

The gonads—testes in males and ovaries in females—produce the sex hormones, or *steroids*. There are three major steroid groups: estrogens, progesterones, and androgens. They share a common molecular structure that is also found in some hormones produced by the adrenal glands. Generally, we think of the first two as "female" hormones and the third as a "male" hormone. Actually, all three groups are found in both men and women, although the proportions differ. It is more accu-

rate to think of estrogen and progesterone as feminizing hormones, in that they exert an influence that is commonly considered female on the body. Similarly, androgens are masculinizing hormones, and cause physical changes that are considered masculine. For instance, estrogens are involved in breast development, while androgens are necessary for the development of facial hair.

Since normal females have some androgens and normal males have a certain amount of estrogens, the physical differences between the sexes cannot be explained merely by the type of hormones present. Rather, the critical factor seems to be the proportion of masculinizing to feminizing hormones. For instance, testosterone, the strongest androgen, is found at levels ten times higher in men than in women. However, a weak androgen called androstendione is found at higher levels in women than in men. A woman in the ovulatory phase of her menstrual cycle has about eight times the amount of estradiol found in a postmenopausal woman or in a normal male. Thus development in a male or female direction requires that masculinizing and feminizing hormones be present in the correct proportions. If this balance is disturbed, maturation and reproductive processes are likely to be delayed or abnormal.

Puberty

In Chapter 2, we noted that the unborn child has extremely high levels of steroid hormones. These hormones are crucial in the differentiation of male and female sexual organs. After the differentiation process is completed, steroid hormone levels drop dramatically and remain low until the pubertal process begins. We know that rising hormone levels are asso-

ciated with the beginnings of puberty because we can measure the breakdown product of these hormones in the urine. These measurements indicate that steroid hormones reappear at about the age of 8 years. Thus, there is an interval of several years between their reappearance and the time that they produce the obvious physical changes of puberty. The steroid hormones steadily increase until, between the ages of 20 and 40, they reach a maximum level.

What causes puberty to begin? We do not yet understand the exact mechanism that sets the pubertal process in motion. John Money and Anke Ehrhardt (1972) suggest that there is a "biological clock" of puberty that is programmed in the brain, causing the hypothalamus to send out messages that are passed on to the pituitary gland and gonads. We do not know what causes this "clock" to start. We do know, however, that the average age at puberty has been decreasing over the past 150 years (see Figure 6.2). For instance, in 1833 the average age at first menstruation was about 17, while at present, it is closer to 12 or 13. One popular explanation for this change is improved dietary patterns. Also, the age at first menstruation is correlated with body weight — the higher a girl's weight, the earlier she is likely to menstruate. However, the variable of body weight is probably influenced by a number of factors in addition to dietary patterns. Thus, it seems likely that the initiation of puberty is determined by an extremely complex interaction between the body and the external environment.

FEMALE PUBERTY

In girls, the changes we consider a part of puberty begin at about the age of 11 years. The first signs of puberty vary, but they often include the growth of the breasts and nipples. Gradually, the shape of the body changes — the pelvis widens, and fatty tissue is distributed to form feminine contours. Pubic hair becomes visible, as does axillary (underarm) hair. There is a spurt in both height and weight that typically occurs before there is a similar spurt for same-aged boys. Generally, the first menstrual cycle, called *menarche*, takes place about 2 years after the first signs of puberty, at the age of 12 or 13 years. Along with the menstrual cycle, there is a growth of the external genitals and the internal sexual organs, including the uterus and vagina.

These changes in appearance are produced

FIGURE 6.2

Graph showing the decline in the age of first menstruation (menarche) in various Western countries. *(Tanner, 1962)*

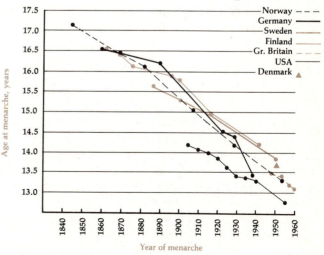

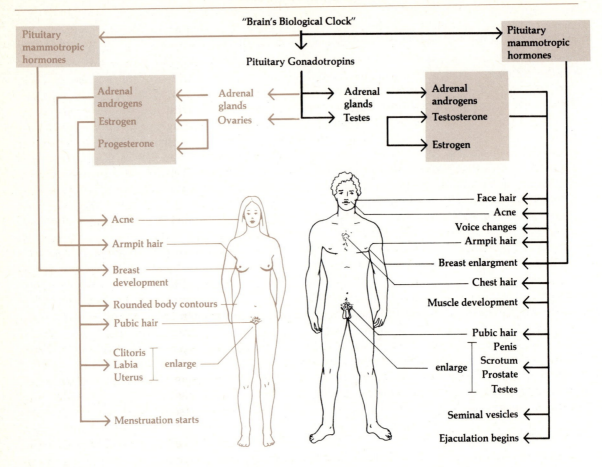

FIGURE 6.3

Schematic representation of the effects of sex hormones on pubertal development in the male and female. *(After Gagnon, 1977)*

when the endocrine glands, stimulated by releasing factors from the hypothalamus, begin to secrete various hormones. The pituitary gland secretes the two gonadotropic hormones, LH and FSH. LH stimulates the ovaries to produce and release estrogens, while FSH stimulates the process of ovulation. The estrogens are carried by the bloodstream to their sites of action—the breasts, uterus and vagina, pelvic bones, and fatty tissue (see Figure 6.3). In addition, small amounts of androgens produced by the adrenal glands are involved in the growth of pubic and axillary hair, and enlargement of the clitoris. At about the time of menarche, the levels of various hormones begin to rise and fall in a rhythmic pattern. This pattern will continue until the menopause.

MALE PUBERTY

In boys, the pubertal process begins about 2 years later than in girls, and sexual maturation tends to take longer. One of the earliest signs of puberty is an increase in the size of the penis and testes. These changes are initiated by the pituitary gland's release of the gonadotropins LH and FSH. (As noted earlier, LH is often called ICSH in males because its site of action is the interstitial cells in the testes.) LH stimulates the testes to produce testosterone, while FSH is involved in the production of sperm.

As the testes enlarge under the influence of LH and FSH, they are capable of producing greater amounts of testosterone. In turn, increased testosterone levels produce a variety of physical changes. The testes and penis enlarge further, and pubic hair appears. The voice becomes deeper, and the chest and shoulders take on a masculine contour. Axillary hair appears later, as do the beginnings of facial hair. Height and weight increase rapidly during a "growth spurt" but may continue to increase slowly until about the age of 20 years.

Although penile erection and orgasm are possible before puberty, the first ejaculation usually does not occur until a boy is about 12 or 13 years old. Nocturnal emissions, or "wet dreams," become more frequent. Mature sperm are present in the ejaculatory fluid from about the age of 15 years.

PROBLEMS AT PUBERTY

The physical changes that take place during puberty have many social and psychological consequences. As the adolescent enters a period of reproductive maturity, there are the beginnings of a change in status from childhood to adulthood. The pubertal adolescent must learn to cope with physical alterations in appearance and function that may not be welcome. The young girl may resent the restrictions imposed on her by her menstrual cycle, while the young boy may feel awkward and uncomfortable with his uneven physical development. Although puberty is usually considered to be the time when dating becomes appropriate, the adolescent's new physical maturity does not always signify a corresponding social maturity. Thus, many adolescents find themselves thrust into dating and social activities for which they are unprepared.

Even when puberty proceeds according to the "normal" sequence of physical changes, there are likely to be difficulties with personal and interpersonal adjustment. The normal sequence of changes includes a great deal of variation between girls and boys, and among members of the same sex (see Figure 6.4). We know that girls generally experience the first effects of puberty about 2 years before boys show any obvious signs of sexual maturity. This time lag between males and females may present interpersonal difficulties—the 12-year-old girl is likely to be taller, heavier, and more sexually developed than her male counterpart. The appearance of the first sign of female puberty—breast development—may set her apart from former male friends who are not yet mature enough to cope with this symbol of sexual development.

At the same time as girls and boys are restructuring their relationships with one another, they must also adjust to uneven rates of growth among members of their own sex. While normal pubertal development occurs within a set time span, there are wide individual differences in the onset and extent of sexual maturation. Certainly, young girls and boys will compare their own growth with that of members of their peer group. The girl whose breasts develop first may be envied by members of her class, or she may feel awk-

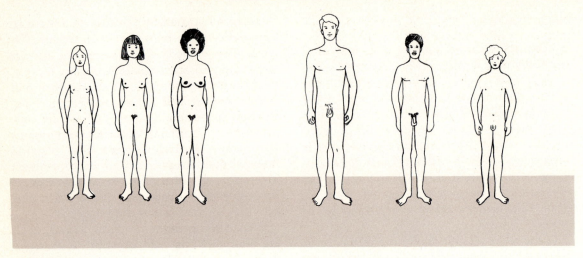

FIGURE 6.4
Pubertal development varies widely among boys and girls of the same
age. The three girls in the upper row were all between 12 and 13 years of
age, the three boys in the lower row between 14 and 15 years of age.
(After Tanner, 1977)

ward and strange because she is "different." Similarly, the boy whose growth spurt is delayed a year longer than that of his friends will feel at a disadvantage. Normal variations in pubertal development may cause the adolescent intense worry about whether he or she is actually normal.

Some of the psychological difficulties of puberty can be eased by providing the adolescent with factual information about what to expect. Sex education can take the form of biological data supplemented with a healthy dosage of reassurance and understanding. The girl who knows about menstruation and approximately when it will happen is probably better equipped to integrate this physical change into her self-concept. (Those of you who saw the movie *Carrie* will be aware of the possibly dire consequences of not understanding the meaning of menstruation.) However, sex education cannot ease all the prob-

lems of puberty unless it also addresses the *meaning* of pubertal changes in the adolescent's life. Puberty presents the child with a real change in social status, and as such, it is an extremely crucial transition, or "passage," into adult sexuality.

Puberty does not always proceed along the "normal" path. It may be delayed, precocious, or incomplete for a variety of reasons. For instance, *precocious puberty* (see the boxed extract on page 69) occurs when there is an excess of hormones before the normal age of puberty. In such cases, the child may develop secondary sexual characteristics—breasts or a beard or a deep voice—long before the age when these changes usually occur. Similarly, if there is a delay in the secretion of the steroid hormones, pubertal changes will not occur within the normal time span. A boy who is deprived of androgens, perhaps through castration or as a result of the androgen-insensitivity syndrome, will not follow the usual course of masculinization. He will retain a soprano voice, have no facial hair, and have disproportionately long arms and legs. His genitals will remain small, and he is likely to be apathetic about sexual activities. However, he will grow pubic and axillary hair, as these changes are caused by hormonal secretions from the adrenal glands, not the testes. Hormonal supplements will speed the pubertal process except in cases where the boy is insensitive to the effects of androgens.

A relatively common "error" in male puberty is *gynecomastia*, a condition in which the breasts become enlarged. Gynecomastia is usually caused when the testes secrete too much estrogen, and it generally disappears within a few years. While the boy who has this condition is likely to be disturbed and upset about his appearance, it will not cause him to doubt his gender identity as a male.

Money and Ehrhardt (1972) note that there are no relationships between the masculinity or femininity of body type during puberty and adult sexual behavior or orientation. In other words, the broad-shouldered and muscular adolescent boy will not necessarily grow up to become a "Romeo," and the thin and "effeminate" boy will not necessarily become sexually indifferent or dysfunctional. Similarly, the size of a girl's breasts does not tell us anything definite about what her sexual activities as an adult will be. However, it does seem that society has different sexual expectations for muscular as compared with thin boys, and for large-breasted as compared with flat-chested girls. These physical variations, which have little predictive value in and of themselves, may be associated with real behavioral differences under the exacting pressure of cultural expectations.

Hormones and Female Sexuality

Hormones continue to play an important role in the female life cycle after the beginnings of puberty. Such life processes as menarche, pregnancy and delivery, and the menopause are all affected by hormones. However, the feelings and behavior of a woman who is going through one of these milestone events will be influenced to a great extent by the cultural and social context. Hormonal changes will lead directly to certain physical effects, but the accompanying emotional changes will usually be determined by a complex interaction of environmental and biological variables. For example, the first menstruation, or menarche, has vastly different meanings in different cultural groups. Although the hormonal event is the same, it may be associated with a wide range of customs, emotions, and behav-

iors. In India, the menarche is seen as an occasion for rejoicing, and the menarchal girl may be presented with gifts, washed with ceremonial oils, and visited by friends and relatives for feasting and celebration. Hindu tradition treats menarche as an occasion of rebirth, and the rites of menarche are structured to fit this view. Among other cultures, menarche is seen as a time when the girl has powers that are dangerous to her tribe. The aboriginal peoples of South America commonly conduct "purification" rituals to alleviate these dangers (Delaney *et al.*, 1976). Thus while hormonal changes set the stage, the event is interpreted within a cultural context, and a woman's experiences cannot but be influenced by prevailing societal views.

Clearly, social factors shape our reactions to

hormonal events. This emphasis on social factors should, however, be balanced with the recognition that hormones do have strong physical effects. Additions to or subtractions from the "proper" hormone mixture will result in real physical changes. Hormones play a key role in our physical maturation and in our reproductive functioning. Their importance to our sexual behavior, however, is far from clear-cut.

THE MENSTRUAL CYCLE

The menstrual myth. The female menstrual cycle has long been a subject of myth, misunderstanding, and confusion. While we now have a fairly clear understanding of the hormonal changes that regulate the menstrual cycle, many of the myths persist. In most primitive tribes, the menstruating woman is considered taboo—among the Arapesh of New Guinea, she is segregated in an isolated mountain hut; among the Eskimos, she is thought to bring bad luck to the hunter; and among some groups in India, she is forbidden to prepare food.

While severe restrictions on the menstruating woman are not common in industrialized societies, they have often been replaced by "protective" limitations and concerns. The menstrual cycle has been used to rationalize restrictions on women's work activities and responsibilities. Women are often considered to be unsuitable candidates for important positions because of the "menstrual handicap." Some opponents of the Equal Rights Amendment, by suggesting that women require special consideration and treatment, are perpetuating the myth that menstruation is a handicap.

Sexual behavior has not escaped the influence of menstrual myths.

The attitudes taken by members of different so-

cieties toward menstruation furnish an excellent example of one way in which social forces influence human sexual life. In very few societies is the menstruating woman regarded as a suitable sexual partner. (Ford and Beach, 1951, p. 211)

Although some cultures permit intercourse when the woman is menstruating, the majority regard her as "unclean." In most cases, these prohibitions are designed to protect the *husband* against ill health.

There is no evidence that intercourse during menstruation is harmful to either female or male. However, the menstrual myth of danger has been replaced, in many modern societies, by "aesthetic" prohibitions. Our culture has reinforced the notion that menstruation is messy and embarrassing. The menstruating woman is told, through advertising, that she has a secret that can be concealed only by using the proper tampons and vaginal deodorants. Thus, the menstrual myth persists in our modern world.

How the menstrual cycle works. Only in the twentieth century has medical science developed a clear and accurate picture of how the menstrual cycle works. Early explanations were often distorted by male prejudice and medical ignorance. In an interesting cultural history of menstruation titled *The Curse*, the authors review some of these explanations (Delaney *et al.*, 1976). One theory, originating with Aristotle and remaining popular for over two thousand years, was that menstrual blood is the unformed matter that, combined with sperm, assumes a bodily shape. There was no knowledge of the female egg, so the female role was limited to providing the raw material that only the male sperm could give direction to. Other menstrual theories included the notion that women have too much blood—either because of an internal defect or because they engaged in less physical activity. The menstrual cycle was considered a method of eliminating this excess. That this elimination took place through the uterus was thought to be because this was the weakest part of the body. While we now understand the physiological basis of menstruation, we are left with the unfortunate legacy of these theories — that menstruation is in some sense an illness or an unnatural process.

As noted earlier, the menarche occurs at about the age of 12 or 13 in our society. Prior to the first menstrual cycle, hormone levels have been rising steadily for about 2 years. At the menarche, they begin to rise and fall in a regular monthly pattern that will continue until the menopause — unless interrupted by pregnancy or illness stress. There are wide individual differences in the length of the cycle, but the average is about 28 days. The length of the cycle may be affected by such factors as illness, drug use, and physical deprivation. It can also be altered by psychological factors — anxiety, stress, or change may either lengthen or shorten the cycle. There are also differences in the duration of menstruation, the average being about 5 days. During this time, approximately 57 to 85 grams (2 to 3 ounces) of menstrual fluid are released, made up of the discarded uterine lining and blood.

The menstrual cycle is regulated by the hypothalamus, the anterior pituitary, and the ovaries. Each of these organs is sensitive to circulating hormone levels and signals other glands to secrete the appropriate hormones at the correct times. The effect of the hormones is to cause the maturation and release of an egg, the build-up of the lining of the uterus, and finally, if there is no pregnancy, the shedding of this lining. Although eggs are matured during this process, they have been present in the ovaries since before birth. Between 300,000 and 400,000 immature eggs are available, but only 300 to 500 will be released during a woman's reproductive years. The remainder will degenerate before developing fully.

The menstrual cycle can be divided into three overlapping phases. During the *proliferative* phase, the pituitary secretes the hormone FSH (follicle-stimulating hormone), which travels through the bloodstream to the ovaries and stimulates the growth of an egg follicle. In turn, cells in this follicle, called the *Graafian follicle*, secrete increasing amounts of estrogen, causing a build-up of the *endometrium* that lines the uterus.

Just before mid-cycle, the pituitary releases a sudden burst of LH (luteinizing hormone). *Ovulation*, or the release of the egg from the ovary, takes place about 36 hours after this LH burst. On average, ovulation occurs about 14 days after the start of the last menstruation, and about 14 days before the start of the next menstrual period. It is possible for more than one egg to be released, which may result in multiple births. Thus, fraternal twins result when two different eggs are released and fertilized by two different sperm cells. In contrast, identical twins develop from a single fertilized egg that immediately divides, resulting in two individuals with identical genetic make-ups.

During the *secretory* phase which begins after ovulation, LH causes the ruptured Graafian follicle, which is still in the ovary, to become the *corpus luteum,* or yellow body. The corpus luteum secretes both estrogen and progesterone. Under the influence of these hormones, the endometrium secretes substances that will nourish a fertilized egg.

An egg must be fertilized within about 36 hours of its release from the ovary. If fertilization takes place, the corpus luteum will continue to secrete estrogen and progesterone to maintain the pregnancy. If the egg is not fertilized, however, the corpus luteum will begin to disintegrate, producing decreasing amounts of these hormones. When this happens, the endometrium can no longer be maintained, and it begins to be shed at the beginning of the *menstrual* phase of the cycle.

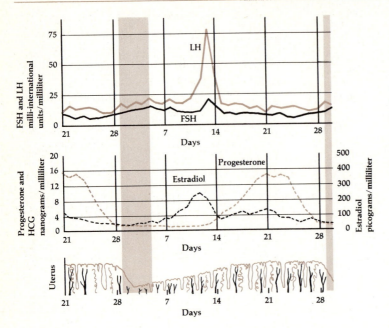

FIGURE 6.5
(above) Hormone levels during the menstrual cycle. (below) Changes in the uterine lining during a typical cycle. The rise in FSH level early in the cycle causes the ovaries to secrete estrogen. The LH peak brings on ovulation and the development of the corpus luteum. The latter secretes estrogen and progesterone in the second part of the cycle. If conception does not occur, the corpus luteum disintergrates, causing the endometrium to be shed. *(Data from Christoper A. Adejuwon of the Population Council)*

Typically, this phase lasts from about 3 to 7 days. At this time, low levels of estrogen will again trigger the pituitary to secrete FSH, beginning the cycle anew (see Figures 6.5 and 6.6).

The premenstrual syndrome. The notion that women's moods fluctuate with the hormonal changes of the menstrual cycle has long been an accepted part of our cultural folklore about menstruation. The most distressing changes, believed to take place in the week before menstruation begins, have achieved the status of a syndrome—the *premenstrual syndrome* or PMS. The response to PMS varies; it has been treated as a physical disease requiring medication by some and ignored as the psychosomatic carrying-on of neurotic women by others. Actually, the scientific status of PMS is uncertain at present. Arguments center on

whether it exists and, if it does exist, what it is and how many women experience it.

Research on the existence and characteristics of PMS has been severely criticized for its methodological shortcomings and biases. Mary Brown Parlee (1976), in a review of this research, maintains that there is no established proof that PMS even exists according to strict scientific criteria. For example, she notes that data on this topic are frequently in the form of self-reports that may well be influenced by cultural beliefs and attitudes toward menstruation. When women are asked specifically to give retrospective reports about premenstrual symptoms, they tend to provide more evidence for PMS than they do if asked simply to provide daily records of mood changes.

Another source of data used to support the existence of PMS is correlational studies that relate the phase of the menstrual cycle with specific behaviors. A review of this research (Dalton, 1964) found that the premenstrual woman was more prone to accidents and injuries, more likely to enter a mental hospital, and more likely to call in sick at her place of employment. Parlee (1976) criticizes these correlational studies on several grounds. First, she suggests that many researchers assume, mistakenly, that correlations between the premenstrual phase and the occurrence of various behaviors prove that the hormones cause the behavior. Given that psychological stress can alter the menstrual cycle, it seems equally likely that the behavior might be affecting the menstrual cycle. Further, Parlee points out

that correlational data obtained from a specific population of women—say, criminals— should not be generalized to all women: "From knowing, for example, that crimes are likely to have been committed during certain phases of the cycle, it is not possible to assume the truth of the inverse—that women in these phases of the cycle are more likely to commit crimes" (1976, p. 34). Finally, Parlee notes that few studies on this subject employ a control group or attempt to obtain baseline measures. Rather than viewing the premenstruum as a time when moods such as irritability increase, we could just as easily view the mid-cycle as a time when irritability decreases. She concludes that although many women spontane-

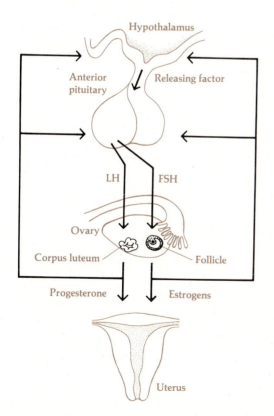

FIGURE 6.6

Feedback mechanisms controlling the female reproductive cycle. Note that the hypothalamic secretions stimulate the pituitary gland to secrete FSH and LH. FSH causes one or more follicles in the ovary to develop and produce estrogen. The LH triggers ovulation and the formation of the corpus luteum. In turn, hormones secreted by the corpus luteum cause the hypothalamus and pituitary to inhibit or stimulate further secretions.

ously report the occurrence of PMS, the syndrome has not been validated through rigorous scientific research.

Karen Paige (1976), in contrast, claims that ample evidence exists regarding mood and behavior changes during the course of the menstrual cycle. However, she disagrees that these changes are caused solely by fluctuating hormone levels, referring instead to the social and cultural responses to menstruation. As support for this view, she cites the results of her research with fifty-two women who were using the contraceptive pill. The pill provides constant dosages of synthetic estrogen and progesterone, thereby minimizing hormonal fluctuations during the menstrual cycle. One side effect of the pill, experienced by some but not all users, is reduced menstrual flow. Paige hypothesized that PMS was linked to menstrual bleeding, not hormone levels, and that women who experienced a reduced flow would show less of the "premenstrual blues." She found that women with reduced flow did in fact show less anxiety than women whose flow remained normally heavy. In addition, she found that the Catholic and Jewish members of her sample, whose religions tend to view the menstruating woman as "unclean" and an unsuitable sexual partner, showed more premenstrual anxiety than did Protestant women.

Although many studies have reported cyclical mood changes, few of them suggest that all women experience these changes. For example, one researcher (Moos, 1969) used a "menstrual distress questionnaire" to assess the symptoms experienced by the wives of graduate students at a large American university. Of 839 respondents, only about 20 percent complained of moderate to severe symptoms of irritability, mood swings, or tension in the premenstrual phase. Further, women showed differing types of distress: some women experienced pelvic cramps but no

emotional changes, whereas others felt little physical distress but did notice irritability and emotional liability. Researchers vary in the number of women they believe experience PMS. Some have suggested that only 15 to 20 percent of women show signs of PMS; others believe the number to be as high as 90 percent. Many find that if the self-reports of a large group of women are averaged together, there is evidence for cyclical mood changes; but if these self-reports are examined for each individual woman, there are few who experience the "classic" premenstrual pattern.

One study suggests that the negative attitudes of male researchers have biased the outcome of many studies on PMS:

We believe that with a more positive attitude toward female processes, researchers could begin to view PMS in an altogether different framework. In the case of the Menstrual Distress Questionnaire, . . . the title reveals quite clearly that the attitudes will be negative. Of the forty-seven items in the questionnaire, only five predict positive results. . . . The questionnaire, because of its overwhelmingly negative emphasis, is bound to show negative results. (Delaney et al., 1976, p. 87)

The authors suggest a "menstrual joy questionnaire," in which women are provided with positive options to describe their premenstrual feelings.

Arguments about whether PMS is "real," that is, of physical origin, or psychologically induced remain unresolved. Those in favor of a physical etiology hypothesize that cyclical changes are caused by shifting levels of estrogen and progesterone. A side effect of these shifts is water retention, a symptom that might perhaps be related to other types of premenstrual discomfort. However, it seems likely that theories relying solely on hormonal shifts will not be able to explain why only some women experience PMS, why their symptoms differ, and why social factors influence PMS. On the basis of the available data, the following conclusion seems valid: Hormones set the stage for PMS insofar as they regulate the menstrual cycle, but psychological and social factors shape women's attitudes toward menstruation. Since our culture expresses negative attitudes toward menstruation and expects the premenstrual phase to be a time of distress, it is not surprising that some women do indeed feel distress at this particular time.

The existence and etiology of PMS is a hotly debated issue because it is related to the status of women in our culture. Since PMS is often the underlying rationale for denying women positions of authority, many feminists prefer to disclaim its existence. Others claim that while PMS may exist, it is taught to women by a sexist society. Still others, angered that PMS is viewed as being "all in a woman's head," claim that premenstrual symptoms have real physical causes. From the data presently available, it is not possible to accept or reject any of these views conclusively. However, as Paige (1976) points out, although we still have no definite answers, we are, at last, beginning to ask the questions. Perhaps by asking the right questions, we will finally unravel the confusing theories surrounding PMS.

The menstrual cycle and sexual behavior. Menstrual cycles—defined as the periodic shedding of the uterine lining—occur only in humans, apes, and some species of monkeys. Lower mammals have *estrus* cycles, in which estrogen levels increase as the time for ovulation approaches. During this estrus cycle, the female is receptive to sexual activity only at the times when impregnation is possible. Increases in estrogen produce a sexual odor that makes her more attractive to males. She may even actively seek a mate at this time. However, her sexual urges are rigidly tied to her reproductive function, and mating rarely occurs when impregnation is not possible.

After ovulation, estrogen levels decrease and the female becomes sexually inactive. The majority of mammals are sexually receptive, or "in heat," for only one or two short periods each year.

Among nonhuman primates, sexual behavior is less dependent on reproductive processes. Captive chimpanzees, gibbons, and orangutans will mate throughout the year and do not restrict themselves to the female's fertile period. Although the female does show a well-defined period of sexual desire corresponding to the high-estrogen phase of the cycle, she will mate with a preferred partner at other times. Chimpanzees do show clear preferences for particular partners. A female who is not in her ovulatory phase may accept the sexual approaches of one male and reject those of another. At ovulation, she will usually accept the approaches of all males. While males generally prefer to mate with a female in the ovulatory phase of the cycle, they will approach a cooperative or favored female at other times.

Sexual behavior among nonhuman primates provides a transition from the instinctive and hormonally controlled mating of lower animals to the largely socially controlled sexual behavior of humans. The sexual behavior of lower mammals is dominated by the influence of hormones: when hormone levels are "right," mating will occur at the time when impregnation is most likely, and at all other times, sexual advances will be rejected. With apes, sexual behavior is less rigidly tied to hormone levels; although hormones still have a major influence, other factors, such as partner preferences, begin to affect sexual patterns. Among humans, the importance of these social factors is at its peak and may well mask any hormonal influences on sexuality.

In some cultures, there are clear expectations that a woman's sexual desire will be strongest at specific times during the menstrual cycle. For example, members of the Masai society believe that a woman's responsiveness is lowest just before menstruation and rises sharply just after her period. The Hopi Indians believe that a woman is most ardent just before and just after menstruation. Few cultures suggest mid-cycle as the height of sexual responsivity, although this is the phase in which pregnancy is most likely to occur. There are also few claims that menstruation is a time of enhanced sexuality, a fact that is not surprising considering that few cultures even permit intercourse during the menstrual period.

In terms of species survival, hormonal influence should dictate a sexual peak at mid-cycle, when pregnancy is most likely. Social factors, however, suggest increased sexual activity just before and just after the menstrual period. The woman who expects to have no sexual contact during her period may well show heightened desire before and after, as a way of compensating for her socially dictated abstinence. Social factors may also influence sexual behavior in other ways, for example, intercourse rates may drop at mid-cycle precisely because this is the time when pregnancy is most likely to occur. Changing hormone levels may influence sexual behavior in that they affect general mood and feelings of well-being, which result in variations in sexual interest in the course of the cycle.

In a summary of current research on female sexual response, the authors (McCauley and Ehrhardt, 1976) conclude that most data support a sexual activity peak just before and just after menstruation. Early studies, reviewed by Ford and Beach in 1951, generally reported a similar increase in erotic desire at these times of the cycle. Desire seems to be strongest at times when a woman is least likely to conceive. In contrast to other primates, hormones in human beings do not appear to heighten sexual desire at ovulation, or if they do have this effect, it is far outweighed by social influences. McCauley and Ehrhardt conclude that hormonal contributions to human sexual behavior are minor when compared to the importance of the effect of attitudinal and emotional factors.

These findings are in contrast to those reported by J. Richard Udry and Naomi Morris (1968). These researchers studied the sexual behavior of 40 working-class and forty-eight middle-class women. For both these groups, they found an increase in coital rates at mid-cycle and a second increase just before menstruation. Their other major finding is a "luteal depression," that is, a decrease in coital rates at the time when the corpus luteum is secreting large amounts of progesterone, several days after ovulation. They suggest that the probability of sexual activity is increased by estrogen and decreased by progesterone. Udry and Morris also correlated menstrual cycle changes with the women's husbands' reported interest in sexual intercourse (see Figure 6.7).

A rise in sexual activity at the time of ovulation was also found in a more recent study (Adams et al., 1978), in which the experimenters carefully controlled for sexual activity initiated by the female subjects versus sexual activity initiated by their husbands. With this control, it became clear that ovulation increased *female-initiated*, but not male-initiated, sexual activity. The authors also found that this effect did not occur in women using oral contraceptives, which is most likely due to the fact that in these women estrogen and progesterone levels are much less variable during the menstrual cycle.

In attempting to relate hormone levels to sexual activity, however, we should recognize that there are enormous variations among women. One researcher (Whalen, 1975) argues

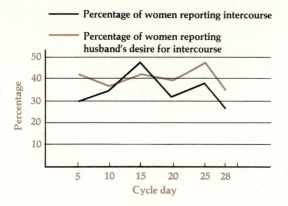

— Percentage of women reporting intercourse

— Percentage of women reporting husband's desire for intercourse

FIGURE 6.7

Graph showing a rise in intercourse rates at mid-cycle as reported by married women (solid line), compared to reports of husbands' sexual interest (dashed line) over the course of the menstrual cycle. *(Adapted from Udry, Morris, and Waller, 1973)*

that there are striking individual differences in both the amount and timing of hormonal secretions. In other words, we should not assume that because two women have cycles of equal length they also have similar patterns of hormone release. The only way to verify hormone levels is to use the considerable technology that exists for measuring hormones in the bloodstream. Not only do hormone levels vary among women; they also appear to vary among different ethnic populations. In a study that compared hormone levels in Bantu, Japanese, and Caucasian women of similar age and economic status, it was found that there was considerable variation among the groups (Hill *et al.*, 1976). The Bantu and Japanese women had higher estradiol levels in both the early follicular and the late luteal phases than did the Caucasian women. The authors attribute this difference to varying dietary patterns.

Given that there is such variability among women, it is not surprising that hormone levels and sexual activity are not more strongly related. Clearly, the probability that sexual behavior will take place is a function of many factors besides hormonal secretions. The availability of an attractive partner, general feelings of health and well-being, the time and place to have a sexual encounter, and the opinions of others are just a few of the influences that contribute to sexual activity. If all these factors remained constant, we might see hormonal influences on sexuality more clearly. However, since these factors do vary, they may well mask whatever hormonal influences exist.

PREGNANCY, HORMONES, AND SEXUAL ACTIVITY

Pregnancy is accompanied and maintained by a series of hormonal changes. These changes include a temporary end to menstrual cycling and high levels of estrogens and progesterone until after delivery. It has been suggested that progesterone acts to relax the uterus, while estrogen is believed to control the growth and function of the uterus. In addition, about 10 days after impregnation, the placenta begins to produce a hormone called human chorionic gonadotropin or, HCG. Levels of HCG rise rapidly for the next 20 days and remain high through the first trimester, dropping off in the second and third trimesters (see Figure 6.8). HCG works to stimulate continued production of progesterone in the corpus luteum. The placenta also begins to secrete a series of hormones, including estrogens, progesterone, and small amounts of androgens.

What happens to sexual behavior during pregnancy? Ford and Beach (1951) report that

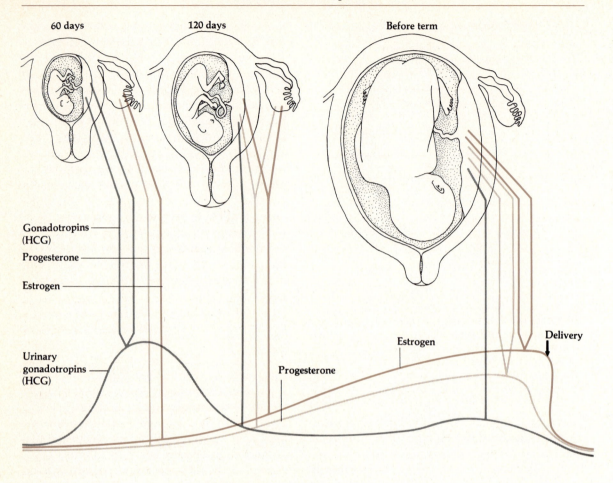

FIGURE 6.8

Schematic representation of hormonal fluctuations during pregnancy. Note the production of gonadotropins during the first trimester, followed by rising levels of estrogen through the remainder of the pregnancy.

among most animals, sexual activity during pregnancy is almost unknown. Cultural attitudes toward intercourse during pregnancy vary from a belief in total abstinence to total permissiveness. In their survey of sixty primitive societies, Ford and Beach (1951) report that about 70 percent permit intercourse during the second month of pregnancy, but only about 25 percent permit it during the ninth month.

In our own culture, women have received mixed messages about the advisability of sexual intercourse during pregnancy. Some physicians continue to voice concern about possible danger to the fetus, although many restrict this concern to the last few months of pregnancy, or suggest coital positions that will minimize pressure on the woman's abdomen. This seems to be a way of "playing safe" in the absence of conclusive information that intercourse will *not* harm the fetus. Masters and Johnson (1966) found that of 101 pregnant women in their sample, 77 had been forbidden by doctors to have intercourse during the last trimester of their pregnancy. A large number of women ignored this prohibition, with no apparent harmful effects to either themselves or their babies. (This issue is discussed more fully in Chapter 10.)

Does pregnancy and its associated hormonal changes effect a woman's desire for sexual contact? While this question is discussed in detail in Chapter 10, most research shows that a woman tends to become less sexually active as her pregnancy becomes more advanced. There are, of course, exceptions to this general rule; some women remain sexually active up to the time of delivery, while others abstain from sex soon after their pregnancy is confirmed. A variety of factors can play a role in a woman's level of sexual desire and activity during pregnancy: for example, fear of harming the fetus, feelings of physical well-being or discomfort, changes in body image and attractiveness, and the husband's level of sexual interest.

MENOPAUSE, HORMONES, AND
SEXUAL ACTIVITY

Thus far, we have reviewed hormonal events that occur during the childbearing years. The weight of the evidence indicates that hormone levels during these years have little or no direct relationship to sexual activity. The likelihood that sexual activity will or will not occur depends far more on external factors— the availability of time, space, and most of all, a desired partner—than on hormone levels

alone. In examining the evidence for women past the menopause, we see a more direct relationship between hormones and sexuality but are still left with the impression that social factors play a dominant role in shaping sexual behavior.

Menopause, derived from the Greek words for month and cessation, means simply the end of the menstrual cycle. However, our culture has given it many other meanings. The stereotype suggests that menopausal women are upset, capricious, impulsive, irrational, and depressed. Menopause has mistakenly been viewed as a time of decreased physical vigor, and a period when femininity declines. Finally, the menopausal woman is mistakenly thought to have lost her capacity and desire for sexual activity. These myths, though currently under wide criticism, are bound to have some effect on the experiences of menopausal women.

Although menopause refers only to the end of the menstrual cycle, the *climacteric,* or "change of life," generally takes place over a period of one or more years. During this time, the ovaries gradually cease functioning. The menstrual cycle may become increasingly irregular, with longer intervals between periods; menstruation may cease for months and then reappear. Menopause is rarely an abrupt change from regular menstrual periods to a complete absence of menstruation. Along with a decrease in the amount and frequency of the menstrual flow, there is a gradual decrease in circulating levels of estrogen and progesterone.

The age at menopause varies widely, with the average being about 50, and the normal range extending from 40 to 60 years. Premature menopause, before the age of 40, is experienced by about 8 percent of all women. It is generally caused by some sort of hormonal imbalance, either natural or surgically induced. For instance, a woman who undergoes ovariectomy at the age of 30 will experience a premature menopause. In a small percentage of women, menopause occurs after the age of 60.

The timing of the onset of menopause is not well understood. There is some indication that it may vary with national or geographic origin, but there are no proven correlations between age at menopause and socioeconomic status. The age at which menopause begins also appears to be unrelated to the age at menarche. While nineteenth-century explanations of early menopause included female employment, alcohol use, and "excessive sexual indulgence" as possible causes, none of these factors appears to have any influence at all.

There are two major physical changes resulting from the decreased estrogen supply after the menopause. The first, commonly called hot flashes, is generally described as intermittent sensations of heat, usually in the upper body, followed by feelings of chill and sweating. Hot flashes are unpredictable and momentary, most often occurring at night. It seems likely that secondary symptoms such as tiredness and irritability are a result, in part, of sleep being disrupted by hot flashes. We do not yet understand what causes this symptom, although there are several possibilities. Hot flashes may be the result of estrogen withdrawal or deprivation in a woman whose body has become accustomed to relatively high levels of estrogen. At the menopause, her body must readjust to lowered estrogen levels, and it may be a temporary imbalance until the adjustment has been made that results in hot flashes. Also, at this time the pituitary increases its secretion of FSH in response to the low circulating levels of estrogen and progesterone, and it may be that these large amounts of FSH upset the hormonal balance of the body.

The second major symptom of decreased estrogen at the menopause is vaginal dryness, sometimes accompanied by decreased vaginal elasticity. Vaginal dryness may result in painful intercourse and can cause irritation and increased susceptibility to infection. Artificial lubricants may provide a satisfactory solution. Although these are the only menopausal symptoms that are clearly linked to hormonal changes, a small percentage of women may experience other problems: palpitations, dizziness, anxiety, fatigue. While these symptoms are often considered to be "psychosomatic," it seems equally likely that they are a result of the body's attempt to cope with altered hormone levels.

Although the menopause is a natural and normal part of the aging process, our society often views it as a disease, and it may be "treated" with tranquilizers, sleeping pills, and antidepressants. For women who are experiencing extreme discomfort, these medications may be extremely helpful. However, it is a mistake to assume that all women experience physical or mental symptoms that require medication.

The most controversial technique for treating menopausal symptoms is estrogen replacement therapy. Synthetic estrogen may be taken in the form of pills, creams, surgical implants, or injections. The physician who considers menopause to be an "estrogen deficiency disease" is likely to prescribe replacement therapy as a long-term treatment. Other physicians are likely to use it as a short-term treatment to ease the transition to postmenopausal hormone levels. At the present time, a more cautious approach is being used in the prescribing of estrogens. The woman receiving estrogen replacement has an increased risk of blood clots, uterine and cervical cancer, and "breakthrough" bleeding from the uterine lining. Estrogen replacement therapy will not be prescribed for a woman who has a medical history of these disorders.

Estrogen replacement has been hailed as a

"fountain of youth," a magical hormone that will keep a woman "feminine forever" (Wilson, 1966). Actually, there is little evidence that estrogen retards the aging process. It does, however, lessen the severity of the two symptoms associated with lowered estrogen—hot flashes and vaginal dryness. Although estrogen has also been used to treat other symptoms, such as insomnia and depression, there is little medical evidence to support this practice. Since these symptoms are not directly caused by estrogen deficiency, it is unclear why they should be cured by estrogen replacement.

The sex life of postmenopausal women has been neglected by most researchers. As noted, the only direct effect of the menopause on sexual functioning is a tendency toward vaginal dryness and lack of elasticity—a condition easily remedied with artificial lubricants. However, the menopause brings other changes in a woman's life. She no longer has to be concerned with contraception—a change that might be expected to increase her sexual interest and activity. On the other hand if, as is likely, her culture considers the menopause to signal the end of sexuality, that myth will probably have a negative effect on her sexual interest—and that of her partner.

Most studies on this subject find that for the

It is important for women to know that, even though hormonal changes do occur during menopause, their potential for intercourse and orgasm continues throughout the lifespan. (© *Joel Gordon 1979*)

majority of postmenopausal women, there is little change in sexual interest. One researcher (Neugarten, 1963) interviewed 100 women from working-class and middle-class backgrounds; 65 percent reported no changes, while the remainder were equally divided into groups experiencing increased and decreased sexual interest. A study of menopausal and postmenopausal women conducted by members of the Boston Women's Health Collective (1976) obtained similar results: about half of the women noticed no change in their sexual desire, and the remainder were equally divided between those reporting increased desire and those reporting decreased desire.

While sexual interest may remain largely unchanged, women over the age of 60 often experience a decline in sexual activity. In part, this decline may be related to the husband's lessening sexual interest. It may also be related to the mistaken cultural expectation that sexual activity is not necessary or dignified for older people. However, women retain their potential for intercourse and orgasm throughout the life span. The hormonal changes of the menopause are not sufficient, of themselves, to alter this potential. Once again, expectations and personal history play a major role in the sexuality of women experiencing hormonal changes. (See the essay "Sex and Aging," pp. 121-127)

OVARIECTOMY, HORMONES, AND SEXUAL ACTIVITY

Ovariectomy is the equivalent of male castration. The surgical operation consists of the removal of the ovaries and should not be confused with tubal ligation (in which the Fallopian tubes are cut) or hysterectomy (in which the uterus is removed). With ovarian removal, circulating levels of estrogen and progesterone fall, and the menstrual cycle is halted. The adrenal cortex continues to se-

crete small amounts of these hormones.

The vast majority of research indicates that ovariectomy does not alter female desire or capacity for orgasm. According to Ford and Beach (1951), any decrease in desire found after ovariectomy is a result of suggestion and expectation, rather than of physiological change. In other words, a woman who expects that ovariectomy will decrease her sexual activity may be more likely to experience this effect, while a woman with a pleasurable and fulfilling sex life may find little difference in her desire for sexual activity.

The major effect of ovariectomy, and the consequent lowering of hormone levels, is vaginal dryness. As with menopause, this problem may be solved in several ways: the use of artificial lubricants such as oils, creams, and jellies, or the prescription of synthetic estrogens to supplement lowered endogenous levels.

While ovariectomy has no definite adverse effects on sexuality, researchers have found evidence that removal of the adrenal cortex at the same time does cause changes. (Waxenburg *et al.*, 1959). Women who had had their ovaries *and* adrenal glands removed showed a decrease in sexual drive, activity, and responsiveness. There are several possible explanations for these findings. First, decreased desire may result because with the removal of ovaries and adrenal glands, the body is deprived of both of its sources of estrogen. Second, removal of the adrenal glands deprives a woman of her major source of androgens. Finally, these surgical procedures may cause health problems that indirectly interfere with sexual functioning.

THE EFFECT OF ANDROGENS ON WOMEN

From pubescence through the menopause, women have small amounts of masculinizing hormones, or *androgens*, circulating through the bloodstream. The primary source of these androgens appears to be the adrenal gland. The adult female has testosterone levels that are approximately one-tenth of those found in the adult male. These natural, or endogenous, androgens appear to vary along with the menstrual cycle. One study reported that one of the androgens, testosterone, is highest at around mid-cycle or ovulation, with a second peak occurring during the luteal phase (Goebelsmann *et al.*, 1974). The highest levels of testosterone always corresponded with the mid-cycle peak in LH. However, there was great variation among individual women. In many cases, the day-to-day variations in serum testosterone were greater than the differences among average follicular, mid-cycle, and luteal phase values.

Several researchers have suggested that some low level of androgens is necessary to maintain female sexual interest (Kaplan, 1974). Support for this notion comes mostly from research in which exogenous androgens are administered to women. There are several situations in which it is medically necessary to do this. For example, androgens may be given to genetic females with ambiguous genitalia who are being reared as males, in order to promote masculine development at puberty. Androgens are also given to female-to-male transsexuals to develop masculine appearance. Breast cancer patients may be given androgens to suppress malignant growth. Finally, androgens have been used to increase sexual desire in women with low sex drive.

When androgens are given to a female before puberty, she will develop as a normal-appearing male. Muscular development, voice pitch, and facial and body hair will be masculine. If androgens are not given until after puberty, the physical changes will be less dramatic. The voice will deepen, and some facial and body hair may develop; but the female pelvic structure will not be altered, and breast development will not be reversed. Giving androgens to a female obviously cannot cause her to grow a penis, but she may experience an increased sensitivity and enlarging of the clitoris.

Although androgens do not change a woman's sexual orientation, they frequently seem to intensify desire (Money and Ehrhardt, 1972). Other researchers have noted this effect. Helen Kaplan (1974) considers testosterone to be a highly effective aphrodisiac for women, particularly in cases where the ratio of androgens to estrogen has been somewhat low. She states that some women who are given androgens for medicinal purposes, as in the treatment of cancer, find that they are more easily sexually aroused. Whereas previously their sexual interest had been restricted to a loved sexual partner, they may tend to become sexually interested in men outside the context of an affectional relationship.

While androgens do seem to increase female sexual desire, the mechanisms involved are not clear. Kaplan suggests that androgens enhance libido by activating cerebral sex centers. An alternative explanation is that the critical factor is the heightened sensitivity of the clitoris under the influence of androgens—a suggestion that seems feasible since the clitoris plays such an important role in female sexuality.

Hormones and Male Sexuality

It is commonly believed that the male sexual drive is fueled by the masculinizing hormones, or androgens. Actually, the relationship between male sexual interest and androgens is extremely complex. Low levels of androgens do not necessarily indicate low sexual interest, nor do high androgen levels always ensure high sexual interest. Once again, we find that hormones affect sexuality within a larger context that includes individual differences in experience, expectations, and physiology.

PATTERNS OF HORMONE RELEASE

We are accustomed to thinking that only females show cyclical patterns of hormone release. While males do not have a well-defined cycle comparable to the menstrual cycle, they do show both rhythmic and nonrhythmic patterns of hormone release. In prepubertal boys, plasma testosterone levels average about 20 to 80 ng./100 ml.*—about the amount found in adult women. After puberty, these levels rise to from 400 to 1,400 ng./100 ml. These levels are not stable in a single individual. Studies that continuously monitor testosterone levels have found the levels to be characterized by irregular and abrupt increases, suggesting that androgens are released in spurts (Schiavi and White, 1976).

Clearly, measuring testosterone is vastly more difficult than measuring weight. A man who weighs 150 pounds in the morning is likely to be about the same weight at night. However, testosterone levels are constantly varying.

The increase/decrease pattern of hormone release may be as short as 30 minutes or considerably longer. For instance, there is a circadian, or 24-hour, rhythm: levels increase as a man sleeps, generally reach a peak early in the morning, decrease during the day, and reach their lowest levels in the late evening. This is particularly interesting when we consider that the late evening, when testosterone is lowest, is when sexual intercourse is most likely to

take place. However, there are large individual differences, and while one man's testosterone level may peak at 8 A.M., another may not reach a peak until 11 A.M. Further, the short-term oscillations in testosterone contribute additional variation. Any study that relies on a single blood sample to measure testosterone must be regarded with some skepticism. These variations in testosterone release patterns are of importance when we review research that correlates hormone levels with some measure of behavior. Most studies standardize the time at which blood samples are taken in order to minimize the effects of circadian variations. It has also been suggested that men have annual cycles, with peaks in the summer and early autumn, and lowest levels in the winter and early spring, as well as regular increases and decreases in testosterone levels in cycles ranging from 8 days to over a month.

Plasma testosterone level is the measure most frequently used to study male hormones. However, hormonal influence is also determined in part by the receptivity of the target tissues. Consider, for example, the extreme case of the genetic male with androgen insensitivity syndrome. He has adequate amounts of testosterone in his bloodstream, but his body tissues are unable to make use of it. Thus while his plasma testosterone levels may be normal, his appearance is not that of a normal male. It is also likely that there are individual differences in the capacity of various sexual tissues to make use of testosterone. It is important to remember that plasma testosterone measures do not tell the whole story.

Additionally, we know that testosterone levels may be influenced by changes in the external environment. Both physical and emotional stress have been shown to lower testosterone levels. Under stressful conditions, the hypothalamus sends chemical messages to the pituitary to cease stimulating the testes. Re-

*ng./ml. = nanograms per milliliter.

searchers at the Walter Reed Army Medical Center compared the plasma testosterone levels of troops in Vietnam with those of soldiers in basic training or on noncombat duty. The Vietnam group had lower testosterone levels than the other groups. They also studied men in officer candidate school. At the beginning of the course, when emotional pressure was greatest, testosterone levels were at their lowest. As the pressure decreased, testosterone levels increased.

Kaplan (1974) also notes that there is a strong relationship between androgen secretion and psychological state. Increased androgen levels tend to be associated with sexually attractive opportunities, stimulation, and activity. Decreases are associated with depression, defeat and humiliation, and chronic stress. Other researchers have described a relationship between testosterone level and aggressiveness. For example, one study (Rose *et al.*, 1972) found that in monkey colonies, the more aggressive males tended to have higher plasma testosterone levels than their nonaggressive peers. A drop in plasma testosterone was noted after the dominant male monkey lost his position as leader of the group. However, this does not permit us to conclude that aggressive males have higher testosterone levels, or that testosterone causes the aggressive behavior. A study of male convicts (Kreuz and Rose, 1971) reported no relationship between plasma testosterone and aggressive behavior or self-assessments of aggressiveness.

Finally, a more recent study at UCLA (Houser, 1979) looked at the relationship between male hormones and mood states over a 10-week period, during which time a large number of blood tests and psychological questionnaires were administered. When the averages for all the subjects were compared, it was found that mood states correlated negatively with testosterone level—that is, the higher the testosterone level, the more hostile and anxious the subjects felt. However, Houser also found considerable variability in this relationship from one subject to the next, and it is not possible to predict for any one individual how hormones will influence mood.

HORMONE LEVELS AND SEXUAL ACTIVITY — CAUSE OR EFFECT?

While conventional wisdom dictates that hormone levels trigger sexual desire, there is some evidence that the converse is true: that is, that sexual desire and activity increase hormone levels. Increased levels of testosterone have been found after mating in several species of mammals, including monkeys, bulls, rabbits, and rats. One study (Rose, 1972) evaluated hormonal changes in male rhesus monkeys after sexual activity. Male monkeys were put with receptive females, and testosterone levels were measured before and after mating. Increases after mating ranged from 109 percent to 247 percent of baselines obtained before exposure to the females. Within one week, testosterone levels had fallen back to baseline.

The finding that hormone levels are altered by sexual activity has been replicated for human males. In one study (Kraemer *et al.*, 1976), twenty normal males aged 20 to 28 and all with regular sexual partners were asked to keep diaries of their sexual behavior for two months. Each man gave a blood sample at 8 o'clock every second morning. The authors report that testosterone levels were extremely variable both among and within subjects. That is, the average values for the subjects varied, and measures of the same subject on different days also varied widely. There was no overall relationship between the mean testosterone level over the 2-month period and the frequency of sexual contacts. Men with high testosterone levels were not more likely to have sexual intercourse, and men with low average levels were not less likely to have intercourse. In fact, there was a slightly negative relationship between hormones and the number of sexual contacts: the more sexual activity, the lower the mean testosterone level.

Each subject's testosterone level on mornings following sexual activity and mornings following no sexual activity were compared. A majority of subjects had significantly higher testosterone levels *after* sexual activity. In other words, increases in testosterone were a result rather than a cause of sexual behavior. The authors suggest a plausible but unproven hypothesis to explain this finding. When testosterone falls below a critical threshold, the body attempts to raise this level by increasing the probability that sexual behavior will occur. In contrast to the common view that high testosterone levels cause increased sexuality, these results suggest that it is low testosterone levels that have this effect.

Support for these findings was provided by a study on the effects of masturbation on male hormone levels (Purvis *et al.*, 1976). A group of thirty-four young male volunteers provided blood samples immediately before and after a masturbatory session. To control for the possibility that the anticipation of masturbation was affecting hormone levels, eleven of the volunteers were called back and told that they would participate in a similar study. However, after the first blood sample was taken, they were merely asked to wait for a period of time equivalent to their masturbatory session, and then a second blood sample was taken. The results indicated that while masturbation produced several significant changes in hormone levels, the anticipation of masturbation had no effect. Masturbation resulted in a significant increase in several androgens, including testosterone. The pattern of steroid increases suggests that masturbation has the greatest effect on hormones secreted by the adrenal glands, and a lesser effect on those hormones secreted primarily by the testes.

A review of research on this subject (Schiavi and White, 1976) concludes that the relationship between sexual activity and hormone levels is not clearly understood. While some researchers have found elevated hormone levels after sexual behavior, others have failed to find this relationship. Some studies have suggested that it is sexual arousal, rather than activity, that causes elevated hormone levels. For example, males who are shown a sexually arousing film but have no opportunity for sexual behavior show increases in testosterone that peak after 60 to 90 minutes (Pirke *et al.*, 1974).

HORMONE LEVELS AND SEXUAL COMPETENCY—CAUSE OR EFFECT?

We have already discussed the complexity of the data that suggest a relationship between sexual activity and hormone level in normal men. In using the word "normal," we are including an extremely large range of testosterone levels. One man may have three times the testosterone level of another, yet show no difference in masculine appearance, sexual virility, or frequency of sexual contacts. Thus knowledge of a man's testosterone level will usually not enable us to predict the quality or quantity of his sex life.

However, men with abnormally low testosterone levels have been shown to be more susceptible to sexual dysfunction. Once again, this is not a consistent finding, and not every researcher has reported this relationship. For instance, one study compared the sexual experiences of hormonally normal men with men known to have a physical condition that lowers testosterone to below-normal levels (Raboch and Starka, 1973). Results indicated

The effect of testosterone on male sexuality is unclear. Sexual disinterest, or impotence, as well as other sexual problems, are both psychological and physiological in origin. (© *Joel Gordon 1980*)

that there were no differences in the reported coital frequencies of these two groups. In fact, men with testosterone levels as low as 300 ng./100 ml. reported having intercourse from two to three times per week. The authors conclude that circulating testosterone levels are much higher than is necessary to maintain sexual competency, even in men with abnormally low levels. They also suggest that tissue sensitivity, rather than hormone levels in the bloodstream, is the critical factor in affecting sexuality.

Several studies have investigated the relationship between testosterone levels and sexual dysfunction. The sexual problems most commonly examined are low sexual interest and impotence. Although men suffering from one might be more likely also to feel the effects of the other, the two problems are not identical. The impotent man may be normal in his sexual interest but unable to maintain an erection. Conversely, the man with low sexual interest may, in his limited sexual behavior, be quite capable of maintaining an erection.

One study compared testosterone levels of impotent or sexually disinterested men with normal men (Raboch *et al.*, 1975). They found that while dysfunctional men tended to have lower hormone levels, this difference reached statistical significance only for men aged 41 to 45. However, men with physical conditions that lower testosterone to levels similar to the dysfunctional men in this study usually con-

tinue to function normally. Therefore, it seems that testosterone deficiency is not the critical factor in either sexual disinterest or impotence. These researchers suggest that the chronic stress of being dysfunctional may in fact have been responsible for lowering some men's testosterone levels. They conclude that testosterone level is probably a less important factor in male sexual function than has previously been believed.

A review of the results of several studies that investigated the relationship between testosterone levels and potency disorders (Schiavi and White, 1976) found a great deal of overlap in testosterone levels between normal and dysfunctional men in about half of the studies. That is, some men who are impotent have higher testosterone levels than some men who have no potency problems. In contrast, a significant relationship was found in a study evaluating testosterone levels in two groups of impotent men (Cooper *et al.*, 1970). "Constitutional impotence" was characterized by an insidious and progressive development of the problem, with a gradual decline in sexual interest. "Psychogenic impotence" was defined by a high sex drive, an acute onset of potency problems, and evidence of such sexual outlets as masturbation. These researchers reported that men in the "psychogenic" group had significantly higher testosterone levels than men in the "constitutional" group. The results indicate that impotence is a complex problem with several possible contributing factors. However, it is not clear whether the low testosterone values found in the "constitutional" group were a cause or an effect of their sexual problems. Some of these men were given supplementary testosterone for up to 4 months after completion of the study, and still failed to show any improvement in their sexual functioning.

TESTOSTERONE SUPPLEMENTS

Treating potency disorders with hormone supplements is a controversial issue. There is little evidence that impotent men with normal testosterone levels are aided directly by supplements. However, when impotence is associated with below-normal testosterone levels, replacement therapy may reverse the problem. Research investigating the effectiveness of this form of treatment has yielded mixed results. Many studies use a mixture of substances with the testosterone supplement. For instance, a drug called Afrodex, frequently

Is There a Male Climacteric?

In recent years, the notion that men experience something analogous to the female menopause has achieved some popularity. The male experience has been given several names, including "male menopause," "male climacteric," and "mid-life crisis." The symptoms of this experience vary and may include a loss of sexual interest and potency, changes in temperament and behavior, and a series of physical changes such as fatigue and sleeplessness.

Female menopause is marked by clear changes in ovarian function. The physical changes in "male menopause" are less clear-cut. We do

used in the treatment of potency problems, also contains "aphrodisiac" substances such as yohimbine. In cases where Afrodex is effective, we cannot be sure that testosterone was the responsible ingredient. In addition, there may be a large placebo effect. Men who are told that they are taking a powerful male hormone that will "cure" their potency problems often do find relief from their difficulty, even if they are given only a sugar pill.

When testosterone does work to alleviate potency problems in men whose testosterone levels are within normal limits, we are not sure of the cause of its success. Kaplan (1974) thinks that the cause of success may lie in the temporary physiological boost that testosterone administration gives the patient, which may serve to interrupt a vicious psychological circle. In other words, testosterone does not

know that there is a gradual drop in testosterone levels as men grow older. These hormonal changes may have some role in a man's "change of life," as his body adjusts to lowered levels of certain hormonal secretions. However, most "menopausal" men have testosterone levels that are well within the normal range. Thus, it seems that hormone changes are only one of several possible contributing factors.

The "male crisis" generally occurs at about the same time in life as does female menopause. Not all men experience it, and the severity of the symptoms also vary. While almost all women cease menstruation in mid-life, we know that few of the symptoms commonly associated with menopause are directly caused by hormonal changes. It seems likely that both men and women are subject to similar pressures at mid-life, and that these pressures contribute to menopausal symptoms. Men are susceptible to the expectation that their sexual potency will decline, and this fear is often sufficient to cause actual sexual difficulties. In addition, both men and women must face the fact of their declining physical energy and the changes that are part of the aging process. Mid-life is often a time to take stock of one's life, to examine what has been accomplished, and to plan for the future. While hormonal factors may be an additional element in this process, the "male menopause" is increasingly being viewed as a natural mid-life transition, a developmental "passage" toward greater maturity and adjustment. The impetus for this passage is less clear for men than it is for women, since the female climacteric has easily identifiable physical correlates. However, the forces that push us to reevaluate ourselves at mid-life are basically the same.

work directly to produce erections. Rather, it provides a general feeling of well-being that indirectly may improve sexual function.

THE EFFECTS OF MALE CASTRATION

Much of our information about the role of androgens in male development and functioning comes from research on the effects of castration. Farmers have long known the effect of castration on their livestock and have used the procedure to make their animals more docile. Castration has been a requirement for membership in certain religious sects—for example, the Skoptsy of Russia—and was employed in eighteenth-century Europe to enable boy singers to retain their soprano voices as adults. More recently, castration has been used in some countries, such as Sweden, as punishment or treatment for the male sex offender.

The major effect of *castration*, defined as the removal or destruction of the testes or of testicular function, is a drastic reduction in testosterone levels. In the past, castration was performed surgically, and this technique is still used with animals. Nowadays, the functional effects of castration can often be achieved with the use of drugs that block or counteract the effects of testosterone. This is usually called "chemical castration," and its effects may be reversed once drug use is halted.

The foundation of modern knowledge about castration comes from laboratory research with rats. In the castrated rat, testosterone disappears from the bloodstream within a few hours of the operation. However, sexual behavior may continue for days or even weeks. In longer-lived species, sexual competency may continue for months and years. It has been suggested that small amounts of testosterone secreted by the adrenal glands are responsible for maintaining sexuality; but this seems unlikely, as removal of the adrenal glands has little effect on the persistence of sexual behavior after castration.

After sexual behavior does cease, it may be reinstated by giving testosterone injections. There is a relatively long time lag between the injection of testosterone and the reappearance of sexual activity, and the length of the lag seems to be related to the length of time that has elapsed since castration. If testosterone replacement is begun immediately, sexual behavior will reappear much more quickly than if replacement is delayed for some period of time. According to one researcher (Davidson, 1975), this indicates that when the "target tissue" is deprived of testosterone, it develops an insensitivity to the hormone. The longer the period of deprivation, the longer it takes for resensitization to occur. Davidson also reports that the amount of testosterone needed to reinstate sexual behavior is considerably less than the amount present in the animal before castration. In other words, there is a large "margin for error" in circulating testosterone levels, which implies, again, that most men have much more testosterone than is necessary to maintain their sexual competence.

The effects of castration differ depending on whether it is performed before or after puberty. Usually, the boy who is castrated before puberty retains a high voice and does not develop facial hair. The body will not have masculine contours, and there will be no male pattern of balding. However, he will have both pubic and axillary hair, as these characteristics are under the control of hormones secreted by the adrenal glands. There is very little information available about the sex lives of men castrated before puberty. According to Money and Ehrhardt (1972), most prepubertal castrates who do not receive hormone replacement therapy will, more likely than not, be apathetic about sexual activity as adults. However, there are exceptions to this general rule. Some prepubertal castrates appear to be capable of erection and orgasm, although they cannot ejaculate. This makes sense when we recall that some young boys are capable of orgasm before they reach puberty. While testosterone is clearly necessary for ejaculation to occur, it seems possible that orgasm requires little or no male hormone.

The effects of castration after puberty are extremely variable. In some men, sexual drive and capacity may diminish and disappear within weeks. For others, sexual interest may persist, in spite of a decline in the ability to have erections and orgasm. Finally, some men are able to maintain both sexual interest and ability for years after castration; however, the amount of ejaculate when orgasm does occur will diminish and ultimately disappear. A study that illustrates the variability of male response to castration was performed in Norway on 157 men, ranging in age from 25 to 54, who had been castrated for medical or legal reasons (Bremer, 1959). Over two-thirds of these men showed a complete loss of sexual activity and interest within one year of the operation. In the remaining third, interest and activity persisted for over a year, and in some, potency was retained for as long as 10 years.

Why are responses to castration so variable? Several factors may play a role in determining the sexual aftereffects of castration. For instance, the adult male castrate may have had considerable sexual experience before the operation, and the memory of past sexual contact may prolong sexual capacity. The availability of a supportive sexual partner is also likely to be important. Further, psychological and physical health are probably related to the sexual outcome of castration, as is the context of the operation. For example, a man who is castrated to curtail criminal sexual behavior may react differently from a man castrated to halt the spread of cancer. Finally, a man's attitude is likely to have a great effect on his reaction. If he is convinced that the procedure will leave him sexually dysfunctional, this conviction may prove to be a self-fulfilling prophecy. However, if he expects to be able to continue to function normally, this expectation may help to maintain his sexual ability.

Chemical castration has effects similar to those described above. There are several types of hormones that will functionally castrate the male. For instance, use of either estrogens or progesterone will have a "castrating" effect. Both of these hormones have additional side effects for men. Progesterone causes the testes to become reduced in size, while estrogen may cause the breasts to develop. Even if the female hormones are withdrawn, breast growth will remain unless surgically removed. Other steroids that have a "castrating" effect are called antiandrogens; they either inhibit the uptake of testosterone at the receptor sites or inhibit the gonadal production of testosterone. Generally, antiandrogens cause a rapid decline in potency and also a decrease in erotic fantasies and desire. They are most often used in the treatment of habitual sex offenders, a topic that will be discussed in detail in Chapter 12.

HORMONES AND HOMOSEXUALITY

Hormones have been linked to male homosexual behavior in several ways. It has been suggested that homosexual orientation is "caused" by hormones in the prenatal environment, but there is no support for this position as yet. Other theories suggest a relationship between sexual orientation and hormone levels, with homosexuals having lower testosterone levels than heterosexuals. Among those who view low hormone levels as the cause of homosexuality, there have been attempts at "treatment" by providing testosterone supplements.

Research attempting to relate homosexuality with hormones has produced a complex picture. Some studies identify clear hormonal differences between heterosexual and homosexual males, others find no differences at all. Many studies find a great deal of overlap in the hormone levels of the two groups: some homosexual males have higher testosterone levels than some heterosexual males, and some heterosexual males have higher estrogen levels than homosexual males. Clearly, low testosterone values and high estrogen values are not a predictor of homosexually oriented behavior.

Among studies that do report a hormonal difference related to sexual preference, the most well-known was performed by Robert Kolodny and his colleagues in 1971. They compared the plasma testosterone levels of thirty male homosexual students with a control group of fifty heterosexual males. Both groups consisted of healthy young men with a mean age of about 21 years. All subjects were ranked on the Kinsey Sexual Orientation Scale: 0 represents exclusively heterosexual behavior, 6 exclusively homosexual behavior. The points between 0 and 6 are values along this continuum, with 3 representing a completely bisexual orientation, that is, equal attraction toward men and women. Only one blood sample was taken from each subject.

The results indicated that males rated 2, 3, and 4 on the Kinsey scale were not different in plasma testosterone levels from the control group, all of whom were rated as either 0 or 1. However, males rated 5 or 6 did have a significantly lower plasma testosterone level than the controls. Kolodny and his colleagues do not suggest that these results mean that homosexuality is caused by an endocrine dysfunction or that homosexual males have any endocrine abnormality. Rather, they suggest that depressed testosterone levels may be a secondary result of a homosexual life style. For example, the stress and anxiety of being an open homosexual could well have the effect of lowering testosterone levels. Also, as noted earlier, the variation in testosterone levels is so great, both among and within individuals, that one blood sample is probably insufficient to establish the presence of hormonal differences.

The search for hormonal correlates of homosexual behavior is based on assumptions that require further examination. First, it assumes that the direction of sexual drive is based on the type of hormones. Thus, male hormones are supposed to lead to a preference for female partners, and female hormones to a preference for males. Most of the evidence reported in this chapter does not support this notion. For instance, we know that giving androgens to a heterosexual woman will not make her a lesbian. Instead, it seems to intensify her interest in heterosexual activities. Similarly, giving female hormones to a heterosexual male does not cause him to become homosexual. Rather, he seems to lose interest in any form of sexual activity. Finally, low levels of testosterone do not seem to imply anything about a male's sexual orientation, although they may appear to indicate a general disinterest in sexuality.

According to Money and Ehrhardt, the sex drive is neither male nor female. Rather, it is "undifferentiated . . . an urge for the warmth and sensation of close body contact and genital proximity" (1972, p. 317). If homosexuality were linked to a deficiency in male hormones, then testosterone supplements could be expected to alter sexual orientation. Instead, it seems that administering testosterone to homosexual males has the effect of intensifying their homosexual behavior or desires.

Another assumption that requires reexamination is the notion of homosexuality as a single entity. As noted in Chapter 3, it is difficult to define precisely what we mean when we label someone as "homosexual." Do we mean an exclusive and continuous preference for same-sex partners? Are we referring to any man who has ever had a homosexual contact? If so, the group we are labeling as homosexual is very large, since Kinsey (1948) reported that about one of every three men in his sample had had some homosexual experience during his lifetime. How do we categorize the man who is exclusively homosexual during a period of confinement, as in prison, and exclusively heterosexual outside of this situation? Given the variety of ways in which one can be homosexual, it is not surprising that there are no consistent relationships between homosexuality and hormone levels.

Perhaps the questions that are being asked — for instance, do homosexuals have different hormone levels from heterosexuals — are bound to produce contradictory and confusing results. Nearly 30 years ago, Ford and Beach summed up the subject of hormones and homosexuality in a way that still seems relevant today:

The fundamental error . . . is the unjustified assumption that gonadal hormones determine the character of the sexual drive in human beings. This is not the case. The reproductive hormones may intensify the drive but they do not organize the behavior through which it finds expression . . . human sexual behavior is controlled and directed primarily by learning and experience. (1952, p. 236)

Summary

Hormonal influences on sexuality can be examined from a number of differing perspectives. For example, hormones have a relatively clear and direct effect on physical maturation at puberty, as well as on reproductive function after it. The effects of hormones on sexual behavior, however, may be indirect and subtle, and in contrast to most of the animal kingdom, human sexual activity seems to be largely independent of hormone levels. In addition, social factors play an important role in the experience of hormonal events; a woman's sexual responsiveness after menopause, for instance, depends to a large extent on cultural and personal expectations about sexuality during this particular stage of the life cycle. To summarize:

1. Hormones are released into the bloodstream by the endocrine glands. In turn, the endocrine glands are supervised by the hypothalamus, a brain structure that regulates the internal environment of the body. It is this connection between the endocrine glands and the brain that allows the stresses of the external environment to affect the hormones circulating within the body.

2. Men and women have both masculinizing hormones (androgens) and feminizing hormones (estrogens and progesterone). It is the proportions of these hormones, rather than the types, that determine reproductive function and secondary sex characteristics.

3. At puberty, an enormous increase in sex hormone levels brings the adolescent to reproductive maturity. Accompanying the changes in body shape, size, and appearance, there are often adjustment difficulties as the adolescent copes with a new body image and the beginnings of adult sexual status.

4. Pregnancy and menopause are two major hormonally determined events in the female life cycle. Although hormones clearly alter physical functioning at these times, the sexuality of both the pregnant and menopausal woman can best be understood by looking at social and psychological factors as well as biological changes.

5. The relationship between hormone levels and male sexuality is complex: to date, most research shows that when testosterone is within the normal range, there is no direct relationship between testosterone level and sexual potency. In addition, hormone levels do not appear to relate to sexual orientation.

6. Female sexual desire and activity seem almost completely independent of the level of feminizing hormones, but are often heightened by the administration of masculinizing hormones. Male sexual desire and activity seem unrelated to the level of masculinizing hormones but are substantially decreased by the administration of feminizing hormones, such as estrogens.

3

SEXUAL FUNCTION AND DYSFUNCTION

SEVEN

Sexual Behavior I: Solitary and Interpersonal Scripts

Overview

What causes us to label a particular behavior sexual? From a reproductive viewpoint, sexual behavior is defined as an activity that can lead to impregnation. But since we know that there are many nonreproductive motives for sex, this definition is inadequate to describe the full range of human sexual activities. Similarly, the common assumption that a behavior is sexual if it involves genital stimulation or orgasm is inadequate: many sexual activities—for example, petting or foreplay—can be nongenital and nonorgasmic. Even so basic a behavior as kissing can be sexual in some situations and nonsexual in others. Perhaps the best way to define a behavior as sexual, then, is in terms of its subjective *meaning*—if the person or persons involved think an activity is sexual, then it is.

Given the complexity of all human behavior, it is not surprising that there are almost an infinite number of ways in which we can express our sexuality. Because sexual behavior tends to be more controversial than nonsexual behavior, however, we are often less tolerant about sexual variations than we might be with respect to, say, variations in the ways we dress or speak. While we accept speech patterns as a product of varying personal and social factors, we mistakenly believe that all sexual patterns are natural or instinctive. Actually, learning plays as important a role in sexual behavior as it does in most other types of human activity.

Sexual behavior represents the end product of sexual learning and decision making. We are exposed to a wide range of sexual options at each stage in the life cycle, and we select—

without necessarily being aware or conscious of this decision-making process—from this range of sexual alternatives. Our sexual choices are influenced by many factors: what we learn about our sexual selves, what we learn from our partners, and what our culture tells us are acceptable and unacceptable sexual behaviors.

The basic purpose of this chapter is to present the range of sexual behaviors that lead up to, or serve as alternatives for, genital intercourse. There is no question that intercourse occupies a unique position in our sexual repertoire—indeed, for some people, sex *is* intercourse. The decision to relegate the discussion of intercourse to the second of our two chapters on sexual behavior does not repre-

sent a value judgment as to what is "better" but an attempt to dispel the myth that intercourse is the *only* satisfying form of sexual interaction possible.

Before turning to the range of sexual behaviors, we will discuss the notion that all sexual activities are to some extent planned, or "scripted." We approach any sexual situation with some preconceived ideas of what should happen, with whom, where, and when—even how we will feel. Although there may be some overlap, we each have our own individual script or scripts for sexual behavior. So once again, we must recognize that variation is the rule rather than the exception in human sexual behavior.

The Organization of Sexual Behavior: Sexual Scripts

Much as we would like to think of ourselves as being spontaneous in our actions, there is little about human behavior that is random. We approach almost any situation with a mental plan, or *script*, that helps us to organize our own behavior and to understand the behavior of others. This is certainly true of sexual situations: "Without the proper elements of a script that defines the situation, names the actors, and plots the behavior, nothing sexual is likely to happen" (Gagnon and Simon, 1973, p. 19). For example, the meeting of two attractive people under even the most romantic circumstances will not end in sex unless one or both of them see this situation as sexual and organize their behavior in sexual ways.

Gagnon and Simon define the term "script" as having two dimensions: the external and the internal. By external, they mean those elements of the script that regulate our behavior in a sexual situation. In the same way that

actors follow the script of a play when they perform their roles, people follow mental plans of how the action should proceed. From the script, an actor learns who the characters are, how they will behave, and the sequence of their actions. Similarly, the sexual script acts as a plan or code for directing sexual action, allowing people in an interpersonal situation to anticipate one another's next moves. In this sense, a sexual script is simply a set of sexual conventions. When we are invited to a formal dinner party, we are aware of certain expected conventions: we must dress in a particular way, use the silverware properly, and eat the various courses of the meal in a prescribed sequence. The conventions of a sexual situation may also be well-defined; for instance, we may expect to be undressed, to be in a bedroom, and to move through a sequence of sexual acts. Without such guiding rules, our external behavior might be disorganized and inappropriate. This is not to deny the importance of novelty, experimentation, and improvisation in sexual encounters. But just as a musician or an actor who is very familiar with a melody or the script of a play is more comfortable in improvising, it is also true that familiarity with a sexual script facilitates sexual improvisation.

The internal dimension of the sexual script relates to how we feel about our sexual behaviors and what they mean to us. The relationship between sexual partners, the circumstances of their encounter, and their respective motivations all influence the meaning of a script. For example, a passionate or romantic script might have strong emotional meaning, whereas sex for money—the prostitution script—may be physiologically intense but without any emotional significance. Similarly, two people might masturbate in exactly the same way, but the meaning of that act will differ if one of them scripts masturbation as a positive form of self-pleasuring whereas the other scripts it as a shameful substitute for intercourse itself.

The work of sex researchers such as Kinsey emphasizes the external aspects of the sexual script—type of behavior, number of orgasms, and so on—but generally ignores the emotional significance of these behaviors. Yet human sexual behavior can be a complex form of emotional communication involving non-sexual as well as sexual motivations. When sex is used to communicate love, for instance, it becomes the central focus of an intimacy script that brings out intense emotions. On the other hand, a sex-for-reproduction script expresses our most basic biological role.

In a sense, then, our scripts reflect our sexual motivations; in turn, we express these motivations with a set of specific sexual acts. Some of these acts, however, are sexual only when they take place in the context of a sexual script. Kissing, for example, has an almost un-

limited range of meanings, depending on the script in which it takes place. Kissing is a particularly strong example of a behavior in which the motives of the actors are relatively ambiguous or open-ended. To take an example from the other end of the continuum, when we learn that a man and a woman have enjoyed anal intercourse together, we tend to assume that their relationship is very intimate. The more ambiguous the behavior, the more we must depend on context and script to interpret its meanings.

MAJOR SCRIPT DIMENSIONS

We can look at both the internal and the external aspects of our sexual scripts as varying along several dimensions. One such dimension is simplicity-complexity. In general, animals have more simple scripts than human beings, children have more simple scripts than adults, and most people have more simple scripts for masturbation than for intercourse. Not only the complexity of the behavior but also the feelings attached to that behavior can vary. For example, while anal intercourse is relatively simple to define on a physical level, the meanings attached to this act may be emotionally powerful and complex.

Flexibility-rigidity is a second important script dimension. A flexible script is one in which variations in time, place, or behavior will be accepted. In contrast, a rigid script follows a predictable pattern. A script may be rigid in one way—for instance, in regard to setting—but flexible in another—such as who plays the ''passive'' role.

Sexual scripts may also vary on a dimension of passionate-dispassionate, or romantic-unromantic. A script may be more or less emotionally charged depending on the intentions of the participants. Women are stereotyped as having romantic scripts, whereas men are

ments about which is the "best" script, it is
probably more realistic to accept that for reasons of learning and experience, some scripts
work better for some people than others. And
even for those people they work better at some
times than at other times. Thus while a dominance script may be totally unacceptable to
some people, it may be very satisfying to
others.

Finally, we can classify sexual scripts according to a functional-dysfunctional dimension based on the degree of sexual satisfaction
they provide for the participants. Dysfunctional scripts will be considered in depth in
Chapter 9; in this chapter, we will focus only
on the more functional scripts—those that
achieve the goal of stimulating sexual arousal.

THE SEQUENCE OF SEXUAL BEHAVIOR

Just as a play begins with the raising of the
curtain, a sexual encounter begins with the
process of initiation. The rise of the curtain
serves as a signal to actors and audience that
the play is about to start; the words or gestures
used to initiate a sexual encounter signal the
beginning of the sexual script. Initiation usually serves the additional function of inviting
the participation of a partner, an invitation
that may be either accepted or rejected. Under
noncoercive circumstances, initiation is the
start of a sexual communication that continues
until the encounter has come to an end.

The word "foreplay" is often used to describe
the next stage of the sexual script. Caressing,

expected to prefer a less romantic approach.
But there are far too many exceptions for this
to be a valid generalization.

Another dimension involves dominance-
reciprocity. In some scripts, sex is used as a
way of controlling or being controlled by one's
partner; in others, the goal may be mutual satisfaction. While it is tempting to make judg-

kissing, undressing, and touching of the nongenital areas are used in most Western societies to set the stage for genital contact. Foreplay also plays an important role in establishing trust and intimacy, and in overcoming inhibitions against touching or being touched. Some people respond sexually and become aroused during the early stages of foreplay; others prefer more extended contact. Many people enjoy the intimacy and affection of foreplay for its own sake, without feeling the necessity to proceed any further. For this reason, the word "foreplay" is often criticized because it implies that something else ought to follow.

Oral or manual stimulation of the genitals can be seen either as advanced aspects of foreplay or as the main act of the sexual script. For example, a person wishing to avoid intercourse, pregnancy, or the loss of virginity might find these forms of stimulation a satisfactory alternative to genital intercourse. When used as foreplay, these techniques can prepare the male for intercourse by providing him with a firm erection; they can also aid the female in having adequate vaginal lubrication.

For most people in our society at the present time, penile-vaginal intercourse is the central or culminating act of the sexual script. According to Clellan Ford and Frank Beach (1951), intercourse is the most preferred sexual activity in all cultures, although the particular position, timing, and so on, will vary from one culture to another.

In general, the sexual equivalent of the falling curtain in a play is the male orgasm. That is, most people define male orgasm as the end of the sexual script. However, this script may be altered as male and female roles are redefined in our society. Also, some couples may incorporate a period of *afterplay* into their script, so that sexual contact continues, in the form of touching and kissing, after one or both partners have reached orgasm.

This sequence of sexual behaviors—initiation, foreplay, intercourse, afterplay—is in many ways the most typical and socially approved of sexual scripts; but it is certainly not the only one. People can and do vary the sequence, and the variations may be obvious—as in using a new technique—or subtle—as in the feelings associated with that particular technique.

If a script represents a sequence of sexual behaviors, then a person's range of scripts could be called their *repertoire*. A person with a large repertoire of sexual scripts might have experienced masturbation, oral sex, and anal sex, in addition to intercourse. On the other hand, a limited repertoire might include only masturbation or only intercourse.

Masturbation: A Solitary Script

No other sexual act has been so widely condemned while at the same time being so widely practiced as masturbation. Historically, medical, religious, and even sexual authorities have frowned upon masturbation, although it is a commonly practiced behavior in most human societies and among most animal species. This double standard of attitudes toward masturbation is partly due to the fact that it is generally performed as a solitary sexual act—masturbation can be practiced in private while it is condemned in public.

Only recently have scientists and the public alike begun to reexamine our historical prohibitions against masturbation. Past statements about the moral and medical dangers of masturbation seem unconvincing in the context of today's sexual attitudes. However, many people have inherited a legacy of guilt about masturbation. While we have discarded the more obvious masturbation myths—such as the early notion that there was a direct link between masturbation and insanity—we may still feel slightly uncomfortable about the subject. Masturbation remains an almost universal sexual activity, but one that is surrounded by confusion, misinformation, and shame.

Our negative attitudes toward masturbation are founded in the Judeo-Christian tradition, which disapproves of all sexual activity that does not lead to reproduction (see the boxed extract on page 242). Among many religious groups, bodily pleasures are seen as interfering with spiritual growth; masturbation, which is pleasurable without procreative intent, has no place within such belief systems.

The religious prohibitions on masturbation received strong support from medical authorities in the eighteenth and nineteenth centuries. For example, the highly respected Swiss physician Tissot published a major textbook on the diseases caused by "onanism." When his work became available in the United States in the 1830s, it had a powerful impact on the medical profession. Medical educators such as William Alcott maintained that masturbation affects the health not only of the masturbator but of his offspring as well. In fact, masturbation became one of the favorite scapegoats for a wide variety of physical, mental, and sexual problems. The renowned psychiatrist Krafft-Ebing was convinced that masturbation caused insanity and sexual perversion, and Alcott believed that it could lead to a weakening of all bodily functions.

Freud and his followers took a somewhat less harsh view of masturbation; they tended to see it as a "narcissistic" and immature form of sexual behavior. Children were expected to practice masturbation, but the mature adult

was supposed to lose interest in this sexual act. Thus in the Freudian tradition, adult masturbation was sometimes considered a sign of incomplete sexual development.

In 1948, Kinsey and his associates summarized contemporary attitudes toward masturbation as follows:

Throughout history, both the Jewish and Christian churches have condemned masturbation as either immoral or unnatural. In more recent years, with an increase in public respect for science, the moral arguments have been supported with statements concerning the physical and mental harm supposed to come from the continuance of such a habit. . . . Every conceivable ill from pimples to insanity, including stooped shoulders, loss of weight, fatigue, insomnia, general weakness, neurasthenia, loss of manly-mindedness, genital cancer and the rest, was ascribed to masturbation. (Kinsey *et al.*, 1948, p. 513)

Opposing this strong antimasturbation tradition, Kinsey presented an impressive array of statistics showing that masturbation is an extremely common and essentially normal sexual behavior. More recent sexual surveys—such as Morton Hunt's in the 1970s—continue to report that nearly all males and a very high proportion of females have masturbated at some time. Perhaps more important, Hunt found that attitudes toward masturbation did not correspond to the traditional view that it was a dangerous and immoral act. When asked to agree or disagree with the statement "Masturbation is wrong," male and female subjects over the age of 35 were twice as likely to disagree as to agree. Among subjects under the age of 35, about 80 percent disagreed with the view that masturbation is wrong. This apparent rejection of the notion that masturbation is sinful does not mean, however, that we now accept masturbation unconditionally: Hunt cautions that "most people who masturbate remain more or less guilt-ridden about it, and nearly all of them are extremely secretive about their masturbating and would be horribly embarrassed to have anyone know the truth" (1974, p. 66).

That masturbation might have beneficial effects on our sexual and social adjustment is a relatively new idea in our culture. One of the first therapists to see masturbation in this way was Wilhelm Reich—he believed that it was a useful technique for helping patients who were experiencing sexual problems. In the past decade, many therapists have reported that masturbatory instruction is a successful method for overcoming female orgasmic difficulties (McMullen and Rosen, 1979). Further, there is evidence that masturbation improves the capacity for orgasm during intercourse for females (Kinsey *et al.*, 1953).

Relatively few individuals in our society today consider masturbation to be unnatural or immoral behavior. Even fewer people believe that masturbation has serious negative effects on physical well-being. Instead, our doubts tend to focus on the criteria of psychological adjustment: we still wonder if masturbation is "healthy," how it might effect our sexual and psychological relationships, and how much is "too much."

IS MASTURBATION HARMFUL?

Although we reject the idea that masturbation can cause blindness or insanity, some people still express fears that masturbation may change the shape or appearance of the genitals. This mistaken belief may have originated in the work of early sexologists such as Dickinson, who thought that "excessive" masturbation caused recognizable changes in genital structure. Although some men and women blame genital "deformities"—for instance, enlarged labia in the female or an angled penis in the male—on masturbatory habits, there is no evidence that masturbation alters genital ap-

pearance in any way. The following is a quote from a respondent in the Hite survey:

I pulled one of my labia minora when I was masturbating when I was eleven. It got long and I thought that was the reason. The other got almost as large, later. . . . My mother said my labia majora were separated because I had "touched" myself. (Hite, 1976, p. 240)

A more complex question is whether masturbation may cause psychological harm. When masturbation is accompanied by anxiety or guilt, it may be harmful. For example, boys or girls who are punished severely for masturbation can develop sexual inhibitions that extend beyond masturbation into all aspects of sexual behavior. Feelings of guilt and anxiety may also cause masturbatory activities to take place hastily and secretly. In males, this pattern of extremely rapid ejaculation may transfer to sexual activity with a partner, causing problems with intercourse. In some cases, men with erection problems teach themselves to masturbate to orgasm with only partial erection; the habit of ejaculating without erection may lead to or exacerbate erectile problems during intercourse. Further, men and women who develop extremely unusual methods of masturbation—for instance, stimulation of the urethral canal—may have difficulty duplicating this pattern during intercourse, and therefore experience orgasmic difficulties with a partner. In all these cases, however, masturbation is not intrinsically harmful—rather, it is the habits accompanying masturbation that may cause problems.

Even sexologists who view masturbation as healthy and positive are likely to warn against the dangers of compulsive masturbation. The term "compulsive" is not easy to define, but it generally refers to masturbation that seems uncontrolled and "excessive" (another vague term)—that is, masturbation that is a compulsion in much the same way as excessive hand washing or other ritualistic behaviors.

After masturbation, many individuals feel a release of sexual tension. *(Emmet Gowin, Courtesy Light Gallery, New York)*

Finally, masturbation may be considered harmful when it occurs as a means of avoiding sexual interaction or as a way of expressing hostility toward a sexual partner. For example, men who are afraid of or feel hostility toward women may use masturbation as a substitute for forming sexual relationships. Within a relationship, one partner may masturbate in order to reject or avoid the other. Once again, it is not masturbation per se that causes harm; instead, the problem comes from using masturbation to avoid interpersonal difficulties.

To balance this review of the possible harm that may be associated with masturbation, there is a long list of potentially healthful and beneficial effects. Masturbation is usually the primary and most basic way that we learn about our own sexuality. It is an important means of relieving sexual tension, particularly for those men and women who do not have an available sexual partner. Within the marital relationship, masturbation may be seen as an acceptable form of sexual variety, or as an activity that reconciles the different sexual needs of the partners. Masturbation presents no risk of pregnancy or venereal disease and is thus a safe means of experiencing sexual pleasure. It is often an important and effective adjunct of sex therapy programs. Masturbation has even been described as a way to achieve, without the use of drugs, an altered state of consciousness—in fact, among certain Eastern religious groups masturbation is used as a technique for achieving mystical awareness (Masters, 1967).

How does masturbation affect sexual desire? Many cultures, including our own, believe that we have a limited amount of sexual energy; by using this energy for masturbation, it is thought that the desire for other forms of sexual contact will be decreased. Perhaps one of the more common reasons why people abstain from masturbation is the mistaken notion that it will "use up" sexual desire. While it is true that many adolescents, particularly males, use masturbation as a way of relieving sexual tension, later in life masturbation can be an effective means of stimulating sexual energy. We have tended to accept the analogy that sexual desire is like the gasoline in an automobile—the more we drive, the less gasoline we will have. A better analogy would be to compare sexual desire with the battery of the automobile—if the automobile is left undriven in the garage, the battery is certain to run down. While the immediate effect of masturbation may be to decrease sexual desire, the long-term effect is usually a continuing and stable interest in sexual activity.

MASTURBATION FACTS AND FIGURES

Our most complete set of statistical figures on masturbation (and most other sexual activities) comes from Kinsey and his associates (see Chapter 1). Although his work provides us with a great deal of information about masturbation, it is information of a very specific sort. Kinsey, a zoologist, was most interested in the classification and demography of masturbation—for example: how common it is within each social class, how often it occurs in different age groups, and what proportion of total sexual activity it forms. The key defining question of masturbation in Kinsey's interview was, "Does it lead to orgasm?" Kinsey did not inquire into the emotional aspects of masturbation—that is, the feelings and motives surrounding the behavior or the fantasies that frequently play an important role. Thus from Kinsey's work we know a lot about Who? and How often? but relatively little about Why?

The second major source of information about the demographics of masturbation, published about 20 years after the work of Kinsey, is the Hunt survey (1974). Both Kinsey and Hunt took care to break down the statistics on masturbation incidence by age, marital status, educational level, religious background, and a variety of other variables. Table 7.1 shows some of the key findings from these surveys. Although there were some changes over the years, a surprising number of statistics have stayed the same. For example, both Kinsey and Hunt found that more than 90 percent of males and more than 60 percent of females masturbate at some time in their lives. However, the males and females in Hunt's survey were likely to have their first masturbatory experience at an earlier age than those in Kinsey's time. In addition, while Kinsey found a rather large difference between male and female masturbation incidence and frequency, Hunt's survey showed that the gap between the sexes was narrowing. However, even in Hunt's study nearly 30 percent of the women that were interviewed had never masturbated to orgasm.

Kinsey's statistics on masturbation surprised and shocked many members of the scientific community and the public. Three of his findings had particular impact: that fully 93 percent of the male population masturbated at some time, that women who masturbated were more likely to achieve orgasm in marriage, and that masturbation was most common among the well-educated.

A common myth holds that young men who masturbate frequently during adolescence, when their sex drive is high and they are denied other sexual outlets by society, will cease masturbation completely once they have married or begun to have intercourse on a regular basis. Although there was some support for this myth in the Kinsey finding that masturbation frequency declined considerably for men who had married, the more recent Hunt survey found that 72 percent of the married men aged 30 and over were still masturbating. There was a higher incidence of masturbation among unmarried women aged 30 and over in the Hunt survey as compared to those in Kinsey's, but 68 percent of the married women in that age group were still masturbating.

TABLE 7.1

Comparison of Kinsey and Hunt Data on Masturbation Incidence and Frequency

	Males		Females	
	Kinsey	Hunt	Kinsey	Hunt
Total accumulative incidence	93%	94%	62%	63%
Incidence by age 13	45% *	63%	15% *	33%
Unmarried incidence:				
Age 18–24	86%	86%	30% *	60%
Age 30+	80%	90%	50% *	80%
Unmarried frequency:				
Age 18–24	49 times/yr.	52 times/yr.	21 times/yr. *	37 times/yr.
Age 30+	30 times/yr. *	60 times/yr.	16 times/yr.	not reported
Married incidence:				
Age 30+	40% *	72%	33% *	68%
Married frequency	6 times/yr. *	24 times/yr.	10 times/yr.	10 times/yr.
Incidence for grade school education	89%	about the same as Kinsey	34%	somewhat higher than Kinsey
Incidence for college educated	96%	about the same as Kinsey	57%	somewhat higher than Kinsey
Incidence and religious adherence:				
Regular attenders	slightly less than Hunt	92%	much less than Hunt	51%
Nonattenders	slightly more than Hunt	93%	much more than Hunt	75%

"Accumulative incidence" refers to the total number of individuals who have ever performed the activity; "incidence" refers to the number engaging in masturbation at the time of the survey. Hunt's criteria for incidence are more stringent than Kinsey's, and the increases in several categories are therefore conservatively estimated.
Asterisks indicate major differences.
Source: Derived from A. C. Kinsey et al., *Sexual Behavior in the Human Male* (Philadelphia: Saunders, 1948); A. C. Kinsey et al., *Sexual Behavior in the Human Female* (Philadelphia: Saunders, 1953); and M. Hunt, *Sexual Behavior in the 1970's* (New York: Dell, 1974).

MOTIVES FOR MASTURBATION

While statistical facts and figures of masturbation have been well-researched, we know relatively little about precisely why people masturbate. Usually, this question is not included in sexual surveys; where it is included, people often have difficulty in expressing their motivation for masturbation. However, certain broad categories of reasons can be described.

Instinctive self-stimulation. According to Ford and Beach (1951), self-stimulation of the geni-

tals is extremely common among most mammalian species. In the lower mammals, stimulation often takes the form of self-cleaning, or grooming; in nonhuman primates such as apes and monkeys, self-stimulation seems to be directed at producing orgasm. It seems likely that among humans, manipulation and exploration of the genitals is a somewhat spontaneous and instinctive act. When genital manipulation is followed by the pleasurable sensations of orgasm during childhood or adolescence, masturbation becomes a source of conditioned sexual gratification. That is, the pleasure of orgasm becomes associated with the act of masturbation, so the act is repeated. Among adults, the most common reason mentioned for masturbation is the pleasurable release of sexual tension (Hunt, 1974).

Expression of unacceptable desires. Sexual fantasy is an important aspect of masturbation for many individuals. Although most masturbation fantasies follow such acceptable themes as love and romanticism, some men and women develop fantasies that they cannot or will not act out in real life. In such cases, masturbation becomes a way of experiencing novel or unconventional sexual scripts vicariously, that is, it serves as a "safety valve" for the expression of socially unacceptable desires. Masturbation scripts often involve reading erotic literature or viewing explicit photographs.

Altered state of consciousness. The search for altered states of consciousness is a theme that extends throughout history: drugs, alcohol, meditation, fasting, chanting, and many other techniques have been used for this purpose. The psychological experience of orgasm appears to be yet another technique to alter consciousness. One way to account for the persistence of masturbatory behavior despite, at times, heavy social sanctions, is in terms of the special mental effects of masturbation and sexual fantasy. For instance, R. E. L. Masters (1967) proposed that masturbation produces, in some individuals, a "trancelike or hypnoid state." Psychophysiological research has confirmed that orgasm is accompanied by a unique set of changes in brain waves (Cohen et al., 1976) — as was discussed in Chapter 5.

Nonsexual motives. Masturbation is not always performed for sexual reasons. For instance, some of the men in the Hunt survey masturbated to relax or to overcome insomnia.

Some women masturbated as a means of easing menstrual cramps. The feelings of calm and relaxation that most people experience after orgasm is an effective way of coping with tension.

Some nonsexual motives for masturbation are not so positive. For example, some men or women use masturbation as a demonstration of hostility toward a sexual partner or as a means of avoiding any kind of interpersonal sexual contact.

MASTURBATION STYLES AND SCRIPTS

Masturbation is not always a simple and predictable behavior. There is a large range of masturbation fantasies, scripts, and techniques. Men and women, heterosexuals and homosexuals, young and old, may all have different masturbation needs and modes of expression. In fact, the same individual may try different masturbation styles at different times in the life cycle, and no two people will masturbate with exactly the same thoughts, setting, or pattern of stimulation.

Masturbation scripts. Because masturbation has historically been viewed as a shameful act, very few people feel relaxed enough to do it in other than a completely private setting. The major exception to this rule is the young male; it is not uncommon for adolescent boys to learn to masturbate within a group setting. However, for most men and women masturbation is an intensely private activity, and often we find it difficult or impossible to masturbate in the presence of even the most intimate sexual partner. Nevertheless, some couples report that they are able to incorporate masturbation into their sexual script, where it may serve as a source of variety or a way to reconcile differences in sexual desire.

Because of traditional views of masturbation, we often do it in ways that minimize the chances of discovery. Children whose parents punish them for masturbating, or who simply fear being caught, learn to masturbate behind closed doors and as rapidly as possible. This pattern often continues into adulthood. Unfortunately, secretive and hasty masturbation patterns may have a negative effect on sexual activities with a partner. To counteract this effect, certain therapists and writers (e.g., Barbach, 1974) have suggested that people devote more time and thought to masturbation settings; for example, anorgasmic women are instructed to take a warm bubble bath, play music, light candles, and so on, in order to make the masturbation script more pleasurable and appealing.

Masturbation fantasies. Kinsey found that 72 percent of males and 50 percent of females usually fantasize during masturbation. Masturbation fantasies were most common among males with higher educational levels. Kinsey did not inquire about the content of these fantasies, but he believed that fantasy was far less important for arousing desire in females than it was for males (for data on the sex surveys, see Table 1.1).

Gagnon and Simon (1973) have focused on the qualitative differences between male and female masturbation fantasies. In their view, female fantasies center on specific sexual acts that have already occurred, in the context of such social arrangements as love, marriage, and social attachments. In contrast, the typical male fantasy appears to neglect relationship factors while centering on specifically erotic themes.

More recently, Hunt and other researchers have found that males and females show considerable overlap in fantasy content during masturbation. For instance, Hunt reported that 75 percent of men and 80 percent of women mentioned thoughts of intercourse

with a loved partner as their most common fantasy during masturbation. Other relatively common themes included intercourse with strangers, sex with more than one person of the opposite sex at the same time, and performing sexual acts that would be taboo in reality. Young people were likely to use a greater variety of fantasies, and fantasies of a more daring nature, than older people. Hunt concluded that the sex differences observed by Kinsey 20 years earlier were culturally conditioned, noting that "women today are far more likely to be aroused by erotic materials and fantasies, and to utilize fantasies while masturbating, than was true only a generation ago (1974, p. 92).

There are very few generalizations that can be made about masturbation fantasies: some people will have the same fantasy consistently throughout their sexual lives, others continually invent new and different fantasies. Some masturbation fantasies are extremely elaborate and complex, involving large casts of characters and exotic settings, others are simple images of the genitals. Sometimes, fantasies center on the socially unacceptable or forbidden—such as sadism, masochism, homosexual relations, or rape—other fantasies focus on traditional positions of intercourse with an opposite-sex partner. Finally, some people find that they are unable to masturbate without fantasy; others have never used any fantasy during masturbation. Perhaps the greatest variability in fantasy styles occurs in women—whereas some women make use of explicitly erotic themes and can even reach orgasm through fantasy alone, other women have never fantasized while they masturbate.

Masturbation techniques. Most men and women have never had the opportunity to observe another person masturbating, so it is not surprising that we have many misconceptions about specific masturbation techniques. We

FIGURE 7.1

Female masturbation. The most common technique among women is manual stimulation of the outer genitals (labia and clitoris) while lying on the back. Sex therapists often recommend that a woman who is learning to masturbate use a small mirror to locate the different anatomical parts and observe her own responses.

tend to believe that all males masturbate by manually stroking the penis, and that all females masturbate by inserting some form of penile substitute into the vagina. While these stereotypes are somewhat accurate for the male, they are not accurate for the female.

Kinsey found that females employed a greater variety of masturbation techniques than males. Only 20 percent of the women in his sample reported using some form of vaginal insertion during masturbation. In addition, about 10 percent of women masturbated by rubbing or squeezing their thighs together, without any use of the hands to touch the genitals. A very small number of women could reach orgasm through fantasy alone, or through breast stimulation alone. However, the majority of women masturbate by rubbing the labia or the clitoral shaft with a firm and rhythmic motion that usually increases in pressure or intensity as orgasm approaches.

Hite (1976) categorized the masturbation techniques of the women in her sample into six basic types. The most frequent, used by 73 percent of the women, involved stimulating the outer genitals by hand while lying on the back. Others were manual stimulation while lying face down, pressing the genitals against a soft object, rubbing the thighs together, water massage over the genitals, and vaginal penetration. Massagers and vibrators were also used by some women. Hite found that 11 percent of her sample tried more than one method of masturbation. In addition to these basic masturbation techniques, there were

The Story of Onan: The Biblical Origin of the Masturbation Taboo

Perhaps the primary source of the historical taboo on masturbation is the Judeo-Christian tradition. The origin of this taboo can be found in the Old Testament story of Onan:

And Er, Judah's firstborn, was wicked in the sight of the Lord: and the Lord slew him.
And Judah said unto Onan, Go in unto thy brother's wife, and marry her, and raise up seed to thy brother.
And Onan knew that the seed should not be his; and it came to pass, when he went in unto his brother's wife, that he spilled it on the ground, lest that he should give seed to his brother.
And the thing which he did displeased the Lord; wherefore He slew him also. (Genesis 38:7–10)

The confusion that has almost always surrounded the subject of masturbation is evident in the traditional interpretation of this story. Onan's crime was actually far more complicated than the simple act of masturbation. According to ancient Jewish law, when a woman's husband died, the husband's brother was expected to assume the role of husband. However, any children born to the woman were considered to be the offspring of the dead husband and not of the brother. Onan refused to accept responsibility for fathering children who would bear his dead brother's name; thus, during intercourse with his brother's widow, he withdrew before ejaculation and "spilled it on the ground."

The act of masturbation—defined as solitary sexual activity—does not occur in the story of Onan. What does take place, however, is sexual activity that cannot lead to reproduction. Thus Onan's crime can be interpreted more broadly than the act of masturbation—rather, it may be seen as engaging in sexual intercourse that would not lead to procreation. In fact, as recently as 1976 the pope issued a strongly worded condemnation of masturbation, and the Catholic church continues to prohibit the use of all methods of contraception except the "rhythm method."

The simplest and most literal interpretation of Onan's crime is simply that he did not assume the marital responsibilities of his dead brother. Nevertheless, the term "onanism" has been used, until quite recently, to describe masturbation as an immoral and sinful act.

---

many variations of bodily position, site of stimulation, and intensity and rhythm of stimulation. For example, some women needed to have their legs apart while masturbating, others wanted their legs together, and still others preferred to have their knees bent. It seems likely that these preferences develop early in a woman's masturbation history and often continue to be important throughout her sexual life.

Male masturbation techniques appear to be less varied. Most often, males perform a rhythmic stroking of the shaft of the penis; however, a small number of men masturbate without manual stimulation—for example, some can reach orgasm by lying face down and rubbing the penis against a sheet or bed cover while simulating the movements of intercourse. Once again, there are individual preferences as to body position—some men must lie down, others are capable of masturbation in a standing position.

Interpersonal Scripts

TOUCHING

The primary way in which we express our sexual feelings is by touching and being touched. In a sense, all the sexual behaviors to be described, ranging from kissing to intercourse, are based on our sense of touch. Indeed, Ashley Montagu (1971) has suggested that the skin may be our most basic organ of perception and communication. In addition to erotic stimulation, skin contact provides us with feelings of intimacy, comfort, safety, and love. Touch is so important that our language is filled with expressions that use "touching" metaphors:

We speak of "rubbing" people the wrong way, and "stroking" them the right way. . . . We get into "touch" or "contact" with others. Some are "thick-skinned," others are "thin-skinned," some get "under one's skin," while others remain only "skin-deep." . . . Some people are "touchy," that is, oversensitive or easily given to anger. (Montagu, 1971, p. 110)

A series of studies by Harlow and his associates (1959; 1972) has shown that adult sexual and emotional behaviors are related to early physical contact. Harlow removed newborn monkeys from their mothers and provided two types of mother surrogates: an uncovered wire mesh structure and a similar structure that was covered with soft terry cloth and kept warm with a light bulb. Monkeys reared with a terry-cloth surrogate spent much more time clinging to their "mothers" than those reared with a wire structure. Further, monkeys given the opportunity to cling to the cuddly mother surrogates and to play with other infant monkeys developed completely normal adult sexual and social behavior. In contrast, infants reared with the wire-mesh surrogates showed serious inadequacies in their adult behavior.

Physical contact between animals often takes the form of "grooming"—that is, touching that serves the function of improving health and cleanliness and also reinforces important social bonds. Apes and monkeys spend considerable amounts of time scratching and licking each other and removing insects or dirt from each other's fur. Sometimes this grooming behavior is a secondary sexual activity that leads to intercourse. For instance, the female baboon in estrus frequently grooms the "head male" as a way of ensuring his sexual attention. In the same way, a low-status male chimpanzee may groom a female as a way of currying favor with her (Ford and Beach, 1951). Grooming as a sexual prelude is not, however, restricted to animals. Among some cultures, couples spend hours cleaning, primping, and touching one another before sexual intercourse begins.

In our own culture, sexual touching can be viewed in two perspectives: as an end or goal in itself or as a prelude to intercourse. When sexual touching does not continue to intercourse, we usually call it necking or petting. Touching that does lead to intercourse is often labeled foreplay. We tend to think of petting as an adolescent or premarital behavior, whereas foreplay characterizes the sexual behavior of adults. Although there may be some truth to these stereotypes, many exceptions also exist: for instance, some married adults may enjoy the variety of petting without intercourse, while some adolescents use touching only as foreplay for intercourse.

Petting. Petting can be defined as the tactile stimulation of any part of the body, but it most usually involves the face, hair, neck, breasts, and genitals. Hunt describes such behavior as a compromise established in twentieth-century America between those who insisted on premarital chastity and those who tended to-

ward sexual liberalism. He also notes that "in most societies petting without intercourse has been either unknown or practiced only during a very brief transitional stage of the life cycle" (1974, p. 132). At the time of Kinsey's surveys, however, petting was both common and frequent among many respondents. In particular, Kinsey found that petting experience was related to educational level; among males, about 88 percent engaged in petting at some time, but petting frequencies were higher for college students than for those with a grade school education. Among females, the highest petting incidence and frequency was found for women of the younger generation and those with higher educational levels, with 94 percent reporting at least some kind of petting experience.

Despite the prevalence of petting, Kinsey seems to have had mixed feelings on the subject. On the positive side, he noted a correlation between adolescent petting experience and subsequent sexual adjustment in marriage—perhaps because petting provides a useful training in sexual communication, especially for women. For women with no petting experience, sex after marriage could be a traumatic experience for which they had no preparation. On the negative side, Kinsey was concerned that "such arousal as petting provides may seriously disturb some individuals, leaving them in a more or less extended nervous state unless the activity has proceeded to the point of orgasm" (Kinsey *et al.*, 1948, p. 542). While some men reported little discomfort after extended petting without orgasm, others did experience pain unless they masturbated soon after leaving the female partner.

According to Hunt, petting is now more acceptable than in Kinsey's time but also is less important. Most of the men and women in his survey approved of petting, particularly in an affectional relationship, and the frequency of petting was slightly higher than that found by Kinsey. Also, a larger proportion of petting sessions led to orgasm. However, whereas the women in Kinsey's study had reported an average of about eight petting partners before marriage, the women in Hunt's study averaged only three premarital petting partners. Hunt relates this change to the fact that in the 1970s, women were less reluctant to form a premarital relationship that included intercourse. It seems that petting fills the interval between the start of dating and the start of intercourse — an interval that was much longer in Kinsey's time.

This is not to suggest that petting is an insignificant step in adolescent sexual development. In his study of adolescent sexual behavior, Robert Sorenson (1973) notes that most teen-agers begin their sexual activity with some form of petting. Sorenson reported that among sexual beginners — that is, those girls and boys who engage in sexual activities other than intercourse — petting usually begins with the boy touching the girl's breasts, and moves to genital stimulation. Males tend to stimulate their female partners' genitals at an earlier age than when they themselves first experience genital stimulation by a female partner. Sorenson concludes that males are more active and less hesitant in initiating sexual contact.

Foreplay. As we have already mentioned, sexual contact as a preliminary to intercourse is usually called foreplay. Such contact serves several important purposes: it stimulates penile erection and vaginal lubrication, and it allows for emotional intimacy and psychological arousal. However, many people criticize the label we have given to this wide range of erotic activities. Zilbergeld, for instance, notes that "the very term we use to describe these other activities — foreplay — clearly indicates their lowly status relative to intercourse" (1978, p. 43). Kissing, hugging, stroking, and oral stimulation are all viewed simply as events that occur before the main act of intercourse. Zilbergeld believes that males are particularly susceptible to the myth that foreplay is a relatively unimportant preliminary. He reasons that since men are brought up to be goal-oriented, and most men see the goal of sex as intercourse and orgasm, it is not surprising that men "tend to ignore or not fully

participate in the process of sex (it is 'only foreplay') and therefore miss out on experiences that might well be stimulating and pleasurable" (p. 37). To get back "in touch," Zilbergeld suggests massage as one way by which men can overcome these goal-oriented attitudes (see the boxed extract on p. 248).

The notion that foreplay is not second-class sex is a relatively recent one. In fact, at the beginning of this century there was disapproval of foreplay even as a preliminary to intercourse. Since sex was justified only as a means of procreation, techniques of foreplay had no place in a "moral" sexual relationship. When Kinsey questioned married men about precoital contact, he found little or no foreplay at all among the less-educated. Foreplay was most common and of longest duration among college-educated males; but even within this group, it was likely to last only 5 to 15 minutes. Hunt found, in contrast, that noncollege men estimated their duration of foreplay at about 15 minutes.

A cross-cultural look shows great variety in the amount and type of foreplay before intercourse. For instance, Ford and Beach (1951) found that whereas some tribes condone only the physical contact of intercourse, other tribes approve of precoital touching that lasts for several hours. In much the same way, some animal species proceed to intercourse very quickly whereas others require extended contact and "courting" before they are ready to mate. Even within a single species there are individual preferences in the amount of foreplay; Ford and Beach note that some male apes "appear to enjoy a protracted period of gentle play followed by intercourse, whereas others habitually rush to the female and attempt to copulate without indulging in any preparatory measures" (1951, p. 42).

For animals, foreplay activity serves the purpose of ensuring that both partners are physiologically ready to mate at the same time. Of course, among humans it also serves this purpose, but animal and human foreplay differ in one major respect: human foreplay is a deliberate and conscious attempt to arouse one's partner and to become aroused. Humans become sexually aroused not only by being touched, but also by touching their partners. For instance, Kinsey observed that a man who caresses a woman's breasts may become more aroused by his experience of touching a "forbidden" part than she is by his sometimes clumsy efforts. In other words, the sexual meanings of touching can be just as arousing as the physical stimulation of being touched.

Types of touching. Which types of touching feel good? To a large extent, the experience of touch as pleasurable depends on learning factors. A particular type of touch—say, anal stimulation—may be arousing to the individual who sees this activity as "normal," and unpleasant to an individual who sees it as "abnormal" or improper. Moreover, men and women often develop preferences for a pattern of touching that is associated with past sexual experiences or that most closely duplicates the stimulation they use during masturbation. These individual differences highlight the importance of communication during foreplay; while we would like to assume that the "perfect lover" knows intuitively how to arouse his or her partner, guidance of some sort is usually necessary for pleasurable touching.

The need for communication is especially important in genital stimulation. For instance, women in the Hite survey report preferring very different patterns of clitoral stimulation—some liked a soft touch, others wanted firm pressure; some liked direct clitoral stimulation, others found direct touching to be uncomfortable or even painful. In the same way, men learn to prefer particular patterns of penile stimulation, which must be communicated to their partners. Comfort (1972) suggests that

one way of communicating these preferences is by watching one's partner masturbate and then trying to duplicate that pattern of stimulation. While this may be the most direct way of communicating touch preferences, it is not the only way—both verbal and body language are common means of expressing sexual pleasure or displeasure.

In general, we think of sexual touching as involving soft movements of the hands over the body of one's partner. However, some individuals respond to more extreme types of touch, such as scratching, tickling, and biting. While we tend to consider a positive response to painful stimulation as "masochistic," in other societies the conventional sexual script may include pinching, scratching, and biting by both male and female. Ford and Beach emphasize the role of learning in the enjoyment of painful stimulation; they suggest that we are all born with the physiological capacity to respond erotically to mild degrees of pain, and that this capacity is shaped by childhood experiences. When a culture teaches its children that biting or pinching can bring sexual satisfaction, and when these behaviors are seen as an essential part of the sexual script, then they will be perceived as sexually pleasurable. As Ford and Beach point out, however, cultures that approve a mild amount of painful stimulation also emphasize mutuality and lack of coercion; the woman who allows her partner to bite her will usually enjoy the opportunity to reciprocate.

Tickling is another form of touch that can be either sexually exciting or inhibiting depending on one's learning history. We do not really understand why some people are ticklish and others are not, but we do know that there are strong individual differences in the erotic value of being tickled. Perhaps the giggling, laughing, and playful struggling that often result from being tickled are ways of building emotional intimacy and therefore work to enhance sexual desire and arousal. For the person who is very ticklish, however, the sense of being out of control can be very uncomfortable and may inhibit sexual response.

Whatever form of touching is preferred, there can be no doubt that touch is a primary form of sexual and nonsexual communication.

Touch is an end in itself. . . . It bridges the physical separateness from which no human being is spared, literally establishing a sense of solidarity between two individuals. Touching is sensual pleasure, exploring the texture of the skin, the suppleness of muscle, the contours of the body, with no further goal than enjoyment of tactile perceptions. (Masters and Johnson, 1970, p. 238)

KISSING

Once he drew, with one long kiss,
My whole soul through my lips—as sunlight
    drinketh dew. (Alfred Lord Tennyson)
The sound of a kiss is not so loud as that of a
cannon, but its echo lasts a great deal longer.
(Oliver Wendell Holmes)

Perhaps the most widely accepted of all sexual behaviors, and the only sexual act that can be performed in public without causing raised eyebrows, is the kiss. Indeed, we tend to assume nowadays that all sexual relationships will include kissing, and most recent sex surveys do not even bother to include questions on this subject. Kissing seems such a normal, instinctive, pleasurable, and desirable way of expressing affection that we take it completely for granted. This accepting and even somewhat jaded attitude toward kissing has not, however, always prevailed.

Until fairly recently, most Western societies have revered the kiss as the ultimate expression of romance and love. Earlier in this century, when more extensive sexual contact was

The Kiss. This 1930s Art Deco-style illustration is taken from the 1936 book, *The Art of Kissing*, reprinted in 1977.

unthinkable before marriage, the kiss assumed a significance that is difficult to imagine in today's world. Contrast the explicitness of present-day sex manuals with a 1936 volume called *The Art of Kissing*, a book that was well-received and very popular in its day. *The*

(continued on page 250)

The Art of Massage

FIGURE 7.2
Massage is recommended as a form of foreplay, for relaxation, and for improving nonverbal communication, as well as for a variety of other purposes.

According to one source, the word "massage" is derived from the Arabic word "mass," which means to touch. Massage does, indeed, involve a great many types of touch, including rubbing, kneading, and even slapping. Athletes resort to massage for relaxation after a hard workout or for relief of muscle strain. Massage has also been used as a form of healing or therapy for emotional problems. In the context of a close relationship, massage is often used to enhance sensual and sexual communication. For some people, massage is an art, a discipline that requires serious attention, study, and practice.

There are several important "schools" of massage including Swedish, Japanese Shiatsu, and California-Esalen (from the Esalen Human Potential Institute in California, where massage is used to heighten self-awareness). The so-called massage parlors that have appeared in recent years are usually intended for the sale of sex rather than serious massage. This association between massage and prostitution is unfortunate because it reinforces the myth that all touching leads to sex or orgasm. For someone practicing Swedish or Japanese massage, the focus is on touching the whole body, not on stimulating the genitals.

Sensate focus is a form of massage recommended by Masters and Johnson (1970) to develop relaxation, trust, and intimacy in a sexual relationship. This approach can be particularly effective for men or women who are troubled by sexual inhibitions or performance anxiety. Sensate focus techniques are nondemanding, slow, and relaxed—focused on sensation rather than on performance.

Receiving a massage can be as much of an art as giving one. Some people are uncomfortable in a situation where they are expected to relax and "let go." If a massage is to be successful, the receiver must trust the giver, accepting rather than resisting the sensations experienced. For those who can accomplish this, the feeling of being "in touch" with body sensations is often very rewarding, and the experience of trust and intimacy can enhance and strengthen a relationship.

Is there a "right" way of doing massage? While there are many forms of massage, certain methods are more recommended than others. In one of the best books on this subject, Downing (1972) provides the following general guidelines:

1. Apply pressure when you do massage, unless your partner complains that it hurts or feels too sensitive.

2. Relax your hands—this may be quite difficult if you are also trying to apply pressure.

3. Mold your hands to fit the contours over which they are moving. The fingers and palms of the hands should remain in contact with the body as much as possible.

4. Maintain an even speed and pressure—jerking or other sudden movements can be very distracting.

5. Do not, however, be afraid to vary both speed and pressure—too little variety can be monotonous.

6. Use your weight rather than your muscles to apply pressure; to achieve greater pressure, if this is desired, it is better to lean your body weight forward than to strain the muscles of your hands or arms.

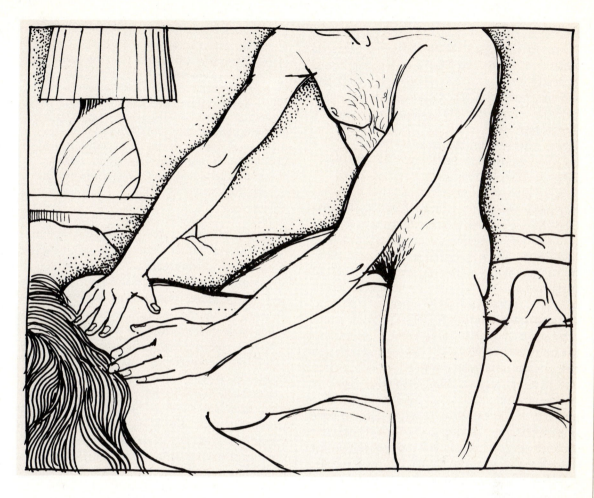

7. As much as possible, contact should be maintained throughout the massage.

8. Pay attention to how you are standing, sitting, or kneeling—although massage can be performed in many positions, some positions offer greater freedom of movement and less strain on the person performing the massage.

9. Remember always that you are massaging a person and not an intricate muscle-and-bone machine. Massage is a form of communication, and the needs and feelings of the receiver should be considered at all times.

Finally, there are certain aids and devices that can be used to enhance or vary the massage experience. For example, oil or cream is useful in reducing friction and increasing sensitivity. Natural oils such as coconut oil have the added advantage of conditioning the skin. Electric vibrators may also be included in the massage script as a way of increasing sensation and relaxing the muscles.

Art of Kissing did indeed elevate the act of kissing to an art. It included such chapters as "How to Kiss Girls With Different Sizes of Mouths," "Enjoy the Thrills of Kissing," and "Variation Kisses Are the Spice of Love." The author concluded, in rapturous tones, that "only mankind has the reason, the logic, the happy faculty of being able to appreciate the charm, the beauty, the extreme pleasure, the joy, the passionate fulfillment of the kiss" (Morris, 1977, p. 105).

If we look at the customs of other cultures, however, we can see that there is nothing "natural" about the kiss. Like most other forms of sexual behavior, the sexual value of the kiss is more a matter of learning and experience than it is a matter of instinct. Of the 190 primitive societies studied by Ford and Beach, only 21 mentioned any form of kissing. Among the remaining societies, a great many considered mouth-to-mouth contact to be unpleasant, unhealthy, even disgusting: "When the Thonga first saw Europeans kissing they laughed, expressing this sentiment: 'Look at them—they eat each other's saliva and dirt'" (1951, p. 49). Even those societies that approve of some form of kissing do not always use the techniques common in Western cultures: for example, the Arapesh touch lips and inhale, while the Lapps kiss the nose and mouth at the same time (Tiefer, 1978). Further, the absence of kissing does not necessarily mean that a society is sexually restrictive. The Mangaian people of Polynesia are sexually permissive and train young women to reach orgasm, but kissing of any sort was unknown before Western culture appeared (Marshall, 1971).

How do we learn to associate sexual pleasure with kissing? In the Freudian view, early gratifications such as breast feeding teach the child that the mouth is a source of pleasure. The kissing games of adolescence also serve as a common way to learn the kissing script.

American children and young adolescents begin their kissing education with games in which mouth-to-mouth kisses are exchanged in an otherwise nonsexual situation. "Spin the bottle" and "post office" are among the most popular of these, but dozens of local variants dot the nation. If you watch children at a kissing game (or if you remember your own experiences), you will usually find more giggling, blushing, and derision than sexual desire. The social rewards of such kissing games, rather than providing sensual pleasure, ensure that the rehearsal will continue. (Tiefer, 1978, p. 36)

Not only is kissing usually the first step toward adolescent petting, but it also remains the "curtain raiser" for most adult sexual scripts. The kissing games of adolescents usually begin with closed lips and no tongue contact. With time, the petting script usually evolves to include deep kissing and kissing of other parts of the body. As with all aspects of sexual behavior, individual preferences develop with experience—some people prefer light, soft contact, others prefer more pressure.

There are many variations to the sexual kiss—in fact, the German language has about thirty different words to describe different types of kisses. For example, the word *abküssen* means giving little kisses to different parts of the face. "Soul kissing" or "French kissing" are terms commonly used to describe deep kisses with the tongue active, while the "butterfly kiss" refers to fluttering movements of the eyelashes against a lover's cheek.

Desmond Morris reminds us that not all kisses are sexual.

You kiss your lover on the lips, an old friend of the opposite sex on the cheek, an infant on the top of the head; if a child hurts a finger, you kiss it "to make it better"; if you are about to face danger, you kiss a mascot "to bring you luck"; if you are a gambler, you kiss the dice before you roll them; if you are the best man at a wedding, you kiss the bride; if you are religious, you kiss the bishop's ring as a sign of respect; if you are bidding someone farewell and they are already out of reach, you kiss your own hand and blow the kiss towards them. (1972, p. 135)

ORAL SEX

As one of the "optional" elements of the sexual script, oral sex is often the subject of controversy and disagreement. From one culture to another, there are enormous differences in the degree to which oral sex practices are accepted. Even within the same culture, there are often strong differences in how people feel about oral sex. Kinsey noted that some husbands and wives reported major conflicts on this issue, including "several instances of wives who have murdered their husbands because they insisted on mouth-genital contacts" (1948, p. 578). Kinsey placed oral sex with masturbation and homosexual relations as the three primary sources of personal sexual conflict.

We can tell something about a culture's attitudes toward oral sex by examining the words it uses to describe oral sex behaviors. In our own culture, the general term "oral intercourse" can be used to describe any sexual contact in which the genitals of one partner are stimulated by the lips, tongue, or mouth of the other partner. Our technical terms for oral sex come from Latin: *fellatio* (from *fellare*, meaning to suck) describes oral stimulation of the penis) and *cunnilingus* (from *cunnus*, meaning vulva, and *lingere*, meaning to lick) refers to the oral stimulation of the female genitals.

In addition to these technical terms, we have numerous slang expressions to describe oral sex, such as "blow-job," "giving head," and "going down." Such terms tend to be both misleading — for example, a "blow-job" involves more sucking than blowing — and pejorative. In an attempt to avoid the negative connotations of most terms for oral sex, Van de Velde coined the expression "the genital kiss" — an expression also used by current sex educators such as Alex Comfort (1972). Other cultures have also developed positive terms to describe oral sex practices. Perhaps the most beautiful description of cunnilingus is the Sanskrit expression: "licking a lotus blossom." In the same way, the Japanese use the attractive metaphor of "playing the flute" to describe the act of fellatio (Edwardes and Masters, 1962).

Incidence: what the surveys tell us about oral sex. The Judeo-Christian tradition contains powerful prohibitions against oral sex, and in some states oral-genital contact, even between husband and wife, is still illegal. However, survey data show that in a statistical sense, oral sex is in no way "abnormal." In fact, most surveys have found that oral sex is practiced by a large segment of our society.

The first systematic survey data on oral sex came from the Kinsey reports. Citing the work of Ford and Beach (1951), Kinsey noted that oral-genital contact is common among other mammals and is also freely discussed in the literature and folklore of many modern and ancient civilizations. However, Kinsey cautioned that taboos against oral sex in the United States of the 1940s probably led to some "cover-up" on the part of his respondents; he believed that his data represented minimum incidences of oral sex. With this qualification, Kinsey reported the following findings:

Close to 60 percent of all males had experienced oral sex at some time as either the "active" or "passive" partner.

The incidence of oral sex was related to educational level; among males, 72 percent of the college group, 65 percent of the high school group, and 40 percent of the grade school group had had some experience with oral sex.

Among married females, about 50 percent had experienced oral stimulation by their partners, and a similar number had practiced fellatio.

Among unmarried females, the incidence of oral sex was related to both educational level and coital experience; 62 percent of the better-educated and sexually experienced women reported oral contact with the male genitals, 46 percent reported having experienced cunnilingus.

In the 20 years between the Kinsey and Hunt surveys, oral sex has become more generally accepted in our society. About 70 percent of the married couples in Hunt's survey saw oral sex to be a common part of the sexual script. In addition, Hunt found that the less-educated men and women were more accepting of oral sex than were those of Kinsey's generation. Perhaps the most dramatic change found by Hunt was the experience of the younger age groups—among men and women in the under-25 age group, about 90 percent had tried oral sex at least once. Looking at the changes that had already taken place since the recording of Kinsey's data, Hunt predicted that in the next generation oral sex would be a part of almost all American marriages.

The authors of *The Redbook Report* reached essentially the same conclusions as Hunt: "Today it is clear that if the sexual revolution has occurred anywhere, it is in the practice and acceptance of oral sex. Among people under age 25, it is virtually a universal part of the sexual relationship" (Tavris and Sadd, 1977, p. 87). More than 90 percent of the women responding to the *Redbook* survey had tried oral sex. Even among religious women—a group that Kinsey found was unlikely to engage in oral sex—more than 80 percent interviewed reported having experienced oral-genital contact.

Not only did most women report having tried oral sex, but they also rated their reactions to this activity as positive. For instance, 62 percent stated that cunnilingus was "very enjoyable," while only 10 percent rated it neutral or unpleasant. Women tended to be slightly less positive about fellatio, with 72 percent considering it "somewhat enjoyable," and 28 percent rating it neutral or unpleasant. Interestingly, women who enjoyed oral sex and practiced it frequently were most likely to rate their marriages and sex lives as excellent. Conversely, women who strongly rejected oral sex tended to report less satisfactory sexual adjustment and more sexual inhibition. The authors suggest that it is the willingness to experiment with sex—rather than the practice of oral sex per se—that contributes to more satisfying sexual relations.

The Hite Report provides us with information about how women *feel* toward oral sex. Hite found that 42 percent of the women in her study reported being able to reach orgasm through cunnilingus, and she suggests that this figure might be considerably higher if men would view oral sex as a goal in itself, rather than as simply a foreplay technique. Many women in Hite's study complained that oral sex was too brief. On the other hand, many women were reluctant to allow their partners to perform cunnilingus for two major reasons: concern about the partner's feelings—"Is he really enjoying it?"—and negative feelings about their own genitals—for instance, "Do I smell bad?"

Women also reported some reservations about performing fellatio. For example, many were reluctant to take semen in their mouths if the male should accidentally or deliberately ejaculated during fellatio; some women expressed uncertainty about whether to swallow the semen or spit it out. Also, some respondents were ambivalent about mutual oral sex, or the "69" position, mentioning such problems as the awkwardness of finding a comfortable body position and the difficulty in concentrating on both giving and receiving pleasure.

Attitudes toward oral sex. Although the incidence of oral-genital contact has certainly increased over the past decades, it is not clear that our attitudes have kept pace with our behavior. While Kinsey pointed out that oral sex activities had been recorded "from every culture in the history of the world," he also recognized that such activities were the subject of deep and widespread taboos and often caused "bitter condemnations" and even "violent disturbance." Nowadays, even though oral sex has become a relatively common part of the sexual script, there are still some remnants of our Victorian heritage in our attitudes toward it. Negative attitudes are usually based on one or more of the following objections:

Oral sex is seen as unclean, unsanitary, or a health risk. Typically, those who reject oral sex on these grounds are concerned with taking such bodily fluids as urine, semen, or vaginal lubricant into the mouth. Actually, such fluids are harmless in a healthy individual, and there is little danger to health unless one of the partners already has some venereal disease. Of course, any intimate contact can lead to the transmission of germs that are already present, but in this regard, oral sex presents considerably less risk than kissing—a behavior that is rarely labeled unclean or unsanitary.

Oral sex is considered objectionable from a religious, moral, or aesthetic point of view. The Judeo-Christian emphasis on sex for procreation rather than for pleasure leads to the labeling of oral sex as an unnatural or immoral behavior. Further, we tend to learn as children that our genitals are to be kept hidden, so it is not surprising that as adults we feel embarrassed about the way our genitals look, smell, or taste. This embarrassment is not common to all cultures—for example, the Japanese consider mutual oral sex to be the highest and most sacred expression of love (Edwardes and Masters, 1962). Until recently, however, the Japanese considered mouth kissing to be dirty and obscene. In contrast, Western cultures have tended to praise and elevate the mouth kiss, while assigning negative or pejorative meanings to oral sex.

An objection that was common in the past, although it is less prevalent today, is the issue of modesty. At a time when female sexual modesty was highly valued, women who showed an obvious interest in oral sex were likely to be labeled immodest or even perverted. The otherwise relatively liberal Van de Velde, writing in the 1920s, cautioned that women should refrain from oral sex during the first few years of marriage and thereafter take care not to cross the thin borderline between "supreme beauty" and "hideous ugliness." Even though we now recognize that women have sexual needs and desires, a woman who is concerned about modesty might still feel inhibited about oral sex.

Arguments against oral sex have been countered by those who see such behavior as normal and acceptable. Kinsey presented the biological argument that the mouth and the genitals are the most erotically sensitive parts of the body; he suggested that oral sex is a simple and instinctive sexual act that has been inhibited by cultural restrictions: "The human is exceptional among the mammals when it abstains from oral activities because of learned social proprieties, moral restraints, or exaggerated ideas of sanitation" (Kinsey et al., 1953, p. 588).

The following are some additional arguments in favor of oral sex:

Oral sex is an effective form of foreplay, serving the dual function of stimulating the genitals and providing the natural lubrication of saliva.

There is no risk of pregnancy with oral sex.

Oral sex does not require an erection from the male or vaginal lubrication from the female. For this reason, it is often recommended to individuals who are experiencing sexual problems. It has proved effectual in cases of vaginismus, an involuntary contraction of the muscles around the vagina that makes intercourse difficult if not impossible (see Chapter 9 for a detailed discussion).

Oral sex is often recommended for older couples. As a normal and predictable part of the aging process, men may experience occasional erectile failure, and women after menopause may find that there is less vaginal lubrication. For older couples who wish to maintain an active sex life in spite of these changes, oral sex can provide a good alternative to intercourse. In addition, older men and women often report that the intensity and variety of sensations coming from careful oral stimulation are of value in reaching adequate levels of sexual arousal. Finally, individuals with physical disabilities such as arthritis may find it more comfortable to substitute oral sex for intercourse (Comfort, 1973).

Oral sex provides the opportunity for variety and experimentation in a sexual relationship. Some people find that a single sexual script that includes only intercourse can become boring; introducing oral sex can help to stimulate renewed sexual interest.

Oral sex and pleasure—learning or instinct? There is no question that oral sex is pleasurable when practiced by people who are free of cultural inhibitions and who use careful and considerate techniques. Aside from the physical pleasure of oral stimulation, the psychological *meaning* of the act is important as well. A woman in the Hite sample explained:

I enjoy cunnilingus immensely for the obvious physical reason and for a mental reason as well. The male is exhibiting positive feelings to my femaleness. Its particular odor and architecture is as attractive to him as it is to me. (1977, p. 241)

For many men and women, receiving oral stimulation is emotionally meaningful because it shows the partner's love and caring. On the other hand, the *giving* of oral sex can also be intrinsically pleasurable—that is, some men and women are aroused simply by per-

forming the act of oral sex. Further, the giver may derive pleasure from watching the responses of the receiver.

Often, the feelings about oral sex have been discussed on a continuum of dominance-submission with the assumption that it is the submissive partner who "gives" and the dominant partner who "receives." Actually, feelings of dominance and submission depend to a great extent on subtle characteristics of the sexual script. Some women experience performing fellatio as an act of dominance because they are able to control the intensity and pace of their partner's response. On the

FIGURE 7.3
Oral sex can be performed in many different positions; it offers several advantages—either as a form of foreplay or a satisfying sexual experience in its own right.

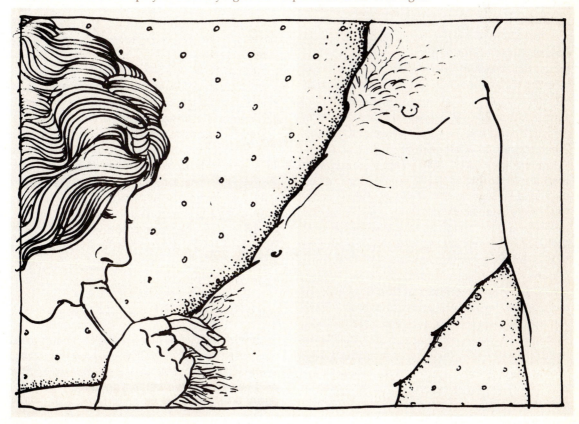

other hand, the man who is receiving fellatio may feel dominant because his partner is acting in ways that give him pleasure. Similarly, cunnilingus can be perceived as an act of male submission or male dominance. In most cases, the issue of dominance during oral sex will reflect the couple's relationship in nonsexual situations; if dominance plays an important role in their other interactions, it is also likely to be a factor during oral sex.

Is the pleasure of oral sex a matter of instinct or learning? Those who stress the importance of instinct, such as Kinsey, point out that oral-genital contacts are prevalent in most mammals, especially the higher apes (Ford and Beach, 1951). It is possible that odors or pheromones released from the genitals of either sex may stimulate a reflexive licking response in both animals and humans. Also, "grooming" behavior is very common among most animal species. There is danger, however, in applying observations about animal behavior to humans. Because two species are observed performing the same behavior does not mean that the behavior has the same function; for instance, although oral sex has an erotic meaning among humans, it may be a nonsexual grooming response in other mammals.

Kinsey speculated that while oral sex was instinctive, cultural inhibitions were often powerful enough to overcome instinct. Learning plays a role in creating inhibition by teaching us, for instance, that the genitals are dirty. However, learning can also be important in helping to overcome our cultural inhibitions. John Gagnon and William Simon (1973) have commented on this dual role of learning in our attitudes toward oral sex. First, our society provides us with a set of messages that the substances and fluids from "that" part of the body are unclean and undesirable. Then, we learn that proficiency in oral sex is part of the expected repertoire of the sexually competent and mature individual. Gagnon

and Simon speculate that it is the interpersonal rewards of oral sex—that is, feedback from the partner that oral sex is enjoyable—that motivates us to overcome our learned aversion to oral-genital contact.

If we accept the notion that the pleasures of oral sex are learned, then we must also recognize the value of learning specific techniques of oral stimulation. Sexual anatomy and preferred patterns of stimulation vary from one individual to the next. In general, men express a preference for firm and rhythmic pressure around the penis, whereas women prefer gentle tongue movements over the labia and clitoral shaft (Hite, 1977). However, Comfort (1972) has pointed out the importance of individualizing techniques of oral sex to fit the needs of one's partner. What is pleasurable to one person may well be unpleasant to another, and good communication is necessary if partners are to recognize and meet each other's needs.

In fact, there is no one "right" way of performing oral sex, and the ability to learn from one's experience is probably the key element in developing effective oral sex techniques. It would be unfortunate, however, if the new acceptance of oral sex in our society was to lead to a new set of performance demands. Performance and failure are two sides of the same coin, and demands for perfect performance are sure to lead to stress. When oral sex is viewed as an act of intimate emotional experience, however, it can do much to enhance a sexual relationship.

ANAL SEX

Although attitudes have changed greatly over the past decades, stimulation of the anus for sexual purposes remains a source of conflict and confusion for many couples. *Anal sex* is condemned in the Judeo-Christian tradition and is illegal in many states. Although the statutes seldom mention anal sex specifically, laws against "sodomy" are often worded to include the placing of "unnatural objects" into "unnatural orifices." However, legal prosecutions for anal sex are rare, and probably it is social learning, rather than religious or legal prohibitions, that creates conflict about anal sex. As Gagnon and Simon (1973) point out, Western concerns with body odors and cleanliness must be overcome in order to engage in anal sex. Further, health authorities have done much to reinforce the belief that anal sex presents serious health risks, and most sex educators emphasize the importance of washing to avoid infections.

In spite of these problems, anal sex seems to be more acceptable and widespread now than it was during the time of Kinsey's surveys. Kinsey reported that while there was some anal play—that is, touching of the anus—among married couples, anal intercourse was infrequent. In contrast, Hunt reported that about half of the young married respondents in his survey would accept anal play with someone they loved. Among unmarried respondents, well over half of under-35 males and females had tried anal play at least once. Only about 25 percent of men and women agreed with the statement "Anal intercourse is wrong." The incidence of anal intercourse was correlated with subjects' ages: very few people over the age of 45 but about 14 percent of those aged 35 to 44 and nearly 25 percent of those under the age of 35 had tried anal intercourse in the past year. However, only about 6 percent reported engaging in anal intercourse sometimes or often. For the remainder it was a rare occurrence.

In the *Redbook* survey, less than half of the women reported having tried anal sex, but 21 percent had tried it often or occasionally. Among those women who had tried anal intercourse, 41 percent reported that it was enjoyable; the rest rated it as neutral to unpleasant. As in the Hunt study, younger women were more likely to try anal intercourse than older women. Further, the authors reported that women who experiment with anal sex are more likely to rate their sex lives as very good than women who are not willing to experiment; here again, however, it is not anal sex per se but "the uninhibited willingness to experiment, to explore all realms of sexuality, that makes for happy sex" (Tavris and Sadd, 1977, p. 94). The major motivating factor for performing anal intercourse was the woman's curiosity and her strong desire to please her partner.

There are both physiological and psychological reasons why stimulation or penetration of the anus can be perceived as pleasurable. Kinsey (1953) emphasized the rich nerve supply to the anal entrance, which, like the vaginal entrance, is much more sensitive than the interior part. He also noted that since the anal and genital areas share certain muscles, stimulation of one area may arouse the other area. For instance, contractions of the anal sphincter—the tight ring of muscle that holds the rectum closed—also produce contractions in the male and female genitals.

According to Kinsey, it is the attitude of the individual that is principally responsible for whether anal sex is experienced as pleasant or unpleasant. Some people are strongly attracted to anal sex because it has been regarded as taboo or forbidden. Anal sex has been the subject of much "psychologizing," and it has often been linked to the themes of dominance and submission. Although anal intercourse may demand a special degree of abandonment on the part of the female, Hunt emphasized that "it does not, as some may think, represent the brutalization and abuse of wives by sadistic husbands, but generally a more or less free choice by both partners of something they want to do together" (1974, p. 204).

In the Hite survey, slightly less than half of the women reported that they enjoyed "rectal contact" at least sometimes. Of those women who did enjoy such contact, however, less than half said that they enjoyed anal intercourse. The majority preferred gentle touching or, at most, finger penetration of the anus.

There is little information available about the number of women who reach orgasm during anal intercourse. Gagnon and Simon (1973) suggest that while orgasm may occur for some women, it is more likely to occur for males. Female orgasm frequencies are probably higher if clitoral or breast stimulation is added to anal stimulation.

Even among those women who find anal intercourse to be an erotic idea, however, there may be some difficulties in the practice of this activity. Perhaps the major difficulty is that if the anal muscles are not relaxed, penetration can cause discomfort or pain and may even result in injury to the tissues in the anal area. Because of this danger, Comfort goes so far as to make an exception of anal intercourse as a form of sexual experimentation: "Unlike almost any other common sexual practice, this one does have drawbacks. Usually the first try is painful . . . and extreme gentleness on the man's part is needed" (1972, p. 150).

THE SEXUAL BEHAVIOR OF HOMOSEXUAL MEN AND WOMEN

Homosexuals are often the subject of a number of contradictory sexual myths: that they are more sexually active that heterosexuals, or that they are less active; that they use a greater variety of sexual techniques than heterosexuals, or that their sexual repertoire is restricted; that they rigidly adopt "active" or "passive" roles, or that they are flexible in their role taking. In reality, it is as difficult to characterize the sexuality of homosexual men and women as it is to theorize about heterosexual behavior. The sexual activity of homosexuals is shaped and influenced by a wide variety of factors—age, experience, the duration of the relationship, individual sexual preferences, and so on.

In a culture where penile-vaginal intercourse is equated with the term "sex," it is difficult for most people to imagine what homosexuals do. But according to Hunt, "there's really very little that's strange or unusual about [homosexual sex acts] except that they're performed by two persons of the same sex. Most of the same physical acts are also used by the majority of straight persons, usually as preliminaries to heterosexual intercourse but sometimes in place of it" (1977, p. 81). Kinsey noted that female homosexuals used many techniques common to heterosexual petting. In describing their behavior, he reported that some women used only kissing and generalized body contact. Among women with extensive homosexual experience, kissing and manual stimulation of the breasts and genitals were nearly universal, while oral-genital contacts were reported by 78 percent. In addition, slightly more than half used "genital appositions which were designed to provide specific and mutual stimulation" (1953, p. 467). Contrary to popular myths, very few women used *penile substitutes*, or *dildos*. Interestingly, Kinsey found that experienced homosexual women had higher orgasm rates than heterosexual women who had been married for 5 years. He attributes this difference, in part, to the notion that two people of the same sex are better able to understand each other's sexual and emotional needs. For instance, both homosexual and heterosexual women tend to prefer general body stimulation, but the heterosexual males in Kinsey's sample were often unable to meet this need. But, as Kinsey points out, "It is, of course, quite possible for males to learn enough about female sexual responses to make their heterosexual contacts as effective as females make most homosexual contacts" (1953, p. 468).

Hunt (1974) found little change in the sexual activity of homosexuals since Kinsey's time. For instance, among active female homosexuals, the majority used mouth-breast contact and half used oral-genital stimulation. The most popular technique, used by 80 percent of the women, was general body-to-body contact. Once again, only one of six respondents had ever used a dildo.

Among active male homosexuals, about 66 percent had experienced fellatio as the "insertor," and 50 percent as the "insertee." Also, about half had experienced anal intercourse. The most popular and widely used technique was reciprocal manual masturbation. Hunt concludes that there is little evidence of "great freedom" in the sexual activity of homosexuals. He cautions, however, that his sample may not have reached a more sophisticated homosexual population that is as sexually experimental as the more "liberated" heterosexual groups.

Additional information on homosexual behavior is presented in a more recent study by

The lesbian sexual script typically involves a variety of body caresses. From a woodcut by Suzuki Morondadaba.

Alan Bell and Martin Weinberg (1978). They interviewed 293 women and 686 men from the San Francisco homosexual community. Subjects were recruited from a variety of sources: public ads, bars, personal contacts, gay baths, homophile organizations, mailing lists, and so on. Each subject was asked 528 questions in a Kinsey-like interview that lasted from about 2 to 5 hours.

Each male subject was asked whether he had performed any of the following sexual techniques in the past year: body rubbing to orgasm, masturbating or being masturbated by a partner, performing or receiving fellatio, performing or receiving anal intercourse. Almost all of the men had used five or more of these techniques, and about 25 percent had used all seven. Fellatio was the most common type of sexual contact and the one used most often by respondents; it was also reported as the most preferred sexual technique. Manual masturbation was second in use, followed by anal intercourse, and body rubbing.

Female subjects were questioned about their use, in the past year, of the following sexual techniques: body rubbing to orgasm, masturbating or being masturbated by their partner, performing or receiving cunnilingus. More than 75 percent of the women had used at least three of these techniques, and about 25 percent had used all five. Masturbation was both the most common and the most frequently used sexual technique, although the most preferred type of sexual contact was cunnilingus.

The influence of a subject's age on his or her sexual behavior was the same as is usually found for heterosexual samples—that is, the younger the subject, the greater the sexual repertoire employed. Bell and Weinberg hypothesize that younger homosexuals, like their heterosexual counterparts, are more sexually experimental and less inhibited than older homosexuals. They also suggest the pos-sibility that the older group may have used a greater variety of techniques in past years but, with increasing age, narrowed their repertoire to a few favorite techniques.

From these studies, it appears that homosexual techniques do, in general, follow the same patterns as heterosexual foreplay. Perhaps the major exception is anal intercourse, which occurs far more frequently among homosexual males than in heterosexual relationships. However, although the behaviors seem essentially the same, some people question whether the meaning of those behaviors can be identical when both partners are of the same sex.

In the traditional view of heterosexual contact, it has been assumed that the male plays the "active" and the female the "passive" role. This perspective has of course been challenged by many people, and there is evidence that the notion of rigid roles is somewhat less common now than in the past. In considering homosexual relationships, however, there is still a tendency to assume that the partners play rigid roles. "Straight people, in trying to understand what homosexuals do, naturally assume that in a sexual situation one gay person plays the masculine role and the other plays the feminine role" (Hunt, 1977, p. 89). Although such roles do exist in some homosexual relationships, Hunt suggests that this is the exception rather than the rule and may be a function of "special emotional problems" rather than a natural outgrowth of homosexuality. Roles among heterosexuals are often affected by a couple's moods, personal preferences, and individual needs, and there is no reason to think this is not also the case with homosexuals. "Like the majority of modern heterosexuals, they take turns starting things, are sometimes aggressive and sometimes yielding, will sometimes play one role and sometimes another, and at other times will play both" (Hunt, 1977, p. 92).

Conclusion

The list of sexual behaviors presented in this chapter is long, but it is by no means exhaustive. We have described several broad categories of behavior—such as oral sex—but there are obviously a vast number of ways of including this behavior in the script. One important characteristic of human beings is the ability to be creative, and this creative ability makes the list of sexual behaviors potentially limitless. So while we can identify certain behaviors or scripts as more frequent than others, there is no way that we can specify all possible human sexual scripts.

In discussing this broad range of sexual behaviors we have purposely avoided such terms as "right" or "wrong." Even "better" and "worse" seem inappropriate words in the context of studying human sexuality. Value judgments do, of course, play an important role in our personal decisions about sexuality, but they cannot easily be applied to the behavior of others. An old Latin maxim makes this point rather well: *de gustibus non est disputandum*, or, "In matters of taste there can be no debate."

Summary

1. Sexual behavior tends to be organized into mental plans, or scripts, that include both a sequence of specific sexual activities and the emotions associated with those activities. Scripts have a number of dimensions: for instance, simplicity-complexity, flexibility-rigidity, and romantic-unromantic.

2. Masturbation has been condemned by religious and medical authorities, but remains a near universal sexual activity. Fears that it will cause physical harm have lessened, but there is still some concern that, in certain situations, masturbation may be a cause or effect of psychological difficulties. In the twenty years between the Kinsey reports and the Hunt survey, incidence of masturbation among married men and women increased; at the same time, there was a decrease in the age at which masturbation began.

3. Interpersonal scripts include such activities as touching, petting, kissing, oral and anal stimulation. Attitudes toward these activities vary from one culture to another, and in our own culture, behaviors such as oral sex have become quite a bit more acceptable in the past 20 years.

4. Homosexual scripts tend to include many of the same behaviors that are found in heterosexual foreplay. The notion that homosexuals tend to assume masculine or feminine roles in a sexual interaction is open to question. Just as heterosexual couples may vary their sexual script in order to meet their personal needs and preferences, so may homosexual couples be flexible in the sexual roles they choose to play.

EIGHT

Sexual Behavior II: Intercourse

Overview

How many synonyms for "intercourse" can you think of? There is probably no other human activity for which we have as many different slang and scientific labels as sexual intercourse. Each culture has its own preferred terminology, and every age and period of history has seen the development of a new set of popular expressions. In Chaucer's time, the word "swive" was a common expression for intercourse. Another old English term that has disappeared from our vocabulary is "jape," which also meant to joke or trick. The still popular term "fuck" began to appear in English ribald verses during the sixteenth and seventeenth centuries, and the term is probably derived from an old Germanic verb for penetrate.

Most scientific terms for intercourse are derived from Latin words. For example, the word "coitus" comes from the Latin word *coire*, which means coming together. Similarly, the word "copulation" is derived from the Latin word *copulare*, which means fastening together or linking. The word "intercourse" itself is also derived from a Latin term —*intercurrere*—which means to run between. The word "intercourse" can also be qualified to mean something other than insertion of the penis into the vagina. The expression "oral intercourse" is sometimes used for cunnilingus or fellatio, and "anal intercourse" for insertion of the penis into the anus. "Femoral intercourse" means rubbing the penis between the partner's thighs and is synonymous with the slang expression "dry humping." When the word "intercourse" is used without qualification, however, it generally means penile-vaginal intercourse.

Many people feel that the "proper" terms for intercourse are unsatisfactory.

The words that people use for sex start with *conjugation*, which is what lower organisms do, and *copulation*, which is for higher animals. *Sexual intercourse* is for people. Scientists call it co'-i-tis, although if it makes them nervous they sometimes call it co-igh'tus, but co'-i-tus is what it is. *Sexual union* is something you can talk about in front of an audience, but only on Sunday. . . .

The trouble with all the words above is that they seem cold and dry and sterile even though they are not. Conjugation sounds like making a fire by rubbing two eggs together. Copulation sounds wet but slightly repulsive, while coitus sounds sticky, like walking through molasses in a pair of sneakers. Sexual intercourse is an okay phrase to use in public or in writing, although it sounds too sensible to be much fun. (Berne, 1970, pp. 2–3)

The act of intercourse undoubtedly occupies the center stage of our sexual script. Perhaps the major reason for this is that intercourse, unlike the many other forms of sexual behavior presented in the previous chapter, is the means to impregnation and the reproduction of our species. Although the widespread use of contraception in our society has gone a long way to separate the procreational from the recreational uses of intercourse, we continue to attach a special significance to penile-

vaginal sex. A popular expression of adolescents, "going all the way," expresses the distinction we draw between intercourse and other forms of sexual expression.

Patterns of intercourse in our society have undergone significant changes in the past century. In the atmosphere of sexual prudery that characterized the Victorian period in Europe and America, sexual intercourse was often referred to as "carnal indulgence" — an activity that was intrinsically demeaning or degrading to those who practiced it. Medical authorities of the time frequently cautioned the public about the physical and mental dangers of "overindulgence" and suggested that even intercourse between married couples could be harmful if practiced in excess. For example, Dr. William Alcott, a prominent New England physician of the pre–Civil War era who was generally regarded as a "moderate" on sexual matters, advocated that married couples should engage in sexual intercourse no more than once a month.

In this chapter we review the results of a number of scientific surveys which show the dramatic changes that have taken place in the past few decades, and consider the effects of the so-called sexual revolution on the various dimensions of intercourse — such as age of first experience, frequency, and duration. Finally, we consider ways in which the intercourse script varies from one culture to another, and how men and women in our own society feel about the central act of the sexual drama.

An Evolutionary Perspective

Let us begin by comparing the sexual intercourse patterns of human beings with those of other mammals. In all mammalian species, impregnation depends on ejaculation of the male sperm-semen into the female vagina,

and heterosexual intercourse is the means through which this goal is achieved (unless one wishes to include such asexual means of conception as those used for "test-tube" babies). Intercourse is therefore a sexual behavior that is directly linked to the all-important process of reproduction and survival of the species; without intercourse, the history of a species would be that of a single generation. Because of this link between sexual intercourse and reproduction, it is meaningful and important for us to consider the effects of natural selection on patterns of intercourse. From an evolutionary perspective, the key question becomes: "How does a particular pattern of intercourse contribute to reproductive success in a particular species?"

Intercourse behavior in lower mammals is almost totally under the control of the estrus cycle of the female. Estrus is brought on only by a rise in estrogen levels as the time for ovulation approaches, and it usually results in physical changes that make the female sexually attractive to the males of her species. A female is likely to seek out suitable mating partners only during the period that she is "in heat." After ovulation, estrogen levels decline and sexual receptivity generally ends until the next cycle begins. Control of sexual intercourse by means of the estrus cycle is highly adaptive, as it ensures that the frequency of copulation is highest at those times that fertilization of the egg is most likely to occur.

Human beings have lost this dependence on the estrus cycle, and estrogen levels in the human female seem to play a relatively insignificant role in determining when intercourse will occur (see Chapter 6). We can view this freedom from hormonal control as either an advantage or a disadvantage from a reproductive point of view. A lower mammal female will go for months in between estrus cycles without copulating, and human beings therefore have higher rates of intercourse overall. On the other hand, human intercourse is much less "efficient," in that it often occurs at times when there is no possibility of impregnation. This loss of reproductive efficiency, which comes with untying sexual intercourse from the hormone cycle, has led psychologist Frank Beach to conclude that "compensatory modifications had to occur which would ensure that a sufficient number of matings

According to Beach, human beings are differentiated from other animals by their capacity for symbolic behavior. Sexually, this means that they can be aroused by pictures that are not themselves directly sexual. *Nomad* by James Rosenquist, 1963. *(Albright-Knox Art Gallery, Buffalo, New York. Gift of Seymour H. Knox)*

would take place when [human] females were about to ovulate and thus could be impregnated" (1976, p. 356).

From Beach's point of view, human intercourse patterns have evolved primarily as a way of coping with this reduction in reproductive efficiency. For example, he speculates that the human capacity for symbolic behavior is one way in which we compensate for the loss of hormonal signals. Human beings can be sexually stimulated by words, pictures, and a variety of sounds and gestures. The development of the nuclear family based upon heterosexual pair-bonding is another way of meeting this need:

Development of the family may be viewed as an adaptive change tending to encourage frequency and regularity of heterosexual coitus. It is a reasonable assumption that existence of the family with the associated intensification and prolongation of interpersonal bonds and dependencies would promote more frequent intercourse than would be likely to occur in the absence of family structure. (Beach, 1976, p. 360)

A third evolutionary development to compensate for the lack of estrus, Beach suggests, is the female orgasm. Sexual orgasm in females of other species, if it occurs at all, seems to have little or no effect on mating behavior during estrus. Desmond Morris points out that orgasm would even be a possible disadvantage for a female animal in heat: "While they are in heat, there is no time to lose, they must keep going at all costs. If they experienced intense orgasms, they would then waste valuable potential mating time" (1967, p. 78).

Human females certainly have the capacity for orgasm, even though many women do not achieve this potential, and orgasm during intercourse is an important source of gratification for many women. Further, as Beach notes, since orgasm does not depend on the state of the hormone cycle, in human females it acts as

a continuously motivating factor for sexual intercourse.

How did the specific capacity for female orgasm during intercourse evolve? There are several factors that might account for this evolutionary development. First, an important effect of the upright posture that evolved as human beings developed bipedalism (walking on two legs) was that the human pelvis became tilted more to the front. As a result, the human vagina lies at a different angle than the vaginas of other species, which means that human intercourse is possible in a face-to-face position. The typical position of intercourse for all other land mammals is rear-entry, with the male usually standing or crouching behind the female. According to Beach, human intercourse in the face-to-face position, with either the male or the female on top, is important in allowing for continuous clitoral stimulation during intercourse. And because the clitoris is the sexual organ most sensitive to stimulation, the development of this position of intercourse may have been an important factor in the evolution of female orgasm.

Not all experts agree with Beach that human intercourse patterns and the capacity of human females to experience orgasm have evolved as compensations for the lack of estrus control. In fact, a radically different point of view has been proposed by well-known psychiatrist Mary Jane Sherfey. According to Sherfey (1973), the effect of civilization is not to promote greater frequency of intercourse, as Beach suggests, but to restrain and control the potentially "insatiable" demands of female sexuality. Sherfey maintains that the females of other species (especially primates) are capable of orgasm but are limited in this respect by the controls of estrus and inadequate clitoral stimulation during intercourse. Human females, on the other hand, have a highly developed sexual capacity and a freedom from

Most animals typically mate in the rear-entry intercourse position. (© Fran Allan/Animals Animals)

direct hormonal control, in addition to the potential for multiple orgasms—all of which, according to Sherfey, have contributed to the evolution of "an inordinate cyclic sexual drive" in women. To support her claims, she presents evidence that in preagricultural times it was not uncommon for women to dominate society and to engage in much higher rates of intercourse than we find today. The conclusion of her theory is that modern patriarchal societies are based on the suppression of female sexuality:

It is conceivable that the *forceful* suppression of women's inordinate sexual demands was a prerequisite to the dawn of every modern civilization and almost every living culture. Primitive woman's sexual drive was too strong, too susceptible to the fluctuating extremes of an impelling, aggressive erotism to withstand the disciplined requirements of a settled family life. (1973, p. 138

At the present time there is no direct way of proving or disproving either of these two theories. Although Beach's arguments are based on more extensive scientific research, we must consider Sherfey's point of view as a challenging and controversial alternative. Finally, these evolutionary theories can be seen to have important sociopolitical implications. Beach's idea that the pair-bond relationship is necessary for adequate reproduction can be used to defend maintaining the status quo of the nuclear family. Alternatively, Sherfey's arguments can be used to defend the right of women to greater social and sexual freedom.

First Intercourse and Premarital Sex

Among most mammalian species, the timing of first intercourse coincides with the development of physical maturity. The female typically does not display any sexual behavior until the estrus cycle begins; the male may engage in sex play but cannot ejaculate until puberty. Primates are an exception to the rule — for example, chimpanzees often engage in a range of sexual behaviors, including attempts at intercourse, before they are capable of reproduction.

The timing of first intercourse among humans is governed primarily by social, rather than biological, factors and rules. Like other primates, humans are capable of having intercourse before puberty, but few human societies condone such behavior. Ford and Beach (1951) found that in many societies sexual intercourse is forbidden until the female has reached puberty, but after the menarche she is free to have intercourse with any number of partners. In the same way, many African societies enforce male chastity until the boy has undergone some form of puberty ceremony or initiation rite, but after this ceremony, the male is free to have intercourse because he has achieved adult status. In some cultures, however, intercourse is prohibited until marriage or betrothal has taken place. To enforce this prohibition, males and females may be kept apart, placed in different living quarters, and strictly chaperoned until after the wedding date. Generally, females are monitored more closely than males. Among the Hopi Indians, for example, girls and boys are separated from the age of 10 until marriage, and girls are expected to remain chaste. Boys are less restricted in their behavior and may attempt to have intercourse before marriage. When an unmarried couple is caught having intercourse, it is the female who must take the blame for their illicit behavior.

In many ways, our own culture has followed a similar pattern for regulating the first intercourse experience. According to the Judeo-Christian tradition, young men and women are expected to abstain from intercourse until marriage, and failure to uphold this rule is usually blamed on the female. Since most boys and girls reach puberty in their early teens,

and most marriages do not take place until the late teens or early twenties, there is a gap of from 5 to 10 years when intercourse may be desired but is considered socially inappropriate.

As is often the case among humans, however, our attitudes toward sexuality do not necessarily reflect our sexual behavior. Thus in spite of popular condemnation of premarital intercourse, a large percentage of men and women have their first intercourse experience before marriage or outside of a marital relationship. In addition, the trend has been toward having first intercourse at an increasingly early age (see the boxed extract).

In 1948, Kinsey reported a strong relationship between a male's age at first intercourse and his social class. More than half of all males with no college education had had their first intercourse experience by the age of 16 years. But only 15 percent of college-educated males had had coital experience by the age of 16 years. Among 20-year-old males, more than 80 percent of the high school-educated but only 44 percent of the college-educated had experienced intercourse.

For females, Kinsey found that the age of first intercourse related both to educational level and to age at marriage. Although women with less education tended to start having intercourse at an earlier age than those with college education, the important factor appeared to be the earlier age of marriage for less-educated women. For instance, grade school–educated women started having intercourse about 5 years earlier than women with higher education. However, grade school–educated women also tended to marry several years earlier than more-educated women. Thus Kinsey noted that "among the females who had married at a given age, approximately the same percentages had had premarital coitus, irrespective of whether they belonged to high school, college, or graduate

groups" (Kinsey *et al.*, 1953, p. 294). In other words, about half of all women had had intercourse before marriage; lower-class women, who married earlier, had also had intercourse earlier in their lives.

How much have things changed since Kinsey's reports? According to Hunt, a dramatic series of changes have occurred, dating from about 1965: "To some extent the younger generation of American men, and to a very marked extent the younger generation of American women, are rapidly adopting a standard of behavior different from that of their elders" (1974, p. 150). Indeed, Hunt goes so far as to suggest that "only a tiny minority of females and an even smaller one of males, consisting of the deeply religious, the emotionally disturbed and the personally undesirable, will remain virginal through their teens or will be virginal at the time of marriage" (p. 150).

This is certainly a strong statement, but considerable survey data back it up. Among the married respondents to Hunt's survey, 95 percent of 18- to 24-year-old males and 81 percent of similarly aged females reported having had premarital intercourse. Among college-educated males—the group Kinsey found was least likely to have premarital intercourse—fully half had had premarital intercourse by the age of 17 years. For females, dramatic increases occurred at all educational levels. In a survey of 15- to 19-year-old females (Zelnick and Kantner, 1972), almost half of the 19-year-old women reported having had premarital intercourse.

The results of the *Redbook* survey also confirmed a dramatic shift in female premarital sexual activity. For example, among married

women of all ages, only two of every ten were virgins at the time of their marriage. When the age of the respondent was taken into account, the shift was even more evident, as shown in Table 8.1. Educational level had no effect on

TABLE 8.1

Premarital Sex in Relation to Age

Age	Percentage Reporting Premarital Sex
Under 20	96
20–24	91
25–29	84
30–34	74
35–39	74
40 and over	68

Source: C. Tavris and S. Sadd, *The Redbook Report on Female Sexuality* (New York: Delacorte Press, 1977), p. 34.

(continued on page 272)

The First Time

I knew what was going to happen to me, and I wasn't scared, because I trusted him. I knew that he wouldn't hurt me. But I was just kind of in shock, you know. I remember he was asking me: "Are you okay?" I just lay there. It doesn't make me feel bad or anything even though I was pretty young.

I was thirteen and she was ten. We were trying out having sex for the first time. She was my very best friend's sister. It happens, believe me. I know a lot of ten- or eleven-year-old girls who are pregnant now. Anyway ours lasted for one or two years. But we really didn't mean much to each other. We had nothing.

These statements were made by two of the subjects in Robert Sorenson's (1973) study of adolescent sexuality. In this study, Sorenson constructed an extensive questionnaire to be administered to 13- to 19-year-old males and females. A national sample of 2.042 households from 200 city, suburban, and rural areas was selected. In about 60 percent of these households it was possible to obtain parental permission to have the adolescent complete the questionnaire. Finally, the data from 411 completed questionnaires were computer analyzed for inclusion in the survey.

Sorenson found that 52 percent of the adolescent participants in his study had experienced intercourse and that for many of these individuals the experience of first intercourse was a memorable one. Even when the event had taken place several years prior to the research study, most subjects could vividly recall the experience and were able to report their feelings in some detail. The results of this study are very revealing about how "the first time" feels to boys and girls of different ages and different levels of sexual experience.

First, it is clear that the male subjects, on the average, had looked forward more to their first intercourse experience and generally felt better afterward.

Many [boys] feel that a milestone has been reached and that they are closer to being adults after the first intercourse encounter. Boys report twice as frequently as girls that they experienced feelings of maturity, joy, and thrill after their first intercourse. (p. 189)

On the other hand, about two-thirds of the female subjects reported feeling afraid at the time, and about one-third felt guilty, embarrassed, or worried. However, when the reactions of the girls are broken down by age, a somewhat surprising finding emerges—the younger the age of the girl at the time of first intercourse, the more positively was the event experienced by her.

Girls fifteen and younger report twice as frequently as girls sixteen and older that they were excited, and four times more frequently that they were joyful. Younger girls report only half as frequently as older girls that they felt hurt, foolish, or disappointed. (p. 205)

A possible explanation for this finding is that girls who preserve their virginity by resisting intercourse during the early years of adolescence might build up greater anxiety or guilt than those who engage spontaneously in intercourse at an earlier age.

Another significant difference between the first intercourse experience of boys and girls is in their perceptions of the partner relationship. Table 8.2 shows that the majority of girls (57 percent) were either going steady with the boy, or had plans to marry him. On the other hand, 44 percent of the boys hardly knew their partners at the time of first intercourse. It is interesting to note, however, that none of the boys in the Sorenson study had their first experience with a prostitute. For many young men of the previous generation, prostitution was either a necessary or a preferred recourse for sexual initiation (Hunt, 1974).

TABLE 8.2

Relationship with First Sex Partner Prior to Intercourse

	Percentage of Boys	Percentage of Girls
My wife/husband after we were married	0	2
A girl/boy I was going steady with and planned to marry	7	36
A girl/boy I was going steady with but had no definite plans to marry	18	21
A girl/boy I knew well and liked a lot, even though we weren't going together	31	25
A girl/boy I knew slightly and was more or less friendly with	19	5
A girl/boy I had met only a little while before the time we had sex together	25	10
Someone who raped me	—	1

Source: R. C. Sorenson, *Adolescent Sexuality in Contemporary America* (New York: World Publishing, 1973), p. 198.

Why is the partner relationship so much more important in the first sexual experience of girls than boys? According to Sorenson's findings, many girls rationalize their decision to have intercourse on the basis of their affection for the partner and often commit themselves to intercourse in the hopes of further strengthening the relationship. Boys tend to view their virginity as more of a liability than an asset and often initiated the first intercourse experience as a way of enhancing their masculinity. In some instances, boys specifically avoided intercourse with a girl whom they felt would take it as a commitment to marriage.

An additional difference between boys and girls is in their preference for first intercourse with a partner who is more or less sexually experienced than themselves. As one might expect, the boys in Sorenson's study generally preferred to have their first intercourse with a female partner who was also a virgin—presumably because a more experienced female partner could arouse feelings of insecurity or inadequacy. Most girls, on the other hand, chose a male partner who was at least a year or two older and generally more sexually experienced—presumably because girls generally feel more secure and trusting with a more experienced partner.

Finally, it is rather disturbing to note that most adolescents do not use any form of contraception during their first intercourse experience. Sorenson reported that only 32 percent of his adolescent subjects used some form of birth control for their first intercourse. For the younger age group, for whom the consequences of unwanted pregnancy could be the most damaging, the proportion was even lower—only 26 percent.

the chances of having premarital sex, but religious devoutness did have some influence. Although those reporting strong religious conviction were less likely to have premarital sex, fully 61 percent of those who said they were "strongly religious" and 78 percent of those who said they were "fairly religious" also had experienced premarital sex. Tavris and Sadd point out that it is difficult to know whether strong religious conviction prevents premarital sex or whether those who have premarital sex are likely to become less religiously devout. Clearly, young women who believe strongly in religious prohibitions against sex but nevertheless are subject to strong peer pressure toward premarital sexual activity are placed in an awkward emotional position. Some may choose to ignore social pressure while maintaining their religious convictions, others may modify their religious beliefs to accommodate premarital sex. However, a large number probably live with the guilt and conflict produced by trying to combine two irreconcilable sets of standards.

Concerning the age of first intercourse, Tavris and Sadd found that the effects of religion and education were in contrast. Whereas education did not affect the total number of women having premarital intercourse, college-educated women did tend to wait longer to have their first intercourse experience than those with a grade school education. For example, by age 15, 59 percent of women with a grade school education had had intercourse; in contrast, 20 percent of high school graduates and only 7 percent of college graduates had had intercourse by age 15. In contrast, religious devotion did affect the total number of women having premarital intercourse, but it did not seem to influence the age at which intercourse began. In other words, if a religious woman was going to have premarital intercourse, she would probably have this

experience at about the same age as her nonreligious sister.

Survey research over the past 10 years leaves little doubt that premarital intercourse has become normative and may become close to universal in the future. For some people, this trend is a rational and acceptable alternative to the standards of the past; for others, premarital sex brings fears of widespread promiscuity and moral decline. Little can be done to reconcile these differing points of view, but it is worthwhile to look more closely at the specifics of the situation.

Examination of the data on premarital sexual intercourse reveals little evidence that the "average" woman who is sexually active before marriage is in any sense promiscuous. In Kinsey's study, more than half of the women who had premarital intercourse did so with only one partner—the man they later married. Similarly, Morton Hunt found that 54 percent of the females with premarital sexual experience restricted themselves to a single partner. Finally, 51 percent of comparable women in the *Redbook* survey had had a single premarital sexual partner.

Among women having more than one premarital sexual partner, the vast majority had had from two to five partners. Thus there is little evidence of casual sex among most young people. Indeed, while premarital intercourse has become acceptable to most adolescents, it is acceptable only in the context of emotional commitment or closeness. Certainly, some individuals have accepted a "swinging" sexual life style, but such people do not tend to come from the young and unmarried groups; according to Hunt, "swingers" are more common among the male and female members of older single, separated, or divorced groups. Therefore, Hunt concludes that "while today almost any 'nice girl' will do, before marriage, what only the daring girl would do a generation ago, today's 'nice girl' is still guiding herself according to romantic and historically rooted values'' (1974, p. 152).

What of young males? Hunt notes that while they tend to have a greater number of sexual partners before marriage than do females, males are also subject to constraints that include ''firm emotional ties, conventional stand-ards regarding fidelity and a definite social identity as a couple'' (1974, p. 153). Thus while the sexual revolution has deeply touched one aspect of our sexuality—the likelihood of having premarital intercourse—it has not greatly altered our feeling that sexual intercourse is appropriate only within the context of emotional commitment.

Frequency of Intercourse

On the basis of cross-cultural research, it is clear that no ''standard'' frequency of sexual intercourse exists. Biology does impose some constraints on the potential for intercourse and orgasm, as does the aging process, but the major influences on coital frequency appear to be social in origin. For example, the male refractory period may limit intercourse frequency, and in older males this refractory period tends to lengthen; nevertheless, in some cultures the older male is more sexually active than is the adolescent male in our own society.

Different cultures have vastly different expectations about what constitutes a ''normal'' frequency of intercourse. Among the Mangaians of Polynesia, for instance, intercourse and orgasm are seen as important and necessary. Males under the age of 30 report having intercourse from five to seven nights per week, with an average of two to three orgasms per night. Older males report one orgasm per night, but still note that they have intercourse from two to four nights per week. Although the Mangaians are sexually active before marriage, even among the married it is expected that intercourse will occur almost every night (Marshall, 1971). In contrast, the Capaya tribe of Latin America appears to operate at considerably lower sexual levels.

While the Capaya admire and emphasize the importance of male virility, the average coital frequencies reported by newly married males is usually about once or twice per week (Altschuler, 1971).

From their cross-cultural survey, Ford and Beach (1951) concluded that in most societies, adults normally engage in intercourse once a day during the periods when sex is permitted. Indeed, some groups expect that younger males and females will have intercourse many times on the same day; and among polygamous tribes, a man may be expected to have intercourse with each of his wives in a single night. Even in the most sexually active cultures, however, on numerous occasions intercourse is taboo. For instance, some cultures forbid intercourse with a woman who is menstruating, pregnant, or nursing a child. An intercourse taboo may also be applied in connection with certain religious rites, at times of war, and for men and women performing certain occupational roles.

Compared to most primitive cultures, intercourse frequencies in the United States are fairly low. A 1931 survey (Dickinson and Beam) reported that the most common frequency for married couples was between two and three times per week. Less than 15 percent of couples reported having intercourse on a daily basis, with a similar number reporting intercourse less than once per month. Despite the "sexual revolution" of the 1970s, there appear to have been few changes in this rate over the past 50 years (see Table 8.3).

It seems clear that our relatively low rates of sexual intercourse do not reflect a biological limitation, since many primitive peoples have intercourse frequencies considerably higher than our own. Further, it is unlikely that widespread social taboos can account for our lower coital frequencies: most surveys focus on coital frequency for the married, and marriage is the one context in which sexual intercourse has complete social approval. Indeed, marital coitus is considered an important, valuable, and highly satisfying aspect of the marriage relationship. Why, then, are our marital intercourse rates fairly low in comparison to the rates found for other cultures?

One factor that appears to have played a role in setting rates for marital intercourse is religious devoutness. Kinsey reported that religiously active Protestant males had intercourse at rates that were 20 to 30 percent lower than inactive Protestants. He explained this difference as resulting from religious inhibi-

tions against premarital sex; even after marriage, Kinsey suggested, these sexual prohibitions continue to inhibit marital intercourse. Interestingly, Kinsey did not find a relationship between coital rates and religious devotion for married females. Devout Catholic women aged 26 to 30 reported having intercourse a median of 2.2 times per week; for inactive Catholic women in the same age group, the median was 2.1 times per week.

According to Kinsey, the reason why male religious devotion affected coital rates whereas female devotion did not was because it was the male who determined rates of marital intercourse. In Kinsey's time the responsibility and indeed the motivation for having intercourse came primarily from the male; thus the intercourse rate was likely to be determined by the husband's, rather than the wife's, religious beliefs. Twenty years later, Hunt found that there was still a relationship between religious devotion and marital intercourse rates, with religion continuing to exert an inhibitory effect on coital rate. However, Hunt found it was the woman's religious devoutness, rather than the man's, that tended to depress coital frequency. To explain this reversal, Hunt suggests that women are now playing a more active role in setting the rates for intercourse in marriage.

Another interesting change that has occurred in the interval between Kinsey and Hunt is the discrepancy between husbands' and wives' estimates of coital frequency. According to Kinsey, wives were likely to report a higher rate of intercourse than were their husbands:

Studies of paired spouses indicate that females estimate the frequencies of their marital coitus a bit higher than males estimate theirs, evidently because some females object to the frequencies of coitus [want it less often] and therefore overestimate the amount they are actually having. Males, on the other hand, often wish that they

TABLE 8.3

Marital Coitus in the United States: Frequency per Week, 1938–1949 and 1972

1938–1949		1972	
Age	*Median*	*Age*	*Median*
16–25	2.45	18–24	3.25
26–35	1.95	25–34	2.55
36–45	1.40	35–44	2.00
46–55	0.85	45–54	1.00
56–60	0.50	55 and over	1.00

Source: Morton Hunt, *Sexual Behavior in the 1970's.* New York: Dell, 1974, p. 196.

were having coitus more frequently, and consistently underestimate the amount they actually have. (Kinsey *et al.*, 1953, p. 349)

In contrast, Hunt found that if any discrepancy existed between husbands' and wives' estimates of coital frequency, it was in the direction of the men providing higher estimates than their mates. This was especially so among younger couples. Hunt interprets this discrepancy as indicating that it is the young women who now perceive their coital rates as too low.

Results from the *Redbook* survey also contrast with Kinsey's suggestion that in 1953 women were having intercourse more often than they wanted to. Tavris and Sadd found that only 4 percent of the women in their sample expressed dissatisfaction about having intercourse too often; 38 percent felt that they were not having intercourse often enough. According to Tavris and Sadd, "one of the most remarkable findings from the Redbook study is the dramatic shift away from the 'she won't let me' lament of the male and the 'he's oversexed' complaint of the female. Today's marital dilemma is ''He doesn't want to''' (1977, p. 68).

One factor that is consistently associated with marital intercourse rates is male and female age—the older the couple, the less often they have intercourse. Kinsey reported that among women who married in their late teens, the median frequency of intercourse was 2.8 times per week; this figure dropped to 2.2 times per week for women who were 30 years old, 1.5 times per week for 40-year-old women, and once per week for those aged 50 years. This decrease, Kinsey notes, is not paralleled by a steady decline in any other aspect of female sexual activity.

Almost 25 years later, this decrease in intercourse frequency with increasing age was still evident in results from the *Redbook* survey. For instance, about one-fourth of newly married

Word Job. (© *Jules Feiffer*)

women reported having intercourse more than four times per week; among women married 1 to 4 years, this percentage dropped to 12 percent, and among women married 8 or more years, only 5 percent had intercourse more than four times per week. While older women clearly tended to have less active sex lives, this did not necessarily mean that they were less satisfied with their intercourse rates. Older women were no more likely than young women to express dissatisfaction with coital frequency. Thus it seems likely that with increasing age we expect that we will become less sexually active, and our behavior tends to conform to this expectation.

Although Hunt emphasizes that marital intercourse frequencies have increased since the time of Kinsey—he reports a median of 2.55 times per week among those aged 25 to 34, as compared with 1.95 in the Kinsey study—it is clear that this higher rate is still low when compared with data from other cultures. Factors such as age, length of marriage, and religious conviction do seem to play a role in setting our intercourse rates, but they do not provide a sufficient explanation for why our intercourse rates overall are only about one-third of those found in Polynesia. According to Gagnon (1977), a better explanation for our coital rates is to be found in two factors: how our culture prepares us for marital sex and the conditions of our sexual lives within marriage.

Whereas we spend a great deal of time learning to find and attract a mate, we pay relatively little attention to remaining attractive after marriage. In addition, the presence of children tends to complicate marital sexuality—for instance, a man may find it difficult to reconcile his mate's roles as sexual partner and mother. Further, boredom may result from repetition of the same sexual script and become an inhibiting factor for some couples, although other couples may find such repetition comfortable and satisfying.

A final but very important factor in regulating intercourse frequency is individual differences. Every sex researcher, from Kinsey through Hunt and the *Redbook* survey, has noted the huge individual differences in coital rates. Hunt, for example, reported that although the median rate of marital coitus for 35- to 44-year-old men was just under 100 per year, some men in that group had intercourse with their wives only two or three times in a year, others several hundred times. With such enormous variation among individuals, it becomes difficult to generalize about coital frequencies. Just as we cannot evaluate our society's sexuality by comparing it with that of a vastly different society—say, that of the Polynesians—it makes little sense to compare ourselves individually with people of differing age, sexual history, and personal preferences.

Duration of Intercourse

In most mammalian species, including human beings, the amount of time spent in the act of intercourse depends to a large extent on the time required for the male to ejaculate after intromission. Among apes and chimpanzees, for example, ejaculation usually takes place in less than 30 seconds, although males of other primate species, such as the macaque monkeys, will delay ejaculation by dismounting a number of times before they ejaculate (Ford and Beach, 1951). The "kings of the jungle"—the lion and the elephant—both ejaculate in less than 30 seconds. According to Ford and Beach the longest intercourse durations have been recorded for the mink and the sable. It seems that these animals are able to continue intercourse for up to 8 hours, and even though the males ejaculate a number of times during this period, intromission is maintained.

Intercourse durations also vary a great deal from one culture to another. For example, among the traditional sexual scripts of China and India considerable emphasis is placed on the protraction of intercourse through techniques of delayed ejaculation:

In ancient and esoteric Taoist and Tantric doctrine, the utmost prolongation of the act of sexual intercourse is said to be spiritually, physically, mentally, and supernaturally beneficial to both male and female. (Edwardes and Masters, 1962, p. 105)

According to these same authors, Muhammad practiced prolonging intercourse for several hours without ejaculation ("coitus reservatus") in order to build his physical strength and mental prowess. The people of Bali believe that hasty intercourse results in a deformed child. In contrast, the men of Ifugao, an island in the South Pacific, rarely engage in foreplay and ejaculate almost immediately after penetration.

The concept of prolonging intercourse through delayed ejaculation—sometimes referred to as "Karezza"—has met with a mixed response in the West. Van de Velde, for example, vehemently opposed it on the grounds that prolonged tumescence would lead to genital congestion and "emotional irritability." Van de Velde originated a trend still common among Western sex experts of emphasizing the physiological and psychological release and relaxation functions of both male and female orgasm. However, it is our view that the factors that determine the duration of intercourse have little bearing on physiological criteria; rather, they are closely linked to social conventions and prevailing sex role expectations. For example, because lower-class males in the Kinsey survey generally adhered to a concept of masculinity that involved a rapid, goal-oriented approach to intercourse, with little concern for the satisfaction of the female partner, many of these men ejaculated within 2 minutes of intromission.

There is an emerging historical trend in our society toward longer duration of intercourse. Several factors appear to account for this trend, including greater recognition of the sexual rights of women, more variety in conventional sexual scripts, and a current tendency to view a man's ability to control and delay ejaculation as an indication of sexual competence. Statistics on average duration of intercourse show a dramatic change in the years since the Kinsey studies. Precise comparisons are difficult to draw for three reasons: (1) Kinsey failed to obtain very clear information on this subject beyond the fact that half or more of his male sample ejaculated within 2 minutes of intromission, and this statistic was not assessed directly in the female study. (2) Kinsey's sample included a substantial proportion of lower-class males, who, as we have noted, were more likely to ejaculate rapidly and show little concern with prolonging intercourse. (3) Subjective estimates of the duration of intercourse are often unreliable (see the boxed extract). Although recognizing these problems of comparison, Hunt nevertheless drew the following conclusion:

We find an increase in the median duration of coitus of such magnitude as to make most of our other indicators of change pale into insignificance. . . . The increase in typical duration reflects the more relaxed enjoyment, greater mutuality, and increased variety that now characterize marital coitus. (1974, p. 204)

Hunt based his conclusion on the finding in the *Playboy* survey of a mean intercourse duration of *10 minutes* (approximately five times as long as Kinsey's mean duration). In addition, Hunt discovered a lack of significant difference in the mean duration of intercourse for different socioeconomic and educational groups. In fact, he even reported a slight tendency for lower-class men to prolong intercourse more than college-educated controls—a surprising reversal of the trend shown in the Kinsey study. Hunt also found that younger persons in the sample reported taking more time in intercourse than did older respondents, data that contradicts the notion of rapid

Estimating the Duration of Intercourse

Most surveys of sexual behavior assume that respondents are able to provide reasonably accurate estimates of the duration of sexual intercourse. However, the circumstances of intercourse are such that very few survey respondents have actually timed themselves in the act, and estimates of intercourse duration are always based on retrospective recall. When researchers at the Indiana University School of Medicine (Levitt and Duffy, 1977) conducted an experiment on time estimates of sexual behavior, some interesting findings emerged.

The subjects in this experiment were all sophomore medical student volunteers—88 males and 25 females. Instead of estimating the time of their own sexual behavior, the students were all shown a classroom film in which a young couple act out a complete foreplay and intercourse script. At the time of watching the film, the subjects were not aware of the purpose of the experiment and were given no specific instructions other than to pay close attention to the movie.

When the students returned to the lecture room 24 hours later, they were all asked to estimate how long the foreplay and intercourse parts of the film had lasted. Half of the group were to put down their answers in minutes or seconds, the other half were to judge whether the times were above or below "average." The results of the study were further broken down by whether the subjects were male or female, and married or unmarried.

The most interesting finding of the study was that students were able to estimate the time of foreplay in the movie with much greater accuracy than the time of intercourse. Both male and female subjects tended to significantly *overestimate* the duration of intercourse, and unmarried subjects of both sexes overestimated the most. Another interesting finding was that the married subjects tended to rate both the duration of foreplay and the duration of intercourse as "above average," whereas the unmarried subjects generally rated both as "average" or "below average."

How do we explain these results? If we assume that the act of intercourse has a greater emo-

ejaculation occurring due to the hyperexcitability of the younger male. Specifically, Hunt reports median durations of intercourse about 3 minutes longer for the younger than the older group.

Prolonging intercourse is often believed to be important if the woman is to achieve orgasm. One of the common myths of male sexuality is that it is possible to bring any woman to orgasm during intercourse if the

man is able to hold off his ejaculation indefinitely. While it is certainly true that some minimum period of time is necessary for most women to reach orgasm, duration of intercourse is not the only determinant of female orgasm. Hite (1976) reports that the kind of stimulation the woman receives is more important, overall, than the time factor alone. For example, women who receive adequate clitoral stimulation during intercourse may be

tional impact than the various aspects of fore-play shown in the movie, it is understandable that overestimation was greatest for the intercourse part. Subjective estimates of time are easily affected by any intense emotion — positive or negative. When we are very afraid, for example, seconds may seem like hours. Although the subjects in this study were only viewing a classroom film, the amount of overestimation observed suggests that there may be an even greater bias in surveys that ask subjects to rate the duration of their own intercourse experiences. Especially if subjects are very actively involved and experiencing intense emotional feelings, significant overestimation is likely.

Why did the married subjects rate the times as "above average" and the unmarried subjects as "average" or "below average"? This finding could be explained by assuming that most subjects were comparing the times of foreplay and intercourse in the movie to their own typical script. Unmarried subjects were probably used to a fairly lengthy period of foreplay, especially if the partners were in the early phase of a relationship. Unmarried partners might also make more of an effort to prolong the duration of intercourse. On the other hand, foreplay and intercourse tend to become more routinized for married partners and therefore take less time. This would explain why married subjects might

view the movie script as taking more time than their own and consequently rate it as "above average."

Returning to the question of how reliably survey respondents are able to estimate the duration of intercourse, several tentative conclusions can be drawn. First, a general tendency exists in both men and women to overestimate the duration of emotional events — respondents would probably give much more accurate answers to questions about how long they take over preparing dinner than how long they take over sexual intercourse. Subjects who are more sexually experienced (generally the married subjects) are likely to overestimate less, perhaps because they are less emotionally involved than sexually inexperienced subjects. Finally, when asked to estimate how long a sexual experience lasts, we seem to measure against a particular inner standard, or ideal, and again it seems that married, or more experienced, subjects will tend to use a different internal standard of comparison than less experienced, or unmarried, subjects.

able to reach orgasm in less than 5 minutes, whereas a woman who is inadequately stimulated might never reach orgasm no matter how long intercourse is continued.

The desire to prolong intercourse leads many couples to try distraction techniques, anaesthetic creams, and a variety of sex therapy treatments to counter "premature ejaculation" (see Chapter 9). While these may be of some value for a small number of individuals,

we believe that there is danger of an exaggerated concern with this one aspect of sexual performance:

Too many people have become fixated on how long a man lasts. It is time that we stopped judging our sex lives with a stop-watch. It's also time we stopped keeping score of our orgasms. We know when a sexual experience has been gratifying, and it's rarely just a matter of timing. (Rosen and Rosen, 1977)

Positions of Intercourse

There are probably an infinite number of ways in which a male and female may arrange their bodies during sexual intercourse. Some variations—such as the angle at which an elbow is bent—may have relatively little significance to the act; other variations—such as those portrayed in Tantric sex manuals—are all but impossible to perform. Nevertheless, we are left with four or five basic positions, plus variations, to select from. How, then, do we select from these possible positions for sexual intercourse?

Certainly, individual preferences play some role. Because of our own particular sexual architecture, we may find some positions more comfortable or satisfying than others. Also, physical constraints such as pregnancy may influence our choice of position. Perhaps most important, we are influenced by cultural values and preferences; in subtle and not so subtle ways, our culture gives us messages about which positions are "natural" and which "unnatural," which positions are "sexy," what is awkward and what comfortable, and what is approved or disapproved.

A CROSS-CULTURAL PERSPECTIVE

A survey of other cultures shows that the value of different positions, and even the importance of using different positions, has varied greatly. Among those ancient cultures that Bullough (1976) labels as "sex positive"—for example, the Hindus of ancient India and the Buddhists of ancient China—there was often great emphasis on appropriate variations in intercourse position. Since these cultures viewed sex as important to both physical and spiritual health, they were naturally concerned with instructing their members in the full range of positional possibilities. While we do not know whether the average person actually practiced all these intercourse variations, we do know, through art and literature, that such variations were portrayed, explained, and taught. For instance, ancient India had many sex manuals, the most famous of which is Vatsyayana's *Kama-sutra*. This book describes eighty-four different positions of intercourse; it was not expected that every couple could perform all these variations, and some positions required enormous physical flexibility as well as practice. Each position was named after an animal—the "congress of the cow" or "tiger," for example—and couples were encouraged to make the appropriate animal noises while performing these positions. Positions were also categorized according to postures—sitting, reclining, and so on—and the movements accompanying each position were also described: in "spinning the top," for example, the woman was on top and spun around like a wheel. Couples were encouraged to attain the more difficult positions through exercise and practice.

In China, a group of sex manuals called *fang-chung-shu*—literally, "the art of the bedchamber"—were popular. These books also described and illustrated intercourse positions with such exotic names as "silkworm spinning a cocoon" and "bamboos near the altar." Within Chinese philosophy, Bullough writes, "the male above, and the female below was part of the cosmic orientation in lovemaking" (1976, p. 286). But the Chinese also recognized that other positions were natural, acceptable, and desirable.

In her analysis of coital positions in ancient Greece, ancient Rome, and modern America, Carol Marks (1979) points out that every culture appears to have one basic intercourse posture. Further, she suggests that this posture in some way reflects the psychological

Tantric intercourse position portrayed in a nineteenth-century Indian miniature. Tantric sex techniques were regarded as a highly evolved form of Yoga and involved maintaining a position such as the one illustrated for an hour or more.

concerns of that culture — for instance, the relative status of and relationships between men and women. In ancient Greece, where the highest form of love was a platonic relationship between two males, the preferred coital position was supposed to be the rear-entry position. But in ancient Rome, where women could wield considerable power within the home, the position most frequently depicted in art and literature is the female-superior, or woman-above, position. Marks notes, however, that males were probably ambivalent about female power, and thus, in about half the portrayals of this position the female is facing away from her male partner.

Cultural preference for a single position is also described by the findings of Ford and Beach (1951). They note that while the male-superior, or man-above, position is normative in many cultures other than our own, there are many variations as well. For instance, among the Masai the preferred position is side-by-side and face-to-face; among the Palau the most common position has the woman squatting on top of the male. Interestingly, Ford and Beach note that the rear-entry position is not the preferred one for any of the cultures surveyed. They also point out that while a single position may be preferred, most cultures use and approve of a number of other postures.

CHANGES IN OUR OWN SOCIETY

In our culture, there have been some marked changes in attitudes toward varying coital positions over the past decades. Although the Judeo-Christian tradition does not specifically prohibit the use of particular intercourse postures, its general emphasis on intercourse for procreational, rather than recreational, purposes has had considerable influence on our behavior. The man-above position had, for many centuries, the status of the only "normal" posture for intercourse. Since women were expected to be sexually passive and indifferent, this position dominated the Victorian era. It came to be called the "missionary position" when missionaries working in the South Pacific during the nineteenth century showed their disapproval of the variety of postures commonly used by the Polynesians and, instead, instructed the natives that the man-above position was the only proper and moral coital technique.

To some extent, this attitude persisted into the twentieth century. However, this century has also seen the appearance of sex manuals that in some way resemble those of the ancient Oriental world. For example, even so seemingly conservative a sex educator as Van de Velde, originally writing in 1926, described a variety of intercourse positions. Admittedly, his terms for these positions — the "posterior-lateral attitude," the "ventral attitude," and the "flexed attitude from behind" — were much less poetic than those created by the Chinese. His intentions, however, were in many ways the same — to enhance sexual pleasure and to allow for variations in genital architecture. In addition, Van de Velde was concerned with describing intercourse positions that maximized or minimized the chances of conception.

In Kinsey's time, few members of the general population had accepted Van de Velde's views that variations in intercourse position were normal and desirable.

Universally, at all social levels in our Anglo-American culture, the opinion is held that there is one coital position which is biologically natural, and that all others are man-devised variants which become perversions when regularly engaged in. However, the one position which might be defended as natural because it is usual throughout the Class Mammalia, is not the one commonly used in our culture. The usual mammalian position involves, of course, rear entrance, with the female more or less prone, face down, with her legs flexed under her body, while the male is above or to the rear. (Kinsey *et al.*, 1948, p. 373)

In his 1948 volume on male sexuality, Kinsey wrote that the man-above position was probably the exclusive coital position for as many as 70 percent of the general population. The second most popular position, in which the female was above the male, was being used frequently by about 35 percent of college-educated males but only by 17 percent of males with a grade school education. In fact, variation and experimentation with coital positions were generally more common among those with higher levels of education. However, Kinsey found that sitting, standing, and rear-entry positions were relatively rare at this time.

The same basic trends are reported in Kinsey's 1953 volume on female sexuality. For example, the man-above position was most common among the entire sample of women, and was used exclusively by 16 percent of the women born before 1900. Among those born after 1900, the exclusive use of this position was less common and there tended to be a greater variety in coital positions. The female-above position, for instance, was used by 35 percent of women born before 1900, but by 52 percent of women born between 1920 and 1929. Obviously, there is a clear trend toward

TABLE 8.4

Percentage of White Married Couples Often Using Specified Variant Positions, by Age

Position	18–24	35–44	55+
Female-above	37	29	17
Side-by-side	21	15	15
Rear-entry	20	8	1
Sitting	4	2	1

Source: Adapted from Morton Hunt, *Sexual Behavior in the 1970's* (New York: Dell, 1974), p. 203.

greater variety of positions among the younger generations.

According to Hunt, this trend has certainly continued into the 1970s. Nearly 75 percent of the couples in Hunt's survey at least occasionally used the female-above position, and more than half used the side-by-side position. Positions described by Kinsey as rare—sitting or rear-entry, for instance—were fairly common among Hunt's respondents. Unlike Kinsey, Hunt found that the willingness to vary coital position was unrelated to educational status. However, like Kinsey, Hunt found that the younger generations were more likely to use a variety of coital positions than the older generations (see Table 8.4).

THE BASIC INTERCOURSE POSITIONS

There is little point in trying to specify all of the possible ways in which two human bodies can be juxtaposed in intercourse. Alex Comfort suggests that the total (including the very exotic Oriental positions) adds up to more than 600 possible positions. For most people, however, the script extends to four or five variations. In describing the most commonly used positions, we have been careful to avoid value judgments as to which is the most desirable or "best" position, as this will always be a matter of personal preference.

Face-to-face, man-above. The face-to-face, man-above position—most often referred to as the "missionary position"—is called the "matrimonial position" by Alex Comfort, who recommends its advantages as follows:

Chiefly it's unique in its adaptability to mood; it can be wildly tough or very tender, long or quick, deep or shallow. It is the starting point for nearly every sequence . . . and the most reliably mutual finishing-point for orgasm. (1972, p. 124)

Historically, this position has dominated the sexual script of most Western societies (Ford and Beach, 1951). In the 1948 Kinsey report, 70 percent of the sample reported no experience with any other position. Today this position is still preferred by many men and women, although it is rarely used on an exclusive basis (Hunt, 1974).

A major advantage of this position is the opportunity it provides for eye contact, kissing, and other forms of intimacy during intercourse. Numerous variations can add to the comfort or intensity of stimulation—the woman's legs can be wide apart and the knees drawn up for deeper penetration, or the woman's legs can be close together if less penetration is desired. Discomfort can be caused for the woman if the man fails to support his weight ("A gentleman always leans on his elbows") and for this reason the position can be tiring for the man after a period of time. In addition, the position is not recommended for pregnant women.

At one time it was believed that the technique of "riding high"—elevating the male pelvis to press against the woman's pubic mound—would produce greater clitoral stimulation and increase the possibility of female orgasm. While this technique is enjoyed by some, it is not necessarily effective in produc-

FIGURE 8.1
Face-to-face, man-above intercourse position. This is the most common intercourse position in our own and most other societies.

FIGURE 8.2
Face-to-face, woman-above intercourse position. This position may facilitate orgasm for the female partner.

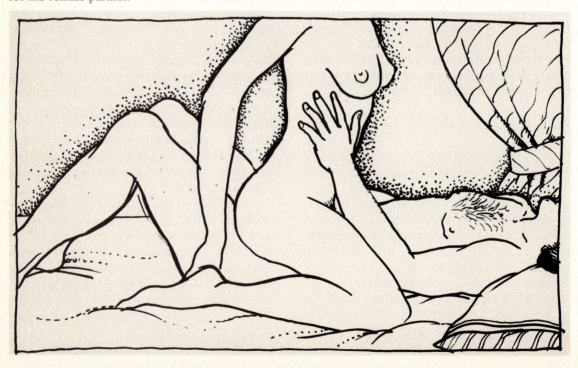

ing orgasm and might even be uncomfortable for some individuals.

Face-to-face, woman above.

If the matrimonial is the king of postures, the queen is her turn on top, "riding St. George." . . . for her it is unique, giving her total freedom to control movement, depth and her partner. She can lean forward for breast or mouth kisses, back to show herself to him, touch her own clitoris as she moves, delay if she wishes, for emphasis—the lot. (Comfort, 1972, pp. 145–146)

Many couples develop a preference for the face-to-face, woman-above position because they find that it helps the male to delay ejacu-

lation or conversely, it may help the female to achieve orgasm more rapidly or more efficiently. As with the male-above variation of the face-to-face, numerous additional options are possible. The woman may face toward her partner's head or toward his feet, she may lie flat, bend forward from the waist, or sit in an upright position. An important advantage of this position is that it allows the man relatively free use of his hands. Kissing and eye contact are also possible in this position. The position is often recommended by sex therapists for couples with sexual dysfunctions.

Rear-entry. The major recommendation for the rear-entry position is the intense stimula-

FIGURE 8.3

Rear-entry intercourse positions can be achieved in a number of different ways. The woman may be in a kneeling posture or lying face down. The male partner may either kneel behind her or crouch over her as in this illustration.

FIGURE 8.4

Side-by-side intercourse position, with woman half on top of the man. This position is sometimes called the *flanquette*.

tion it can provide for the male partner—the tactile stimulation of deep penetration and the contact with the woman's buttocks—as well as the feeling of dominance that the man may derive from the position. Unfortunately the position sometimes evokes negative feelings as being too "animal-like" or as having homosexual connotations. The advantage to the woman of this position is that either partner can provide manual stimulation of the clitoris. A common name for this position is "doggy-style." The position is good for the late stages of pregnancy.

Side-by-side. The side-by-side position can be performed with the couple face-to-face or using a rear-entry approach—the "spoons" position. In the side-by-side, face-to-face position, the intimacy of kissing and eye contact are possible and some of the same advantages of the female-above position apply. In the "spoons" variation, the male achieves penetration from a rear-entry position with both partners lying on their sides. The side-by-side positions can be very relaxed and some couples enjoy remaining in a side-by-side position as they fall asleep after intercourse.

The side-by-side positions can be further varied by having either the male or female partner lift one leg up and over the hips of the other. Comfort uses the French term *flanquette* to describe the position in which the woman is half on her side and half on top of the man, with one of his thighs between her legs. Some women enjoy the additional clitoral pressure from the man's thigh in this position. *Cuissade* is the French word used by Comfort to describe a similar position in which the man enters from the rear, with one of the woman's legs drawn up so that he can insert a thigh between her legs.

Sitting and standing positions. Erotic illustrations from India (especially of Tantric Yoga) often show intercourse positions in which both male and female are seated and facing each other. These illustrations are meant to demonstrate the Tantric goal of minimizing body movement during intercourse—the woman was supposed to be so skilled in her control of the vaginal muscles that she was able to stimulate the penis sufficiently without any other body movement. To emphasize the poise and control attained in this position, the man or woman is sometimes represented as holding a musical instrument or bow and arrow during intercourse in this position.

In our own culture, sitting and standing are among the least frequently used intercourse positions. For instance, Hunt (1974) found that 4 percent of the couples aged 18-24 in his sample had used this position, and among those over age 50, only 1 percent had used it. Perhaps one of the reasons that sitting or standing positions are not more widely used is that active thrusting may be difficult to

FIGURE 8.5

Standing positions also are a variation on the intercourse script.

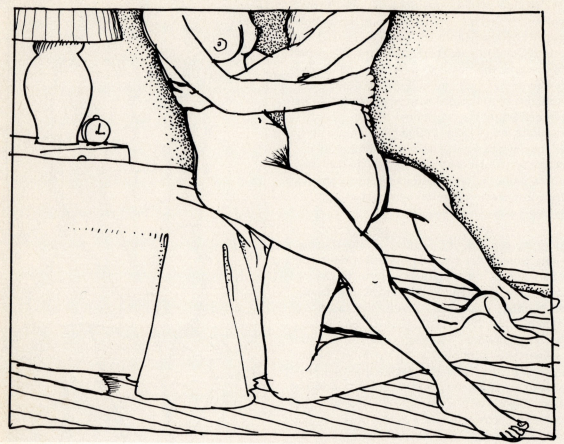

FIGURE 8.6

Sitting positions are sometimes used to vary the intercourse script, although they tend to become uncomfortable if continued for more than a few minutes.

achieve. In addition, these positions are not part of the intercourse script in our culture.

VARIETY AND EXPERIMENTATION

If intercourse is always performed in the same position and with the same pattern of movements, boredom for one or both partners may ensue. Many couples complain that their intercourse patterns have become mechanical or predictable, and that routine has replaced spontaneity. On the other hand, some individuals use sexual intercourse as a form of athletic competition in which the goal becomes the attainment of ever more unusual and more demanding intercourse techniques. Neither of these extremes is recommended; too little or too much experimentation can each detract from the full enjoyment and emotional intimacy of sexual intercourse.

While rigidity and routine in sexual matters are undoubtedly bad, there is no special magic in ever-varying athletic contortions. Nor is there such a thing as the ultimate, superior, or even natural or normal position for coitus. . . . Detailed descriptions of such positions are unnecessary and may even be harmful because they tend to encourage a mechanistic view of coitus. (Haeberle, 1978, p. 217)

Albert Ellis, a well-known clinical psychologist, has frequently criticized the compulsive way in which we approach most aspects of sexual interaction. Human beings, according to Ellis, have an irrational overconcern with "doing the right thing," and this greatly limits the freedom of sexual expression. Men and women are equally affected by these compulsive attitudes, although they express them in different ways. For example, many men believe that deep thrusting during intercourse is an effective form of stimulation, and they continue this practice even with a partner who does not care for it at all. On the other hand, many women cling to the irrational idea that they should not initiate changes in the position or movements of intercourse and end up waiting in vain for the male partner to find the right approach.

One of the most important reasons for varying the pattern of intercourse is to enhance *sexual communication*. According to Alex Comfort intercourse positions are a form of body language: "Play it the way you enjoy it, and test your further responses by occasional sessions devoted simply to variety — a language is no good unless you speak it constantly" (1974, p. 77). Comfort also advocates a trial-and-error approach, because "describing sexual positions is a bit like trying to tell someone how to put up a deck chair." Pictures and descriptions may help in providing general guidelines, but they cannot substitute for personal experience.

Some people believe that experimentation with intercourse positions increases the probability of impregnation. This belief is generally tied to unfounded or superstitious expla-

nations of infertility. For example, there is an Arab belief that problems of conception are due to a "displaced uterus," which can be remedied by having intercourse in a side-by-side position. As far as we know, no scientific basis exists for this belief. Some authorities (e.g., Goldstein, 1976) feel that the male-above (missionary) position increases the chances of impregnation, as this position causes the semen to form a pool at the rear end of the vagina. Positions in which the woman is on top could lead to the semen leaking out more rapidly and perhaps decrease the overall chances of impregnation. However, the relationship between intercourse position and the probability of impregnation has not been adequately studied to date.

Just as there is a great variety of possible intercourse positions, there is also a variety of possible coital movements. The rhythm, pressure, and speed of pelvic thrusting can all be varied to increase the stimulation for either partner. While most males tend to concentrate on in-and-out motions and deep thrusting, women frequently report great pleasure from slow rotations of the penis inside the vagina. Another common preference of women is to rub or grind the pubic bone against the partner during intercourse, thereby producing additional clitoral stimulation. Just as habitual use of the same intercourse position can lead to monotony and routine in love making, a lack of variation in the movements of intercourse can also detract from overall enjoyment of the experience.

The ideal intercourse script is one in which the positions and movements are varied and adapted to the mutual needs of the partners. Unfortunately, many couples fail to achieve this ideal because of the belief that sexual initiative is entirely the male's prerogative. Traditional sex role stereotypes can act as a major barrier to effective sexual communication and may involve an intercourse script such as this one:

Usually he hunts for, finds the vaginal outlet, and inserts the penis; yet, the woman could have accomplished the insertion with greater facility, for she certainly would not have had to hunt and find. He selects coital positioning, usually without consultation as to his partner's preference, and she almost always defers to his decision. He predominantly sets the thrusting pattern and presumes that she will respond and will be pleased. And usually she makes every effort to cooperate with his thrusting pattern whether she is pleased or not. (Masters and Johnson, 1979, p. 220)

This is clearly not the way to make intercourse a mutually rewarding experience. During intercourse, both partners should take responsibility for communicating their needs and desires, and men should not assume that they know how the woman feels and what she desires. Conversely, a woman who fails to openly express what her preferences are, is depriving herself and her partner of the means to a fuller and more complete sexual experience.

Orgasm During Intercourse

It has long been an accepted fact that all men will, and should, experience orgasm and ejaculation during intercourse. In contrast, the notion that females should also experience orgasm during intercourse is relatively new. But as most sexual surveys show, female orgasm during intercourse is not universal — indeed, some researchers have found that a large proportion of women are not coitally orgasmic. These findings have created a great deal of concern and are often thought to indicate that sexual dysfunction, or at least sexual dissatisfaction, are very widespread in our society. Blame for this "failure" has been placed on female sexual inhibition, male sexual technique, and the general sexual misinformation that is so common in our culture. As we shall see, however, the assumption that intercourse and orgasm must always go together in a sexually healthy individual is simply that — an assumption. At other times and in other cultures, orgasm has not been the primary goal of intercourse.

In modern-day America, female orgasm has become a primary goal of intercourse, and researchers such as Hunt have argued that it is virtually synonymous with female sexual pleasure and satisfaction. Since women expect to be coitally orgasmic, he notes, they will naturally be disappointed and disturbed if they do not experience orgasm. Further, many males accept responsibility for the orgasm, or absence of orgasm in their female partners. So, the goal of female orgasm during intercourse can lead to quite considerable tension, doubt, anxiety, and unhappiness for both males and females.

In this regard, the statistics tend to be rather encouraging. That is, over the past decades there seems to be a real increase in the number of women who always or almost always experience orgasm during intercourse. For example, a 1931 study by Dickinson and Beam showed that less than half of a sample of 442 married women reported experiencing orgasm during intercourse. By the 1940s, Kinsey found half of the women surveyed reporting regular orgasm during the first year of marriage, and as many as 64 percent reporting coital orgasm by the twentieth year of marriage. In addition, women born in later decades were more likely to be orgasmic. Finally, in the 1970s, Hunt found that as many as 75 percent of the married females in his sample

FIGURE 8.7

Manual stimulation of the clitoris during intercourse. Many women find that additional clitoral stimulation is required for them to experience orgasm during intercourse.

had frequent or regular orgasms during sexual intercourse.

These data contrast sharply with those reported by Hite (1976). It is true that Hite's sample was not representative of the general population. Nevertheless, her report describes the experience of a considerable number of women, and only about 30 percent of these women stated that they regularly had orgasms from intercourse *alone*. When manual stimulation of the clitoris was added during intercourse, the proportion increased by 19 percent, providing a figure—49 percent—that is

closer to the findings of other researchers. In addition, many women in the Hite sample were not married, and other researchers have found that married women seem more likely than the unmarried to be orgasmic during intercourse. Finally, it is possible that some women in the Kinsey and Hunt samples were using manual stimulation during intercourse but, since they were not specifically questioned about this practice, did not mention it.

From Hite's perspective, female orgasmic capacity during intercourse is really something of a political issue, and not simply a function of a woman's sexual or psychological adjustment.

Insisting that women should have orgasms during intercourse, from intercourse, is to force women to adapt their bodies to inadequate stimulation, and the difficulty of doing this and the frequent failure that is built into the attempt breeds feelings of insecurity and anger. (1976, p. 162)

In other words, Hite believes that a woman's sexual architecture is simply not designed for coital orgasm without the addition of more direct clitoral stimulation. By denying this fact, many women, and their male partners, are simply setting themselves up for a continuing round of disappointments and sexual failures.

Not all women are easily able to accept this notion. Years of emphasis, in sex manuals and the media, on female orgasm through penile stimulation alone, have made many women reluctant to accept anything less. In response to their needs, a variety of sex therapy programs have been developed that, by and large, are successful in teaching the woman to duplicate, during intercourse, the pattern of stimulation that brings her to orgasm during masturbation. Using such techniques, many women can be taught to experience coital orgasm; there is some question, however, as to whether coital orgasm is always a necessary or meaningful goal.

In terms of reproductive function, it is obvious that only male ejaculation during intercourse is absolutely necessary. But only a small proportion of intercourse experiences are actually reproductive in intent. More often, male ejaculation is a contraceptive problem and it would be most convenient if males ejaculated only when they actually desired to impregnate their partners. As we pointed out in Chapter 5, some men are able to have orgasms without ejaculation (Robbins, 1978). It is unlikely, however, that men are capable of

learning *reliably* to have orgasms without ejaculation. Clearly, female orgasm is unnecessary for reproductive purposes. Thus in the majority of cases no reproductive necessity exists for a link between intercourse and orgasm.

Why have we developed this link? In part, arguments for regular orgasm during intercourse have a physiological basis. Starting with Van de Velde, many sex authorities have stressed the harmful consequences of sexual excitement without the sexual release of orgasm. For instance, Van de Velde wrote that "every considerable erotic stimulation . . . that does not terminate in orgasm, on the woman's part, represents an injury, and repeated injuries of this kind lead to permanent—or very obstinate—damage to both body and soul" (1975, p. 194). Van de Velde strongly condemned the practice of coitus interruptus, which he labeled "conjugal fraud." By using it, Van de Velde contended, the man is depriving his partner of her right to a coital orgasm and leaving her in a state of "vain, unsatiated, unrelieved longing which becomes a positive malaise and pain" (p. 195). Nor should the male think he escapes unharmed by withdrawing before ejaculation; Van de Velde believed that the male also might suffer severe physical consequences from coitus interruptus. In the view of Van de Velde and many later sex researchers, a satisfactory sexual relationship must include regular orgasm during intercourse for both male and female. Today, this view is seen as so obvious as to be taken for granted. And the experience of orgasm—particularly simultaneous orgasm—during intercourse has, for many years, epitomized the heights of sexual gratification.

In some cultures, however, there is no orgasm-intercourse link. That is, orgasm is *not* the goal of intercourse. Perhaps the best example is the Taoist philosophy practiced in ancient China. While the Taoists were extremely concerned with female satisfaction, they also placed considerable stress on the regulation of male ejaculation. Ejaculation was seen as both stressful and fatiguing for the male physique, particularly for men of more advanced age. "The ancient Taoists taught that male orgasm and ejaculation were not one and the same thing. Fewer ejaculations in no way meant a man was sexually inadequate nor that he would experience less sexual pleasure. Calling ejaculation 'the climax of pleasure' is really just a habit. And a harmful habit at that" (Chang, 1977, p. 21). The Taoists believed that a man should regulate his ejaculations according to his age and health. A young man might ejaculate on most coital occasions, whereas an older man would be wise to limit himself to ejaculating only once of every ten or more occasions. In this way, the male can be available for more frequent love making and will be better able to satisfy his partner. Contrast the view of Van de Velde — that after ejaculation a man is relaxed, calm, and at peace — with the view of an ancient Chinese Taoist text:

After ejaculation a man is tired, his ears are buzzing, his eyes heavy and he longs for sleep. He is thirsty and his limbs are inert and stiff. In ejaculation he experiences a brief second of sensation but long hours of weariness as a result. And that is certainly not a true pleasure. On the other hand, if a man reduces and regulates his ejaculation to an absolute minimum, his body will be strengthened, his mind at ease and his vision and hearing improved. Although the man seems to have denied himself an ejaculatory sensation at times, his love for his woman will greatly increase. It is as if he could never have enough of her. And this is the true lasting pleasure, is it not? (Chang, 1977, pp. 21–22)

Clearly, the Taoist view of male ejaculation is diametrically opposed to the Western view. We do not include this differing view in order to change anyone's mind but simply to illustrate that our perspective — orgasm during intercourse is good and necessary — is simply one of many possible viewpoints.

Afterplay

"I like a man to hold me after intercourse.
There doesn't have to be a lot of conversation,
just a few tender words, some physical
intimacy, some contact that tells me that the
closeness is still there even after the orgasm is
over."
"I resent a man who, after orgasm, jumps up
and says 'Now on to the important events of
the day.' " (Zilbergeld, 1978, p. 192)

Afterplay is the last act of the intercourse script. Just as the final scene of a play or movie often leaves a lasting impression on the audience, the way we wind down after intercourse can do much to influence the way we feel about the experience. When afterplay is brief

or perfunctory, the result can be a feeling of distance at a time when most people have a strong need for intimacy and closeness. On the other hand, words of affection and gentle expressions of tenderness are especially meaningful at this time. The exertions of intercourse may leave one or both partners feeling anywhere from slightly weary to completely exhausted, and the need to rest and relax during afterplay is also important.

The feelings that men and women experience after intercourse can be greatly affected by whether or not orgasm has been achieved. For one thing, the physiological aftereffects of orgasm can produce a special feeling of satisfaction (see Chapter 5). But the temporary loss of control during orgasm may also produce feelings of embarrassment or vulnerability, which make the need for intimacy and affection during afterplay all the more important. For the man or woman who is unable to reach orgasm during intercourse, there may be a residual feeling of frustration or disappointment, and words of reassurance and comfort need to be offered. This is clearly a time when a special concern for one's partner's needs is called for.

It is often said that men have a tendency to be selfish or insensitive to a woman's needs during this important time. The man who simply rolls over and falls asleep immediately after intercourse may arouse strong feelings of resentment and hostility in his partner. The woman may feel rejected at a time when she desires her partner's affections the most. But as Zilbergeld explains:

The time after sex can be difficult for men to handle since there is no longer any agenda or format. There is no task to be done, no goal to be reached, and nothing to be accomplished. We men are not trained to deal comfortably with such situations. There's just you and this other person and nothing in particular to do except relate. (1978, p. 207)

Finally, we would like to emphasize again that the sexual script need not necessarily end with the male's ejaculation. Some couples view afterplay more as an intermission between sexual acts than as a final curtain. If the female partner has not yet reached orgasm, it may be worthwhile for the man to continue manual or oral stimulation after he has ejaculated. Furthermore, it is not uncommon for younger men to regain their erection within an hour of the first ejaculation, in which case further intercourse may be desirable. On the other hand, when both partners feel fully satisfied and relaxed, the focus of attention will naturally shift away from further sexual interaction, leaving behind the warm afterglow of emotional intimacy.

Summary

For many people, sexual intercourse is synonymous with sexual behavior. Intercourse differs from the sexual behaviors described in Chapter 7 in one major respect—it is directly linked to reproduction and survival of the species. In lower mammals, intercourse is rigidly tied to this reproductive function; among most primates, and particularly among humans, intercourse patterns have social as well as hormonal sources. To summarize:

1. There has been an increase in the number of women experiencing premarital intercourse. For the majority of these women, premarital intercourse occurs within a committed, emotional relationship and often is restricted to the future marital partner.

2. The "normal" frequency of intercourse differs greatly from one culture to another, with the United States scoring relatively low when compared with cultures such as the Mangaians. Intercourse rates tend to decrease with advancing age and length of marriage. The duration of intercourse, though difficult to measure, also seems to be influenced by cultural and individual factors.

3. Preferences for a particular intercourse position are common both for individuals and cultural groups. In our own culture, the male-

above position was considered the only "normal" or "natural" position for many years. However, sexologists such as Van de Velde in the 1930s, and Comfort in the 1970s, have emphasized the importance of variation and experimentation regarding intercourse positions. In addition, research shows that people are more likely to use a variety of positions today than they were in Kinsey's time.

4. In recent years the goal of intercourse is orgasm for both males and females, although some controversy exists as to how many women are orgasmic through intercourse alone. The social pressure to be orgasmic during intercourse — and particularly the goal of simultaneous orgasm — may sometimes lead to the sexual problems that are discussed in Chapter 9.

Overview

NINE

Sexual Problems

Overview

At a time in history when there is a new openness toward all aspects of sexuality, it is not surprising that some of the frustrations and anxieties of the sexual experience have also come "out of the closet." A woman of the Victorian era was unlikely to request help for a sexual dynsfunction for a number of reasons: she had low expectations about the pleasures of sex, her very interest in sex would probably label her as a woman of doubtful morals, and there was simply no one available to provide sexual counseling. In contrast, men and women today expect sexual activity to be satisfying and can consult a wide range of health professionals for help with their sexual difficulties. To be sure, some stigma is still attached to admitting a sexual problem for many individuals. By and large, however, our soci-ety has come to accept that the sexual relationship is not always a "bed of roses," and that a sexually distressed individual is often in need of professional assistance.

The kinds of problems discussed in this chapter are usually referred to as "sexual inadequacy," "sexual dysfunction," or more simply, "sexual behavior problems." These terms are used more or less interchangeably to describe the difficulties experienced in some aspect of sexual desire or performance. The term "hyposexuality" is also sometimes used to describe a person who is unable to function sexually.

Almost every man and woman will experience sexual problems at some stage of the life cycle. In fact, it would be surprising if an activity which is interwoven with so many facets of our everyday lives did not respond to pressures from other areas. In many cases, a period of sexual inadequacy will be followed by a return to normal sexual functioning. In other cases, however, sexual dysfunction can become a chronic and debilitating problem.

Defining Sexual Problems

THE LABELING OF SEXUAL PROBLEMS

Sexual problems can be labeled in either very general or very specific terms. For most purposes, the more specific the label, the more valuable it will be. The traditional labels "frigidity" and "impotence" are very vague and nonspecific terms that convey little information about sexual dysfunction. In addition, such labels have pejorative connotations; "frigidity" implies that the women is cold and unresponsive, whereas in fact she may be warm and accepting. Similarly, "impotence" implies that a man has no power, strength, or masculinity. Fortunately, both terms have now been almost completely discarded by professionals.

Nor does giving a sexual problem a medical-sounding label necessarily improve our understanding of it—for example, using "hypogyneismus" (Musaph and Abraham, 1977) as another way of saying "frigid," or "impotentia ejaculandi" (Cooper, 1969) to denote the inability to ejaculate, or "ejaculatio praecox," the traditional medical term for premature ejaculation. Such labeling serves only to make sexual dysfunction seem to be both mysterious and inaccessible.

Fortunately the current trend in labeling sexual dysfunction is to use terms that are specific and easily understood—for example, *anorgasmia* to refer to lack of orgasm, *delayed ejaculation* to describe an ejaculation that takes longer than normal, *erectile impotence* meaning the inability to achieve or maintain an erection, and *ejaculatory impotence* to denote the inability to ejaculate. Defining sexual dysfunctions in ways that are simple and precise offers a number of important advantages: (1) the dysfunctions become more understandable to the public, (2) professionals concerned with the diagnosis and treatment of dysfunction can communicate more easily about their work, (3) it facilitates scientific study of the causes and treatment of a dysfunction, and (4) it removes much of the shame and stigma associated with such labels as "frigidity" and "impotence."

SEXUAL DYSFUNCTION AS A CONTINUUM

Describing a sexual dysfunction is very different from diagnosing a physical disease. In diagnosing disease, it is usually appropriate to think of dichotomous categories: healthy or sick, normal or abnormal. However, because no absolute standard exists for sexual function, *dysfunction* should be understood as referring to a *continuum* or range of possible capacity/incapacity. There are many degrees of sexual incapacity, and the word "dysfunction" may have meaning only for a given individual in a given context. Some sexually dysfunctional individuals have severe problems in all areas of sexual activity; others have minor problems that interfere with only a small segment of sexual behavior.

The degree of an individual's sexual incapacity depends on a number of factors. One such factor is the extent of *genital function.* For instance, injury or illness may cause loss of erectile capacity in a male. However, this does not necessarily mean a loss of desire for sex or inability to enjoy certain aspects of the sexual script.

CASE: David H., age 28, suffered a serious injury to his spinal cord in an automobile accident. After the accident, he found that he was unable to get an erection, although his doctor told him that there was no reason he could not experience orgasm. Both David and his wife had been sexually active before the accident and were concerned that his erectile dysfunction would seriously threaten their marriage. They sought help from a sexual counselor who suggested that although their sex life would obviously change, it did not have to cease. They were instructed to try out new sexual scripts: for instance, they learned to replace intercourse with manual or oral stimulation. Although the change in David's physical capacity required some readjustment, both members of the couple found that they could nevertheless still maintain satisfying and pleasurable sexual interaction.

Another dimension of sexual incapacity is *attitude toward sex.* Attitudes that provoke anxiety, guilt, or embarrassment about sex can be more damaging to sexual function than physical incapacity. Perhaps the most damaging attitude of all is an individual's belief that he or she *must* be able to perform and that any sexual dysfunction is a sign of personal failure.

CASE: When Steve and Elaine M. (aged 24 and 22) sought therapy, their rate of sexual activity had declined to less than once per month. On the surface, their problem appeared to be Steve's inability to maintain an erection long enough for intercourse. But more intensive questioning revealed that Elaine had never been able to reach orgasm during intercourse, although she was easily orgasmic with manual or oral stimulation and was not particularly upset about her "problem." Steve, however, seemed to feel that her lack of orgasm during intercourse was his fault and related to some deficit in his sexual technique. He blamed himself, felt guilty about sex, and tried hard to "perform" in ways that would bring her to orgasm. In the end, he became so anxious about her orgasm that he had difficulty in maintaining an erection.

Defining sexual dysfunction in this case required consideration of the interaction between the couple. Steve's difficulties in maintaining an erection were directly related to Elaine's anorgasmia, and it was the *couple* as a unit, rather than either individual, that was

Sexual dysfunction within a relationship always involves both partners. *(Anestis Diakopoulos/ Stock, Boston)*

sexually dysfunctional. Overcoming the problem required the acceptance of mutual responsibility by both partners.

The continuum of sexual dysfunction is also affected by current cultural expectations of adequate sexual performance. Cultural concepts of masculinity and femininity play a major role in defining our sexual goals. For example, young men in our society often perceive their masculinity in terms of whether they can delay or control their ejaculation.

CASE: Martin V. (26 years old) had masturbated frequently during adolescence and showed a strong interest in sex from the time he began dating in high school. He had engaged in petting to orgasm with several girlfriends before meeting Carol. They began dating seriously in their junior year in college and were married shortly after graduation. Although they both enjoyed foreplay and intercourse, Martin usually ejaculated 3 or 4 minutes after intromission. The couple sought counseling for Martin's "premature ejaculation." There was no question that Carol was orgasmic — she enjoyed both manual and oral stimulation to orgasm during petting. However, the couple had oriented their sexual script entirely to orgasm during intercourse, placing a considerable demand on Martin to delay his ejaculation until his wife reached orgasm. This goal was impossible for them to achieve. When it was suggested that they experiment with a different script, in which Carol would reach orgasm through manual or oral stimulation *before* beginning intercourse, the results were dramatic. Martin expressed a great sense of relief that he could relax and enjoy his ejaculation without struggling to delay it, and Carol no longer had to cope with the frustration of sex without orgasm. Ironically, with the pressure off, Martin found it much easier to control his ejaculation although their new sexual script worked perfectly well without it.

The young couple in this case both enjoyed sex and were sexually responsive; they were experiencing a sexual dysfunction only in the sense that they perceived themselves as failing to meet certain cultural criteria for adequate sexual performance. Sexual problems of this kind can usually be overcome successfully if the couple are willing to suspend their cultural stereotypes and experiment with new sexual scripts.

SEXUAL DYSFUNCTION AND SELF-ESTEEM

Perhaps the most common side effect of sexual dysfunction is a loss of self-esteem. While we may accept our failure to play winning tennis and excuse ourselves if we are not able to jog 5 miles, we are usually very hard on ourselves when we perceive our sexual performance as deficient in some way. For some people, a sexual problem can become an unforgivable failure that leads to intense shame and anxiety; in turn, these reactions to sexual dysfunction will probably make the problem worse.

Sexual problems do not invariably lead to a sense of failure or to personal unhappiness. In fact, many couples and individuals learn to make some adjustment to their sexual limitations and report leading a satisfying sexual life. One study (Frank *et al.*, 1978) examined the sexual life of 100 satisfied married couples. The mean age of the wives was 35 and 37 for the husbands. None of these couples had sought professional help for sexual dysfunction, and over 80 percent reported that their sexual and marital experiences were happy and satisfying. Yet their self-report questionnaires indicated that about 40 percent of the men had at least occasional erectile or ejaculatory dysfunction and that 63 percent of the women experienced some difficulty in becoming aroused or reaching orgasm. In addition, a majority of the respondents reported such sexual difficulties as lack of interest, inability to relax, and too little foreplay. Clearly, these couples were able to tolerate a large number of sexual dysfunctions and difficulties without feeling that they had serious problems.

Understanding and Coping With
Sexual Problems

Sexual problems are not esoteric events that happen to only a small minority of people in our society; they can be serious obstacles to sexual growth and satisfaction that have far-reaching effects on an enormous number of people. An individual's sense of self-esteem depends to a large extent on how well he or she is able to cope with a number of important life roles, including those of husband/wife and sexual partner. Such problems as erectile failure and lack of orgasm can lead to a sense of failure or incompetency and thus a greatly diminished sense of self-worth. For this reason, it is important to discuss in some depth the nature of sexual problems — specifically, the causes of such problems and the best available means for overcoming them.

Since the publication of *Human Sexual Inadequacy* (1970), the major work by Masters and Johnson on sexual problems, a new era in our understanding and approach to sexual problems has begun. In this book, they challenged many previous concepts of sexual dysfunction, particularly the notion that a sexual problem is always a sign or symptom of some deeper problem. In the past, professionals had been reluctant to approach sexual problems in a direct way, believing that it was necessary to focus on underlying emotional and interpersonal conflicts. The specific sexual problem was considered to be merely the "tip of the iceberg."

Nowadays, professionals are likely to see the value of providing sexual information and directive counseling for individuals or couples experiencing sexual difficulties. Although the origins of a specific problem may well lie in the remote past, more than ever we are concerned with factors in the here and now in order to understand and cope with these types of problems.

GENERAL CAUSES
OF SEXUAL DYSFUNCTION

Suppose we were to ask an individual the question, "Why can't you have an orgasm?" We might get such answers as: "Because I'm too anxious" or "Because I have a hard time 'letting go.'" These simple answers may, in fact, apply to the problem, but we should recognize that they are superficial responses lacking in specific detail. In reality, human behavior is determined by a multiplicity of factors, and we can attempt to highlight only some of the more common or obvious causes of sexual dysfunction, while acknowledging that some or all of these causes may not apply to a specific individual.

One approach to explaining sexual dysfunction is to separate immediate causes (such as fear of failure) from remote causes (such as early family dynamics). Kaplan (1974) suggests that by considering both immediate and remote factors, we may avoid the danger of superficial explanations. In the following sections, we begin by considering immediate causes, such as physical health and relationship factors, and then go on to a discussion of the role of remote causes, such as childhood sexual experiences.

Physical health. Any condition that impairs physical health may also interfere with normal sexual functioning. Our sexual performance depends on a delicate state of balance in the communications network of the body — the nervous system and the endocrine system. When this balance is upset by illness, trauma, stress (either physical or mental), or drug use, sexual functioning can suffer.

In the case of certain physical conditions such as diabetes, the effects may be felt directly on the physiological capacity to respond.

Such traumas as spinal cord injury may also directly impair sexual capacity. With other physical conditions, however, the effect may be an indirect one that is mediated by psychological factors. For example, a debilitating health problem such as mononucleosis can lead to a depressed mental state, which in turn can cause a loss of interest in sex. Also, physical conditions that are associated with body-image problems—for example, removal of a limb or body part—may indirectly inhibit sexual expression.

Long-term use of certain drugs or medications can also have negative sexual effects. For instance, certain medications commonly prescribed in the treatment of hypertension can lead to erection problems or loss of sexual interest if taken in large doses for an extended period of time. Major tranquilizers such as the phenothiazines can also impair sexual performance. The abuse of such nonprescription drugs as alcohol or heroin can have a similar effect. (The effects of drugs and illness are discussed fully in Chapter 12.)

Immediate psychological causes. In the category of immediate psychological causes are a number of emotional, cognitive, and general psychological factors that can directly contribute to sexual distress. Attitudes, beliefs, and feelings about sexual performance can, in and of themselves, present major obstacles to overcoming sexual problems. The most important example of this effect is the *performance anxiety*, or fear of failure, that is so often associated with long-standing sexual dysfunctions. Masters and Johnson use the term "spectatoring" to describe the mental set of an individual who is always somewhat detached from a sexual situation; while involved in sex, the "spectator" watches himself or herself and so cannot fully respond to sexual stimulation. In almost all cases, spectatoring is directly attributable to high levels of performance anxiety and serves to maintain or even worsen the sexual problem. Frequently, there is a vicious cycle, in which an initial failure is reinforced by fears of further failure, turning commonplace difficulties into much more serious dysfunctions.

Ignorance or misinformation can also cause or aggravate sexual problems. Perhaps the most damaging myth is that sex should come "naturally" if two people care for each other sufficiently. Unfortunately, love is not always enough to ensure sexual compatibility and satisfaction. Ignorance about methods of sexual stimulation can lead to serious sexual communication difficulties. For instance, it is surprising how many men (and women) are still ignorant about the importance of adequate clitoral stimulation in achieving female sexual arousal and orgasm.

Another damaging sexual myth is that men and women have a fixed amount of sexual energy that can be "wasted" by masturbation or sexual fantasy. It is not uncommon for the individual experiencing sexual difficulties to avoid masturbation or fantasy in order to "save" sexual energy. However, these attempts to store up sexual power often backfire, leaving the individual with less rather than more energy for sex. The analogy we often use in counseling is that of a car battery: if the charge in the battery is low, leaving the car in the garage for a period of time is the least useful approach to take. The best way to recharge the battery is to run the car. Similarly, the person who thinks about or engages in sexual stimulation will develop more and not less sexual energy. The myth of saving sexual energy, which results in the avoidance of sex, is often a major contributing factor to long-standing sexual dysfunctions.

Relationship factors. Masters and Johnson have stressed the very important concept that "there is no such thing as an uninvolved partner in any marriage in which there is some form of sexual inadequacy." The interaction between two members of a relationship is a major determinant of the sexual difficulties experienced by either one of them. Even in situations where it appears that one partner alone has the sexual problem, closer examination of the situation often reveals ways in which the behavior or attitudes of the "uninvolved" partner are actually contributing to the problem. Sexual problems can be either the cause or the result of conflicts within the relationship—determining which came first is usually like trying to solve the riddle of the chicken and the egg.

Feelings of mistrust or hostility between the partners are common causes of sexual disinterest or dysfunction. For most people, such feelings are directly antagonistic to the feelings of intimacy involved in sharing a sexual experience. When one partner rejects the other's sexual advances, the problem may be compounded even further. Kaplan has compiled an interesting list of the subtle (and not so subtle) ways in which an individual's sexual desires may be frustrated:

He likes her to swing her hips—she lies motionless.

He needs to be made to feel loved and desired—she "does him a favor."

She likes to move actively—he pins her down.

He is very stimulated by touching her breasts—she feels "ticklish" and cannot bear to have her breasts touched.

She is aroused by having her breasts caressed—he does not want to bother and/or implies that her breasts are not attractive.

She likes to talk with him a bit first to relax her before sex—he plunges wordlessly in.

She hates TV—he always watches TV before making love.

She wants and needs clitoral stimulation—he im-

"What is it, really—the book's so good you can't put it down, or I'm so awful you can't get it up?"
(© Modell/Playboy)

plies that his other lovers didn't need that sort of thing.

He likes to experiment—she thinks that everything but "straight" missionary position is perverted.

She is very turned on by oral sex—he is disgusted by the odor of women's genitals.

He craves oral sex—she is repelled by the drop of secretion or it "gags" her to swallow the semen.

He has his best erections in the morning—she insists on sex at night only.

He would like to try anal stimulation—she is horrified by the idea. (Kaplan, 1974, p. 165)

In some instances, there is no conscious intent to frustrate the sexual desires of the partner, but the couple simply has incompatible "script" preferences. If open and direct communication is possible, these incompatibilities may often be resolved over the course of time. However, when sex is a taboo subject of discussion, an escalating cycle of rejection and frustration can lead to major sexual problems between the couple.

The role of conditioning and childhood sexual experiences. Few people doubt that early learning and experience play an important role in adult sexual behavior. According to the Freudian view, all children experience incestuous sexual desire for the parent of the opposite sex during the phallic stage of development. Freud also hypothesized that in boys, the incestuous desire for the mother led to "castration anxiety" and fears of retaliation from the father. For girls, the problem was seen as "penis envy." Normal sexual development was thought to require identification with the parent of the same sex, and failure to resolve childhood sexual conflicts was believed to be the cause of adult sexual dysfunction.

Modern theories of learning tend to emphasize the effects of reward and punishment on the conditioning of sexual responses. The release of tension during orgasm is assumed to act as a natural reinforcer for any behaviors that are practiced consistently just before orgasm takes place. For instance, if a man develops the habit of stroking his penis vigorously during masturbation, and this habit is reinforced by the occurrence of orgasm, then he may become conditioned to and dependent upon that particular pattern of stimulation in order to reach a climax. Likewise, men who have the habit of masturbation to orgasm with a partial erection, sometimes develop erection problems during intercourse.

Cultural learning and conditioning may also play a role in sexual dysfunction. Much of our social learning takes place through "modeling," or imitation, and books, movies, and television in our culture provide abundant role models. Unfortunately, the attitudes toward sexuality that are modeled in this way are not always conducive to solving sexual problems. In many cases, cultural pressures have the effect of setting up new performance standards and demands, which in turn lead to further sexual difficulties. According to Masters and Johnson (1970), religious orthodoxy is another major cultural determinant of sexual dysfunction—in some cases, early religious indoctrination may lead to equating sex with sin, resulting in a deep-seated fear of sexual pleasure.

MODERN APPROACHES TO COUNSELING

We are fortunate to have available the work of Masters and Johnson (1970) and Kaplan (1974) as very detailed descriptions of the methods and procedures for overcoming sexual dysfunction. Prior to Masters and Johnson, behavior therapists Wolpe (1958) and Lazarus (1963) had described the value of behavioral treatment of anxiety in overcoming common sexual problems. James Semans, a urologist, had also developed a direct training approach to overcome problems of rapid ejaculation. However, first Masters and Johnson and later Kaplan described a complete structure and format for dealing with a wide variety of sexual dysfunctions, and integrated earlier work into their approaches. In this respect, their work has profoundly affected professionals and the public alike.

Many large universities and medical schools now provide specialized sexual counseling services. These facilities, providing treatment for a range of sexual problems, can be a real asset to the communities they serve. Even though some controversy exists about the proper qualifications for a sex counselor, therapists are usually well-trained health professionals. In addition to offering basic clinical services for dysfunctional individuals, such programs typically provide educational and consultation services as well.

Sexual counseling programs vary somewhat in the techniques they use. Nevertheless, certain common elements form the basis of the modern approach to overcoming sexual dysfunction. The following summary of these elements is based on LoPiccolo (1977):

1. Mutual responsibility: It is generally advisable for the sexual partner of a dysfunctional individual to be included in the counseling program, because often the partner's behavior is reinforcing the problem. The formation of male/female therapy teams can be helpful in encouraging the involvement of both partners.

2. Information and education: In some cases of dysfunction, providing information and education is by itself sufficient to overcome the problem (McMullen and Rosen, 1979). In virtually all cases, it is a necessary first step.

3. Attitude change: The destructive effect of sex-negative attitudes was repeatedly emphasized by Masters and Johnson (1970). The development of more positive attitudes toward sex is an essential aspect of counseling in such cases.

4. Eliminating performance anxiety: In the first stage of counseling, couples are usually instructed to refrain from intercourse. Instead, they are instructed in techniques of nondemanding touching and caressing that teach them to relax in a sexual situation.

5. Improving communication and sexual technique: The couple are encouraged to communicate with each other regarding the types of sexual stimulation each finds most effective — for example, by guiding the hand of the partner in direct genital stimulation. They are also encouraged to invent and discuss new mutually acceptable sexual scripts, to share their sexual fantasies, and to observe the partner during masturbation.

6. Giving sex a chance: The conditions under which most couples attempt sexual intercourse are usually far from ideal. Physical or mental fatigue, financial or family concerns, or the frequent absence or preoccupation of one or both of the partners — all reduce the chances of regular and satisfying sexual relations. Masters and Johnson dealt directly with this problem by insisting that a couple undertaking their therapy program move into a motel in St. Louis for the full 2 weeks of the course. Most counseling programs are carried out while the couple live at home, but sex is given high priority while therapy is in progress.

7. Easing sex role inhibitions: Maintaining rigid sex roles — such as dominant male and submissive female — inhibits progress. Counselors usually encourage couples to share responsibility for initiating sexual experiences and to suspend their usual sex role expectations during the course of the therapeutic experience.

8. Directive counseling: In addition to a general program of therapy along the lines described, a counselor will usually, at appropriate stages in the course of therapy, recommend specific techniques for dealing with the couple's particular problems. (In the sections on specific male and female dysfunctions we present details of a number of these techniques.)

LEVELS OF COUNSELING

Not all sexual problems require intensive therapy or referral to a specialist. When short-term sexual difficulties are accepted as a normal part of life, they often disappear with the passage of time. In other cases, a physician, nurse, or minister, or even a sympathetic friend or family member can be of great help. In addition, many excellent self-help guides are available for women (Barbach, 1975; Heiman *et al.*, 1976) and for men (Zilbergeld, 1978). However, long-standing or complicated sexual dysfunctions will usually require specialized help from a qualified professional. Within the general framework of sex therapy a number of different levels of intervention might be required in any individual case. A useful description of these levels has been provided by Annon (1975), who has proposed the "P-LI-SS-IT" model:

Permission to engage in certain behavior (for instance, masturbation) or reassurance is all that is needed in some cases. "Am I normal?" is a question that can provoke a great deal of sexual anxiety. Any sensitive professional can deal with sexual problems at this level.

LI Limited information may be needed to provide the individual with specific facts relevant to his/her particular problem—for example, information about orgasm, the role of the clitoris in sexual stimulation, and differences in male and female sexual response. Although this level of intervention also requires no specialized training, a sound knowledge of human sexuality is important.

SS Specific suggestions should be offered only after a complete sexual history has been obtained. If it appears that a problem might be overcome by a specific change in behavior, this level of therapy may be sufficient. Professionals with lim-

ited experience in the field of sexual dysfunction may still be able to offer help at this level.

IT Intensive therapy should be necessary only in a small minority of cases. If the above three levels have failed to overcome the problem, or if the sexual dysfunction is associated with serious emotional or relationship problems, referral should be made for specialized treatment. Professionals functioning at this level will typically have advanced degrees in clinical psychology, psychiatry, or social work. Intensive therapy will usually require at least several months, and sometimes years, to be completed.

Male Sexual Problems

Very few men go through their entire lives without experiencing some form of sexual difficulty. Most men have learned to accept that their sexual performance is not always under their own control. In Chapter 5 we noted that the sexual responses of erection and orgasm

depend to a large extent on the autonomic nervous system, which is primarily related to the expression of emotion. Any condition or situation that upsets the delicate balance of the autonomic nervous system can temporarily interfere with erection and orgasm. For example,

Anxiety or tension may affect sexual responses. (© *Burke Uzzle/ Magnum*)

drug and alcohol use or physical illness may sometimes lead to a temporary sexual dysfunction, as may the emotional stress of anxiety, anger, or depression.

A onetime or infrequent sexual problem is usually not considered to be a sign of dysfunction and should be accepted as a normal part of living. When the problem persists, however, and the man is unable to cope with his own sexual difficulty, one or more of the following labels may apply.

ERECTILE PROBLEMS

Helen Kaplan (1974) estimates that approximately 50 percent of the adult male population experience occasional erectile problems as a normal part of male sexual development. In contrast, the most serious erectile problem—sometimes called *primary impotence*—involves a lifelong failure to achieve either heterosexual or homosexual intercourse. Fortunately, cases of this degree of severity are quite rare, accounting for less than 5 percent of the Masters and Johnson (1970) clinical sample.

If a man has been successful in maintaining enough of an erection for intercourse on at least one occasion, the problem is described by Masters and Johnson (1970) as *secondary impotence*. Other writers (e.g., O'Connor, 1976) favor using the terms *total* and *partial* to distinguish between the man who is totally unable to become erect and the man who has partial or intermittent erectile failure. The most clear-cut cases of total erectile dysfunction are those in which a physical trauma or disease, such as a spinal cord injury, has permanently blocked the erection response.

Within these broad categories is a very wide range of erectile problems:

Some men cannot achieve an erection during foreplay. Others attain an erection easily, but lose their erection and become flaccid subsequently at specific points in the sexual response cycle, e.g., at the moment before entry, or upon insertion, or during intercourse. Other men are impotent during intercourse, but can maintain an erection during manual manipulation or oral sex. Some men can have an erection while clothed, but become flaccid as soon as their penis is exposed to view. Some men become excited and have erections during foreplay when they know that intercourse is not possible, but lose their potency when they are involved in situations where intercourse is not only feasible but expected. Some men can erect only if the woman dominates the sexual situation, while others become impotent if their partner tries to assume control. Some suffer from "total" impotence, i.e., they cannot achieve even a partial erection with any partner, under any circumstances. Others suffer from purely situational impotence and experience erectile difficulties only under specific circumstances. (Kaplan, 1974, p. 256)

Even partial or situational erectile problems can cause great distress to the man experiencing them. Because the ability to perform sexually is so often linked to feelings of masculinity, and because erectile problems are so obvious to both partners, the dysfunction usually presents a serious threat to the man's self-esteem. If a woman is insufficiently lubricated she may still be able to go through the motions of intercourse; but when the man's erection is lost, intercourse usually becomes impossible. Men who experience erectile difficulties often compound their problem by withdrawing from all forms of sexual interaction (Zilbergeld, 1978).

CASE: Max T. had been married for 28 years when his wife died of cancer. After mourning her death for several months, he gradually began to date again. When dating progressed to the point of sexual intercourse, he found himself repeatedly unable to maintain an erection long enough for penetration. The harder he tried, the worse the problem became. His doctor reassured him that he was physically healthy and suggested tranquilizers for his problem. As Max's fear of sexual failure increased, he began to avoid any sexual relations and even broke off with two active dating partners. This process of sexual withdrawal was finally reversed when Max decided to attempt masturbation for the first time in more than 20 years. To his surprise, he discovered that he still had the capacity to maintain an erection and reach orgasm. This experience gave him sufficient confidence to begin dating again, and gradually he was able to overcome any erectile problems during sexual intercourse.

Simple and complex causes of erectile failure. Erectile problems are usually considered to have two major types of causes: *psychogenic* and *organic,* meaning that the problem is due to either psychological or physical determinants. Among the organic causes are any diseases or disorders that affect the male hormone balance, nerve pathways, or blood supply to the penis. Masters and Johnson have listed more than forty potential organic causes of erectile problems; however, they found that among 213 cases of secondary impotence only 7 cases could be attributed to physical factors.

There is no doubt that most erectile difficulties are due to psychogenic factors. This does not mean that potential physical causes should be overlooked, and in some cases there may be an interaction between mental and physical causes. Since admitting to emotional or psychological inadequacies carries a great stigma in our society, men with these problems frequently search for physical explanations for their problem as well as physical cures, such as hormone injections.

In addition to specific diseases, medical texts often mention the side effects of certain medications as potential causes of erectile problems, the most commonly mentioned being major tranquilizers (e.g., Mellaril) and antihypertensive drugs. High doses of alcohol also impair erectile function (Farkas and Rosen, 1976), and chronic alcoholism frequently leads to serious sexual problems.

By far the greatest number of erectile problems are caused by psychological or emotional factors. *Performance fears*, and particularly the fear of failure, are common to almost all cases of erectile dysfunction. For example, suppose a man first experiences erectile failure due to overconsumption of alcohol. On the next occasion that he attempts intercourse, the memory of the previous failure and his fear that the experience will be repeated can be sufficient to cause further erection problems. He begins a vicious cycle in which each failure confirms his fear and increases his chances of subsequent failure. When a man has experienced erectile dysfunction on several occasions, performance anxiety alone will be sufficient to maintain the problem, regardless of the original cause.

The psychogenic causes of erectile failure can be divided into those that are immediate and those that are remote (Kaplan, 1974). Among the immediate causes are fear of failure, the demands of the sexual partner, disagreements with the sexual partner, fears of premature ejaculation, factors that prevent the man from feeling relaxed, and emotional stress from nonsexual activities such as work. The possible remote causes of erectile failure are also numerous. For example, childhood conditioning and the early learning of negative attitudes toward sex can certainly affect a man's sexual responses. A man who has been taught to believe that masturbation is harmful, for example, will not use it as a natural remedy for an instance of erectile failure. Masters and Johnson (1970) list religious indoctrination, the effects of maternal or paternal dominance on feelings of masculinity, and repressed or conflicting homosexual feelings as possible remote causes of erectile dysfunction.

A well-known sex therapy team (Lobitz and Lobitz, 1978) have developed a useful flow chart to illustrate the interaction of factors causing erectile dysfunction, ranging from the

The pressures to be 'masculine' in our society can sometimes cause erectile dysfunction. (© *Hazel Hankin 1980*)

man's attitudes and life style to the immediate effects of performance anxiety. This chart demonstrates the complexity of factors that may be present in a case of erectile dysfunction of psychogenic origin: A man who is achievement-oriented and believes that he should be able to get an erection on demand will probably try even harder to get an erection after he fails; in turn, this "trying" makes him less receptive to sexual pleasure and more likely to experience erectile failure.

Overcoming erection problems. A man who has experienced an erectile problem faces a wide range of possible causes and solutions. For the individual who has experienced the problem only once or twice, the obvious remedy is simply to try again, if possible under more favorable and less demanding circumstances. Unfortunately, the natural tendency is often to avoid all types of sexual activity after the occurrence of erectile failure, and once a pattern of avoidance is established, the problem is likely to become progressively worse. Open communication with the sexual partner concerning sexual feelings can also help to overcome erectile problems of short duration; but once again, many men are reluctant to discuss with their partners what they perceive as "failure."

When the erection problem is persistent and appears to grow severer with the passage of time, professional help is highly recommended. The first step is to consult with a physician (usually a urologist) to rule out the possibility of organic causes. Physical examination and routine laboratory tests are normally sufficient for this purpose. If the physician's findings indicate that the problem appears to be of psychogenic origin, a referral may be made to a psychologist, psychiatrist, or qualified sex therapist. Professional counseling usually proceeds along the following lines:

1. A full sex history is taken in order to determine the possible role of family and early sexual experiences. If a sexual partner is involved, she or he also contributes a sexual history. Relationship factors such as guilt and hostility are also discussed and evaluated.

2. The individual (or couple) is instructed *not* to attempt intercourse for several weeks. Instead, the focus is placed on sexual tasks and assignments that minimize performance demands on the male and at the same time maximize a relaxed, sensual interaction between the partners. Masters and Johnson use the term *sensate focus* to describe the specific tasks they use for this purpose. Sensate focus exercises usually begin with nongenital massage and gradually progress to include more specific genital stimulation exercises.

3. Overcoming the fear of failure is an important, often difficult, step in counseling. Even when the stimulation exercises of the sensate focus program are successful in producing erections, the man may retain his fear that the erection will not last. The therapeutic gain may be undone by the obsessive thought that the erection, once lost, will not return—which easily becomes a self-fulfilling prophecy. To overcome this fear, Kaplan (1974) and Zilbergeld (1978) both strongly recommend exercises in which the man and his partner practice getting erections and then deliberately *losing* them by withdrawing the stimulation. Developing a relaxed and playful attitude is important also in this regard. If there is sufficient confidence by the man in his erection, it can be regained with further stimulation.

4. Once sufficient confidence in the erection has been established, the man is instructed to attempt intercourse, but in a very specific way—for instance, that he should lie down in a comfortable position, and that after a period of manual or oral stimulation, his female partner should kneel over him and insert his penis slowly into her vagina. Some counselors suggest that the first time this is done, the couple should content themselves with experiencing the sensations of the penis inside the vagina without attempting any thrusting or orgasm. Only after the man has become relaxed and confident with the penis inside the vagina should he attempt other positions or active thrusting to orgasm.

5. In addition to the above four steps, Zilbergeld (1978) strongly recommends the use of fantasy and masturbation exercises for increasing the control of erection. For instance, during masturbation the man is advised to practice losing and regaining his erection several times before reaching orgasm. It is important that he not ejaculate until full or almost full erection is reached, since many men with chronic erection problems acquire the maladaptive habit of ejaculating with only partial erection.

Following this type of sex therapy program takes a great deal of commitment on the part of the dysfunctional man and his partner. For a man who is unwilling to follow these steps, there may be more appeal in the use of medical/technological solutions, such as hormone injections or a penile implantation (prosthesis).

Implants are tempting to many men. Surgery seems so much simpler than thinking about conditions and how relaxed you are, considering whether or not you want sex, talking to your partner—all the silly human things. Just have an operation and—barring equipment failure—you're all set. This logic appeals to many men who are accustomed to technological solutions for all problems. (Zilbergeld, 1978, p. 247)

In those rare cases where erection is permanently lost through trauma or disease, penile prosthesis—the surgical implantation of an inflatable or semirigid device inside the penis (see Figure 9.1)—can be a very valuable form of sexual rehabilitation. For example, a man whose spinal cord had been permanently damaged in an automobile accident suffered greatly from his inability to obtain an erection sufficient for intercourse. Since the nerve fibers critical for erection had been damaged by the accident and no hope of his recovering normal erectile capacity existed, his urologist surgically fitted him with a penile prosthesis. For such an individual, the implant is an important and justifiable last resort for regaining sexual capacity.

Another form of medical treatment is the prescription of testosterone injections or pills. When laboratory tests indicate the existence of a deficiency in male hormone levels, such treatment can be of considerable help in restoring erectile function (Sobotka, 1969). However, hormone supplements are frequently given to men who show no indication of a hormone deficiency. In such cases, positive treatment results may well be due to the placebo value of the injection or pill. In one study (Benkert *et al.*, 1979) a group of twenty-nine older men experiencing erectile dysfunction were treated for 2 weeks with a placebo drug; then, thirteen of the men were given daily supplements of a form of testosterone while the rest continued to take the placebo. At the end of this period, eight of the placebo subjects reported improvement compared to only five of the subjects receiving hormone supplements. Further, the authors report that the hormone supplements decreased the overall levels of plasma testosterone. They conclude that for men who show no androgen deficiency, androgen supplements are no more effective than placebo treatment in restoring erectile capacity.

A more recent study (Spark *et al.*, 1980) has caused considerable controversy over the role

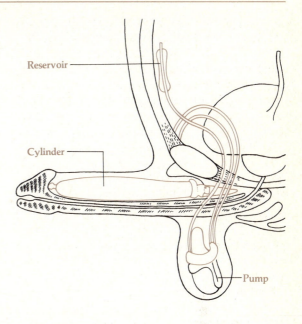

FIGURE 9.1

Penile prosthesis with pump for inflation. (*American Medical Systems, Minneapolis*)

of organic (hormone) factors in male erectile dysfunction. The authors of that study question the traditional wisdom that 90 percent of erectile failure is due to psychological factors, suggesting instead that subtle hormonal deficits or endocrine imbalance may be responsible for a much higher percentage of cases. In examining 105 men complaining of erectile problems, they found through hormonal assays that 37 of the men had a previously undetected disorder in hormonal function. Further, 33 of the men showed improvement in sexual capacity in response to hormonal treatment. Unfortunately, several methodological problems may limit the value of this research. First, the men who participated in the study were referred for hormonal assay by family physicians or internists — it may well be that the physician was more likely to refer a patient in whom a suspicion of hormonal difficulty existed than a patient whose problem seemed clearly psychogenic. Second, the authors used no control group; it is possible that even among a group of men with no erectile dysfunction there might be some who had a subtle hormonal imbalance that did *not* interfere with sexual function. Finally, the authors had no placebo group, so it seems likely that some of the patients were so relieved by a physical diagnosis of their problem that they improved in response to the placebo value of the hormone supplements.

The administration of hormones to men with erectile dysfunction has one major psychological drawback: if the patient is told that he has received impressive amounts of powerful male hormones and he then continues to experience sexual difficulties, he is likely to feel completely hopeless about the possibility of successful treatment. Often, men who have received unsuccessful hormone therapy for erectile problems experience much greater difficulty responding to subsequent psychological counseling.

Evaluation of treatment programs. How successful are these treatments for erectile dysfunction? It is difficult to draw any definite conclusion about effectiveness for two reasons: (1) With so many different reasons for erectile failure, the subjects in one study may be so unlike the subjects in another study as to make comparison of the results impossible. (2) Most of these techniques are relatively new, and long-term follow-up studies are few and far between (Reynolds, 1977). In fact, thus far the only study to include a 5-year follow-up of patients treated for erectile dysfunction is that of Masters and Johnson (1970). They found that

of all the problems they had treated, erectile dysfunction had the least certain outcome. Of patients with primary impotence — that is, no history of successful intercourse — 40 percent failed to overcome their problem. The initial failure rate for men with secondary impotence was 26 percent, but after 5 years, this rate had increased to 31 percent.

A number of individual characteristics seem to predispose a more favorable outcome to therapy. After reviewing all the studies completed to date, Reynolds (1977) proposed the following list:

1. Some history of successful sexual behavior

2. Sudden onset of the problem, as opposed to slow onset

3. Short duration of the problem

4. Motivation to seek and follow counseling

5. An affectionate and cooperative partner

6. The absence of deeper psychological problems

In cases where all these factors are present, counseling is often effective in a relatively short period of time — between 3 and 8 weeks. On the other hand, some erectile problems can take months and even years of counseling to overcome, particularly if the problem is related to underlying psychological difficulties. Unfortunately, many men become impatient when immediate results are not forthcoming, and premature termination of therapy accounts for a considerable number of treatment failures.

RAPID (PREMATURE) EJACULATION

Rapid, or *premature, ejaculation* is often considered to be the single most prevalent sexual dysfunction among males. However, the prevalence of this dysfunction depends, to a large extent, on how we define "premature." If we include all healthy, sexually responsive young males, and if we count only the time from penetration to first ejaculation, then there certainly are a large number of "premature ejaculators" in our society. We would definitely apply this label to men who ejaculate so rapidly that they do not penetrate their sexual partner. But if we were to use Masters and Johnson's definition of prematurity—the inability to delay ejaculation until the female partner has reached orgasm during at least 50 percent of intercourse occasions—then we might apply the label to a man who ejaculates after 20 minutes of intercourse if his partner requires 40 minutes to reach orgasm. In situations where a man ejaculates within a period of minutes following intromission and rapid thrusting, the problem might have more to do with a limited script than with any physical or psychological problem on the part of the male.

CASE: Maxwell C., a 34-year-old engineer who had been married for 6 years, consulted a psychologist for help after losing his erection for the second time during intercourse. His wife had been complaining a great deal about his rapid ejaculation, which seemed to occur more and more quickly as Maxwell became increasingly anxious about his problem. Finally, his anxiety increased to the point of causing him to lose his erection before penetration could take place.

Rapid ejaculation as a normal response: Kinsey's argument. In his study of male sexuality, Kinsey argued that rapid ejaculation might be a normal or even a preferable response for certain men.

On the present issue [premature ejaculation], it is to be emphasized that in many species of mammals the male ejaculates almost instantly upon intromission, and that this is true of man's closest relatives among the primates. . . . It would be difficult to find another situation in which an individual who was quick and intense in his responses was labelled [sic] anything but superior,

and that in most instances is exactly what the rapidly ejaculating male probably is, however inconvenient and unfortunate his qualities may be from the standpoint of the wife in the relationship. (1948, p. 580)

A great deal of criticism has been directed at Kinsey for focusing too much on the reproductive functions of sexuality. While rapid ejaculation may have some advantages for reproduction, it can be a major drawback when considering the recreative functions of sexual intercourse. For the man who feels that he cannot control his own ejaculation, much of the pleasure of intercourse may be lost. Kaplan (1974) defines premature ejaculation primarily in terms of lack of control, rather than in terms of time; thus a man may be perceived as having an ejaculation problem regardless of whether intercourse lasts for 10 seconds or 10 minutes. According to Kaplan, the goal of therapy should be to develop a sense of control over the ejaculatory reflex.

There is a real danger of extending the concept of "prematurity" too far, and Kinsey's point of view should serve as a restraining influence in this respect. For a highly aroused young man to ejaculate quickly can almost always be viewed as a sign of sexual health and not of dysfunction. Typically, such a man will have a short refractory period; thus, it makes more sense for him to attempt more than one ejaculation during a session of love making than to focus all his attention on slowing his response.

On the other hand, Kinsey's view should be qualified for those men who cannot enjoy sexual intercourse because of persistent and uncontrollable rapid ejaculation. Most men tend to show improved ejaculatory control as a normal part of the aging process, but in a few cases, the problem becomes worse instead of better with time. Anxiety and guilt feelings usually play a role in these chronic cases of premature ejaculation, and sex therapy with a qualified professional is indicated to deal with the problem.

Specific causes of premature ejaculation. The sexual response patterns that lead to premature ejaculation are often established during adolescence. Early sexual behaviors—including both masturbation and intercourse—are generally accompanied by the fear of being caught, and so the young man learns to reach orgasm as quickly as possible. Some young men learn to reach orgasm even before they have a full erection.

There are very few physical or medical causes of rapid ejaculation—the problem is almost always due to psychogenic factors (or, according to Kinsey, to healthy sexual responsivity). In rare cases, prostatic or urethral infections can lead to uncontrolled ejaculations. Also, a few drugs may increase the speed of ejaculation—for example, drugs that stimulate the central nervous system. There is also a popular myth that the glans of the uncircumcised male (because it is covered by foreskin) is more sensitive and so responds more quickly to stimulation, which sometimes results in premature ejaculation. However, no scientific support exists for this belief, and circumcision usually offers no help to the man who ejaculates rapidly.

Because the ejaculation reflex is controlled by the sympathetic branch of the autonomic nervous system, emotional factors can and often do affect the control of ejaculation. For example, a state of fear or anxiety will cause an overreaction of the sympathetic nervous system, and this can trigger ejaculation. As with erectile dysfunction, rapid ejaculation is often accompanied by a "performance anxiety" that further compounds the problem. The more the man thinks about his problem, the more anxious he becomes, and consequently, the faster he ejaculates.

When premature ejaculation is associated with marital discord, it is sometimes believed to be an expression of hostility on the part of the husband; by ejaculating rapidly, he is able to deprive his wife of adequate sexual stimulation. However, the problem also occurs frequently in marriages where there is no hostility. On the other hand, persistent premature ejaculation often leads to hostility on the part of the wife, who is repeatedly left frustrated and disappointed by her sexual experiences. It is not unusual for a serious and long-standing ejaculation problem on the male's part to be accompanied by an orgasmic problem on the part of the female partner. Thus Masters and Johnson (1970) recommend viewing the problem as a sexual dysfunction of the marital unit.

Treatment of premature ejaculation. Our sexual folklore is filled with "home remedies" for rapid ejaculation. Some men attempt to distract themselves from the excitement of the sexual experience with mental techniques—reviewing the stock market, counting sheep, or remembering an unpleasant incident. Others use creams or lotions that numb penile sensation. Still others believe that cold showers or strenuous physical exercise will slow their ejaculatory response. All of these techniques may have some success, but they also have a major limitation—they distract the man, either mentally or physically, from the experience he seeks to enhance.

Professional counseling typically proceeds initially along the same general lines as for erectile dysfunction. A complete sexual history will be taken from the man and, if available, from his sexual partner. Their relationship will be evaluated, as will their sexual history as a unit. Then the man will be instructed *not* to attempt intercourse for a stipulated period. The role of performance anxiety will be discussed, and steps will be taken to minimize this anxiety.

Perhaps the most effective technique for dealing with premature ejaculation was developed by James Semans in 1956. The *Semans technique* is based on the idea that the male's stimulation threshold for ejaculation is too low —that is, he requires only very low levels of sexual stimulation in order to reach orgasm. To increase this threshold, the following steps are followed:

1. The man stimulates his penis until he feels that he is about to ejaculate.

2. He stops the stimulation and waits for the sensation of high arousal level to decrease.

3. He then resumes stimulation of his penis.

This procedure is repeated again and again until the man can experience high levels of arousal without feeling the need to ejaculate. With continued practice, as he learns to tolerate high levels of stimulation without needing to ejaculate, he should need to stop stimulation less often.

This basic procedure has been modified by Masters and Johnson (1970) to include the female sexual partner and is called the *squeeze technique*. At the point when the male feels the urge to ejaculate, his partner is instructed to

In any sexual therapy, the marital history of the couple as a unit is an important guide to their sexual problems. *(Alisa Wells Witteman 1970)*

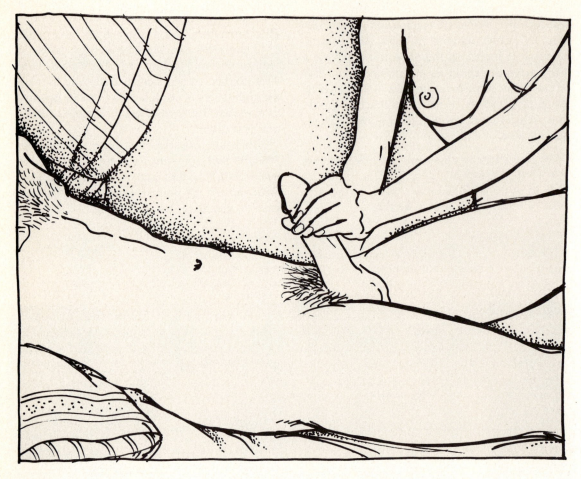

FIGURE 9.2

The Semans procedure for treatment of premature ejaculation. The man is instructed to lie on his back and to focus on the sensations produced by his partner's manual stimulation. He is to signal her when ejaculation is approaching. This procedure is repeated several times in each session.

squeeze firmly around the frenulum of his penis. The squeezing movement is intended to eliminate the urge to ejaculate and may cause a partial loss of erection. Then, the female continues to stimulate her partner until the next "squeeze" becomes necessary. A crucial part of this technique is that the male must recognize when ejaculation is imminent and communicate his awareness to his partner.

Although both the Semans technique and the squeeze technique are quite effective, there are some advantages in making use of self-masturbation before involving the female partner. If the male is attempting the exercise himself, he can focus exclusively on his own sensations and learn to recognize the "point of inevitability," when orgasm cannot be forestalled; he does not have to worry about communicating this information to his partner. Further, by practicing alone, he may build up confidence and reduce his anxiety. When he feels confident enough that he can control his ejaculation, he may attempt to teach his partner to cooperate in applying the technique that he has learned.

Once the man has gained control of his ejaculation with his partner applying manual or oral stimulation, the therapist might suggest that they attempt intercourse. Usually, the female is instructed to guide his penis into her vagina while sitting astride him but to remain completely stationary. Gradually, the couple may begin to attempt active thrusting. If at any time the male feels he cannot control his response, the couple are instructed to move back to a less demanding sexual interaction. Although intermittent failures may occur, this program is successful in solving a large majority of ejaculatory problems.

DELAYED (RETARDED) EJACULATION

Just as some men do not have sufficient control to delay their ejaculation for a reasonable span of time, other men are overcontrolled and cannot ejaculate when they would like to. In those cases where a man is completely unable to ejaculate, Masters and Johnson (1970) label the problem *ejaculatory imcompetence*. For some men this label may be felt as humiliating.

Delayed ejaculation can be further identified as either primary — present from the first sexual experience — or secondary — developing after some period of satisfactory sexual function. Kaplan (1974) has added the term "partial retarded ejaculation" to describe cases in which ejaculation does occur but is accompanied by little sensation or muscular contraction associated with orgasm. The common element in all these forms of delayed ejaculation is a sense of being unable to ejaculate in the right way or at the right time despite the presence of a firm erection and a willing partner.

Causes of delayed ejaculation. Delayed ejaculation has traditionally been regarded as one of the more rare forms of male sexual dysfunction. In Masters and Johnson's clinical sample, less than 5 percent of the couples coming for treatment complained of this problem. However, there is some indication that the frequency of delayed ejaculation is increasing, perhaps because of the pressures placed on young men to hold off ejaculation for longer and longer periods of time. In attempting to delay ejaculation, some men lose ejaculatory ability altogether. Generally, such cases of secondary delayed ejaculation are far more amenable to treatment than the long-standing or primary cases.

CASE: John S., a 38-year-old sales representative, had been married for 9 years. At the insistence of his 32-year-old wife, the couple sought counseling for their sexual problem — his inability to ejaculate during intercourse. During the early years of the marriage, his wife had experienced difficulty reaching orgasm until he learned to delay his ejaculation for a long period of time. To do this, he used mental distraction techniques and regularly smoked marihuana before making love. Initially, John felt very satisfied that he could make love for longer and longer periods of time without ejaculation and regarded his ability as a sign of masculinity.

About 3 years prior to seeking counseling, after the birth of their only child, John found that he was losing his erection before he was able to ejaculate. His wife suggested different intercourse positions, but the harder he tried, the more difficulty he had in reaching orgasm. Because of his frustration, the couple began to avoid sex altogether. John experienced increasing performance anxiety with each successive failure, and an increasing sense of helplessness in the face of his problem.

Many psychogenic factors can play a role in causing delayed ejaculation. For example, religious fears or strong sexual taboos can be involved, as can fear of making the female partner pregnant. In addition, men who are emotionally overcontrolled in general might experience difficulty in "letting go" and allowing ejaculation to take place. Such men may develop great skill in satisfying the sexual needs of their partners, but because of their constant desire to be in control, they are unable to reach orgasm themselves. In other cases, relationship conflicts can lead to withholding of ejaculation on the male's part as an expression of hostility or anger toward his partner (Kaplan, 1974).

Maladaptive sexual learning patterns can also play a role. Jay Mann (1976) has discussed the importance of unusual methods of masturbation in some men who develop delayed ejaculation. The major difficulty seems to be that the pattern of stimulation provided by intercouse is too different from the stimulation provided by the unusual masturbation technique suggested.

For example, one man would masturbate by striking the shaft of the penis forcefully with the heel of his hand; another lightly stroked the urethral meatus with a throat swab; a third stimulated only one spot on the shaft with rotary movements of the index finger. Thus, these individuals had succeeded in conditioning the ejaculatory response to forms of stimulation not provided by coitus. (Mann, 1976, p. 4)

In addition, men who masturbate with very unusual fantasies (often masochistic) may experience some difficulty ejaculating inside the vagina.

Although it is very unusual for physical factors to be the direct cause of delayed ejacula-tion, certain drugs and diseases may play a role. For instance, major tranquilizers such as Mellaril work by inhibiting the sympathetic nervous system and can lead to "dry" ejaculation or delayed ejaculation in some men. Any disease, injury, or drug that affects the sympathetic nervous system or the specific nerves controlling ejaculation may be a factor in causing delayed ejaculation.

Overcoming retarded ejaculation. As with other male sexual problems, the first goal of therapy is to confront and relieve performance anxieties. Structured tasks such as the sensate focus program are very useful in diverting the man's attention away from his problem and onto the pleasurable sensations experienced in various parts of his body. Men with this problem are characteristically preoccupied during intercourse with thoughts about ejaculation. In turn, this preoccupation reduces the physical pleasure that they feel and thus the likelihood of their reaching orgasm. Establishing a relaxed mental set is, therefore, the first important step for a man in overcoming retarded ejaculation.

Some men with this problem are able to ejaculate with masturbation or with manual or oral stimulation provided by a partner. In such cases, the method of *behavior shaping*, derived from behavior modification principles, can be very effective. To use this technique, a series of intermediate behavioral goals, starting from the point at which the man can function, are set up; he then proceeds step by step toward the ultimate goal of ejaculation during intercourse. The typical steps in this program are as follows:

1. Male masturbates to ejaculation in private.

2. Male masturbates to ejaculation with partner present.

3. Female places her hands over male's hand while he masturbates to ejaculation.

4. Female masturbates male to ejaculation.

5. Female stimulates male orally to ejaculation.

6. Female inserts penis into vagina for several minutes, followed by manual or oral stimulation to ejaculation.

7. Female stimulates penis almost to point of ejaculation several times before inserting penis into the vagina. After several repetitions of this last step, the male will usually experience his first intravaginal ejaculation.

It is important to note that some of these steps, such as oral stimulation to ejaculation, may be hard for either partner and may need to be modified. A behavior-shaping program will be most effective if the attitudes and feelings of the sexual partners are explored first, and any negative feelings resolved. As mentioned earlier, delayed ejaculation can sometimes be an expression of fear, distrust, or hostility on the part of the male towards his partner. For example, one man became unable to ejaculate during intercourse after discovering that his wife was having an affair. It was essential to resolve his feelings about this affair before the behavior-shaping program could begin.

How effective are these treatments in overcoming delayed ejaculation? In the Masters and Johnson clinical sample, less than 20 percent of delayed ejaculation problems were unresolved at the end of therapy. However, this finding requires cautious interpretation since the sample comprised only seventeen couples. More recently, Mann (1976) has reported statistics from the University of California program that are much less optimistic —about 40 percent of men with this problem were unsuccessful in therapy. Some cases of delayed ejaculation are related to deeply ingrained interpersonal problems and may require very extended counseling before significant progress is seen. Factors such as the duration of the problem, the health of the partner relationship, and the overall psychological adjustment of the individual are all important determinants in predicting the chances of success.

Female Sexual Problems

Our cultural concepts of female sexuality have undergone enormous changes in the past century, and particularly in the past 20 years. The work of sex researchers such as Havelock Ellis, Kinsey, Masters and Johnson, and others have succeeded in liberating us from the Victorian denial of female sexual potential. It is now accepted that the modern woman has a legitimate right to sexual gratification; however, this right brings with it a series of new conflicts and dilemmas. For example: Can a woman be both "feminine" and sexually assertive? Is it "normal" for a woman to want sex more than her male partner does? Should every woman be capable of having multiple orgasms? These and other questions create self-doubts that may be an important source of many sexual problems. Additionally, the recent explosion of information on sexual function and techniques has set up a new group of sexual performance demands to which women are just as susceptible as men. "Sex—once evil, then a conjugal duty, then psychologically dangerous —[has] come to be an expected accomplishment" (LoPiccolo and Heiman, 1978, p. 62).

In view of these cultural changes and demands, it is not surprising that a considerable number of women experience dissatisfaction with some aspect of their sexual performance.

ANORGASMIA (LACK OF ORGASM)

In his study of female sexuality, Kinsey (1952) found that about 10 percent of the women he surveyed had never experienced orgasm through either masturbation or intercourse. In a more recent study, Hite (1976) reported that about 11 percent of the women who responded to her questionnaire were anorgasmic. Although the proportion of orgasmic women tends to increase with length of marriage and with age, as many as 25 percent of women in the Kinsey sample were anorgasmic at the end of their first year of marriage. Orgasmic ability seems to peak between the ages of 30 and 45, with a gradual decline following in the 50s and 60s. Kinsey's early findings have been confirmed by more recent research (Hunt, 1974). The obvious conclusion to be drawn from these studies is that anorgasmia, or lack of orgasm, effects a considerable number of women in our society.

Anorgasmia can be categorized in a number of ways. Masters and Johnson (1970) use the term *primary orgasmic dysfunction* to describe a woman who has never experienced orgasm from any means of stimulation — manual, oral, or intercourse. Barbach (1975) labels this same group as *pre-orgasmic* to emphasize their future potential for developing orgasmic ability. The woman who can experience orgasm in some, but not all, situations is described by Masters and Johnson as having a *situational orgasmic dysfunction*. Typically, the women in this group have difficulty reaching orgasm during intercourse but have no difficulty with manual or oral stimulation. Anorgasmia, like male erectile dysfunction, can also be classified as *primary* or *secondary* — that is, the problem may have always existed or be of more recent origin.

Kaplan (1974) cautions that anorgasmia should not be confused with disinterest in sex or with difficulty in becoming sexually aroused. "As a general rule, women who suffer from orgasmic dysfunction are responsive sexually. They may fall in love, experience erotic feelings, lubricate copiously, and also show genital swelling" (p. 343). Also, Barbach (1975) has worked with a number of "pre-orgasmic" women who were experiencing major self-esteem problems because of their sexual frustration and disappointment. However, probably some women for whom orgasm is not an important goal, feel contented without it.

According to Kaplan, failure to reach orgasm during intercourse is not necessarily a dysfunction at all, although it may be a major disappointment: "It is difficult to believe that the millions of otherwise responsive women who do not have coital orgasms are all 'sick' " (Kaplan, 1974, p. 398). Kaplan suggests that for some women, the inability to reach orgasm during intercourse is a normal variation of female sexuality. Since women require different amounts and types of stimulation to reach orgasm, it seems likely that for certain women, the stimulation provided by intercourse is not enough to trigger the orgasm reflex.

CASE: Margaret D. grew up in a conservative middle-class home in which sex was a taboo subject. A virgin at the time of her marriage, she enjoyed sex with her husband despite a consistent feeling that "something was missing." After the birth of her second child, Margaret decided to return to her teaching career. Although she was proud of her roles as teacher and mother, her sex life remained disappointing and frustrating. A pattern emerged in which her husband would ejaculate after several minutes of intercourse with no orgasm on her part. Her husband blamed himself for his inadequate sexual technique and became increasingly defensive in their discussions of the problem. At the suggestion of Margaret's gynecologist, the couple decided to seek sexual counseling.

Causes of anorgasmia. Margaret's case is a

For women who have trouble attaining orgasm, the use of sexual fantasy can be an effective stimulus. (© *Susan Shapiro*)

typical example of anorgasmia problems of the simplest kind, deficit in learning—the woman simply has not learned how to experience orgasm. While learning to ejaculate seems to happen naturally for the vast majority of males, women do not inevitably learn how to reach orgasm. Perhaps this is due to their differing reproductive functions—male ejaculation is required if conception is to occur, female orgasm is not. Other major causes of anorgasmia are psychological inhibition and relationship factors.

Learning/experience deficits. Kaplan (1974) has proposed the existence of a continuum of orgasmic ability: sexual fantasy alone is sufficient to trigger orgasm in some women; others require intense and prolonged clitoral stimulation. Discovering the appropriate level and type of stimulation to trigger an orgasm is often a matter of trial and error. Kinsey (1953) found that most women discover masturba-

tion accidentally while exploring their genitals. He also reported that women who masturbated to orgasm before marriage were more likely to be orgasmic within the marital relationship. While it is not clear that the experience of masturbation *causes* orgasmic ability during intercourse, it is very likely that masturbation is one very important way for a woman to learn how to achieve orgasm. Hite (1976) found that anorgasmia was five times higher among women who had never attempted masturbation.

Many women have little awareness or information about their own sexual anatomy. The sex counselor is frequently asked such questions as: Where is the clitoris? Is my husband's penis too short for me to reach orgasm? What is an orgasm? How will I know when I've had one? Ignorance about sexual anatomy and function can prevent a woman from acquiring the necessary sexual skills to reach orgasm.

Lack of experience and knowledge on the part of the male sexual partner can further compound the problem.

Psychological inhibition. Although orgasm is a physiological reflex, it can easily be inhibited for a variety of psychological reasons. One possible cause of psychological inhibition mentioned by Masters and Johnson (1970) is a strict religious upbringing. About 20 percent of the women in their clinical sample who had never experienced orgasm were from strictly religious families. Orthodox Catholic and Jewish backgrounds were more common in this group than Protestant. However, a number of other studies do not find that religious upbringing per se correlates with orgasmic ability (Morokoff, 1978). It is difficult to reconcile these findings except by suggesting that perhaps only a particular subgroup of women are affected by religious prohibitions.

Another source of inhibition is the fear of losing control. This fear may take a specific form—for instance, Barbach (1975) found that some women anticipate fainting, screaming, or other involuntary reactions if they were to experience orgasm. For other women, it is important to remain in emotional control during a sexual interaction, and their inability to let go acts as a major impediment to orgasm. It is normal for a woman (or man) to experience a momentary loss of consciousness during orgasm, but for some women the fear of losing touch is sufficiently strong to inhibit orgasm. One interesting theory (Fisher, 1973) is that women who experience male love objects (e.g., father, husband) as undependable will have greater difficulty in giving up control to sexual sensations and therefore be more likely to show orgasmic inhibition.

Orgasmic inhibition can easily be *learned*, so that even though the original reasons for holding back are no longer present, the conditioned inhibition can be strong enough to block orgasm. For instance, a woman who

grows up believing it is "unfeminine" to show sexual excitement will tend to inhibit her sexual response. Her attitudes toward showing sexual excitement may subsequently change, but her habit of inhibiting orgasm may be too powerful to be easily reversed. At this point, *performance anxiety* may also play a role: the harder she tries to reach orgasm, the more anxious and inhibited she becomes, and the less likely she is to have an orgasm. In many ways, her experience may parallel that of the man whose performance anxiety is inhibiting the erectile response.

Relationship factors. There are two ways that the relationship between a woman and her sexual partner may affect her ability to have orgasms. First, nonsexual problems in the relationship such as lack of trust or poor communication can lead to a pattern of sexual withholding. The woman need not require to be highly aroused to take part in intercourse, but her negative feelings toward her partner may prevent sufficient emotional involvement to achieve orgasm. Masters and Johnson (1970) found this to be particularly true in situations where the wife had lost respect for her husband and felt she had a "second-best" mate.

The second relationship factor important to a woman's orgasmic ability is her partner's level of sexual functioning. For example, obvious difficulties will exist if the male partner has serious erectile or ejaculatory control problems. If he loses his erection before or during intercourse, the woman will naturally find it difficult to reach orgasm. Similarly, in cases of extremely rapid ejaculation the woman may not be sufficiently aroused before her partner ejaculates. Even in the absence of male dysfunction, a male who does not use proper techniques can prevent his partner from reaching orgasm by failing to provide the necessary stimulation.

The role of the husband as an effective and nondemanding sexual partner for his wife is ob-

A woman who has lost respect for her partner may experience difficulty in functioning sexually with him. (© *Joel Gordon 1979*)

Johnson's results (1970) showing that most women (about 80 percent) could learn to become orgasmic without undergoing extensive psychotherapy or major personality change. By removing performance demands and providing direct instruction in techniques of genital stimulation, Masters and Johnson developed a program that was usually successful in a short period of time.

LoPiccolo and Lobitz (1973) augmented the Masters and Johnson approach by developing a guided masturbation training program for women who had never experienced orgasm. More recently, group methods (Leiblum and Ersner-Hershfield, 1977) and self-help manuals (Barbach, 1975; Heiman *et al.,* 1976; McMullen and Rosen, 1979) are commonly recommended for women with this problem.

The LoPiccolo program (1973) for becoming orgasmic consists of nine steps to be followed in sequence:

1. Self-exploration of the genitals with the aid of a hand mirror. Identification of the external genitals—the "looking" phase.

2. Start of tactile stimulation of the genitals—the "touching" phase.

3. Further tactile stimulation, focusing on areas of greatest sensitivity. Start of clitoral stimulation.

4. Intensive stimulation (masturbation) of the most sensitive areas. This step is usually continued for some time, with the use of artificial lubricants (e.g., K-Y jelly) to minimize discomfort from extended stimulation.

5. If orgasm does not occur in step 4, additional fantasy or the use of an electrical vibrator might be introduced into the program. Masturbation is

viously crucial in orgasmic dysfunction, especially secondary orgasmic dysfunction. In one sense it can be argued that if a woman can produce orgasm for herself through masturbation, but cannot have orgasm with her husband, he is the dysfunctional one. . . . The principle of mutual responsibility, however, points out that such a woman has failed to train her husband to be an effective lover for her. (LoPiccolo, 1977, p. 1240)

Becoming orgasmic. One of the most significant developments in the field of sex therapy has been the development and growth of programs designed specifically to help women become orgasmic. The first step in this direction came with the publication of Masters and

continued for up to 45 minutes per session until orgasm is reached.

6. For women who have difficulty in letting go, role playing of orgasmic reaction may be used to desensitize embarrassment and fears of loss of control.

7. The woman masturbates to orgasm with her partner present. He is instructed to pay close attention to her stimulation techniques.

8. The male partner attempts to do for her what she has been doing for herself. He applies either manual or vibrator stimulation to the point of orgasm.

9. The couple attempts intercourse for the first time. Intercourse positions are recommended in which the woman can receive manual or vibrator stimulation at the same time to maximize the probability that orgasm will occur during intercourse.

It is interesting to note that women who have never before achieved orgasm tend to be more successful at learning to have orgasm during intercourse than those women who are situationally anorgasmic. In the Masters and Johnson study, a 25-percent rate of failure was

FIGURE 9.3

Direct clitoral stimulation during intercourse. For some women, the thrusting of the penis alone is insufficient to produce orgasm during intercourse, and positions such as this one are recommended by sex therapists.

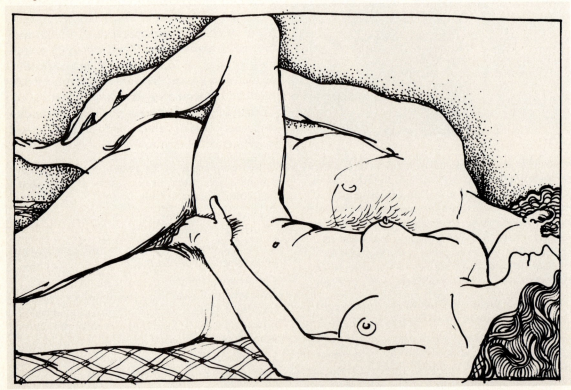

reported for the situational problems after 5 years, in contrast to an 18-percent failure rate among women who had never experienced orgasm in any situation prior to therapy. One possible explanation for this difference is that a woman who has never experienced orgasm may have little difficulty in transferring her newly learned response to intercourse. On the other hand, a woman who is orgasmic during masturbation only may have learned a particular pattern of stimulation that is difficult to transfer to the intercourse situation.

Among women with situational orgasmic problems, a large number find it difficult or impossible to reach orgasm during intercourse without additional clitoral stimulation. According to the traditional Freudian point of view, these women are "fixated" at the stage of "clitoral orgasm" and need to develop emotionally until they can experience the mature "vaginal orgasm." Evidence reviewed in Chapter 5 indicates that no real differences exist between clitoral and vaginal orgasms, however, and most authorities have come to reject the traditional Freudian point of view. Instead, many sex therapists accept the notion that women have different orgasmic thresholds; women with low thresholds respond orgasmically to relatively low levels of stimulation, whereas those with high thresholds require intense clitoral stimulation. These different thresholds seem to represent a normal variation in female sexuality, and no amount of therapy will cause a high-threshold woman to reach orgasm without clitoral stimulation.

There is increasing recognition of the importance of concurrent clitoral stimulation during intercourse as a means to female orgasm. In Hite's (1976) study, only 30 percent of the women were able to reach orgasm during intercourse without some form of additional stimulation. Nevertheless, many women continue to feel distressed by their inability to reach orgasm during intercourse.

One woman in the Hite study expressed her feelings as follows:

I would like manual clitoral stimulation during intercourse, but feel shy about asking for it since I have a fear of making the man feel shut down about the effectiveness of his penis. Equally, or more important, I have felt I ought to be able to do without it. (1975, p. 256)

PENETRATION PROBLEMS: VAGINISMUS AND DYSPAREUNIA

Vaginismus is the term applied to a condition in which penetration is difficult or impossible because of involuntary contraction of the muscles around the vagina. When the male sexual partner attempts intercourse, a muscular spasm occurs that effectively closes the entrance to the vagina and makes penetration impossible. In most cases, vaginismus occurs involuntarily, in the sense that the woman has no control over her response. *Dyspareunia* refers to pain or discomfort during intercourse and is sometimes, although not always, the cause of vaginismus. While both conditions lead to major problems with intercourse, vaginismus is usually psychogenic in origin, whereas dyspareunia is often caused by physical problems.

Causes of penetration problems. The critical first step in evaluating penetration problems is physical examination, preferably by a gynecologist. In severe cases of vaginismus, the physician may find that spastic contractions of muscles surrounding the vagina make the normal pelvic examination impossible. In less severe cases, it may be possible to insert a speculum or two fingers for examination purposes.

When dyspareunia is the complaint, the physician will usually examine for the following conditions:

Vaginal infections such as monilia or trichomoniasis

Endometriosis and infections of the cervix or uterus

Scar tissue in the vagina due to infection or surgery

The most common cause noted by Masters and Johnson (1970) was inadequate lubrication of the vagina, for either physical or psychological reasons. The absence of adequate lubrication can lead to intense sensations of burning, itching, or aching during intercourse. Since women who have passed the menopause produce less lubricant, they tend to be more susceptible to this problem. When dyspareunia appears to result from lubrication problems, most professionals recommend the use of an artificial lubricant.

Vaginismus is usually associated with negative sexual learning or specific fears about intercourse. For example, women who have suffered the psychological trauma of rape will sometimes develop vaginismus. Exaggerated fears of pregnancy or injury from intercourse are other important factors (Kaplan, 1974). Strong religious taboos against sex are also found in some cases. Finally, Masters and Johnson (1970) report that a number of cases of vaginismus are associated with serious erection problems on the part of the male partner. In some cases, the male's repeated failure to penetrate his wife, and the resulting frustration, had caused the male erection problem. In other cases, however, the erection problem seemed to precede the vaginismus and may have been caused by the female's response to repeated frustration during intercourse. Whatever the original cause, authorities agree that vaginismus is a serious sexual problem that, if uncorrected, can lead to complete disruption of the sexual relationship. Often, it plays a role in marriages that remain unconsummated for many years.

A woman with vaginismus may be capable of both sexual arousal and orgasm, although not intercourse. Some woman adjust to this problem by achieving sexual satisfaction through manual or oral stimulation. In other cases, the difficulty and frustration with intercourse can lead to a general loss of interest in sex. The response of the woman's partner will determine, to a large extent, her adjustment to the problem.

Counseling for vaginismus. A woman being counseled for vaginismus must first learn to relax completely in the presence of sexual stimulation. This can be accomplished in a number of ways, one of them being the sensate focus program developed by Masters and Johnson. Behavior therapists may use deep muscle relaxation techniques as a first step. Muscle relaxant drugs, deep breathing, and relaxing imagery are also sometimes used for this purpose.

Once the woman is able to relax completely, the second step is to desensitize her gradually to increasing amounts of vaginal penetration. The therapist might begin by asking her to imagine inserting a tampon or finger into her vagina, then gradually progress, through imagination, to intercourse. When she is comfortable with these images of penetration, a carefully structured program of actual insertion is started. For instance, vaginal dilators of increasing thickness may be inserted (usually in a gynecologist's office) or the couple can practice insertion at home, using only the wife's or husband's fingers. Several repetitions of each step may be necessary before the woman is relaxed enough to proceed from one step to the next, and this may require considerable patience from both members of the couple. The final step in this desensitization program would be for the woman to sit astride her partner and slowly insert his penis into her vagina. Most women need several weeks or even months of practice before they are ready to attempt this step.

In addition to desensitization, some counselors suggest the use of specific exercises (Kegel, 1952) to improve control over the vaginal muscles. For example, the woman is instructed to practice a pattern of urination in which she stops the flow of urine for several seconds, starts again for several seconds, and then stops again. Starting and stopping the flow of urine in this way leads to an increased awareness and control over the pelvic muscles. Once the woman has learned to identify the muscles involved, she can practice voluntary contraction and relaxation of these muscles several times per day. Although a number of women have reported a greater sense of con-

fidence after performing these exercises, there is an unfortunate lack of research documenting their real effectiveness.

Both Kaplan (1974) and Masters and Johnson (1970) report complete success when the methods to counter penetration problems are carefully applied. However, many women with vaginismus do not seek counseling, or they terminate treatment prematurely. Among women who are successful in overcoming the problem, many find that their future sexual relationships are devoid of further problems. In some cases, however, overcoming the vaginismus problem will reveal additional sexual or interpersonal problems that had previously been masked by the absence of intercourse (Kaplan, 1974).

Sexual Desire Deficits in Males and Females

The category of sexual desire deficits includes sexual dysfunctions that are the most difficult to define, and also the most difficult to overcome. Dysfunctions within this category may range from a diminished desire for sex to an apparently total absence of sexual feelings. Men and women with low levels of sexual desire may show the normal responses in a sexual situation — such as lubrication in the female and erection in the male — yet have little urge to initiate or participate in sexual activities. Some men and women may go through the motions but experience little sexual pleasure; others actually find the experience very unpleasant and avoid it completely. Finally, some men and women find sexual interaction pleasurable but prefer to engage in sexual behavior at far lower rates than those of the general population.

Traditionally, low sex drive and low sexual responsiveness were thought of as an exclusively female problem. While more women than

men may show desire deficits, it is now recognized that males can also exhibit disinterest in sexual activity. In fact, the individual who is sexually disinterested may not perceive herself (or himself) as having a problem at all. Deficits in desire or responsiveness are most likely to become problematic within the context of a relationship in which one partner has greater sexual needs than the other.

Low sexual interest may be a chronic condition — that is, existing throughout the sexual life cycle — or it may become apparent only after some specific life event or phase. For example, some women complain that after the birth of a child their sexual interest decreases dramatically, for reasons that are difficult to explain. Often, these acute lapses in sexual interest will disappear once the external environment changes.

There are important gender differences in how people deal with their low sexual interest or lack of responsiveness. A man with no desire for sex will typically avoid it out of fear of erectile failure and the consequent inability to perform during intercourse. In contrast, since a woman need not necessarily be sexually aroused or motivated in order to participate in intercourse, women with sexual desire deficits are less likely to avoid sex. Further, many women are willing to engage in sex for nonsexual reasons — for example, the opportunity for closeness and intimacy.

CAUSES OF DESIRE DEFICITS

Physical stress or illness can often lead to a loss of interest in sex, as can any physical condition that places an unusual strain on the nerv-

ous system. Certain drugs, especially sedatives and narcotics, can produce central nervous system depression and consequently a reduction in sexual desire. In addition, illness or certain surgical procedures such as mastectomy can lead to secondary psychological stress reactions causing long-term sexual unresponsiveness.

Lack of interest or unresponsiveness may also be related to another, more specific form of sexual dysfunction. For example, a woman who is anorgasmic or a man with erectile dysfunction might gradually lose interest in sex because of repeated frustration and disappointment. In these cases, the lack of desire may sometimes persist even after the primary difficulty has been overcome.

Traumatic early sexual experiences or strong sex-negative learning can sometimes lead to chronic sexual disinterest. Even painful or traumatic rejection experienced in adulthood may lead to a defensive denial of sexuality (Kaplan, 1977). For example, a woman whose mate consistently rejects her sexual advances may decide that sex simply is not important. In addition, sexual unresponsiveness may sometimes be associated with loss of respect for the partner.

According to Kaplan (1977), men with unusual sexual preferences — ranging from exhibitionism and fetishism through strong sadomasochistic fantasies — may find that they are unresponsive and disinterested in more conventional sexual settings.

Childhood traumas often affect one's sexual functioning as an adult. The writer Virginia Woolf was molested as a child by her half-brother. As a married woman, she remained disinterested in sexual relations with her husband. *(Culver Pictures)*

APPROACHES TO COUNSELING

There is no generally agreed upon approach to the set of problems encompassed by the label "sexual desire deficit," in part because of the broad range of difficulties and their intrinsically subjective nature. In contrast, such problems as vaginismus are easy to delineate and therefore comparatively easy to overcome through a structured and standardized sex therapy program. Sexual desire problems seem to be among the most difficult to modify, and Kaplan (1977) has noted that they account for a significant number of failures in her sex therapy program. However, when the problem seems to be related to a specific change in the overall life pattern — such as pregnancy or change of job — then sexual interest often reappears with the passage of time.

Rosen and Leiblum (1976) have advocated a counseling approach based on compromise. Recognizing that low sexual interest may be more of a problem for the rejected partner than for the individual who is actually experiencing it, they suggest that frank communication might lead to certain options acceptable to both partners. For example, mutual masturbation, oral sex, or massage might be included as substitute sexual activities, and the couple might compromise on a rate of sexual activity. A mature recognition and acceptance of the differences in sexual need between members of the couple is a great advantage in coping with this problem.

When lack of sexual interest in a partner follows a general loss of interest in the relationship, both the causes and the solutions for the problem are likely to be more complex. Specifically, a range of factors from simple boredom with the relationship, to deep-seated hostility toward the partner can lead to both emotional detachment and loss of sexual desire. For some marital counseling or extended therapy can help overcome problems. In many other cases, however, increasing dissatisfaction, and ultimately separation, results. And in still other circumstances, a marriage or relationship without sex can be the result.

Current Trends and Future Directions

The past decade has seen an enormous increase in our knowledge about the causes of and solutions to common sexual problems. But concepts are changing rapidly in this field, and many of the methods being used today will probably become obsolete in the next decade. Unfortunately, research is lagging far behind clinical practice, and many new techniques are being introduced and used without adequate scientific evaluation. Perhaps the most encouraging trend in the field of sex therapy, however, is the growing number of institutions that are supporting research and evaluation programs.

Following the maxim that "an ounce of prevention is worth a pound of cure," there is also an encouraging trend toward emphasizing sex education with the goal of improving sexual function. Mary Calderone (1978), one of the most important figures in the field of sex education, has stressed the value of sex education in promoting sex-positive attitudes and providing sex information — both being factors that go a long way toward the prevention of sexual problems. In addition, several books published over the decade (e.g., Boston Women's Health Collective, 1975; Barbach, 1975; Zilbergeld, 1978) have presented the causes of and solutions to common sexual problems in language that is readily accessible to the public.

Several new and innovative approaches to sexual counseling appear to hold promise for the future. For instance, many advantages are apparent in the use of *group* methods for treatment of sexual dysfunction. Group methods have been found effective in counseling anorgasmic women (Barbach, 1975), men with rapid ejaculation problems (Kaplan *et al.*, 1974), and couples with a variety of sexual problems (Lieblum *et al.*, 1976).

The *weekend workshop* format also appears to have a number of advantages in overcoming sexual problems (Leiblum and Rosen, 1979). Although long-standing sexual dysfunctions may not be reversed in such a short span of time, the weekend workshop can be a useful tool in stimulating major attitude changes and improved marital communication. Also, the group experience can be a powerful motivating force.

The most controversial innovations in treatment involve the techniques of nude encounter and sexual contact with the therapist. For example, Hartman and Fithian (1974) use a number of these controversial techniques in their Southern California sex therapy program. During the so-called sexological examination, therapists will touch and stimulate the breasts and genitals of the patient in order to determine responses to stimulation and areas of maximum sensitivity. Such techniques have a great potential for abuse on the part of the counselor, and they have been rejected by most professionals in the field. Likewise, the use of *surrogate partners* — individuals who are paid to provide real-life sexual instruction to the dysfunctional individual — has been abandoned by Masters and Johnson and by most other sex therapists because of the potential for abuse.

The growth of sex therapy as a specialized form of treatment has been accompanied in recent years by the demand for a set of professional standards and training qualifications. AASECT (the American Association of Sex Educators, Counselors, and Therapists) began a program of sex therapy certification in 1974. Anyone wishing to inquire about the credentials of a sex therapist can do so through the organization's office in Washington, D.C. Although we still have a long way to go in developing comprehensive and generally accepted licensing procedures, a definite trend is noticeable toward greater consumer protection from unqualified individuals who advertise themselves as sex therapists.

Summary

This chapter began with a consideration of how sexual problems are defined and the changes that have taken place with regard to how we label our sexual difficulties. The vague and pejorative labels "frigidity" and "impotence" have generally been superseded by a new terminology for sexual dysfunction. Nowadays, we tend to think more of a continuum of sexual competence or capacity, rather than in such absolute terms. Also, there are a number of important approaches to explaining sexual problems and a variety of specific self-help and counseling techniques available today. Specifically, the following points have been emphasized:

1. Sexual problems can be influenced by many causal factors, some of them more immediate and some of them more remote. Physical health can play a role, and we have considered a number of physical causes of sexual

dysfunction. For most men and women, however, the evidence suggests that attitudes, emotions, and interpersonal relationships are the source of the major difficulties.

2. Masters and Johnson (1970) have greatly emphasized the importance of couples working together to overcome sexual problems. Rather than singling out the dysfunctional individual, they suggest that both partners in a relationship need to be involved and to take responsibility.

3. Among the most common male problems are primary and secondary impotence, rapid or premature ejaculation, and delayed ejaculation. There are a number of differing counseling approaches to male problems with erection and ejaculation. Men with long-standing sexual problems such as these are often anxious and demoralized, and may seek relief through physical solutions such as hormone injections or penile implants.

4. In considering female sexual problems, it is important to remember the changing attitudes in our culture towards female sexuality. Women are no longer expected to participate passively in sexual relations, and many women now experience the same pressures to perform as men do. Among the most common female problems are anorgasmia (lack of orgasm) and penetration difficulties.

5. Certain general observations can be made on the basis of our experience in counseling men and women with a wide range of sexual problems such as these. Although there are many valuable techniques for dealing with these problems, there is no panacea or one method that will work in every case. Patience and perseverance are extremely important in overcoming long-standing sexual dysfunction. Problems such as lack of desire are especially difficult to overcome and may require compromise solutions. On the other hand, there are many common sexual problems that cause unnecessary personal suffering and relationship conflicts and are maintained because of ignorance and apathy.

Sex on the College Campus

As part of a human sexuality course offered at a large university, students were invited to share their feelings in a small group discussion. Like most students in such situations, this group needed some time to overcome their initial feelings of self-consciousness and embarrassment. With the help of an instructor who conducted some "warm-up" exercises and told the group about the problems that had troubled her during her college years, the discussion rapidly opened up and the students discovered many common themes in their experiences.

One of the first issues discussed was contraception. Anne, a 19 year old sophomore, related her feelings of humiliation and resentment at her treatment by the college health service when she sought a prescription for oral contraceptives: "I can't understand why they needed to know how many different sexual partners I had, and the nurse's look when she asked what I wanted made me feel so embarrassed." Robin, aged 18, said that she was too frightened by the idea of a gynecological exam to even ask for contraceptives although she was sexually active. Peter, a freshman, told about the first time he had gone to a drugstore to purchase condoms—and left with a box of cough drops instead.

Another issue that concerned the students was homosexuality. One young woman told about her brother's recent "coming out" and the problems that this had created in her family. A male student described his feelings of conflict and surprise when his roommate came out as gay: "Mike is still my friend, but I look at him differently now—there are certain things we just can't talk about, and I guess I'm always a bit concerned about how he feels about me."

Both male and female group members felt that the college environment pressured them to become more sexually experienced: "I'm afraid to admit that I'm still a virgin," commented Nancy, "since I assume that I'm the only one left in my dorm." Fears of being sexually inadequate—of not reaching orgasm at the "right time", for example, or being unable to get an erection—were also common. Many students admitted that their sexual activity conflicted with their religious views, family upbringing, or romantic notions about love and commitment.

Group discussions such as this are becoming increasingly common on campuses across the country. The so-called best years of your life can also be a time of great personal conflict and confusion. From a life cycle perspective, the college years are an important transition period between the dependence of living at home and the emergence of autonomous adulthood. The college campus is a special kind of social environment in which students are exposed, often for the first time, to issues and influences such as contraception, abortion, sex roles and feminism, homosexual rights, and in-depth sex education. At the same time, they have more opportunity to experiment and make sexual decisions. It is not surprising that many students feel considerable stress in their social and sexual relationships. As one group member put it: "By the end of my freshman year, I was much more concerned and involved with my sex life than with my grades."

THE "SEXUAL REVOLUTION" AND THE COLLEGE CAMPUS

College students, according to conventional wisdom, represent the vanguard of social change; we expect them to be more daring and experimental than other social groups, although this stereotype is certainly questionable. Our information about sexual changes comes primarily from a series of surveys, beginning in the 1940's, in which students from a variety of colleges have responded to interviews and questionnaires on a wide range of sexual topics. Before presenting this information, however, it is important to keep certain methodological cautions in mind. For instance, what are the characteristics of the college being surveyed? The size of a college, its geographical location, and the types of students it attracts will certainly influence the outcome. Also, since very few of these studies present the type of 100 percent sample employed by Kinsey (in which every member of the group responds), it is important to know which students participated and which refused to participate. Finally, among those that did participate, it is necessary to recognize the possibility of response bias—some students who feel that everyone else is sexually active may hesitate to admit their own inexperience, for example.

Despite these research problems, a number of consistent findings have emerged over the past four decades, and the magnitude of the changes that have occurred might be great enough to be called revolutionary. Perhaps the most significant finding is the number of unmarried students who become sexually active (have intercourse) during the college years. Table 1 summarizes the major findings on virginity rates on college campuses from the 1940's to the 1970's. Three major conclusions can be drawn:

1. More males are sexually active now than in the 1940's. For instance, while about 45 percent of male students had experienced intercourse in the 1940's (Finger, 1947; Kinsey et al., 1948), about 80 percent of college males were nonvirgins in the 1970's (King and Sobel, 1975; Playboy Magazine, 1976).

2. More females are sexually active now—indeed, the changes are even more striking than for males. While only about 25 percent of females surveyed by Kinsey and his colleagues (1953) were sexually active, recent studies have

shown that the number has tripled (Bauman and Wilson, 1972; Sarrel and Sarrel, 1974). The differences between males and females on this measure have all but disappeared.

3. There are significant differences in the rates of sexual activity from one campus to another. For instance, intercourse rates for Mormon students in Utah were a good deal lower than at a secular Midwestern college (Christenson and Gregg, 1958). The highest rates of sexual activity tend to be reported from surveys of campuses on the East Coast and in California.

The notion of sexual revolution, however, does not extend to every aspect of college student sexual behavior. For example, relatively little change has occurred in the number of partners with whom the college student has intercourse. During the protest years of the 1960's, a popular stereotype showed the rebellious college student as someone who experimented with drugs and believed in "free love"; the data, however, show that for the vast majority of students, this is a myth. Indeed, there may be a trend towards fewer sexual partners in the college years. In Kinsey's time a small but significant number of college males had intercourse with prostitutes. Today, visits to prostitutes are rare, and the emphasis for most college students is on a primary, committed relationship with the sexual partner.

SEXUAL ATTITUDES AND VALUES ON THE COLLEGE CAMPUS

It seems likely that changing rates of premarital intercourse on the college campus are related to a new set of sexual attitudes and values. Typically, traditional values such as "A woman should save her virginity for her husband" have been replaced by the view that "sexual intercourse is a normal part of a loving relationship". Thus, the student who feels that he or she is in a committed (but not necessarily permanent) relationship is more likely to engage in intercourse than the student of thirty or forty years ago. Also, one study has shown that the transition from virginity to non-virginity is more likely to be made by students who are independent-minded and autonomous, (Jessor and Jessor, 1975).

Of course, not all college students are sexually active before marriage. A variety of factors may be involved in abstaining from intercourse: the absence of a strong relationship, fear of pregnancy or venereal disease, or religious and moral convictions. Unfortunately, the notion of a sexual revolution on campus can place uncomfortable pressures and performance demands on students who choose to abstain: "As students are told more and more that they are in a sexual revolution, those students who do not see their own behavior as either especially liberated or revolutionary may develop uneasy feelings" (King and Sobel, 1975).

Almost all authorities agree that the prevailing sexual mores on today's college campuses cannot be characterized as "promiscuous", that is, multiple sexual partners with minimal emotional involvement. While most college students respond with a liberal attitude to the questions in sex surveys, their behavior cannot be equated with the idea that "anything goes". For example, even in one of the studies reporting high rates of intercourse experience (83 percent of males and 72 percent of females), intercourse experience was clearly related to the student's involvement in a dating or steady relationship (King and Sobel, 1975). And this emphasis on the emotional relationship is certainly not restricted only to female students. Based on their experiences in providing contraceptive and sexual counselling to Yale students, physicians Philip and Laura Sorrel state that "sex just for

the sake of putting a penis in a vagina is something that's out, but sex within a relationship has become an important value for the students" (1974, p. 78).

This increased emphasis on the intimate relationship as a basis for sexual activity has also led to a weakening, although not a complete disappearance of, the sexual double standard. Thirty years ago one set of standards applied to the sexual behavior of college men, and a completely different (and much less permissive) set applied to college women. The past decade, however, has seen a considerable shift towards a single standard for judging the sexual behavior of both men and women. There are still some areas in which male-female differences persist: men still seem to have their first sexual experience at an earlier age; men still seem to take greater initiative, or be more aggressive, in seeking sexual experience; and men are still more likely to have a larger number of sexual partners than are women, although this difference is not as great as it was in the past (Chilman, 1979).

Another major change in attitudes relates to students' feelings towards marriage. Very few students today endorse the belief that "sex is something to be saved for marriage", and in fact, an increasing number of students think that sexual compatibility is an important prerequisite to marriage. And, in fact, an increasing number of students choose to live together (or cohabit) for a period of weeks or years before deciding to marry.

COHABITATION AMONG COLLEGE STUDENTS

Estimates of the number of college students who have cohabited range from 25 (Chilman, 1979) to 33 percent (Peterman et al., 1974). However, it is difficult to know precisely what these figures mean, since there are many definitions of "living together". For example, "sleeping to-gether", meaning sharing the same bed but not necessarily for the purpose of having sex, is one way that students use to express feelings of in-timacy. In some cases, cohabitation may not mean anything more than a steady dating rela-tionship, whereas in other cases it implies that a couple intend to marry. Couples may cohabit for an evening or a weekend, or they may set up a more or less permanent household.

In a study of 1100 undergraduates at Pennsyl-vania State University, several factors contrib-uted to increasing cohabitation rates in recent years (Peterman et al., 1974). For instance, more students were living off campus in rented apart-ments or houses rather than in dormitories. Also, fear of pregnancy was reduced by the availability of effective contraception. In terms of attitudes, most students thought that living together was a natural outgrowth of a love rela-tionship. Since the students' parents generally disapproved of cohabitation, most students con-cealed their living arrangements from them. In contrast, there was relatively widespread support for cohabitation among the peer group. Finally, the authors reported no apparent ad-verse effects from the experience, and found that cohabiting students tended to have more positive self-images and heterosexual relation-ships than those who did not cohabit.

This research seems to suggest that while atti-tudes towards sex have become more liberal, there is still a strong emphasis on the quality of the emotional relationship. Most students seem to equate sex with intimacy and to view sex as a natural outgrowth of a love relationship. Pair-bonding—the need to form stable and commit-ted relationships—is just as important now as it was in the previous generation, but with one important difference: marriage is now seen as only one of many ways to develop a loving, sex-ual pair-bond.

THE EFFECTS OF RELIGIOUS BELIEFS

For many segments of the adult population a negative relationship exists between sexual ac-tivity and religious conviction, and this also ap-pears to be true of college students. For ex-ample, a study of students at the University of Maryland found a clear negative relationship between religious adherence and sexual atti-tudes and behavior (Zuckerman et al., 1976). In-terestingly, while religious female students did have more conservative sexual attitudes than their nonreligious counterparts, the two groups did not differ in the range of their sexual be-havior. In another study, it was found that al-though female students were more likely to at-tend church than male students, the females' sexual behavior and attitudes were more liberal than that of religious males (Mercer and Kohn, 1979). The authors interpret these results by suggesting that many female students attend church for reasons of family and social pressure, and are less ideologically committed than church-attending males. This interpretation is supported by the results of an earlier study (Potkay, 1973) showing that church attendance correlated with conservative sexual beliefs only if it was purely voluntary.

What has been the effect of the recent revival of evangelical and orthodox religious sects on the college campus? Chilman (1979) suggests that for the small segment of the student body that is actively involved in a serious spiritual com-mitment, celibacy and sexual puritanism are a defining characteristic of their lifestyle. Since there appears to be an increase in the practice of fundamentalist religions, this trend toward sex-ual conservatism may, for some students, be-come even more marked in the 1980's.

Although religious practice does not substan-tially effect the sexual choices made by most college students today, evidently feelings of guilt—from both religious and non-religious sources—do exercise a sexually restraining influence. In group discussions such as the one described at the beginning of this essay, it is typical for a number of students to report guilt and shame about certain aspects of their sexual behavior. Psychologist Donald Mosher has proposed that sex guilt can be measured by a personality-type questionnaire and correlated with sexual experiences, attitudes and standards. In a study of unmarried students at the University of Connecticut, Mosher found that students who scored high on a measure of sexual guilt were less likely to engage in intimate forms of sexual activity and, in addition, expressed more conservative sexual views over questions such as the role of oral sex in marriage (1971).

A CROSS-CULTURAL PERSPECTIVE

How do American college students compare with those from other countries? In one large-scale study looking at the sexual attitudes and behavior of college students from Canada, the United States, Bangladesh, and Malaya, it was found that sexual permissiveness varied within the broader cultural context (Perlman et al., 1979). Students in the United States sample (Bard College in New York State) were the most permissive, while students from the Far East were least permissive. In terms of attitudes towards premarital sex, for instance, it was shown that the majority of Malaysian and Bangladesh students believed in sexual abstinence before marriage. In all four countries there was a tendency for males to be more permissive than females, and for students from higher socioeconomic backgrounds to be more permissive than those from less advantaged backgrounds.

Students from the United States are not, however, the most permissive student population. When Danish students were compared with two groups in the United States (Midwestern and Mormon students) it was found that the Danes

had significantly more permissive attitudes and greater sexual experience both before and during the college years (Christenson and Gregg, 1970). In 1968 less than 5 percent of male and female Danish students were virgins, and many students accepted sexual intercourse in the absence of a committed relationship. The United States students had much more limited experience with premarital intercourse, particularly the Mormon group, and also showed much greater discrepancies between male and female attitudes and behavior.

Attitudes towards contraception also vary among college students from other countries. For example, while 83 percent of males and 56 percent of females at a university in Nigeria were sexually active before marriage, only 36 percent reported using contraceptives (Soyinka, 1979), although almost all these students were familiar with family planning and contraceptive use. Among a sample of Ugandan students, 97 percent of the males and 69 percent of the females experienced premarital intercourse, but the majority of sexually active students used no contraceptives at all, and those that did try to limit fertility used only the condom (Kisekka, 1976). One factor that explains these findings is that premarital pregnancy is much more readily accepted in these African countries than it is in the United States.

Finally, while relatively few college males in the United States visit prostitutes for their first sexual experience, this is not the case in many other countries. In many South American countries, for example, prostitution is an accepted and important part of male sexual initiation. A study of male medical students from Colombia showed that 92 percent had had intercourse with a prostitute at some time, and 65 percent had gone to a prostitute for their first sexual experience, (Alzate, 1976). The author suggests that the "machismo" ethic and the sexual double standard play an important role for these students, and explains, in part, why so many of them seek out early sexual experiences with a prostitute while encouraging chastity for their girlfriends.

CONCLUSION

The college student of today differs from his or her counterpart in the 1940's, 1950's, and even 1960's in a number of important ways:

1. He or she is far more likely to experience intercourse before marriage, and the incidence of premarital intercourse for males and females is about equal;

2. Male students are far less likely to visit a prostitute;

3. Students are far more likely to cohabit—that is, live together while unmarried—than in past years;

4. Students generally express far more liberal attitudes towards a variety of sexual behaviors and lifestyles.

At the same time, some things have changed very little in the past four decades:

5. In general, students have about the same number of sexual partners today as they did in earlier years;

6. Perhaps most importantly, most students still believe that sex is appropriate and meaningful only within the context of an emotionally committed relationship.

In some ways, then, today's college students truly are in the middle of a sexual revolution, a revolution that gives them considerable freedom to make sexual choices relatively free of guilt and hypocrisy. We might applaud this new openness, egalitarianism, and rationality in regard to sexual matters, but we should also recognize that sexual freedom exacts a cost among those that exercise it.

When sexual choices are limited and clear, the student may feel restricted but at least the rules that guide sexuality are well understood. In a situation where sexual options are expanded and the guidelines are vague, the student may feel considerable confusion and pressure. For instance, a student who knows that he or she is not ready for a sexual relationship may nonetheless become sexually involved through a desire to please or conform. Some students may come to doubt their own sexuality if they fail to measure up to what they think other students are doing. And, although college students live in a relatively insulated world, they are aware that those outside the campus, and particularly their parents, do not always share their sexual values.

It is not surprising, then, that students participating in discussion groups such as the one described at the beginning of this essay have sexual doubts and questions. As one female undergraduate stated:

Usually, I don't feel that there's anything wrong with my sleeping with my boyfriend. Most of my roommates are sexually involved, or say they are, and they certainly don't disapprove. I also feel very strongly that women should have the same sexual rights as men. But even though my head tells me it's alright, there's another part of me that has questions. For example, my boyfriend and I sometimes have sexual problems, but we're not really mature enough to discuss it rationally. Also, I'm really troubled about contraception; I hate going to the health center for a prescription—I even used my roommate's birth control pills for awhile—and while I worry about their side-effects, I am even more worried that I might get pregnant or catch some type of venereal disease. But I think that what worries me most of all is knowing where to draw the line between what I will and won't do sexually. My parents do not provide any guidance; they think everything sexual outside of marriage is wrong, and I can't follow those rules. But I'm definitely uncomfortable with the idea that 'anything goes'. So I guess that I'll just have to learn by experience, and hope that along the way I don't make any sexual choices that I'll regret in later years.

4

REPRODUCTIVE ISSUES

TEN

Pregnancy and Childbirth

Overview

No other phase of the life cycle has the profound significance and consequences of pregnancy and childbirth. But while the decision to have children causes major and permanent life changes, it was not, until quite recently, even considered to be a decision. Childbearing was considered a natural result of sexual intercourse—a result that has been encouraged in almost all societies. The motivation to have children has been considered so basic as to be one of the few essentially human instincts.

To some extent, however, this view of childbearing as instinct has been questioned in recent decades. With the development of reliable contraceptives, pregnancy is no longer an inevitable result of sexual activity. Childbearing has become an option, a matter of choice. We can decide whether we want children, and

if so, when and how many. This new freedom has obvious benefits, but it also poses some difficult new questions: "Do I really want children?" "Am I ready to be a parent?" "How many children do I want, and can I afford, to have?"

Although fertility rates among married couples have been decreasing over the past 20 years, most people continue to answer the question "Do I want children?" in the affirmative. There are many reasons why we make this choice. On a personal level, we still see parenting as natural and normal, an instinctive validation of our identity as male or female, and proof of our adult status. We expect child rearing to be a source of emotional growth and fulfillment. These pronatalist views do not, however, develop in a vacuum. Our society tends to disapprove of couples with very large families or with no children, but it strongly reinforces the decision to have a family of two or three children.

Not everyone responds to these social pressures. A small but growing number of couples have opted for a life style that does not include any children. Organizations such as NON (National Organization for Non-Parents) provide support for this decision and suggest the many possible reasons for it: concern with overpopulation and limited natural resources, the possibility of passing a hereditary disease to one's children, the demands of a career, or simply a dislike of the responsibilities of raising children. Another relatively recent trend is the growing number of women who decide to

have children outside of the traditional marital relationship.

Along with these changes in childbearing decisions have been numerous changes in the actual processes of pregnancy and delivery. In this chapter, we review both traditional and innovative approaches to conception, treatment of infertility, the experience of pregnancy, and the experience of childbirth. We also look at how pregnancy affects sexual desire and responsiveness. As in other chapters, the emphasis is on the importance of individual differences; while the basic processes of reproduction are determined by human biological architecture, each pregnancy is also a uniquely personal and one-of-a-kind event.

Fertilization

Throughout much of history, the most popular explanation of fertilization was "homuncular theory"—the homunculus is a miniature human being presumed to exist within each egg or sperm cell. Of course, within each homunculus was thought to be an even smaller egg or sperm cell containing another miniature human being, and so on through infinity. The major controversy of this theory was whether it was the male or the female who contained the homunculus; those who believed the homunculus was in the ovum, the "ovolists," reasoned that the sperm cell was necessary only to start the growth of the already-formed human being in the egg. In contrast, the "spermatists" held that the egg was merely a fertile place for the already-formed child in the sperm to grow.

Only in the past hundred years have scientists recognized the equal contributions of the ovum and sperm to the growth of a new human being. Our modern understanding of fertilization is based on the great work of Gregor Mendel (1822–1884), an Austrian monk

who founded the science of genetics. Working with rows of pea plants grown in his monastery garden, Mendel crossbred strains with different characteristics and made his major discovery: each plant inherited characteristics from both parent plants. Even if a particular characteristic was not observable in a "daughter plant," the genetic information was present, and future generations would show that characteristic. The laws formulated by Mendel in his study of pea plants are still relevant to human reproduction: both ovum and sperm contain approximately equal amounts of the genetic information that determines the characteristics of a new individual.

Sperm cells were first observed in 1676 by Anton van Leeuwenhoek, the Dutch lens maker credited with inventing the microscope. He correctly concluded that the millions of "little creatures" he saw had to enter the female for fertilization to occur. A single sperm cell measures about five hundredths of an inch (.06 mm.) in length, and the head of the sperm, which contains the genetic material, is only about one-tenth of this length. The remainder of the sperm is made up of a small middle piece and a long tail, which enables the sperm to move. Sperm cells are so small that there may be about 400 million of them in a single ejaculation.

The single egg cell released at the time of ovulation is about 50,000 times larger than the sperm cell. The mature egg cell contains not only genetic material but also a mass of nutrient substances surrounded by a gelatinous capsule. Normally, it takes between 3 and 5 days for this egg cell to make its journey along the 4-inch (10 cm.) uterine tube to the uterus.

The egg can be fertilized only during the first day of its journey. Of the millions of sperm cells released during ejaculation, relatively few will reach the egg cell during the time that it is located in the outer third of the uterine tube. Millions of sperm are lost if the woman changes her position after intercourse and spills ejaculate out of the vagina. Millions more are killed by the acid environment of the vagina or are lost in the many folds of its sur-

face. Many more will not make it through the cervix or will become lost in the uterus, and half of those that continue on will travel up the "wrong" uterine tube. Among those sperm still in the race, some will get lost within the uterine tube or miss the egg cell by as little as a millionth of an inch. However, thousands of sperm do make it to the outer surface of the egg, and finally one sperm cell succeeds in penetrating to the genetic material in the center of the ovum. Once this happens, the outer layer of the egg becomes hardened so that other sperm cells cannot enter. The tail of the sperm drops off, and its 23 chromosomes combine with the 23 chromosomes in the egg, forming the first cell of the new human being.

During the first week after fertilization, the single nucleus divides into two nuclei, then four nuclei, and so on; but it does not grow in size. At this phase, it is called a *blastosphere*. Usually, the blastosphere takes about a week to travel down the uterine tube (see Figure 10.1). In the second week after conception, it becomes implanted in the uterine wall, and

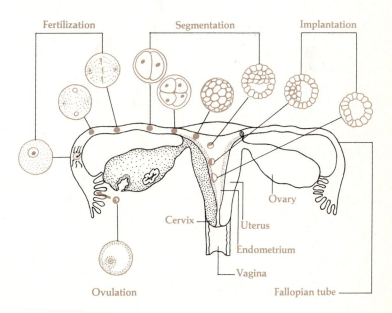

FIGURE 10.1

Schematic representation of the passage of the egg from ovulation (1) to implantation (10). Note that the size of the ovum and the blastosphere has been exaggerated for the purpose of illustration.

begins to grow rapidly in size. In rare cases, the blastosphere does not complete its journey to the uterus and instead becomes implanted in the wall of the uterine tube. This is called an ectopic pregnancy, as are all cases in which the fertilized egg implants somewhere other than the uterus. Since the fertilized egg cannot grow within the tubes beyond the first few weeks of pregnancy, this condition is potentially dangerous in that the tube may burst. This usually happens within 8 to 12 weeks after fertilization and is signaled by a sharp pain followed by internal bleeding. The usual treatment for a tubal pregnancy is surgical removal of the affected tube.

Fertility Problems

It is estimated that about 15 percent of couples in the United States experience some difficulty in their attempt to have children. Fertility problems can be relatively mild and quickly responsive to simple treatment, or they can be severe and untreatable. Sometimes, fertility problems have their origin in early developmental processes; at other times, infertility occurs only after one or more successful pregnancies. Perhaps the most universal characteristic of infertility is the emotional reaction it provokes — while most couples expect that there may be a small number of complications in conception and pregnancy, few are prepared to accept a complete inability to have children. Fertility problems can be an enormous disappointment, and can lead to doubt about our function as males and females.

Fertility can be conceptualized as a continuum: some couples are so fertile that pregnancy occurs even when contraceptives are used, others may try for several years before experiencing a successful pregnancy. Among couples who are trying to conceive and are sexually active, it is expected that about 25 percent of the women will be pregnant at the end of 1 month, about 60 percent within 6 months, and about 80 percent within 12 months. Therefore, most medical specialists suggest that a couple try for at least a year before medical intervention is started. However, many couples who know of others who have conceived quickly will be concerned about their fertility well before a year has even passed.

In the past, infertility was viewed as a female problem — some cultures even allowed a man to divorce his wife on the grounds of "barrenness." To this day, some men refuse to undergo tests of their own fertility. However, recent estimates are that about 40 percent of infertility is due to male factors, and about 40 percent to female factors. In the remaining 20 percent of cases, there is no clear physical cause in either the male or female partner, and it is believed that psychogenic factors may be involved. In some cases, the low fertility of one partner may be counterbalanced by high fertility in the other partner. For instance, a man with a very low sperm count may still succeed in impregnating his wife if she is very fertile. Finally, about 5 percent of "infertile" couples experience a spontaneous recovery.

Fertility problems are much easier to diagnose in the male; it is a relatively simple matter to obtain and examine a semen sample, and the male genitals are more accessible to external examination. In contrast, testing for female fertility may require extensive examination of hormone levels and even exploratory surgery. However, medical intervention tends to be more successful with female fertility problems. Regardless of whether it is the male or the female who shows low fertility, it is important that both partners become involved in efforts to increase fertility.

SEXUAL BEHAVIOR AND INFERTILITY

A surprisingly large number of cases of low fertility are a result of sexual dysfunction, sexual misinformation, or low rates of sexual activity. Thus before beginning medical intervention, it is important for the physician to inquire about a couple's sexual practices. For example, even in this age of supposed sexual enlightenment many couples are unaware of when in the menstrual cycle a woman is most fertile. It is not unusual for a couple concerned with infertility to report that they concentrate their sexual activity during the menstrual period rather than at mid-cycle. Other couples believe that sexual activity as infrequent as once a month should be sufficient for conception. By clearing up such misconceptions, a physician is able to resolve many cases of infertility with no medical treatment at all. Although there is some dispute as to how often sexual intercourse should occur for maximum fertility, most medical authorities suggest that intercourse once every 2 or 3 days should maximize the chances for conception.

Both male and female sexual dysfunction also play a role in fertility problems. For instance, a woman with vaginismus will have

obvious difficulties with conception. Similarly, a man who ejaculates before penetration, or who does not ejaculate at all, cannot impregnate his partner. Erectile dysfunctions may also be involved — a man experiencing difficulty in maintaining an erection during intercourse has little chance of fathering a child. Fortunately, many of these sexual dysfunctions respond to treatment (see Chapter 9). Medical testing and intervention should begin only after the physician is sure that a couple has been maximizing their chances of conceiving a child through adequate sexual performance.

MALE FERTILITY PROBLEMS

In the chapter on sexual anatomy, the male genitals were described as a "sperm delivery system." Through this system, the male must *(continued on page 347)*

Nowadays infertile couples are often referred for counseling and sex education; fertility problems can sometimes be solved by such simple information as when in her menstrual cycle a women is most likely to conceive. Ernst Kirchner. Nudes. Detail, 1908. (The Solomon R. Guggenheim Museum, New York)

Choosing Your Child's Sex

Parents have always wanted to influence the sex of their offspring. Long before scientists discovered that X or Y sperm cells determine a child's sex, people developed theories to explain sex determination. One early theory was that the female had two uteri—a baby growing in the uterus on the right side of the body would be male, on the left side female. Another theory was that sperm from the right testis produced male children, sperm from the left testis female children. Couples were advised that to produce males, they should lie on their right sides while having intercourse. Aristotle believed that both partners produced semen and that the partner who was more vigorous, particularly during sex, would produce a same-sex child. Other beliefs were that boys were more likely if women dressed in male clothing, ate bitter foods, and had intercourse by the light of the full moon.

The discovery that sex was determined by X or Y chromosomes present in the male sperm cell came only around 1950. In 1960, Landrum Shettles published research indicating that X and Y sperm have different shapes: the X sperm is oval and somewhat larger than the Y sperm, which is rounded in shape. Because of these differences in size and shape, Shettles suggested that the Y sperm cells, which are smaller, can move more quickly but have less resistance to vaginal acidity. The larger X sperm move more slowly but can survive for a longer span of time within the female genital system. On the basis of these structural differences, Shettles (1972) believed it was possible to maximize the chances of conceiving a child of the desired sex.

The first step in the Shettles program is to determine when the woman ovulates. This can be accomplished by charting basal temperature, cervical mucus, and any other signs of ovulation, over several months. The timing of sexual intercourse is perhaps the single most important aspect of the program. According to Shettles, the Y sperm (or androsperm) can survive for no more than 24 hours, whereas the X sperm (or gynosperm) can survive for 2 to 3 days. Thus to conceive a male it is necessary to have intercourse on the day when the woman ovulates—this ensures that the androsperm will be alive on the critical day and that their greater speed will help them to reach the ovum before the gynosperm. In contrast, to conceive a female it is necessary to abstain from intercourse for at least 2 days before ovulation—this is supposed to ensure that no living androsperm will be present when the ovum is released, so that fertilization must be accomplished by a gynosperm.

Although timing is the most important aspect of the program, Shettles provides many other suggestions to maximize conception of the desired sex. For example, couples who want to conceive a girl are supposed to maximize vaginal acidity, since acidity is more harmful to the androsperm. Acidity can be maximized if the woman uses a mild vinegar douche before intercourse. To conceive a male, the couple should maximize alkalinity—for example, the woman can use a mild baking soda douche before intercourse. Shettles also offers suggestions as to the proper diet and the appropriate intercourse position for conceiving a male or female.

Little research is available to document the success or failure of Shettles' techniques. Some authorities believe that his method is sound, others remain skeptical about influencing the sex of an unborn child in this way. However, most agree that there is little harm in using the techniques that he suggests. In contrast, a more certain method of determining a child's sex—amniocentesis—has been severely criticized. With this method, a small amount of amniotic fluid is withdrawn through a long needle inserted in the mother's abdomen; cells in this fluid are examined, so that the presence of genetic abnormalities, as well as the sex of the unborn child, can be tested about 4 months after conception. Couples who find that they have conceived an abnormal child or one of the "wrong" sex may opt for an abortion at this time. This method of sex selection is rarely used, for a number of reasons: abortions performed this late in pregnancy carry a greater risk to the mother, many doctors disapprove of abortion simply because the parents want a child of the "other" sex, and most parents would find this kind of procedure morally objectionable.

Sex selection techniques are obviously not appropriate for all couples. Some believe that it is wrong to interfere with any part of the reproductive process. Others find that Shettles' techniques are too mechanical to fit into their particular sexual styles. Finally, some people are concerned that given the opportunity to select a child's sex, most couples will opt for male children, leading to a major imbalance in the population. They base this fear on the fact that throughout most of history and in most cultures, male children are seen as more valuable and desirable than female children. However, several recent studies have shown that rather than desiring only male children, most couples try to have a "balanced" family that includes both boys and girls. For example, Westoff and Rindfuss (1974) found that while most women would prefer a son as their first child, the "ideal" family would contain a daughter as the second child. Thus, it appears likely that the availability of a successful technique for selecting a child's sex would not alter the balance of males and females in our society.

be able to produce an adequate number of healthy sperm and deposit them near the female partner's cervix.

Although a single sperm cell is all that is required for fertilization of the ovum, the healthy male produces between 50 and 125 million sperm in each cubic centimeter of ejaculate, and the average volume of ejaculate is between 2 and 4 cc. (.12 and .25 cu. in.). This vast number appears to be necessary because most sperm cells do not complete their journey to the ovum and are lost within the female internal genitals. Generally, it is expected that men who have less than 20 million sperm/cc. will show low fertility.

An adequate number of sperm is not sufficient to guarantee fertility. The sperm must also show adequate motility—that is, between 60 and 85 percent of the sperm should be active within one hour of ejaculation. Further, between 60 and 85 percent should have normal morphology—that is, normal shape and structure. Finally, the sperm must have vitality—some proportion should be motile at least 24 hours after ejaculation.

Sperm quality and quantity can be evaluated by studying, under a microscope, a semen sample provided by the male through masturbation. Since the number of sperm cells can vary over time, it is usually necessary to obtain more than one sample.

A low sperm count may be caused by a number of temporary factors. For example, since sperm production is most efficient at temperatures slightly lower than the normal body temperature, exposure to heat can be enough to lower fertility temporarily. A man who works in a hot environment—say, a bakery—or who wears tight underwear and takes long, hot baths may temporarily impair his fertility. In addition, sperm production can be depressed by the use of certain drugs, an illness that is accompanied by high fever, or poor general health. In these cases, sperm counts may return to normal if the cause is eliminated.

In more long-term cases of low sperm count, three general factors may be involved: a hormonal disturbance, an impairment in sperm production, or a problem in the sperm delivery system.

The mechanisms of sperm production are not well understood at this time, and the use of hormones to treat low fertility is therefore still in a somewhat experimental stage. When the problem is a blockage in one of the delivery tubes, reparative surgery may be attempted. For example, in a condition called a *varicocele*, varicose veins develop in the scrotal sac and interfere with the production of sperm. Surgical repair of this condition is often successful in increasing sperm counts.

Another treatment approach is to use the low-fertility sperm in ways that maximize the chances of conception. For instance, the couple may be instructed on intercourse positions most likely to lead to conception. Another method is to obtain several semen samples which can be frozen for storage, from the man, and then use the combined samples for *artificial insemination*. In this case, a man's own semen would be used to fertilize his partner, but it would be deposited near the woman's cervix through artificial means at her most fertile time. The rationale is that accumulating several ejaculations will increase the number of healthy, motile sperm cells.

FEMALE FERTILITY PROBLEMS

A large variety of problems can interfere with female fertility: "hostile" cervical mucus, anovulation, hormonal imbalances, blocked or nonfunctioning uterine tubes, and growths or infection in the uterus. Thus the evaluation of female fertility is a complex and lengthy process. But fortunately, many of these problems can be treated successfully with medical intervention.

One of the most common causes of female infertility is the failure to ovulate. In some cases, *anovulation* may be caused by temporary factors that will reverse themselves with time—for example, emotional stress or physical illness can interfere with ovulation, and some women who have just stopped using birth control pills may fail to ovulate for several months. In other women, the hormones necessary to induce ovulation—FSH and LH—are not present in sufficient quantities.

The simplest means of testing for ovulation is the basal temperature chart; when the chart does not show the characteristic temperature rise at mid-cycle, it is likely that ovulation is not taking place. Additional tests may be performed to evaluate hormone levels in the bloodstream. When anovulation is diagnosed, fertility drugs may be used to reestablish an ovulatory pattern. However, fertility drugs also incur a certain number of risks, most notably the risk of multiple births; in recent years, a large number of multiple births have been caused by fertility drugs.

Another common cause of infertility among women is blockage or disturbance of tubal function. The uterine tubes (Fallopian tubes) play several roles in conception—they transport the ovum toward the uterus and also aid sperm in moving toward the egg. Thus if the tube is blocked, or if it does not contain essential nutrients, or if the transport mechanism is disturbed, infertility may result. Tubal blockage can be tested in a number of ways; for example, a small amount of carbon dioxide gas or a saline solution is slowly pushed through the cervix—if the tubes are open, the gas or liquid will travel through the uterus and tubes and be absorbed in the abdominal cavity. However, if both tubes are blocked there will be a build-up of gas or fluid pressure. Other tests involve the use of special dyes inserted through the cervix to give an x-ray picture of the tubes, or surgical exploration of the tubes.

Tubal problems have a number of causes. Sometimes, the tubes are misformed since birth. More often, the problem is due to infection in the pelvic area. For example, untreated gonorrhea may lead to a permanent scarring of the uterine tubes, as may pelvic inflammation or even appendicitis. A condition called *endometriosis*, in which cells from the lining of the uterus become displaced to other parts of the body, is often involved in tubal problems. While the uterus sheds its endometrial lining every month, endometrial cells attached to the ovaries or tubes cannot be shed and may cause scarring and adhesions that interfere with a woman's fertility.

In some cases, tubal blockage may be treated by focusing on the underlying problems of infection or endometriosis. When the tubal damage is not reversible by medication, it may be possible to repair the damage using surgical procedures. The most recent and extreme method of overcoming tubal problems is "test-tube" fertilization. This procedure is still in a highly experimental stage but has been used successfully on several occasions. In cases where the physician has determined that the tubes cannot be opened, an egg may be removed from the ovary by surgical means. The egg is then placed in a "test tube" and fertilized using the husband's sperm. After fertilization, the egg is implanted into the woman's uterus, and the pregnancy then proceeds in the normal way.

Another relatively common fertility problem is "hostile" cervical mucus—that is, mucus that inhibits the movement of sperm from the vagina to the uterus and tubes. Cervical mucus is evaluated through the "postcoital test"; the couple is instructed to have in-

tercourse at mid-cycle, and than a sample of mucus is taken from the cervix, usually within 4 to 12 hours of intercourse. This sample is examined to determine whether the sperm located within the mucus are still active. If the sperm are dead or show little activity, the cervical mucus is considered "hostile."

Since the cervical mucus is normally made receptive to sperm by high estrogen levels at mid-cycle, a possible cause of nonreceptive, or hostile, mucus is an inadequate level of estrogen. Cervical mucus may also become hostile if the woman has a cervical infection.

Another form of cervical mucus hostility occurs when a woman develops antibodies to her partner's sperm cells. The body has a complex set of antibodies, which are crucial in protecting it from infectious agents. When a foreign agent enters the body, antibodies are manufactured to combine with the invader and destroy it. In some cases, a woman may develop immunity to sperm, so that her partner's ejaculate is destroyed by antibodies present in her cervical mucus. Since antibody levels drop when the foreign agent is no longer present in the body, treatment for sperm immunity is usually the use of a condom during intercourse; after several months, levels of sperm antibodies may drop sufficiently to permit conception.

SPONTANEOUS ABORTION (MISCARRIAGE)

Spontaneous abortion, also called *miscarriage*, is a surprisingly common experience—it has been estimated that about 15 percent of confirmed pregnancies end in miscarriage. It is likely that even more conceptions end in miscarriage before the pregnancy has been confirmed. In these cases, a delayed or heavier than usual menstruation may be the only indication that a conception had occurred.

Among confirmed pregnancies, about 75 percent of miscarriages take place within the first trimester, and 25 percent in the second trimester. After the second trimester, an early birth is called a *premature* delivery rather than a miscarriage.

Miscarriage is usually an emotionally distressing experience for a couple who have anticipated the birth of a child and have had no indication of any problems. It may also be a physically stressful experience for the woman, depending on the stage of pregnancy at which the abortion takes place. Very early miscarriages may resemble a heavy menstrual period; miscarriages occurring at the end of the first trimester may involve cramps and bleeding for several days. A late miscarriage—that is, one occurring during the second trimester—may resemble labor, including uterine contractions and dilation of the cervix.

A spontaneous abortion may be caused by several factors. Thus, many such abortions occur because the fetus is defective in some way; sometimes, there is a genetic defect such as Down's syndrome, in other cases, an illness during early pregnancy causes harm to the fetus. In a "blighted pregnancy," there has been an accident in the early division of the chromosomes, resulting in a defective fetus. In these cases, miscarriage is the body's way of preventing the birth of a defective child, and very little can or should be done to halt the process. The chances of having a blighted pregnancy are random, so it is likely that a following pregnancy will be normal.

In other cases, a normal fetus is aborted because it has not been well implanted into the uterine wall. For instance, if the fetus becomes implanted at the lower end of the uterus, it may become detached as the uterus grows. Miscarriage of a normal fetus may also occur due to an incompetent cervix—that is, a cervix that dilates prematurely because of the growing weight of the uterus. This condition is sometimes corrected by wrapping a circle of surgical suture material around the cervix, thus preventing it from opening before the expected date of delivery.

A third set of factors that may cause miscarriage involve hormonal problems. During the first 10 weeks of pregnancy, the corpus luteum secretes large amounts of progesterone to maintain the pregnancy, a process that is then taken over by the placenta. Miscarriage may occur if the corpus luteum does not secrete sufficient amounts of progesterone. Until fairly recently, it was common for women prone to miscarriage to be given synthetic progestins. However, there has been some controversy over the effectiveness of this treatment, and there is evidence that progestins are associated with malformations of the fetus. At present, natural progesterone, which is considered more safe than synthetic varieties, may be given to those women who are prone to miscarriage because of their low hormone levels.

The possibility of miscarriage exists whenever there is bleeding or cramping—or both—during pregnancy. However, these signs sometimes develop for other reasons and may disappear on their own. In the past, the woman who threatened to miscarry was told to remain in bed until the bleeding stopped; but subsequent research has indicated that bed rest has no effect on the course of most pregnancies. In addition, many physicians recommend sexual abstinence during threatened miscarriage. When miscarriage does occur, it is not uncommon for a woman or couple to search for reasons in their own behavior to explain the abortion, and many feel guilty about their sexual activity. However, there is no conclusive evidence that sexual activity can cause miscarriage. Generally, once the process of miscarriage has begun, and particularly if it is due to a defective fetus, there is little that can be done to halt the process.

Pregnancy

SIGNS OF PREGNANCY

Pregnancy is accompanied by a number of physical and behavioral changes. Some of these changes can also occur when a woman is not pregnant, others are considered a definite indication of pregnancy. In addition, some indications of pregnancy can be detected by the woman herself, whereas others may require medical detection or laboratory tests.

For most women, the first presumptive sign of pregnancy is a missed menstrual period. However, a menstrual period can be delayed or missed for a wide variety of reasons—emotional stress, physical illness, a change of climate or diet—and is certainly not a definite sign of pregnancy. In fact, some women who are pregnant experience bleeding during the early months of pregnancy.

Usually, a missed menstrual period will lead a woman to seek a pregnancy test. The most commonly used pregnancy tests evaluate the level of *human chorionic gonadotropin*, or HCG, in the urine. HCG is a hormone secreted by the newly formed placenta; it helps to maintain the corpus luteum, which in turn secretes hormones to maintain the pregnancy. About 4 weeks after conception—or about 2 weeks after the missed menstrual period—small amounts of HCG are excreted in the urine of the pregnant woman. In the past, technicians tested for HCG by injecting a small amount of the woman's urine into an immature female animal; if HCG was present, an autopsy on the animal would show egg development in its ovaries. Nowadays, it is no longer necessary to use rabbits or other animals to detect HCG—instead, immunologic tests are used. These tests are considered more than 95 percent accurate, but they can yield a "false negative" if performed too early, that is, before there are sufficient levels of HCG in the urine. Some women may require several tests at least 2 weeks after the missed period before a positive outcome is accurately recorded. Accurate pregnancy test kits of this type have now become available "over the counter" for women who want to perform their own tests.

Another recent development in pregnancy detection is a blood test that can be used even before a missed menstrual period. This blood test, which measures an HCG-like substance that may be produced by the fertilized egg, seems to be a reliable indicator of pregnancy as early as 4 to 6 days after conception—even before the fertilized egg has implanted in the uterus and the placenta begun to develop.

There are a variety of symptoms that may be experienced during early pregnancy. For example, sometimes the high level of hormones secreted during pregnancy causes tenderness or swelling of the breasts, and the nipples and areolae may darken in color or become enlarged. Also, some women experience nausea and vomiting that ranges from very mild to quite severe. A woman may notice that she needs to urinate more frequently, or that she feels more tired than usual. Although these changes are fairly common among pregnant women, they can also occur for reasons other than pregnancy, so they are not definite signs that a pregnancy has occurred.

The growth of the fetus within the uterus provides the physician with a number of definite signs of pregnancy. For example, increased hormone levels cause the uterus to "soften" at the site of implantation early in pregnancy; by 8 weeks, this softening can be detected in both the uterus and the cervical area. By the third month of pregnancy, the uterus shows definite changes in size and shape. Finally, fetal movement and heartbeat can usually be detected some time in the fourth month of pregnancy.

PHYSICAL AND PSYCHOLOGICAL CHANGES DURING PREGNANCY

There is no question that pregnancy is a time of profound physical and psychological change. Some authors even suggest that all women experience pregnancy as a psychological crisis, a time when emotional liability is the norm rather than the exception (Colman and Colman, 1971). The term "crisis" is not used in a negative sense but refers to the adjustments that are necessary for women and men to become mothers and fathers.

Although the physical and emotional changes of pregnancy can be discussed separately, it seems likely that the two dimensions often influence one another. For instance, a woman who experiences severe physical discomfort during pregnancy may well have a different psychological attitude from a woman who has little or no discomfort. Likewise, a woman who is emotionally upset about her pregnancy might be prone to greater physical discomfort. However, each pregnancy is unique, and it is difficult to generalize from one woman to another. Physical discomfort is not a sign that a woman is unhappy about her pregnancy, nor is happiness a sign that the pregnancy will be trouble-free.

Physical changes. The average pregnancy lasts about 270 days and is usually discussed in terms of three trimesters, or three-month periods. Although certain physical changes tend to be associated with each trimester, it should be stressed that not all women will experience all of these changes.

During the first trimester, the most common physical side effects include breast swelling and tenderness, increased urination, nausea, fatigue, and constipation. At this time, the body is adjusting to high hormone levels, which cause many of these symptoms. The pregnancy usually does not become visible until the second trimester, when the uterus grows rapidly and weight gain becomes more obvious. Some time around the fourth or fifth month comes the moment of "quickening," when the woman is first able to feel the movements of the fetus within her uterus. Also, the breasts may begin to secrete a yellowish substance called colostrum and can become fuller and heavier (see Figure 10.2). A deeper skin color may develop around the nipples, the line between the navel and the pubic hair, and on the face. This skin pigmentation usually disappears from the face after delivery, but it tends to remain around the nipples. Common physical symptoms during the second trimester include indigestion, heartburn, and constipation. Retention of water in the body—called edema—may lead to swelling of the face, feet, and hands.

Many of these symptoms continue into the third trimester; the uterus, which is now large and firm, exerts pressure on other pelvic organs. The uterus may also tighten in what are called "Braxton-Hicks" contractions, which

FIGURE 10.2

Stages of fetal development during a typical pregnancy.

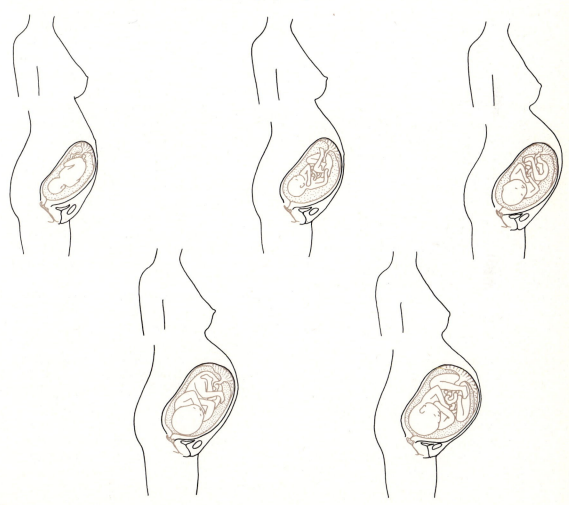

are thought to strengthen the uterine muscles. Due to the increased weight of the fetus, there may be fatigue or backache. Also, there may be difficulty breathing as the uterus presses up against the diaphragm.

Many doctors are understandably hesitant to prescribe drugs to counteract these symptoms. Instead, the focus has been changing to common sense health measures: for example, an adequate and balanced diet, sufficient rest, and appropriate forms of exercise. Pregnancy symptoms should not, however, be dismissed as "all in the mind"—they are real physical changes that at times may actually warrant medical intervention.

Of course, the physical changes experienced by the expectant mother are only half the story of pregnancy. At the same time, the fertilized egg is growing from a single cell to the millions of complex cells that make up a human being (see Figure 10.2). Fetal development is a fascinating and exciting process; to explain it adequately would require more space than is available here. It should be noted, however, that the more the expectant mother knows about her child's development, the better she will be able to understand and accept her own experiences during pregnancy.

Psychological changes. A popular image of pregnancy is the woman who develops cravings for strange foods in the middle of the night. Pregnant women are expected to be somewhat eccentric in both their desires and their moods, and this eccentricity is tolerated as if it were a physical side effect of pregnancy. Actually, the psychological experiences of the pregnant woman are complex and far more profound than a craving for pickles or strawberry ice cream.

A vast number of physical, personal, interpersonal, and cultural factors influence the psychological experience of pregnancy. On the

(continued on page 356)

Couvade: Male Roles in Childbearing

Until quite recently, most literate societies denied the husband any role in his wife's childbearing. Pregnancy and birth were almost exclusively "women's business," and men were expected to remain uninvolved until some time after the birth. When childbearing became a medical specialty, a male doctor was often present at birth, but the husband still had no role other than distributing cigars in the hospital waiting room. With the popularization of "natural childbirth" over the past decade, some husbands welcome the opportunity to "coach" and help their wives during birth, but many men still believe that their proper place is well away from the delivery room.

In contrast, some men in nonliterate societies take an important and even primary role in childbearing. *Couvade* (from the French word *couver,* meaning to brood or hatch) refers to childbirth rituals, in which the man may take the starring role. Before birth, the husband of a pregnant woman may be expected to rest, observe certain dietary restrictions, and remain in seclusion. When labor starts, the pregnant woman may quietly go off with a female companion to deliver her baby while her husband lies in bed and mimics the pains and stresses of birth. He may take a considerable amount of time to recover, remaining in his bed and eating special foods while he receives visitors.

Several explanations for these couvade customs have been proposed. One theory is that the couvade ritual enables a man to demonstrate and affirm his paternity of the newborn child (Paige

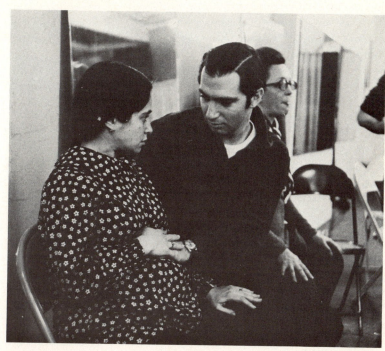

Many couples today feel the importance of the husband's involvement during pregnancy and birth. © *Shelly Rusten 1971)*

and Paige, 1973). In modern societies, a man may use legal or scientific means to establish his paternity; and in some primitive societies, the severe restrictions placed on women by highly organized male groups are considered sufficient to make paternity unambiguous. However, in tribes where women are relatively unrestricted, the social or legal father has no simple means of proving that he is also the biological father. By following rituals of couvade, he is telling his tribe that he claims the newborn child as his own offspring.

Another explanation of couvade is that it fills a psychological need, enabling the husband to feel he is an important part of the mystery of birth. Rather than feeling envious of his wife's creative role, he has a role of his own that gives him status and satisfaction. Such rituals may also facilitate the transition to active fatherhood and child care—as among the Arapesh, where

men and women are expected to share the care of infants and children.

A third explanation of couvade involves the belief in sympathetic magic found in some preliterate societies. When the physiology of pregnancy and birth are not well understood, people may develop complex rituals to ensure the birth of a healthy child. For instance, they may believe that the pregnant woman should avoid certain sights, foods, or activities. (Even in cultures where the facts of birth are understood, as in our own, superstitions may develop—that sex is harmful to the fetus, for example, or that a frightening sight can cause spontaneous abortion.) In societies where parents are trying to protect their unborn child from evil spirits, the father may mimic the activities of pregnancy and birth as a way of fooling these spirits and diverting them away from the mother.

physical level, a woman must cope with side effects as well as her changing physical appearance. Some women enjoy the visible signs of pregnancy; others, recognizing the social standard that "slim is beautiful," may try to hide the pregnancy as long as possible. The restrictions that pregnancy puts on movement and activity may also influence a woman's emotions.

Personal feelings about becoming a mother are also important. Positive emotions include feeling special, feeling fertile and womanly, and feeling excited and impatient. Among the negative emotions, which are natural and should be dealt with, are feelings of fear, exhaustion, worry about the health of the child, and concern about one's ability to cope with motherhood. For some women, doubts about potential motherhood disappear early in pregnancy or at the time of quickening; for others, these doubts continue past the time of delivery.

Another factor in the experience of pregnancy is the reaction of those around the woman. If she has a male partner, his response to the pregnancy can be very important. To some women, pregnancy is a time of vulnerability when male support is necessary. However, men are susceptible to the same anxieties as women and may not be able to meet the supportive needs of the mother-to-be.

Social forces play an important role in the psychological experience of pregnancy. According to Judith Laws and Pepper Schwartz (1977), society has relatively ambiguous expectations as to how the pregnant woman should behave. In other words, there are few clearly defined rules for the pregnant woman to follow. Laws and Schwartz suggest that as a way of resolving this ambiguity, some women decide to play the "sick role," that is, a role that exempts them from normal role responsibilities and a sense of personal responsibility for the "illness." Some women do, indeed,

treat pregnancy as an illness, and research shows that those around her tend to regard the pregnant woman as "nonnormal" or as a "novel stimulus." To some extent, there is also pressure from physicians for the pregnant woman to act as though she had a medical condition. Thus pregnant women learn to play a sick role in our culture even though the physical changes of pregnancy do not necessarily dictate this role. Laws and Schwartz speculate that this sick role may be avoided if the pregnant woman is surrounded by a network of family and friends who provide a different set of expectations for her behavior.

Many couples view prospective parenthood as "a rite of passage out of adolescence into adulthood" and experience a considerable change in their sense of who they are. "Expecting children affects the way we see the world and the way the world sees us in enriching and complicating ways. We begin to watch and react to the lives of parents and families. . . . Our friends see us in a new light. . . . We experience being seen and treated as mothers and fathers" (Boston Women's Health Collective, 1978, pp. 34–35, 39). Becoming a mother or father is indeed a major change in status, and in this sense, pregnancy is a profound transitional "crisis" in the life cycle.

SEXUAL BEHAVIOR DURING PREGNANCY

Among most mammalian species, sexual activity is rigidly tied to reproductive processes: when the female becomes pregnant she is no longer receptive to sexual advances, and usually, she is no longer an attractive sexual partner to the male of the species. Sexual activity is somewhat more flexible among nonhuman primates—for example, certain female apes may submit to the sexual advances of insistent males—but usually, the sexual behavior of a pregnant female is sporadic and unpredictable. Only among human females is sexual activity both common and sought after during pregnancy.

In their cross-cultural survey of sexual behavior, Ford and Beach (1951) report that there is a wide range of attitudes and rules concerning sexual activity during pregnancy. Members of the African Masai tribe demand abstinence after the woman has missed one or two menstrual periods. Women of the Crow Indian tribe are expected to abstain from intercourse as soon as they feel the first movement of the unborn child. Other tribes permit intercourse almost until the time of delivery, or for as long as the woman can comfortably participate in sexual activity. "In general, the demand for sexual abstinence during part or all of pregnancy applies exclusively to the wife. Many societies make some provision for alternative sources of outlet as far as the husband is concerned" (Ford and Beach, p. 217). Where prohibitions against intercourse exist, the rationale is usually fear that it will harm the unborn child in some way.

In our own culture, there is also a wide range of sexual responses during pregnancy. Perhaps the best-known research on this topic was that conducted by Masters and Johnson (1966); they interviewed 101 women on subjective sexual responses during pregnancy and, in addition, obtained direct physiological recordings from six pregnant women.

Masters and Johnson stress the importance of increased blood supply to the pelvic region during pregnancy; sexual arousal further increases this pelvic engorgement. The six subjects studied during pregnancy all reported that they were aware of "increased levels of sexual tension" during the third or fourth months of pregnancy. Moreover, these women reported experiencing strong sexual interest and multiple orgasms during their second trimester. Both vaginal lubrication and vasocongestion increased as pregnancy pro-

gressed. By the third trimester, the vagina became so engorged with blood that vaginal contractions during orgasm were barely observable, although the women reported experiencing the subjective feelings of orgasm. However, third trimester orgasms produced a very strong uterine response; instead of regular contractions, the uterus was sometimes observed to go into a spasm that lasted as long as 30 minutes. The resolution phase tended to last longer as pregnancy progressed; also, it was slower in women for whom this was not the first pregnancy. By the third trimester, the pelvic area remained congested even after the resolution phase, and the women noted that although orgasm was intense and pleasurable, it did not relieve their feelings of sexual tension for a substantial period of time.

Among the 101 women interviewed during various stages of pregnancy, there were several differences between those having their first child (primiparas) and those who already had children (multiparas). During the first trimester, many women experiencing their first pregnancy reported a decrease in sexual interest, whereas those with children reported little change in sexual interest. In the second trimester, a majority of women in both groups noticed an increase in sexual interest, activity, fantasy, and even erotic dreams. By the third trimester, a majority of women in both groups reported that they were less sexually interested or active. This third trimester decrease was probably influenced by a number of external factors. For instance, many of the women's physicians recommended sexual abstinence at this time, and many of the women's husbands reported that they were less interested in sexual relations as the pregnancy progressed.

Masters and Johnson explain this pattern of changing sexual interest during pregnancy as follows: During the first trimester, many women, and particularly those having their first child, are disturbed by a variety of physical discomforts—nausea, weight gain, breast tenderness—that inhibit sexual interest. By the second trimester, most woman are comfortable with their pregnancy, and the increased blood flow to the pelvic area often seems to enhance sexual responsiveness. Just before delivery, the physical awkwardness of sexual intercourse plus a fear of injuring the child result in decreased sexual interest and activity.

Not every study has found this pattern of change in pregnant women. For example, Naomi Morris (1975) found a gradual decrease in sexual activity, with no second trimester increase, among a sample of 114 women from Thailand. Until the seventh month of pregnancy, these women reported intercourse rates that were similar to a larger group of nonpregnant women. By the ninth month, however, about 70 percent of the pregnant women reported complete sexual abstinence. There were large differences between individuals—some couples abstained as soon as the pregnancy was confirmed, others continued sexual activity up to the time of delivery.

This same pattern of sexual activity was confirmed in a more recent study (Solberg *et al.*, 1978). The researchers interviewed 260 women in the immediate postpartum period. The mean age of the sample was 26, and most of the women were middle-income and well-educated; 65 percent were multiparas, the remainder were experiencing their first pregnancy. Results indicated that in terms of the frequency of intercourse, there was a steady decrease over the course of pregnancy. About 5 percent of the women abstained during the first and second trimesters; by the seventh month, 10 percent were abstaining, and this increased to 20 percent in the eighth month and 60 percent in the ninth month. Sexual intercourse was most frequent among those women who were young, those who had not

been married long, and those who experienced orgasm most consistently. By the third trimester, many women reported that orgasm was less intense or that intercourse was less likely to lead to orgasm. However, a number of women reported a steady increase in orgasmic intensity throughout pregnancy.

The general decrease in intercourse frequency was usually accompanied by a decrease in other forms of sexual activity. For instance, most women reported decreased rates of masturbation and of oral or manual stimulation as pregnancy progressed. Among those who continued intercourse throughout pregnancy, there was a tendency to use coital positions that maximized the woman's comfort—for instance, couples were less likely to use the man-above position and more likely to use a side-by-side position.

Women gave various reasons for their decreased sexual activity: about half cited the physical discomfort of intercourse during pregnancy, about 25 percent were frightened of harming the baby, 23 percent noted a loss of sexual interest, and 8 percent reported that they were following the physician's recommendations. This last statistic indicates that a considerable number of women disregarded the physician's advice, since about 30 percent had been told to abstain from all sexual activity for the final 2 to 8 weeks before their delivery dates.

A considerable amount of controversy surrounds medical warnings against intercourse in the last weeks or months before delivery. The prohibition is based, in part, on fears that the intense uterine contractions accompanying orgasm may prematurely start the process of delivery. Research on this question has yielded mixed results—some studies show more frequent orgasm after 32 weeks of pregnancy among those who deliver prematurely, other studies show no such relationship. In the study conducted by Solberg and associ-

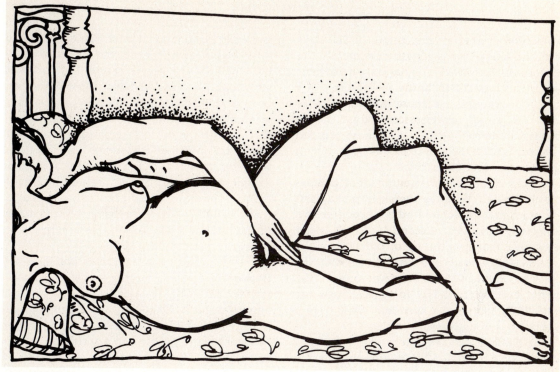

FIGURE 10.3

During pregnancy, many couples find the side-by-side intercourse positions the most comfortable.

ates, the prematurity rate was the same—about 6 percent—for women who abstained from sex and those who continued to have orgasms after the seventh month of pregnancy. It seems likely that for the vast majority of women experiencing a normal pregnancy, intercourse presents no danger to the fetus. However, in certain cases—for instance, if there is pain or bleeding—it may well be safer to avoid sexual contact for the remainder of the pregnancy.

Richard Naeye has further fueled the abstinence-during-pregnancy debate with his controversial study (1979) indicating that women who are sexually active during pregnancy are more likely to show amniotic-fluid infections than those who abstain from sexual intercourse. Such infections account for about 17 percent of fetal and neonatal deaths, usually because the infection leads to premature delivery. In his analysis of 26,886 pregnancies, Naeye reported that coitus increased both the frequency and the severity of amniotic fluid infections; further, coitus during the second trimester was more strongly associated with infection than coitus in the third trimester. It should be noted, however, that these data were gathered between 1959 and 1966; it is possible that today there is less risk of mortality from this type of infection. Certainly, this subject deserves further investigation before the results can be considered conclusive.

Childbirth

About 266 days after conception, or 280 days from the start of the last menstrual period, the process of birth begins. Although it is valuable for a woman to be aware of her "due date," she should also know that this date is only an approximation—266 days is the *average* gestation period, and most women give birth within 2 weeks of this date, but in some cases, labor can begin earlier or later. The exact changes that start the labor process are not known, but it seems likely that a variety of hormones secreted by both mother and fetus are involved. Recently, it has been suggested that it is the fetus, rather than the mother, that actually initiates labor. When the fetus has reached its full development, it secretes hormones; these, in turn, cause the mother to secrete the hormones that trigger the process of delivery.

The mother may experience several signs that labor has started. One such sign is the "bloody show"—the expulsion of the mucus plug that has kept the cervix sealed throughout the pregnancy, accompanied by a small amount of bleeding. Another sign that delivery is imminent is rupture of the amniotic membrane, causing the watery fluid surrounding the fetus to leak from the vagina. In addition, some women experience diarrhea in the days preceding delivery—this sign may be seen as nature's way of emptying the bowels to provide more room for passage of the baby through the birth canal. However, the clearest sign that labor is occurring is strong and regular uterine contractions.

At the time that labor begins, the fetus is usually about 20 inches (50.8 cm.) long and weighs around 7 pounds (3.2 kg.). Some time within the last month of the pregnancy, the baby's head drops down into the pelvis, a process called lightening because removal of pressure against the mother's stomach can make her burden feel lighter. Since the baby is quite heavy at this time, the pressure of its head against the cervix causes the cervix to stretch and become irritated. Most babies are born in this head down position—however, a small number are in the "breech" position—that is, with the buttocks emerging first. Even less common is the "transverse" presentation, with the baby lying crosswise and an arm or leg entering the birth canal. When the breech or transverse positions occur, the physician may attempt to rotate the baby while it is still in the uterus; if this fails, a Caesarean section if usually performed.

The duration of labor varies considerably from one woman to another and may also vary for the same woman in different pregnancies. However, the average labor for a woman having her first child is between 12 and 14 hours. For women giving birth to a second or subsequent child, labor averages about 7 hours in duration. In rare cases, birth can occur in a matter of minutes or take as long as 30 hours. With very short labors, there is danger that the mother's tissues have not stretched sufficiently to accommodate the passage of the baby, and some attempt may be made to slow down the process. Long labors can be risky because of the great physical stress they place on both mother and child, and most physicians will intervene surgically if the labor seems unduly prolonged.

THE STAGES OF LABOR

Labor is usually divided into three stages. During the first and usually longest stage, the cervix, which has remained tightly closed throughout pregnancy, must open up to a width of approximately 10 cm. (3.9 in.) to accommodate the passage of the baby's head (see Figure 10.4).

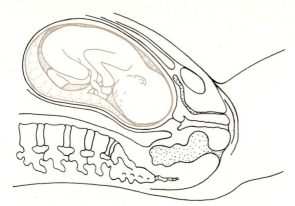

1. Fetus ready to be born

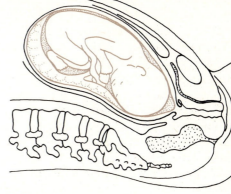

2. Cervix dilating

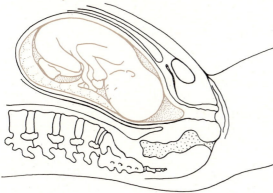

3. Cervix completely dilated

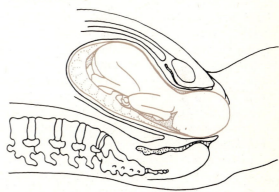

4. Head appearing

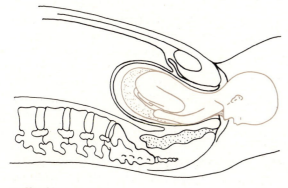

5. Shoulders appearing

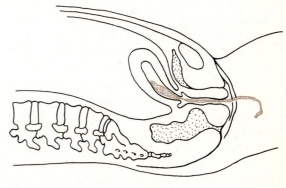

6. Placenta separating from uterus

FIGURE 10.4

The birth of a baby: schematic representation of the birth process, from
before the beginning of labor to delivery and afterbirth.

Cervical dilation is accomplished by the muscular contractions of the uterus. As described in Chapter 4, the uterus has three layers. The outermost layer consists of muscles that run lengthwise, and the innermost layer contains the circular muscles that hold the uterus closed. In the middle are muscles containing a rich supply of blood vessels. During the first stage of labor, contractions start from the outer, longitudinal, layer and move downward toward the cervix, causing it to open up. These contractions are involuntary—in much the same way that a muscle cramp is—and take a different form for each woman. In general, however, all contractions are wave-like—they start slowly, build to a peak, and then decline slowly.

First-stage labor is often divided into three substages. The first—called *early* labor—lasts until the cervix is about 4 cm. (1.6 in.) wide. Contractions at this time are usually between 10 and 20 minutes apart, with each contraction lasting about 30 seconds. It is during this phase that most women identify their labor and go to the hospital. The contractions are not usually too uncomfortable, and the woman has enough time between contractions to rest and relax. Most doctors agree that the more relaxed a woman is, the more quickly this phase will pass.

In the next phase, called *late* or *active* labor, the cervix dilates to a width of 8 cm. (3.2 in.). Contractions become stronger and are spaced more closely together in time. The discomfort is usually greater than in early labor, although this phase does not last as long.

The final phase of first-stage labor, called *transition*, is often called the most difficult part of childbirth. At this time, the cervix dilates to a full 10 cm. (3.9 in.). The transition phase usually lasts about an hour; typically, there are about nine to twelve enormously powerful contractions, with only a minute's pause between contractions. Women commonly report feelings of nausea and intense irritability, and may tremble or have chills. Toward the end of transition, the pressure of the baby's head on the mother's pelvic area causes her to feel the urge to push. If she pushes too early, however, there is danger of harming herself and the baby, so it is necessary that she resist the urge to push until the cervix is fully dilated.

Up to this point, the mother's role has been to relax as much as possible while the involuntary uterine contractions work to open the cervix. In the second stage of labor, she can take a more active role in pushing the baby out. At the beginning of this stage, the baby's head starts to move from the uterus down into the birth canal; it moves forward with each contraction and slides back slightly in between contractions. As the baby inches down the birth canal, the mother bears down with each contraction, causing the baby to move further. Toward the end of this stage, the baby's head "crowns"—that is, it can be seen at the vaginal opening. At this point, the baby is usually facing toward the mother's back; with a few additional contractions, the baby's shoulders rotate so that it is facing sideways. The baby may take its first breath or cry before it has emerged completely. After it is born, the umbilical cord, which stretches from the baby's navel to the placenta, will be cut. The second stage of labor normally lasts between 1 and 2 hours, although it may be considerably shorter for some women who have already had one or more children.

In the third and final stage of labor the uterus continues to contract, causing the placenta to become detached from the uterine wall and be delivered—this is the *afterbirth*. The placenta, which has nourished the baby throughout pregnancy, weighs about one pound and is rounded in shape. The inner surface, which faced the baby, is smooth; the surface that was attached to the uterus appears fibrous. Normally, the placenta emerges within an hour of the baby's arrival. The doctor may place mild pressure on the mother's abdomen, or tug gently on the umbilical cord, to speed this process. Also, many doctors administer an oxytocinlike hormone to stimulate contractions. However, if the mother is permitted to breast feed her child immediately, the sucking of the baby causes the release of oxytocin within the mother's body, and this hormone will naturally stimulate the uterus to contract and expel the placenta.

METHODS OF CHILDBIRTH

The Bible tells us that because Eve tempted Adam to bite from the forbidden apple, all women were punished: "I will increase your labour and your groaning, and in labour you shall bear children" (Genesis 3:16). The Romans called childbirth the *poena magna* — the great pain or punishment. Throughout history, in both civilized and primitive cultures, images of pain and suffering have surrounded the act of giving birth. Adrienne Rich (1977) goes so far as to suggest that in many cultures a woman's passive suffering during childbirth was considered the very purpose of her existence.

Since Eve's curse dictated that childbirth must be painful, there were few attempts in Western society to alleviate that pain until the nineteenth century. Then a Scottish physician named James Simpson found that newly discovered anaesthetics such as ether and chloroform could relieve the pains of labor. His work was greeted with opposition because most religious authorities believed pain was necessary and even desirable for the laboring woman. This opposition began to wane when Queen Victoria, an extremely conservative force in most aspects of English history, performed the radical act of accepting anaesthetics for the birth of her seventh child. Her act

had historic overtones — to this day, the use of painkillers is an integral part of the childbirth experience for most women. Painkillers are considerably more sophisticated than in the days of Queen Victoria, but the principle that attempts should be made to minimize pain is generally accepted.

But exactly how painful is childbirth? There is no doubt that giving birth is a stressful and powerful experience — the stretching of tissues and the pressure of the baby's weight are bound to cause discomfort. However, there are other ways of viewing such pain than as a passive and overwhelming experience of suffering that is beyond our personal control:

A woman preparing to swim the English Channel, or to climb in high altitudes, is aware that her system will undergo stress, her courage will be tested, and her life may even be in danger; but despite the demands to be expected on her heart, her lungs, her muscular coordination, her nerves, during such an effort, she thinks of it primarily in terms not of pain but of *challenge*. (Rich, 1977, p. 150)

The experience of pain is a real part of most births, but few women can see this pain as a challenge. This is because almost everything in our culture teaches us to fear pain, particularly the pain of childbirth. Until very recently, most birthing women had little information about what actually happened during labor except that they should expect pain. Birth was a mysterious process surrounded by fear: fear of the unknown; fear of suffering; fear generated by countless descriptions of childbirth, in folklore and literature, as an agonizing experience. It is not at all surprising that women have feared childbirth — even the normal muscular contractions of labor were labeled "pains" until a few decades ago.

Two general approaches have evolved to deal with the pain of childbirth. One approach, used in most hospitals, is the administration of drugs to lessen pain. A second approach, pioneered by the English physician Grantly Dick-Read, is generally termed "natural childbirth." He reasoned that the fear of pain causes muscular tension, which in turn maximizes the sensations of pain and leads to more fear. To break this vicious cycle, Dick-Read and others have suggested a variety of "natural" ways for a woman to conquer her fear and tension. Some people believe that a "natural childbirth" cannot take place within the confining regulations of a traditional hospital setting. Others think that it may be possible to combine the best elements of hospital service with a more natural approach to childbirth. Indeed, over the years many hospitals have modified their procedures to accommodate those desiring a more natural birth. Perhaps most important, women now have a greater degree of freedom in choosing how they want to give birth.

The traditional hospital birth. Not all hospitals treat birth in exactly the same way, but certain elements, if not standard, are at least relatively common. These elements arise to a certain extent from the view that the birthing woman is a patient — she is in a place where people are cured of illness and is subject to a variety of medical interventions that streamline or hasten the resolution of what is seen as a medical problem. In exchange for the safety of the hospital, she may have to sacrifice some of her individual needs and desires to hospital procedures.

Shaving of pubic hair. In most hospitals, the first procedure after admission is shaving the woman's pubic hair. Although this is done to minimize the risk of infection, there is some question as to whether just clipping the hair or sterilizing the pubic area might better serve this purpose.

The enema. Preliminary procedures often include an enema, with the intention of emptying the bowels so as to increase space within the lower pelvis. For women who have experienced the natural occurrence of diarrhea in the days preceding labor, this procedure seems unnecessary.

Intravenous solutions. Once a woman is admitted to the hospital, she is unlikely to be given any food until after delivery of her child. This is done for two reasons: so that she will not vomit during labor and, more important, so that she will not vomit if anaesthesia becomes necessary. To supply her with necessary fluids, and to be sure that a vein is open in case of emergency, an intravenous glucose solution is often administered. Although this procedure is not painful, it does have the disadvantage of limiting the woman's mobility at a time when she may feel the need to move around.

Induction of labor. If the physician feels that labor is proceeding too slowly, or if the baby is "overdue," he or she may make use of a number of techniques to start or speed up the labor process. One such technique involves rupturing the amniotic membrane. Another technique is the administration of an oxytocin substitute — commonly, pitocin — to stimulate uterine contractions.

Labor induction can be an extremely valuable procedure when there is some problem in the birth — for example, if there are signs that the baby could not survive a long labor, or if the mother has a condition such as diabetes. Unfortunately, labor induction is often performed for the convenience of mother and doctor, as a way of "scheduling" the birth. In some cases, this may not be harmful; however, there is always the chance that labor will be induced before the baby is "ready" — sufficiently developed — to be born. Further, the contractions caused by pitocin can be extremely powerful and unexpected, leading to the use of painkilling drugs that might not have been necessary if labor had been allowed to proceed normally.

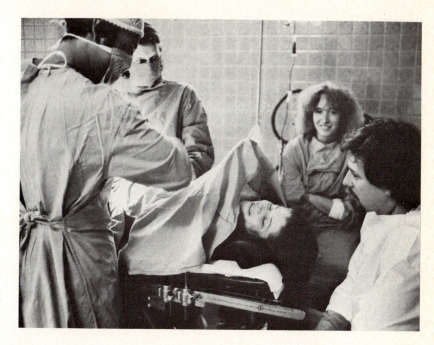

Although most births still take place in a hospital, this birth is a little unusual in that it is a Caesarian. (© Irene Barki 1979/ Woodfin Camp & Assoc.)

Medication. The wholehearted and enthusiastic acceptance of painkilling drugs has changed, to some extent, over the past decade. Although most women will make use of some form of painkiller during labor, there is now a trend toward using the mildest types of drugs and as little as possible of them. Nevertheless, most hospitals make painkilling drugs freely available to the birthing woman and may even encourage her to use them.

Two categories of drugs are commonly used: analgesics, which are given during labor, and anaesthetics, which are given during delivery. Among the analgesics are such drugs as tranquilizers (e.g., Valium), narcotics (e.g., Demerol), and barbiturates (e.g., Seconal); these substances work to reduce the sensations of pain and to relax the mother. In contrast, anaesthetics remove the sensation of pain entirely, either by numbing the anaesthetized area, or by inducing sleep. General anaesthesia, which causes complete unconsciousness,

is most often used when there are serious complications such as those leading to Caesarean section. Partial anaesthesia, however, is fairly common; it numbs a specific part of the body, depending on where the drug is administered: for example, spinal anaesthesia numbs the entire body below the waist, a pudendal block numbs only the external genital area. Two other regional anaesthetics, the caudal and epidural blocks, require the placement of a catheter into the spinal cord so that drug administration is continuous.

There is no doubt that these drugs can work to minimize pain during labor and delivery, and for this reason their use is likely to continue. Further, drugs play an important role where there are complications—in cases requiring forceps delivery, Caesarean section, or if maternal illness occurs. However, the trend toward minimizing drug use is based on a strong foundation—researchers have found that all drugs can cross the placenta and affect the baby. Sometimes the effects may be relatively minor, but there is a fair chance that the baby born to a drugged mother will be more sluggish and less responsive than the baby of an undrugged mother. (It has even been suggested that the slap given to the bottom of a newborn baby is necessary only to counteract the effects of drugs passed from mother to child.)

While drugs do minimize pain, they can also have some negative effects on the mother. For the woman attempting some form of natural childbirth, even small drug dosages can lead to a feeling of loss of control—instead of being aware and "on top of" labor, the woman may fall asleep between contractions and awaken only when the contraction reaches its peak.

A final drawback of painkilling medication is that it may interfere with the emotional bonds that develop between mother and child in the first few hours of life: "Obviously, a drugged mother and a drugged baby have a hard time relating to each other during the first few days" (Newton and Modahl, 1978, p. 48). Moreover, there is evidence that as long as one year after birth, babies born to drugged mothers are not performing as well as babies of undrugged mothers—the degree of behavior impairment seems to be related to the types of medication used, with some drugs having more severe effects than others (Brackbill, 1978).

Episiotomy. Episiotomy refers to an incision made in the perineum just before the baby's head emerges from the vagina. Two types of incisions are used: a median cut, extending from the vagina down towards the anus, or a mediolateral cut, extending obliquely from the vagina. Usually, a local anaesthetic is given just prior to the episiotomy, and the incision is repaired after delivery of the baby.

There are several reasons for this medical intervention. First, after an episiotomy there is more room for passage of the baby's head. When there is a need to speed delivery because of fetal distress, or if the perineum cannot stretch sufficiently to accommodate the baby's head, an episiotomy helps to prevent harm to mother and child. A second reason commonly given for episiotomy is that the regular cut made by the physician is easier to repair than a jagged tear that might result if episiotomy were not performed. Finally, some physicians suggest that without episiotomy the vaginal tissues may become permanently stretched, interfering somewhat with future sexual pleasure.

Episiotomy is so common in traditional hospital births as to be almost a standard procedure. It has been estimated that more than 80 percent of women have this incision. Further, a woman who has had one episiotomy is likely to require the incision at each subsequent birth in order to prevent tearing of the original incision. Although episiotomy is considered sound medical procedure in the United States, it is far less common in other Western countries. For example, only about 15 percent of birthing women in England have episiotomies, and the rate is even lower in Holland and Denmark.

Why are episiotomy rates so high in the United States? In part, they are performed as a type of preventive medicine—that is, as a way of preventing tearing even before it is clear that a perineal tear will occur. However, statistics from Europe indicate that for the majority of women, a tear will not take place. In these countries, several techniques are used to prevent the need for episiotomy. For instance, massage of the perineal area or the application of hot compresses may facilitate natural stretching of the perineal area. Further, the position of the mother during childbirth seems to have an effect on the need for episiotomy. The *lithotomy* position—in which the birthing woman lies flat on her back—is most often used in American hospitals, and it places the most stress on the perineum. When women are permitted to assume a semiupright position, the force of gravity may operate in such a manner as to eliminate the need for any episiotomy.

For some women, episiotomy is a necessary and valuable procedure that increases the safety of birth. However, the medical description of this procedure as a "tiny cut" ignores the discomfort it may cause for some women. Although the incision generally heals within 2 weeks of birth, it can make walking and sitting very uncomfortable and may severely restrict the new mother's mobility. Stiz baths and heat treatments may be required to reduce her discomfort. Thus while few people would argue that episiotomy should be eliminated, there are many who believe that steps should be taken to minimize its use.

Alienated labor. Adrienne Rich uses the term "alienated labor" to describe a birth taking place outside the context of natural experience. Of course, it is not easy to define what the natural experience of birth is, since every woman feels differently about her pregnancy and labor. However, "the experience of lying half-awake in a barred crib, in a labor room with other women moaning in a drugged condition, where 'no one comes' except to do a pelvic examination or give an injection, is a classic experience of alienated childbirth" (Rich, 1977, p. 172). Many aspects of traditional hospital delivery promote the feeling that the woman is having an abnormal experience that is beyond her control, rather than a normal life event in which her active participation is required.

The exclusion of family and friends, the early separation of mother and newborn, the use of drugs and medical technology, and even the lithotomy position can all contribute to the sense that labor is not a normal part of life. Fortunately, some of these hospital procedures have become more "humanized"—for example, most hospitals now permit the father to be present during birth. Other hospitals permit "rooming in"—allowing the baby to remain in the mother's room. Still others focus on making the hospital environment more homelike. With these changes, the new mother may feel more relaxed and less fearful of birth as an experience outside the range of normal life events.

Natural childbirth. The term *natural childbirth* encompasses a wide variety of techniques, procedures, and attitudes aimed at making birth a more rewarding and less painful experience. Although there are many methods of natural childbirth, they all tend to emphasize three factors: the importance of educating parents about the birth process; the value of a trusted companion or "coach" during labor; and the use of techniques that minimize pain and at the same time encourage the woman to be an active participant in the birth.

The modern era of natural childbirth can be dated with the work of British obstetrician Grantly Dick-Read. His books—*Natural Childbirth* (1932) and *Childbirth Without Fear* (1944)—challenged the popular notion that birth must be accompanied by anxiety and pain. Dick-Read, who had been trained in the traditional obstetric tradition, describes his "discovery" of natural childbirth as follows:

I had plowed through mud and rain on my bicycle between two and three in the morning down Whitechapel Road, turned right and left, and innumerable rights and lefts, before I came to a low hovel by the railway arches. . . . There was a pool of water lying on the floor; the window was broken; rain was pouring in; the bed had no proper covering and was kept up at one end by a sugar box. My patient lay covered only with sacks and an old black shirt. . . .

(continued on page 370)

The Home Birth Movement

A small but growing number of couples have become disenchanted with childbirth procedures in the typical American hospital: routine enemas, shaving of pubic hair, sterile and uncomfortable environments, routine episiotomies, administration of drugs, separation of mother and child, and other medical interventions that interfere with the natural rhythms of delivery. As an alternative, these couples are opting for home birth — delivery of the child in the home, attended by a physician or trained nurse-midwife. Compared to a century or even 50 years ago, very few births are taking place at home. Compared to 10 years ago, however, the number of home births has shown dramatic increases. Between 1972 and 1975, for example, reported out-of-hospital births increased by 60 percent (Parfitt, 1977). The home birth movement seems most popular in the Western states, particularly California.

In general, the home birth movement has been severely criticized by the medical profession. Doctors, who are trained to view birth as an event that may require medical intervention, believe that home birth represents an unnecessary risk to the health of both mother and child. They stress the importance of hospital technology to deal with last-minute complications in birth; and there is no doubt that thousands of lives have been saved by the skills and equipment available in the hospital delivery room. Finally, even the rare physician who approves of home birth will have difficulty participating in the event, since he or she may lose hospital privileges or insurance coverage by becoming involved in a home delivery.

Home delivery is also considered unacceptable by the vast majority of expectant parents. Looking back over the history of childbirth, most people conclude that the movement from home to hospital delivery has lessened the overall risks for mother and child. Further, we have become accustomed to the notion that birth requires medical intervention. By delivering in a hospital, we place the responsibility for the health of mother and child in the hands of the physician; in contrast, home delivery places a high level of responsibility on the parents.

Parents whose home birth has a less than successful outcome are usually in for some blame from society, unlike parents who have given over management of the birth experience to an institution and suffer a similar outcome. Parents of an infant born at home who dies may be prosecuted for negligence. (Parfitt, 1977, p. 148)

Aside from criminal prosecution, an unsuccessful home delivery will probably lead to feelings of guilt and self-blame.

Given these disadvantages, why should any couple opt for home birth? According to Suzanne Arms, author of *Immaculate Deception,* routine hospitalization of the birthing woman presents several problems:

Besides the threat of damage to mother and infant, hospital birth causes strain on the average family's budget, enforces rigid separation of family members and of mother and child after birth, and results in long isolation of mother and infant from siblings, all of which place unusual strain upon the healthy family unit. (1975, p. 186)

In contrast,

Home birth offers a woman the opportunity to labor in familiar surroundings; to choose her own attendants; to follow rituals and actions which soothe and encourage her. At home she avoids the annoying, and sometimes dangerous, hospital routines. At home, birth is a family event, with the father, grandparents, older children and friends all welcome to share the wonder of birth and greet the new baby. Once her task is accomplished, the new mother can relax in her own way, eat the food she likes, and get to know her new baby without regard for an institution's schedules. (Boston Women's Health Collective, 1976, p. 269)

From this perspective, home birth sounds very alluring indeed. However, almost all parents are willing to sacrifice some degree of comfort for the assurance of a healthy baby and mother. Thus, the important question is, How safe are home births? Unfortunately, the answer is unclear. In such countries as Holland and England, where home birth is relatively common, infant mortality rates are lower than in the United States. Medical personnel trained in home birth are available, and back-up emergency procedures are well-established. Such assistance is not generally available in the United States.

Perhaps the single most important factor in maximizing the safety of home birth is *screening*; expectant mothers with any risk of birth complications should not try home delivery. NAPSAC (the National Association of Parents and Professionals for Safe Alternatives in Childbirth) provides a number of medical and nonmedical criteria for safe home birth. For example, the mother should be less than 10 miles from a hospital and be willing to go to that hospital immediately if complications should arise. Further, she should locate a pediatrician who could see the infant soon after birth, attend childbirth preparation classes, be well-informed about birth, and agree to prepare her home for the delivery. Among the medical criteria, there should be no chance of prematurity, malpresen-

tation, multiple births, blood incompatibility, or disproportion between the baby's head and the mother's pelvis, and no history of complications in previous births. Finally, the mother should have no history of illnesses such as hypertension, severe anemia, or diabetes; she should not have had more than four previous deliveries; and she must be in good general health. Through active prenatal care and screening, the vast majority of high-risk mothers should be identified and discouraged from home birth. However, even with the most stringent screening procedures, there is always a slight risk of last-minute complications, and the couple contemplating home delivery must weigh this risk against the benefits they expect.

Although a small number of women will continue to reject hospital delivery in favor of home delivery, the home birth movement is not likely to gain widespread popularity in our culture. Nevertheless, the home birth movement may have some important indirect effects. By opting for home birth, women are expressing some basic discontents with the hospital birth experience; a less extreme alternative than home birth could eliminate these discontents while maximizing safety. A recent trend is the establishment of maternity centers—pleasant and homelike settings where women can give birth knowing that medical help and equipment are available if needed but will not be used indiscriminately. Even the traditional hospital birth has changed somewhat in response to pressures from expectant parents: for instance, fathers are often permitted in the delivery room, and drug-free births are accepted and even encouraged. Further, some women are delivering their babies in a hospital but spending their recovery period at home. These are relatively new options for childbirth and reflect the same basic needs that led to the rediscovery of home birth.

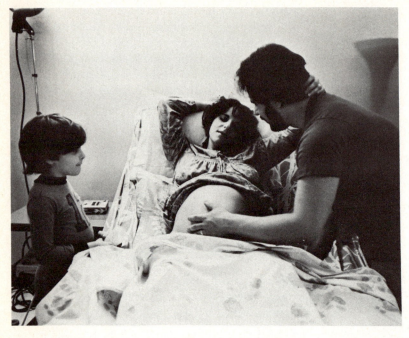

An increasing number of women
are opting for natural childbirth.
The presence of one's family is
seen as one part of a reassuring setting. (© *Lawrence Frank 1980*)

In due course, the baby was born. There was
no fuss or noise. Everything seemed to have been
carried out according to an ordered plan. There
was only one slight dissension; I tried to persuade my patient to let me put the mask over her
face and give her some chloroform when the head
appeared and the dilatation of the outlet was obvious. She, however, resented the suggestion and
firmly but kindly refused to take this help. It was
the first time in my short experience that I had
ever been refused when offering chloroform. As I
was about to leave some time later, I asked her
why it was she would not use the mask. She did
not answer at once, but looked from the old
woman who had been assisting to the window
through which was bursting the first light of
dawn; then shyly she turned to me and said: "It
didn't hurt. It wasn't meant to, was it, doctor?"
(1944, pp. 17–18)

In his travels through Africa, and in his
practice in Britain, Dick-Read saw many
births that confirmed his belief that childbirth
"wasn't meant to hurt." He also saw births in
which women experienced a great deal of

pain. From these observations, Dick-Read
concluded that fear and the anticipation of
pain were the true causes of painful childbirth. He noted that in most "civilized" cultures, women are brought up to expect birth to
be painful; in turn, their fear of pain causes
muscular tension that interferes with birth
and increases the pain. Dick-Read reasoned
that "if fear, tension and pain go hand in
hand, then it must be necessary to relieve tension and to overcome fear in order to eliminate
pain" (1944, p. 24).

Dick-Read offered many suggestions to deal
with the "fear-tension-pain syndrome." He
advised that all people should be educated
that childbirth is strenuous but not painful.
Pregnant women should be aware of the physiology of pregnancy and delivery. Doctors and
other birth attendants should work with the
birthing woman to reduce her fear and tension. Dick-Read stressed the importance of exercise and breathing techniques to promote
relaxation, both before and during delivery.

Although he believed that anaesthesia was valuable and justified in some births, Dick-Read emphasized that for the vast majority of women for whom labor and delivery are uncomplicated, birth should be a spiritual and not a medical experience.

The second major figure in the acceptance of natural childbirth was Fernand Lamaze, a French obstetrician, who published *Painless Childbirth* in 1958. Lamaze based his method on the Russian technique of "psychoprophylaxis"—that is, the prevention of pain through psychological means. In the *Lamaze method*, a woman spends the months before birth practicing a set of specific breathing techniques. Then when labor begins, she uses these techniques as a focus for her attention, rather than focusing on feelings of discomfort or pain. As labor progresses, she uses more complicated and involving breathing techniques to cope with more intense pain. A coach—usually the husband—encourages her to use the techniques and provides emotional support.

Many methods of natural childbirth have been developed and popularized in the past two decades. Each of these methods discusses the importance of education, preparatory exercises, minimal medical intervention, and the absence of painkilling drugs. There is no doubt that the natural childbirth movement has done a great deal in expanding a woman's options during birth. However, the movement is not without its problems. Perhaps the most general criticism of natural childbirth is that it does not work for every woman—pain thresholds vary, as do physical and emotional needs. Women who have been trained in natural childbirth and expect a painless delivery are often disappointed with themselves when they find that they want medication. According to most methods, a woman who cannot deliver without drugs is a "failure" in some way, and there is little provision made for an unusual birth experience such as Caesarean

section. Although the promise of a painless birth is certainly inviting, it will not always be fulfilled; three months of education and training cannot be expected, in all cases, to overcome a lifetime of fear and anxiety about birth.

Caesarean section. Caesarean section involves delivery of a baby through a surgical incision made in the mother's abdomen and uterus. The trend nowadays is to make the incision horizontally just above the pubic hair line. The operation can be performed under either general or local anaesthetic. Since a Caesarean section is considered to be major surgery, the recovery time—typically 1 to 2 weeks—is considerably longer than recovery from a vaginal delivery.

In some cases, a doctor can predict well before delivery that a Caesarean section will be necessary—for instance, if it is clear that the infant's head is too large to pass through the birth canal. Expectant mothers who suffer from a complication such as high blood pressure or diabetes, or mothers who have already had one Caesarean section in the past, are often informed that a Caesarean will be safer than vaginal delivery. In other cases, however, the decision to perform a Caesarean section is made after delivery has started. The following are conditions that may require performance of a Caesarean: if the placenta has become detached, if the umbilical cord has prolapsed, if the baby is in a breech position, or if the mother or child show signs of distress. Further, the physician may opt for a Caesarean section if labor seems unduly prolonged.

There is no question that Caesarean section is often a life-saving procedure for both mother and child. As with other technological advances, however, there are questions as to whether or not this operation is performed more frequently than is absolutely necessary. The attending physician must evaluate two

(continued on page 374)

Birth Without Violence:
The Leboyer Method

During birth, almost all physicians focus their attention on the physical health of mother and child. In addition, the physical comfort of the mother is a concern, and drugs may be used to lessen pain. A lesser concern, but one that is gaining in importance, is the mother's psychological comfort—efforts are being made to "humanize" the birth experience by providing pleasant surroundings and permitting the husband to attend the birth. But one aspect of the birthing process continues to be neglected: the psychological needs of the newborn infant.

Our traditional script for a successful birth reads as follows: after a cooperative and relatively painless labor, the baby emerges and is "caught" by a physician who holds the child upside down and smacks its bottom. The child starts to scream; it is weighed, measured, and cleaned, and then is placed in a sterile environment separate from its mother. At the sound of the infant's first cries, everyone in the delivery room smiles, believing that this is the normal and healthy way that life must begin.

Frederick Leboyer, a French physician, challenges this birthing script. In his book *Birth Without Violence* (1975), Leboyer looks at birth from the newborn's point of view and finds it a traumatic and agonizing experience. But he notes that it need not be so, and he offers many suggestions to "humanize" birth for child as well as parents.

As a first step, Leboyer reinterprets the "birth cry" that brings such joy to new parents. Usu-

ally, a crying child or adult is thought to be in pain or distress; but when the cry comes from a newborn, we don't consider that it may signal pain, because we do not yet view the newborn as a "real person." According to Leboyer, however, the newborn experiences the world in a uniquely intense way: "Birth is a tidal wave of sensation, surpassing anything we can imagine. A sensory experience so vast we can barely conceive of it. The baby's senses are at work. Totally. They are sharp and open—new. What are our senses compared to theirs?" (pp. 15–16).

Leboyer imagines what life must be like for the fetus before birth. For the first half of pregnancy, it is enveloped in a warm, spacious, fluid environment. Then in the second half of pregnancy, the space becomes more confined as the fetus grows larger. One day, the walls of the baby's environment begin to contract and labor begins. The fetus is squeezed, crushed, and pushed from its home. At the end of this terrifying experience, the infant emerges into a world that is very different from its former home. Instead of warmth, softness, quiet, darkness, and closeness, it experiences a cold, hard, and noisy world. The typical delivery room environment contributes to this painful contrast.

There are many ways, Leboyer says, to ease the trauma of birth. First, there is no need for bright lights in the delivery room, nor for loud voices. Second, instead of holding the baby upside down, listening for a cry, and then cutting the umbilical cord, the child should immediately be placed on the mother's stomach. In this way, the child can feel the warmth and closeness of the mother while it begins to breathe on

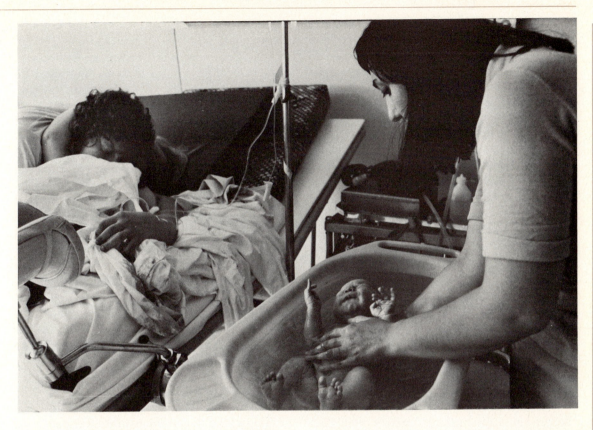

its own. By leaving the umbilical cord attached for 4 or 5 minutes, the baby is ensured of an adequate oxygen supply as it makes the transition to independent breathing.

After the umbilical cord is cut, the child is softly and gently massaged by its mother. Next, the child is separated from its mother for a short time and placed in a water bath heated to body temperature. In the bath, the infant reexperiences the warmth and support of its fetal environment, but with one difference—it has sufficient room to explore movement, flexing its arms and legs as it relaxes against the support of the water. Finally, the infant is wrapped in warm, soft materials and left alone for a short while to discover its own stillness and im-

mobility. Since the infant's birth has been designed to minimize pain, fear, and shock, it is calm enough to enjoy this moment of tranquillity.

Leboyer's method of birth without violence is not possible in all cases. He notes that if there is any complication in the birth—for example, if the umbilical cord has become wrapped around the child's neck—then every technique must be used to start the child's breathing as soon as possible. Also, a child that is listless or drugged may require special attention. However, in an uncomplicated and undrugged birth, Leboyer's method is a thoughtful and interesting alternative to our traditional script for the newborn baby.

sets of risks: the danger of harm to mother and child if the operation is not performed, and the dangers presented by the operation itself. Although Caesareans are certainly much safer than they were in the past, they have been associated with major complications in a small percentage of mothers.

Caesarean section rates tend to be higher in the United States than in other Western countries, and they have been rising over the past 10 years. According to a national survey, about one child in eight was delivered by Caesarean in 1977—a rate that is three times as high as in 1967 (Brody, 1978). Rates tend to be even higher in teaching hospitals, where as many as one child in four may be delivered through the abdomen. As a result of these high rates, medical authorities have begun to reassess the need for Caesarean sections in some cases.

A couple who have been informed, in advance of delivery, that a Caesarean will be necessary have time to learn about the procedure and adjust to what will happen. In contrast, last-minute Caesareans are often a severe shock and disappointment to expectant parents; the mother may feel inadequate because she could not deliver vaginally, and both parents may feel "cheated" of a natural birth experience. To counteract these disappointments, some health facilities have started support groups for women trying to adjust to a Caesarean birth. Further, childbirth classes have begun to educate expectant parents about Caesarean procedures and about the possible last-minute need for such surgery.

After Birth: The Postpartum Period

RECOVERY AND ADJUSTMENT

The time after the birth of a child is often both exhilarating and stressful for the new parents. For the mother, there are enormous changes in hormone levels and other physical functions. Also, there is the psychological stress of assuming complete responsibility for the well-being of the newborn. Where these caretaking chores devolve primarily on the mother, the new father must also adjust to the presence of a newcomer for whom he has financial responsibility. In families where caretaking responsibilities are shared, the new mother and father must often develop complex schedules to balance the needs of their child with the needs of the work world.

The postpartum period may be seen as having at least two stages: the first stage includes the days immediately following birth, and is often spent in a hospital. Several major physical changes are taking place at this time. For example, the new mother usually experiences "afterpains," which result as the uterus contracts to a smaller size. The hormone that causes these contractions, called *oxytocin*, is secreted in larger quantities if the woman breast feeds her child, since sucking stimulates the release of oxytocin. Afterpains are often more intense in women having a second or subsequent child, since the uterus has to work harder to regain its normal size. For most women, the uterus has returned to its prepregnancy size and shape within 6 weeks of birth, and for many this occurs even earlier.

A variety of other physical events take place at this time. As the uterus heals, there is a discharge, called lochia, which continues for several weeks. Also, the episiotomical incision heals, and the sutures needed to repair it are removed. Further, on the second or third day following delivery, the breasts usually become full and tender as they fill with milk. This engorgement will be relieved if the mother decides to breast feed; if, however, she decides not be breast feed, her milk production can be suppressed by the administration of estrogen.

In the past, women were expected to spend as long as 2 weeks in the hospital to recover from the stress of childbirth. Nowadays, the trend is toward shorter and shorter periods of "confinement." The average hospital stay is about 3 days, and the mother is often out of bed within a day of delivery. Indeed, there is some evidence that women who get on their feet quickly are less likely to suffer from bladder and bowel problems, and more likely to have a short recovery time.

The second postpartum stage includes the first few months of caring for the infant at home. At this time, the mother continues to undergo both physical and emotional stress. For example, her body must adjust to decreased blood volume and metabolic changes. Also, the high levels of estrogen and progesterone to which the body had adjusted during pregnancy are no longer present. Some women respond to these physical changes with little discomfort, others experience a variety of unpleasant side effects: sweating, constipation, loss of appetite, and so on. Perhaps the most common physical side effect is fatigue — the demands of caring for a newborn baby, combined with the stress of childbirth and returning to a nonpregnant state, often produce a feeling of tiredness that may last for several months.

Accompanying the physical stress of the postpartum period are a number of emotional or psychological changes. The term *postpartum depression* is used to describe a variety of emotional reactions following delivery. For many women, there is an emotional letdown in the days immediately following delivery that has been labeled the "baby blues"; this response — which may include crying, nightmares, and fears or worries about the baby — is usually relatively shortlived. However, some women may experience mild or even severe depressions that last for several months. Finally, for a very small number of women, the stresses of the postpartum period can precipitate a psychotic reaction. But it is likely that in such cases, pregnancy and delivery was only one of a number of possible stresses that could lead to severe psychological disturbance.

Researchers have accounted for postpartum depression in several ways. Perhaps the most common explanation is that depression is caused by the dramatic drop in hormone levels after delivery. However, while all women experience this drop, not all women respond with psychological depression. Laws and Schwartz (1977) point out that investigations of postpartum depression tend to ignore the psychological implications of the fact that in giving birth to a child a woman becomes a parent. This new role of mother, they suggest, is sufficient of itself to produce a depressive response.

In a society where motherhood is seen as both natural and rewarding, we tend to overlook the fact that there may also be negative aspects to the mother's role. For instance, many women report feelings of "entrapment" after the birth of a first child, a response that is understandable considering that the mother is viewed as the best, and often the only, caretaker of the newborn child. Postpartum depression seems to be particularly common among women who have a strong commitment to work or career, since the role of mother is usually seen as incompatible with the role of worker (Laws and Schwartz, 1977). Finally, one of the most predictable consequences of motherhood, and one that is often overlooked, is loss of sleep. Almost all new mothers can expect to be deprived of uninterrupted sleep for

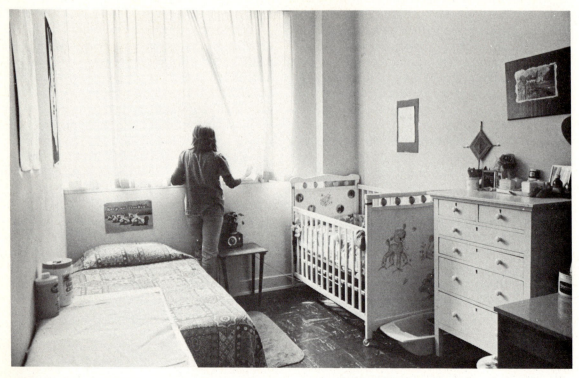

Postpartum depression is common to many women. (© *Janet Fries 1977/Icon*)

a considerable period of time, and scientists have shown that sleep deprivation often results in psychological distress. However, relatively few researchers have attempted to relate postpartum depression with this predictable loss of sleep.

In the past, postpartum depression has been viewed as a biological event, a rejection of the "feminine role," or simply as neurotic moodiness. The authors of *Our Bodies, Ourselves* suggest another perspective—that postpartum depression can be seen as a maturational crisis, in much the same way that puberty and menopause are crises in the process of maturation. Delivery, particularly of a first child, can be expected to result in numerous stresses: fear of being an inadequate parent, feelings of

entrapment, a new relationship with one's partner, and a new life style that incorporates many restrictions on time and freedom. Some of these stresses may be eased if parents feel free to talk about their emotions and to compare their responses to those of other parents. Information and the support of family and friends can also help. "We are entitled to give ourselves the psychic space for the growing pains of giving birth to ourselves as parents" (Boston Women's Health Collective, 1978, p. 43). Rather than feeling guilty or distressed about postpartum emotional difficulties, it would be better for the new parents to accept these reactions as natural ones and use them as a means toward personal growth and maturation.

THE POSTPARTUM PERIOD AND SEXUAL FUNCTION

In the animal kingdom, where sexual activity is usually determined by the female's estrous cycle, most species do not resume intercourse until breast feeding has been completed. This is because the act of breast feeding tends to suppress the hormones necessary to restart the reproductive cycle. Among the subhuman primates, however, the menstrual cycle may recommence during the later stages of breast feeding, so sexual intercourse can resume before the young are weaned.

Although breast feeding tends to suppress the menstrual cycle in human females also, we know that human sexual behavior is relatively free of hormonal influence. Thus many women in the postpartum period will be ready to resume sexual intercourse long before they are ready for a second pregnancy. (It should be noted that breast feeding is *not* a reliable contraceptive technique. Even though ovulation may be delayed for the woman who breast feeds, it is often delayed for only part of the breast-feeding period. The appearance of the first menstrual period is not the best signal for resuming contraception, since it is possible for ovulation to precede menstruation.)

While there is no hormonal basis for delaying sexual intercourse after childbirth, most cultures have developed some rules for when a couple may properly resume sexual activity. Ford and Beach (1951) note that some primitive tribes approve of sexual intercourse as soon as one week after delivery, whereas others insist on abstinence for as long as several years. Some tribes forbid intercourse until the child has reached a particular developmental stage—for example, until the baby can sit up, or until it can walk. In a number of tribes, the intercourse prohibition lasts throughout the breast-feeding period; the rationale for this prohibition is that a second pregnancy would diminish the mother's supply of milk and therefore harm the child that she is nursing. For still other tribes, intercourse may be forbidden but other forms of sexual activity be considered acceptable.

Our own attitudes toward postpartum sexuality have changed considerably in the past century. In 1866 a physician named William Alcott, author of about fifty books on sex and health, wrote that the proper time to resume sexual intercourse was when the infant's first teeth appear. This view, which seems excessively strict by modern-day standards, was actually somewhat lenient in Alcott's time. Most of his contemporaries believed that intercourse should be forbidden throughout the time of breast feeding. Indeed, Alcott noted that "sexual commerce" deprived the nursing child of its "rightful nourishment" by decreasing both the quantity and quality of the mother's milk.

A more recent standard in our culture is that intercourse may be resumed 6 weeks after delivery. By this time, it is argued, the episiotomy is fully healed and uterine bleeding has stopped. Actually, for many women the traumas of childbirth have healed long before the 6-week period, and there is little risk of infection if the lochia discharge has stopped and there is no vaginal discomfort. The 6-week prohibition seems somewhat arbitrary—most physicians schedule a postpartum checkup at this time and approve the resumption of intercourse if physical healing has been normal. Masters and Johnson (1966) strongly disapprove of this 6-week "blanket medical interdiction of coital activity," suggesting that each case needs to be individually assessed; if a woman is physically and psychologically ready for intercourse before 6 weeks have passed, she should be encouraged. In fact, many women in their study had resumed sexual activity 3 weeks after delivery, contrary to their physicians' instructions.

Just because a woman is physically healed, however, does not mean that she is psychologically ready to resume intercourse. About half of the women in the Masters and Johnson study reported little or no interest in sexual activity at an interview conducted in the third month postpartum. Many of these women were concerned that intercourse could cause them physical harm; other reasons for delaying sexual activity included fatigue and weakness, and vaginal pain or discharge. In addition to these physical reasons, the Boston Women's Health Collective points out the importance of psychological factors: "Low sexual interest may also be caused by the trauma of having your life tipped upside down; of having the needs of a new baby, a mate, possibly other children, to consider while your needs go unmet" (1976, p. 301).

Masters and Johnson report that the remaining 50 percent of the women in their sample did experience sexual interest during the 3-month postpartum period. Some women noted that within 3 weeks their sexual interest had returned to prepregnancy levels; others found that sexual interest was considerably higher than it had been before pregnancy. Interestingly, these high levels of sexual tension were most likely to occur in women who were breast feeding their children. Not only were nursing mothers the most eager to resume intercourse with their husbands, but some also noted high levels of sexual arousal, and even orgasm, while breast feeding their infants.

Although sexual interest may return to high levels within several weeks of delivery, Masters and Johnson found that the physiology of sexual response took considerably longer to recover. Among the six women in their study who underwent physiological tests, all showed a diminished sexual response at 6 to 8 weeks after delivery. For example, there was less vaginal lubrication, blood flow into the genitals took longer, and orgasmic contractions were shorter and less intense than before pregnancy. By 3 months postpartum, however, sexual physiology and response had returned to normal. The diminished sexual response in the early postpartum period did not affect the women's subjective perceptions of sexual satisfaction—that is, they felt as satisfied by an orgasm occurring 4 to 6 weeks postpartum as one occurring after 3 months and were not able to describe any differences between the two orgasmic experiences.

Summary

Reproduction is, of course, a biological event, but it involves personal, interpersonal and social factors as well. In some cultures, the pregnant woman is restricted by special rules and regulations as to where she may go, what she may eat, and how she may act sexually. In other cultures, she is cast in the role of someone who is sick. In still others, she is seen as different, but normal. The experience of pregnancy, then—as well as the experience of birth—is determined by both biological and social forces.

1. Fertility problems exist in about 15 percent of couples who are trying to conceive, and are equally common among males and females. Many of these problems can be solved through sexual counseling or by medical intervention.

2. Little medical evidence exists that sexual activity is harmful during a normal pregnancy. Rates of sexual intercourse vary depending on cultural expectations, physical and psychological feelings of well-being or discomfort, and previous level of sexual activity.

3. Expectations about the birth experience, and the actual setting and experience of giving birth, vary a great deal from one culture to another. In our own society, there has been a shift from the Biblical notion that birth should be painful, to the use of painkilling drugs, to the idea that birth pain can be lessened with relaxation and education. At present, the birthing woman can choose from a number of medical and nonmedical birthing techniques.

4. We have evolved an extensive technology for birth that includes artificial insemination, test tube fertilization, amniocentesis, fetal monitors, surgical procedures, and drugs to numb or ease pain and to speed up or slow down the labor process. These developments have both benefits and drawbacks; in some cases, their use can save lives, but at other times, they may succeed only in alienating a woman from the experience of giving birth.

5. The postpartum period presents a variety of physical and emotional stresses to the new mother. The resumption of sexual activity will depend on a variety of factors: the couple's adjustment to the strains of parenthood, the woman's physical health, and the role of sexual activity in the couple's life before pregnancy and birth took place.

ELEVEN

Contraception and Abortion

Overview

Our bodies are designed for reproduction. If we do not interfere with this design, the natural outcome of sexual intercourse will be conception, pregnancy, and childbirth. In a sense, then, contraception is actually a process of redesign — an attempt to interrupt what comes naturally, to separate sexuality from its reproductive consequences. We have accomplished this goal with some, but not complete, success; we have yet to discover the "perfect" contraceptive.

Birth control is not a new idea. The attempt to control fertility has existed throughout history. But effective, widespread, and socially approved contraceptive use is a relatively recent phenomenon. Our present contraceptive freedom is a product of slowly changing social, sexual, economic, and political conditions. We tend to view contraception as a right and even a duty, but this attitude has developed gradually; it was not too long ago that contraception was considered immoral, unhealthy, and socially destructive.

The availability and acceptance of contraception has not put an end to unplanned and unwanted pregnancy. In the second section of this chapter, we discuss the contraceptive problems of women at different stages in their "fertility career." The most serious problems seem to occur among sexually active adolescents, but there are also contraceptive failures among adults. The mere availability of effective contraception does not guarantee its use; many personal and social factors may interfere with effective birth control, and a contraceptive must fit well into the user's life style if birth control is to be effective.

Next, we discuss the contraceptive options available to the user. Since we do not have a perfect contraceptive, we are forced to choose among a variety of methods having different advantages and drawbacks. That is, we make a contraceptive compromise—for example, we decide that the effectiveness of the pill compensates for its health risk, or that the inconvenience of the diaphragm is balanced by its safety. In general, the more effective a contraceptive technique, the more risk it presents to health. Unfortunately, several of the techniques that were used quite successfully by our parents—the condom and diaphragm, for instance—are now downplayed in favor of the more technological methods.

Abortion is discussed in the final section of the chapter. Although abortion is not, strictly speaking, a contraceptive method—it limits fertility *after* conception has taken place—it is the most widely used means of birth control in the world. From a physical standpoint, abortion performed early in pregnancy is both safe and effective. Unlike other methods of birth control, however, abortion is not viewed as desirable. Most people accept abortion only as a "necessary evil" when other methods of contraception have failed. The negative view of abortion in the United States is not shared throughout the world; in some countries, abortion is seen as a primary and acceptable way of controlling fertility.

The Contraceptive Revolution

Although ours is a generation that, historically speaking, makes the greatest use of contraceptive techniques and devices, the notion of birth control has been with us since the beginning of recorded history. As the men and women of ancient civilizations became aware of the connection between sexual intercourse and pregnancy, they attempted to find ways to limit their fertility. For example, Egyptian writings dating back to about 2000 B.C. describe the use of vaginal suppositories to prevent conception, and paintings of the same era show men wearing penile sheaths, perhaps the first condoms. In the Bible, God condemns Onan for "spilling his seed," a practice we now call coitus interruptus or withdrawal. The ancient Romans wrote that to avoid conception, a woman should hold her breath, rise immediately from her bed, squat down, and try to sneeze. When these techniques failed, the ancients practiced abortion or infanticide to limit family size.

The present generation has seen a "contraceptive revolution" in two areas: first, we have seen the development of medically sophisticated contraceptives that are close to 100 percent effective in preventing conception. Second, and more important, the vast majority of our society accepts the use of contraceptives as a valid and desirable means of limiting fertility. Only in the second half of the twentieth century have contraceptive information and devices become accepted by and available to almost all people in industrialized nations. This attitudinal change represents a substantial break with the past. Before this century, contraceptive knowledge was often the privilege of a restricted few—physicians, prostitutes, and the upper classes of certain cultures. In most cultures, the limitation of fertility was discouraged by legal, religious, and social codes of behavior.

Nowadays, we tend to view the ability to limit fertility as a necessary and even indispensable part of modern life. Most of us have become so accustomed to the notion of birth control as an "inalienable right" that it is somewhat difficult to understand why previous generations struggled over this issue. To understand that struggle we should remember that although birth control is, in the final analysis, a personal choice, individuals make the decision to limit fertility within a social context. According to Linda Gordon (1976), birth control has always been socially regulated because fertility has such important consequences for society. For instance, population size is directly related to the use of contraceptives; thus a society that sees advantages to expanding its size is likely to prohibit contraceptive measures. In addition, a culture that limits contraception has a greater degree of control over the sexual activity of its members because the consequence of disapproved sexual conduct—pregnancy—will be unavoidable. Therefore, while the individual may see a personal advantage in limiting fertility, the actual decision to use contraceptive techniques is also influenced by what may be overwhelming social, economic, and religious pressures.

Our modern-day concern with "overpopulation" is a relatively recent phenomenon. In the past, most societies had the opposite concern—how to increase population levels. Many factors were in operation that kept population levels low: a higher rate of infant mortality, a shorter lifespan, disease, famine, higher maternal mortality during childbirth, and so on. From a political standpoint, then, most societies were best served by high birth rates. Western religious traditions supported this need; for instance, Christian authorities generally condemned all sexual behavior that was not procreational in intent. As recently as 1968, a papal encyclical on birth control reaffirmed the rhythm method as the only acceptable form of contraception within the Catholic church. In keeping with the desire to encourage population growth, many societies have prohibited the dissemination of birth control information. In the nineteenth century, both the United States and England declared such information to be "pornographic"; and the United States passed the Comstock Law, which made it illegal to provide any birth control information or devices to the public.

This public ban on contraceptive information did not, however, mean that individuals abandoned their private attempts to limit fertility. As Table 11.1 shows, family size in the United States has been decreasing since 1800 in spite of the ban on dissemination of birth control information. While some of this decrease probably reflects lowered infant mortality rates—it was no longer necessary to have seven children in order to ensure that two or three would survive to adulthood—there is no doubt that individuals did try to limit their family size. In the face of restrictive laws, it

TABLE 11.1
Estimates of Live Births Among White Women in the United States, 1800–1950

Year	Births Per Woman	Year	Births Per Woman	Year	Births Per Woman
1800	7.04	1860	5.21	1920	3.17
1810	6.92	1870	4.55	1930	2.45
1820	6.73	1880	4.24	1940	2.19
1830	6.55	1890	3.87	1950	2.
1840	6.14	1900	3.56		
1850	5.42	1910	3.42		

Source: Adapted from A. Coale and M. Zelnick, *New Estimates of Fertility and Population in the United States* (Princeton, N.J.: Princeton University Press, 1963), p. 36.

seems that contraceptive information simply went underground and was passed around by word of mouth.

The issue of overpopulation (see Figure 11.1) is considered to have originated with the work of Thomas Malthus, an English economist and sociologist. In his classic book, *An Essay on the Principle of Population*, first published in 1878, Malthus argued that the human race was driven by a powerful sexual urge that would lead to overpopulation relative to the available food supply. The only checks on population growth were war and famine. To avoid these miseries, Malthus advised that reproduction must be kept under control. He did not, however, advocate the use of contraceptives to achieve this end. Instead, he suggested the use of self-control: men were advised to marry as late as possible in their lives and to restrain their sexual behavior even within marriage. A group called the neo-

Malthusians shared Malthus' fear of overpopulation but believed that effective contraception was the solution to the problem. They wrote books and pamphlets describing the use of condoms, vaginal sponges, and coitus interruptus to limit family size. Their work did not receive widespread public acceptance for several reasons. First, since it was illegal, it had a limited impact on the public. Second, most medical authorities in the nineteenth century believed that contraception was unhealthy and even dangerous. Finally, the moral ethic of the time viewed sexuality as an instinct to be restrained and not encouraged. Thus the encouragement of sexual abstinence was more socially acceptable than was the use of contraceptives (Bullough, 1976).

The birth control movement in the United States has gone through many stages and transformations. Gordon (1976) suggests that the first stage, in the second half of the nine-

FIGURE 11.1

Graphs of world population. (a) The rise in the overall world population over the centuries. (b) Projected population growth, by region, 1975-2000. The greatest increase is taking place in the poorest countries.

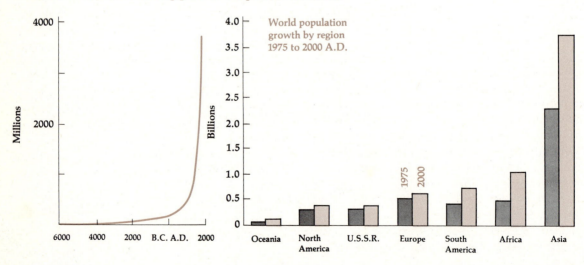

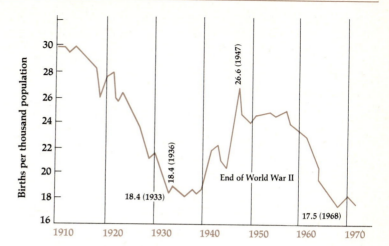

FIGURE 11.2

Graph showing birth rates in the United States since 1910. The birth control movement has received widespread public acceptance in the twentieth century.

teenth century, was the acceptance of the notion that motherhood should be a voluntary activity. Members of the voluntary motherhood movement stressed the importance of choice in childbearing but did not advocate using contraceptives to make this choice; they saw abstinence as the best technique for limiting family size. With time, however, the view of birth control devices as unhealthy and unnatural began to change. Two women had a great deal to do with this change: Margaret Sanger in the United States (see the boxed extract) and Marie Stopes in England.

The concept of birth control finally received widespread public acceptance in the twentieth century (see Figure 11.2) — for several reasons. Urbanization and industrialization undoubtedly played an important role. Whereas the rural farmworker's children were a source of labor and financial support, the urban industrial worker found that children were a financial drain. City living was more comfortable when there were only a few children to feed, clothe, and educate. Even now, countries with large agricultural populations are less successful than industrialized nations at motivating

their citizens to limit family size. (See the boxed extract on contraception on page 390.)

The *eugenics* movement also played a role in the public acceptance of contraception. "Eugenics" is a term coined in 1885 by Francis Galton, a cousin of Charles Darwin. It refers to an applied biological science concerned with increasing intelligence levels from one generation to the next. At the time this idea developed, it was thought that intelligence was entirely a hereditary trait, and proponents of eugenics hoped to use "selective breeding" to raise intelligence levels. The eugenics banner was taken up by many political groups who saw an advantage to limiting fertility in certain racial groups. For instance, the upper classes of New York, concerned with the large families raised by poor immigrants, found themselves willing to provide birth control information to these groups. While the eugenics movement clearly played upon the racial prejudices of the well-off, it did serve the important purpose of bringing contraceptive information to the public.

A final factor in the public acceptance of
(continued on page 387)

Birth Control: A Cross-Cultural Perspective

In some cultures, contraceptive measures are in such great use that birth rates are stable or even declining; in others, population control is proving to be very difficult. According to Giele and Smock (1977), we can best understand these differences by examining the role and status of women within the particular culture.

EGYPT

Improved health care has increased the Egyptian life span, but there has been no corresponding decrease in birth rates. Although the government has tried to limit fertility by providing free birth control services, as of 1970 only 12.6 percent of all eligible couples had made use of these services. Religion does not seem to play a major role in the failure to limit birth rates — Islamic authorities generally oppose only abortion and surgical sterilization as contraceptive measures. Islam does stress, however, the importance of early marriage and family life. The major source of respect and status for the Egyptian woman is motherhood, and very few women plan a life that does not include childbearing. Thus the issue becomes not whether to have children but how many to have. The most important factor in determining family size appears to be educational status: women who have graduated from college have half as many children as women who are illiterate. The educated, urban Egyptian woman is more aware of the costs of having a large family, and is also more likely to have expanded life opportunities such as a career.

BANGLADESH

Bangladesh has one of the most severe overpopulation problems in the world. Women report that the "ideal" family size is about six children. With high infant and child mortality rates, this means that women must spend most of their adult lives bearing children, usually at considerable cost to their health. Although it has been reported that 85 percent of the population is aware of the government's birth control program, only about 3.7 percent of those eligible used any contraceptives in 1968–1969.

In Bangladesh's largely agricultural society, the benefits of large families, particularly many male children, seem to outweigh the costs. Children are important for their labor to the family. In addition, women have few options other than childrearing for gaining status and security. The more secluded a woman is, the larger her family is likely to be. Muslim women who are secluded in purdah (a practice in which married women see no men other than immediate family members) have more children than the freer Hindu women.

JAPAN

Japan has seen a major drop in family size during the past 35 years; the number of births per woman has declined from 5.14 in 1940 to about 1.69 in 1967. Japan's success in controlling population is due in part to government intervention — there are many birth control clinics, and the cost of birth control is covered by government health insurance. The Japanese people have been extremely responsive to changes in government policy. In addition, contraception does not conflict with Japanese religious or moral traditions. Legal abortions are easily available and carry no moral or social stigma.

The condom accounts for about 90 percent of contraceptive use, with the rhythm method and the IUD also in use.

FRANCE

Although it is many years since women were granted legal rights in France, contraceptives became freely available only in 1967, and abortion was legalized in 1974. Birth rates began to decline in France long before contraceptives were easily available, putting the government in the position of encouraging rather than discouraging childbearing. The techniques formerly used to limit fertility—rhythm, coitus interruptus, and condoms—have retained their popularity.

POLAND

Poland also experienced a dramatic decline in birth rates before contraceptives became freely available. About 50 percent of married women report using some form of contraception, but use of the pill or IUD is not widespread. Abortion, which has been legally available since 1956, is extremely common, and it has been estimated that there is one abortion for every 1.9 live births. While the government wishes to increase the birth rate, it also needs to keep women in the work force; thus Poland encourages fertility by making childbearing compatible with work—for instance, by providing adequate maternity and day-care services.

Source: Derived from Giele, J. Z., and Smock, A. C. *Women: Roles and Status in Eight Countries.* New York: Wiley, 1977.

contraception is the changing role of women. The sexual double standard—that women should remain chaste or faithful to their marital partners while men were permitted to indulge in necessary sexual wandering—clearly worked against the acceptance of contraception. After all, the faithful wife who saw sex simply as a route to motherhood had little need for birth control. While motherhood is still the primary role for many women, our culture has been establishing the right of women to take on other roles as well. Women now have the legal right to control their own fertility, either through the use of contraceptives or through abortion. In turn, such control expands women's life options in many areas—education, career, family structure, sexual behavior, and so on.

Perhaps the most recent attitudinal change of the contraceptive revolution is the acceptance of birth control for the unmarried. Until the past decade, contraceptive use was considered proper only for the married and birth control information was provided in the context of "family planning." Many states had laws against the dissemination of birth control devices to the single woman, and she was often placed in the uncomfortable position of having to lie to her physician in order to obtain what she needed. The assumption that giving contraceptives to the unmarried will lead to promiscuity and the "breakdown of the family" is still prevalent, but recognition of the contraceptive rights of the unmarried has helped to change discriminatory laws. In addition, concern with out-of-wedlock pregnancies has directed attention to the contraceptive needs of the single woman. This concern has eliminated the last legal barrier to access to contraceptives, establishing the right of the unmarried female—including the teenager—to birth control information.

Unfortunately, the contraceptive revolution has not brought an end to unwanted and

Although motherhood is still the primary role for many women, the women's movement has caused a reevaluation of female roles. (© *Kenneth Siegel 1980*)

unplanned pregnancies. Although birth control technology is legally available to all, there are still many emotional, informational, and social barriers to effective contraception.

Contraceptive Use and Disuse

Many factors in our society push us toward the use of birth control techniques. We have a wide variety of sophisticated contraceptives available to us, and we are part of the first generation to use the birth control pill—a method that when used correctly is close to 100 percent effective in preventing pregnancy. At the same time, we live in an era in which contraceptives are legally available, inexpensive, and socially approved. Our culture supports the idea of limiting family size and spacing childbearing over time, while strongly disapproving of births that take place out of wedlock. Given all these conditions, it is easy to understand why individuals would want to use contraceptives. What is difficult to understand is why there are still so many unwanted and unplanned pregnancies.

The failure to use contraceptives (or to use them correctly and consistently) is most obvious when we examine pregnancy rates among unmarried teen-aged females. According to Reiss (1976), illegitimacy rates—that is, the number of children born to unmarried females—increased dramatically between 1940 and 1970. For example, among a random sample of 1,000 women aged 15 to 19, there were about 7.4 illegitimate births in 1940, 15.3 in 1960, and 22.4 in 1970. In 1973, about 400,000 illegitimate births were recorded in the United States, about half of them involving teen-aged mothers.

Illegitimacy rates show only the tip of the iceberg when we look at adolescent contraceptive failure. For every child that is actually born to an unmarried teen-aged mother there are probably several teen-age pregnancies that do not result in an out-of-wedlock birth—first, because a large number of teen-age pregnancies are terminated by legal abortion; second, because teen-aged women are more likely than older women to have a spontaneous abortion of their pregnancy (miscarriage); and finally, because many teen-agers resolve the problem of out-of-wedlock pregnancy by marrying before the child is born. It has been estimated that as many as 60 percent of all births occurring to teen-agers in 1970 were conceived before marriage (Zelnick and Kantner, 1974). While it is difficult to state exactly how many conceptions occur among young, unmarried women, it is clear that the existence of effective contraceptives has not eliminated unwanted pregnancies in this population.

It is even more difficult to estimate contraceptive disuse or failure among older, married women, since all births in this group are recorded as legitimate. For married women, contraceptive error can take two forms: first, a woman may become pregnant before she wants to—a *spacing* or *timing* failure. Second, a woman may have more children than she had planned—a *number* failure. The statistician who examines the birth rates of married women has no way to distinguish these contraceptive errors from planned pregnancies. Further, among the married an unplanned pregnancy does not always produce an unwanted child. A couple faced with an unexpected pregnancy often decide that their life style can accommodate an additional family member.

A woman's *fertility career* can be divided into three stages: adolescence, young adulthood, and older adulthood (McCormick *et al.,* 1977). At each of these stages, a woman will have different fertility concerns and desires, and her contraceptive needs will also differ. The costs of childbearing—not only the financial, but also the emotional, social, and physical consequences of motherhood—will vary. For instance, the unmarried adolescent who becomes pregnant pays a higher price for contraceptive failure than does the married woman whose pregnancy is unplanned but not unwanted. At the same time, the emotional and social barriers to effective birth control are often more severe for the unmarried adolescent. In view of these and other differences in the contraceptive needs of women as they pass through their fertility careers, it makes sense to discuss contraceptive success and failure as it occurs in each of the three stages of the fertility career.

THE ADOLESCENT

Our culture is most concerned about contraceptive failure in the young and unmarried. It is also most conflicted about how to deal with the contraceptive needs of the sexually active adolescent. This conflict is understandable if we examine the gap between our attitudes toward premarital sexuality and the actual frequency of this behavior.

Data gathered over the past few decades show a clear trend toward greater adolescent

Margaret Sanger (1883–1966): Pioneer in Birth Control

A key figure in the history of modern contraception is Margaret Sanger, who probably devoted more energy and enthusiasm to the cause than any other modern figure. Although her abrasive personal style elicited criticism from many sources, her efforts to publicize the issues did much to bring about modern public policies toward contraception.

Sanger was born in the factory town of Corning, New York; the sixth of eleven children. She left home to become a nurse at the age of 15, and at the age of 19 married a young architect, William Sanger. For the next 10 years, she played the role of a traditional housewife—including moving to the suburbs and having three children. Dissatisfied with the isolation this brought, the family moved back to New York City, and Margaret began work as a nurse in the poorer

neighborhoods of the Lower East Side. In her work there, she became increasingly concerned about the lack of contraceptive knowledge among the poor immigrant women, which inevitably led to illegal and dangerous abortions.

From this time on, Margaret Sanger adopted birth control as her personal cause. Although not the first spokesperson for these issues, she was nevertheless able to attract considerable public attention to her activities. After a widely publicized trip to France in search of contraceptive information, Sanger returned to New York and began publishing a magazine called *Woman Rebel*. The magazine was based on her political ideals, and it included articles on socialism, class divisions, and women's rights. She was charged in court with violating the Comstock Law, which prohibited the transportation and mailing of "obscene, lewd, and lascivious articles." In fact, although Sanger had written a pamphlet containing explicit contraceptive information, intending to create a legal test case, she had not yet begun to distribute the pamphlet at the time she was arrested for publishing *Woman Rebel*. Because her plan had back-

sexual activity—in spite of substantial social disapproval of such activity. In a national sample of women aged 15 to 19, Zelnick and Kantner (1977) found that unmarried females were more likely to be sexually active in 1976 than in 1971. As shown in Table 11.2, 26.8 percent of the total sample studied in 1971 reported having had intercourse; in 1976, this figure had risen to 34.9 percent. Among 19-year-old females, those reporting intercourse over the 5-year time span increased from 46.8 to 55.2 percent. In addition, females in the 1976 sample tended to have had more sexual partners than the 1971 group and also reported a higher frequency of intercourse. However, it should be noted that in both samples more than half the women had sexual intercourse

TABLE 11.2

Percentage of Never-Married Women Aged 15–19 Who Have Ever Had Intercourse

Age	1976			1971		
	All	White	Black	All	White	Black
15–19	34.9	30.8	62.7	26.8	21.4	51.2
15	18.0	13.8	38.4	13.8	10.9	30.5
16	25.4	22.6	52.6	21.2	16.9	46.2
17	40.9	36.1	68.4	26.6	21.8	58.8
18	45.2	43.6	74.1	36.8	32.3	62.7
19	55.2	48.7	83.6	46.8	39.4	76.2

Source: Adapted from M. Zelnick and J. F. Kantner, "Sexual and Contraceptive Experience of Young Unmarried Women in the United States, 1976 and 1971," *Family Planning Perspectives*, Vol. 9, No. 2 (1977), p. 56.

fired, she decided to pay a visit to Britain in 1914.

Her time in England was well spent meeting with leaders of the British birth control movement. Havelock Ellis, for example, advised her to concentrate her efforts on the issue of contraception and to moderate her political radicalism. On returning to New York the following year, she found the government unwilling to prosecute her case because of the considerable publicity it had received as a free speech issue.

Sanger then focused her attention on the establishment of a birth control clinic in a poor area of Brooklyn. These activities led to her arrest for distribution of birth control information. At this time, she became aware that her advocacy of birth control as a means of *helping* the poor was not receiving widespread public support. She therefore changed her tactics and stressed the need for birth control as a means of *managing* the poor.

She showed great courage in her efforts to convince both the medical establishment and the Congress that contraception should be viewed as a woman's personal right. As a measure of her success, the American Medical Association issued a report in 1937 stating for the first time that birth control was of value for reasons other than the prevention of disease. Her struggle with government was less successful. Her opponents resorted to denouncing birth control as a "Soviet plot," and she was unable to effect significant changes in federal policy toward contraception. However, the battle continued in the state courts and resulted in each state reaching its own position on the issue.

Her years of struggle did not make Sanger a popular or well-liked figure. Unfortunately she alienated many potential allies with her political maneuvers, her vehement style, and her inability to compromise. The birth control movement benefited from the support of Eleanor Roosevelt, an enormously popular public figure, who made "child spacing" a part of public health programs.

with only one male partner, and about 80 percent with three or fewer partners.

What role does contraception play in this trend? According to one view, the availability of contraception directly contributes to the rise in premarital intercourse; that is, by allowing teen-agers access to birth control measures, we are actually encouraging them to be sexually active because we are removing that age-old deterrent to intercourse, the fear of pregnancy. People who take this perspective often suggest that the best way to discourage adolescent sexual behavior is to withhold contraceptive information.

An opposing view holds that contraceptive information should be made *more* available to sexually active adolescents; since so many teen-agers are already sexually active, it is more realistic to provide them with contraceptives than to force them to suffer the consequences of an out-of-wedlock pregnancy. Proponents of this view point out that there is little evidence that contraceptives directly cause premarital intercourse. For example, Reiss (1970) found that a woman's decision to engage in or abstain from such behavior is based on her entire background of attitudes and values; the availability of birth control devices is incorporated into her value system without actually changing it. Thus a woman who strongly disapproves of premarital sex will tend to abstain even when a highly reliable contraceptive is available. In contrast, a woman who accepts the idea of premarital sex may well act on her beliefs without regard to whether or not contraception is available to her.

As already noted, teen-age sexual activity and out-of-wedlock pregnancies have both been increasing. Combining these two facts, we might conclude that teen-agers are not making full use of the contraceptive devices available to them, and a number of studies have shown that this conclusion is accurate. However, there has been a dramatic shift toward greater contraceptive use. In 1971, Zelnick and Kantner found that 17 percent of sexually active 15- to 19-year-olds had never used any type of contraceptive; and among those using contraception, only 45.4 percent said they had made use of it for their most recent intercourse experience. In 1976, 63.5 percent had used a contraceptive for their most recent intercourse experience, and 30 percent reported always using some form of contraception. However, a substantial number of women still reported never having used any birth control technique (Zelnick and Kantner, 1977).

There has also been a trend toward increasing use by 15- to 19-year-olds of coitus-independent techniques—specifically, the birth control pill and IUD (see Table 11.3). Zelnick and Kantner (1977) report that the pill has more than doubled in its popularity since 1971, with about half of the women in the 1976 sample using it at the time of their interview. The two most common methods of 1971—the condom and withdrawal—both showed great loss of popularity by 1976, although a large number of women continued to rely on them. Unfortunately, fewer than half the women in the samples could correctly identify the time during the menstrual cycle when they were most likely to become pregnant; but about 14 percent of the 1976 sample did report using the rhythm method.

While there is a trend toward more and

TABLE 11.3

Method of Contraception Most Recently Used by Unmarried Women Aged 15–19

	15–17	18–19
1976		
Pill	36.4	58.5
IUD	2.4	4.3
Condom	27.6	14.2
Douche	3.8	3.2
Withdrawal	24.7	9.0
Other	5.1	10.8
1971		
Pill	15.4	32.1
IUD	0.6	2.3
Condom	40.6	23.7
Douche	6.6	5.0
Withdrawal	31.8	29.7
Other	5.0	7.2

Source: Adapted from M. Zelnick and J. F. Kantner, "Sexual and Contraceptive Experience of Young Unmarried Women in the United States, 1976 and 1971," *Family Planning Perspectives*, Vol. 9, No. 2 (1977), p. 63.

better use of contraception, there are still a substantial number of women who use contraception inconsistently, incorrectly, or not at all. Therefore, it is important to examine the barriers that interfere with effective contraceptive use.

Contraceptive barriers

Lack of information. In this age of increasing sexual freedom, there is still considerable ignorance about how our bodies work and how contraceptives should be used. In general, the younger a woman, the less she will know about the contraceptive facts of life. Many adolescents severely underestimate their chances of pregnancy; actually, the young teen-aged girl does have a relatively small chance of becoming pregnant in the first few years after the menarche, but she may mistakenly assume

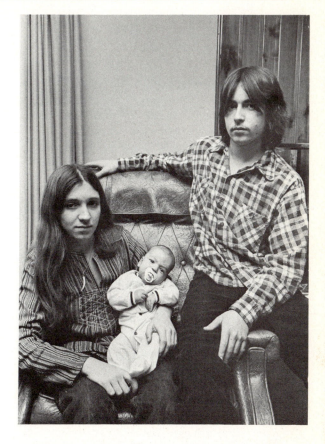

that this relative safety will continue as she grows older. As already noted, only about half of teen-aged girls can identify the period of greatest risk of pregnancy during the menstrual cycle. Sex education, in both the home and the school environment, usually takes the form of explaining the menstrual cycle, but there is rarely any explicit information about how to use contraceptive devices. Thus a girl may *think* that she is protected if she uses one of her mother's birth control pills, if she has intercourse only in certain positions, or if she uses a spermicidal foam after intercourse.

Emotional obstacles. The sexual "double standard," though in modified form, still plays a major role in the contraceptive decisions of many young women. On the one hand, women are given the message that premarital sex is improper and shameful and should not be planned for. On the other hand, they must bear most of the unpleasant consequences when an unplanned sexual encounter leads to pregnancy. In this double-bind situation, the woman is blamed for using contraceptives and for not using them. If she carries a diaphragm in her purse or takes a birth control pill every evening, she is admitting that her sexual behavior is planned and intentional. However, the woman who believes that premarital intercourse is morally wrong cannot easily accept this responsibility and may permit sexual activity only when it is spontaneous and unintentional—and therefore contraceptively unplanned.

Since planned contraception requires taking personal and sexual responsibility for oneself, it is not surprising that women who use contraceptives in a consistent fashion differ from noncontraceptors. For example, one study (Reiss *et al.*, 1975), involving a survey of 482 women attending a Midwestern university, found that women who had made use of a birth control clinic were more self-assured and more tolerant of diverse sexual life styles than women who did not use the clinic. This finding was replicated in a survey of unmarried teen-aged girls seeking birth control, abortion, or delivery of an illegitimate child (Goldsmith *et al.*, 1972). The birth control seekers were more accepting of sexuality, more self-assured, and more positive about the prevention of pregnancy than either of the other two groups.

Our discussion has centered on the female's role in contraception because, by and large, it

The Male's Role in Contraception

Nowadays, contraception is seen as primarily the female's responsibility. Some women object to carrying the full burden of birth control and would like to see their male partners share some of this responsibility; others believe that their independence requires complete contraceptive management and dislike the idea of any male involvement. The vast majority of birth control clinics focus their efforts on females, as do the many popular sex and health self-help books currently available. What is the role of the male in this predominantly female-oriented contraceptive era?

According to Bernard Zilbergeld, a psychologist who has written about male sexuality, "Con-traception is a subject boys and men used to think about but in recent years have learned is none of their business" (1978, p. 164). In past years, when the condom was a primary means of birth control, men at least recognized that contraception had something to do with them. Many men carried a spare condom in their wallet, discussed the advantages and disadvantages of different brands, and practiced putting them on. With the widespread use of the pill and IUD, however, and the media-conveyed impression that all women use one of these two techniques, male involvement in birth control has dropped sharply. "Not surprisingly, men have gotten the message, and many indicate no interest in, or concern about, contraception. Why should they, given their impression that women have taken care of the subject?" (pp. 164–165).

Zilbergeld does not believe that males should dissociate themselves from the contraceptive process. They should be aware of whether their

is the woman who suffers the consequences of premarital conception. However, the emotional context of a sexual relationship plays a major role in the use or nonuse of contraception. Even in a close, romantic relationship, there are often communication problems regarding contraception. For young adolescents, discussions of birth control may be embarrassing and difficult. If the male does not assume contraceptive responsibility, perhaps by refusing to use a condom, the female may not feel able to assert her own contraceptive needs (see the boxed extract). On the other hand, the male might assume that since his partner has no objections to intercourse she must have her own form of contraception. This type of miscommunication is probably most frequent among young, sexually inexperienced men and women; but it can also occur among older adults having sexual contact with an unfamiliar partner.

External obstacles. In theory, contraceptives are available to everyone. In practice, however, access to contraceptives is often blocked for the adolescent. Since there is still some stigma attached to female premarital sexual activity, the unmarried woman often conducts her search for contraception with an eye toward privacy. But the most effective contraceptives can be obtained only through the public act of visiting a clinic or physician and revealing her needs to a stranger. Should this stranger show disapproval for her request, she may become discouraged from further attempts to find an effective contraceptive. Many women will lie to a physician about their marital status in order to avoid such dis-

female partner is using some contraceptive device — contrary to the popular impression, not all women use the pill or an IUD, and many would like to negotiate contraceptive decisions with their male partners. Male involvement in contraception does not necessarily mean using a condom; what it does mean is sharing and participating in contraceptive decisions. The male role should involve discussing contraceptive options, providing support and advice when contraceptive problems arise and, perhaps, sharing the cost of contraceptive supplies or medical care. While there is no way to equalize the consequences of contraception for male and female — it is, after all, the female who suffers most directly from contraceptive failure — it is important that men take their role in contraception as a serious consideration.

approval. Kantner and Zelnick (1973) reported that among 15- to 19-year-olds, married women are far more likely than single women to obtain contraceptives from a physician and twice as likely to use the pill or an IUD; single women of the same age are more likely to obtain their contraceptives from a drugstore, in the form of such methods as spermicidal foam — presumably because of the stigma of admitting premarital sex to a physician.

We should not underestimate the importance of embarrassment in obtaining contraceptive protection. Even when contraceptives are available over the counter, as with the condom, embarrassment can defeat the contraceptive seeker. Gemme (1977) studied the availability of condoms in the pharmacies of Montreal and found that although the vast majority of the stores did stock the item, more

than half kept their supply hidden behind the counter, making it necessary for the customer to request them from the pharmacist. When storekeepers were asked why condoms were not kept in a self-service area, many responded by citing reasons of "morality." Thus, the teenager who senses strong disapproval from the contraceptive supplier may well have sized up the situation correctly.

While birth control clinics are increasingly common, they are not always accessible to all potential users. Although the government supports many clinics, far more money is spent on the care of unwed mothers than on the prevention of pregnancy. This ambivalence about birth control is often shared by religious authorities and by the school systems that are supposed to educate teen-agers about sexuality. Thus while general policy seems to be in favor of birth control, the specifics of delivering contraceptive care — that is, staff attitudes, and accessibility in terms of time, distance, and financial cost — are often less than optimal.

THE YOUNG ADULT

At the second stage in a woman's fertility career, young adulthood, her contraceptive concerns are often substantially different from what they were during adolescence. Most important, this is the time of life when children are likely to be welcomed. Although a small number of women delay childbearing until their thirties or decide not to have any children, the majority of women complete their families while in their twenties. Even when a pregnancy is unplanned, the married adult does not have to face the problems of an illegitimate birth. Further, in her search for effective contraception, the married woman does not incur medical and social disapproval; in our society, the need for contraceptives is legitimized by marriage. However, the single adult woman will probably find that she too has an easier time obtaining contraceptives, as she becomes more confident and self-assured about her sexual and social life style.

Certain costs and benefits are associated with childbirth. In our society, couples are likely to recognize that large families present a heavy financial burden—for example, it has been projected that it will cost about $98,000 to send today's infant to college. Large families also require an emotional and time commitment that may be incompatible with a couple's career plans. Further, the large family has become unfashionable in view of the recent concern with overpopulation. The rewards of raising a family, however, continue to motivate the majority of couples to have children. The ideal family size is usually reported as two children, and couples make use of contraceptives in order to attain this ideal. In addition, most couples use contraceptives to space their children so that one birth does not quickly follow another. Within this group, then, contraceptive failure usually takes the form of more than the ideal or intended number of children, or too short a span of time between births.

How successful are young adults at using contraception to plan the timing and number of births they will have? According to Ryder (1973), couples who intend to *delay* pregnancy are less successful than those who seek to *prevent* pregnancy, regardless of the specific contraceptive technique that is used. In other words, the intentions of the user play an important role in contraceptive success for all methods of birth control. Ryder's data suggest that the newly married couple is especially susceptible to an unplanned pregnancy and that the woman who marries relatively young is more likely to have an unplanned pregnancy than women who marry when they are older. There does, however, seem to be a trend

toward the use of contraceptives, particularly the pill, to delay the birth of a first child; about 70 percent of young married women are practicing some form of birth control, so that the first birth occurs an average of 27 months after marriage (Rindfuss and Westoff, 1974). In terms of the birth of subsequent children, two factors seem to play a role. First, there has been a trend toward the use of more effective contraceptive techniques—for example, the pill, IUD, and vasectomy—and a decrease in the use of unreliable methods—such as withdrawal and douche. Second, couples who want to end childbearing tend to have intercourse less frequently than couples who are seeking to delay the birth of their next child (Westoff, 1974).

In his analysis of the results of the 1970 National Fertility Study, Westoff (1974) also found a clear relationship between a couple's choice of contraception and their coital frequency. As shown in Table 11.4, the mean number of intercourse experiences in the preceding month for couples using any form of birth control was 8.8. Intercourse frequency for users of the pill, IUD, vasectomy, or diaphragm was at or above that mean; in contrast, for users of the less reliable means of birth control—such as withdrawal, foam, or douche —it tended to be below the mean. When Westoff examined these data in terms of contraceptive techniques that were coitus-independent (e.g., the pill), coitus-dependent (e.g., the condom or diaphragm), or coitus-inhibiting (e.g., rhythm or withdrawal), he found the same basic patterns. That is, couples practicing coitus-independent contraception had the highest intercourse frequency, couples using coitus-inhibiting techniques had the lowest intercourse frequency. (The one exception to this pattern was female sterilization, a coitus-independent and extremely effective technique that is associated with *low* coital frequency. Westoff suggests that this is due to the characteristics of women who are likely to undergo surgical sterilization — typically, they tend to be poor, less-educated and the mothers of large families; often they are sterilized because of illness. A somewhat lower coital frequency is associated with each of these characteristics. While these data do show a relationship between effective contraception and sexual activity, it is not possible to distinguish cause from effect: in other words, we do not know whether the availability of such methods as the pill leads to a more active sex life, or whether sexually active women tend to select more effective contraceptive techniques. It seems likely that both these factors are in operation.

THE OLDER ADULT

Most women have completed their families by the time they reach their mid-thirties; since menopause usually takes place at about the age of 50, this leaves a span of 15 years during which a woman who wants no more children will remain fertile. Thus the contraceptive problem of the older adult is how to bridge this time span without becoming pregnant. Increasingly, the solution has involved surgical sterilization.

The major advantage of sterilization to the couple whose family is complete is that it removes the need for all future contraceptive decisions and behavior. Its major disadvantage is that at present the procedure is considered irreversible. While surgical reversals have been successfully performed, the couple who are considering sterilization are told to assume that future childbearing will be impossible. At present, an individual who requests sterilization must wait for 30 days before the operation will be performed — this delay is intended to provide time for a thorough consideration of the decision. If either member of a couple has doubts about the procedure, it is best that they continue using a less permanent means of contraception.

Sterilization has been reported as the fastest-growing method of contraception among all married couples (see Figure 11.3). About 5 million sterilizations were performed in the United States during the 5-year period 1969–1974; and in Puerto Rico, one in three couples rely on this method of birth control. In the 1960s, male sterilization, or vasectomy, was far more common than female sterilization; but the balance has now shifted, mainly because surgical advances have made female

TABLE 11.4

Age-Standardized* Mean Coital Frequency in the 4 Weeks Prior to Interview, by Type of Contraceptive, 1970

Type of Contraceptive Used	Mean
All types	
Wife sterilized	7.6
Husband sterilized	9.6
Pill	9.2
IUD	8.9
Diaphragm	8.8
Condom	8.5
Withdrawal	8.6
Foam	8.5
Rhythm	7.6
Douche	7.6
Coitus-independent	9.3
Coitus-dependent	8.2
Coitus-inhibiting	7.5

Source: Adapted from C. F. Westoff, "Coital Frequency and Contraception," *Family Planning Perspectives*, Vol. 3, No. 6 (1974), pp. 136–141.
*Scores are age-standardized to eliminate the effects of age on method of contraception and coital frequency.

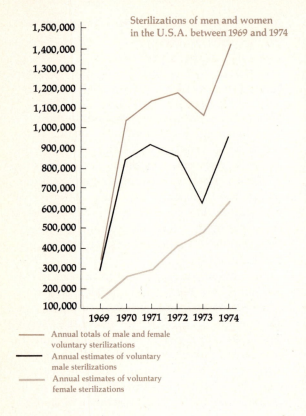

Sterilizations of men and women in the U.S.A. between 1969 and 1974

Annual totals of male and female voluntary sterilizations

Annual estimates of voluntary male sterilizations

Annual estimates of voluntary female sterilizations

FIGURE 11.3

Sterilizations of men and women in the United States, 1969–1974.

sterilization an easier and safer procedure than it was in the past.

Among older couples who do not choose sterilization, a variety of factors tend to reduce fertility. For example, older women are usually less fertile and more likely to have a spontaneous abortion than women in their twenties. In addition, the frequency of sexual relations usually declines among older couples. Finally, the older woman has had many years of experience with contraceptives, knows how to use them, and has easy access to family planning resources (McCormick *et al.*, 1977).

"CONTRACEPTIVE FIT"

To summarize, we have seen that contraceptive patterns tend to change over the life cycle. Contraceptive failure is most common among the young and unmarried, a group that often makes use of nonmedical and less effective birth control methods. Contraceptive success increases with age, as does the use of those methods that are considered extremely effective. The single most effective technique, sterilization, is likely to be used only by the older adult whose family is viewed as complete. We can see, then, that contraceptive needs and behavior change considerably with age. For contraception to be successful, it must suit these changing needs and behavior.

We can make use of the concept of "contraceptive fit" in answering the question posed at the beginning of this section—that is, given the availability and acceptance of contraceptives, why are there still so many unwanted and unplanned pregnancies? Moore (1977) suggests that a major reason why women fail in their contraceptive use is that they have selected or been given a method of birth control that does not suit their needs. When there is a poor fit between the individual's needs and the contraceptive that has been selected, it is not surprising that the individual will discard that contraceptive—which often means being left without any protection from pregnancy.

Every contraceptive technique has both advantages and disadvantages. For example, the pill, which offers almost complete protection, is often associated with unpleasant side effects and the risk of more serious complications. For young women who are willing to take those risks and who do not suffer from the pill's side effects, hormonal contraceptives may be a very acceptable means of birth control. The particular advantage of the pill for the young is that it is independent of coitus, so that the young woman who is not skilled at asserting her contraceptive needs is relieved of that responsibility at the time of intercourse. On the other hand, the pill may not fit well with the needs of the older woman, who is at greater risk of side effects and may be more adept at suggesting and using coitus-dependent techniques such as the diaphragm.

A contraceptive that fits well into a woman's life style is simply that contraceptive she is most likely to use both correctly and consistently. Women who dislike touching their own genitals will probably not do well with a diaphragm; women who are disturbed by a heavy menstrual flow will probably dislike an IUD. In the same way, a man who believes that condoms interfere with his sexual pleasure will object to using them. The married woman who uses contraceptives to delay pregnancy will often tolerate a birth control method that offers a small risk of pregnancy; a woman whose health or age prohibits further childbearing requires a method that guaran-tees complete protection. Thus a contraceptive that fits well into one phase of the fertility career may be unacceptable at another phase.

Unfortunately, contraceptives are often prescribed or selected with little thought as to how they match the individual's needs. Many doctors will routinely prescribe the same type of contraceptive for any woman who visits their office. The time pressures of a medical practice may reduce the chances for a full discussion of each woman's contraceptive options and preferences. In addition, medical experience may lead doctors to make certain generalizations about contraception—such as that young women are not responsible enough to use a diaphragm and should therefore be given a coitus-independent method such as the IUD. While it is understandable that doctors should develop their own contraceptive preferences, even the most effective contraceptive will not work if it does not match the individual's needs and preferences.

Contraceptive Methods

A large and bewildering array of contraceptive methods is available to the individual in need of birth control. We can easily list ten different techniques commonly used in the United States today, and each of these techniques may encompass several subtechniques—for example, there are several types of IUD, many surgical sterilization procedures, and a wide variety of hormone dosages in birth control pills. In order to make an intelligent selection, the contraceptive consumer should be aware of both what is available and what best suits his or her individual needs.

There are many ways to classify modern contraceptive technology. Most devices are suited for women, a few are designed for men, and some require the cooperative effort of both. We might present the range of contraceptive alternatives in terms of their historical development or in terms of the prevalence with which they are used. Or we might choose to arrange them according to the reversibility of their effects; for instance, the contraceptive effects of sterilization are generally considered irreversible, the effects of the pill or IUD are considered to be reversible after some period of time, and the effects of the condom or diaphragm are immediately reversible. Further, contraceptives can be classified according to their relationship with sexual activity; thus abstinence or the rhythm method tend to be associated with some decrease in sexual behavior, whereas the pill has been related to increased coital frequency. Since contraception is intimately related to sexual activity, we have chosen to classify birth control techniques in terms of their being coitus-inhibiting, coitus-dependent, or coitus-independent.

None of the contraceptive techniques and methods to be described is perfect. The ideal contraceptive would incorporate at least the following four characteristics: (1) it would be completely effective—that is, there would be no instances of unwanted pregnancy, (2) it would have no negative effects on physical or psychological health, (3) it would be easily and immediately reversible, and (4) it would fit well into the user's personal and sexual needs —that is, it would be convenient, easy to obtain and use, and inexpensive. All of the methods described in this section fall short of the ideal in some way, although the specific shortcomings differ from one method to another. Until a perfect contraceptive is developed, if ever it is, the user is forced to make a selection on the basis of tradeoffs; for instance, greater effectiveness often means greater risk to health, while less harmful methods tend to be more disruptive of sexual spontaneity. The contraceptive user must compromise in some way, accepting the disadvantages of a method if that method's advantages are highly valued.

CONTRACEPTIVE EFFECTIVENESS

A question of prime importance to the contraceptive user is the *effectiveness* of various birth control techniques: how well does each technique protect against pregnancy? There are two types of statistics used to describe contraceptive effectiveness. *Theoretical effectiveness* refers to how well a method should work if it is used consistently and correctly. *Actual effectiveness* takes into account that most methods are not used consistently and correctly, and that some methods are more prone to user error than others. Thus, actual

effectiveness rates are derived from studies that evaluate the number of pregnancies occurring in the real world among users of different contraceptive techniques. For instance, while the pill is generally thought to be 100 percent effective when used correctly, its actual effectiveness is often lower, depending on the conscientiousness of the user.

Although these two types of effectiveness statistics are often presented interchangeably, they are clearly quite different, particularly for certain types of contraceptives. Generally, the more a specific technique depends on user motivation and skill, the lower its actual effectiveness will be, regardless of its theoretical effectiveness. The diaphragm, for instance, has a high theoretical effectiveness but is usually considered to be relatively ineffective because it is easily subject to user error; it may be inserted improperly, removed too soon, or worst of all, left in a drawer. In contrast, the IUD is relatively immune to user error—once it is in place, the user has no further decisions to make. Actual effectiveness may be related, in part, to the number and type of decisions required of the contraceptive user. For instance, surgical sterilization, which requires only a single decision, is completely effective, whereas the diaphragm or condom, requiring a decision at each act of intercourse, is more subject to user error. However, even the contraceptive techniques most subject to human error can be highly effective when used by a knowledgeable and determined individual.

The providers of contraceptives tend to give biased answers when questioned about the relative effectiveness of various birth control techniques. A survey of physicians, nurses, health educators, and medical students revealed a tendency to give theoretical effectiveness rates for the pill and IUD but actual effectiveness rates for most other methods. In fact, these contraceptive providers often exaggerated the theoretical effectiveness of the pill and IUD while underestimating the actual effectiveness of such methods as the condom, diaphragm, and foam (Hatcher *et al.*, 1976). Needless to say, the contraceptive seeker cannot make an intelligent choice without access to accurate and unbiased information about effectiveness.

The theoretical and actual effectiveness of the most commonly used contraceptives are presented in Table 11.5. The formula used to calculate effectiveness is as follows:

pregnancies per woman-years = 1300 × total number of failures per total number of cycles.

Effectiveness is usually presented in terms of 100 woman-years—that is, in a single year 100 women can be expected to have a total of 1300 menstrual cycles. Thus, if 100 women used combined oral contraceptives correctly and consistently for a full year, the failure rate of the pill would be .34, or less than a single pregnancy for the entire group. However, taking

TABLE 11.5

Approximate Number of Pregnancies Per Year Per 100 Nonsterile Women

Method	Theoretical	Actual
Abortion	0	0
Abstinence	0	?
Tubal ligation	.04	.04
Vasectomy	.15	.15
Combined oral contraceptive	.34	4–10
IUD	1–3	5
Condom	3	10
Diaphragm (with spermicide)	3	17
Condom (with spermicide)	1	5
Spermicidal foam	3	22
Coitus interruptus	9	20–25
Calendar rhythm	13	21
Chance (sexually active)	90	90

Source: After R. A. Hatcher et al., Contraceptive Technology: 1976–1977. New York: Irvington Publishers, 1976.

user error into account, this same group of 100 women could expect between 4 and 10 pregnancies per year. In the same way, correct use of the diaphragm with spermicide would produce 3 pregnancies per year per 100 women; but actual effectiveness, taking user error into account, results in about 17 pregnancies. We should keep in mind that these statistics are derived from studies with many different user populations; the results of studies with young, inexperienced contraceptors are averaged with those of older, more experienced users. Thus, for example, taking diaphragm users as a group, it is possible that those of them who are highly motivated and are given thorough instructions and continued support will show a higher actual effectiveness rate than the average, whereas those of the group who are unmotivated and poorly informed will show a lower than average effectiveness rate.

COITUS-INHIBITING TECHNIQUES

The most obvious means of avoiding pregnancy is to abstain from sexual intercourse. While lifelong abstinence tends to be restricted to members of certain religious groups, many people experience periods of temporary abstinence. They may be abstinent because they have no suitable sexual partner. They may practice abstinence for a short time within each month, as in the rhythm methods. Or they may abstain from only a small part of sexual activity—the male's ejaculation within the female's vagina—as do couples who use coitus interruptus, or withdrawal, as a means of birth control.

Rhythm methods. The traditional rhythm method relies on the calculation of a "safe period" within the menstrual cycle, during which a woman cannot become pregnant. Called *calendar rhythm*, this method is based on two assumptions: first, that ovulation occurs about 14 days before the onset of the next menstrual period, and second, that sperm remain capable of fertilization for only about 48 hours. A woman can calculate her fertile period by recording the length of her menstrual cyles for at least 6 months and then subtracting 14 from the longest and the shortest cycles. For instance, if the shortest cycle was 26 days and the longest cycle 32 days, her fertile period would be from 12 to 18 days after the onset of menstruation. However, since sperm entering the vagina can survive for several days, a margin of safety is gained by adding several days onto this fertile period, and it would be safer to abstain on days 8 to 21 of her cycle. Obviously, the longer the abstention period, the lower the chances of pregnancy.

While calendar rhythm is far from an infallible technique, its effectiveness is certainly increased if the user knows how to calculate her fertile period. Unfortunately, many adolescent women use this technique without having a clear idea of when the fertile period is. The technique also requires self-control and a cooperative and understanding sexual partner. Even under the best of conditions, however, calendar calculations of fertility are risky. Very few women have a completely regular menstrual cycle, and information gained from past cycles may be misleading since emotional or physical stress can often alter the pattern.

There are several methods of calculating fertility that are more reliable than calendar rhythm. One method, called *temperature rhythm*, is based on the fact that basal temperature (the lowest body temperature reached during waking hours) follows a monthly pattern. Body temperature changes are very small, and the measurement of basal temperature requires a special thermometer that is marked off in tenths of a degree. Basal temperature must be taken immediately upon awakening, since getting out of bed and moving

around, taking a drink or smoking a cigarette will change the temperature. If a woman takes and records her temperature every morning at about the same time, she will probably notice that there is a drop in temperature around the middle of her cycle followed by a sustained rise until her next menstruation (see Figure 11.4). These temperature changes seem to be related to ovarian hormone levels; these are low for the first half of the menstrual cycle and increase after ovulation occurs. About 3 days after a sustained temperature rise, the egg can no longer be fertilized and intercourse is safe.

While this technique is more precise than calendar rhythm, it has several disadvantages. First, not every woman shows the clear pattern of temperature changes that are necessary to pinpoint the day of ovulation. Such factors as illness or emotional upset may cause difficulty in interpreting the temperature changes. Second, the technique is accurate in determining the safe period *after* ovulation, but it does not enable the user to predict when ovulation will occur. Thus, it requires abstinence for about half of every menstrual cycle, a time span that may be unacceptably long to many couples.

A third type of rhythm method involves the evaluation of changes in *cervical mucus* during the menstrual cycle. At about the time of ovulation, this mucus tends to become thin and white or transparent and is a hospitable environment for sperm. At other times in the cycle, the mucus tends to take on a recognizably different consistency and color. By learning to recognize these changes, a woman might be able to predict when ovulation is about to occur. Once again, there are drawbacks with this technique — not every woman will have a clear pattern of mucus changes, and such factors as illness or diet may alter the ovulation pattern.

The practitioner of "natural birth control" must be a devoted student of her own body. She must learn to identify all those physical

Days of menstrual cycle

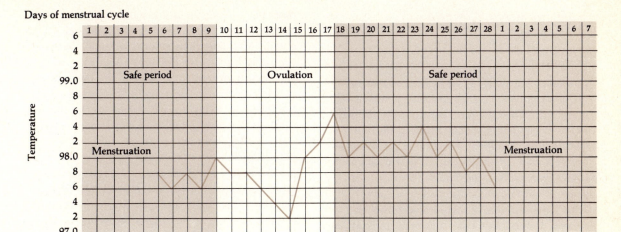

FIGURE 11.4

Basal body temperature graph showing variations during
a model menstrual cycle.

changes that are part of her menstrual cycle: temperature, mucosal secretions, cervical size and shape, mood, sexual arousal, water retention and swelling, "Mittelschmerz" (a cramping feeling associated with ovulation in some women), and so on. Since each woman has a different pattern of signs and symptoms, there is no substitute for personal experience. Ideally, this experience can lead to birth control requiring no external contraceptives and only a short period of abstinence; or rhythm methods can be combined with such temporary methods as the diaphragm during the fertile period. At present, however, it should be used only by women who are willing to put in the work that is required and who are able to tolerate the risk of an unwanted pregnancy.

Although the rhythm methods are the only contraceptive technique considered acceptable by the Catholic church, data from the 1975 National Fertility Study indicate that only 5.9 percent of married Catholic women were using this method. Its popularity for married women of other religions and for unmarried women had also declined to about this level. In recent years, however, there has been a small movement among people who, dissatisfied with conventional techniques such as the pill, advocate a return to contraception that works in harmony with the body (see the boxed extract).

Coitus interruptus (withdrawal). Removing the penis from the vagina before ejaculation, or coitus interruptus, is perhaps the oldest method of birth control, and it remains popular in certain parts of the world to this day. Its obvious advantage is that it requires no preparation, planning, or devices. Theoretically, if a man withdraws his penis before ejaculation, there should be no chance of impregnation. In reality, the failure rate of withdrawal is

Natural Birth Control

Contraception seems to be headed in two vastly different directions. One direction is increasingly technological—birth control pills for men, hormonal implants, and attempts at reversible sterilization. The other direction is a movement "back to nature"—birth control that works with, rather than against, our bodily functions. At present, our knowledge of how to use the body's own rhythms for contraception is extremely limited, but a small number of "natural birth control" advocates persist in their search.

Perhaps the most revolutionary approach is described by Louise Lacey in her book *Lunacep-*tion (1974). After the pill began to have negative effects on her health, she began a personal search for "nature's own form of female human contraception": "Our universe abounds with rhythms in an immense dance to the measures of the stars, the sun and moon, the seasons, and the tides" (p. 83); since we cannot control these rhythms, we must learn to be in harmony with them. Lacey noted that cycles of light and dark play a crucial role in behavior, and that the moon causes light-dark cycles of about the same time span as the human menstrual cycle. She concluded that light, and specifically the light of the full moon, was the trigger for ovulation to take place. The presence of artificial light in our modern environment, Lacey believes, is confusing our natural tendency to ovulate at the full moon and menstruate at the new moon. She uses this information to bring her own menstrual cycle into rhythm with the moon by alter-

relatively high. The man is required to predict his ejaculation accurately and to maintain sufficient self-control to remove his penis in time. Impregnation is possible if he ejaculates near the vagina, and some authorities believe that a small amount of "preejaculate" containing sperm cells is released before the actual ejaculation. While some men may become comfortable with their ability to withdraw before ejaculation, others find that this is a tense and distracting method of birth control. The woman, who has almost no control over this process, may also find that she is too tense and worried to enjoy sexual activity.

Coitus interruptus has the advantages of being free, reversible, and without physical side effects, and of requiring no medical intervention. It has the disadvantages of disrupting the flow of sexual behavior and of being relatively ineffective when compared with other techniques. Like the rhythm methods, it re-quires skill, restraint, and a certain high level of motivation.

COITUS-DEPENDENT TECHNIQUES

The methods described in this section do not require sexual abstinence, but they do demand some action at or before the time of intercourse. Perhaps that is why these techniques, which have high *theoretical* effectiveness rates, have been seen as relatively ineffective when used in the real world.

The diaphragm. Credit for the invention of the diaphragm is generally given to Wilhelm Mensinga, a German doctor who presented his discovery in the 1880s. The diaphragm was hailed by family planning advocates such as Margaret Sanger as the birth control technique that would finally free women from unwanted pregnancy. Generations of women used this

ing the amount of light in her bedroom, and she then simply avoids sexual intercourse when the moon is full. We are certainly not recommending "lunaception" as a general means of birth control; however, Lacey's work is an interesting and thought-provoking challenge to traditional views of contraception.

Another challenge to technological contraception is "natural family planning" (Garfink and Pizer, 1977). This approach is based on observations of a woman's physical changes during the menstrual cycle, in an attempt to predict ovulation. Typically, natural family planning combines observations of basal temperature and cervical mucus to determine the fertility period; once a woman becomes well-acquainted with these rhythms, she can, during "peak fertility," abstain from intercourse, engage in other types of sexual activity, or use a temporary contraceptive method such as the diaphragm.

A promising development for natural birth control is the *ovutimer*, a device that measures the thickness of cervical mucus. Since the mucus becomes thin at the time of ovulation, the ovutimer makes it possible to identify precisely the time of fertility. The ovutimer is not presently available, but it is being tested and may become available in the near future (Seaman and Seaman, 1977).

method with considerable success. However, in the 1960s the availability of the pill and IUD led to a sharp decrease in the popularity of the diaphragm, and it began to receive a bad press — we were told it was messy, difficult to use, and ineffective. More recently the well-publicized side effects of the pill and IUD seem to be causing a small but growing number of women to return to the physical safety of the diaphragm.

The *diaphragm* is a dome-shaped rubber cup that is designed to cover the cervix (see Figure 11.5). Diaphragms come in a variety of sizes (from 50 to 105 mm.) and types, depending on the construction of the spring that maintains the diaphragm's shape. The function of all types of diaphragms is to hold a spermicidal (sperm-killing) cream or jelly over the cervix. However, there is some disagreement as to when the diaphragm should be inserted and how much spermicide must be used. The conservative view, presented by most authorities, is that a diaphragm should be inserted no more than 2 hours before intercourse and should remain in place at least 8 hours after intercourse. If there is repeated intercourse within the 8-hour period, the user is instructed to use a special applicator to insert additional cream or jelly for each sexual act, but to leave the diaphragm in place. While it is advisable to follow these conservative directions, some researchers have suggested that the spermicide has more power than it is being given credit for and that a single application may be sufficient to prevent pregnancy for up to 24 hours. Until this confusion is cleared up through further research, it would be safest to follow the standard instructions.

The diaphragm can be obtained only by medical prescription, since it must be fitted professionally. Generally, the health professional will prescribe the largest size that can

FIGURE 11.5
The diaphragm is gaining in popularity among women who are unwilling to risk the side effects of the pill or IUD. The application of spermicidal jelly to the diaphragm. The jelly must be used every time the diaphragm is inserted. (left) The insertion of the diaphragm into the vagina. (right)

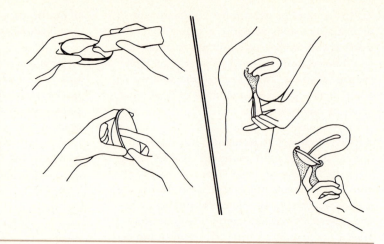

be used comfortably. Once the diaphragm is in place, the woman should not be able to feel its presence. Changes in size may be necessary after a woman bears a child or if there are alterations in vaginal muscle tone. Most diaphragms must be inserted by hand, although some types come with a notched plastic inserter that may make insertion easier. Once the diaphragm is in place, a woman is advised to check its position to be sure it is inserted correctly; this can be done by making sure that the front rim of the diaphragm is tucked behind the ridge of the pubic bone and the cervix can be felt through the dome of the diaphragm. If a diaphragm is well cared for, it should last about 2 years, but its fit should be checked on a yearly basis.

Perhaps the major reason the diaphragm has become less popular is "aesthetics"—a generation that has grown up with the convenience of the pill is likely to view diaphragms as messy and intrusive. (Actually, many diaphragm users have discovered that they can enhance sexual aesthetics by using the diaphragm for intercourse that takes place during menstruation, a practice that is completely safe.) The woman who uses a diaphragm must

either be prepared to plan her sexual activity in advance or interrupt the flow of activity to insert her diaphragm. It is necessary that she insert her diaphragm, check its position, and remove and clean it several hours later. While many sex manuals suggest that the male partner can and should become involved in this process, the woman must be prepared to accept complete responsibility if her partner is not cooperative. Although some men do report that they can feel the diaphragm during intercourse, this typically does not present a problem. However some men object to the taste of the spermicidal jelly or cream if they want to engage in oral sex. It may be necessary to try several different brands of spermicides until both partners have selected a type that is nonirritating and acceptable.

While the diaphragm has some obvious drawbacks, it also has several clear advantages over other contraceptive methods. Most important, it has virtually no physical side effects. Other than the rare allergy to a particular brand of spermicide, it is a completely safe and easily reversible birth control technique. It can be used by almost all women, excepting only those who have a severely displaced uterus or some structural problem in the vaginal area.

The effectiveness of the diaphragm in preventing pregnancy is extremely high when it is used correctly and consistently. But the method must be well suited to the user's personal needs and attitudes. It has been suggested that the most important factor in predicting the diaphragm's effectiveness is the motivation of the couple who are using it. Highly motivated couples are likely to find it an extremely effective method, but couples who are ambivalent about its use may find that their carelessness leads to an unplanned pregnancy.

Several other factors enter into the effectiveness of the diaphragm. First, is the difficulty a would-be user might find in obtaining the professional assistance necessary to begin using the device. It must be fitted correctly, but some physicians who were trained during the age of the pill have little experience with this method of birth control. Many physicians assume that their patients would rather use the pill or IUD, and they permit their biases to interfere with contraceptive prescriptions. More than any other birth control technique, the diaphragm requires professional instruction and support if it is to be used successfully. Thus the doctor who prescribes a diaphragm must be prepared to spend some time explaining its use and being sure that a woman knows how to use it correctly. This investment of time on the part of the medical staff in a busy clinic may actually be the deciding factor in recommending an "easier" form of birth control, such as the pill.

The cervical cap. The *cervical cap,* or *pessary,* is presently available as an "investigational device" in the United States although it was used here in the past and is popular in many European countries. Since there is no clear reason for the cap's restricted use in this country, we mention it in the hope that it will again become available in the future.

The cervical cap operates on the same basic principle as the diaphragm—that is, it is designed to block the cervical opening. It is smaller than the diaphragm; shaped like a thimble, it is typically made of plastic or rubber and should fit snugly over the tip of the cervix. In Europe the cap is fitted by a physician, who may take an impression of the woman's cervix so that she has a completely personalized cervical cap. But the majority of women can be fitted using standard sizes. It is not clear whether spermicidal agents are necessary with use of the cervical cap, and many women report high effectiveness without any creams or jellies (Seaman and Seaman, 1977). The additional advantage of the cervical cap over the diaphragm is that it can be left in place for several weeks at a time, and there is no special advantage to inserting it just prior to sexual intercourse. A disadvantage is that some women find the cap more difficult to insert and remove than the diaphragm.

Foam. Foam is a spermicidal agent used in aerosol form. It works on the same basic principle as the diaphragm, that is, a spermicide blocks the cervix and kills sperm in the vagina. However, since foam is not held in place by a diaphragm, it requires no medical prescription and can be obtained over the counter from most pharmacies. The user shakes the aerosol can, transfers the foam into an applicator, and uses the applicator to deposit the foam into the vagina.

There are several other types of spermicides, usually in the form of creams or jellies, that are used in the same way as foam. These other techniques are considered less effective than foam and are less recommended. Foam works well because it disperses throughout the vagina, spreading over the cervical opening and distributing into vaginal folds and creases. Creams, jellies, and spermicidal suppositories disperse less efficiently and therefore provide less protection.

Foam seems to be about as effective as the diaphragm but has several additional drawbacks. It remains effective for a shorter span of time and so must be applied almost immediately before intercourse and reapplied each time intercourse is repeated. It should not be washed out until about 8 hours after the last intercourse experience. Some men and women report allergic reactions, and there are wide variations in the effectiveness and appropriate dosages of different brands. Finally, foam is disliked for aesthetic reasons—it may leak from the vagina or have an unpleasant taste. However, it also has major advantages; it is easily available and requires no medical intervention. Particularly for the adolescent female whose sexual activity is infrequent, foam may be a good fit to her contraceptive needs. In addition, foam seems to decrease the likelihood of both venereal disease and vaginal infection (Seaman and Seaman, 1977). Finally, when it is used in combination with the condom, foam is about as effective as the medically controlled contraceptive methods.

Condoms. The *condom* has a long and varied history. Pictures dating back to 1350 B.C. show that Egyptian men wore penile sheaths as a form of decoration. In Europe during the eighteenth century, the condom was used as protection against the venereal disease that was widespread at the time, although its use was restricted to prostitutes. Only in the nineteenth century was the condom recognized by the general population as an effective means of regulating fertility. At that time, condoms were generally constructed of sheep cecum (intestinal tissue) and were bulky and expensive. When the process of vulcanization of

rubber was discovered in 1843, it became possible to mass-produce a thinner, less-expensive condom, and the popularity of the device increased. In this century, further technological advances have improved the reliability, comfort, and availability of the condom.

Like other coitus-dependent methods of birth control, the condom has gotten a bad press in the era of the pill. However, many countries having low birth rates—for instance, Japan and Sweden—rely quite heavily on the condom for contraception. In fact, among the Japanese the condom and rhythm method account for 90 percent of all contraceptive use (Giele and Smock, 1977). Part of the reason for the condom's success in Japan seems to be that it is designed with sexual pleasure in mind—Japanese condoms are thinner than American condoms and come in a variety of sizes and pretty colors. In Sweden, condoms are advertised for their ability to prevent venereal disease. In the United States, the advertisement of condoms as "sensuous" or health-protecting is a relatively recent phenomenon, and most newspapers, magazines, and television stations refuse to carry any kind of advertising for the condom.

In an age when most contraceptives are designed for females, many men object to the condom for aesthetic or "sensitivity" reasons. However, it has many advantages: it is quite effective when used correctly, particularly if it is used in combination with a female method such as foam. It has the added bonus of providing protection from venereal disease, is easily reversible, and has no side effects on health. Since it does not require a medical prescription, the condom is available to the sexually active adolescent. Moreover, the condom is the only reversible contraceptive method that allows the man direct control and responsibility for birth control. Finally, the decreased sensitivity caused by the condom during intercourse may actually benefit the young man who is concerned that his sexual response is too rapid.

COITUS-INDEPENDENT TECHNIQUES

Contraceptive techniques that operate independently of coitus—that is, provide protection from pregnancy without special preparations at the time of intercourse—include surgical sterilization, the pill, and the IUD. Each of these technologically advanced methods is highly controversial and subject to continued scientific evaluation for adverse effects on health.

Surgical sterilization. According to an article in the *New York Times* (May 22, 1977), sterilization has been performed on about one of every ten couples of childbearing age in the entire world. In the United States, the figure is about one in four married couples, a total of approximately 7 million men and women between the ages of 15 and 44. In the early 1970s most sterilizations were performed on men, since the procedure for women was more complex and dangerous. With the development of simpler procedures for female sterilization, about half the sterilization operations now performed are on women.

The obvious advantages of sterilization are that it is completely effective and requires no further action on the part of men or women who are sure they want no more children. On the other hand, its major disadvantage is that it is considered irreversible. While it is sometimes possible to reverse surgical sterilization, people who contemplate this form of birth control are encouraged to think of it as permanent. Even if the male surgical procedure can be reversed, there is recent evidence that the male who has undergone vasectomy may build up antibodies to his own sperm, leaving him infertile in the future.

While both male and female sterilizations are almost always safe and effective, their lack of reversibility means they should not be undertaken lightly. The United States government recently instituted a waiting period for all couples or individuals requesting sterilization, so that they might seriously consider their decision. During this time period, the couple should ask themselves the following questions: Are we positive that we will never want another child under any circumstances? Will the operation be completely voluntary? Do we think we will feel the same about ourselves and each other after the operation? Do we think this procedure will solve our marital difficulties? The individual who has any doubts about sterilization should not use this technique of birth control. The ability to have children is often seen as part of the cultural definition of what it means to be a woman, while many men view their masculinity in terms of being able to impregnate a female. Such beliefs are not compatible with surgical sterilization.

The most controversial aspect of sterilization is its potential for coercion or abuse. For instance, a marital partner or physician may put pressure on the individual who is considering sterilization. There have been several publicized instances in which the procedure was performed on women who did not understand its consequences and would not have consented to it if they had understood. In India, the government's sterilization program was halted when it was discovered that gifts and money were being used to persuade men to have vasectomies. Needless to say, sterilization should be carried out only on people who are fully informed and fully consenting.

Female sterilization. In the past, the most common technique for female sterilization was *hysterectomy* (removal of the uterus). While hysterectomy will effectively prevent

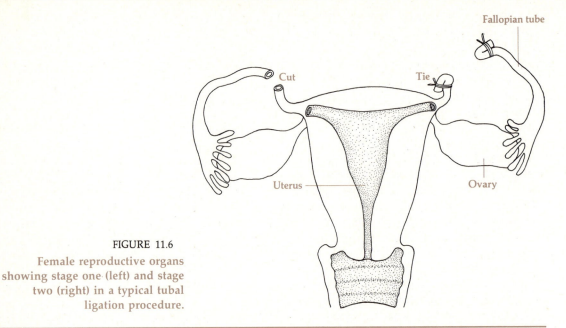

FIGURE 11.6

Female reproductive organs showing stage one (left) and stage two (right) in a typical tubal ligation procedure.

pregnancy, it is not necessary in the absence of other health problems. It is more risky than other sterilization techniques and will have many more side effects on health. Similarly, removal of the ovaries will provide permanent contraception, but it is not advisable because it also deprives the body of hormones.

Tubal ligation now seems to be the technique of choice for female sterilization. In the tubal ligation procedure, the Fallopian tubes, which carry eggs from the ovaries to the uterus, are either cut and tied or cauterized (see Figure 11.6). Since eggs can no longer be fertilized or reach the uterus, they simply dissolve within the Fallopian tube. The ovaries and uterus remain completely intact, and the normal menstrual cycle and hormone levels are not disrupted. Tubal ligation can be performed in several different ways. The Fallopian tubes can be approached through the vagina, a technique that is generally performed under general anaesthetic in a hospital. The major disadvantage of the vaginal approach seems to be a

higher incidence of complications such as infection and hemorrhage. At present the most popular method in the United States is the abdominal approach, specifically *laparoscopic sterilization*. In a laparoscopy, one or two small incisions are made in the abdomen and carbon dioxide is pumped into the abdominal cavity. The purpose of the carbon dioxide infusion is to provide the surgeon with a better view of the Fallopian tubes. Then a small tube with mirrors and lights is inserted through one incision, and after the Fallopian tubes have been located they are cut. Although this procedure is sometimes performed with a general anaesthetic, it can also be done on an out-patient basis in a physician's office. Laparoscopic sterilization has been called a "Band-aid operation" because the incisions made in the abdomen are small enough to be covered with adhesive strips.

The effectiveness and safety of tubal ligation is greatly dependent on the skill of the attending physician. In rare cases, the severed Fallopian tubes grow back together again and pregnancy occurs—a situation that may be extremely serious if the pregnancy is ectopic (that is, if the fertilized egg implants itself within the Fallopian tube instead of in the uterus). Although serious complications resulting from tubal ligation are rare, they do occur in the form of damage to other organs, infection, or hemorrhage.

Male sterilization. The male sterilization procedure, *vasectomy*, is less complicated than female sterilization. It is almost always performed in a physician's office and usually takes about 30 minutes. After a local anaesthetic has been applied, an incision is made in the scrotum and the surgeon cuts or blocks the vas deferens, the duct that carries sperm from the testes to the penis during ejaculation (see Figure 11.7). These are no physical changes caused by vasectomy, other than the absence of sperm in the ejaculate, and the procedure is considered both safe and reliable. However, about 50 percent of men develop antibodies to their own sperm after vasectomy, a condition that is not dangerous but precludes the possibility of fertility in the future. In addition, some men report temporary side effects that include swelling, pain, and skin discoloration; these conditions can all be treated and generally disappear within a few weeks of the operation.

The emotional effects of vasectomy vary depending on the man's prior commitment and attitude toward the procedure. The more sure a man is that he wants a vasectomy, and the better informed he is about its effects, the more likely that he will be satisfied with the outcome. In fact, the vast majority of men who have had vasectomies report that they are completely satisfied with the procedure.

Vasectomy has been reported to have a failure rate of about .15 pregnancies per 100 men. Failure may occur in two ways; first, there are rare cases in which the vas deferens recon-

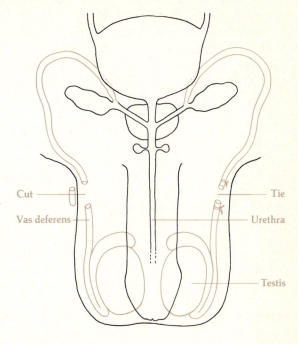

FIGURE 11.7
Male reproductive organs showing stage one (left) and stage two (right) of the vasectomy procedure.

nects; sperm will then again be carried through the penis during ejaculation. Second, immediately after vasectomy the reproductive tract may still contain some sperm capable of impregnation. Thus the vasectomy patient is generally advised to use some form of contraception until the reproductive tract is completely cleared of sperm—usually for about ten ejaculations after the operation. Then a fertility test can be given to ascertain whether unprotected intercourse is completely safe.

The intrauterine device (IUD). The origin of the modern IUD is generally dated at 1909, when a German physician named Richard Richter developed a device made of silkworm gut that was inserted into the uterus. His techniques were not dissimilar to those used today. Following Richter's work, scientists all over the world began testing the effectiveness and safety of IUDs made from a variety of materials. In the United States, IUDs became widely available in the early 1960s. At present, about 15 million women throughout the world use some type of IUD.

IUDs come in many sizes and shapes, and are made of many different types of materials. The first modern IUDs were brought to the United States by German scientists at the time of World War II and were extensively tested before being distributed to the public. Two of the original IUDs were the Dalkon Shield and the Lippes Loop. Few women use these devices today. The majority of new IUDs are models containing small amounts of copper. While copper IUDs seem to be more effective in preventing pregnancy than the older, plastic models, the long-term effects of copper on the body are not well understood and could be harmful. Another type of IUD that is increasing in popularity contains small amounts of progestins that are slowly released into the uterus. Unlike the earlier models, both the copper and the progestin-releasing IUDs must be replaced on an annual or biannual basis.

We are not sure exactly how the IUD works to prevent pregnancy. The most commonly accepted explanation is that since the IUD is a foreign object, it causes an inflammatory response within the uterus, which prevents a fertilized egg from implanting itself in the uterine wall. Unlike other methods of contraception, the IUD does not prevent conception (that is, the meeting of egg and sperm); what it does is halt the development of a fetus. The copper-releasing IUDs seem to give added protection by altering the enzymes that are necessary for implantation to occur.

The effectiveness of IUDs is usually estimated at between 1 and 7 failures per 100 woman-years. Effectiveness varies with the particular type of IUD used, the ease of insertion, the physician's experience, and the likelihood of expulsion. A large number of women who request an IUD will expel it spontaneously; others will request its removal because it causes them discomfort or pain. According to some sources, no more than two-thirds of women retain the device for a full year, and after 4 years only one in three women still have their IUD in place (Seaman and Seaman, 1977). The likelihood of expulsion is increased if a woman has just had a child or if she has recently had an abortion; yet IUDs are often inserted at such times because the woman is highly motivated to avoid another pregnancy. It appears safest to insert an IUD during the menstrual period, since the cervix is already somewhat dilated and there is almost no chance of pregnancy at the time of insertion.

Procedures for inserting an IUD vary with the particular type being used. Women who have such uterine abnormalities as a very small uterus, endometriosis (a pathological shedding of the endometrium), or severe dysmenorrhea (painful menstruation) are not suitable candidates for an IUD. Before insertion, it is necessary for the physician to measure the depth and shape of the uterus so that an appropriately sized device can be selected. Generally, the IUD is placed in an inserter (shaped like a thin plastic straw) which passes through the cervical opening and deposits the IUD within the uterus. There is usually a great deal of discomfort at the time of insertion, and there may be bleeding and severe cramps following insertion, as the body tries to rid itself of the foreign object. If these symptoms persist, it is important to return to the physician for possible removal or adjustment of the IUD. Most IUDs have a string attached to them that is left hanging in the vagina so that the woman can check whether or not the IUD is still in place.

The most frequently reported side effect of the IUD is *dysmenorrhea*, that is, an exaggerated menstrual period. Menstruation is likely to be longer than normal, the menstrual flow heavier, and cramping more severe. A large number of women request removal of their IUD because of these problems. Others take vitamin and iron supplements to compensate for the loss of blood. A less common but more serious complication of the IUD is pelvic inflammatory disease or infection. Women with a history of pelvic infections are advised not to use the IUD because it seems to make them more susceptible to future infections and also makes it more difficult to treat existing infections. The greatest risk of infection occurs within the few weeks immediately following IUD insertion, when unsterile conditions might introduce infective organisms into the uterus and vagina. However, pelvic infections may also occur after the IUD has been in place for months or even years. One type of IUD, the Dalkon Shield, was withdrawn from the market because the type of string attached to it was believed to aid the passage of bacteria from the vagina up into the uterus. Another IUD-related problem is *perforation*—the device can puncture the uterine walls and even enter the abdominal cavity. Perforation is usually the result of faulty insertion by the physician and necessitates removal of the device.

The long-term effects of the IUD are not clear. There is some concern that the IUD should not be left in place for more than 4 or 5 years because it may cause permanent structural changes in the lining and muscles of the uterus. It is not surprising that changes in cell structure should occur if we recall that the IUD appears to work by causing a chronic inflammation of the uterus.

Although the effectiveness of the IUD is high, infrequently a user does become pregnant while the IUD is still in place. About 50 percent of such pregnancies end in spontane-

ous abortion. Some physicians recommend that a therapeutic abortion be performed if pregnancy occurs with the IUD in place, as there is an increased risk of serious infection. If a woman wishes to maintain her pregnancy, the physician will probably attempt to remove the IUD. Contraceptive failure is more likely to occur when a woman thinks that her IUD is in place but it has actually slipped or been expelled and she is not protected from pregnancy. This is why it is important for women using the IUD to check the vaginal string on a regular basis.

Hormonal contraceptives (the pill). All the birth control techniques described thus far have existed, in some form, for hundreds of years. The development of hormonal contraceptives, however, represents a true break with the past—if there has been a contraceptive revolution in the twentieth century, it is certainly the ability to control fertility with synthetic hormones. In the first decade of its use, the pill was hailed as the perfect solution to contraceptive problems, a technique that gave women safe and complete control over childbearing decisions. Since then, however, hormonal contraceptives have come under increasing scrutiny because of their general effects on health; in a generation that seems somewhat suspicious about all medically prescribed drugs it is not surprising that there is also distrust of the pill. While the pill still provides the most effective reversible protection from unwanted pregnancy, it is no longer viewed as the ultimate solution to our contraceptive needs.

Hormonal contraceptives could be developed only after scientists had a clear idea of how the menstrual cycle works—even in the early part of this century the safe period was mistakenly identified as occurring at midcycle. By the 1930s, researchers had acquired sufficient information to understand the relationship between changing hormone levels and ovulation. (This information was reviewed in Chapter 6.) It remained to find ways to intervene in the menstrual cycle so that ovulation would be prevented. A major breakthrough was the discovery of the means to synthesize estrogens and progesterones in the laboratory. By the 1940s, scientists had developed inexpensive sources of synthetic hormones and learned to use these hormones to inhibit ovulation. In 1956, the first commercially marketed birth control pill, called Enovid, was given large-scale testing trials in Puerto Rico, and its success led to the use of hormonal contraceptives in most parts of the world. At present, about 10 million American women use the pill.

There are many varieties of hormonal contraceptives, but all rely on the influence of estrogens or progestins—or both—to disrupt the normal processes of ovulation and pregnancy. Estrogenic agents have two major effects on the menstrual cycle. First, we know that in the normal menstrual cycle, low levels of estrogen trigger the release of FSH, the pituitary hormone that stimulates the development of the egg cell. When a woman takes external estrogens, her body has more than the usual estrogen level at the beginning of her cycle. Thus there is no message to the pituitary to secrete FSH, and the egg cell does not develop. In most cases, the added estrogen is sufficient to prevent ovulation. As pills containing very low levels of estrogen are not always successful at preventing ovulation, there is also a second, backup protection provided by estrogen—when taken in high dosages just after mid-cycle it inhibits implantation of a fertilized egg.

Synthetic progestins also provide two major contraceptive effects. In the normal menstrual cycle, the plug of mucus covering the cervix becomes hospitable to sperm at the time of ovulation. When small amounts of progestins

are taken every day, this cervical mucus remains inhospitable to sperm throughout the entire menstrual cycle. Second, progestins inhibit the lining of the uterus from developing, so a fertilized egg would not be able to implant itself.

Types of hormonal contraceptives. The most widely used hormonal contraceptive is the *combined pill.* It contains constant amounts of estrogens and progestins to be taken for 21 consecutive days, stopped for 7 days, and then resumed again. Since the combined pill contains both estrogens and progestins, it works by inhibiting ovulation, maintaining a thick cervical mucous plug, and inhibiting the development of the uterine lining. While the normal menstrual cycle shows shifting hormone levels before, during, and after ovulation, the pill user's hormones remain relatively stable throughout the month. Thus, the pill user will not see the changing basal temperature levels described in the section on rhythm methods. Further, since pill users do not build up a normal uterine lining, they do not, strictly speaking, have a menstrual period; instead, several days after they stop taking the pill they experience what is called "withdrawal bleeding." In fact, there seems to be very little reason for the 3-weeks-on, 1-week-off pattern of pill use other than that it seems more like a normal menstrual cycle. The pill user could just as easily take her pills for 4 or 5 weeks, since withdrawal bleeding will always occur about 4 days after the pills are withdrawn. This absence of "true menstruation" is the reason why the pill user's bleeding tends to be shorter and more scanty than the nonuser's.

In addition to the combined pill, there are two other types of hormonal contraceptives, each of which provides both estrogens and progestins. The *sequential pill,* which is rarely used today, provides only estrogens for about 14 days and then both estrogens and progestins for about 7 days. Since the primary action of sequential pills is to prevent ovulation, they usually contain higher levels of estrogen than are found in combined pills. With the discovery that estrogens were the primary cause of physical side effects and complications, the sequential pill was considered to present an unnecessary risk, and most physicians prefer to prescribe the lower estrogen dosages found in the combined pill. The other form of estrogen-plus-progestin contraceptive is the *once-a-month* pill, developed because it is more convenient than daily pills. The combination of estrogen and progestin is rapidly absorbed by the tissues of the body and then slowly released into the bloodstream.

Women who experience negative side effects from the estrogen in combined pills may be switched to the *mini-pill*, which contains only progestins. Although mini-pills are less likely to produce side effects, they are also slightly less effective than combined pills. The major complication produced by mini-pills is irregular bleeding and spotting in mid-cycle. The decreased effectiveness is due to the fact that the primary action of the mini-pill is the build-up of hostile cervical mucus, and not the inhibition of ovulation. Mini-pills contain constant levels of progestins, and unlike other pills, they are to be taken every day throughout the entire cycle.

Another form of contraception based only on progestins is the *long-acting progestin injection*. With this method, a woman receives an injection of progestins about once every 3 months. Long-term progestin effects can also be obtained by implanting capsules containing progestins under the skin, by the use of a vaginal ring containing progestins, or by including progestins in certain types of IUDs. In each of these methods, the progestin is released slowly into the bloodstream.

A final type of hormonal contraceptive is the *morning-after pill*, designed for use when a woman has had unprotected intercourse in the middle of her menstrual cycle. Morning-after pills are to be considered as an emergency measure; they should not be used on a regular basis because they can have severe side effects. The estrogen-based morning-after pill usually contains *diethylstilbestrol*, commonly called DES, the same drug that has been associated with increased risk of cervical cancer in the daughters of women who used it while pregnant. Doctors no longer prescribe DES to pregnant women (in the past, it was thought to prevent miscarriage), and if the morning-after pill fails to prevent pregnancy, the woman is strongly advised to have an abortion. DES, which works by inhibiting the implantation of a fertilized egg in the uterus, must be administered within 72 hours of unprotected intercourse and is usually taken for 5 consecutive days. It can have severe side effects, including nausea and vomiting, headaches, visual blurring, menstrual irregularities and breast tenderness. Although DES is a relatively effective contraceptive, the potential danger of this technique is so great that it is recommended for use only in emergencies; even then, some physicians will hesistate to prescribe it. A safer morning-after pill containing only progestins is currently being tested by researchers.

Effectiveness of the pill. The theoretical effectiveness of the combined pill is nearly 100 percent; the effectiveness of progestin-only pills seems to be slightly lower. However, pills that must be taken every day are subject to user error, and it has been estimated that the actual failure rate of the pill is between 5 and 10 pregnancies per 100 woman-years (Hatcher *et al.*, 1976). There are two major types of error: if a woman misses taking several pills, particularly in the first half of the cycle, she may be unprotected from pregnancy. Second, women who dislike the side effects of the pill will often stop taking it without having a backup means of contraception. Women who miss several pills, and women who are just starting to use the pill should have available a secondary means of protection. However, there are rare cases in which a woman who has used her pills correctly and consistently still becomes pregnant. If a woman does become pregnant while using the pill, the increased chances of fetal malformation usually lead to a recommendation of therapeutic abortion.

Reversibility: pregnancy after the pill. In the 1960s, general opinion had it that the pill user who wanted to conceive a child would be especially fertile after she stopped taking the pill. Research has not supported this opinion. While most women who stop taking the pill have little difficulty resuming the normal menstrual cycle and becoming pregnant, a small number of women do experience problems, commonly called the *oversuppression syndrome* — that is, the pill has suppressed ovulation for so long that there is some difficulty in resuming the normal menstrual cycle. The oversuppression syndrome is most likely to occur in those women whose menstrual cycle was irregular before they began using the pill. In fact, irregular menstruation is usually one of the contraindications for pill use. In such women, normal menstruation and ovulation may not resume for some time, and they are therefore temporarily infertile. These women are often treated with fertility agents such as Clomid — a powerful hormone that is usually successful in inducing ovulation but has also been associated with a higher-than-

average frequency of multiple births. Even when a woman has no difficulty resuming a normal menstrual cycle, she may be cautioned to wait several months before trying to become pregnant. There appears to be a greater risk of miscarriage just after stopping pill use, and the waiting period is recommended so that there will be no synthetic hormones left in the body during pregnancy.

Side effects of the pill. In contrast to local methods of contraception such as the condom or diaphragm, the pill's synthetic hormones reach all areas of the body, and their effects are by no means restricted to the reproductive system. Generally, the unpleasant or "nuisance" effects of the pill are referred to as side effects, whereas potentially life-threatening

A variety of factors affect a woman's psychological response to a miscarriage. Hugo Robus. *Despair.* (Collection of the Whitney Museum, New York)

changes are called *complications*. Side effects are relatively common among pill users; complications are much less frequent but are a far greater cause for concern.

According to *Contraceptive Technology* (Hatcher *et al.*, 1976), about 40 percent of pill users will experience some types of side effects. There is some disagreement about this estimate. Some physicians believe that side effects are largely psychosomatic—that is, women read or hear that pill users are likely to suffer from, for instance, severe headaches and then actually experience this side effect. In fact, to minimize worry and psychosomatic complaints, many physicians do not fully inform their patients about potential side effects. On the other hand, it is possible that many women fail to report side effects because they simply do not know that these symptoms can be caused by the pill. We do know that as many as half of all women who start using the pill will discontinue its use within the first year; presumably, many of these women are experiencing unpleasant side effects.

Among the negative side effects reported most frequently are nausea, weight gain, headaches, spotting (slight bleeding between periods), greater susceptibility to vaginal infections, depression, and mood changes. Some of these side effects, such as nausea, seem to get better with continued pill use; others, such as headaches during the week the pill is not taken, tend to get worse with longer usage. Such symptoms as fatigue and mood changes seem to remain constant over time. Some women also report decreased sexual interest and difficulty in having orgasm.

Sometimes these symptoms may be eliminated by switching to another brand of pill; but if the side effects persist, it may be necessary to use a completely different type of contraceptive. For some women, nausea and weight gain might be experienced as a relatively small price to pay for the effectiveness and convenience of the pill. In addition, many women report that the pill has some positive effects along with its contraceptive value. For instance, shortened and lighter withdrawal bleeding is often welcomed in preference to regular menstruation. Pills also seem to lessen premenstrual discomfort and cramping. Since they regularize hormone levels through the cycle, pills may eliminate the drastic mood swings and physical symptoms experienced by some women. Finally, some women report that the pill increases their sexual interest—an effect that may simply be due to removal of the fear of pregnancy.

Complications and risks of the pill. When the pill first appeared on the birth control market it was greeted with such enthusiasm by pharmaceutical manufacturers, physicians, population experts, and the public that for many years it was difficult to gain a forum for opposing views. Most people simply did not want to be disabused of the notion that the pill was completely safe. In recent years, however, a growing number of studies have shown that the pill can present serious health hazards to certain users.

The woman who is considering taking the pill is now faced with a bewildering array of statistics showing her chances of dying or becoming seriously ill from a variety of pill-related complications (see Table 11.6). The overall risk is very small, and pill supporters frequently point out that in terms of health, it is safer to take the pill than to become pregnant and deliver a child. Antipill forces disagree; they state that preventing childbirth through early abortion is safer than using the pill. Further, they say that many of the pill's serious complications are not yet known and will only become apparent over the next 10 or 20 years. Finally, selecting a contraceptive with "death rates" in mind seems an unacceptable approach to birth control.

TABLE 11.6

Annual Mortality Risk per 1,000,000 Women Associated With Control of Fertility

| | Age Group | | | | | |
Method of Contraception	15–19	20–24	25–29	30–34	35–39	40–44
A. No birth control: Birth-associated deaths	56	61	74	139	208	226

B. Traditional contraception (condom and diaphragm):
  With abortion backup:
    Method-associated deaths
	2	2	3	3	3	2

With no abortion: Birth-associated deaths	11	16	20	36	50	42
C. IUD with no abortion: Birth-associated and method-associated deaths	9	10	12	14	20	19

D. Pill with no abortion:
  Nonsmokers:
    Birth-associated and method-associated deaths
	13	14	14	22	45	71

Smokers: Birth-associated and method-associated deaths	15	16	16	108	134	589
E. Abortion only: Method-associated deaths	12	16	18	17	19	12
Deaths due to automobile accidents	236	190	130	124	118	124

Source: Adapted from Luvia, Z., and Rose, M. *Psychology of Human Sexuality* (New York: Wiley, 1979), p. 273.

Actually, the overall risk rates for pill users are confusing and sometimes deceptive. For instance, the pill is clearly associated with increased risk for the following disorders: heart attack, blood clots, stroke, high blood pressure, severe headaches, gall bladder disease, diabetes, liver tumors, and hepatitis. However, the risk is not shared equally by all pill users. For instance, it appears that women with blood type O are less susceptible to clotting disorders than women in other blood groups. Similarly, pill users with a history of hypertension are more likely to suffer heart attacks than those with normal blood pressure levels. For some women, then, the health risks of the pill are probably smaller than the averages usually presented; for other women the risks of illness or death are actually much greater than the statistics indicate.

Since some women are clearly more suscep-tible to serious complications than others, it is of utmost importance to screen out those at greatest risk and provide them with an alternative form of contraception. At present, we know that the pill is most risky to women who

Are over the age of 35

Smoke cigarettes

Have a predisposition to diabetes or are diabetic

Have a history of blood clotting disorders or stroke

Have a history of heart attack or hypertension

Have impaired liver function or gall bladder disease

Have migraine headaches

Have cancer or a family history of breast or genital cancer

The relationship of the pill to cancer is under intense study at this time. There is no evidence that the pill causes cancer, but scientists have known for some time that estrogen speeds up the growth of existing cancers. Thus, any woman who has ever had cancer or who is considered at high risk for cancer should not use the pill. Since pill users are more likely to show changes in the cell structure of the sexual organs, it is important that they have at least annual checkups for breast and cervical cancer.

Advantages of the pill. Even the most fervent critic of the pill must admit that it has several advantages: when used correctly it is the most effective temporary form of contraception, it does not intrude on the sexual experience, it is convenient, and it may produce some positive side effects. In view of these advantages, many women will continue to use the pill.

The decision to take the pill should be made only by a woman who is fully informed about its benefits and risks. Unfortunately, all too often the pill is dispensed automatically to any woman entering a family planning clinic or physician's office. A woman who is fully aware of the health risks of the pill may decide to use it anyway because it meets her contraceptive needs better than other available birth control options. Once a woman and her physician decide that the pill is appropriate, they share a continued responsibility for checking and monitoring the user's health for as long as she takes the pill.

Abortion

Most of the birth control techniques discussed thus far are truly contra-ceptive — that is, they prevent conception, the meeting of egg and sperm, from taking place. A few techniques, such as the IUD or the "morning-after" pill, permit conception but do not allow a fertilized egg to become implanted in the uterine wall. Abortion differs from all these methods because it is the only birth control technique that disrupts fertility *after* implantation of the fertilized egg. This basic difference makes abortion an extremely controversial procedure. Whereas most people accept the desirability of preventing unwanted conceptions, the termination of a verified pregnancy presents a moral dilemma to many who approve of contraception. Some people continue to fight the United States Supreme Court decision of 1973 — that first-trimester abortion is a private matter between a woman and her physician. Other people accept this decision but find it personally offensive. Still others believe that abortion should entail no more guilt or moral concern than any other existing means of fertility control.

Abortion is of two types: *induced* abortion is the voluntary and deliberate termination of pregnancy; *spontaneous* abortion (which is described in Chapter 10) is an unintentional interruption of pregnancy due to illness, injury, or some other factor. Since spontaneous abortion is not a voluntary form of birth control, we will restrict our discussion to induced abortion.

Abortion is usually defined in terms of the *viability* of the fetus — that is, whether the fetus is capable of survival outside the uterine environment. In the past, viability was thought to be reached when the fetus weighed about 1,000 g. (35 ozs.), usually after 28 weeks of gestation. More recently, improvements in medical technology have led to a redefinition of viability as beginning at the twenty-fourth or even the twentieth week of gestation.

Although induced abortion has been for centuries the most widely used method of birth control throughout the world (Tietze, 1977), its legal and moral status has varied and continues to vary in different parts of the world. Tietze estimates that as of 1976, 8 percent of the world's people live in countries that forbid abortion for any reason, 15 percent in countries where abortion is permitted to save the life of the mother, 12 percent in countries where broad medical grounds are considered, 23 percent in countries where social factors are considered, and 36 percent in countries where first-trimester abortions are permitted on request. (The remaining 6 percent are unaccounted for but probably live in countries where abortion is forbidden or severely restricted.) Among the countries with high rates of legal abortion are China, Japan, and the USSR. Abortions are most likely to be legally restricted in countries with strong Catholic traditions—for instance, most South American countries forbid abortion. However, these restrictive countries often have extremely high rates of illegal abortion.

Although abortion is presently a hotly debated issue in the United States, this has not always been the case. Abortion was once widely tolerated, both in the United States and in Europe, as long as it occurred before "quickening"—the mother's first perception of fetal movement, usually between 16 and 20 weeks after the last menstrual period. The Catholic church formerly took the position that the fetus gained a soul, and hence human status, only 40 days after conception if a male and 80 days after conception if a female. (It is not clear how they predicted whether the fetus was male or female.) Abortions occurring before these dates were considered acceptable until 1868, when Pope Pius IX radically changed church policy by making all abortions punishable by excommunication.

Abortion was first prohibited in Britain in 1803, and the United States gradually followed suit. New York was the first state to regulate abortion, in 1829; over a span of about 100 years each state adopted its own individual laws, with the majority forbidding abortion unless it was necessary to save the mother's life. It has been suggested that these early laws were not created to protect the life of the fetus; surgical conditions in the nineteenth century presented a serious danger of infection, and restrictive abortion laws were originally intended to protect the life of the pregnant woman (David, 1973). Laws against abortion have certainly not prevented the procedure from taking place—while about 8,000 legal abortions per year were performed in the 1960s, it is estimated that 50 to 80 times this number were performed illegally. The affluent were able to obtain abortions that were certified as legal or to travel to places where legal abortion was permitted or to obtain an illegal abortion from a competent physician. The poor were often forced to resort to unsafe illegal abortions—often self-induced.

The first European country to legalize abortion, in 1920, was the USSR; that law was rescinded in 1936 and then reinstated in 1955. To this day, abortion is a widely used means of birth planning in the Soviet Union and other Communist countries such as Poland and East Germany—at least partly because the availability of other contraceptive techniques is very limited. Japan was the first country to use abortion to deal with an overpopulation emergency; whereas abortion was strictly forbidden before 1948, pressures to limit family size and a law permitting abortion on request led to a tenfold increase in the number of abortions performed between 1949 and 1958. Since then, the greater availability of con-

Grounds for abortion in countries recently liberalizing their laws						
Risk to:	Mother's physical health	Mother's mental health	Health of fetus	Unwanted pregnancy due to rape, incest	Social or socio-medical	On request
Argentina	●			●		
Australia		●				
Austria		●	●			●
Brazil	●			●		
Britain	●	●	●		●	
Bulgaria	●		●	●		
Cameroon	●			●		
Canada	●	●				
China						●
Costa Rica	●					
Cuba	●		●	●		
Czechoslovakia	●			●		
Denmark	●	●	●	●	●	●
Ecuador	●			●		
Ethiopia	●					
Finland		●	●		●	
France	●	●	●			●
Germany W.	●	●	●	●	●	
Germany E.	●	●	●		●	●
Ghana	●					
Greece	●			●		
Honduras	●					
Hungary	●		●	●		
Iceland		●	●	●		
India	●		●	●	●	
Italy	●					
Japan		●	●	●		
Jordan				●		
Kenya	●					
Korea S.	●					
Mexico				●		
Morocco	●					
New Zealand	●	●				
Norway		●	●	●	●	
Poland		●	●	●	●	
Rumania		●		●	●	
Sierre Leone		●				
Singapore	●	●	●	●	●	●
Sweden		●	●	●	●	●
Switzerland	●					
Thailand	●			●		
Tunisia	●	●	●	●	●	●
Turkey	●		●			
Uganda		●				
Soviet Union						●
Uruguay	●			●	●	
Vietnam						●
Yugoslavia	●	●	●	●	●	

FIGURE 11.8
Chart of countries that have liberalized their abortion laws in recent years. It also shows the grounds on which abortion is now permitted by these countries.

traception has led to a decrease in the number of abortions performed in Japan.

In the United States, restrictive laws against abortion began to be challenged in the early 1960s. The American Law Institute suggested a model penal code in which abortion was legal if the physical or mental health of the mother was threatened, if the child might be born with a serious physical or mental defect, or if pregnancy was the result of rape or incest. The abortion issue was brought to the attention of the public with the case of Sherry Finkbine, an Arizona mother of four who had taken thalidomide during her pregnancy. When this drug was linked to serious birth defects, she requested and was granted the right to a therapeutic abortion at a local hospital. However, when the case was publicized by the news media, there was a hostile reaction, the hospital withdrew its permission for an abortion, and she was forced to travel to Sweden to obtain a legal abortion. The publicity following this and similar cases led to the gradual liberalization of abortion laws in a few states, with most laws following the guidelines set forth by the American Law Institute. In the early 1970s many women seeking a legal abortion traveled to states, such as New York, where abortion was available to residents and nonresidents on demand. Abortion became available in all states in 1973, when the Supreme Court ruled that abortions occurring before "viability" were a private matter between woman and physician.

This landmark decision has not ended the abortion controversy. There have been numerous attempts to overturn the decision permitting abortion, including the proposal of a constitutional amendment. While surveys reveal that the majority of the American people view abortion as essentially a private decision, a highly vocal and well-organized minority continue to press for laws repealing the right to abortion. Few people accept the use of abor-

tion as a primary method of birth control, but an increasing number have come to regard it as a valid backup for contraceptive failure.

TECHNIQUES OF THERAPEUTIC ABORTION

There are many medical procedures for abortion, with more efficient and safer techniques being developed all the time. The specific procedure selected depends largely on the duration of the pregnancy that is being aborted — basically, the shorter the duration of pregnancy, the quicker and safer the abortion will be. Physicians usually calculate the length of pregnancy from the woman's last menstrual period, or LMP, and not from the estimated date of conception. Thus if a woman receives confirmation of pregnancy 2 weeks after she missed her menstrual period, she is considered to be 6 weeks pregnant (assuming a 28-day cycle), even though conception probably occurred about 4 weeks ago.

Abortion within the first trimester. Although most physicians prefer to wait for a positive diagnosis of pregnancy before performing an abortion, it is possible to perform *menstrual regulation* even before pregnancy has been identified as the cause of a missed period. This technique, also called *endometrial aspiration*, is usually performed within 6 weeks from the LMP. A thin, flexible plastic tube is inserted through the cervix into the uterus, and the contents of the uterus are removed through some form of suction — created either with a small pump or with a syringe. With this procedure, it is not necessary to dilate or stretch the cervical passage. The suction pump removes the lining of the uterus, or *endometrium*, and a small amount of fetal tissue if the woman actually is pregnant. While this procedure is considered to be very safe and usually takes only a few minutes, it has one major disadvantage; since the fetus is so small, it is hard to be sure that the pregnancy has in fact been terminated, and it is advised that the woman take a pregnancy test a week after the procedure to be sure that the abortion was successful.

If pregnancy has not been terminated within 6 weeks from the LMP, a technique called *vacuum suction* or *uterine aspiration* can be used (see Figure 11.9). This relatively new technique may be performed any time within the first trimester and is based on the same principle as endometrial aspiration. It is often necessary to dilate the cervix, however, since a nonflexible tube has to be inserted into the uterus. The size of the tube usually depends on the duration of the pregnancy, with larger sizes necessary to evacuate the greater volume of uterine contents in a longer pregnancy. The tube is attached to a mechanical or electrical suction pump, and it is possible to examine what has been removed from the uterus to be sure that it includes all the fetal tissue. A local anaesthetic is usually given with this procedure, and the abortion may be completed within 10 minutes.

The more traditional technique for first trimester abortions is called *dilatation and curettage*, or D and C, and it is still performed by many physicians who are unfamiliar with the suction techniques. A D and C involves the insertion of a sharp metal curette, rather than a plastic suction tube, into the uterus to loosen the uterine lining and remove the fetal tissue. Within 12 weeks from the LMP, this procedure is considered less safe than vacuum suction, although complications are still relatively rare. The major risk appears to be perforation of the

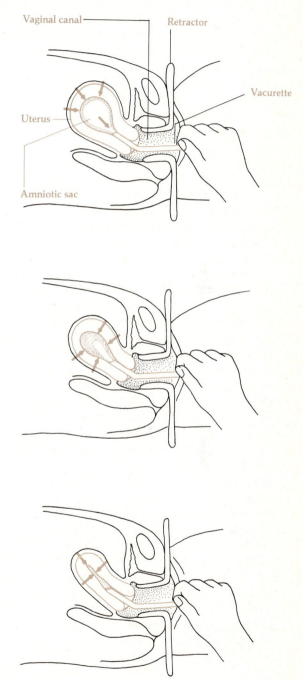

FIGURE 11.9

Schematic representation of the three stages of abortion by uterine aspiration.

uterus with the metal curette and resulting hemorrhage. However, when the D and C is performed between 12 and 15 weeks from the LMP, it is considered to be safer than the second-trimester techniques. Since the cervix must be dilated more extensively than with the vacuum suction technique, this procedure may be more painful and require a greater amount of local anaesthetic, or even a general anaesthetic.

Second-trimester abortions: induced labor. Second-trimester abortion is more dangerous than an early abortion and must be performed in a hospital setting. Changes in the size and structure of the uterus, as well as the growth of the fetus, make it impossible to terminate pregnancy with vaginal evacuation methods. After about 16 weeks from the LMP, the preferred abortion method is to induce labor so that the fetus can be removed through a "natural" delivery. Labor is usually induced in one of two ways. In *saline abortion*, a part of the amniotic fluid surrounding the fetus is withdrawn, through a needle inserted into the mother's abdomen, and is replaced with a saline solution. This causes the fetal heartbeat to disappear within 2 hours, and labor usually starts 12 to 36 hours later. A second technique for inducing labor is called *prostaglandin abortion*; prostaglandins may be administered into the amniotic fluid or through the bloodstream. These hormonelike substances occur naturally when a woman is giving birth, and they induce labor much more quickly than the saline abortion. The disadvantages of prostaglandin abortions are that they have a greater number of side effects and are considered somewhat more dangerous. In addition, there is a small chance that the fetus will show some signs of life for a short time after the delivery.

Second-trimester abortions: surgical proce-dures. Surgical procedures are rarely used to terminate an unwanted pregnancy and are usually performed only for very late abortions. In a *hysterotomy*, the fetus is removed through a small incision in the abdomen. Hysterotomy is similar to Caesarean section. The hysterotomy is a major surgical procedure requiring general anaesthesia and prolonged recovery, as is hysterectomy, the surgical removal of the uterus. Neither of these procedures is likely to be used merely for the purpose of abortion; they are usually restricted to situations in which either surgical sterilization or removal of the uterus will also be performed.

PHYSICAL RISKS OF ABORTION

The physical risks of abortion are directly related to the length of time a woman has been pregnant. Tietze (1977) reports that the mortality rate of legal abortions performed before 8 weeks of pregnancy is 0.4 deaths per 100,000 abortions; this rate increases to 17 deaths per 100,000 abortions after 16 weeks of pregnancy. Since most legal abortions are performed early in pregnancy, it has been estimated that there are 3.2 deaths per 100,000 legal abortions (Hatcher *et al.*, 1976). As is often pointed out, this figure is considerably lower than the mortality rate for women who carry their children to delivery, estimated at 16 deaths per 100,000 live births. In fact, the risk of death from early abortion is equal to or lower than the risk of women who are completely protected from pregnancy by using birth control pills. These figures have led some authors to conclude that the safest method of contraception is the use of a diaphragm or condom, with abortion as a backup method for contraceptive failure (Seaman and Seaman, 1977).

The second major factor relating to the physical risk of abortion is its legal status.

When abortion is illegal—performed in unsterile conditions by untrained persons or self-induced—the risk of death or complications is clearly many times higher than when it is performed by trained persons in medical settings. We do not have precise statistics about the risk of illegal abortion, for the obvious reason that illegal abortions are not reported and come to medical attention only when there are serious complications. We do know that between 1958 and 1962 there was an average of 292 deaths per year from illegal abortions. This figure dropped to 154 deaths in 1969 and 24 deaths in 1974—that is, as legal abortion became increasingly available, deaths from illegal abortion declined.

The physical complications of abortion are usually divided into three types: *immediate* complications—which are very rare with legal abortions—include the risk of uterine perforation from the instruments used in vacuum and D and C abortions, damage to the cervix, hemorrhage, and negative effects from local or general anaesthesia. The most common *delayed* complications are retention of placental tissue resulting in bleeding, and infection. We know little about the *late* complications of abortion, but there is some concern that repeated abortions may increase the risk of miscarriage or premature birth in subsequent pregnancies. Research has not shown consistent results—some investigators have found fertility problems in women who have had abortions, others have not found any problems.

PSYCHOLOGICAL FACTORS

Unlike other methods of birth control, abortion is often a highly emotional experience. Some authors believe that abortion presents a major risk to mental health, and according to the World Health Organization, "there is no doubt that the termination of pregnancy may precipitate a serious psychoneurotic or even psychotic reaction in a susceptible individual" (quoted in Tietze, 1977). However, the vast majority of women who have had an abortion continue to lead normal lives, and there is little evidence that abortion necessarily presents long-term psychological problems. For many women, it has the positive and practical value of eliminating the stress of an unwanted pregnancy (David, 1973). Further, the emotional stress of abortion may be far less damaging than the stress of bearing and rearing an unwanted child.

Several factors will influence a woman's response to her abortion. For instance, early abortions seem to cause less emotional stress than abortions occurring later in pregnancy: the medical procedures are simpler, recovery time is shorter, and the woman has spent less time as a potential mother. The surroundings in which the abortion takes place are also important—a legal abortion in a specialized clinic will be much less traumatic than an illegal abortion performed in a clandestine location. Finally, a great many personal factors are involved: Does the woman have the support of friends and family? Is she being pressured into having an abortion or is her decision completely voluntary? What is her relationship to the man who impregnated her? Does she feel that abortion is morally wrong, or does she view it as acceptable under certain circumstances? All these factors will contribute to her psychological response. While most women feel tremendous relief, there are also many negative feelings—sadness, regret, anger, guilt—that may be experienced. Since we live in a culture that tends to place strong negative values on abortion, it is not surprising that these values shape and color the personal experience of abortion.

Summary

Contraception is an idea as old as human history; even before human beings were aware of the link between sexual intercourse and conception they attempted to limit fertility through superstition and magic. Present day contraceptive efforts are more successful and sophisticated but the use and choice of a birth control technique is still problematical for many people.

1. The United States has seen a "contraceptive revolution" in two areas of birth control behavior. First, several highly effective methods have become available in the past three decades. And second, most people have come to accept contraceptive use as both necessary and desirable.

2. Despite the forces working toward effective contraception (such as concern with overpopulation and an emphasis on the rights of women to control their reproductive lives), a substantial number of unplanned or unwanted pregnancies still occur. Contraceptive failure is of greatest concern among unmarried adolescents; although this group tends to be making greater use of contraceptives in the past decade, several problems remain. For instance, sex information is often inaccurate, and many adolescents are emotionally unable or unwilling to take responsibility for contraceptive use.

3. In the absence of a perfect contraceptive — one that is effective, easy to use, and physically safe — it is necessary to make a contraceptive compromise by selecting a technique that best fits into a particular user's needs and life style.

4. Each contraceptive technique has both advantages and disadvantages. Some methods, such as rhythm or coitus interruptus, require a degree of sexual abstinence. Other methods — the condom, diaphragm, or foam — necessitate contraceptive action at the time of intercourse. The newest methods — the pill, IUD, and surgical sterilization — operate independently of sexual activity. In general, the more effective the technique, the more likely that it interferes in some way with physical functioning.

5. Abortion, unlike other methods of birth control, raises emotional and moral issues as well as technical problems. Legal abortion is safe and effective, particularly if it is performed very early in pregnancy. However, few people accept abortion as a primary birth control technique, and family planning professionals have attempted to decrease abortion rates through better contraception and sex education programs.

5

CURRENT ISSUES
AND CONCERNS

Overview

TWELVE

Sex Offenders and Offenses

Overview

There has never been a culture that permitted its members complete and unlimited sexual freedom. Throughout history, all societies have placed restrictions on sexual behavior, although the nature of these restrictions has varied greatly. It is not surprising that sexual rules and prohibitions are part of the basic foundation of all social systems. Human sexuality is generally viewed as a powerful instinct, which if unchecked, would result in anarchy and chaos. Thus each society maintains and enforces the standards of sexual conduct that it considers acceptable.

However, as the work of Clellan Ford and Frank Beach illustrates, there is little agreement among cultures as to which behaviors are socially acceptable and which unaccept-

able. Perhaps the only sexual conduct that is almost universally prohibited is incest, and even here, there have been exceptions. Among the royal families of such ancient civilizations as the Egyptians and Incas, marriage between brothers and sisters was encouraged to preserve the purity of the ruling family. Definitions of incest vary within different cultures: some groups define incest only in terms of the immediate family members, others extend the definition to include second or third cousins or even all the members of one's tribe.

Whereas homosexuality is stigmatized in most parts of our country today, the ancient Greeks viewed man as bisexual and approved of a close, sensual relationship between a young boy and his teacher. In addition, both

Greek vase showing a homosexual relationship between a youth and an older man. (Cup, *Man and Boy, Attic Black Figured. Gift of E. P. and Fiske Warren. Courtesy, Museum of Fine Arts, Boston)*

male and female prostitution was an accepted part of Greek life. The ancient Hebrews, Greeks, and Romans all recognized two classes of prostitutes: the companion-courtesan, who was often well-educated and accorded high status, and the mercenary prostitute. Further, whereas monogamy is the sexual standard in most Western cultures, the ancient Hebrews often had several wives, and polygamy still exists in certain Muslim groups, for example, today.

How does a culture enforce its norms of sexual conduct? Obviously, some sexual norms attain the status of law—for instance, sexual contact with children, rape, and exhibitionism are criminal offenses punishable by imprisonment. However, we should keep in mind that the laws against many types of sexual behavior are rarely if ever enforced. Many of these laws refer to sexual acts that take place between consenting adults, such as sodomy, adultery, and so on. The private nature of these sexual behaviors makes enforcement almost impossible, and there is some question about whether such acts even deserve the attention of the legal system. Other laws against sexual acts are enforced sporadically and in-

consistently. For example, crackdowns on prostitution often seem to alternate with legal indifference, and the streetwalker is at far greater risk of arrest than the woman who works in a massage parlor.

We are beginning to look at many nonnormative sexual behaviors as variant life styles rather than as offenses. Although it is difficult to draw a clear line between sexual acts that are "variations" and those that are crimes, we attempt to do so. In this chapter, we discuss only sexual acts or life styles that are *legally prohibited.* And we do not include those acts that are illegal but rarely or never prosecuted —such as adultery, sodomy, cohabitation (living together without marriage), homosexuality, and so on.

In general, the law intervenes with respect to three areas of sexual conduct: (1) when there is a lack of legal consent—as in rape and child molestation; (2) when a social nuisance is created or public standards of decency are offended—as in exhibitionism and voyeurism; and (3) when sex is used for commercial purposes—as in prostitution. These are the types of behaviors that are most accurately labeled sex offenses.

We discuss sex offenses from two basic perspectives. They can be seen as an individual problem—that is, as acts committed by individuals, usually male, who are psychologically disturbed. This disturbance may take many forms; such labels as "emotionally immature" or "socially inadequate" are often conferred upon the individual sex offender, and treatment typically focuses on correcting these problems. However, the sex offense is also a social problem. The behavior of the sex offender affects his victims, his family and friends, and the entire society in which he lives. Sex offenses take place within a social context, and the sex offender's behavior is both shaped and reflected by the society in which he lives.

Introduction

DEFINING SEXUAL DEVIANCE

Standards of what is "acceptable" sexual conduct are present in all cultures, although the actual content of these standards may differ from one society to another. Implicit in the concept of sexual standards is the notion that there is a set of sexual behaviors that are "normal"; all sexual behaviors falling outside of this standard are, by definition, "deviant" or "abnormal." The dividing line between what is normal and what is abnormal is not as clear as we might like it to be, however, and prominent sexologists such as Albert Ellis (1956) acknowledge that we have no absolute criterion of what constitutes sexual normality.

There are many approaches to defining normality, and although each approach provides us with a fairly straightforward means of separating normal from abnormal, no single approach can encompass the totality of human sexual behavior. Perhaps the most restrictive is a *moral* approach: in our religious tradition, moral sexuality includes only those sexual behaviors that can lead to childbirth within marriage. All other sexual acts are immoral and are referred to in extremely negative terms— as perverted, debauched, aberrant, unnatural, and so on. There are several problems with a moral approach to defining "normal" sexuality—for one thing, we know that what is morally acceptable in one culture may be strongly disapproved of in another. For example, many cultures do not share our tradi-

tional moral objection to premarital intercourse; in fact, among some groups in the Scandinavian countries, premarital intercourse is considered both moral and necessary. In addition, some of the behaviors defined as immoral in our own culture and practiced by a majority of our population. For example, Alfred Kinsey and his associates found that the "immoral" acts of premarital intercourse and masturbation occurred in more than half of their sample.

Another way of defining normality is by using a *statistical* approach; that is, normal sexuality is average, or statistically common, sexual behavior. If we adopt this approach, we would have to consider premarital and extramarital intercourse, masturbation, oral sex, homosexual behaviors, prostitution, and even child molestation as "normal," since all these acts occur with high frequency in our society. Further, we would have to recognize that what is statistically normal in one culture may be extremely unusual in another culture— because statistically normal behavior is to a large extent *made* normal by the attitudes prevalent in a culture and the widespread practice of such behavior in that culture (Ellis, 1956). In other words, a statistical definition is as variable, from culture to culture and from time to time, as a moral definition.

A third approach to sexual normality and abnormality uses a *psychological* definition of acceptable sexual behavior. Psychologically healthy sexuality is assumed to be mature, well-adjusted, and personally and interpersonally fulfilling, and it should not lead to such negative emotional states as anxiety or guilt. Unfortunately, many people who engage in so-called normal sexual behaviors do experience negative emotions; and in contrast, some people practicing "deviant" sexuality may experience personal satisfaction and little guilt or anxiety. Often, the extent to which we feel disturbed about our sexual behavior has more to do with our social training than our specific sexual acts. For instance, many people who engage in the statistically normal act of masturbation still feel shame and guilt about their behavior; does this mean that masturbation is psychologically abnormal?

If psychologically normal sexuality is evident in the mature and well-adjusted individual, then we might assume that abnormal sexuality has its roots in psychological disturbance. In fact, sexual deviance has often been defined in medical/psychiatric terms: the sexual deviant is seen as a "sick" individual whose illness is manifested in sexual symptoms. This psychological definition assumes that a "healthy" individual would not commit a sexual offense and that such offenses are a direct result of an underlying psychological "disease" or maladjustment.

Many attempts have been made to classify sexual offenses within a psychiatric framework. The first such attempt was made by Krafft-Ebing in his volume *Psychopathia Sexualis*. At the end of the nineteenth century, psychiatry was concerned with little more than taxonomy and classification, and Krafft-Ebing compiled an impressive, if somewhat horrific, compendium of all known forms of sexual deviance. The most interesting thing about his presentation of symptoms and cases is the almost random way in which brutal sex murders are described alongside of innocuous shoe fetishes. From Krafft-Ebing's language, it would seem that he regarded these offenses as equally abhorrent.

Krafft-Ebing's work, and the psychiatric classification systems developed after him, are all based on the notion that abnormality in sexual behavior is directly linked to some form of mental illness. However, a problem with defining sexual deviance in terms of psychological variables is that "deviant" behavior always takes place in a social context. Often, it is the process of being labeled as deviant by society, rather than the specific sexual behavior, that causes psychological problems. By labeling a sexual act deviant, we are defining the person who commits that act as an outsider, someone who has broken one of society's rules. Typically, we respond to the "deviant" with social ostracism, imprisonment, or some form of therapy. For example, most of our society continues to label the man or woman with homosexual preferences deviant; although homosexuals are not frequently imprisoned, they are often the subject of social disapproval and may be severely stigmatized. These social pressures, rather than the actual homosexual behavior, may be a major factor in producing psychological difficulties.

A final approach to defining normality and abnormality is via our criminal and legal systems. That is, we can define any sexual behavior that might lead to arrest and imprisonment as abnormal or deviant. According to this *legal* definition, however, many married couples in the United States would be classified as deviant, since many states still have laws against all sexual acts except coitus, even among the married. Similarly, there are laws against adultery and fornication (sexual contact between unmarried people). While such sexual acts are illegal, law enforcement agencies rarely show any interest in prosecuting for these offenses. In general, sexual contacts between consenting adults, although legally deviant, are not a subject of legal concern. In fact, certain legally prohibited sexual behaviors occur with such frequency that they have been described as "normal deviance" (Gagnon, 1974).

If we were to restrict our legal definition of abnormality to include only those sexual acts for which people are actually arrested and prosecuted, we would still have some definitional problems. For instance, we would find that homosexuality is abnormal in some communities and acceptable in others. Similarly, the pornographer or prostitute is subject to inconsistent and variable legal treatment. In contrast, some legally defined sex offenses, such as incest, which occur with some frequency in our society, rarely come to the attention of legal authorities.

In reviewing the various ways that people define normal and abnormal sexual conduct, we can see that no single standard of behavior applies to all facets of human sexuality. In fact, there may be as many definitions as there are individuals, since we each tend to develop our own personal criteria about what is normal and what is deviant.

THE CAUSES OF SEX OFFENSES

Why do people commit sexual crimes? Early nineteenth-century explanations made frequent use of such concepts as "moral degeneracy," and even today, there are many people who view the sex criminal as the "sick" product of a permissive society. The growth of Freudian psychiatry replaced the old notion of moral degeneracy with the concept of "unconscious motivation"—that sex crimes are committed when we are unable to control our strong "primitive" sexual instincts. Another psychiatric concept frequently used to explain deviant sexual behavior is "psychopathy"—

the sex offender is assumed to lack basic social concern for the rights of others.

The most recent trend in psychology is to explain sex offenses in terms of faulty learning and conditioning. According to this view, sexual preferences must be practiced before they become truly habitual. Some researchers suggest that the primary means of practicing sexual preference is masturbation:

While it has frequently been suggested that sexual deviations are learned, the learning has usually been thought of as taking place during one traumatic experience. From a study of 45 sexual deviants, the authors believe that it is often a more gradual process occurring during masturbation to a memory, which need not have been sexually stimulating at the time of the initial experience and which often alters with the passage of time. (McGuire *et al.*, 1965, p. 185)

In other words, these researchers are suggesting that the sex offender is not suddenly drawn to children, clothing, or other objects as a source of sexual arousal. Instead, these inappropriate sexual choices may develop over a long span of time, in which they gain power because they have become associated with masturbation and orgasm. For example, a boy might have his first masturbatory experience in a bathroom in which his mother's stockings are drying on a curtain rod. The next time he masturbates, he may recall the stockings as part of his masturbatory fantasy. If his fantasies develop in such a way that the stockings become the crucial and necessary element for orgasm, it is possible that he will develop a "stocking fetish"—that is, stockings will be the only fantasy connected with orgasm. Within this same framework, it is possible that persistent sexual fantasies about young children will lead to pedophilia, and that violent masturbatory fantasies will lead to rape.

The conditioning theory is a valuable addi-

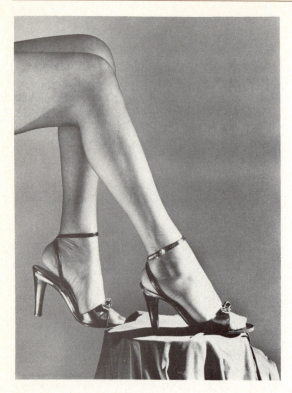

A person with a sexual fetish can be aroused by inanimate objects such as shoes. (© *Joel Gordon 1980*)

tion to our understanding of the psychology of the sex offender. However, psychological factors are only one level of explanation for why people commit sex offenses. We cannot answer this question without making use of information from many other fields of study. Some researchers have investigated the physiology of the compulsive sex criminal, attempting to discover if biological differences exist between those who practice deviant sexuality and non-deviant sexuality. One such study (Rada *et al.*, 1976) compared the plasma testosterone levels of rapists, child molesters, and normal control subjects. The rapists were categorized in terms of the amount of violence used during the commission of the act of rape. The researchers found that the most violent rapists had significantly higher testosterone levels than members of any of the other groups. They conclude that while it is unlikely

that the aggressive act of committing rape is determined by testosterone levels, it is possible that unusually high testosterone levels are associated with extreme violence during rape.

Other researchers have pointed to the importance of social influences in the commission of sex crimes. According to this view, we cannot explain deviant behavior only in terms of an individual's particular psychology or physiology. Deviance takes place within a social context, and many criminologists discuss deviant behavior as a direct product of prevailing social conditions.

An example of this social-learning approach to the causes of sexual deviance is provided by the work of sociologist John Gagnon (1974). Gagnon believes that all sexual conduct, including deviant behavior, is a result of social learning. In his view, we develop our sexual values, attitudes, techniques, and behaviors over a period of time spanning from early childhood through the marital and child-rearing years. Most people learn the elements of a conventional sexual life style that leads to a socially acceptable expression of sexuality. However, the learning process is complex, and there are many occasions for error—that is, the conditions of conventional development contain the origins of unconventional or deviant patterns. Thus deviant behavior is motivated by the same basic set of social conditions and processes as conventional behavior.

In the view of social-learning theorists such as Gagnon, a sexual crime such as rape is not the result of the rapist's poor control over his raging sexual instincts, but the outcome of confused learning. "Sexual relationships themselves are fraught with ambiguity since it is a rare set of persons who can sequence communication in such a way that the man's desire and the woman's desire are directly coordinated" (1974, p. 261). In our conventional sexual scripts, we tend to view the male as the aggressive seeker of sexual contact, the female as more hesitant and needing to be convinced or seduced into having sexual relations. This conventional script sows the seeds for rape: the male believes that he can safely ignore his female partner's lack of consent, since he sees his role as overcoming her natural hesitancy to engage in sexual relations. Rape occurs when he interprets her refusal as "I need to be convinced" rather than as "I definitely do not want to have sexual relations." In this analysis, rape is the result of a miscommunication between male and female.

This social-learning explanation of rape would probably not be accepted by all experts in the field. For one thing, rape almost always involves an element of violence, and the degree of coercion does not appear to be on the same continuum as the typical "seduction script." Further, a number of research studies have shown that the rapist seems to be interested in a completely different script, namely one that involves highly aggressive behavior toward a female victim.

It is unlikely that we will find a single answer to the question What causes sexual offenses? For one thing, there are many different types of sexual deviance, and each type probably has its own particular influences and causes. The causes of violent sexual crimes such as rape may be quite different from the causes of a so-called victimless crime such as prostitution. Second, human sexual conduct, like all human behavior, has many sources; biological, cognitive, emotional, and social factors all play a role. We must refer to all these sources in order to understand the causes of sexual offenses.

WHO IS THE SEX OFFENDER?

Even if we limit our definition of "sex offender" to include only the individual who commits sexual acts that frequently lead to arrest, we will have considerable difficulty identifying a "typical" offender. The vast majority of sex offenses never come to the attention of legal or scientific authorities — for instance, it has been estimated that for every reported case of rape, from five to ten cases go unreported. The same is likely to be true for such offenses as child molestation and incest.

Of the sex offenses that are reported to the police, only a small percentage actually result in arrest. Further, among those arrested for sex offenses, only some will actually be convicted, and among those convicted, only some will be imprisoned. Since most of our knowledge about sex offenders is based on studies of those who have been imprisoned, we can see that this sample is far from representative of the entire population of sex offenders. We can assume that the offender who is caught by the police, convicted, and sentenced to prison is a less successful and resourceful individual than one who escapes punishment after committing the same crime.

Perhaps the best-known study of convicted and imprisoned offenders is a volume produced by Kinsey's research group, *Sex Offenders: An Analysis of Types* (Gebhard et al., 1965). This research is based on interviews conducted with incarcerated offenders in the early 1940s and 1950s. The authors define several different types of sex offenders:

1. The assaultive type, accounting for about one-third of the sample, includes men who use unnecessary physical violence to gain sexual contact. Generally, these men commit sexual assaults with no accomplices and are unacquainted with their victims. Violence appears to be a necessary component in their sexual gratification, and in fact, violence may actually be a substitute for coitus, since many men in this group have erectile dysfunctions.

2. The *amoral delinquent* is typically a young man who is not sadistic but has little concern for the rights of his victim and disregards all forms of social control. While such men are not particularly hostile toward women, they will use force if a woman refuses to fulfill what they see as her role as a sexual object.

3. The *drunken offender* is the man who will commit sexual offenses of various types only while under the influence of alcohol. Intoxication may result in ineffectual attempts at "seduction," or it may, in certain instances, precipitate more violent forms of sexual assault.

4. The *explosive offender*, accounting for about 10 or 15 percent of the sample, is typically a man whose prior life shows little indication that he will commit a sexual assault. Many of these men appear to be average citizens who suddenly "snap" under stress. While their violence appears to be totally unexpected, many explosive offenders do show signs of emotional disturbance before the assault actually takes place.

5. The *double-standard offender*, accounting for about 10 percent of the sample, is a man who categorizes all females into two groups: the "good woman," who is entitled to respect, and the "bad woman," who is considered fair game for sexual assault since she is seen as "asking for it." A man in this group might classify the female hitchhiker as someone who has forfeited her right to refuse coitus, but refrain from coitus with his fiancée because he wants to marry a virgin.

6. The remaining offenders in this sample, constituting almost one-third of the total, are mostly a mixture of the above types. The few exceptions are men who seem to be mentally defective or psychotic.

We can learn more about the "typical" imprisoned sex offender from a study conducted by Albert Ellis and Ralph Brancale (1956). These researchers interviewed and examined the records of 300 convicted sex offenders in the New Jersey State Diagnostic Center at Menlo Park. The men in this sample had been convicted for a wide variety of offenses, including sexual assault and forcible rape, incest, exhibitionism, disseminating "obscene" material, and homosexual relations. Psychiatric evaluations indicated that 14 percent were "normal," and 64 percent were "mild" or "severe" neurotics; the remainder were classified as psychotic, brain-damaged, mentally deficient, or psychopathic. Further, more than half of the 300 offenders were considered to be sexually inhibited rather than oversexed. In fact, the sexually inhibited offenders seemed more likely to behave in the way described earlier as the "explosive" offender—that is, individuals who normally hold their sexual needs in check but might suddenly begin to overreact in a sexual situation.

Ellis and Brancale classified 91 percent of the offenders as "emotionally immature," and the group was more than twice as likely to show "subnormal intelligence" as the general population. Alcohol played a role in the sex offenses of 32 percent of the men, although the overall rate of alcoholism was not appreciably different from the general population. About 21 percent used force or duress in the commission of a sex crime.

But as these researchers point out, the findings regarding sex offenders who are caught and convicted may have little or no relevance to the many individuals who violate sex statutes without ever being found out or convicted. In other words, the portrait of the sex offender as sexually, emotionally, and cognitively disturbed may be appropriate only for the small number of offenders who actually reach the criminal justice system.

There is only one statement we can make with complete certainty about the typical non-incarcerated sex offender: the odds are that this average offender is male. Except for female prostitutes, women are extremely unlikely to commit sexual offenses. They are almost completely absent from the ranks of rapists, exhibitionists, voyeurs, pedophiles, etc. This may be due, in part, to our social conventions—for instance, the exhibitionistic female may be paid to work as a nude model, whereas often her male counterpart has no such outlet for his sexual desires. Other explanations have relied on the male's greater vulnerability to all kinds of sexual disorders, including transvestism and transsexualism (Money and Ehrhardt, 1972). From a social-learning point of view, the conventional female sex role does not easily lend itself to aggressive sexual behaviors. The woman who has learned to be subtle and passive about her sexual needs is not likely to try to force those needs on others, as the male rapist does.

Offenses Involving Lack of Consent

RAPE

Defining rape. Rape is generally defined as *the crime of forcing a female to submit to sexual intercourse.* While this definition seems relatively straightforward and simple, it is actually just a starting point for understanding the act of rape. It is an act surrounded by myths, stereotypes, and misinformation. Rape has been described as a political act in the subjugation of women, a criminal behavior committed by maladjusted men, a natural outcome of the "innate masochism" of women, and the expected result of our socialization into male and female roles. It is an act often sensationalized in books, newspapers, and movies, and may play a considerable role in our sexual fantasies. Cultural attitudes toward rape vary from fear and anger to curiosity, indifference, and even approval.

Little social consensus exists as to how to define "force" in the act of rape. A not insubstantial segment of the population believes that rape, defined as forcible sexual intercourse, is impossible. (In the words of Honoré de Balzac, a nineteenth-century French novelist, "You can't thread a moving needle.") This rather cynical and insensitive view of rape may be further compounded by the cultural belief that every woman secretly desires to be raped. Because of these common myths, the rape victim often becomes an object of disbelief and scorn. Rape may be the only crime in which the victim seems to bear an even greater burden of guilt and responsibility than the offender.

In recent years, many of our archaic beliefs about rape have been changing, in response to increased research and media coverage of the facts of rape. Researchers have provided us with data about the topography of rape—a detailed description of when, where, how often, and who is involved—while feminists have forced us to reevaluate our attitudes toward rape. Robin Morgan, for example, has suggested that "rape exists any time sexual intercourse occurs when it has not been initiated by the woman, out of her own genuine affection and desire" (1977, p. 165). In this broad definition of rape, Morgan sees any element of pressure—be it fear, economic insecurity, or guilt—as constituting "force." While many might disagree with this definition, it does provoke us to rethink our concepts about the meaning of rape.

A persistent theme in the legal history of rape is concern for the falsely accused man. This concern with unjustly punishing an innocent man influences the legal disposition of many rape cases. The notion that women cry

Scene from *Rashomon*, a film by the Japanese director, Kurosawa (1950). The film shows the complex meanings and motives for rape. Other well-known films about rape are *The Virgin Spring*, by Ingmar Bergman and *Clockwork Orange*, by Stanley Kubrick. (*The Museum of Modern Art/Film Still Archive*)

rape out of vengeance, anger, fear, or simply as a means of avoiding responsibility for a sexual act is fairly common in our culture. Little factual information is available about the extent to which women lie about rape. Many states still require that there be *corroboration* to an act of rape—that is, a woman is expected to provide a witness to her sexual assault.

The legal system often seems to act in ways that protect the guilty rather than the innocent. For example, when a charge of rape is reported to the police, they make a judgment as to whether the charge seems to be "founded" before they will actually search for and arrest the accused man. A charge of rape is most likely to be viewed as credible if the victim and rapist were strangers, if the rapist used physical violence, if the victim has physical scars to prove her resistance, if the victim has a "good reputation" or is seen as respectable. Thus, the police will be likely to investigate the rape of a woman who is white, married, badly bruised, and assaulted by a stranger. In contrast, the complaint of a black

woman who is unbruised, unmarried, and of doubtful respectability may well be ignored, particularly if she was acquainted with the accused rapist. Charges of rape brought by a woman against her husband are also likely to be ignored; in fact, in many states it is legally impossible for a man to rape his wife, as the criminal justice system is reluctant to intervene in such "family problems." Similarly, if a woman had previously consented to having sexual relations with a man, she will have great difficulty charging him with rape on a later occasion. Since the victim's reputation for sexual promiscuity is often considered by the legal authorities, a prostitute will have considerable difficulty in making a charge of rape.

Our legal codes tend to provide the benefit of the doubt to all accused criminals, believing that it is better to free a guilty man than to imprison an innocent one. Thus accusations of rape that are seen as doubtful by the police or the court system are not followed up, leading to a relatively low conviction rate for cases of rape. In fact, many of the convictions that are obtained are for *statutory rape*, defined as sexual intercourse with a female who is below the legal age of consent, even if she has given her personal consent. The intention of statutory rape laws is to protect females considered too young to make sound judgments about their sexual behavior. Actually, these protective statutory rape laws are often inconsistent and irrational. The legal age of consent varies from 14 in some states to as high as 21 in others. In fact, some states allow a female the legal right to a marriage license before they permit her the right to consent to sexual intercourse! Some authorities have suggested that the legal age of consent be lowered to 12, on the grounds that many young females lead active sex lives when in their teens, and it is pointless to prosecute men who have obtained a female's personal consent. However, the legal system continues to "protect" females who, by reason of age, are considered incompetent to make sexual choices. While statutory rape charges might also be brought against a woman who is of the legal age and has had sexual intercourse with a male who is below the legal age, such charges are far less common.

Although rape has traditionally been seen as a sexual violation of females, we are beginning to recognize the prevalence of male sexual assaults against men. Many states restrict the legal definition of rape to forcible sexual intercourse with a female, but male sexual attacks against other men can be prosecuted as "sexual assault." It appears that such assaults are most likely to occur within two settings: prison populations and segments of some homosexual communities. The nature of these settings and the extreme humiliation often felt by the male victim of sexual assault make it likely that male rape is an even more underreported and legally prosecuted offense than female rape.

The history and mythology of rape. In her powerful book *Against Our Will* (1975), Susan Brownmiller presents her thesis that rape has been an integral, if underemphasized, part of all cultures since the beginnings of recorded history. Until recently, rape was seen not as a crime against the person of the victim but as a violation of property. A woman has traditionally been viewed as the property of her father until marriage and then as the property of her husband. Thus rape was a crime against the property of a male, and the punishment for an act of rape reflected this view. In the Bible, rape was a crime only if committed against a virgin, and the rapist was often required to reimburse the victim's male guardian for the decrease in her value on the marriage market. The rape of a married woman was treated as an act of adultery, and the rapist and his victim were equally liable to punishment. In medieval English law, the rape of a propertied virgin was a crime punishable by death unless the victim resolved her family's shame by marrying her rapist. In this case, the rapist gained title to his victim's wealth as a result of his sexual assault. Thus the capture and rape of highborn virgins became a common means of upward social mobility in medieval England. Only in the thirteenth century was the legal concept of rape expanded to include the violation of wives, widows, and nuns. Even in these cases, the burden of responsibility to prove rape was placed on the victim; she was seen as the "prosecutrix," since she and not the court was charged with proving her assault.

Traces of these views of rape remain to this day. We have noted that in many states it is not a crime for a husband to rape his wife. The concept of a wife being her husband's property implies that he has the right to do as he wishes with what is already his by law. "Only recently has it been recognized that rape is a crime, not against the men associated with the woman, but to the woman herself" (Gagnon, 1977, p. 308).

Brownmiller (1975) suggests that our cultural notions about rape contribute to the development of a "victim mentality" in women. She cites the following as among the most powerful myths about rape:

That all women want to be raped

That no woman can be raped against her will

That she was asking for it

That if you're going to be raped, you might as well relax and enjoy it

The idea that all women secretly desire rape is a theme that appears continuously in movies, books, and pornography. It also plays a prominent role in the work of Helene Deutsch, author of the psychoanalytically oriented *The Psychology of Women:* "Woman's entire psycholgical preparation for the sexual and reproductive functions is connected with masochistic ideas. In these ideas, coitus is closely associated with the act of defloration, and defloration with rape and the painful penetration of the body" (1944, p. 277). According to Deutsch, rape forms a substantial part of women's fantasies and dreams. However, while it is true that many women include rape in their sexual fantasies, most of them have no interest whatsoever in being raped in real life. No factual basis exists for the notion that all women secretly want to be sexually assaulted.

"She was asking for it" is one of the most pervasive myths about rape. The victim is accused of causing her own rape—by hitchhiking, walking in unsafe places, leaving her door unlocked, wearing "seductive" clothing, or being "provocative" in her behavior. In this way, the responsibility for the act of rape is transferred from the rapist to his victim, and rape is seen as a victim-precipitated behavior—that is, the victim has contributed to her own rape. The National Commission on the Causes and Prevention of Violence describes victim-precipitated rape as occurring "when the victim agreed to sexual relations but retracted before the actual act or when she clearly invited sexual relations through language, gestures, etc." (1969, p. 226). Using this definition, they reported that only 4.4 percent of rapes were victim-precipitated. It is likely that the notion that victims cause their own rape is a natural outcome of our sex role socialization: females are taught to be attractive and seductive by a culture that values these qualities, while males are encouraged to believe that the attractive woman is "fair game" for aggressive sexual advances.

Women are often advised to avoid rape by being extremely cautious in social situations. However, statistics show that about half of all rapes occur in the victim's home. While women are also advised that attractive appearance may provoke the rapist, statistics show that rapists often select their victims with little regard for physical attractiveness. The mythology of rape encourages us to imagine a beautiful, romantic heroine submitting to the handsome, virile man whom she has secretly desired. This fantasy is very different from the reality of the act of rape.

Gagnon (1977) has pointed out our dual and conflicting portraits of the rapist and the rape victim. The rapist may be seen as a sadistic maniac—a man with psychopathic tendencies and an abnormal sex drive. On the other hand, he is often viewed as a healthy, law-abiding man with normal sexual desires who has been understandably provoked by the attractive women in his environment. The first view allows us to place the rapist outside of society because he is obviously "sick"; the second view allows us to believe that the victim bears responsibility for rape. In the same way, the rape victim has been portrayed either as the pure and innocent virgin or as the sexually promiscuous woman who has provoked the attack because of her immorality; thus, we have either a completely innocent victim or a "loose woman" who is getting what she deserves. Neither of these polarities of opinion gives us much insight into the act of rape, but they do illustrate the ambivalence of our society in assigning responsibility for it.

If we reject both stereotypes—that rape is caused by oversexed women tempting men beyond normal endurance or by lust-crazed men driven by abnormal sexual urges—what explanations can be offered? Many individu-

als now feel that rape is not a sexual crime at all but an act of *aggression* directed against women. In fact, evidence exists that, for some rapists, the gratification associated with rape has little to do with sexuality. Thus we might argue that rape should be treated as a violent act of assault rather than as a sexual crime.

The incidence of rape. The statistics most commonly cited on the incidence of rape are those compiled by the Federal Bureau of In-

Violent rape is the subject of this painting by the Japanese artist, Uemura Shoen. Although not all rapists are motivated by sadistic needs, many rapes involve physical and/or psychological domination of the victim.

vestigation in the *Uniform Crime Reports*. These reports include national statistics on the four major classes of violent crimes: murder, rape, assault, and robbery. (Statutory rape is not included in these figures.) In 1973, 51,000 cases of forcible and attempted rape were reported; by 1975, the figure had risen to 56,000. Rape is considered to be the fastest-rising of the four major crimes of violence.

Yet these figures represent only those cases of reported rape that the police considered valid—that is, cases in which they believed the victim. Approximately 15 percent of all rape complaints are considered to be "unfounded" and receive little or no investigation by the police. According to *Uniform Crime Reports, 1973*, about half of all those suspected of committing rape in that year were arrested. Among those arrested, only 76 percent were actually brought to trial; and of these, 47 percent were eventually acquitted or had their cases dismissed. With a few simple calculations, we can see that of the 51,000 reported rapes in 1973, only about 8,000 cases led to a court verdict of guilty.

Rape is widely believed to be the most underreported crime. A study of criminal victimization (Ennis, 1967), in which interviewers approached a sample of U.S. households and asked whether any family members had been raped in the past year, reported a rate of 42.5 rapes per 100,000 people. In the same year, the *Uniform Crime Reports* calculated a rate of 11.6 rapes per 100,000 people. From these figures, it appears that for every rape that is reported to the police, at least three others are unreported. Even this is probably an underestimate, since people responding to the victimization study may have been unaware of the rape of family members or hesitant to discuss the subject with an unknown interviewer.

The generally accepted figure is that only 20 percent of all rapes are reported, indicating that more than 250,000 women are raped each year. It is not difficult to understand why rape continues to be underreported. Women are reluctant to undertake the strenuous and often humiliating procedures necessary to convict the rapist. The rape victim must be prepared to recount her experiences to the police, to the medical authorities, and finally, in court. She must be ready for court cross-examination that will suggest that she provoked the attack; and in many states, she may be asked to describe her previous sexual experiences. Attempts have been made to ease this process for the victim, particularly by training men and women to be sensitive to the rape victim's problems as she enters the criminal justice system. Even under the best of circumstances, however, it is likely that rape will continue to be an underreported crime.

The rapist.

Typically, the rapist is about 26, is from a low income, culturally deprived background, and is mentally retarded or of dull-normal intelligence. He is likely to have had emotionally unstable parents and a weak, often alcoholic father; the majority of rapists, however, come from broken homes. The rapist is usually emotionally immature, received little supervision from his parents in his youth, and is frequently unattractive. (McCary, 1973, p. 400)

The typical American rapist is not a weirdo, psycho schizophrenic beset by timidity, sexual deprivation, and a domineering wife or mother. Although the psycho rapist, whatever his family background, certainly does exist, just as the psycho murderer does exist, he is the exception and not the rule. The typical American perpetrator of forcible rape is little more than an aggressive, hostile youth who chooses to do violence to women. (Brownmiller, 1975, pp. 191–192)

These two conflicting portraits of the "typical" rapist highlight our cultural ambivalence toward rape. On the one hand, as we have stated, it is viewed as a deviant act performed by maladjusted men; on the other, as a not unusual response to our socialization as males and females. Actually, these two descriptions can be reconciled to some extent if we examine the sources of the information. The first description relies on information obtained from studies of the incarcerated rapist; the second is based on the rapist outside of prison. It seems likely that the man imprisoned for rape has less personal, social, and economic resources than the man who escapes punishment; thus the description of the incarcerated offender as tending to be maladjusted is probably accurate. However, the majority of rapists are not incarcerated.

Among convicted rapists, the majority are between the ages of 15 and 25 and come from the lower socioeconomic groups. According to the *Uniform Crime Reports,* 51 percent of rapists are black and 47 percent are white. About 40 percent of convicted rapists are married, and about half have been arrested for rape or other criminal offenses in the past. Alcohol is thought to have been involved in about 50 percent of the rapes. The rapist often shows little or no concern for the rights of others and violates a woman in the same way that he

might violate property (Gebhard *et al.,* 1965). Rapists tend to believe that their female victims secretly desire to be or enjoy being raped. About one-third of the incarcerated rapists studied by Gebhard had sexual interactions with women that usually included threats of violence and were also violent in other areas of their lives.

A study of rape in Philadelphia (Amir, 1971) reported that about 71 percent of all rapes were planned in advance. The rapist may have selected a particular victim or simply have decided that any victim would do. This statistic goes against the popular notion that rape is a spontaneous act provoked by the appearance of an attractive woman. The study also found that in 43 percent of the cases, two or more rapists were involved with a single victim. Often, a group of male friends planned a rape in advance but left the selection of a specific victim to chance. The men studied tended to belong to a generally violent subculture, rape being only one manifestation of their aggressive and antisocial behavior.

In an attempt to understand the motivation for rape, one study (Abel *et al.,* 1977) evaluated the components of sexual arousal in the rapist (see Figure 12.1). Rapists and normal control

FIGURE 12.1

A comparison between nonrapists' responses (left) and rapists' responses (right) when listening to audio-tape descriptions of normal intercoutse and rape. Notice that the nonrapists responded only to the rapes describing normal intercourse, whereas the rapists responsed to both. *(Adapted from Abel,* et al., *1977, p. 898)*

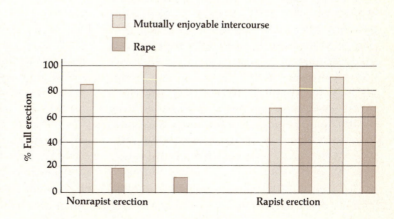

subjects were presented with audiotapes describing either mutually enjoyable sexual intercourse or intercourse forced on a woman. While the men listened to these tapes, the magnitude of their penile erection was measured on a polygraph. The researchers found that rapists as a group showed some degree of erection to both tapes, whereas the control subjects showed significantly less sexual arousal to the tapes describing rape than those describing mutually enjoyable intercourse. But some of the rapists had almost no response to tapes of mutually enjoyable intercourse, although they did respond to tapes describing rape. These same men showed a sexual response to other tapes describing aggression against women even when there was *no* sexual component at all. In other words, some rapists were not aroused by tapes with sexual interaction unless there was violence, and this violence alone was often sufficient to provoke a sexual response.

The role of violence in rape was also examined in a study (Rada *et al.*, 1976) that measured the plasma testosterone levels of fifty-two rapists institutionalized in a state hospital. As a comparison group, the researchers selected twelve men charged with nonviolent child molestation. Alcohol played a part in 44 percent of the rapes committed, and 38 percent of the rapists were classified as alcoholic. The rapists were subdivided into four groups, depending upon the amount of violence displayed in their sexual attack: group 1 included men who used only verbal threats of violence; group 4 included men who had inflicted some physical injury on the victim. The results of blood samples taken from each subject indicated that the range and mean of plasma testosterone of both rapists and nonviolent child molesters were within normal limits. However, when the values were examined for each of the rapist subgroups, the plasma testosterone levels of group 4 (the most violent

group) were significantly higher than those in normal men, the child molesters, and the other three rapist subgroups. In addition, the alcoholic rapists were found to have significantly higher testosterone levels than the nonalcoholic rapists. The authors point out that young men with a history of violent criminal behavior often show elevated testosterone levels. Thus, while plasma testosterone is not associated with the act of rape as such, it does seem to be related to the commission of violent rape.

The rape victim. Although women of all ages have been raped, women between the ages of 15 and 25 seem to be at greatest risk of rape. Further, greater risk exists for the woman who lives in an urban, lower socioeconomic community that also has high rates of nonsexual crimes. Since the majority of rapes occur within the rapist's neighborhood, it is not surprising that the typical victim belongs to the same race and socioeconomic group as her attacker.

What is the relationship of the victim to her attacker? According to one source, 53 percent of victims were total strangers to their attackers, 30 percent were slightly acquainted, 7 percent had a family relationship, and 3 percent had a previous close association but were not related (National Commission on the Causes and Prevention of Violence, 1969). These figures probably overestimate the proportion of "stranger" rape cases. It is possible that women who have been raped by a family member or close acquaintance are less likely to report the crime to the police. In addition, the police are more likely to consider as "founded" the complaint of a woman who does not know her attacker. Therefore, the stranger-rapist is more likely to be convicted and become a member of the imprisoned offender population—which is the population most frequently studied.

According to one study (Amir, 1971), about 55 percent of rape victims responded to their attackers with submissiveness; another 27 percent reported screaming or trying to escape, and 18 percent fought back by hitting, kicking, or throwing objects. The extent of a woman's resistance depended on the rapist's show of force; rapists who carried weapons were most likely to elicit submissive behavior in their victims, and a group of rapists encountered less resistance than a single rapist. However, these statistics apply only to completed acts of rape—that is, acts in which penile penetration took place. The *Uniform Crime Reports, 1973*, state that about 25 percent of all reported rape attempts were incomplete and were recorded instead as "assault with intent to commit rape." It is possible that some of these attempted rapes were incomplete due to male impotence, but it is also likely that female resistance played a role in avoiding rape.

A study of 92 victims of forcible rape admitted to Boston City Hospital for emergency treatment (Burgess and Holmstrom, 1974) reported a biphasic rape trauma syndrome. The women—who represented all age, ethnic, occupational, and socioeconomic groups—all showed both an *acute phase* and a *long-term reorganization process* in reaction to the assault. In the acute phase, victims experienced a great deal of disorganization in their life styles. Women who were interviewed several hours after the attack showed two emotional styles: about half the women displayed their feelings of fear and anger by crying, smiling, or acting tense or restless. The remaining women maintained an outward appearance of composure and control. In the weeks following the attack, victims showed a variety of physical reactions, including tension headaches, disturbed sleep patterns, edginess, appetite changes, and genitourinary disturbances such as vaginal itching, burning, or pain. Emotional responses ranged from fear and humiliation to anger and thoughts of revenge. Some women blamed themselves for the attack, and searched their memories for ways in which they might have avoided the attack.

Burgess and Holmstrom report that the length of the acute phase varied among the women, and they suggest that the speed of recovery depends on such factors as ego strength, social support, and the treatment received as a victim. In the long-term reorganization or coping phase, 44 of the 92 victims changed their place of residence. Many of the women switched their telephone numbers, visited family or friends for emotional support, and took trips to other states or countries. Twenty-nine women reported upsetting dreams or nightmares about rape. In addition, some women developed "traumatophobia"—a phobic reaction to a traumatic situation that has also been described among war victims. For example, women assaulted while at home were afraid of remaining home, while women attacked outdoors felt safe only while at home. Most women were afraid to be alone, and many experienced some difficulty in resuming sexual relations with boyfriends or husbands.

In this study, rape was viewed as a life-threatening event that is expected to have traumatic effects on the victim. Crisis counseling was directed at speeding recovery by helping the women to cope with what had taken place. The authors report that women showing a "silent rape reaction"—that is, victims denying the attack or refusing to talk about it—carry a psychological burden that impedes recovery. Therefore, it is important that the counselor actively initiate discussion and that clinicians be sensitive to cues that an unreported rape has occurred.

Homosexual rape. The limited information we have on homosexual rape comes from male prison populations. It has been estimated that between 40 and 50 percent of imprisoned males will have some homosexual contacts (Gagnon and Simon, 1973); for most of these men, such contacts are not typical of their sexual behavior outside of the prison environment. Several explanations have been proposed for this change in behavior. First, it has been suggested that the pressure of sexual needs, combined with the absence of women, leads imprisoned men to select male sexual partners. However, this does not explain why imprisoned men avoid masturbation, a simpler and less threatening means of sexual release. Homosexual contacts in prison serve a variety of functions besides the purely sexual; they may be a means of developing emotional relationships, asserting and affirming masculinity, maintaining a hierarchy of power among the prisoners, or defying prison authorities. Typically, a clear division exists between male and female roles in these homosexual contacts—the "jocker" assumes the active, male, "inserter" role; the "punk," the passive, female, "insertee" role.

As with heterosexual rape, often some question arises as to when a forcible rape has actually taken place. For instance, young prisoners may be "seduced" by older inmates offering various goods and services—cigarettes, food, the promise of special privileges, or protection from other inmates. The provider of these services expects sexual favors in return, and if the young prisoner refuses, rape may result. Gagnon and Simon (1973) suggest that homosexual rape, like heterosexual rape, may often result from a seduction that has gone wrong.

Another parallel between heterosexual and homosexual rape is that both are extremely underreported crimes. One study of sexual assault in the Philadelphia prison system (Davis, 1970) estimates that of 2,000 assaults that occurred, only 96 were actually reported to the prison authorities. Victims hesitated to report rapes because they were afraid of retaliation from other prisoners; generally, the prison authorities discouraged complaints and were slow to act on them. Sexual aggressors tended to be older, taller, and heavier than their victims; however, both victims and aggressors were younger than the average inmate. Typically, victims looked young for their age and tended to be less athletic and more attractive than their aggressors. In many of the rapes, several aggressors attacked a single victim. Finally, aggressors tended to have been charged with crimes that were more serious and more violent than those committed by their victims.

Davis draws several conclusions from this study. First, he suggests that the majority of sexual aggressors do not view their behavior as homosexual—they continue to define themselves as male as long as they assume the active, aggressive male role. Second, the primary motive for homosexual rape is not the need for sexual release; rather, it is a need to conquer and degrade the victim. Third, sexual assault is the only means for men who have failed in traditional avenues to success to assert their masculinity and power in an environment that denies them all other opportunities to do so.

CHILD MOLESTATION (PEDOPHILIA)

The child molester is generally categorized as a *pedophile*—literally, a lover of children. Sexual contact with children is defined as a crime because a child has not reached the legal, or statutory, age of consent. However, when the victim is an adolescent girl or boy, the offender is usually charged with statutory rape or "impairing the morals of a minor." Thus the term "pedophilia" is most commonly applied when the victim is under 13 years of age.

Child molestation includes a wide range of behaviors. The nature of the sexual contact may vary from obscene language and casual touching to actual coitus with a young girl or homosexual acts with a young boy. The age of

Child molestation may involve such acts as casual touching of a young child by an adult. *(Leonard Speir 1979)*

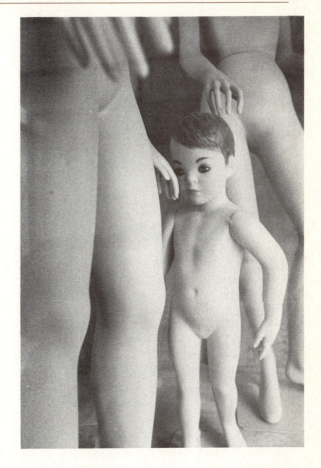

the offender varies, as does the age and gender of the victim. The term *hebephilia* is used when the victim is a young adolescent beyond puberty. Homosexual hebephilia — that is, sexual contact with a boy in his early teens — is a form of pedophilia with special significance. Among the ancient Greeks, "boy-love" was recognized as a unique social institution: "Fathers paid little attention to their own male children but instead left their upbringing to an adult male whose relationship as lover of the son was a 'union far closer' than what bound parents to children. Public opinion, and in some cases even the law, held the lover morally responsible for the development of his beloved. Pederasty came to be considered the most beautiful, the most perfect form of education" (Bullough, 1976, p. 109). In contrast, our own society severely condemns such forms of behavior.

We know little about the incidence of child molestation, and it is likely that incarcerated pedophiles are only a small proportion of the total number of men committing such offenses. Several reasons explain why acts of child molestation are likely to go unreported. First, a child's understanding of what is sexual is very different from the adult view. Thus, the child may be unsure that improper behavior has actually taken place. The very young child, in particular, will have some difficulty in distinguishing purely affectionate behavior from a sexual approach. When the child recognizes an improper advance, it is generally because the act is seen as immodest, frightening, or anxiety-provoking, not as sexual. Improper behavior on the part of strangers is more likely to be reported, since most children are

taught to be suspicious of unknown adults; sexual advances from family or friends are more confusing to the child and are probably reported less often. Second, even when children do recognize an improper advance, they do not always tell their parents or other adults about it. If open lines of communication exist between child and parent, the event may be reported; but if the child fears parental reaction, the information may be kept private.

Finally, if a child does report sexual advances to parents, the parents must decide whether to report these charges to the police. Several considerations enter into this decision. There is a natural hesitancy to expose the child to the stress of legal proceedings. Often, the unsubstantiated testimony of a young child is not legally acceptable—that is, an adult witness must be found. As an alternative to bringing the child to court, Israel and several other countries employ specially trained professionals to take testimony from the child. In addition, the parents of a molested child, like the rape victim, must consider the chances that the offender will actually be caught and imprisoned. Realistically, the chances are quite low, and parents often decide that protection of their children from courtroom procedures is more important than imprisoning the offender.

When a child molester is convicted, he is typically referred to either a psychiatric or a correctional facility. However, first offenders are often given a probationary sentence lasting from 1 to 5 years; during this time, the offender is expected to attend some form of "pretrial intervention" program of psychiatric rehabilitation. The repetitive offender is more likely to be sent to a prison with no psychiatric services, although a few states, such as New Jersey, have recently instituted special sex offender programs for rehabilitation of the repetitive child molester (Vuocolo, 1969).

The child molester. A major Canadian study (Mohr *et al.*, 1964) provides us with some insight into the kinds of individuals convicted for child molestation. The researchers reviewed data collected in several studies in the United States and Canada, and summarized their results as follows:

Child molesters tend to fall into three distinct age groups: (1) the adolescent pedophile, who may be only a few years older than his victim; (2) the middle-aged pedophile, constituting the largest group; and (3) the aged pedophile, who is often senile and a first offender. The middle-aged group shows the most serious marital and social-adjustment problems.

Child molesters are similar to the general population in intelligence and educational levels.

Between 15 and 30 percent of offenders are related to their victims.

Pedophiles do not differ from the general population in terms of occupation, geographic location, race, religion, family size, birth order, or marital status. However, pedophiles do tend to marry later and to report severe marital problems.

The majority of child molesters seek immature forms of sexual gratification, such as looking at or touching the genitals without intercourse or stimulation to orgasm.

Some confusion exists about the mental status of the child molester. While all child molesters are placed in the psychiatric category of pedophilia, there may be considerable variability in their mental health and social and sexual adjustment. According to Paul Gebhard and his associates, most child molesters do not present any gross pathology—that is, they are not more likely than most people to be psychotic or mentally defective (Gebhard *et al.*, 1965). Generally, molesters were diagnosed as having some form of personality disturbance—such as immaturity, inadequacy, or delinquency. The pedophile is often viewed as a man who uses children as sexual objects because he is afraid of, or anxious with, adult females. Such a man may have considerable nonsexual concern and liking for children but find that in certain situations he is unable to control his sexual impulses.

The pedophilia victim. Pedophiles have been classified as heterosexual, homosexual, or undifferentiated—that is, choosing as their sexual object only girls, only boys, or children of either gender. According to one study (Mohr *et al.*, 1964), heterosexual pedophiles are most likely to molest a girl between the ages of 8 and 11; homosexual pedophiles select boys between 12 and 15, the age when puberty is taking place. Undifferentiated pedophiles, who seem to be the smallest group of child molesters, tend to select the youngest victims—boys and girls between the ages of 4 and 7. In addition, an inverse relationship is apparent between the age of the victim and the age of the offender—the older the offender, the younger the victim. Finally, contrary to the popular stereotype of the "unknown assailant," the majority of child molesters are known to their victims. The child molester is frequently a relative, neighbor, or casual acquaintance.

It is difficult to draw any firm conclusions about the effect of child molestation on the victim. With the exception of cases involving violence or force, which are fortunately rare, the damage to the child is thought to depend primarily on his or her emotional status and feeling of security (Mohr *et al.*, 1964). Some children may even respond positively to a mild sexual contact with a familiar adult who provides them with attention and affection. The child is likely to be disturbed by such a contact to the extent that he or she has been taught that it is "wrong" or "bad." It has been suggested that it is not the sexual contact per se, but its aftermath, that is most likely to harm the child. Children may be traumatized by their parents' strong emotional reactions to the event and by the need to tell their story to the police and legal authorities.

INCEST

Perhaps the only universal sexual taboo is the prohibition against incest. Ford and Beach found that all of the 190 cultures they surveyed forbade sexual relations between parent and child. They believe that this taboo is of a psychosocial nature: "Regulations against incest serve to protect the integrity and effectiveness of the nuclear family group" (1951, p. 112). The family could not easily survive the jealousies and stresses that might result from

incest. In addition, the prohibition serves the important biological function of avoiding the congenital deformities that might result from an incestuous conception. Incest taboos have been observed even among nonhuman species such as the chimpanzee (Jensen, 1973).

Legal definitions of incest vary with respect to the degree of familial proximity tolerated by the law. Certain primitive cultures place restrictions on marriage even to very distant relatives, and even to in-laws of relatives. Most authorities agree that incest between siblings occurs more frequently than parent-child incest. However, legal prosecutions are most often for father-daughter incest; remarkably few cases of mother-son incest are reported.

The concept of the "typical incest family" is changing rapidly. Early studies showed a high proportion of incest offenders coming from poor families in rural areas (Gebhard *et al.*, 1965), leading to the stereotype of the uneducated, backwoods incest family. However, a recently established incest treatment program established in Santa Clara County, California, has received the bulk of its cases from middle-class suburban neighborhoods. Thus it seems that incest can occur at all levels of society. Further, the number of cases referred to this program far exceeds the usual estimate of incidence, which is between 1 and 1.5 cases per million population. The public's awareness of incest is clearly limited by underreporting of the offense.

Before the establishment of the Santa Clara program, an incest conviction usually resulted in the father receiving a long prison sentence, the child being removed from her family and placed in a state shelter, and the wife and remaining children being left to cope with the enormous emotional and financial problems. Currently, the incest offender in Santa Clara County is often given a 6-month sentence in an open institution—that is, he is allowed to work in the community by day, but spends nights and weekends in the treatment program. At the same time, his wife and family are given special counseling and support from families who have lived through similar experiences. While Santa Clara's approach seems both humane and sensible, it is the only program of its type; incest offenders arrested outside of Santa Clara County are usually offered no alternative to either long-term probation or incarceration.

Incest may occur as a short-lived and relatively uncomplicated sexual relationship between two family members. For example, preadolescent siblings often engage in sexual play that terminates naturally, as they begin to transfer their sexual interests outside of the family. If the incest is discovered, parents are likely to react quite strongly, although they will probably not involve the law. However, when incest between a father and daughter is discovered, the consequences are usually more serious. Longstanding sexual relationships between fathers and daughters are often associated with major family disruption once the relationship becomes known to the mother.

While incest offenders seem to come from all economic, racial, and environmental groups, one study (Ferracuti, 1972) lists several predisposing factors they often have in common: the real or psychological absence of the mother from the family, alcoholism, the father's depression, and provocation or toleration by the daughter. The incest offender usually has no prior criminal record. Often, the relationship between husband and wife is poor and the couple have little sexual contact; in such cases, the husband may turn to his daughter for support or rationalize his behavior in terms of the daughter's "seductiveness."

The "Nuisance" Offenses:
Voyeurism, Exhibitionism, and Transvestism

Voyeurism, exhibitionism, and transvestism are typically labeled minor sex offenses because they do not involve physical or sexual contact with a victim. However, these nuisance offenses do violate social norms and laws regulating public decency. Exhibitionism, for instance, is usually prosecuted under the laws covering indecent exposure. Voyeurs are sometimes arrested for trespassing or burglary when their offense is committed on private property. Laws against disturbing the peace may also be invoked against the voyeur or the exhibitionist.

The courts tend to view the nuisance offenses as evidence of psychiatric disturbance or delinquency and therefore will often refer the first-time offender to a specialist for treatment. In the case of repeated offenders, however, custodial detention in either a correctional or a psychiatric facility may be imposed. The decision as to whether to impose a punitive or a rehabilitative sentence on the nuisance offender may depend on whether the judge views the offense as a criminal or a psychiatric problem. This arbitrary element in the judicial process has led to a call for more rational and comprehensive administrative procedures for dealing with minor sex offenders (Brecher, 1978).

How do we distinguish the exhibitionist, voyeur, and transvestite from the individual who simply enjoys "showing," "looking," and "dressing up"? The behaviors demonstrated by the nuisance offenders have some parallels in conventional life—for instance, men have the opportunity to undress and view others who are undressed at "nude beaches" or nudist camps. However, the true nuisance offender does not typically restrict himself to these socially acceptable occasions. His conduct is considered to be *compulsive* rather than elective — that is, he is unable to control his urge to expose himself, watch others, or cross-dress, and will perform these behaviors even in settings that are likely to lead to arrest.

VOYEURISM

Voyeurism can be defined in several ways. The term can be applied to someone who has no significant psychiatric or criminal problems but is sexually stimulated by viewing others. Sagarin (1974) has argued that modern media technology has created a "nation of voyeurs" — through newspapers, magazines, and books, we can learn about the sexual secrets of the famous. Sagarin prefers the term "peeper"

or "Peeping Tom" to describe the pathological voyeur observing others in a way that invades their privacy. The origin of the phrase "Peeping Tom" is a thirteenth-century English legend about the famous bareback ride of Lady Godiva: in one version of the legend, Lady Godiva rode naked through the market of Coventry to protest against unreasonable taxation. Out of respect for her, most citizens of the town remained behind locked doors; however, one young man, named Tom, could not resist temptation and peeped out from behind the shutters. He is said to have been struck blind for his crime (Bullough, 1976).

The peeper may be distinguished from the "normal voyeur" in several ways. He is compulsive in his voyeuristic behavior, peeps regularly, and may take considerable risks in doing so. Typically, he gains sexual satisfaction only from the act of looking and will not attempt closer contact with his victim. Finally, the peeper's excitement depends, to some extent, on whether the scene he is viewing is for-

Sexual orgy in the late 18th century. At the right, a voyeur secretly observes homosexual intercourse. (*Collection Gérhard Nordmann.*)

Case Study of a Peeping Tom

William V. is a 28-year-old computer programmer who currently lives alone. He grew up in a rural area within a conservative family with strong religious values. He has two younger brothers and an older sister. William began to masturbate at age 15; his first masturbatory experience took place while he watched his sister urinate in an outdoor toilet. Despite considerable feelings of guilt, he continued to masturbate two or three times a week while having voyeuristic fantasies. At the age of 20 he left home to spend 2 years in the navy.

On a summer evening at about 11:30 P.M., William was arrested for climbing a ladder and peeping into the bedroom of a suburban home. Just before this incident he had been drinking heavily at a cocktail lounge featuring a topless dancer. When he had left the lounge at 11:15 P.M. he had intended to return to his home. Feeling lonely and depressed, however, he had begun to drive slowly through a nearby suburban neighborhood, where he noticed a lighted upstairs window. With little premeditation, he had parked his car, erected a ladder he found lying near the house, and climbed up to peep. The householders, who were alerted by the sounds, called the police, and William was arrested. Although this was his first arrest, William had committed similar acts on two previous occasions.

The police referred William's case for immediate and mandatory psychological counseling. William described a lonely and insecure life style to his therapist—6 months before the arrest, he had been rejected in a long-term relationship, and he had not recovered from this emotional rejection. As an unassertive and timid individual, he had responded by withdrawing from social relationships and increasing his use of alcohol. His voyeuristic fantasies, which were

---

bidden—he must see without being seen. For this reason, the peeper will not be satisfied with the sights provided at nudist camps or pornographic movies (Sagarin, 1974; Gebhard et al., 1965).

Conventional wisdom portrays the peeper as an excessively timid individual who would never harm his victim in any way. This may be an accurate description of someone who is never apprehended by the police because he is able to keep his presence hidden from his victim. However, among arrested peepers, researchers have identified a type who is sadistic and aggressive, and may go on to commit burglary, assault, or rape (Yalom, 1960; Gebhard et al., 1965). About one-third of those arrested might be labeled offensive peepers.

What sort of person becomes a peeper? Evidence suggests that voyeurs often have significant interpersonal problems (see the boxed extract). On the basis of research with convicted peepers, Gebhard and his associates concluded that the majority of voyeurs have little heterosexual experience, are shy with females, and have strong feelings of inferiority (1965). Habitual peepers often have sexual performance problems during intercourse, and they avoid watching females who are not strangers. Their voyeuristic behavior is often reinforced by masturbation to orgasm after the peeping incident—that is, some peepers do not masturbate at the time of the offense but will use their memory of the incident as a masturbation fantasy at a later time.

present to begin with, became progressively more urgent as William's self-esteem deteriorated. His arrest had come as a great personal shock, although he recognized that his behavior was both irrational and self-destructive.

William falls clearly into the category of voyeurism associated with inadequate or insecure self-image and interpersonal relationships. Although he was able to perform sexually with a suitable female partner, he experienced considerable guilt over his sexual behavior, particularly masturbation. No evidence showed any more serious aggressive or antisocial tendency. William was helped greatly by counseling methods that focused on increasing his self-esteem and assertiveness, providing sexual information, and promoting self-control. A year after therapy began, he had entered a stable and satisfying relationship with a female partner and had not been involved in any further peeping incidents.

EXHIBITIONISM

The act of exposing the genitals in public can occur in various situations that are not properly defined as exhibitionistic — as in the case of the drunk who urinates on a streetcorner or the man whose zipper comes undone without his knowledge. An act of true *exhibitionism* must meet two important criteria: (1) It must occur in a public place or without the consent of the victim; (2) The offender must *deliberately* expose his genitals, usually with the intention of obtaining sexual stimulation. Although the legal offense of "indecent exposure" might be applied to the drunk or the man with the broken zipper, these are not examples of exhibitionism because the intention of gaining

sexual satisfaction is not present. A relatively high arrest rate exists for exhibitionism, due both to the public nature of the offense and the fact that many exhibitionists continue their compulsive and repetitive patterns of exposure until they are caught (Rosen, 1965). Where the term "peeper" is applied to the arrested voyeur, the word "flasher" is now used to describe the arrested exhibitionist. Exhibitionism accounts for about one-third of all sex offenses.

In 1920, Freud added the following footnote to his *Three Essays on the Theory of Sexuality:*

The compulsion to exhibit . . . is also closely dependent on the castration complex: it is a means of constantly insisting upon the integrity of the subject's own [male] genitals and it reiterates his infantile satisfaction at the absence of a penis in those of women. (p. 23)

In contrast, behavioral scientists have emphasized a major conditioning factor, in which the exhibitionist combines fantasies of exposure with repeated masturbation to orgasm (Evans, 1968). The first act of exposure often occurs accidentally, and subsequent masturbation fantasies about the incident serve as additional reinforcement for the behavior. Neither of these explanations, however, is completely satisfactory in accounting for all cases of exhibitionism.

The majority of incarcerated exhibitionists are *habitual* or compulsive offenders. Research with this group reveals the following characteristics (Mohr *et al.*, 1964):

Among exhibitionists brought to court, about 25 percent have previous convictions for a sex offense. The high rate of recidivism for this offense seems to be related to its compulsive nature.

The highest proportion of convicted exhibitionists are in their mid-twenties. Although they tend to be slightly above average in intelligence, they are often underachievers academically, occupationally, and personally. They do not differ from the general population in their ethnic or religious background.

Little can be learned from the family patterns of exhibitionists. Fathers were absent from the home in about one-third of the cases, but a very close father-son relationship existed in some families.

Although most of the offenders were married, many experienced significant marital or sexual adjustment problems. Exposure was frequently noted just before or after the birth of a child.

The victim is usually a complete stranger, and the exhibitionist rarely seeks further contact. For some offenders, the primary motive is to shock or embarrass the victim; for others, exhibitionism also involves masturbation to orgasm.

Exhibitionism overlaps with pedophilia when the offender exposes himself to a victim who is under the statutory age. Some exhibitionists obtain particular gratification from revealing their genitals to young girls or boys, an offense that is usually deemed by the court system more serious than exposure to an adult. However, young children often do not view exhibitionism as a sexual assault—in fact, they may consider it silly or funny if they are unaware of the angry or outraged response of their parents.

The current behavioral approach to exhibitionism emphasizes the offender's inability to control his urge to expose (Rooth and Marks, 1974). Exhibitionists frequently experience difficulty in situations requiring interpersonal assertiveness and will fall back on the primitive act of exposing the genitals to reaffirm

Females too can be exhibitionistic. A nineteenth century Victorian brothel is illustrated here. *(Gichner Foundation for Cultural Studies)*

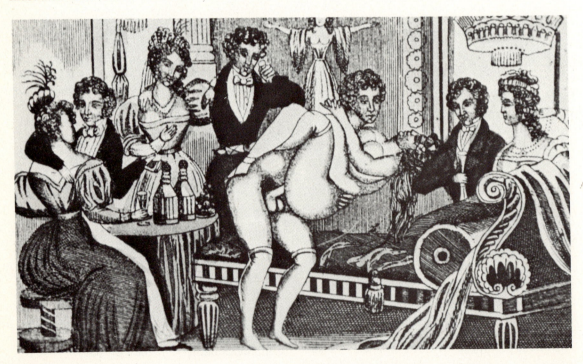

their self-worth or masculinity. The guilt or anxiety produced by the act can lead to a further feeling of inadequacy, thus locking the individual into a vicious cycle of compulsive exhibitionism. Behavioral treatment methods attempt to break this cycle by the development of self-control strategies along with assertiveness training for more effective handling of interpersonal stress. Some exhibitionists join nudist camps or visit nude beaches in order to satisfy their urges in socially acceptable ways.

Can a female be exhibitionistic? We know that females are almost never arrested for this offense, but this might be explained by the social norms of our culture. Consider the following situation: A man walks past a suburban house late at night and stops to watch a woman undressing. If a police officer should pass by, the man would be arrested for peeping. Now, reverse the situation: A woman walking down the street stops to watch a man undressing. The police officer is again more likely to arrest the man, this time on a charge of "flashing." In both cases, the male's behavior is more likely to be seen as offensive. However, we cannot explain all male/female differences in arrest rates for nuisance offenses in terms of leniency toward the female. While the female does have more latitude in the expression of various sexual desires, her socialization usually does not encourage exhibitionism. For one thing, she learns a greater emphasis on modesty and the privacy of sexual contacts than does the male. Further, she rarely sees the exposure of her genitals as an affirmation of her self-worth or identity; instead, she is taught that a more subtle form of exposure—wearing "sexy" clothing—will give her the sexual power and identity a male might get from directly showing his genitals. Moreover, the woman who does desire to expose herself might find an acceptable outlet such as becoming a topless dancer or a stripper, but such opportunities are rare for men.

TRANSVESTISM

Our moral prohibition against cross-dressing, or *transvestism*, comes from the Bible: "No woman shall wear an article of man's clothing, nor shall a man put on woman's dress, for those who do these things are abominable to the Lord" (Deuteronomy 22 : 5). Yet the modern trend toward unisex dressing has blurred many of the distinctions between male and female clothing, and the sight of a woman in a traditionally male outfit is today both common and acceptable. The man who prefers female attire, however, would be wise to stay away from skirts and dresses, although he is permitted to wear shoes with heels, lacy shirts, and clinging sweaters.

Actually, only a very small proportion of transvestites are arrested, since the act of cross-dressing is almost always performed in solitary or at least private settings. Arrest is most likely to occur for the habitual transvestite who develops the desire to pass as a woman in public. When arrested, the transvestite is most usually charged with impersonation—if he is caught in a women's toilet or dressing room—or with creating a public disturbance (Sherwin, 1977). Of the nuisance offenders, transvestites seem to present the least risk to society, and they are rarely sentenced to anything more serious than a fine or probation. We can learn very little about the phenomenon of cross-dressing by studying it as a sex offense, primarily because so few transvestites break the law while pursuing their sexual preferences. Only the most exhibitionistic type of transvestite is likely to fall into the category of sex offender (see the boxed extract).

Case Study of a Transvestite-Exhibitionist

John W. is 45 years old and has been working as a janitor in the same school for the past 17 years. He has been married for 22 years and has two teen-age children. He was referred to the clinic after being arrested and charged for exposing himself in female clothing in a public parking lot. Although this was his first formal arrest, he had been apprehended by the police twice during the previous year. Nine months before this last incident, he had undergone a 3-month period of insight-oriented therapy, with no apparent reduction in his cross-dressing or exposure.

The client lost his mother at 12 years of age. Prior to her death, he recalls playing frequently with her underclothing. Tactile sensations generated by the silken cloth produced erections and ultimately ejaculation through masturbation. By the onset of puberty, John was wearing his mother's clothing whenever the opportunity presented itself. Throughout adolescence he masturbated frequently, using available female garments in a fetishistic manner. During his freshman year in college, his father died, and soon thereafter John joined the service. At this time he met his future wife, and later they were married. She was completely unaware of his sexual proclivities at the time of the wedding.

When his wife learned of his cross-dressing (3 years ago), she was morally outraged and demanded that he never again do it in their house. In response, John began cross-dressing in the

This case study draws our attention to three important developmental stages leading to John's arrest. (1) By combining the tactile experiences of his mother's lingerie with the reinforcement of masturbation, he developed a *fetish* for female clothing. (2) Later, in adolescence, his masturbation script evolved to include the visual aspects of dressing up and then watching himself as he masturbated. (3) As his sexual relationship with his wife deteriorated, he progressed to a public, exhibitionistic phase. Although his cross-dressing was accompanied in each phase by masturbation, the specific sexual stimulus, or "trigger," changed considerably over time.

Most transvestites restrict their dressing-up activities to a limited part of their lives. From his clinical studies with transvestites. John Money concludes that "the transvestite's compulsion is a fetishistic addiction to the clothes of the other sex, and to impersonating the other sex, but on an episodic, not a full-time basis" (1977, p. 924). Money notes that for a small number of adolescent transvestites, cross-dressing may be a precursor to transsexualism—that is, such men may go on to impersonate the female on a full-time basis and request sex-change surgery. Although some females also request surgery in order to live the life of a male, such women do not seem to develop a particularly fetishistic attraction to men's clothing. We should emphasize that the vast majority of transvestites—those who periodically cross-dress—are not transsexuals. The transsexual desires to make a permanent and total gender change.

In its simplest form, transvestism is part of a masturbation script in which female clothing

back seat of his car. At first he chose to do this in deserted parking lots. As time progressed, however, he began exposing himself to passing men. It should be stressed that he did not intend to have sexual contact with any of these men but was sexually stimulated by the act of exposure in the female clothing.

An important facet of the background information was the marital and sexual relationship between John and his wife. She had been anorgasmic throughout their marriage. Although they had maintained regular sexual contact, the level of sexual satisfaction was consistently low. At times, John appeared to be compensating for inadequate sexual relations by frequent masturbation with transvestite fantasies, cross-dressing, and periodic exposure. His wife appeared to have no alternative outlets. Neither had engaged in extramarital relations.

The case is of interest as a rare example of the development of both transvestism and exhibitionism in an individual who is clearly neither transsexual nor homosexual. The case further demonstrates the complex but crucial relationship between marital sexual adjustment and the incidence of cross-dressing and subsequent exposure.

Source: Adapted from R. Rosen and S. Kopel, "The Use of Penile Plethysmography and Biofeedback in the Treatment of a Transvestite-Exhibitionist," *Journal of Consulting and Clinical Psychology,* Vol. 5, No. 45 (1977), pp. 908–916.

is used as a sexual stimulus. More complex social reinforcements come into play for female impersonators who belong to organized groups and attend special transvestite activities. Finally, for the homosexual transvestite, or "drag queen," cross-dressing may be a means of soliciting sexual attention from other men. When transvestites were interviewed about the reasons for their behavior, they gave a variety of explanations:

Perhaps it's all hormonal. I don't know—so many people say that it's all in the blood. Maybe I inherited it. It's part of me—it comes and goes—might as well live with it.

Everyone said it started in childhood. Little kids don't know what they're doing. They're just having fun. It kind of catches on and you can't stop. It doesn't hurt anyone.

Most transvestites start cross-dressing by having

been dressed as a girl for disciplinary purposes, or by a mother who wanted a girl or by sisters wanting playmates.
(Quoted in Feinbloom, 1976, p. 95)

Authorities generally agree that the transvestite has a special relationship with his mother, and often the cross-dressing behavior is reinforced—intentionally or unintentionally—by the mother. According to the psychoanalytic view, the transvestite does not have an adequate identification with his father.

Most forms of psychotherapy seem to have little or no effect on the *desire* to cross-dress, although some success has been reported in helping the transvestite to control the public aspects of his behavior. Transvestism appears to be a deeply ingrained pattern of sexual behavior, originating either before or during puberty. Some adult transvestites come to

In recent years, many tranvestites have "come out," and transvestite bars and clubs are increasingly common in our large cities.
(© Charles Gatewood)

terms with the pattern and gain social support for their activity by joining transvestite groups—much like the homosexual person who joins a gay community group. Such subcultures tend to stabilize the activities of the "deviant" group, aid the members in accepting their own behavior, and work to remove the stigma placed on the group by the wider society (Plummer, 1975). In contrast, the transvestite who cannot confide to a sympathetic listener about his behavior may experience intense guilt, shame, and a lack of self-esteem.

Prostitution

There is some question about whether the selling of sex should be considered a legal offense or simply an alternative expression of human sexuality. Those who believe that prostitution should be legalized argue that the private sexual behavior of consenting adults has no place in our legal codes. Prostitution has been described as a "victimless crime," since the buyer and seller of sexual services are voluntary participants in a commercial transaction. Opposing these views are individuals who believe that prostitution has harmful effects on society at large. They argue that such acts lower moral standards, provoke criminal sexual behavior, and undermine social structures such as the family.

FEMALE PROSTITUTION

Traditionally, prostitution has been viewed as the selling of sex in an overt and straightforward fashion: the stated contract between customer and prostitute is the exchange of money for sexual services. Typically, the prostitute is female and the customer is male, although there is increasing recognition of the male prostitute who provides sexual services for male and, less frequently, female customers. The business of prostitution is assumed to operate in accordance with the economic law of supply and demand—as long as customers are willing to pay, prostitutes will be willing to provide their services.

Actually, prostitution is far more complex than a simple business transaction; it is intimately enmeshed with the social values of the culture in which it takes place. The career and status of the prostitute has varied markedly in different societies and at different times in history. The geishas of Japan, the courtesans of the Renaissance, and the hetaerae of ancient Greece often were granted considerably more independence and freedom than married women. Many cultures have encouraged "sacred" (religious) prostitution—for example, in the temples of ancient Greece young girls often acted as prostitutes, with the proceeds of their work going to maintain the religious establishment. The Greek historian Herodotus related that in the fifth century B.C., all Babylonian women were expected to prostitute themselves once and donate their earnings to the temple. After this single occasion, they were expected to resume their chaste home life. Religious prostitutes in Egypt and India were often accorded some status and were trained to provide entertainment—music and dancing—as well as sexual services.

Prostitutes, like other members of society, have been accorded status depending upon their social background, personal skills, and professional success. Whereas the hetaerae were typically the respected companions of upper-class men; the Greek prostitute, working in the brothels that serviced the lower class-

es, had little status or independence. Similarly, the status of the prostitute today varies depending on her position in a hierarchy that ranges from the streetwalker to the call girl. The successful call girl works only for a select group of clients, is highly paid, and is relatively safe from the police. In contrast, the streetwalker actively solicits unknown customers or is available to their invitation, receives less money for her services, and may have to cope with repeated arrests. In the middle of this hierarchy are prostitutes who work in brothels or massage parlors and who serve a diverse clientele.

The legal status of prostitution is varied and often unclear. In the United States, prostitution is legal only in certain parts of Nevada; and there, it is subject to state regulation. The arrested prostitute is usually charged with soliciting, that is, making an active proposition to exchange money for sexual services. In order to avoid such charges, many prostitutes use vaguely worded invitations and are careful not to ask for money explicitly. The prostitute's folklore also has it that a police officer who has disrobed while with the prostitute cannot then make a valid arrest; thus many prostitutes will take note of a client's distinguishing physical characteristics. However, these precautions do not necessarily protect the prostitute from arrest, since enforcement of laws against solicitation are often at the discretion of the police.

Police crackdowns are rarely intended to eliminate prostitution completely. The police are aware that the vast majority of arrests result in little more than a fine or a night in jail, with the woman free to resume her trade the next day. They are most likely to intervene when prostitution becomes too public or moves into a neighborhood where residents will make a strong complaint. The result of such arrests may simply be to force prostitutes to move to another area.

Although the laws against solicitation apply to both solicitor and solicited, it is almost always the prostitute and not her customer who is arrested. Organized groups of prostitutes in cities such as San Francisco and New York have begun to protest this discriminatory treatment at the hands of the law. They claim that if prostitution is a crime, then the males soliciting their services should share the responsibility for it. It may well be that the arrest of a customer, who wants to protect his reputation, would be more effective in eliminating prostitution than the "revolving door" arrest of the prostitute.

The moral status of the prostitute is even more vague than her legal status. Gagnon and Simon (1973) suggest that most of our notions about prostitution are derived from the attitudes of the upper class in Victorian England. The Victorians placed an extremely high value on the sexual "virtue" of women, insisted on virginity at marriage, and did not believe that the "good" woman had any interest in sex other than as a means of bearing children. At the same time, they thought that men had a strong sexual nature and sexual needs that must be satisfied. Since the Victorians disapproved of masturbation as a means of sexual release, they turned to prostitutes. Within this system of beliefs, "the function of the bad women was to protect the virtue of those who were good" (Gagnon and Simon, 1973, p. 221). The typical "bad woman" was young and from the lower classes—she may have been seduced or coerced into prostitution, or driven to it because of extreme poverty. It was estimated that in the London of the 1850s, one house in every sixty was a brothel, and one women in every sixteen a prostitute (Pearson, 1972). In their efforts to protect the "virtuous" woman from their sexual needs, the men of Victorian England supported one of the most extensive networks of prostitution in history.

This Victorian legacy is still with us today.

The stigma of prostitution is still almost entirely on the woman—we stereotype her as "immoral," "shameful," or in the vocabulary of modern psychiatry, "mentally disturbed." At the same time, the "fallen woman" is a subject of powerful mystery and intrigue; according to Simone de Beauvoir, "she incarnates the Femininity that masculine society has not sanctified and that remains charged with harmful powers. . . . Since she is a kind of pariah, living at the margin of a hypocritically moral world, we can also regard the 'fille perdue' as the invalidator of all the official virtues" (1974, p. 219). Our conflicting views of the status of the prostitute do not extend to her client—he is simply seen as a normal man satisfying his natural sexual needs.

The client. Kinsey reported that while 69 percent of adult males had some experience with prostitutes, only 15 or 20 percent had such experiences more than a few times per year (Kinsey *et al.*, 1948). Single men visit prostitutes more frequently than the married, and men from lower educational and socioeconomic levels do so more frequently than educated and middle-class men. Kinsey stated that the number of men that had ever visited a prostitute had not changed between the two world wars; however, the frequency of contacts—that is, the number of times a prostitute is visited—had decreased by as much as one-half.

Hunt (1974) reported that this trend had continued into the 1970s and suggests that these changes are related to the emancipation of women. In his view, as women more readily consent to premarital and extramarital intercourse, men have less need of prostitutes. Further, the once common ritual of a group of male friends having an "outing" at a brothel has largely disappeared from our culture.

Even though contacts with prostitutes have declined among the general population, they

Election Night. *1954 Jack Levine. (The Museum of Modern Art. Gift of Joseph Hirshorn)*

still play a substantial role in the sexual lives of some men. Thus we might ask why men continue to visit prostitutes. Martha Stein (1977) interviewed 64 call-girl prostitutes in New York City and concluded that the prostitutes served a variety of symbolic and fantasy functions for her client. The encounter between prostitute and client is a "scene" in which both participants may play certain roles: opportunist/hooker, adventurer/playmate, lover/romantic partner, slave/dominatrix, friend/confidante. In Stein's analysis, the prostitute provides far more than a simple sexual service. For instance, some men demand a form of emotional relationship, others require sexual education or "therapy," and most customers expect sexual imaginativeness, variety, and enthusiasm. These men tend to be middle-aged, professional, or in

business, and many have no other sexual outlets. Thus Stein concludes that prostitution may often operate as an "underground sexual health service" that aids men with various sexual and emotional needs. However, we should recall that she is describing the service provided by the relatively elite call girl; possibly the streetwalker provides a less complex set of services.

The prostitute: offender or victim? It seems likely that if a victim exists in the transaction that constitutes prostitution, it is the prostitute. She is the object of both police scrutiny and social stigma. Further, she may be victimized by a large number of people peripheral to her work—the pimp, the brothel or hotel owner, the bartender or cabdriver who *(continued on page 464)*

(continued on page 464)

Roberta Victor: Profile of a Prostitute

You never used your own name in hustling. I used a different name practically every week. If you got busted, it was more difficult for them to find out who you really were. The role one plays when hustling has nothing to do with who you are. It's only fitting and proper you take another name.

The favors I granted were not always sexual. When I was a call girl, men were not paying for sex. They were paying for something else. They were either paying to act out a fantasy or they were paying for companionship or they were paying to be seen with a well-dressed young woman. Or they were paying for somebody to listen to them. They were paying for a *lot* of things. Some men were paying for sex that *they* felt was deviant. They were paying so that nobody would accuse them of being perverted or dirty or nasty. A large proportion of these guys asked things that were not at all deviant. Many of them wanted oral sex. They felt they couldn't ask their wives or girl friends because they'd be repulsed. Many of them wanted somebody to talk dirty to them. Every good call girl in New York used to share her book and we all knew the same tricks.

Roberta begins her self-description with the characteristic cynicism of the prostitution subculture. Prostitutes invariably develop a cynical sense of superiority over their clients, the "Johns," which in time they generalize to most or all of humanity.

I was about fifteen, going on sixteen. I was sitting in a coffee shop in the Village, and a friend of mine came by. She said; "I've got a cab waiting. Hurry up. You can make fifty dollars in twenty minutes." Looking back, I wonder why I was so willing to run out of the coffee shop, get in a cab, and turn a trick. It wasn't traumatic because my training had been in how to be a hustler anyway.

I learned it from the society around me, just as a woman. We're taught how to hustle, how to attract, hold a man, and give sexual favors in return. The language that you hear all the time "Don't sell yourself cheap." "Hold out for the highest bidder." "Is it proper to kiss a man good night on the first date?" The implication is it may not be proper on the first date, but if he takes you out to dinner on the second date, it's proper. If he brings you a bottle of perfume on the third date, you should let him touch you above the waist. And go on from there. It's a marketplace transaction.

Somehow I managed to absorb that when I was quite young. So it wasn't even a moment of truth when this woman came into the coffee shop and said; "Come on." I was back in twenty-five mintues and I felt no guilt.

Roberta goes on to describe her childhood. As an overweight, but precociously intelligent and sensitive child, she sought appreciation and attention from men by offering her body as a sexual reward. Using sex as a form of manipulation fitted in naturally with her prostitution life style:

The call girl ethic is very strong. You were the lowest of the low if you allowed yourself to feel anything with a trick. The bed puts you on their level. The way you maintain your integrity is by acting all the way through. It's not too far removed from what most American women do — which is to put on a big smile and act.

It was a tremendous kick. Here I was doing absolutely nothing, *feeling* nothing, and in twenty minutes I was going to walk out with fifty dollars for twenty minutes' work? Folks work for eight dollars take-home pay. I worked twenty minutes for fifty dollars clear, no taxes, nothing! I was still in school, I was smoking grass, I was shooting heroin, I wasn't hooked yet, and I had money. It was terrific.

At the beginning I was very excited. But in order to continue I had to turn myself off. I had to disassociate who I was from what I was doing.

It's a process of numbing yourself. I couldn't associate with people who were not in the life—either the drug life or the hustling life. I found I couldn't turn myself back on when I finished working. When I turned myself off, I was numb —emotionally, sexually numb.

Almost all the call girls I knew were involved in drugs. The fast life, the night hours. At after-hours clubs, if you're not a big drinker, you usually find somebody who has cocaine, 'cause that's the big drug in those places. You wake up at noon, there's not very much to do till nine or ten that night. Everybody else is at work, so you shoot heroin. After a while the work became a means of supplying drugs, rather than drugs being something we took when we were bored.

The process of deterioration began for Roberta with her increasing dependence on drugs. As her physical attractiveness declined she began to work off the streets and to face the inevitable risks of this lower echelon of the prostitution world.

For the first time I ran the risk of being busted. I was never arrested as a call girl. Every once in a while a cop would get hold of somebody's book. They would call one of the girls and say, "I'm a friend of so-and-so's." They would try to trap them. I never took calls from people I didn't know. But on the streets, how do you know who you're gonna pick up?

I never approached anybody on the street. That was the ultimate risk. Even if he weren't a cop, he could be some kind of supersquare, who would call a cop. I was trapped by cops several times.

I once really got trapped. It was about midnight and a guy came down the street. He said he was a postal worker who just got off the shift. He told me how much money he had and what he wanted. I took him to my room. The cop isn't supposed to undress. If you can describe the color of his shorts, it's an invalid arrest. Not only did he show me the color of his shorts, he went to bed with me. Then he pulled a badge and a gun and busted me.

As a result of her arrest and subsequent conviction, Roberta served a prison sentence of almost 4 years. After her release, she inevitably went back to the world of prostitution and heroin:

You become your job. I became what I did. I became a hustler. I became cold, I became hard, I became turned off. I became numb. Even when I wasn't hustling, I was a hustler. I don't think it's terribly different from somebody who works on the assembly line forty hours a week and comes home cut off, numb, dehumanized. People aren't built to switch on and off like a water faucet.

Source: From Studs Terkel, *Working* (New York: Avon Books, 1972), pp. 91–103.

The primary motivation for most prostitutes is economic—for some women, prostitution may seem to be their only means of survival. (*Charles Gatewood*)

The majority of prostitutes seem to be recruited from among the poor, minority groups, or females labeled delinquent by the police and social agencies. The appeal of prostitution as a profession is largely economic, since few of these women could earn a comparable amount of money in a "straight" job. However, prostitutes are often drawn from more conventional populations—such as housewives or college students who need extra income.

Perhaps the heaviest toll exacted from the prostitute is emotional; the woman who has learned to view sex as a commercial transaction may have a difficult time breaking this connection in her personal life. (See the boxed extract.) Personal accounts of some prostitutes reveal that they develop an emotional numbness or a disdain or dislike for their customers, in order to protect themselves from their work situation.

MALE PROSTITUTION

The incidence of male prostitution serving a female clientele seems to be relatively rare. When such contacts exist, they usually seem to parallel the relationship of a man who supports a "mistress"—that is, a woman will provide financial rewards to a male who provides her with both sexual services and some form of companionship. But, the majority of male prostitutes work for male customers.

Although the male prostitute who performs homosexual services may actually be homosexual, available research indicates that he is far more likely to be heterosexual in orientation. In fact, the male prostitute's success as a

sends her customers. She tends to become part of a subculture of prostitutes even when her working hours are over, since she feels, justifiably, that only another prostitute can share and understand her work experiences. As the prostitute becomes more isolated from conventional society, it is increasingly difficult for her to quit the prostitute life style for a traditional job. In this regard, it is interesting to note that in Denmark the sale of sexual services is not prohibited as long as the woman also has *another* occupation; the intent of this law is to maintain the prostitute's ties to the conventional world (Gagnon and Simon, 1973).

"hustler" often depends on his ability to present himself as exclusively heterosexual (Gagnon and Simon, 1973). Most male prostitutes do not consider themselves to be homosexual, and the etiquette of the contact between male prostitute and male customer is carefully structured to maintain this self-perception (Hoffman, 1972).

The basic similarity between female and male prostitutes is that both provide some form of sexual service in exchange for money. However, many differences also are evident. The male prostitute is less likely than the female to earn all of his income in this way and tends to work as a prostitute for a shorter span of time (Kinsey *et al.*, 1948). In addition, a basic difference exists in the nature of the sexual interaction. "The female prostitute is paid so that her client can have an orgasm, while in nearly all of the cases the male prostitute is paid for his orgasm" (Gagnon and Simon, 1973, p. 166). In other words, the male prostitute almost always assumes a passive sexual role, and is paid to allow the male client to bring him to orgasm. This places a limitation on the number of contacts the male prostitute can have each day; while the female prostitute can fake sexual arousal and orgasm, the male prostitute who cannot become erect and reach orgasm is not fulfilling his contract with his customer. Interviews with male prostitutes have shown that some can ejaculate as many as five or six times per day (Kinsey *et al.*, 1948). This may be one reason why male prostitutes tend to be young men—the young being more capable of repeated orgasm. In addition, youth

and attractiveness, which are important for success in the conventional world, are also valued by the customer of the male prostitute.

Another difference is in the prostitute-client relationship:

Like prostitution in the heterosexual world, there are elements of erotic degradation in paying for a sexual encounter. However, unlike the heterosexual world where the paying of money degrades the woman—making her into a more erotic object to which anything can be done without consequence—in the homosexual world the payment of money often has the effect of degrading the customer." (Gagnon and Simon, 1973, pp. 167–168)

The importance of the male prostitute's heterosexuality may be related to this symbolic self-degradation on the part of the customer. The more powerful and masculine the prostitute appears, the greater the apparent risk to the customer. In addition, the homosexual customer may experience greater satisfaction from his power to "seduce" a stereotypically masculine prostitute.

The sexual contact between a male prostitute and his customer is usually brief and restricted to fellatio or manual masturbation. In order to maintain his self-image as heterosexual, the male prostitute forbids any form of intimacy with his client and may use heterosexual fantasy in order to reach orgasm. It is likely that he has had no sexual contact with males outside of the prostitute-customer context. He cannot risk even the minimal emotional involvement of some female prostitutes.

Society's Response to the Sex Offender

Throughout most of Western history, society's response to the sexual deviant has been harsh and punitive. A variety of sexual offenses—ranging from adultery and consensual homo-

sexuality to child molestation and rape—have been legally punishable by execution, although this extreme sentence may have been carried out infrequently. In keeping with

Krafft-Ebing's view of the sex offender as genetically defective, little or no attempt at rehabilitation or therapy was attempted. The convicted offender was seen as a "sex fiend" and was properly sentenced to a long prison term for the protection of society.

In some ways, the media continue to reinforce the notion of the sex offender as a fiend, someone unable to live within the moral code of his culture. The media tend to report only the most sensational sex crimes — such as brutal and sadistic assaults on children. The public, understandably horrified by such stories, often responds by attempting to increase the penalties applied to sex offenders. While this punitive approach may be appropriate for the violent sex criminal, we should recall that the vast majority of sex offenders do not physically harm their victims.

In the twentieth century, a growing tendency has been to treat the nonviolent sex offender as a psychiatric rather than a criminal problem. In general, this trend is welcome. Courts are reluctant to imprison nuisance offenders, particularly for a first arrest; probation and referral to a treatment facility seem to be a more humane option than criminalization. Researchers have explored all aspects of the offender's life in an attempt to find "causes" and "cures" for sexual deviance. Much of this work has taken place within the *medical model* — that is, sexual deviance is seen as a disease or illness: it can be treated, as physical illness is treated, once the cause is discovered and an appropriate "medicine" found.

This disease model of sexual deviance is based on the notion that the man who commits a sexual offense is different from the general population. However, this belief does not always jibe with our most recent evidence about the background and life style of the sex offender. Often, the exhibitionist, child molester or rapist is indistinguishable from his law-abiding neighbor, with the single exception of his unacceptable sexual conduct. The non-violent sex offender is subject to the same pressures, anxieties, and insecurities as many other members of this cultural group. According to this view, the sex offender differs from his neighbor only in that he copes with normal frustrations in a socially unacceptable way. Thus attempts at therapy and rehabilitation should focus on providing the offender with social skills, "coping mechanisms," and alternative sexual patterns.

Whether labeled criminal, diseased, or socially deficient, the sex offender has always received special treatment from his society. The act of committing a "sex crime" places him in a different category from the offender whose crime is not of a sexual nature. At times, this distinction between sexual and nonsexual offenses seems reasonable and just — for instance, the man who breaks the laws concerning public decency by exposing his genitals does seem to be a more appropriate candidate for therapy than for prison. At other times, however, the differential response to sexual and nonsexual offenders is more difficult to understand. Consider the offender charged with breaking and entering a private home. If his intention was to take money or other valuables, he will be labeled criminal and may well be sent to prison. If, on the other hand, his intention was to steal a soiled female undergarment, his offense will be considered sexually motivated and he may end up in therapy. He may need some form of therapy, but so may the man who steals more conventional goods.

THE LEGAL RESPONSE

Only a small percentage of the sex offenses ever committed actually result in a criminal conviction. There is a great deal of "fall-out" between these two phases of a sex offense — nonreporting by the victim, lack of follow-up by the police, inability to locate the offender, plea-bargaining (pleading guilty to a lesser charge) by the offender, and finally, a not-guilty verdict by the court. Among offenders who are actually convicted, the specific sentence is usually at the discretion of the court. A judge may decide between incarceration, probation, mandatory treatment, or some combination of these sentences. Typically, the first-time nuisance offender will be treated more leniently than the multiple offender, and violent offenders will receive harsher treatment than those whose crimes were essentially nonviolent.

It is generally agreed that a prison sentence will do nothing in the way of rehabilitation. In fact, it may have the opposite effect—the stigma, humiliation, and frustration of prison life usually increases the difficulty of rehabilitation. Further, the sex offender is frequently placed at the bottom of the prison hierarchy, making him especially susceptible to aggression and sexual abuse.

What are the options to incarceration? According to one study (Brecher, 1978), only about twenty treatment programs in the United States are designed specifically for the sex offender. Most of these programs are small, and only four have been in existence more than 6 years. The twenty programs are located in twelve states; thirty-eight states have no special facilities for treating the sex offender. Some programs are located within an institution—either a prison or a psychiatric hospital; others work with paroled offenders in the community. Although these programs are innovative in their treatment approaches, they are clearly inadequate to deal with the large numbers of sex offenders who pass through the criminal justice system.

THERAPEUTIC RESPONSES

Physical intervention. Two forms of physical intervention are currently applied to the sex offender: surgical and chemical castration. The rationale for these techniques is that the sex offender is pressured into deviant behavior by a powerful and uncontrollable sex drive. Castration, which lowers male hormone levels, is intended to lessen sexual interest and potency. It should be stressed that this extreme form of intervention is rare and is typically limited to violent, repetitive offenders.

Surgical castration involves removal of the testes and produces a permanent lowering of androgen levels. As discussed in Chapter 6, loss of sexual interest and potency after castration is gradual, and some men are capable of intercourse as long as 10 years after surgery. At present, the operation is performed only in certain countries of Northern Europe, particularly Scandinavia. In Denmark, castration is viewed as a voluntary therapeutic technique, and not as a means of punishment. It must be requested by the offender and approved by an attending psychiatrist (Sturup, 1972). However, the sex offender who selects this form of therapy is usually aware that it will end his confinement in a correctional or psychiatric facility, and in this sense, the decision is never purely voluntary.

Although surgical castration of sex offenders is not legal in the United States, the use of androgen-depleting hormones such as Provera is currently under evaluation. Provera is a synthetic steroid that has been used as a "morning-after" birth control pill for women. In men, its effect is a dramatic reduction in testosterone levels. It has also been suggested that androgen-depleting hormones may have a direct effect on the brain cells of the hypothalamus and limbic system (Money, 1970). The male user of Provera typically experiences a decline in sexual interest and potency—the higher the dosage, the more extreme the effect of the drug. When the drug is withdrawn or given in lower dosages, sexual interest and potency gradually return. The erotic apathy caused by the drug may actually be a welcome relief to the offender who has felt driven by his sexual urges; during this phase, some form of psychological counseling is provided. Money (1970) suggests that this type of treatment is likely to be most effective when it coincides with a life crisis caused by sexual behavior, and when the offender and therapist agree that there is no acceptable alternative.

Behavioral approaches. Although insight-oriented techniques and psychoanalysis have been used with the sex offender, these methods are usually too time-consuming and expensive for general use. Behavioral approaches, which focus more directly on the actual sexual behavior than on unconscious motivation, seem to offer a more efficient type of individual therapy. Behavior therapists emphasize the importance of objective evaluation techniques in working with sexual deviance. The measurement of deviant sexual response is viewed as one of the cornerstones of effective treatment, because without objective measurement, it is not possible to assess the therapeutic process (Abel and Blanchard, 1976). Thus, a variety of measurement techniques have been developed, including physiological tests of arousal, and self-report questionnaires. These devices are used at every stage of therapy: to assess the offender's initial sexual preferences, to modify these preferences, and to evaluate the success of therapy.

Behavioral therapists recognize two goals in the treatment of the sex offender: first, to minimize or control arousal to deviant stimuli; second, to enhance arousal to appropriate stimuli. For example, successful treatment of a child molester must include both a decrease in his sexual response to children and an increase in his sexual response to an appropriate adult. This twofold approach is based on the notion that sexual deviance is not caused only by excessive arousal to the "wrong" stimuli; the sex offender may also have problems with the "right" stimuli—that is, he may have deficits in heterosocial skills such as approaching and talking with an adult woman. Within this framework, therapy that eliminates an unacceptable sexual pattern will be successful only if it also substitutes an acceptable and satisfying means of sexual fulfillment.

Another technique commonly used by behavior therapists is *masturbatory reconditioning.* We have discussed the observation that most offenders typically masturbate with fantasies of deviant sexual behavior; the behavior therapist attempts to shape the offender's fantasies in a more socially acceptable direction by means of this reconditioning technique. One of the first reports of the successful use of this technique (Davison, 1968) involved the treatment of a young man with very brutal and sadistic fantasies; the therapist was gradually able to replace his client's fantasies with more acceptable masturbation stimuli (*Playboy* nudes).

Despite the obvious appeal of the behavioral approach—it is both pragmatic and efficient—there are unfortunately very few studies of the effects of treatment over the long term. Our own experience suggests that unless treatment is continued over several months, perhaps even years, the possibility of a relapse always exists (Rosen and Kopel, 1977). Additionally, behavioral treatments might be more appropriate for some offenders than others. Most of these require the active participation of the person being treated, and the treatment is unlikely to succeed with unmotivated, mentally retarded, or psychotic individuals. John Bancroft, a British psychiatrist, has provided the following cautionary note: "Modifying deviant sexual behavior . . . involves considerable commitment for both subject and therapist and should not be undertaken lightly by either" (1974, p. 225).

Summary

The term "sex offender" is most properly applied to someone whose sexual behavior violates the rights of others. Violation may take many forms: it may involve physical assault, as is often the case in rape, or it may involve sexual relations with an individual who is underage and therefore unable to give legal consent. Nuisance offenders, such as exhibitionists, violate social norms of privacy and modesty in sexual matters.

1. The only safe generalization that can be made about the sex offender is that he is male, because the only sex offense for which women are likely to be prosecuted is prostitution, and some argue that prostitution is not a sex offense since there is no complaining victim.

2. The majority of sex offenders never come to the attention of law enforcement authorities. Therefore, research on the personality of sex offenders, which is usually based on prison populations, tends to be biased by the factors determining arrest and conviction. Sex offenders cannot be regarded as unitary, homogeneous groups, and we should take care not to stereotype all rapists or exhibitionists as belonging to a certain social class or personality type.

3. There are many explanations of what motivates the sex offender to commit a sex crime, including masturbatory conditioning, hormones, and social factors. Treatment, which is limited in availability, may take the form of behavior modification, social skills training, or the administration of hormones to curb sexual desire.

4. The victim of the sex offender, like the sex offender, may come from any social class, age group, or personality type. The rape victim, for example, is not necessarily an attractive young woman, nor is the victim of the pedophile necessarily a seductive, coy child. The notion that the victim in some way precipitates the crime has little foundation in fact, and contributes to the myth that it is the victim, and not the offender, who is responsible for the commission of sex crimes.

THIRTEEN

Sex and Health

Overview

For those who have it, physical health is often taken for granted. But for those with health problems or handicaps, nothing may seem as important as good health. The state of our health affects the way we look, the way we feel, and our behavior in both work and play. In regard to sexuality, health problems may have both direct and indirect influences; disease, disability, or drugs can directly alter our physiological capacity for sexual response, or they can act indirectly by affecting our mood and self-image. The link between physical health and emotional well-being, and the effects of both on our sexual lives, is a major theme of this chapter.

Definitions of health, like those of normal-ity, are never absolute—our notions of health are always influenced by cultural expectations and individual values. Among the many lifestyle factors that may be regarded as determinants of health are sensible diet and nutrition, adequate exercise and fresh air, a manageable stress level, moderate consumption of drugs and alcohol, and an absence of chronic disease or disability. While there are few people in our society whose health might be described as ideal, there are even fewer people who are too sick or too disabled to desire and enjoy some form of sexual expression.

Health is a topic of major public concern today. Two of the specific health issues we deal with in this chapter—venereal disease and drug use—have reached into the lives of millions of Americans. Despite enormous government expenditure and the vast resources of the medical establishment, these issues remain controversial, problematic, and clouded by stereotypes and misinformation.

Venereal Disease

We do not like to talk about venereal disease. No other sex-related topic brings such embarrassment, guilt, shame, distress, and confusion as do the "sexual diseases." Indeed, our attitudes toward venereal disease (VD) are the single most important reason why, in the presence of completely effective treatment methods, we are still experiencing an epidemic in the sexually transmitted diseases. We can trace these attitudes to our traditional views of sexuality and illness.

Before technology was developed for the identification of the microorganisms that cause disease, it was not uncommon to think of illness as a punishment for bad or immoral behavior. Nowhere was this view more prevalent than in attitudes to the acquisition of the venereal diseases. Even now, when we are able to pinpoint the precise causes of most types of venereal diseases, we still persist in considering them as punishment for improper sexual activity. Out attitudes toward VD are strongly related to cultural standards of acceptable sexual behavior. In a culture where premarital chastity and marital fidelity are very much the standard, if not the reality, the acquisition of a venereal disease is often seen as proof of sexual misconduct. Indeed, for centuries the possibility of acquiring a venereal disease was thought to be an effective deterrent against sexual "promiscuity." Before the discovery of antibiotics in the 1940s, VD was certainly something to be feared, and it may well have caused some people to think twice about their sexual activity. Nowadays, however, there are effective cures for most types of VD, so that its deterrent value has certainly lessened. In fact, it has been argued that one reason for the latter-day "lapse in sexual standards" is the elimination of that deterrent.

This view, besides being against basic medical ethics, is incorrect. VD is not caused by sexual promiscuity. It is caused by germs. This simple point, long ignored by medical authorities and the public, is crucial to our understanding of and ability to deal with the VD "epidemic." No other group of diseases provides such stigma to the infected individual, nor do we assume that someone with a nonvenereal disease has committed a moral error. Earlier literature—and some that is more current—is filled with references to "promiscuity" in the discussion of VD. Such references do nothing to halt the spread of venereal diseases, and they are likely to be harmful, in that they tend to make these diseases a moral rather than a medical issue.

MYTHS ABOUT VD

In order to obtain a better understanding of VD, it is necessary to take a hard look at the myths and misinformation that are a standard part of our culture.

1. "Nice people don't get VD": Venereal diseases make no distinctions regarding social class, racial or religious background, educational level, marital status, or sexual orientation. Since even "nice" people are likely to have sexual contact, we should all be aware of the signs and symptoms of VD. Of course, multiple sexual partners may in-

crease the chances of acquiring a venereal disease. People who tend to have many sexual partners—such as the young, some segments of the homosexual community, servicemen, and so on—are therefore often at higher risk. Nevertheless, it is possible to acquire these infections within a sexual life style that is relatively conventional. Consider the case of the woman whose husband visits a prostitute while on a business trip and then passes his infection along to his unknowing wife. Or the man who acquires gonorrhea within a monogamous relationship with a woman who does not yet know that she has previously been infected.

Although it seems obvious that all but the completely chaste are susceptible to VD, we have not fully accepted the fact that nice people can and do get venereal diseases. In addition to our moral biases, statistical information has sometimes contributed to this mistaken belief. This statistical information usually comes from the public health service, which is expected to collect data on the number and types of venereal diseases present throughout the United States. For example, estimates of the number of cases of syphilis are derived from the reports of public health clinics, private clinics, and physicians. Although reporting of VD is legally required of all health practi-

tioners, this requirement may not always be met. In fact, it has been estimated that less than half of all cases of the two major venereal diseases, syphilis and gonorrhea, are actually reported to public health authorities. Public health clinics—which tend to treat the economically disadvantaged—are probably the most conscientious in fulfilling their reporting requirements. In contrast, the private physician who attends a long-time client may be hesitant to expose his or her patient to the reporting system. While there is no way to be sure exactly how many cases of VD go unreported, it seems likely that the older middle- or upper-class man or woman is the most likely to escape becoming a statistic.

2. *"You can get a venereal disease only once"*: Unlike many infectious diseases—measles, mumps, and so on—venereal diseases do not provide immunity to subsequent infection. Although most of these diseases can be cured, there are no antibodies sufficient to insure against reinfection. There is no limit to the number of times an individual may be reinfected.

3. *"Venereal diseases are acquired only through sexual intercourse"*: Although the term "venereal" (which comes from Venus, the goddess of love) does imply sexual intercourse, the fact is that ve-

Venereal disease does not necessarily affect only the promiscuous; it affects people of all ages and sexual lifestyles.
(Jim Kalett 1980/Photo Researchers, Inc.)

nereal disease may be acquired through a variety of types of sexual contact. For instance, both oral and anal sex can transmit an infection, as may skin contact with an infected area in the case of syphilis. Few if any cases of VD are acquired through contact with nonhuman surfaces — for example, the legendary toilet seat. While it is possible for certain types of infection to be transmitted without close physical contact, this is certainly the rare exception and not the rule. In general, the microorganisms that cause VD can survive only on skin surfaces that are warm and moist — most typically, the mouth and the genital areas.

4. *"Sexual contact with an infected partner invariably results in VD"*: Although venereal diseases are contagious, single exposure, or even multiple exposures, to the microorganisms that cause these infections does not always lead to infection. When public health officials trace the sexual contacts of someone infected with, say, gonorrhea, they often find that only about half of these contacts have contracted gonorrhea. The rates of contagion tend to differ with the different types of venereal diseases. However, it seems likely that in the long run, the more exposures an individual has to VD, the greater the chances of infection.

The chances of infection also seem to vary with several personal health factors. For instance, women who select birth control pills as their method of contraception seem far more susceptible to gonorrhea than women using other techniques of birth control. In fact, it is possible that women who use spermicidal creams or jellies have lower rates of gonorrheal infection because these contraceptives make the vagina a less hospitable environment for the gonococcus. Also, women are more likely to incur certain vaginal infections during the premenstrual and menstrual periods of their cycles, and during pregnancy.

5. *"The signs and symptoms of VD are always irreversible"*: Fortunately, early treatment of most venereal diseases will completely eliminate the infection. This was not always the case, however; it was only in the 1940s, with the clinical use of penicillin, that diseases such as syphilis and gonorrhea could be cured with 100 percent certainty. After adequate treatment, the microorganisms

causing syphilis and gonorrhea are completely eliminated.

When treatment is delayed, however, the damage caused by these infections cannot be reversed. In the female, for example, gonorrhea can lead to pelvic inflammation and scarring of or damage to the uterine tubes. Once this damage has occurred it cannot be reversed. Similarly, the serious damage caused by late-stage syphilis cannot be reversed. But treatment, even years after the infection was acquired, will halt its progress so that no further damage can take place.

There are a few exceptions to the rule that treatment can completely eliminate venereal infections. The most important exception is herpes genitalis, a viral infection for which there is no known treatment at present. Once a herpes infection is acquired, the virus continues to live in the body and cannot be destroyed. However, during latent periods the virus causes no symptoms and is not contagious. When symptoms do appear, treatment focuses on relieving the symptoms, and not on curing the disease.

6. *"The signs and symptoms of VD are easily recognizable"*: If you acquire a venereal disease, how likely are you to recognize that you are infected? Obviously, such recognition is crucial in order to receive prompt and effective treatment. If you are a male, the chances are that you will know something is wrong in a relatively short span of time. Most, although not all, men do develop warning signs that lead them to seek treatment.

Women, on the other hand, are much less fortunate. While the male genitals are external and easy to examine, females often develop symptoms that are internal and difficult to detect. When the internal male organs become infected, there are usually symptoms of urinary discomfort or discharge. The female urinary tract, however, is separate from the genitals and may not be involved in the infection. Thus, women often develop symptoms in the vagina or on the cervix, and these symptoms are difficult to detect without an internal examination. Even external symptoms may be missed because women tend to avoid examining their genitals. Unless a woman develops pain or vaginal discharge, she may be completely unaware of her infection until the disease progresses to a later stage with severe secondary complications. Because nature has played this unfortunate trick on women, they are very dependent on the honesty and responsibility of their male sexual partners if they are to be aware of an infection. Women do best to rely on periodic tests for venereal disease to be sure they are free from infection. Unfortunately, most physicians do not routinely perform such tests unless specifically requested to do so by their patients.

IS THERE A VD EPIDEMIC?

Are we in the midst of an epidemic of venereal disease? Over the past centuries, there is considerable evidence that VD rates tend to rise and fall in cycles. Generally, in times of war, social stress, or physical deprivation, VD rates have risen; during times of peace and prosperity, VD rates have tended to fall. However, this pattern no longer seems to apply in the Western countries. Although we are relatively peaceful and prosperous, our overall VD rates have been rising in recent years. This does not apply to all forms of VD — for instance, syphilis rates appear to be declining. However, gonorrhea rates are extremely high, and a number of other diseases that can be considered venereal — such as herpes and nongonococcal urethritis — have become increasingly common. What is being done to halt the "VD epidemic"?

At present, efforts are concentrated in a few major areas. First, treatment techniques have been developed that can cure most forms of VD. For example, public health authorities have provided standard treatment regimens for the cure of gonorrhea and syphilis. Second, to ensure that such treatment is available to all those who need it, there are public and private health clinics that dispense appropriate treatment. Treatment is also available from private physicians. Third, regulations require that the sexual contacts of an infected individual be traced, tested, and if necessary, given appropriate treatment. However, such follow-up efforts tend to be time-consuming and difficult. Although all health practitioners who treat VD are required to report each case to a public health authority, this may not always be done. It has been estimated that as many as half of all cases of VD go unreported. Even conscientious reporting does not ensure that the infected individual will honestly and accurately report his or her sexual contacts. And even when all contacts are reported, it may not be possible to trace all of them.

In response to these difficulties, several other techniques for locating infected individuals have been developed. For example, most states require VD testing for those about to be married and for pregnant women. Further, some doctors recommend routine testing for sexually active patients. In addition, public health clinics have conducted large-scale screening projects in which populations at greatest risk — for instance, the young — are all tested. Nevertheless, it is likely that many infected individuals unknowingly slip through this screening net.

Several other approaches to combating the VD epidemic require our attention and support. Perhaps the single most important factor is education: the more we know about VD, the better we are able to deal with it. Such education may take many forms: for instance, some school systems are now educating their students about the causes, symptoms, and cures of VD. But many schools refuse to present such information on the grounds that it will lead adolescents to "improper" sexual behavior. Information about VD has also appeared in the mass media — on television and in magazines and books.

In particular, it is attitudes to VD that need to be changed, because it is our attitudes that often prevent us from seeking help or information. Indeed, the vast majority of people prefer to approach a sexual encounter with little or no thought about the possibility of VD. VD is certainly not in tune with our romantic concepts of sexuality, and it is not easy for sexual partners to discuss this topic with one another. Medical research is certainly important, as are inexpensive and easily available testing and treatment facilities; but we will not succeed in lowering VD rates unless we confront our attitudes toward sexuality and sexually transmitted diseases.

Another approach that warrants more attention is the preventive approach. Medical technology has focused on treatment after the fact, and unfortunately development of a vaccine to immunize us against all venereal diseases seems highly unlikely at this time. Even without a preventive vaccine, are there ways we can decrease the likelihood of acquiring VD?

THE PREVENTION OF VENEREAL DISEASE

Current efforts to eliminate VD focus on treating the symptomatic patient; that is, patient A notices some disturbing symptoms, visits a physician, is diagnosed, and receives the appropriate medication. At the same time, patient A is questioned about his or her sexual contacts. Then, the physician or health service searches for contacts B and C, finds them, and treats them if necessary, and is put on the trail of contacts D, E, and so on.

This system, while effective in curing those patients who come to medical attention, has certain major drawbacks. For instance, many individuals infected with a venereal disease— particularly women—will have no noticeable symptoms, and therefore will not visit a physician. Some asymptomatic individuals will be fortunate enough to learn that they are infected because one of their sexual contacts develops symptoms and reports them. But this "reporting" system may break down for several reasons; the symptomatic patient may be dishonest in giving the names of sexual contacts or may be unable to locate a casual sexual partner. To combat the possibility that an asymptomatic individual remains untreated, many medical sources suggest that we all receive twice-yearly tests for syphilis and gonorrhea. While such tests may protect us as individuals, they do little to decrease the overall number of VD cases.

According to one researcher (Brecher, 1975), the incidence of VD will not decrease with current treatment methods. As we know, the symptoms of a venereal infection usually do not appear until at least one week after sexual contact, and in some cases this time period may be considerably longer. For most women, no symptoms appear. So, the unknowing but infected individual is likely to continue having sex, and to infect someone else, before medical treatment is sought. Thus, even with prompt and effective treatment techniques, the number of people with VD at any one time is unlikely to decrease.

Clearly, the best way to eliminate the venereal diseases is to *prevent* them, rather than to treat them after infection has occurred. Unfortunately, our moralistic attitudes have hampered prevention efforts. Those who see VD as a just punishment for "promiscuity" and believe that fear of VD is an effective deterrent to nonmarital sex are not anxious to develop or publicize preventive measures. However, some such measures do exist. As yet no vaccine has been perfected that will permanently protect us from VD, but some precautions can lessen our chances of infection. None of these precautions provide complete protection, and they do not eliminate the need for personal wariness and medical treatment. But even if a preventive measure is only 50 percent effective, it can do a great deal to decrease the overall incidence of VD in the future.

Condoms. According to many sources, the declining popularity of the condom is one of the major reasons for increasing VD rates in the 1970s. The contraceptive function of the condom has been replaced by the birth control pill, a method that actually appears to increase the chances of contracting certain venereal diseases. For example, women on the pill have much higher rates of trichomonal and monilial infections, and it is also likely that they are at greater risk of acquiring other venereal diseases (Secondi, 1974).

The condom, when used correctly, affords considerable protection from VD. To be effective, the condom must be put on before contact between sexual partners, and it must remain on the penis until the contact is over. Even so, the condom will not prevent VD if the source of the infection is a nongenital area, such as the inner thighs. It has been estimated, however, that a properly used condom will prevent the transmission of gonorrhea over 90 percent of the time (Secondi, 1974).

This protective function of the condom has been known for over 500 years. In countries such as Sweden, health authorities actively publicize the importance of condoms for preventing VD, and during World War II members of the U.S. armed forces were often supplied with condoms when given leave. Recently, however, we have neglected to emphasize, particularly to the young, that the condom has value both as a contraceptive and as a health protection device.

Visual inspection. A visual inspection of the male genitals, the "short-arm" method, is often valuable in detecting signs of venereal infection. This "short-arm" inspection is often used by prostitutes attempting to safeguard their own health. Visual inspection requires some practice before the signs of VD can be easily recognized: generally, these signs include skin sores or eruptions, and possibly some form of discharge from the penis in the case of gonorrhea. As already noted, however, some men show few signs of infection or may

be asymptomatic because they are in a quiescent phase of the infection. Visual inspection of the female genitals seldom reveals signs of infection, since most women are asymptomatic or show symptoms only on the internal genitals.

Vaginal protection. In the same way that we have neglected to publicize the preventive function of the condon, we have also ignored the fact that certain of the vaginal contraceptives currently available — such as contraceptive creams and jellies — afford some protection against VD. A relatively new development is a gel called *Progonasyl* (from "*pro*tection against *gon*orrhea *a*nd *syl*hilis"), which is currently being tested. This substance was used in Nevada's legal prostitution establishments and was found to decrease the chances of these venereal diseases to a great extent. At present, Progonasyl is available only through medical prescription.

Soap-and-water prevention. Another technique that may somewhat reduce the chances of VD is simple washing with soap and water. While washing certainly does not provide complete protection, it may decrease the chances that an infection will be transmitted. To be most effective, both partners should clean their genitals before and after sexual contact.

Urination. Another relatively unknown technique is urination after sexual contact. Since germs may travel up the urethra in both sexes and urine is a sterile but acid solution, germs that are in the urethra may be washed out when a man or woman urinates after sex. However, it is also important not to have intercourse when the bladder is full, since pressure on a full bladder can cause the kind of damage that increases the susceptibility to infection.

Presymptomatic antibiotics. We know that large doses of antibiotics such as penicillin can cure certain venereal diseases. It is logical, then, to suppose that smaller doses, administered before the infection has spread, will prevent certain venereal diseases. This technique, however, is very controversial and is not used by many people. While adequate doses of penicillin, administered either just before or just after sexual contact, will prevent an infection, there are also some dangers with this method. First, it is difficult to know, without a doctor's advice, exactly how large a dose is enough. People who use the leftover antibiotics in their medicine cabinets may take an insufficient dose, in which case they may eliminate some of the symptoms of VD without completely killing off the infection. The discovery of increasingly penicillin-resistant strains of gonorrhea is often blamed on insufficient dosages—the penicillin kills off the weaker germ strains but does not affect the stronger strains. Further, antibiotics have powerful side effects on the body, and overuse may cause other health problems as well as some resistance to the effects of the drug. Finally, sexual contact with an infected partner does not necessarily ensure a venereal infection. Although rates vary with different types of infection, there is usually a better than even chance that the "healthy" partner will not contract the disease. In this case, presymptomatic treatment is an unnecessary use of a potentially dangerous drug.

There are arguments in favor of preventive penicillin use under physician's orders. In the very early stages of infection only a relatively small amount of antibiotic is necessary, in contrast to the massive doses required in later stages of infection. Further, when an adequate dose is given, there should be no need to worry about masking symptoms or causing the development of disease-resistant germ strains. At present, however, most physicians are reluctant to prescribe these powerful drugs unless clear signs of infection are present.

TYPES OF VENEREAL DISEASE

Syphilis. Although syphilis has been the most feared of the venereal diseases, and perhaps one of the most dangerous, it is also becoming increasingly less common in our society (see Figure 13.1). This is not to say that syphilis has disappeared—it has been estimated that there are close to a half million cases in need of treatment in the United States today—but its general incidence has certainly declined in this century. Perhaps the most important factor in this decline has been the effective use of penicillin, beginning in the early 1940s. With the use of penicillin or various other antibiotics, syphilis can be completely cured, although the individual does *not* develop immunity to subsequent reinfection. Before the 1940s, however, there was no reliable cure for syphilis. The standard treatment, dating back as far as the seventeenth century, was the use of mercury or other heavy metals, a treatment that continued well into this century. There is little or no evidence that the mercury treatment worked, although considerable evidence exists that many patients suffered serious side effects or even death as a result of the treatment itself. With the hindsight of modern science it is difficult to understand why this dangerous and ineffective treatment technique was used for so many centuries. One possible reason may be the nature of the disease; since the early symptoms of syphilis disappear spontaneously, those who prescribed mercury may have thought that their treatment had brought about a cure. Another possibility is that mercury treatment was used on patients who did not actually

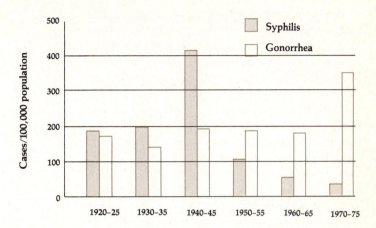

FIGURE 13.1

The incidence of reported cases of gonorrhea and syphilis, 1920– 1975.

have syphilis. It was only in 1906 that a German physician named August von Wasserman developed the first reliable blood test to detect the presence of syphilis.

The venereal disease *syphilis* is usually described as occurring in several stages. During the *primary stage*, the only sign of infection is a painless sore called a *chancre*. Typically, this chancre appears near the place where the bacteria has entered the body—usually on the genitals—after an incubation period of from 10 to 90 days. Since the chancre is painless, the infected individual may not notice it or consider it to be a sign of disease. Further, in women the chancre may develop internally, so that it goes unnoticed. Regardless of whether the infection is treated, the chancre will disappear by itself within 1 to 8 weeks.

During *second-stage* syphilis, the bacteria will have spread from the genital area to many other parts of the body. One of the most common symptoms of second-stage syphilis is a rash or blisters that may appear anywhere on the skin. Like the chancre, this skin rash will disappear without treatment. Other symp-

toms may include headache, fever, loss of appetite, or sore throat. Symptoms may be so mild that they are ignored, or they may resemble a variety of other diseases such as the flu. The syphilis infection is highly contagious at this time.

In the *latent stage*, no additional symptoms may appear for 10, 20, or even 30 years. The disease is usually not contagious at this time, except in a pregnant woman, who may infect her unborn baby. During this latent stage, the syphilis bacteria may attack and destroy various parts of the body, including the circulatory and nervous systems. Finally, in *late* or *third stage* syphilis, this internal damage becomes apparent; it may take the form of cardiovascular disease, paralysis, mental incapacity, or other serious health problems.

At any time in the course of this progression, the disease may be halted by adequate doses of penicillin or penicillin substitutes such as tetracycline. In fact, up to the third stage the disease can be cured with little or no permanent damage, and even here, the damaging effects can be completely halted.

Gonorrhea. Gonorrhea differs from syphilis in several important ways. First, it is far more common in the United States—in 1977, about 23,000 cases of syphilis but over one million cases of gonorrhea were reported to government health authorities. According to some sources, gonorrhea ranks second only to the common cold among widespread infectious diseases. Second, while syphilis can cause destruction to many parts of the body, the effects of gonorrhea tend to be restricted to the genitourinary tract—although it is possible for gonococcal germs to become lodged in the rectal area or the throat. Unlike syphilis, the bacterium gonococcus cannot penetrate the skin; it can only enter the body through warm and moist surfaces.

The symptoms of gonococcal infection appear sometime between 2 days and 2 weeks after exposure. In men, these symptoms tend to take the form of pain during urination and a penile discharge. In women, a vaginal discharge is the primary early symptom. However, while 80 to 90 percent of men experience these warning symptoms, only about 10 percent of women show any symptoms of infection. Thus whereas most men are likely to receive treatment during the early stages of infection, women may be unaware of having contracted the disease until it has caused some serious secondary infection. For example, the most common complication experienced by women is an infection of the pelvic area, called pelvic inflammatory disease, which may cause severe pain, fever, vomiting, and menstrual irregularities. When the pelvic inflammation is extensive, it is possible for sterility to result. Also, in rare instances, an untreated gonococcal infection may spread to the heart, nervous system, and bone joints.

Gonorrhea is usually diagnosed in symptomatic men by making a slide from the urethral discharge and examining the slide under a microscope. For women, the general procedure is to make a culture test, which entails taking a swab from one of the affected sites, placing the swab on a special culture medium, and then permitting the germs to grow under special conditions. It may be necessary to perform several cultures, from several different areas—the cervix, anus, urethra, and so on—before a positive result is found.

Once a positive diagnosis is made, treatment is relatively simple and straightforward. Penicillin is the drug of choice, although other antibiotics are effective for individuals who are allergic to penicillin. In recent years, there has been some concern about the development of penicillin-resistant strains of gonorrhea, but in fact, all types of gonorrhea will respond to penicillin if it is given in adequate doses. To be sure of cure, it is usually recommended that the patient have several followup tests before resuming his or her sexual activity.

Nongonococcal (nonspecific) urethritis. It has been estimated that about half of all men who visit a physician's office complaining of urethral discharge do not actually have gonorrhea. Once the possibility that the infection is gonococcal has been eliminated, the problem is usually diagnosed within the catch-all term of *nongonococcal,* or *nonspecific, urethritis:* that is, a urethral infection that is not caused by gonococcal bacteria.

In the United States, nonspecific urethritis is usually unreported to public health authorities, and we therefore do not have good information as to its prevalence. However, some indications point to it becoming a major health problem and that its incidence is on the rise. In fact, at least as many cases of nongonococcal urethritis may exist as there are of gonorrhea. A study by the national Center for Disease Control, the public health agency

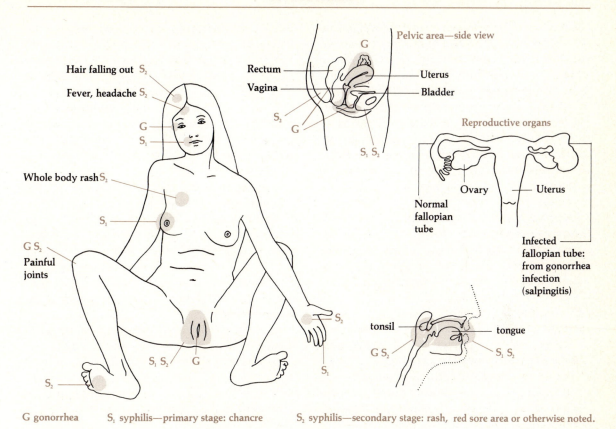

Hair falling out S₂

Fever, headache S₂

G

S₁

Whole body rash S₂

S₁

G S₂
Painful
joints

S₁ S₂   G

S₂

Pelvic area—side view

G

Rectum

Vagina

S₂

G

Uterus

Bladder

S₁ S₂

Reproductive organs

Ovary

Uterus

Normal
fallopian
tube

Infected
fallopian tube:
from gonorrhea
infection
(salpingitis)

S₂

S₁

tonsil

G S₂

tongue

S₁ S₂

G gonorrhea   S₁ syphilis—primary stage: chancre   S₂ syphilis—secondary stage: rash, red sore area or otherwise noted.

FIGURE 13.2

Possible sites of venereal disease symptoms in the female. The various symptoms may take months, or even years, to appear.

responsible for collecting information about infectious diseases, found that between 25 and 30 percent of men reporting to a clinic for treatment of VD had nongonococcal urethritis (*New York Times*, February 20, 1979).

The symptoms of nongonococcal urethritis may be similar to those produced by gonorrhea—that is, a burning sensation during urination and a penile discharge—or they may be mild and barely noticeable. As noted, nongonococcal urethritis is diagnosed by a process of elimination; if a test for gonococcus is negative, then the problem is labeled nongonococcal urethritis. Considerable disagreement exists concerning the causes of this problem. Some specialists believe it to be a viral disease, others point to an organism called chlamydia, and still others discuss the importance of mechanical irritation of the male genitals in stirring up a latent infection.

When untreated, nongonococcal urethritis can produce such complications as an inflamed prostate in males or pelvic inflammatory disease in females. For many infected individuals, however, the only consequences of this disease seem to be mild discomfort. Usually, the treatment of choice is tetracycline, an antibiotic. Unlike gonorrhea, which is completely eliminated with adequate doses of penicillin, nongonococcal urethritis may become a chronic condition in some men — that is, recurrent episodes may continue even in the absence of reexposure to the infection.

Herpes. Like nongonococcal urethritis, herpes is not a reportable disease in the United States. Nevertheless, considerable evidence indicates that herpes is extremely widespread and that it is on the rise. When tests are done for the presence of antibodies to herpes, it is found that about 90 percent of the adult population has been infected by herpes type 1, and about 60 percent have been infected, usually without any symptoms, by herpes type 2.

Herpes is actually a family of over fifty different viruses, but two types are the most familiar in our society: Herpes type 1 causes cold sores on the mouth; herpes type 2 produces infection in the genital area. In the past, it was believed that herpes type 1 could not infect the genitals and that herpes type 2 could not infect the mouth. Recently, however, there is evidence that approximately 10 percent of herpes infections are "crossovers" — that is, genital herpes can sometimes be caused by type 1, while a cold sore may be produced by type 2. It appears that the initial herpes infection is usually, but not always, caused by sexual contact.

The first attack of herpes tends to produce the most severe symptoms. In women, groups of small blisters tend to appear on the cervix, vulva, and sometimes the thighs or buttocks. These blisters may cause an itching or burning sensation and can feel tender to the touch. In men, similar blisters usually appear on the penis, although they may also develop on the thighs or buttocks or in the urethra. In severe cases, both men and women may experience fever, swollen glands, headache, and other flulike symptoms. However, many individuals will have symptoms so mild as to be unnoticeable. For instance, women who develop a herpes infection of the cervix may be completely unaware that they have contracted the disease.

Usually, the symptoms of herpes type 2 will disappear spontaneously within 1 to 3 weeks. Unfortunately, the herpes virus continues to live within the body, remaining out of reach of the protective antibodies in the bloodstream by staying within the cells. Although some people may never experience a return bout of the virus, most people will have recurrences at intervals in their lives. Sometimes these recurrences are linked with emotional or physical stress; in women, they may occur during certain phases of the menstrual cycle. Recurrences are usually less severe than the primary infection and tend to disappear more quickly. Herpes type 2 is contagious only when the blisters are present.

At present, no cure exists for herpes type 2, nor is there a preventive vaccine. Usually, medical treatment focuses on relieving uncomfortable symptoms — for example, a physician may prescribe oral painkillers, surface anaesthetics, sitz baths, or soothing compresses. Since the open blisters increase susceptibility to secondary infection, a doctor might also prescribe an antibacterial medication. To avoid infecting others, it is necessary to abstain from sexual activity until the symptoms disappear.

Although herpes can be physically distressing in its own right, it has received particular attention recently because of its association with cervical cancer. Research has demonstrated that women with cervical cancer have had greater exposure to herpes type 2 than women who do not have cervical cancer. This does not mean that all women who have had herpes type 2 will develop cervical cancer, but it does suggest that such women should have more frequent Pap smears to monitor the health of the cervix. When cervical cancer is caught in its early stages, cure rates are extremely high. Thus it has been recommended that women who have had a herpes type 2 infection should have a Pap smear about twice per year.

Another serious consequence of herpes type 2 is the possibility of passing the infection to a child during birth, with a chance that this infection may cause serious illness or death in the newborn. A child cannot contract herpes if the virus is dormant in the mother, but if the infection is active at the time of delivery, the infection can be transmitted when the infant passes through the cervix and vagina. In cases where the herpes is active, most doctors recommend a Caesarean section so that the child is not exposed to infection in the vaginal canal.

The "minor" venereal diseases. Included with syphilis and gonorrhea as diseases that must be reported to public health authorities are three so-called minor venereal conditions: chancroid, granuloma inguinale, and lymphogranuloma venereum. Discovered about one hundred years ago, these diseases were traditionally thought to be found in tropical climates, among the economically disadvantaged. Recently, however, they have been reported in all social classes and, although more prevalent in tropical climates, in all kinds of environmental conditions.

These three venereal infections are minor in the sense that they are much less common than either gonorrhea or syphilis. They are not at all minor, however, in the discomfort that they may cause. They tend to cause skin lesions and growths on or near the genitals, with intense itching or pain as a result.

Chancroid. Chancroid is caused by a bacterium that infects the genital area. The symptoms may be very like those caused by syphi-

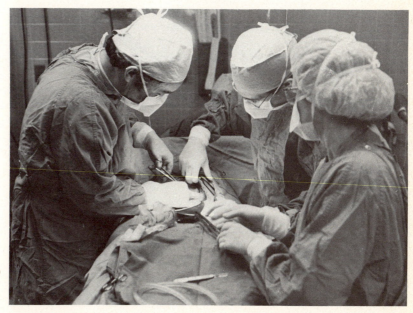

A Caesarean section is recommended for pregnant women who have herpes. *(Jim Harrison/Stock, Boston)*

lis, with one important difference: chancroid remains in the genital region, whereas syphilis spreads through the blood to infect many parts of the body. Chancroid causes a smooth, round ulcer that may look like the primary chancre of syphilis; unlike the syphilitic chancre, however, chancroid tends to be painful. In men, the sore usually appears at the end of the penile shaft; in women, it commonly appears around the vulva. However, infection may show up in other places: for men, around the anus, scrotum, or thighs; for women, in the vagina. Sores may also appear on the hands or mouth. In fighting off this infection, the body sends out white blood cells, which drain the bacteria through the lymph nodes. Thus, the lymph nodes may become infected and may swell, causing abscesses in the groin. The skin lesions may persist and cover the genitals, causing disfigurement and pain.

Treatment for chancroid is relatively simple and extremely effective. Sulfa drugs, given orally, will usually clear up the infection within several weeks.

Granuloma inguinale. Granuloma inguinale is also caused by a bacterium. "Granuloma" refers to the growth of scar tissue in response to the invasion of some microorganisms, and "inguinale" simply means the groin area. When this bacterium invades the body there is a continuous growth of scar tissue on or near the genitals.

Early symptoms are painless ulcers, which may spread from the genitals to the thighs or buttocks. Since the body cannot fight off these lesions, the disease will continue to spread, causing weakness and discomfort. Treatment usually includes the use of various antibiotics. The more advanced the case, the longer it will take to reverse the problem.

Lymphogranuloma venereum. Lymphogranuloma venereum is caused by an organism called chlamydia, which is described as "somewhere between a virus and a bacterium" (Secondi, 1975). The first sign of infection is a small blister that usually goes unnoticed, especially in women, and will disappear by itself. In the next stage, the organism causes the lymph nodes of the groin to swell and become tender or painful. If untreated, the infection may cause enormous and grotesque swelling of the genitals. Once again, antibiotic treatment will halt the progress of the disease, with early treatment being more efficient and effective than delayed treatment.

Venereal warts. Far more common than the three "minor" venereal diseases, and much less serious, is a condition called *condyloma acuminata*, or venereal warts. These warts, found on the genitals, are similar to warts that may be found on other parts of the body. They are caused by a virus that prefers the warm, moist environment of the genitals. Usually, the warts first appear as small, soft, pink or fleshy growths. With time, they may spread and grow to cover more of the genital area. However, for most people the warts tend to remain small, painless, and unnoticed.

If the warts do spread, they may cause itching and irritation, which makes sexual contact unpleasant or painful. Scratching may cause the warts to become infected and inflamed. In many cases, the warts seem to disappear spontaneously.

Since warts, like herpes, are caused by a virus, they are not susceptible to treatment with antibiotics. Thus, treatment is usually local—the physician applies some type of chemical ointment directly to the warts, which destroys them. One common form of treatment is podophyllin, a chemical that "burns" the warts off. In more severe cases, the warts may have to be burned off using electricity or extreme cold. Treatment may require several sessions.

VAGINAL INFECTIONS

Normally, the vagina contains a large number of microorganisms kept in delicate balance by one another and by a healthy vaginal environment. For instance, the vagina is usually too acidic to be hospitable to many types of microorganisms. (In addition, the healthy vagina and cervix produce a nonirritating discharge in response to hormonal changes and sexual excitement.) Thus it is possible for the vagina to contain potentially harmful microorganisms that apparently result in an absence of symptoms.

However, various factors can upset this balance and thus allow the microorganisms to proliferate and produce unpleasant symptoms. For example, the hormonal changes that accompany pregnancy often encourage the development of vaginal infections. In the same way, some women are especially prone to infection just before or during menstruation. The use of antibiotics, birth control pills, and other medications may also upset the ecology of the vagina, as may physical or emotional stress. Finally, it has been suggested that the use of commercial douches and "feminine hygiene" products can cause irritation that may pave the way for vaginal infection.

Are vaginal infections really a venereal disease? We tend not to put them in this category for two reasons: first, vaginal infections are so common that more than one of every four women will experience them at some time; second, vaginal infections are not always the immediate effect of sexual contact. It is possible for women to acquire these infections several years before any symptoms become apparent; symptoms appear only when the vaginal environment permits the microorganisms to multiply. However, vaginal infections are almost always transmitted through sexual contact, and in this sense, they are "venereal" diseases. Males are as likely as females to harbor the microorganisms but very rarely experience any unpleasant symptoms from them.

Trichomoniasis. Trichomoniasis, commonly called "trick," is caused by a one-celled parasite (see Figure 13.3) which tends to live in the vagina, although it may also be found in the urinary tract. This extremely common parasite can be found in over 50 percent of females, most often during the childbearing years. Trichomonas vaginalis may be found in the vagina in the absence of any symptoms, or it may cause acute or chronic discomfort.

The major symptom of trichomoniasis is a foamy vaginal discharge, which may be yellowish or gray and often has an unpleasant odor. This discharge, which may be slight or excessive, tends to irritate the vulva. Thus the vaginal opening and vulva may become irritated and inflamed. Sexual intercourse may become unpleasant or painful because of this irritation. Typically, trichomoniasis is diagnosed by examining a slide of the discharge under a microscope. In men, who usually develop no symptoms at all, trichomoniasis may be diagnosed microscopically or with culturing techniques.

FIGURE 13.3
The *Trichomonas vaginalis* parasite.

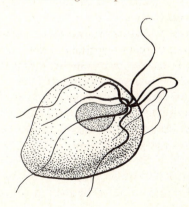

Typically, trichomoniasis has been treated with a drug called metronidazole, which is effective in killing the protozoan. However, it seems possible that this drug, marketed under the name Flagyl, may have some harmful side effects, particularly when taken orally in large doses, and it is not recommended for pregnant women. Other, less severe types of treatment, such as vaginal suppositories, have been found to yield satisfactory results for some women. It has also been suggested that vinegar douches, which increase the acidity of the vagina, can be effective in the early stages of a trichomonal infection. To prevent recurrences, it is important that the male sexual partner receive treatment at the same time.

Yeast infections. Next to trichomonas vaginalis, the most common vaginal infection is caused by *Candida albicans*, a yeast fungus, also called *Monilia albicans*. This yeast fungus is usually present in the vagina, but in quantities so small as to be unnoticeable. When the vaginal environment is disturbed, however, the yeast may multiply and cause physical distress. As with trichomoniasis, the use of antibiotics and birth control pills, and the hormonal changes of pregnancy, are often associated with an increased risk of yeast infections.

The symptoms of a yeast infection, also called thrush, include a discharge that tends to be thick and white; in turn, this discharge may irritate and redden the vulva, and cause intense itching. Diagnosis is usually made from slides or cultures.

Several treatments are available for yeast infections. A drug called nystatin may be used either orally or as a vaginal suppository. Or gentian violet may be applied to the affected areas. As with trichomoniasis, however, yeast infections may either be stubbornly persistent or respond to treatment only to reappear during the next menstrual cycle. Treatment is often complicated because several vaginal infections may occur together.

Hemophilus vaginalis and nonspecific vaginitis. Vaginal infections that are not caused by trichomonas vaginalis or *Candida albicans* are often classified as "nonspecific vaginitis"—a category that corresponds in some ways to nonspecific urethritis in males. As with other infections, symptoms usually include some form of vaginal discharge and vulvar irritation. One type of vaginitis is now attributed to hemophilus vaginalis, a bacterium that can be recognized through microscopic examination. Since this bacterium is transmitted venereally, treatment—usually with antibiotics or sulfa creams—must be given to both male and female sexual partners.

Prevention of vaginal infections. Probably, the only way to avoid totally the acquisition of the microorganisms producing vaginal infections is to lead a completely chaste and solitary life. A more practical approach involves attempting to maintain a vaginal environment that inhibits the growth of these microorganisms. The following precautions have proved helpful in avoiding vaginitis or in minimizing its severity:

Since most microorganisms flourish in warm and moist environments, avoid nylon underwear and tight clothing, which build up heat and moisture.

Wash or bathe at least once a day.

Since sugar tends to encourage the growth of many infections, avoid excessive sugar intake.

Avoid "feminine hygiene" products and douches that irritate the vaginal area.

Since antibiotics tend to destroy the body's natural defenses against vaginal infection, do not use them unless absolutely necessary. Yogurt, which restores some of these defenses, is often recommended.

Sex and Disability

SEX AND THE PHYSICALLY DISABLED

It is difficult for the able-bodied man or woman to understand the sexual difficulties of the physically disabled. Imagine, for instance, that you have recently suffered a heart attack and are concerned that your future sexual activity must be curtailed in order to prevent a recurrence. Or imagine that you have experienced a spinal cord injury that confines you to a wheelchair, and you are worried about how to manage sexual contact when you cannot move your lower body. Generally, the medical profession concerns itself with your physical health but pays relatively little attention to your psychological needs. For many disabled patients, however, the resumption of sexual activity is a primary consideration in adjusting to a physical disability.

It has been estimated that as many as 10 percent of adults in our country suffer from a physical disability that seriously interferes with daily functioning. The range of disabilities is enormous, including such problems as paralysis, heart disease, physical deformities and scars, sight or hearing impairments, arthritis, diabetes, amputations, and developmental abnormalities. Each type of disability presents a particular set of sexual obstacles; in addition, all disabilities may produce certain common sexual problems. For instance, according to a widespread myth, the disabled are not, and should not be, interested in sex. Also, there is the problem of the disabled individual finding a suitable sexual partner. Further, if the disability was not present since childhood, the individual must often cope with a sudden and negative change in body image; for example, a woman who has undergone mastectomy or a man who has had a limb amputated may see themselves as unattractive, and feel ashamed and self-conscious about displaying their bodies. Disabled people may also have to accept sudden limitations in their ability to control their bodies. Thus even when a disability does not directly affect the sexual organs, it is likely to produce side effects that are sexual in nature.

Michael Cole (1975) has attempted to categorize physical disabilities according to how they might affect sexual functioning. For example, disabilities might be classified depending on how conspicuous they are; a cardiovascular condition is easy to conceal, amputation of a leg is not. The individual with an inconspicuous disability may move through society attracting relatively little attention; in contrast, the individual with a conspicuous disability must cope with special treatment not only from friends and family but from everyone he or she encounters. However, this special treatment may be beneficial in the long run; since the paraplegic's condition cannot be hidden, he or she is forced to deal with physical or sexual limitations and may, therefore, be able to develop satisfying adjustments or compromises.

Another way to categorize physical disabilities is according to age of onset and whether the disability is stable or progressive. Disabilities that began early in life will often restrict the socialization process; for example, the handicapped child may have limited contact with other children, less opportunity for dating and sexual learning, and a limited choice of marriage partners. Thus, even such disabilities as blindness or deafness can interfere with sexual maturation. A second category are disabilities acquired suddenly sometime after puberty that are not progressive; spinal cord injuries would be in this group. In such cases, the sexual maturation process has been completed and the individual may have been sexually active before the injury. Many of the disabilities in this category are conspicuous to outsiders, and there may be concern about future sexual and reproductive abilities. A third category includes those disabilities that begin after puberty and are progressive—that is, likely to become worse over time; examples include heart disease and diabetes. This group of disabilities often has a major influence on the patient's sexual partner—there may be concern that sexual activity will harm the patient or even lead to death. The sexual partner of someone with a nonprogressive disease may have to make enormous adjustments, but usually these changes occur all at once; when a disease is progressive, the need for sexual and other adjustments may be continuing and constant. In addition, many progressive disabilities require the use of drugs that can further interfere with sexuality.

Regardless of the nature of the disability, the disabled man or woman is likely to require counseling, information, and reassurance. The person who is most frequently turned to for help is the physician. For this assistance to be available, Alex Comfort (1978) suggests that the "conspiracy of silence" that exists between patient and physician regarding sexuality must be ended.

The "disabled" person has two types of disabilities to contend with in the sexual field: those arising from physical problems which limit activity or response, and those arising from misinformation and lack of social permission. It is the second of these, which the disabled share with the able, which accounts for the major part of the difficulty. (Comfort, 1978, p. 2)

Thus the physician has a double obligation to the disabled patient: first, to provide up-to-date information about the sexual consequences of the disability; second, to help in dispelling sexual myths and stereotypes.

To perform these functions, Comfort suggests that the physician should follow a three-stage pattern of management (1978). Stage one involves a thorough evaluation of the extent of the physical problem: for instance, a "sleep erection test" might be used to ascertain whether erectile physiology is still intact. In stage two, the physician should encourage the patient or couple to widen their sexual repertoire: when erection is impossible, for example, the couple might be educated about oral-genital techniques or the use of sexual aids. Finally, stage three involves the setting of realistic and attainable sexual goals: even when the couple cannot expect to reach predisability levels of sexual activity, they can learn to devise ways of "outwitting" the limitations imposed by the disability. If the physician does not feel capable or comfortable in performing this function, Comfort suggests that he or she is obligated to refer the patient to a qualified sex therapist. Efforts to "protect" the patient from sexual frustration by pretending there is no problem, while well-intentioned, are bound to fail. Disabled persons do have sexual concerns, and so, sexual counseling must be an integral part of the rehabilitation process.

Heart disease and sexuality. One of the most common of all physical disabilities in this country is heart disease—it has been estimated that more than 14 million Americans have some form of heart or blood vessel ailment. Until fairly recently, however, cardiac patients received little advice concerning sexuality; they were usually told to stop smoking and alter their diet, but as for sexual activity, they were left to find their own way. Often, understandable fears led to sexual abstinence or a severe curtailment of sexual expression. In turn, the avoidance of sex was likely to result in marital stress and frustration. Fortunately, research has led to a more realistic evaluation of the cardiac patient's sexual abilities, and medical authorities have been developing guidelines for when sexual activity can safely be resumed. (One limitation of the research surveyed here is that it focuses on male cardiac patients; but, it is likely that the same guidelines can be applied to women.)

Does sexual activity place a great strain on the cardiovascular system? Laboratory results presented by Masters and Johnson (1966) suggest that it does: they observed that the greatest stress was produced during orgasm, when heart rates ranged from 110 to 180 beats per minute and there were also large increases in systolic and diastolic blood pressure. In addition, respiration rates were two to four times as high as in the resting state. From these data, many physicians and patients concluded that sexual activity is dangerous after a heart attack.

It has been argued, however, that Masters and Johnson studied a select population — young, healthy couples — in a specific setting — a physiological laboratory. Thus their results might not apply to a group of older, long-married cardiac patients who are sexually active in their own homes. To test this possibility, two researchers (Hellerstein and Friedman, 1970) studied the cardiovascular effects of sexual activity in a group of heart-diseased and cardiac-prone patients. They concluded that the cardiovascular "cost" of sexual intercourse was considerably lower for middle-aged, long-married men who were measured at home; for instance, the peak heart rate averaged 117.4 beats per minute at orgasm, and this dropped to 85 beats per minute after orgasm. In comparison, the average heart rate during work activity was about 120 beats per minute for these men. In other words, sexual activity with one's wife of many years was not any more stressful than, say, climbing several flights of stairs.

One of the most common concerns of cardiac patients and their wives is that sexual activity will lead to a heart attack. This is a possibility, but it seems to be extremely rare. One study, conducted in Japan, found that the heart attack rate during intercourse was 0.6 percent (Ueno, 1968). Heart attacks were most likely to occur when a man was with an unfamiliar partner, particularly in an unfamiliar setting such as a motel. While intercourse with one's wife is not especially stressful, a new partner seems to cause greater stress and therefore greater risk of a coronary.

When can the cardiac patient safely resume sexual activity? Nathaniel Wagner (1975) notes that while intercourse with a long-standing partner is only moderately stressful, it is still a form of exercise. Thus, it is necessary to take into account the man's previous level of physical and sexual activity, as well as his state of recovery from the heart attack. Cardiac patients are often given programs of systematic physical exercise to improve their overall level of physical conditioning, and the safety of sexual activity is probably related to the ability to perform these exercises. To test his ability to tolerate intercourse, a patient might undergo an exercise stress test that evaluates his cardiovascular response to moderate exercise.

One way to reintroduce sexual activity to the recovering cardiac patient, according to Wagner, is masturbation. For some patients, the urge to masturbate is a positive sign that health and normality are returning. Masturbation has several advantages over intercourse in this situation; for one thing, sexual stimulation is completely under the man's control; for another, he does not have to cope with the anxiety and fear that his sexual partner might feel. Moreover, the ability to masturbate may increase a man's confidence in his ability to perform with his partner.

Even after intercourse has resumed, there are certain recommendations the patient might wish to follow in order to minimize any health risks. For example, one researcher

(Mackey, 1978) suggests that extremes of temperature—either extreme heat or extreme cold—cause additional stress to the heart. Also, since digestion places a strain on the heart, it is best to wait several hours after having a large meal before starting sexual activity. Similarly, large amounts of alcohol or excessive fatigue may cause additional and unnecessary stress on the heart. Of course, these same precautions might be beneficial to those with no history of cardiac problems.

Spinal cord injury and sexuality. As a result of recent advances in medical technology, many men and women with spinal cord injuries can expect a normal life span. However, the com-

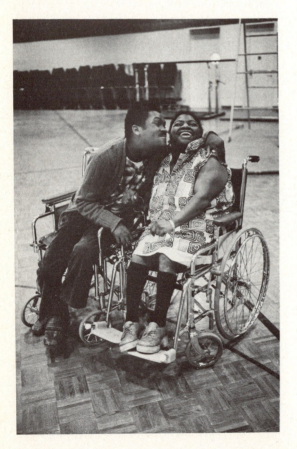

plications of a spinal cord injury may interfere with sexual activity in many ways. For instance, in addition to losing sensation in the lower body, the paraplegic also loses control of the bladder and bowel.

The extent of the paraplegic's sexual disability depends in part on the exact location and amount of spinal cord damage. For example, a large number of males with upper motor neuron lesions are able to experience reflex erections; that is, penile erection will occur in response to physical stimulation, but not in response to psychogenic arousal. Ejaculation is less common than erection but may occur even when the male has no sensation in the genitals. Orgasm is also uncommon, but may be reported even when all nerve connections to the pelvis have been severed.

Some spinal injured adults state that they are able to concentrate on sensation from a neurologically intact portion of their bodies and reassign that sensation to their genitals, thus experiencing it in their fantasy as orgasm. Using that technique, some spinal injured males report multiple orgasms. (Cole, 1975, p. 161)

Although most attention has been focused on males, especially because of the need to rehabilitate veterans of the Vietnam war, women are also likely to experience sexual problems as a result of spinal cord injury. Since the injury does not usually interfere with the menstrual cycle, most paraplegic women are able to become pregnant and have a relatively normal pregnancy and delivery. However, absence of sensation in the genitals will interfere with orgasm in the same ways as

For disabled individuals who are able to make a satisfactory adjustment, the rewards of sexuality need not be sacrificed. (© *Abraham Menashe 1980*)

it does in males. Like males, some women are able to use fantasy and erotic imagery in order to be able to experience orgasm.

Many of the typical responses to sexual arousal described by Masters and Johnson are also present in spinal-injured men and women. For instance, respiration, heart rate, and blood pressure increase in response to arousal; nipple erection occurs; and often a sex flush breaks out on the skin of the trunk, neck, and face. In order to resume sexual activity, however, the injured man or woman must make some major adjustments in sexual attitudes, communication, and behavior. For example, an injured male may have to take a more passive role during intercourse, or be willing to experiment with new sexual techniques. The key points that should be emphasized when working with the spinal-injured adult are "ability to communicate effectively with one's partner, willingness to experiment with sexual options which are pleasing to both partners, use of pleasuring techniques, emphasis upon fantasy, the importance of hygiene, and recognition that the largest component of human sexual excitement and response remains undamaged within the skull" (Cole, 1975, p. 164).

DIABETES

The effects of diabetes on sexual functioning can be severe for many individuals with this chronic disease. Among male diabetics, approximately 50 percent will experience erectile dysfunction—indeed, erectile failure is often one of the early symptoms that brings the diabetic to medical attention. Research has shown that diabetic impotence is not related to the severity or duration of the disease, nor does the diabetic experience a corresponding decline in sexual desire.

The precise cause of diabetic impotence is not clearly understood. In fact, there are probably many different factors that can play a role in this problem. One researcher (Ellenberg, 1971) has investigated the prevalence of neurologic damage among diabetic men; such damage was far more common among those reporting erectile dysfunction than among a control group with no sexual difficulties. As a result of his studies, this researcher discounts the theory that dysfunction is caused by hormonal deficiencies, since most diabetics have normal testosterone levels.

Although it is generally assumed that the diabetic's erectile problems are a physical by-product of his disease, another researcher (Renshaw, 1975) points out that the diabetic is also subject to many psychological pressures. For example, the need to cope with a chronic, debilitating disease might lead to depression, and that, in turn, to sexual difficulties. The researcher also describes "three important A's —Alcohol, Anxiety, and Anger" that may play a role in precipitating or worsening a sexual dysfunction. In such cases, sex therapy is often helpful.

To date, almost all of the research on the sexual side effects of diabetes has focused on males. However, some evidence indicates that female diabetics may also be subject to sexual difficulties—in particular, a lessening of vaginal lubrication and the loss of any sexual desire.

SEX AND THE MENTALLY RETARDED

The mentally retarded, like the aged and the physically disabled, have been subject to many repressive sexual myths and attitudes. Not only do we tend to deny that the retarded have sexual feelings, but we also severely discourage them from becoming involved in any form of sexual activity. In the past it was not uncommon to inflict compulsory sterilization on the retarded and forbid them to marry. Even today, the vast majority of institutions for the retarded prohibit even solitary forms of sexual behavior, such as masturbation, and refuse to provide any type of sex education or discussion for their residents. However, there is increasing recognition that "normalization" is a better goal than segregation—that is, as much as possible, the retarded individual should be encouraged to live within the mainstream of society. As part of this "mainstreaming," new efforts are being made to recognize and deal with the sexual needs and problems of this group.

We are conflicted about the sexuality of the retarded for a number of reasons. Perhaps most important, we do not view them as mature enough to make adult sexual decisions; rather, we see them as children in need of sexual protection. Parents may have real fears that, say, a retarded daughter will be sexually exploited. Another fear is that the retarded will produce children for whom they are unable to care, or they themselves will become involved in an unhappy marriage. Certainly, the ways in which we usually care for the retarded in our society may encourage these unhappy outcomes. Typically, the retarded have been cut off from the types of social interactions that would bring them to some level of social maturity; for instance, they may be closely protected by parents who forbid learning experiences such as dating and other cross-sex interactions. Also, they are usually denied information about sexuality, contraception, and so on.

The term "mental retardation" is applied to a group of individuals with widely differing skills and abilities. Often it is used to describe people whose IQ falls below 70; another criterion is "adaptive behavior"—that is, whether a person is able to show certain levels of personal responsibility and independence. Within this large group of the retarded—

sometimes estimated to be 3 percent of the U.S. population—are some people with relatively mild deficits in intellectual ability and behavior, and others who show severe deficits. In the same way, the sexual maturation of the retarded may reach different levels of competence and ability. Research has shown that a relationship exists between IQ and sexual maturation—the lower the IQ, the slower the sexual development. To the limits of their ability, the retarded will follow the same developmental pattern of sexuality as the nonretarded.

Typically, the first sexual behavior to appear is masturbation. Children are normally sensitive to cues that masturbation is a disapproved activity that should be carried out in private to avoid parental punishment. Retarded children, however, must often be taught that masturbation is a private activity. Because they are watched more closely, the retarded are more likely to get caught and be punished for sexual activity. Given our current attitudes toward masturbation, it is far more common for attempts to be made to eliminate this behavior than to try to teach the retarded child when and where the activity is appropriate.

Things become even more complicated when the retarded show interest in interpersonal sexuality. Our greatest concern is that they will produce retarded children, or that even if they have normal children they will lack the resources to be effective and responsible parents. It is certainly true that parenting requires enormous personal resources, and the retarded may often be unable to undertake this responsibility without considerable outside help. At the same time, we cannot assume that all retarded individuals, regardless of personal skills and outside support, must be inadequate parents. Parenting is, to a large extent, a learned skill, and with proper training it is possible that some retarded men and women can be at least adequate in the role.

It is a cruelty of our society that many people regard the mentally retarded as asexual. *(Mary Ellen Mark/Magnum)*

Even for those who are clearly unable to raise children, there is no reason to deny the opportunity for sexual intimacy. Warren Johnson (1977) suggests that for the retarded we should make a distinction between recreational sex and procreational responsibility. If we recognize that recreational sex is good and valuable in and of itself, then we cannot forbid this experience to the retarded simply because they cannot accept procreational responsibility. Of course, the method of contraception that is selected must be appropriate to the individuals involved; for example, while sterilization may be most appropriate for the severely retarded, it is possible that the mildly retarded can make effective use of reversible techniques such as the pill or IUD.

There is usually little sex education provided to the mentally retarded other than where babies come from and, in the case of females, menstrual hygiene at puberty. . . . Then, when normal heterosexual attachments occur, parents and teachers somehow are convinced that these persons cannot learn to cope with methods of contraception or decisions about marriage and parenthood. The truth is closer to the statement that the retarded have not been adequately educated in these areas. Only after having so educated them can we possibly say that they cannot understand." (Hall, 1975, p. 192)

Sex and Drugs

Both licit and illicit drug use is common in our society. For some drug users, the sexual side effects of drug use are a welcome and intended outcome. For others, sexual side effects may be unpleasant, unintentional, and unwelcome. While the folklore surrounding drug effects on sexuality is enormous, scientific research is relatively scarce to date.

Few drug substances act directly on our sexual organs or physiology. Most drugs act indirectly, affecting the user's mood, energy level, inhibitions, perceptions, and general physical health. Drug effects are subtle, and they often vary from one individual to another, or even for the same individual at different times.

DRUG FOLKLORE:
THE SEARCH FOR APHRODISIACS

We can find myths and folklore about the effects of drugs on sexuality in almost all cultures. The search for the perfect aphrodisiac—a drug that will heighten sexual desire, pleasure, and performance—has been a continuing cultural theme from ancient to modern times (see the boxed extract). The results of contemporary research seem to indicate, however, that this search is in vain. There are few, if any, drug substances that have a direct and positive effect on human sexuality. In fact, it seems far easier to find drugs that are "anaphrodisiacs"—that is, substances that diminish sexual desire and pleasure.

Nevertheless, the search for aphrodisiacs has continued throughout history. Natural substances such as datura, belladonna, and henbane were used in the sexual orgies of ancient fertility cults. Tribes that worshiped the Greek god Bacchus, also known as the "phallus god," used the poisonous psychedelic mushroom *Aminita muscaria* to create sexual frenzy. Marco Polo chronicled the sexual effects of hashish in the Eastern palaces of the eleventh century. Yohimbine has long been used by natives of Africa to increase their sexual powers, and the mandrake plant was popular in medieval Europe for the same purpose.

Certain foods have acquired the reputation of being aphrodisiacs. The list of foods consid-

ered to have sexual powers includes such varied substances as oysters, celery, bananas, and tomatoes. Some societies have placed their faith in animal parts—for example, powdered rhinoceros horn or raw bull's testicles. Natural food advocates may believe in the powers of ginseng root or vitamin E. A sign in a popular New York seafood restaurant reads FISH IS FOOD FOR LOVE.

One of the best-known aphrodisiac drugs is cantharides, also called "Spanish fly," made from a beetle that is dried, powdered, and taken internally. It causes an irritation and inflammation of the genitourinary tract that may produce an unpleasant genital stimulation. However, it does not increase sexual desire and may cause illness. Another well-known drug is yohimbine, taken from the yohimbe tree in Africa. While it does seem to stimulate the nerve centers controlling erection, its effectiveness as an aphrodisiac is questionable. However, it has been used medically, in combination with male hormones, to stimulate sexual drive.

In modern Western society, the two drugs with the most powerful reputations as aphrodisiacs are alcohol and marihuana. At this point, we can say that the effects of either alcohol or marihuana seem to be highly dependent on the amount used, the setting in which use takes place, and the personality of the user. A factor of critical importance for each of the drugs mentioned is the strength of their reputation as sexually stimulating substances. If we really believe in the aphrodisiac powers of, for example, a banana, then it may indeed have sexual significance in our lives.

Why do we continue to search for the "true aphrodisiac"? Perhaps we are looking for a path to instant ecstasy, one that is not blocked by the usual obstacles to sexual fulfillment. Sexuality is a complex and often troubled area of human behavior. We are held back by insecurity, confining sex roles, sexual myths, and

Aphrodisiacs in the Kama Sutra

The Kama Sutra, a classic guide to love-making practices in the East, contains the recipes for many potions that are believed to enhance sexual performance and pleasure. For example:

Now the means of increasing sexual vigour by drinking milk mixed with sugar, the root of the cuchchata plant, the piper chaba, and liquorice. Drinking milk mixed with sugar, and having the testicle of a ram or goat boiled in it, is also productive of vigour. . . .

According to ancient authors, if a man pounds the seeds or roots of the trapa bispinosa, the kasurika, the tuscan jasmine, and liquorice together with the kshirakapoli [a kind of onion], and puts the powder into milk mixed with sugar and ghee, and having boiled the whole mixture on a moderate fire, drinks the paste so formed, he will be able to enjoy innumerable women.

If a man takes the outer covering of the sesamum seeds, and soaks them with the eggs of sparrows, and then, having boiled them in milk, mixed with sugar and ghee, along with the fruits of the trapa bispinosa and the kasurika plant, and adding to it the flour of wheat and beans, and then drinks this composition, he is said to be able to enjoy many women. (pp. 214–215)

---

misinformation. With the use of drugs, we hope to overcome some of these barriers.

DRUG EFFECTS ON SEXUAL FUNCTION

When we speak of drug effects on human sexuality, we must keep in mind that such effects are complex. Drugs may have physical or psychological effects—or both. Further, they may influence different aspects of sexuality. For instance, a drug might increase the desire for sexual experience, but have no effect on sexual performance. Some drug substances are known as "disinhibitors"; that is, they make it easier to initiate sexual behavior by removing feelings of self-consciousness or guilt. However, the same substances might also interfere with sexual performance, perhaps by making it more difficult to reach orgasm. Other drugs might do little to change our objective sexual behavior but cause a major change in our subjective experience of that behavior. For example, just as marihuana may cause time to appear to pass slowly, it may make a sexual experience seem to be longer and more intense. The difference is not in what actually happens, but in what seems to happen.

The effects of drugs on sexuality are far more than a simple chemical reaction. We cannot expect that each person who takes drug X will immediately experience sexual effect Y. The drug user is the all-important intervening variable. That is, the user processes the drug according to his or her own personality, mood, needs, and expectations. So drug X may have an infinite variety of sexual effects, depending on who is using it and why and where it is being used.

If we want to predict the sexual effects of a specific drug, we must keep the following types of factors in mind:

1. *Physiological effects:* Most drugs can be expected to alter our body chemistry in some way. However, few drugs directly effect the sexual organs. An exception would be a drug such as Spanish fly, which acts specifically on the genitourinary tract. The majority of drugs can be expected to act indirectly, perhaps by influencing central nervous system arousal, metabolism, coor-

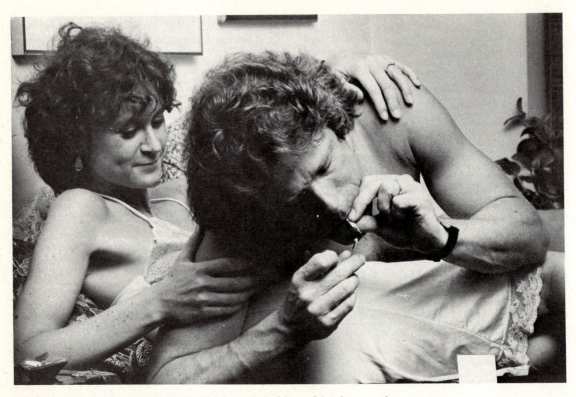

The effect of drugs on sexuality is always colored by subjective reactions.
(© Joel Gordon 1980)

dination, or general health. These physiological changes are rarely sufficient, in and of themselves, to alter sexual behavior radically.

2. *Expectations:* The way we expect a drug to act is a critical factor in the types of effects we actually experience. Generally, if a drug is expected to act as an aphrodisiac, then the user will, indeed, experience heightened sexual arousal. On the other hand, if a drug is expected to have negative sexual effects, the user is more likely to experience sexual difficulties. An interesting example of this "self-fulfilling prophecy" logic is found in the *Report of the Indian Hemp Drugs Commission, 1893–1894.* It reports that cannabis (marihuana) is used in houses of prostitution as a sexual stimulant, and that it is also used by religious ascetics to destroy sexual appetite. In both situations, it

successfully fulfills its purpose. Clearly, cultural expectations play a major role in determining the sexual side effects of drug use.

3. *Setting:* The setting in which a drug is used is important in determining its sexual effects. The same drug may have vastly different effects depending on where it is used. For example, trying LSD in a relaxed setting with a loved partner may have a completely different sexual outcome than using it among a group of strangers. Similarly, a food may acquire an aphrodisiac reputation when eaten at an intimate, candlelit dinner table with an attractive partner. However, the same food will have no sexual effect when eaten in a crowded cafeteria.

4. *Dosage:* Obviously, the effect of one glass of wine will be very different from the effect of an

entire bottle. This dosage relationship can be predicted for almost any drug substance that is taken. Generally, a moderate quantity of almost any substance can have aphrodisiac qualities. A large quantity of most substances, even those that are relatively harmless, is likely to be a sexual obstacle. The simplest explanation of this phenomenon is that low-dosage drug use adds novelty and interest to a sexual situation but does not impair sexual performance. Higher dosages may be disorienting, frightening, and physically debilitating.

5. *Duration of use:* Whether drug use is acute or chronic is a major factor in determining effect on the user. The short-term user remains sensitive to the novelty of the substance. However, the long-term user may be immune to these effects. Further, a chronic user is subject to serious effects on general health, possibly including psychological or physical addiction. Finally, the chronic drug user is more likely to use high dosages, which have a detrimental effect on sexuality.

EXPERIMENTAL RESEARCH ON SEX AND DRUGS

Experimental research on the subject of sex and drugs is a relatively recent phenomenon. Most of our knowledge about the sexual effects of drugs has come from other sources. Writers, law enforcers, and religious authorities have often contributed opinions based largely on their own experiences and observations. While these opinions may have value, they should not be accepted as gospel. Many theories that have commonsense appeal fail the test when they are subjected to laboratory experimentation.

Another source of information about the sexual effects of drugs is the clinical case history. This is often the report of a physician who prescribes a drug to an individual and later notices or is told that a sexual side effect has occurred. While case histories also provide us with valuable information, they have several drawbacks. First, the physician is treating

an individual who is already having some type of physical or psychological problem. Any sexual effects experienced are probably a function both of this problem and of the drug used to treat it. Second, whether or not a sexual problem is reported to a physician is often a function of that physician's attitude. If he or she encourages discussion of sexual matters, the patient is far more likely to report on them. However, if sexual communication is frowned upon, many sexual side effects of drugs will remain unreported. Finally, some physicians may have preconceived notions about the effects of a specific drug on sexuality. They will ask the very questions that reaffirm these preconceptions and at the same time miss information that is new or inconsistent with their existing ideas.

A third source of information about drug effects on sexuality is the survey or interview study. In this type of research, individuals are questioned about their sexual experiences when using a particular drug. This method, too, has both advantages and drawbacks. The advantages lie in collecting firsthand information about drug effects from experienced users. The drawbacks include the possibility that only certain types of people will consent to be interviewed—for instance, individuals who have had positive sexual experiences with drugs. Further, the interviewer may unintentionally influence the subject to provide particular types of information, for example, that a specific kind of drug is detrimental to sexuality.

Finally, we come to experimental research, generally carried out in a highly structured and controlled laboratory environment. The amount of the drug used is controlled, and the sexual outcome measures are as objective as possible. The experimenter has the least chance of biasing the results, although bias is still possible.

There are real dangers, however, in drawing

simplistic conclusions from laboratory experiments. Most experiments on drugs and sex have been conducted with animals. While basic biochemical processes mediating sexual arousal in the rat may have some relevance to human behavior, we must not underestimate the complexity of human sexuality. Second, the laboratory experiment is, by definition, artificial and contrived. Animals or humans may respond completely differently in their natural environments. For example, males who are tested for penile response to an erotic film may find that the unfamiliar and pressured atmosphere of the laboratory interferes with their sexual response.

Studies in which only one or two different dosages are administered may lead to completely false conclusions. If the drug dose is unusually high or very low, the experimental results may not reflect the more typical effects of the drug. Research with animals often tends to use excessively high dosages, whereas research with humans often uses very low dosages, to protect the subject's health. In addition, the previous experience of the user with a particular drug may substantially affect the outcome. In the case of marihuana or alcohol research with human subjects, experienced users may report opposite effects from naive users.

Drug research with humans must be designed with certain legal and ethical concerns in mind. Subjects must be informed about both the drug they will be given and the nature of the experiment. It is, in fact, highly unethical to give drugs to human subjects without their informed consent. If subjects were not informed about the purpose of an experiment, they might become anxious at some change in their sexual responsivity. However, if they are aware of the type of drug being used, they may develop strong expectations about how that drug will affect their sexuality, and respond accordingly.

ALCOHOL AND SEX

Candy is dandy
But liquor is quicker.

(Ogden Nash)

Lechery, sir, it provokes and it unprovokes; it provokes the desire, but it takes away the performance: therefore, much drink may be said to be an equivocator with lechery.

(Shakespeare, *Macbeth*, act 2, scene 1)

Our culture provides us with conflicting messages about the aphrodisiac effects of alcohol. Psychologist Terence Wilson of Rutgers University points out the widespread cultural belief that alcohol exerts a "disinhibiting" effect on our sexual behavior (1977). In other words, many individuals in our society use alcohol to lift the inhibitions that prevent or detract from a sexual experience. Does alcohol really have this effect?

There is no doubt that many people believe alcohol breaks down the sexual barriers and acts as an aphrodisiac. Unfortunately, scientific investigation of this question has been hampered by the moralistic attitudes of our culture toward both alcohol and sex. We have traditionally frowned on research that focuses on pleasure, opting instead for studies with direct relevance to treatment and therapy. Only recently has research on alcohol's effects on sexuality become possible.

In 1970, *Psychology Today* published the results of a survey on sexuality in which 45 percent of males and 68 percent of females reported that alcohol increased their enjoyment of sex (Athanasiou *et al.*, 1970). However, the survey did not relate sexual enjoyment to the amount of alcohol consumed. Possibly the positive expectations of the respondents at low dosages, did indeed increase their sexual pleasure. But at high dosages, alcohol might lead to performance difficulties.

One of the first controlled studies of alcohol's effects on human sexuality used the

The chronic use of alcohol in large doses generally leads to a major disruption in sexual (and social) functioning. (*The Granger Collection*)

Thematic Apperception Test (TAT) (Clark, 1952). Subjects were given alcohol in an informal party situation and then shown erotic slides. Their responses to the TAT, a projective test in which subjects make up stories to fit a series of pictures, were recorded. Clark found that the stories of subjects who had received alcohol had more sexual content than did those of subjects who had not received alcohol. While suggesting that alcohol disinhibits the repression of sexual material, the study contains many methodological flaws, making it difficult to draw any firm conclusions.

Although most research on the sexual effects of alcohol has either been done with animals or has employed indirect measures of human sexual arousal such as the TAT, a series of studies conducted at Rutgers University has directly measured human subjects — that is, they have included precise measurement and administration of alcohol dosage and direct physiological measurement of genital arousal.

The first experiment (Farkas and Rosen, 1976) examined the effects of four different dosages of alcohol on young male volunteers. Each of the sixteen young men in the study received all four alcohol dosages. The amount of alcohol they consumed was disguised in a mixture of alcohol and orange juice. The four alcohol levels used in this study were 0, .025, .050, and .075 percent. The highest level corresponds to approximately five straight drinks but is in fact less than the legal driving limit in the State of New Jersey (.10 percent).

After the subject had reached the desired blood alcohol concentration, he was asked to recline on a bed facing a movie screen. Heart rate electrodes were attached, and the subject placed a penile plethysmograph around his penis. While the subject viewed a 15-minute erotic film, the experimenter recorded his penile response and heart rate on a polygraph in the adjoining room.

The results of this study are pictured in Figure 13.4. The major effect of increased alcohol was suppression of erection, with the greatest

penile response occurring at the lowest blood alcohol level. Increasing intoxication was also associated with a slower penile response and an increase in heart rate. The more rapid heart rate is evidence of the general discomfort that subjects felt at the highest alcohol dosage. Their verbal reports supported these findings. They reported the highest subjective estimates of erection at the lowest alcohol level.

This experiment is historically significant as the first controlled demonstration of the direct effects of specific alcohol dosage on human sexual response. It is important to remember, however, that all subjects were young (under 25) and that the experiment took place under artificial laboratory conditions. It is possible that older subjects would have responded differently, and that subjects might have behaved differently under somewhat more natural conditions.

In addition to alcohol's physiological effects, it is important to determine whether the subject who strongly believes that alcohol will increase sexual arousal does in fact show a greater response. A second study (Bridell and Wilson) investigated the effects of subjects' expectations of how alcohol would affect their sexual response. Half the subjects were told that alcohol would increase their sexual arousal as they viewed an erotic film. The remaining ones were told that alcohol would decrease their arousal. Varying alcohol dosages, ranging from none to six drinks, were given to the subjects, who were unaware of the alcohol content of their drinks. Penile erections were measured during presentation of the film.

The results confirmed the earlier finding— that increased alcohol levels were associated with *less* penile tumescence. However, this study also found that positive expectations noticeably enhanced the subjects' responses. In fact, it seems that when the first group of subjects were told they had consumed alcohol, even if they had not, they showed a greater response to erotic stimuli.

FIGURE 13.4

The relationship between blood alcohol level, penile tumescence, and heart rate. *(Farkas and Rosen, 1976)*

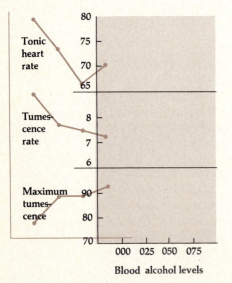

Do women respond to alcohol in the same way? A study using the vaginal plethysmograph described in Chapter 5 (Wilson and Lawson, 1976) measured sexual arousal in female volunteers viewing erotic films. One very interesting finding emerged from this study: expectations and physiological effects of alcohol can sometimes work in opposite directions. The physiological effects of alcohol were similar to those reported for men, that is, increased alcohol dosage was associated with lowered arousal as measured by vaginal blood flow. However, when the women believed they had consumed alcohol, they generally reported verbally that they were more aroused by the films. On the other hand, at high alcohol dosages, subjects reported that they were aroused when in fact their vaginal blood flow response showed very little arousal. In other words, the expectation of consuming alcohol seems to be a more effective aphrodisiac than the actual consumption.

In summary, these studies have shed some light on the effects of alcohol on sexual arousability. We now have conclusive evidence that large amounts of alcohol suppress the sexual response in both men and women. Also, expectations about the effects of alcohol have considerable influence on how we react. In our culture, a widespread belief exists that sex and alcohol "go together," and this belief is evident in subjects' self-reports. Small quantities of alcohol may help to set the mood, without necessarily interfering with the ability to perform sexually. However, large quantities almost invariably lead to some kind of sexual dysfunction.

MARIHUANA AND SEX

In different parts of the world, marihuana is used for warding off fatigue, as a medication for diseases such as glaucoma, and as a part of religious rituals. Within such settings, it has few sexual side effects. In the West, though, marihuana has acquired a reputation as an aphrodisiac. Although it has relatively subtle physiological effects on the user, the strong expectation of increased sexual pleasure is often borne out in the experience of marihuana smokers.

Cultural mythology about the relationship between sex and marihuana has produced lurid tales of sexual orgies, sexual perversion, and debauchery. Marihuana has been described as a "killer weed" that destroys will power and eliminates the line between right and wrong. Such fears have rarely been verified by scientific research. In fact as early as 1944, New York Mayor LaGuardia's Commission on Marihuana reported that the drug was not a direct causal factor in stimulating prostitution, hypersexuality, or sexual debauchery.

Current evidence indicates that both the physical and the psychological effects of marihuana use are, in the potency usually consumed in the West, relatively mild. Nevertheless, the belief that marihuana enhances sexuality persists among both users and nonusers. Its origin may lie in the popular stereotype of the typical "potsmoker"—a rebellious and politically radical hippie, who lives in a commune that encourages free love and uninhibited sexuality. Since the hippie is also seen as a confirmed marihuana user, the conclusion drawn is that marihuana causes this sexual life style.

Research on the sexual effects of illicit drugs is particularly difficult to perform under controlled laboratory conditions. Most research on marihuana has been in the form of questionnaire, interview, or survey studies. We have already reviewed the methodological difficulties of these techniques: first, ensuring that the data are representative of the target population; second, controlling for the great variability in drug potency—the effects of smoking Mexican marihuana may be very different from smoking an equal amount of Asian marihuana. Finally, the marihuana user may also be using other drugs, making it difficult to attribute sexual effects to marihuana use alone.

With these reservations in mind, it is worth reviewing some of the research on marihuana's effects on sexuality. Given the variability among samples, drug potency, and types of questionnaires, there is surprising consistency in the outcome of this research. Erich Goode, after summarizing the results of several studies, reports: "The most obvious and dominant impression is that users overwhelmingly describe their marihuana experience in favorable and pleasurable terms" (1972, p. 51).

An extensive questionnaire study (Tart, 1971) reported the responses of 150 students on the side effects of marihuana. Results indicated that marihuana increased sexual desire in the company of those who would in any case be likely sexual partners.

There is usually no drive toward sex unless the overall situation seems appropriate to the user. Desire is then intensified, sexual sensations enhanced, and feelings of greater contact, responsiveness, sharing and desire to give, and empathy with one's sexual partner are often experienced. (p. 151)

For most users, marihuana was the ideal aphrodisiac. Generally, level of intoxication was positively related to feelings of sexual pleasure. But with very high levels of intoxication, some users reported that their involvement with internal fantasies and experiences began to detract from the sexual involvement.

Another questionnaire study on marihuana use (Koff, 1974), which analyzed the responses of 251 undergraduates, found that 48.5 percent of subjects reported increased sexual desire and 51.3 percent reported increased sexual enjoyment. A significant difference occurred between male and female responses to these questions: females were more likely to report increases in sexual desire; males were more likely to note increased enjoyment. Koff interprets this difference in terms of traditional sex roles: The disinhibiting effects of marihuana are more powerful for the female because she has traditionally been taught to repress her sexual desires. The intensity of physical sensation during sexual activity is more important for the male, whereas the loss of mental control at this time tends to be uncomfortable for females. Finally, the study reported a tendency for higher marihuana dosages to be associated with lessened desire and pleasure.

This pattern of results has been confirmed in several other studies. Goode (1969) found that 50 percent of the females and 39 percent of the males in his sample reported an increase in sexual desire while high. Another study (Halikas et al., 1971) indicated that more than half of the sample had experienced heightened sexual feelings as a result of the drug. It should be noted that the majority of subjects who do not report increases in sexual desire or pleasure report that marihuana causes no change.

The studies described above usually relied on college student samples. A different population—patients at the Haight-Ashbury Free Medical Clinic—was studied by two researchers (Gay and Sheppard, 1973). Fifty subjects, most of whom had extensive drug use histories, were asked about the effects of various drugs on sexuality. Marihuana was mentioned by 80 percent of the subjects as the best drug for sex. The reasons most often mentioned for this sexual enhancement were the disinhibitory and relaxing effects of marihuana and the heightened sensory awareness and time distortion it imparts.

Since marihuana has few direct physical effects that would account for its enormous popularity as an aphrodisiac, it is interesting to note the high proportion of users who report positive side effects. We might suggest an explanation that relies on the set and setting of use: that is, it is not the physical effect of marihuana that increases sexual desire, but rather, the setting in which the drug is used — a room lit by candles, burning incense, music.

Although marihuana does seem to enhance the sexual script for many individuals, concern has arisen that it may interfere with sexual function by altering hormone levels. In 1974, *Newsweek* published the results of a study that found lowered testosterone levels in male users — which caused great public concern. Indeed, some controversy is evident over this issue, with two prominent studies reporting vastly different findings. In the first study (Kolodny *et al.*, 1974), the plasma testosterone levels of male marihuana users were compared with a nonusing control group. The researchers found that users had significantly lower testosterone levels than nonusers, and further, that heavy users had lower levels than light users. In contrast, a second study (Mendelson *et al.*, 1974) found no evidence of a relationship between marihuana use and testosterone levels. In this study, casual and heavy users were confined to a research ward for one month, where they were permitted to smoke marihuana. Blood samples were taken daily and showed no systematic relationship between the amount of marihuana used and testosterone level. Thus it is difficult to arrive at any clear conclusions on this topic; the different outcomes of these two studies may well have been due to methodological differences.

NARCOTICS AND SEX

The narcotic drugs, particularly heroin, have acquired the reputation of being sexual depressants. Although there is an absence of controlled laboratory studies on this subject, the weight of interview data generally confirms this view. Both male and female narcotics addicts have reported that opiates reduce sexual desire. In addition, narcotics have been described as reducing potency and delaying orgasm. Also, reports indicate that narcotics lower testosterone levels in the male addict and interfere with the menstrual cycle of the female addict.

Not all narcotics users report these effects, and the degree of sexual impairment is often associated with the duration of use and the amount used. In fact, some users report that opiates have improved their sexual functioning. As with other drugs, the sexual effects of opiates may vary with the expectations and desires of the user, and with the setting of use.

Narcotics act as central nervous system depressants. Heroin use also seems to act as a sexual depressant in the life style of the addict. The heroin high is usually described as a solitary and deenergizing experience. Most addicts report sedative effects of the drug — "nodding out," being unconcerned with other people and surroundings, and feeling extremely passive. Often, the addict is in poor health, uses drugs of doubtful purity, and supplements his narcotics habit with other drugs. Finally, the user subculture generally views heroin as a sexually incapacitating drug. Heroin use removes the need for sexual performance, and it has been suggested that addiction is in some ways a substitute for sexuality. Hustling for drugs, shooting up, and the subsequent feelings of peace and serenity have analogies in sexual behavior.

As with other drugs, a distinction can be made between the effects of chronic and acute use. Initial experimentation with heroin often produces desirable sexual effects. Ejaculation is delayed, so that intercourse can continue for long periods of time. Ed Brecher (1972) reports that opium was often used in India during the nineteenth century for this purpose. During the "honeymoon" period with heroin, the user often experiences improved and more pleasurable sexuality.

Sexual difficulties usually emerge with continued use. In one study (DeLeon and Wexler, 1973), residents of an abstinence treatment program for addicts were interviewed about their sex lives. Almost all subjects reported a decrease in the frequency of intercourse, masturbation, and nocturnal emissions. Time to ejaculation increased for all heroin users, to a mean of 44 minutes.

A curious phenomenon during detoxification from heroin is the appearance of spontaneous erection and orgasm. The recovery of sexual interest and potency is usually very rapid and may occur in such unlikely environments as hospitals and prisons. Addicts enrolled in abstinence programs usually report normal sexual functioning. Rates of masturbation, nocturnal emission, and orgasm are all significantly improved during treatment, and time to ejaculation decreases.

A large proportion of ex-addicts enroll in methadone maintenance treatment programs. In such a program, the ex-addict receives a daily dose of methadone that is intended to block the craving for heroin without interfering with general functioning. Researchers and ex-addicts have expressed concern about the sexual side effects of methadone.

Research on this question has generally demonstrated an improvement in sexual function relative to the addict's behavior while using heroin. One study (Cushman, 1972) found that 50 percent of the methadone patient sample reported normal sexual functioning, and most reported some improvement. A small percentage reported new or continued sexual difficulties. In another study (Wieland and Yunger 1970), 65 percent of the methadone patients described libido, activity, and enjoyment as being at least average. The study

notes that although methadone generally produces less frequent difficulties than heroin, some subjects experienced worse problems with methadone than with heroin.

There are several reasons why methadone might improve sexual functioning. Generally, it stabilizes the user's life style and health. It is a longer-acting drug than heroin, making the user less susceptible to extreme highs and lows. The dosage is stable, and the drug is relatively pure compared with heroin. It is possible that methadone users who report sexual difficulties had some of these problems before they began their drug use careers. However, methadone is a powerful drug, and as such, it may well have debilitating sexual effects on some users.

STREET DRUGS AND SEX

A variety of illicit drugs have acquired reputations as aphrodisiacs in the past decade. Among them are amphetamines, cocaine, amyl nitrite, LSD and other hallucinogens, barbiturates, and methaqualone (Quaalude). All of these drug types except cocaine and the hallucinogens are also prescribed as medication for certain physical or emotional problems. However, their reputation as sexual enhancers is most likely to come from those who use them illicitly.

One of the difficulties in researching the effects of the illicit use of these substances is the phenomenon of "polydrug use." The user of any one of these drugs is likely to have tried several others, often at the same time. Therefore, distinguishing the effects of each drug individually is difficult. Another problem is the variability of dosages and of quality of the drugs that are used. Very little research has been done that controls for these factors.

Members of drug-using subcultures often have different sexual values from nonusers.

For instance, Goode (1972) found that the number of types of drugs used by members of his college student sample was related to the number of sexual partners they had had. Drug use also corresponded with an increased frequency of intercourse and with an earlier age of first intercourse. Goode cautions against concluding that drug use causes increased sexual activity. He suggests that the student drug user becomes socialized into a sexually permissive milieu and adopts the attitudes of this peer group toward drug use and sexuality.

In reviewing the effects of illicit drug use on sexuality we have little experimental information to rely on. The majority of our data come from the self-reports of experienced drug users, and from our knowledge of the pharmacological actions of these drugs. In examining self-report data, we must be aware that drug users are often influenced by their expectations of how a specific drug will affect their sexuality.

Amphetamines. Various effects have been claimed for amphetamines ("speed") by its users—from heightened sexual interest but decreased ability to perform, to definitely increased powers, to decreased sexual interest, to no effects at all (Cox and Smart, 1972). In other words, there is little consensus among users as to how amphetamines affect sexuality. Some of the variability may be due to differences in dosage, method of administration, and drug experience. Obviously, large individual differences also exist in the ways that users react to this drug.

Methamphetamine has its most powerful effect when taken intravenously. "With intravenous injection an overwhelming total body orgasmic 'flash' or 'rush' was repeatedly described" (Gay and Sheppard, 1973, p. 154). Male users have reported erection simultaneous with injection of the drug. Users frequently note both an increased desire for sex-

ual activity and an increased aggressiveness in the sexual act; but while sexual activity is often prolonged, subjects report that orgasm may become difficult or impossible. Other researchers have also reported that chronic amphetamine use may prevent orgasm without affecting potency. On the other hand, some users report multiple orgasm after amphetamine use. When the chronic user comes off of a "run" of speed use, common symptoms include exhaustion, insomnia, weight loss, and paranoia. These aftereffects are clearly incompatible with any kind of further sexual activity.

Cocaine. In 1884, Freud wrote of the powers of cocaine as an aphrodisiac: "The natives of South America, who represented their goddess of love with coca leaves in her hand, did not doubt the stimulative effect of coca on the genitalia"; and he made great use of the drug to cure his own depression and fatigue. For many drug users, cocaine remains the ultimate mood elevator and energizer. According to some researchers, its use is limited chiefly by its high cost and low availability.

In general, the sexual effects of cocaine appear to parallel those of amphetamines: increased ability to maintain an erection, prolonged sexual activity, and some difficulty in reaching orgasm. When large amounts of cocaine are used, its strongly stimulative nature may result in sexual frustration. Once again, dosage and the individual's predrug level of sexual function appear to play a major role.

Amyl nitrite. Amyl nitrite, commonly known as "poppers," is used as medication for the treatment of anginal pain. It causes expansion of the blood vessels, and therefore a rapid drop in blood pressure. Along with this drop, there are usually feelings of faintness, skin flush, and a feeling of heat in the skin. The relaxation of blood vessels in the brain may

Certain street drugs are believed by users to enhance sexual experiences.
(© *Charles Gatewood*)

cause pressure to build up in the skull, sometimes producing severe headaches. The physical response to amyl nitrite is immediate and intense, and may be extremely dangerous.

Amyl nitrite has been popularized as an aphrodisiac among some homosexual groups, although its use has also spread to heterosexual groups. It appears to be more popular with males than females. Generally, it is inhaled at the moment of orgasm, when it is reported to lead to a prolonged and intensified climax. The effect of the drug is relatively short-lived, usually one to two minutes.

Psychedelics. In 1966, Timothy Leary, the "guru" of psychedelic drug use, discussed the sexual effects of LSD in an interview in *Playboy* magazine. In that article, he stated that LSD was the most powerful aphrodisiac

ever discovered. His use of the word "aphrodisiac" was not in the sense of a drug that releases pent-up sexual energy but as a drug that augments the sexual experience. His statement influenced the expectations of drug users as to the sexual effects of LSD for many years.

From the limited research published on this subject, we know that the effects of psychedelics are very dependent on the setting in which they are used and the empathy that exists between sexual partners. The Haight-Ashbury sample reported that with a compatible partner, psychedelics increased sexual sensitivity, heightened awareness, and improved interpersonal communication. On the other hand, if the user was uncomfortable with the setting, negative sexual experiences were common. Reactions to psychedelics are often unpredictable, although the amount used seems to be a critical variable. At high dosages, subjects were much more likely to report that sex was difficult or impossible.

Barbiturates. The barbiturates have effects similar to those of alcohol, in that both are centrally acting nervous system depressants. If they make the user feel more relaxed, this may increase the likelihood of sexual activity. At higher dosages, barbiturates tend to depress all behavior, including sexual activity. Physical coordination is impaired, as is emotional control. In the Haight-Ashbury sample, the chronic barbiturate user generally had a bad reputation as a lover and as a companion. While barbiturates may decrease inhibition, they usually have negative effects on sexual performance.

Quaalude. Methaqualone, commonly marketed in the United States under the trade name Quaalude, is a sedative-hypnotic drug that is chemically unrelated to barbiturates. While it is a central nervous system depressant, it acts on different brain centers than do other sedative drugs. Quaalude is generally prescribed to produce sleep or relaxation in agitated patients.

While the drug was regarded as an aphrodisiac in the initial stages of its popularity among illicit users, the Haight-Ashbury sample rated its sexual effects as relatively low. Response to it generally varies with dosage. It has been reported to increase desire and break down sexual resistance, but to decrease potency. At high dosages, Quaalude's relaxing qualities are likely to result in sexual difficulty and disinterest.

PRESCRIPTION DRUGS AND SEX

In addition to the drugs described thus far, there are dozens more that are commonly prescribed in medical and psychiatric settings. While it is impossible to review the sexual side effects of all such drugs, there is evidence that many of them can lead to some form of sexual dysfunction. A review of this subject (Story, 1974) lists 118 antihypertensive and psychiatric drugs that have been reported to affect sexuality in some way. The reported side effects include ejaculatory disorders, impotence, low sexual interest, amenorrhea (the absence or cessation of regular menstrual cycles), and gynecomastia (abnormal increase in male breast size).

The sexual side effects of any prescription drug will depend, in part, on the length of use and the dosage taken. It will also be affected by such individual factors as the age, sex, and health of the user. We would expect that a drug that successfully treats an incapacitating physical condition would indirectly improve sexual functioning. Similarly, psychiatric medications that reduce anxiety or depression may well improve sexual abilities in an indirect fashion. If these drugs improve interpersonal relationships, they are likely to facilitate better sexual performance as a function of improved social adjustment.

When a drug can lead to sexual difficulties, the patient should be aware that this is a normal side effect of the drug. If the patient is not informed about potential sexual side effects, he or she is likely to be seriously concerned if a sexual problem appears.

Summary

Throughout this book sexuality has been described as resulting from a complex interplay of psychological and physical factors, with our bodily responses being strongly affected by our attitudes, beliefs, and experience. Certainly this is true of the three major health issues discussed in this chapter. Although venereal disease, disability, and drug use are vastly different health issues, they have in common a relationship to sexual functioning that is both physical and mental. Further, the problems that arise in relation to these three issues have both psychological and physical components; in solving these problems, then, we must make use of techniques that involve our sexual attitudes and information as well as our sexual architecture.

1. In regard to venereal disease, we have made considerable progress in finding appropriate medical solutions. We have been less

successful, however, in tackling the social stigma and psychological discomfort that are attached to VD. Thus while medication is available to cure almost all of the sexually transmitted diseases, VD rates have continued to climb. Perhaps the most important factor in this paradox is our sexual value system; VD continues to be viewed as a moral rather than a medical problem. As long as we see VD as a punishment for promiscuity, and withhold sexual information in the hopes of promoting chastity or fidelity, we can expect to see VD rates that are frighteningly high.

2. In regard to physical or mental disability, we have touched on only a few of the many conditions that can adversely affect sexuality. While this section is by no means exhaustive, it does indicate that the disabled have two types of sexual problems; first, those related to their specific disability, and second, those related to our misconceptions about their sex-ual needs and capabilities. We have tended to ignore that the disabled do have sexual interests and that, in many cases, these interests can be incorporated into a sexual script adapted to the limitations of the specific disability.

3. In regard to drug use, we have briefly discussed what is probably the most common health issue in our society today. It is almost impossible to find an American who has never used alcohol, an illegal drug, or one of the thousands of prescription drugs now available. Unfortunately, we know very little about how the vast majority of drugs interact with our sexuality, and research on this issue is relatively new and controversial. We do know, however, that our expectations and beliefs about the effects of drugs on sexuality play a major role in how they are actually experienced by us.

Views on Pornography and Obscenity

Most discussions of this topic begin with an attempt to define the terms *pornography* and *obscenity.* Although many people may agree with Supreme Court Justice Potter Stewart that, in regard to pornography, "I know it when I see it", the question of definition is complex and has troubled the Court for many years. Dictionary definitions do relatively little to clear up the confusion: Pornography, derived from a Greek word meaning the "writing of prostitutes", carries with it the suggestion of eroticism that results in sexual arousal. Obscenity is a Latin word that conveys the notion of filth or dirt. Thus, the two words are not necessarily tied together—conceivably sexually arousing material may not be obscene, and obscene material may not be sexually arousing.

Indeed, until the past century, the word obscene was more likely to be applied to works of religious heresy rather than to sexual material. The audience for literary pornography was very limited because only a small, privileged segment of the population in Europe and America could read.

Concern with pornography began in the 19th century in England. The rise in literacy, coupled with a concern for the sensibilities of the Victorian woman, led to the passage of the Obscene Publication Act by Parliament in 1857. Obscene material was defined as that which would corrupt or deprave minds open to such influences. The act, which remained in effect for about 100 years, was effectively used to suppress works by such prominent sexologists as Havelock Ellis.

Meanwhile, in the United States, Anthony Comstock, a religious fanatic, founded and led the Society for the Suppression of Vice, a group that saw disasterous consequences in the spread of any sexually oriented materials. Comstock persuaded Congress to pass a law, in 1873, banning from the mails "every obscene, lewd, lascivious or filthy book, pamphlet, picture, paper, letter, writing, print or other publication of an indecent character". (It was under this federal law that Margaret Sanger's birth control efforts were prosecuted.) Indeed, in 1913 Justice Learned Hand was moved to write about whether Americans would "long remain content to reduce our treatment of sex to the standard of a child's library in the supposed interest of a salacious few, or that shame will long prevent us from adequate portrayal of some of the most serious and beautiful sides of human nature".

The definition of obscenity was seriously tackled by the Supreme Court in 1957 in the case of Roth vs. the United States. In this landmark decision, the Court ruled that the right to be obscene was not protected by the First Amendment to the Constitution. Material could be deemed obscene, however, only if "to the average person, applying contemporary community standards, the dominant theme of the material taken as a whole appeals to prurient interest". The Court further refined this decision saying that obscene works must be "totally without redeeming social importance".

In providing these definitions, the Court intended to protect such serious works as James Joyce's *Ulysses,* which had previously been banned. As a result, however, pornographers made use of a technical loophole; a pornographic book might be "redeemed" by including a single quote from Shakespeare or by providing medical captions for blatantly sexual photographs. In 1967, the Court was forced to admit that its earlier definition had not worked, and in the case of Redrup vs. New York, wrote that, if material was not held to be obscene by the majority of the Court, then it was protected by the First Amendment. Since each Justice had his own personal definition of obscenity, this meant that hundreds of local and state convictions had to be reviewed by the Supreme Court. First Amendment absolutists such as William Douglas, who believed that all forms of speech were protected by the Constitution, objected to this procedure, reasoning that since it was impossible to define obscenity, any laws against it were bound to be unconstitutional.

A way out of this dilemma was suggested in the 1969 decision of Stanley vs. Georgia. In this case, the court concluded that "a state has no business telling a man, sitting alone in his own house, what books he may read or what films he must watch". This doctrine of privacy was extended, by pornographers, to include those who produce, sell, or distribute sexual materials. However, the Court retreated from this position in 1973, when it decided that local communities could set their own standards as to what is obscene. With this ruling, a movie that was acceptable in a major city could be prosecuted in a rural area, and a book forbidden in the South might be sold freely in the North. This confusing state of affairs, and the lack of a generally accepted definition of pornography, continues today.

At issue in all these decisions is whether pornography and obscenity are dangerous. There is usually an assumption that society—or at least certain segments of society, such as children—require protection from the effects of pornographic materials. The question of whether or not this assumption is accurate, is receiving attention and angered debate from a variety of scientific and partisan groups. Perhaps the largest effort to answer it was made by the Presidential Commission on Obscenity and Pornography.

THE COMMISSION ON OBSCENITY AND PORNOGRAPHY

The Commission on Obscenity and Pornography was formed in 1968 to investigate the effects of pornography on American society, and if necessary, to recommend corrective actions. The members of the Commission, appointed under President Lyndon Johnson, included a variety of clergymen, teachers, health-care professionals, researchers, and legal authorities. In addition, the Commission was empowered to gather information by funding fieldwork and experimental research projects. The results were published in 1970. Despite the fact that the report reflected the views of the majority of the Commission, it generated a great deal of controversy and protest. The then President Richard Nixon, and many members of his government, publicly rejected and condemned both the Commission and its recommendations.

What were these recommendations that created such great opposition? Perhaps most importantly, the Commission wrote that ". . . there is no warrant for continued governmental interference with the full freedom of adults to read, obtain or view whatever such material they wish" (1970, p. 58). As well, the Commission recommended "that a massive sex education effort be launched", and reported that they had found "no evidence to date that exposure to explicit sexual materials plays a significant role in the causation of delinquent or criminal behavior among youth or adults" (p 59). The results upon which these statements are based, as well as more recent research findings, will be reviewed in the following sections.

EXPOSURE TO PORNOGRAPHY

According to one study using a national sample, about 84 percent of males and 69 percent of females had seen some form of pornography in their lives (Abelson et al., 1970). Forty percent of males and 26 percent of females reported exposure to pornography within the past two years. The group most likely to have seen pornographic materials is made up of young adults, the highly educated, the socially and politically active, and the religiously inactive. Thus, the "typical" user of pornography is male, college-educated, married, 30 to 40 years old, and above average in socioeconomic status. In addition, the majority of those who have seen pornographic materials did not actually purchase them, but rather, had them passed along by a friend or acquaintance. And, even though most males had seen such materials, only a small proportion reported using them regularly.

ATTITUDES TOWARDS PORNOGRAPHY

In the same national survey, respondents were asked about the effects of pornography. Sixty-seven percent agreed with the statement that "sexual materials excite people sexually", and 61 percent thought that "sexual materials provide information about sex." Fifty-six percent agreed that "sexual materials lead to a breakdown of morals", and 48 percent believed that they lead to rape. As well, 34 percent stated that "sexual materials provide an outlet for bottled up impulses", and 27 percent agreed that "sexual materials give relief to people who have sexual problems."

Interestingly, people who had seen sexual materials tended to describe the effects as positive or neutral. And individuals with the greatest exposure to pornography were most likely to describe its effects as desirable. In contrast, those with little or no exposure tended to believe that it was most harmful, although they were unacquainted with anyone who has experienced such negative effects.

The Commission also reported the findings of several studies that investigated the opinions of professionals on the effects of pornography. While the majority of police chiefs thought that sexual materials were important in causing juvenile delinquency, only 12 percent of health care professionals supported this position. And, the vast majority of psychiatrists and psychologists disagreed with the statement that exposure to pornography leads to antisocial sexual acts, an opinion they shared with sex educators.

THE EFFECTS OF PORNOGRAPHY

Research on the effects of pornography tends to be complicated by a number of problems. First, the method of measuring these effects is crucial; most questionnaire studies find that relatively few respondents report sexual arousal on viewing pornography. However, when subjects' sexual arousal is measured in the laboratory, the proportion reporting arousal is much higher. It seems likely that while pornography is sexually arousing to a majority of people, there is some hesitancy to report this arousal, particularly among those who disapprove of sexual materials. Second, the type of sexual material is important. For instance, studies find different arousal rates for literary, pictorial, and film presentations. Also, the theme of the sexual material—that is, whether it is hard-core or romantic, heterosexual or homosexual, portraying familiar or unfamiliar sexual acts—has a major impact on sexual response. Marvin Zuckerman (1976) suggests that

Erotic stimuli are arousing to the extent that the person can put himself into the action portrayed and empathize with the feelings. This means that the portrayed persons, actions, and motivations must be in some part within the range of experience familiar or acceptable to the respondent (pp. 149–150).

Even with these reservations, several generalizations can be made about the effects of pornography:

1. Most people are sexually aroused by exposure to sexually explicit materials;

2. exposure to pornography does not generally increase the amount of sexual activity engaged in;

3. exposure to pornography does not generally change the types of sexual behavior engaged in, nor does it change attitudes about what is sexually acceptable behavior;

4. for the 24 hour period following exposure to pornography, there tends to be an increase in the amount of time people spend talking about sex;

5. evidence exists that repeated exposure to the same types of sexual materials produces a satiation effect—that is, while initial exposure produces increased arousal, long-term exposure decreases sexual interest.

THE DANISH EXPERIENCE

To better understand the consequences of legalizing pornography, many researchers and jurists have examined the experiences of countries that have already lifted all restrictions on sexual materials. Most prominent among these is Denmark. In 1969, the Danish Parliament removed restrictions against the dissemination of pornographic materials to individuals aged sixteen or above. Even before 1969, however, relatively few restrictions existed on both literary and pictorial pornography, which had been produced in increasing amounts in the previous decade. It is a relatively well-accepted fact that the market for such materials among the Danes increased for several years, and then began to decline. Generally, it is thought that the Danes became "satiated" with sexual materials, and the pornography industry was forced to turn to the tourist and export markets in order to maintain its sales.

Several studies have investigated the relationship in Denmark between the legalization of pornography and sex crimes. In the Commission Report, it is noted that all types of sex crimes decreased, with some crimes—such as rape—decreasing less than others—such as exhibitionism. Further, the Report states that ". . . changes in the incidence of sex offenses could not be attributed to legislative change, alteration of law enforcement practices or modified police reporting and data collection procedures" (p 274). In other words, the decrease in sex crimes was perceived by the Commission as a real change, and not one produced by some artifact.

Not all researchers accept these findings, nor is it clear that the Danish experience can be generalized to the United States. Given the enormous complexity of collecting data on sex crimes (see the discussion of rape in Chapter 12) it seems likely that such research has methodological problems. But even if we accept the Danish experience as valid, whether this same experience would take place in the United States is questionable. Denmark is a small, relatively homogeneous country with a particular set of sexual norms and customs; in contrast, the United States is a large, heterogeneous country with a very different sexual history. Thus, the effects of legalization of pornography on sex crimes are extremely difficult to predict.

PORNOGRAPHY, AGGRESSION, AND SEX CRIMES

For many people, the crux of the argument against pornography is the belief that its use leads to antisocial behavior and crime. Recognizing this concern, the Commission Report reviewed the data then available with two questions in mind: Is there a relationship between the availability of pornography and the incidence of antisocial behavior? What is the experience of sex offenders with pornographic materials?

The first question is extremely difficult to answer. While the availability of pornography has clearly increased in recent years, as has the rate of adult arrests for sex offenses, it is not possible to say that these changes are directly related. Indeed, the Commission suggests that since the distribution of pornographic materials increased at a far greater rate than did sex crimes, there is no support for the notion that the two are causally connected. On the other hand, the Commission notes that the data do not rule out such a connection. Clearly, there are many intervening variables—such as changes in law enforcement, the willingness to report certain sex crimes, and even the structure of the family—that might be part of any connection between pornography and crime.

In discussing the second question, the Commission describes one of the most extensive studies of convicted sex offenders (Gebhard et al., 1965), performed by the Kinsey Institute. This study, which compared the sexual histories of sex offenders, non-sex offenders, and a normal control group, found surprisingly few differences in experience with pornography between the three groups. For example, almost all members of each group had seen pornography. When questioned about their arousal to such material, about 33 percent of the controls and 38 percent of the non-sex offenders reported little or no arousal, and about 31 percent of the controls and 36 percent of the non-sex offenders reported strong arousal. Interestingly, the sex offenders were less likely to report strong arousal, and more likely to report no arousal, than the other two groups. The authors explain this finding as follows: arousal to pornography, they reason, depends on imaginativeness and sensitivity. These qualities are found most frequently among the young and well-educated. Since most of the sex offenders in their group were neither young or well-educated, they were less likely to report that pornography was arousing.

A more recent study on this question (Goldstein et al., 1971) compared the experiences of rapists, pedophiles, homosexuals, transsexuals, and control subjects with pornographic materials. In regard to the two offender groups (rapists and pedophiles), the study found less exposure to pornography during adolescence than for controls. The same pattern was evident when the sex offenders were asked about their recent experiences with pornography—that is, rapists and pedophiles reported significantly less use of pornography than normal controls. The authors conclude that "reasonable" exposure to pornography during adolescence reflects normal sexual curiosity and tends to correlate with an acceptable pattern of adult sexual behavior. In contrast, less than average exposure to pornography during adolescence, as was found for the rapists and pedophiles, reflects some developmental problem that may predispose the individual to sex crimes.

In regard to the relationship between experience with pornography and criminal behavior, then, the Commission Report concludes that there is ". . . no substantial basis for the belief that erotic materials constitute a primary or significant cause of the development of character deficits or that they operate as a significant determinative factor in causing crime and delinquency" (p 287). Many prominent theorists, however, including Sigmund Freud, have postulated an intimate relationship between sex and aggression. In other words, it is possible that while erotic materials are not directly related to the commission of sex crimes, they are associated with increased aggression in other ways.

To investigate this relationship, many recent studies employ the following design: subjects, usually males, are made angry in the laboratory and then shown some type of erotic material.

Next they are placed in a situation where they are expected to give electric shocks to a male or female victim as part of the experiment. The number and severity of the shocks they deliver are then compared to subjects who were exposed to a neutral or non-sexual set of stimuli. In general, these studies tend to show that sexually aroused male subjects deliver more intense shocks to male victims than do control subjects but inhibit aggressive responses against female victims (e.g., Meyer, 1972). Subjects who are only moderately aroused by erotic stimuli, however, tend to inhibit aggression towards both male and female victims (e.g., Baron and Bell, 1977). These findings might be explained as follows: high arousal makes the subject feel frustrated and irritated, leading to increased aggression, while low or moderate sexual arousal is pleasurable, and hence, lowers aggressive behavior.

Since aggression against women is a major concern among those concerned with the effects of pornography, it is particularly interesting to note that male subjects tend to be much less aggressive towards female than male victims. To explain this finding, Edward Donnerstein (1980) suggests that male subjects are aware that aggression towards females is socially disapproved, and so, they inhibit it. Thus, Donnerstein modified the experimental situation in ways that he believed would overcome this social inhibition to aggress against females. Indeed, with these modifications he found that aggression against females was increased after exposure to erotic materials. In explaining his finding, Donnerstein writes that: "Given the nature of most erotic films in which women are depicted in a submissive, passive role, any subtle aggressive content could act to increase aggression against females due to their association with observed aggression." To summarize Donnerstein's results: when a male has been angered or stressed, and then views an erotic film that shows some form of aggression against women, he is likely to behave in a more aggressive manner towards a potential female victim. Clearly, this research has implications in the evaluation of pornography's effects. As we shall see in the next section, the portrayal of women as sexual victims or objects of hostility is a major concern among those who argue against the distribution and sale of pornography.

ARGUMENTS AGAINST PORNOGRAPHY: THE FEMINIST PERSPECTIVE

In general, feminists stand firmly on the "liberal" side of most social questions; they tend to support, for example, the right to contraception and abortion, the rights of homosexuals, and the equal rights amendment. This explains the confusion and misunderstanding about the feminist position on pornography that has developed in recent years. In arguing against pornography, such organizations as *Women Against Pornography* seem to be taking the conservative position in regard to our First Amendment rights to free speech. In fact, their position is considerably more complex than a simple desire to increase sexual censorship.

Feminists tend to make a distinction between "eroticism" and pornography. Eroticism, they say, is the portrayal of sexuality in ways that do not encourage exploitation or violence, and this type of material is not objectionable. In contrast, pornography is described as "propaganda against women"; it fosters the view, according to feminists, that violence against women is a normal and acceptable part of sexual expression. It is the violence of pornography, rather than its sexual content, that is of concern:

Most hard-core pornography consists of pictures or graphic descriptions of women being raped, bound, beaten, or mutilated; some of it involves child molestation. Subtler images of women as passive sex toys pervade soft-core pornography and legitimate commercial advertising. The message is clear: sex is power, and women and children are objects for subjugation and abuse. (Statement by Women Against Pornography)

Objections to pornography, therefore, are not directed only at "hard-core" magazines and movies but at all sexually suggestive material that portrays women and children as victims. Women Against Pornography argue that such material is particularly dangerous when it becomes part of our popular culture—for example, in record album covers, movie billboards, and advertisements. While hard-core pornography has a relatively limited audience, each of us is exposed to the images of popular culture.

The heart of the feminist position against pornography is that pornographic materials encourage violence and hostility towards women. Research on sex offenders, however, does not clearly show a direct relationship between the viewing of such materials and the commission of sex crimes. Nevertheless, we cannot simply dismiss the notion that images of women being sexually abused, and even enjoying this abuse, contribute to a climate in which such behavior seems acceptable. The use of these materials may not necessarily lead to rape, but it does encourage a view of sexuality that equates pleasure with power. Although most users of pornography would not consider translating the images of pornography into behavior, recognizing that pornography is fantasy and not reality, possibly these images do color our feelings about sexuality. In particular, feminists argue that images of women as passive sexual objects who enjoy being dominated become part of the fantasy lives of both men and women, so that men think that they should dominate, and women think they should be dominated.

This type of objection to pornography is echoed by many conservative authors, among them psychiatrist Charles Socarides. Socarides also draws a line between erotic realism and pornography; erotic realism is defined as the realistic depiction of sexuality in ways that emphasize the emotional and aesthetic, as well as the physical, aspects of sex. In contrast, pornography is not concerned with reality, but only with provoking a physical response. Socarides writes that, ". . . when sexual excitement is mixed with the desire to humiliate, to degrade, or to befoul—the very element which makes up pornography has been introduced" (1975, p. 63). Pornography is harmful, then, for several reasons: it replaces love and tenderness with aggression and dominance; it offers an unrealistic and exaggerated portrayal of sexuality; and its themes run contrary to our ideals of human dignity and health.

For these reasons, many people, and particularly feminists, believe that access to pornographic materials should be limited. Thus far, the fight against pornography has taken several forms. Women's groups have attempted to "raise our consciousness" by educating people about its implications. At the same time, there have been protests—both legal and economic—against those who produce or distribute offensive materials. Their goal is not censorship in the sense of forbidding all sexual materials, but rather, a redefinition of obscenity—traditionally excluded from protection by the First Amendment—to include violent depictions of sexuality.

Women and men who accept the feminist arguments against pornography face two types of criticism: that they are sexual prudes, and that they are advocating censorship. To the first criticism, they might reply that they have no objections to sexually explicit materials as long as sex is not equated with power. Indeed, certain types of materials previously defined as obscene—such as information on birth control techniques—are seen as absolutely necessary in the feminist perspective. Nevertheless, the new movement against pornography faces the difficulty of distinguishing itself from earlier anti-pornography crusades in which all sexual materials were seen as threatening.

There is no simple reply to the second criticism. For some feminists, the goal of the movement is not so much to ban obscenity in the courts as it is to make such material morally and ethically unacceptable, and thus, unavailable. We know, for instance, that the publication of materials that disparage certain ethnic or religious groups is usually greeted with anger and protest. In the same way, homosexual groups have become outspoken in their objections to movies that portray their lifestyles as potentially dangerous. If we accept the idea that ethnic, religious, or homosexual groups have a right to protest the distribution of such materials, then we cannot deny feminists a similar right to protest materials that they see as threatening or harmful.

CONCLUSION

It has been suggested that pornography is both a cause and an effect of our sexual attitudes and values. On the one hand, it reflects the ways our culture deals with sex, and with relationships. The notion of sex as a marketable product, as a struggle for power, or as a battleground between men and women, each has its roots in our popular culture. On the other hand, pornography may shape how we feel about sex—as a source of sexual information, and given the scarcity of such information, it may exert a powerful influence on our sexual ideas and beliefs.

The problem of pornography, then—whether it should be available, to whom, and in what form—is not easily solvable. There will continue to be people who argue against any form of sexual material, people who want to limit certain types of pornography, and people who believe that censorship of any sort is unjustified. Among the conclusions drawn by the Commission on Obscenity and Pornography, is the strong suggestion that better and more widespread sex education may be the best solution. By providing information that is accurate, honest, and emotionally meaningful, such education may revise the ways that we think about sexuality, and thus, alter or replace the use of pornography.

Epilogue: Sex Education and Personal Growth

The story is often told, in today's sex education classes, of how Alfred Kinsey's research on human sexuality originated in his lectures on the subject of marriage to Indiana University students. The Marriage Course, which Kinsey first taught in 1938, rapidly grew in enrollment from 100 to nearly 300 students within the first two years that it was offered. Perhaps it was his shabby suits and old-fashioned bow ties, or maybe it was Kinsey's non-judgmental and open approach to sexual matters, that endeared him to his students and allowed them to ask personal questions after class. It was through Kinsey's discussions with hundreds of students that the largest study of human sexuality was born. One of the most important things he learned in these discussions was that, unlike the zoology classes he had previously taught, the Marriage Course involved his student's innermost needs and feelings. It is ironic to note that, although Kinsey went on to achieve an international reputation as a sex researcher, he was forced to resign his position as lecturer in the Marriage Course in 1940 due to pressure from conservative elements in the University and the surrounding community. From then on, Kinsey devoted his energies to assembling those facts and figures about human sexuality that he was not permitted to teach.

While the form and content of sex education classes have changed greatly in the forty years since Kinsey first offered the Marriage Course, his observation that this course is qualitatively different from all others remains valid today. Topics such as masturbation, contraception, and homosexuality affect the student very differently than calculus or French. The sex education class must engage the student's emotions, allow for reflection on personal and societal values, and provide a factually sound basis for personal decision-making. As well, many students who enroll in a human sexuality course are at a stage in their development where sexual conflicts and problems present a stumbling block to personal growth and relationships. Perhaps no other university level course addresses such a wide array of the student's personal questions, emotional needs, and immediately relevant personal issues.

Of course, the sex education course is only one of many sources of sexual information, and no matter how well presented, sex education in the classroom has its inherent limits. For example, while the classroom may be a suitable place for the acquisition of ideas and facts, the home remains a major source of values and role-model learning. The media also provides both explicit and implicit messages about sexuality, as does the peer group.

As we shall see, there is still some controversy about the necessity for, and purposes of, classroom instruction in human sexuality.

The notion that sex education can provoke unacceptable sexual behavior—that is, that students will be tempted to act on what they learn—persists among those who disapprove such courses. In addition, there is the argument that sex education removes the mystery from human sexuality, and that some areas of our lives—like love and sex—are best left unstudied and mysterious. But increasingly, sex education is viewed as important and necessary. Among those who argue for its importance there seem to be two groups; the traditional group stresses the connection between sexual ignorance and venereal disease, unwanted pregnancy, and poor sexual adjustment in marriage. A second and more modern group emphasizes personal growth and self awareness as the major goals of sex education. In general, sex education does seem to be moving in the direction of these positive personal goals, and away from the goal of preventing sex-related social problems. As Alan Harris, a British author, puts it:

The ultimate aim of education, I would argue, is the promotion of personal autonomy. The more educated a person is the better he (she) is able to make a responsible and informed choice between possible courses of behavior. (1974, p. 12)

Historical Trends in Sex Education

To put this modern view of sex education in perspective, let us consider some examples of sex education in the past. The formal teaching of human sexuality might be dated back to the 1700's and the ideas of philosopher Jean-Jacques Rousseau (1712–1778) during the so-called Age of Enlightenment. Rousseau believed in the innate goodness and innocence of children before they were exposed to a cor-

rupt world and generally viewed sexuality as one such corrupting influence. Sex education in his time carried this viewpoint to an extreme, with teachers using every possible means to dissuade their students from any sexual experimentation. Haeberle describes the goals and methods of sex education in the late 1700's as follows:

These classes aimed, above all, at creating a sense

of modesty and wholesome fear. Everything had to take place in an atmosphere of utter seriousness. Any suggestion of pleasure or joy was to be avoided. As a matter of fact, it was proposed that students should be prepared for a sex education class with a special and very meager diet which would weaken their bodies and thus prevent dangerous desires from being aroused . . . . In the same somber spirit, some educators also preferred to demonstrate the anatomical difference between the sexes by inviting their students to the morgue and showing them naked male and female corpses. In addition, children were taken to hospitals and insane asylums to observe syphilitic patients and madmen who were described as victims of masturbation . . . . In short, the real purpose behind the whole enterprise was not so much to educate the young about sex as to warn them against temptation. (1978, p. 472)

When, in 1760, the famous Swiss physician Samuel Tissot published *Onanism*, a book that blamed masturbation for causing almost every known physical and mental disease, he started a wave of medical opposition to sex education that lasted well into the present century. English and American physicians in the Victorian era were especially conservative in their sexual attitudes, and filled their writings with gloomy and puritanical warnings about "sexual excess". An example is provided by William Alcott's *The Physiology of Marriage*, first published in 1866. Much of his book is devoted to arguments against frequent "indulgence", which Alcott believed to be dangerous even for the married. As can be seen from the Table of Contents presented, sexuality was seen as fraught with "errors", "penalties", and "crimes".

Twentieth century attitudes towards sex education have been greatly influenced by the ideas of Sigmund Freud, Havelock Ellis, and Alfred Kinsey, all of whom advocated a rational and scientific approach to the subject. Freud, for example, dispelled the 18th century myth of childhood innocence, thus paving the

CONTENTS.

way for sex education aimed at pre-adolescents. At the same time, Ellis was laying the groundwork for a more tolerant and understanding view of the diversity of human sexual behavior. Ellis's books were a major factor in freeing Western thought from the intolerance of the Victorian period. Without this view of sex as a natural function, it is unlikely that Kinsey, Masters and Johnson, and numerous other sex researchers, could have even investigated the parameters of human sexual behavior.

The future of sex education rests, in large part, with such key professional organizations as SIECUS (The Sex Information and Education Council of the United States) and AASECT (The American Association of Sex Educators, Counsellors, and Therapists). These organizations maintain a commitment to progressive sex education and have helped to make it publicly acceptable. Their progressive influence is counterbalanced, to some extent, by the more conservative views of certain political, educational, and parent groups. At present, responsibility for sex education at the public school level—its content at different grades, and whether it should be taught at all —rests largely at the community level. Thus, students in one community may be taught about all aspects of sexuality, whereas in a neighboring town, they may receive no instruction at all. At the university level, sexuality courses may be taught through departments of psychology, sociology, biology, or even political science, with the varied perspectives that these academic disciplines seem to imply.

Sex Education at Home

Does sex education belong in the schools? No, say many parents, who believe that it is their right and responsibility to provide for the sexual education of their children. In contrast, those who believe that the school system should play a major role argue that parents often will not or cannot carry out the task. While parents are concerned that the schools will emphasize sexual facts at the expense of sexual values, educators such as Mary Calderone, President of SIECUS, suggest that: "Sex education by most parents has to date been either nonexistent, actively negative, threatening, frightened, or capricious, and sometimes seductive" (1978, p. 146).

One consequence of this controversy has been a serious effort to evaluate the sources and impact of sexual information on the young. One such study, by John Gagnon and Elizabeth Roberts (1980), reported the results of a survey of parents with children aged three to eleven concerning the manner and content of their communications about sex. Several hundred parents in a large, midwestern city were interviewed in depth, and the results of these interviews confirmed some common-sense predictions, while upsetting some others.

As might be expected, mothers assumed most of the responsibility for sex education in the majority of households. This was true regardless of whether the family had male or female children. About 75 percent of the mothers reported discussing pregnancy, birth, and the physical differences between the sexes with their children. Less than half of the fathers reported a similar discussion.

Another important issue was the age at which children should be told various facts about sexuality. A substantial proportion of the parents believed that it was best to wait for the child to ask a specific question before providing sexual information; that is, they subscribed to the notion that "the child will ask when he or she is ready". Gagnon and Roberts view this as something of a cop-out on the part of parents: some children may never ask questions about sex, while others

Sex Education in Families

Morton Hunt's recent survey (1974) found that 2/3 of men and 4/5 of women interviewed had received no direct sexual information from their fathers. Half of the women and most of the men reported that their mothers had *never* discussed sex with them. A survey of *Psychology Today* readers (mostly middle-class, highly educated) found an even smaller number who had received significant sex education from their parents. Mothers will sometimes introduce the topic of menstruation with their daughters, but will usually ignore other important aspects of sexuality. Sexual communication between father and son is usually limited to warnings about the dangers of pregnancy and VD. The novelist, Ernest Hemingway, describes such a "heart-to-heart" talk between father and son.

'The little bugger,' Nick said.
'Do you know what a bugger is?' his father said.
'We call anything a bugger,' Nick said.
'A bugger is a man who has intercourse with animals.'
'Why?' Nick said.
'I don't know,' his father said. 'But it is a heinous crime.'

Nick's imagination was both stirred and horrified by this and he thought of various animals but none seemed attractive or practical and that was the sum total of direct sexual knowledge bequeathed him by his father except on one other subject. One morning he read in the paper that Enrico Caruso had been arrested for mashing.

'What is mashing?'

'It is one of the most heinous of crimes,' his father answered. Nick's imagination pictured the great tenor doing something strange, bizarre, and heinous with a potato masher to a beautiful woman. . . . He resolved, with considerable horror, that when he was old enough he would try mashing at least once.

His father had summed up the whole matter by stating that masturbation produced blindness, insanity, and death, while a man who went with prostitutes would contract hideous venereal diseases and that the thing to do was to keep your hands off of people.

Source: From "Fathers and Sons" in *Winner Take Nothing* by Ernest Hemingway, Charles Scribner and Sons, 1933.

may receive discouraging signals from their parents if the topic is raised at the wrong time or place. And when children do raise sexual questions, they may be more of the simple type—such as "How are babies born?"—and less of the complex, but perhaps more important, type—such as "Is sex bad if you don't love someone?".

Interestingly, among parents who believed that it was their responsibility to initiate sexual discussions, there was a tendency to delay these discussions until their children were older. That is, parents of three-year-olds intended to discuss sex with them when they were six, while parents of six-year-olds were waiting for their children to reach the age of nine, and so on. Even parents with the best of intentions regarding sex education clearly hesitated about when to actually begin the educational process.

One unexpected finding of this study was that television played an important role in initiating sexual discussion for about one-third of the families. A recent British study also found that a children's sex education program produced by the BBC was likely to stimulate sexual discussion in the home (Rogers, 1974). Although most television sex education programs are currently aimed at an adult audience, television can be quite an effective stimulus for engaging children's interest in sexual matters.

The Effects of Sex Education

As noted earlier, opponents of sex education often suggest that such programs will stimulate sexual behavior. Proponents, in contrast, believe that sex education may help to solve a variety of sex-related health problems such as venereal disease and teenage pregnancies. In fact, no conclusive evidence shows that either of these views is completely accurate. That is, participation in a sex education program does not guarantee that the participant will become sexually active, nor does it always protect the participant from sex-related problems. Of course, the teenager who understands the biology of conception is better equipped to understand, as well, the various methods of contraception. This knowledge in no way guarantees, however, that the sexually active teenager is emotionally prepared to take contraceptive responsibility.

How, then, does the student who completes a course in human sexuality differ from the student who does not take such a course? Certainly, we would expect that the participating student will have access to a variety of sexual facts, figures, and ideas, although this information will not necessarily effect his or her behavior. Perhaps the most important change reported by researchers in this field, however, is related to sexual *attitudes*. For example, one study evaluated a wide range of attitudinal and behavioral changes among students at the University of Delaware (Zuckerman et al., 1976). After completion of a sex education course, both male and female students reported more permissive sexual attitudes than students in a control group did. Their more permissive view, however, was unrelated to an increase in sexual experience. Students in both the sex education course and the control group reported more sexual experience by the end of the semester. That is, changes in sexual behavior seem more directly related to time on campus than to any specific educational process. Interestingly, students who selected a sex education course had more permissive attitudes than control subjects even before the course began. This suggests that students willing to enroll in such a course—and who, it may be assumed, think that sexual learning is important—tend to be more open-minded than those who do not take the course.

Several research studies have confirmed this finding of short-term attitudinal changes among participants in a sex education class. In addition, one recent report (Story, 1979) included a two-year follow-up period in the assessment. Two groups of Iowa students were evaluated: an experimental group who had taken the human sexuality course, and a control group enrolled in a course in communications. When the groups were compared, it was found that students who had taken the sexuality course were more accepting both of their own sexual behavior and the sexual behavior of others. An unexpected finding was that students in the control group actually became less accepting of their own and others' sexual behavior after the two-year follow-up period. The author suggests that community pressure toward more conservative sexual attitudes had a much greater impact on those who did not take the course. An interesting implication of this study, then, is that in addition to becoming more tolerant and accepting, students participating in a human sexuality course may also develop greater confidence in their own attitudes and beliefs.

Obviously, it is impossible to generalize about the effects of sex education without knowing the specific content and orientation of each course. Some schools offer intensive one- or two-week programs; others provide full semester classes. Some courses are taught with a biological orientation; others emphasize social factors. And some classes emphasize values and choices; others stress facts. Finally, and perhaps most importantly, some teachers are comfortable with their own sexuality, whereas others are defensive or easily embarrassed. Implicit in each of these choices is a decision about the purpose of the sex education course: what are the appropriate goals of sex education?

Goals and Values in Sex Education

The most important challenge that sex educators must meet in the 1980's is the definition of their goals and values. Few people would disagree that one goal of sex education should be the teaching of accurate and up-to-date sexual information. The question of sexual values, however, produces considerably more controversy. Sex educators tend to locate themselves somewhere on a continuum between two extreme positions: at one extreme are those who believe that definite rules exist for all aspects of sexual conduct, that sexual behavior is easily categorized as "right" or "wrong", and that each sexual question has a specific and clear-cut answer. At the other extreme is the view that nothing is inherently wrong with any form of sexual expression, that sexual questions can be answered in many ways, and that sexual conduct is "right" or "wrong" only in relation to sexual norms that vary widely from one culture to another.

One approach to this dilemma of "sexual doctrinism" versus "cultural relativism" is provided by Harvard psychologist Lawrence Kohlberg. Kohlberg is best known for his work on the stages of moral development; at each of the six stages he lists, the child or adult tackles moral questions with a different understanding of what morality means. Suppose, for example, that the question is whether or not a man should marry a woman that he has impregnated. At stage 1, an individual might respond that he should act in the way that is most likely to avoid external punishment; at stage 3, the individual would be more concerned with the disapproval of others; at stage 6, the primary concern would be to act in a way that avoids self-condemnation. Sex education, according to Kohlberg, should proceed in a way that stimulates the student to think about such questions from a higher level of moral development. Kohlberg believes that morality is universal, and not tied to any particular culture's standards of right and wrong. Moral principles, however, do not always lead to a clear choice between alternatives in a moral dilemma. Sex education, then, must involve discussion and argument about the solution to sexual problems; in turn, such discussion can be expected to stimulate the student to think about sexual issues from a higher level of moral development.

While Kohlberg stresses the moral development that enables us to make sexual decisions, other sex educators are more concerned with self-awareness, personal growth, tolerance, and values clarification—that is, an understanding of how one makes decisions and what the consequences of the decision-making process are. This is the approach taken by Mary Calderone (1977) and is implicit in the *Basic Values for Sex Education* that follows:

1. That we are born sexual and remain so until death;

2. That our sexuality is of central importance to each of us throughout life;

3. That sexuality itself is morally neutral, but that how we learn or are taught to use it throughout life has heavy moral implications;

4. That the sex education with the most impact is probably that done by parents or their surrogates by the age of fourteen, but especially before the age of five;

5. That this undoubtedly determines or profoundly influences the child's sexuality for the rest of its life;

6. That this influence extends, for good or ill, into the areas of gender identity, gender role behavior, erotic response, and sex object choice;

7. That in the interests of prevention, the institutions of society (educational, religious and health) should be called upon to accept primary responsibility for persuading, educating and helping parental figures to carry out their unique roles as primary sex educators.

Yet another approach is described by the Council of Churches in their *Interfaith Statement on Sex Education* (1974). Their guidelines are:

a) Such education should strive to create understanding and conviction that decisions about sexual behavior must be based on moral and ethical values, as well as on considerations of physical and emotional health, fear, pleasure, practical consequences, or concepts of personality development.

b) Such education must respect the cultural, familial and religious backgrounds and beliefs of individuals and must teach that the sexual development and behavior of each individual cannot take place in a vacuum but are instead related to the other aspects of his life and to his moral, ethical and religious codes.

c) It should point out how sex is distorted and exploited in our society and how this places heavy responsibility upon the individual, the family and institutions to cope in a constructive manner with the problem thus created.

d) It must recognize that school sex education, insofar as it relates to moral and religious beliefs and values, complements the education conveyed through the family, the church or the synagogue. Sex education in the schools must proceed constructively, with understanding, tolerance and acceptance of difference.

e) It must stress the many points of harmony between moral values and beliefs about what is right and wrong that are held in common by the major religions on the one hand and generally accepted legal, social, psychological, medical and other values held in common by service professions and society generally.

f) Where strong differences of opinion exist on what is right and wrong sexual behavior, objective, informed and dignified discussion of both sides of such questions should be encouraged. However, in such cases, neither the sponsors of an educational program nor the teachers should attempt to give definite answers or to represent their personal moral and religious beliefs as the consensus of the major religions or of society generally.

g) Throughout such education human values and human dignity must be stressed as major bases for right and wrong; attitudes that build such respect should be encouraged as right, and those that tear down such respect should be condemned as wrong.

h) Such education should teach that sexuality is a part of the whole person and an aspect of his dignity as a human being.

i) It should teach that people who love each other try not to do anything that will harm each other.

j) It should teach that sexual intercourse within marriage offers the greatest possibility for personal fulfillment and social growth.

k) Finally, such a program of education must be based on sound content and must employ sound methods; it must be conducted by teachers and leaders qualified to do so by training and temperament.

The goal of sex education, according to this group, is to place sexuality within the context of a moral and social framework and at the same time maintain respect and tolerance for the individual.

There is also a growing recognition among sex educators that it is impossible to teach students about sexuality without, to some extent, teaching them about all other aspects of life. Self-esteem, interpersonal relationships, gender identity, moral convictions, and so on are influenced by, and in turn will influence, our sexuality. Sex education must, by definition, address the needs of the whole person. As stated in *The Student Guide to Sex on Campus,* a book written by and for students;

Today's youth culture has become associated with the demand for greater honesty in all personal dealings. In our dress, through our music, and by our tastes, we express a strong need to be treated as total beings. We are not ashamed of our bodies or embarrassed by our sexuality. If we have questions, we want to be counselled and understood; if we have problems, we want help in facing them. (1970, p. 150)

The question for the future is whether sex education will rise to meet this challenge.

References

Abarbanel, A. R. Diagnosis and treatment of coital discomfort. In J. LoPiccolo and L. LoPiccolo (Eds.), *Handbook of Sex Therapy.* New York: Plenum Press, 1978, pp. 241–260.

Abel, G. G., Barlow, D. H., Blanchard, E. B., and Guild, D. The components of rapists' sexual arousal. *Archives of General Psychiatry,* 1977, *34,* pp. 895–903.

_____, and Blanchard, E. B. The role of fantasy in the treatment of sexual deviation. *Archives of General Psychiatry,* 1974, *30,* 467–475.

_____, and Blanchard, E. B. The measurement and generation of sexual arousal in male sexual deviates. *Progress in Behavior Modification.* Vol. 2. New York: Academic Press, 1976, pp. 99–136.

_____, Murphy, W. D., Beckes, J. V., and Bitar, A. Women's vaginal responses during REM sleep. *Journal of Sex and Marital Therapy,* 1979, *5,* 5–14.

Abelson, H., Cohen, R., Heaton, F., and Suder, C. Public attitudes toward and experience with erotic materials. *Technical Reports of the Commission on Obscenity and Pornography, Vol. 6.* Washington, D.C.: U.S. Government Printing Office, 1971.

Adams, D. B., Gold, A. R., and Burt, A. D. Rise in female-initiated sexual activity at ovulation. *New England Journal of Medicine,* 1978, *299,* 1145–1150.

Alcott, W. A. *The Physiology of Marriage.* New York: Arno Press & New York Times, 1972. (Originally published in 1866.)

Altschuler, M. Capaya personality and sexual motivation. In D. S. Marshall and R. C. Suggs (Eds.), *Human Sexual Behavior.* New York: Basic Books, 1971, pp. 38–58.

Alzate, H. Sexual behavior of Colombian male medical students. Paper presented at the International Congress of Sexology, Montreal, October 1976.

Amir, M. *Patterns of Forcible Rape.* Chicago: University of Chicago Press, 1971.

Annon, J. S. *The Behavioral Treatment of Sexual Problems.* Honolulu: Kapiolani Health Services, 1975.

Arms, S. *Immaculate Deception: A New Look at Women and Childbirth in America.* Boston: Houghton Mifflin, 1975.

Asimov, I. Essay on human sexuality. In I. Braun and D. E. Linder (Eds.), *Psychology Today.* New York: Random House, 1979, p. 379.

Athanasiou, R., Shaver, P., and Tavris, C. Sex. *Psychology Today,* July 1970, pp. 39–52.

Bach, G., and Wyden, P. *The Intimate Enemy.* New York: Avon Books, 1975.

Baker, S., and Ehrhardt, A. Prenatal androgen, intelligence and cognitive sex differences. In R. C. Friedman, R. M. Richart, and R. L. Vande Wiele (Eds.), *Sex Differences in Behavior.* New York: Wiley, 1974, pp. 53–76.

Bancroft, J. *Deviant-Sexual Behavior.* London: Oxford University Press, 1974.

Bandura, A., and Walters, R. H. *Social Learning and Personality Development.* New York: Holt, Rinehart, and Winston, 1963.

Barash, D. P. *Sociobiology and Behavior.* New York: Elsevier Press, 1977.

Barbach, L. G. *For Yourself: The Fulfillment of Female Sexuality.* Garden City, N.Y.: Doubleday, 1975.

Barlow, D. H., and Abel, G. G. Sexual deviation. In W. Craighead, A. Kazdin, and M. Mahoney (Eds.), *Behavior Modification.* New York: Houghton Mifflin, 1976, pp. 341–360.

Baron, R. A., and Bell, P. A. Sexual arousal and aggression by males: Effects of type of erotic stimuli and prior provocation. *Journal of Personality and Social Psychology,* 1977, *35,* 79–87.

Bauman, K. E. Volunteer bias in a study of sexual knowledge, attitudes, and behavior. *Journal of Marriage and the Family,* 1973, *35,* 27–31.

Beach, F. A. Characteristics of masculine sex drive: In *Nebraska Symposium on Motivation,* 1956. Lincoln: University of Nebraska Press, pp. 1–32.

_____, and Wilson, R. R. Sexual behavior of unmarried university students in 1968 and 1972. *The Journal of Sex Research,* 1974, *4,* 327–333.

_____. Hormonal factors controlling the differentiation, development, and display of copulatory behavior in the Ramstergig and related species. In E. Tobach, L. Aronson, and E. Shaw (Eds.), *The Biopsychology of Development.* New York: Academic Press, 1971, pp. 249–296.

_____. *Human Sexuality in Four Perspectives.* Baltimore: Johns Hopkins University Press, 1976.

Beigel, H. G. Romantic Love. In A. Montagu (Ed.), *The Practice of Love.* Englewood Cliffs, N.J.: Prentice-Hall, 1975, pp. 136–149.

Bell, A. P., and Weinberg, M. S. *Homosexualities: A Study of Diversity Among Men and Women.* New York: Simon & Schuster, 1978.

Bem, S. The measurement of psychological androgyny. *Journal of Consulting and Clinical Psychology,* 1974, *42*(2) 155–162.

Benkert, O., Witt, W., Adam, W., and Leitz, A. Effects of testosterone undecanoate on sexual potency and the hypothalamic-pituitary-gonadal axis of impotent males. *Archives of Sexual Behavior,* 1979, *8,* 471–479.

Bentler, P. M., and Newcomb, M. D. Longitudinal study of marital success and failure. *Journal of Consulting and Clinical Psychology,* 1978, *46,* 1053–1070.

Berman, E. M., and Lief, H. I. Sex and the aging process. In W. W. Oaks, G. A. Melchiode, and I. Ficher (Eds.), *Sex and the Life Cycle.* New York: Grune & Stratton, 1976, pp. 125–135.

Bernard, J. How to make marital sex more exciting. In L. Gross (Ed.), *Sexual Issues in Marriage.* New York: Spectrum, 1975, pp. 17–18.

Berne, E. *Sex in Human Loving.* New York: Pocket Books, 1971.

Boston Women's Health Collective, *Our Bodies, Ourselves.* New York: Simon & Schuster, 1976.

_____. *Ourselves and Our Children.* New York: Random House, 1978.

Bowlby, J. *Attachment.* New York: Basic, 1969.

Brackbill, Y. Obstetrical medication and infant behavior. In J. D. Osofsky (Ed.), *Handbook of Infant Development.* New York: Wiley, 1978.

Brecher, E. *The Sex Researchers.* London: Deutsch, 1970.

_____. *Licit and Illicit Drugs.* Boston: Little, Brown, 1972.

_____. Prevention of the sexually transmitted diseases. *Journal of Sex Research,* 1975, *11,* 318–328.

_____. Treatment programs for sex offenders. Unpublished manuscript, 1978.

Bremer, J. *Asexualization: A Follow-Up Study of 244 Cases.* New York: Macmillan, 1959.

Bridell, D., and Wilson, G. T. Effects of alcohol and expectancy set on male sexual arousal. *Journal of Abnormal Psychology,* 1976, *85,* 225–234.

Brody, J. E. Personal health. *New York Times,* March 8, 1978, p. C10.

Brownmiller, S. *Against Our Will: Men, Women, and Rape.* New York: Simon & Schuster, 1975.

Bullough, V. L. *Sexual Variance in Society and History.* New York: Wiley, 1976.

Burgess, A. W., and Homstrom, L. L. Rape trauma syndrome. *American Journal of Psychiatry,* 1974, *131,* 981–986.

Burt, J. C. Preliminary report on an innovative surgical procedure for treatment of coital anorgasmia. Paper presented at the International Academy of Sex Research, *1977*, Bloomington, Ind.

Byrne, D. Determinants of contraceptive values and practices. Paper presented at the International Conference on Love and Attraction, Swansea, Wales, September 1977.

_____, and Byrne, L. *Exploring Human Sexuality*. New York: Thomas Crowell, 1977.

Calderone, M. S. The interfaith statement on sex education. In M. S. Calderone (Ed.), *Sexuality and Human Values*. New York: Association Press, 1974.

_____. Human sexuality. (Address at the International Congress of Sexology, Montreal, 1976.) In *Progress in Sexology*. New York: Plenum Press, 1977.

_____. Is sex education preventative? In C. B. Qualls, J. P. Wincze, and D. H. Barlow (Eds.), *The Prevention of Sexual Disorders*. New York: Plenum Press, 1978, pp. 139–158.

Chang, J. *The Tao of Love and Sex*. New York: Dutton, 1977.

Chilman, C. S. *Adolescent Sexuality in a Changing American Society*. Bethesda, Maryland: U. S. Department of Health, Education and Welfare, 1979.

Christensen, H. T., and Gregg, C. F. Changing sex norms in America and Scandinavia. *Journal of Marriage and the Family*, November 1970, pp. 616–627.

Clark, R. A. The projective measurement of experimentally induced levels of sexual motivation. *Journal of Experimental Psychology*, 1952, 44, 391–399.

Cohen, H., Rosen, R. C., and Goldstein, L. Electroencephalographic laterality changes during human sexual orgasm. *Archives of Sexual Behavior*, 1976, 5, 189–199.

Cole, T. M. Sexuality and the spinal cord injured. In R. Green (Ed.), *Human Sexuality: A Health Practitioner's Text*. Baltimore: Williams and Wilkins, 1975, pp. 181–196.

Colman, A. D., and Colman, L. L. *Pregnancy: The Psychological Experience*. New York: Herder & Herder, 1971.

Comfort, A. *Sex in Society*. New York: Citadel Press, 1966.

_____. *The Joy of Sex*. New York: Simon & Schuster, 1972.

_____. *More Joy of Sex*. New York: Simon & Schuster, 1973.

_____. *A Good Age*. New York: Simon & Schuster, 1976.

_____. (Ed), *Sexual Consequences of Disability*. Philadelphia: George F. Stickley, 1978.

Constantine, L. L., and Constantine, J. M. Sexual aspects of group marriage. In R. W. Libby and R. N. Whitehurst (Eds.), *Marriage and Alternatives: Exploring Intimate Relationships*. Glenview, Ill.: Scott, Foresman, 1977, pp. 186–195.

Cooper, A. J. Factors in male sexual inadequacy: A review. *Journal of Nervous and Mental Disease*, 1969, 4 (149), 337–359.

_____, Ismail, A. A., Smith C. G., and Lorraine, J. A. Androgen function in "psychogenic" and "constitutional" types of impotence. *British Medical Journal*, 1970, 3, 17.

Cox, C., and Smart, R. G. Social and psychological aspects of speed use. *International Journal of the Addictions*, 1972, 7, 201–217.

Craig, G. J. *Child Development*. Englewood Cliffs, N.J.: Prentice-Hall, 1979.

Crepault, C. Love as a regulator of premarital sexuality among young French Canadians. Paper presented at the International Congress of Medical Sexology, Montreal, 1976.

Cross, R. *Handbook for Rutgers Medical School Human Sexuality Program*, 1979.

Cuber, J. F. Adultery: Reality versus stereotype. In G. Newbeck (Ed.), *Extramarital Relations*. Englewood Cliffs, N.J.: Prentice-Hall, 1969, pp. 190–197.

_____. Sex in five types of marriage. In L. Gross (Ed.), *Sexual Issues in Marriage*. New York: Spectrum, 1975, pp. 3–10.

Cushman, P. Sexual behavior in heroin addiction and methadone maintenance. *New York State Journal of Medicine*, 1972, pp. 1261–1265.

_____. Some endocrinological aspects of heroin addiction and methadone maintenance therapy. *Proceedings of the Third National Conference on Methadone Treatment*. Public Health Service Publication No. 2172.

Dalton, K. *The Pre-Menstrual Syndrome*. Springfield, Ill.: Charles C Thomas, 1964.

Davenport, W. H. Sex in cross-cultural perspective. In F. A. Beach (Ed.), *Human Sexuality in Four Perspectives*. Baltimore: Johns Hopkins University Press, 1976, pp. 115–163.

David, H. P. Psychological studies in abortion. In J. T. Fawcett (Ed.), *Psychological Perspectives on Population*. New York: Basic Books, 1973, pp. 241–273.

Davidson, J. M. Hormones and sexual behavior in the male. *Hospital Practice*, September 1975, pp. 126–132.

Davis, A. J. Sexual assaults in the Philadelphia prison system. In J. H. Gagnon & W. Simon (Eds.), *The Sexual Scene*. Chicago: Aldine, 1970, pp. 107–124.

Davison, G. C. Elimination of a sadistic fantasy by a client-controlled counterconditioning technique. *Journal of Abnormal Psychology*, 1968, 73, 84–90.

De Beauvoir, S. *The Second Sex*. New York: Vintage Books, 1974.

Delaney, J., Lupton, M. J., and Toth, E. *The Curse: A Cultural History of Menstruation*. New York: Dutton, 1976.

DeLeon, G., and Wexler, H. K. Heroin addiction: Its relation to sexual behavior and sexual experience. *Journal of Abnormal Psychology*, 1973, *81*, 36–38.

DeLora, J. S., and Warren, C. A. *Understanding Sexual Interaction*. Boston: Houghton Mifflin, 1977.

Denfield, D., and Gordon, M. The sociology of mate swapping: Or the family that swings together clings together. *Journal of Sex Research*, 1970, *6*, 85–100.

Deutsch, H. *The Psychology of Women*. New York: Grune & Stratton, 1944.

Deutsch, M. Conflicts: Productive and destructive. *Journal of Social Issues*, 1969, *25*, 7–40.

Diamond, M. Human sexual development: Biological foundations for social development. In F. Beach (Ed.), *Human Sexuality in Four Perspectives*. Baltimore: Johns Hopkins University Press, 1976, pp. 22–61.

Dickinson, R. L. *Human Sex Anatomy*. Baltimore: Williams & Wilkins, 1933.

_____, and Beam, L. *A Thousand Marriages: A Medical Study of Sex Adjustment*. Baltimore: Williams & Wilkins, 1931.

Dick-Read, G. *Childbirth Without Fear*. New York: Harper & Row, 1944.

Dodson, B. *Liberating Masturbation*. New York: Bodysex Designs, 1974.

Donnerstein, E., & Hallam, J. The facilitating effects of erotica on aggression against women. *Journal of Personality and Social Psychology*, in press.

Downing, G. *The Massage Book*. New York: Random House, 1972.

Driscoll, R. A., and Davis, K. E. Sexual restraints, a comparison of perceived and self-reported reasons for college students. *Journal of Sex Research*, 1971, *7*.

Edwardes, A., and Masters, R. E. L. *The Cradle of Erotica*. New York: Bantam Books, 1962.

Ehrhardt, A., and Baker, S. Fetal androgens, human central nervous system differences, and behavior sex differences. In R. C. Friedman, R. M. Richart, and R. L. Vande Wiele (Eds.), *Sex Differences in Behavior*. New York: Wiley, 1974, pp. 33–52.

_____, and Meyer-Bahlburg, H. F. Psychological correlates of abnormal pubertal development. *Clinics in Endocrinology and Metabolism*, 1975, *4*, 207–222.

_____, and Money, J. Progestin-induced hermaphroditism: IQ and psychosexual identity in a study of ten girls. *Journal of Sex Research*, 1967, *3*, 83–100.

Eibl-Eibesfeldt, I. *Love and Hate: The Natural History of Behavior Patterns*. New York: Schocken Books, 1974.

Ellenberg, M. Inpotence in diabetes: The neurologic factor. *Annals of Internal Medicine*, 1971, *75*, 213–219.

Ellis, A. What is normal sexual behavior? In A. Ellis & R. Brancale (Eds.), *The Psychology of Sex Offenders*. Springfield, Ill.: Charles C Thomas, 1956, pp. 120–132.

_____, and Brancale, R. (Eds.) *The Psychology of Sex Offenders*. Springfield, Ill.: Charles C Thomas, 1956.

_____. Rationality in sexual morality. *Humanist*, September–October 1969, pp. 83–86.

Ellis, H. *Studies in the Psychology of Sex*. New York: Random House, 1906.

Ennis, P. H. *Criminal Victimization in the United States: Report of a National Survey*. Washington, D.C.: United States Government Printing Office, 1967.

Erikson, E. H. *Childhood and Society*. 2nd ed. New York: Norton, 1963.

Evans, D. R. Masturbatory fantasy and sexual deviation. *Behavior Research and Therapy*, 1968, *6*, 17–19.

Farkas, G., & Rosen, R. C. Effects of alcohol on elicited male sexual response. *Quarterly Journal of Studies on Alcohol*, 1976, *37*, 265–272.

Federal Bureau of Investigation, *Uniform Crime Reports*, 1973.

Feinbloom, D. H. *Transvestites and Transsexuals: Mixed Views*. Delacorte Press/Seymour Lawrence, 1976.

Ferracuti, F. Incest between father and daughter. In H. Resnick and M. E. Wolfgang (Eds.), *Sexual Behaviors: Social, Clinical, and Legal Aspects*. Boston: Little, Brown, 1972, pp. 169–183.

Finger, F. W. Sex beliefs and practices among male college students. *Journal of Abnormal and Social Psychology*, *42*, 57–67, 1947.

Fisher, C, Gross, J., and Zuch, J. A cycle of penile erection synchronous with dreaming (REM) sleep. *Archives of General Psychiatry*, 1965, *12*, 29–45.

Fisher, S. *The Female Orgasm*. New York: Basic Books, 1973.

Ford, C. S., and Beach, F. A. *Patterns of Sexual Behavior*, New York: Harper & Row, 1951.

Fox, C. A., and Fox, B. Blood pressure and respiratory patterns during human coitus. *Journal of Reproductive Fertility*, 1969, *19*, 405–415.

Francoeur, R. T., and Francoeur, A. K. Hot and cool sex: Fidelity in marriage. In R. W. Libby and R. N. Whitehurst (Eds.), *Marriage and Alternatives: Exploring Intimate Relationships*. Glenview, Ill.: Scott, Foresman, 1977, pp. 302–319.

Frank, E., Anderson, C., and Rubinstein, D. Frequency of sexual dysfunction in "normal" couples. *New England Journal of Medicine*, 1978, *299*, 111–115.

Freud, S. *Ueber Coca*. (1884) Reprinted by Dunequin Press, 1963.

_____. *Three Essays on the Theory of Sexuality.* New York: Basic Books, 1962. (Originally published in 1905.)

_____. The interpretation of dreams. In A. A. Brill (Ed.), *The Basic Writings of Sigmund Freud.* New York: Modern Library, 1938, pp. 181–468.

_____. Some psychological consequences of the anatomical distinction between the sexes. In N. Wagner (Ed.), *Perspectives on Human Sexuality.* New York: Behavioral Publications, 1974.

Fromm, E. *The Art of Loving.* New York: Harper & Row, 1956.

Gadpaille, W. J. *The Cycles of Sex.* New York: Scribner, 1975.

Gagnon, J. H. Sexual conduct and crime. In D. Glaser (Ed.), *Handbook of Criminology.* New York: Rand McNally, 1974, pp. 233–272.

_____. *Human Sexualities.* Glenview, Ill.: Scott, Foresman, 1977.

_____. Reconsiderations. *Human Nature,* 1978, pp. 92–95.

_____, and Greenblat, C. S. *Life Designs: Individuals, Marriages, and Families.* Chicago: Scott, Foresman, 1978.

_____, and Roberts, E. J. Content and Process in Parental Verbal Communication about Sexuality to Preadolescent Children. Manuscript in preparation.

_____, and Simon, W. E. *The Sexual Scene.* Chicago: Aldine, 1970.

_____, and Simon, W. E. *Sexual Conduct: The Social Sources of Human Sexuality.* Chicago: Aldine, 1973.

Galin, D., and Ornstein, R. Lateral specialization of cognitive mode: An EEG study. *Psychophysiology,* 1972, 9, 412.

Gardner, H. *Developmental Psychology.* Boston: Little, Brown, 1978.

Garfink, C., and Pizer, H. *The New Birth Control Program.* New York: Bolder Books, 1977.

Gay, G. R., and Sheppard, C. W. Sex-crazed dope fiends — myths or reality? *Drug Forum,* 1973, 2, 125–140.

Gebhard, P. H., Gagnon, J. H., Pomeroy, W. B., and Christenson, C. V. *Sex Offenders: An Analysis of Types.* New York: Harper & Row, 1965.

Geer, J. H., and Fuhr, R. Cognitive factors in sexual arousal: The role of distraction. *Journal of Consulting and Clinical Psychology,* 1976, 44, 238–243.

Gemme, R. Some new sexological aspects of contraception. Unpublished paper, Université du Quebec à Montréal, 1977.

Gennep, F. O. Sexual ethics in Protestant churches. In J. Money and H. Musaph (Eds.), *Handbook of Sexology.* Amsterdam: Elsevier/North Holland Press, 1977, pp. 1333–1338.

George, L. K., and Weiler, S. J. Aging and sexual behavior: the myth of declining sexuality. *Archives of General Psychiatry,* in press.

Giele, J. Z., and Smock, A. C. *Women: Roles and Status in Eight Countries.* New York: Wiley, 1977.

Gilmartin, B. G. Swinging: Who gets involved and how? In R. W. Libby and R. N. Whitehurst (Eds.), *Marriage and Alternatives: Exploring Intimate Relationships.* Glenview, Ill.: Scott, Foresman 1977, pp. 161–186.

Goebelsmann, V., Arce, J. J., Thorneycroft, I. H., and Mischell, D. R. Serum testosterone concentration in women throughout the menstrual cycle and following HCG administration. *American Journal of Obstetrics and Gynecology,* 1974, 119, 445–452.

Goldsmith, S., Gabrielson, M., Gabrielson, I., Mathews, U., and Potts, L. Teenagers, sex and contraception. *Family Planning Perspectives,* 1972, 4, 32–38.

Goldstein, B. *Human Sexuality.* New York: McGraw-Hill, 1976.

Goldstein, L., Sugerman, A., Marjerrison, E., and Stoltzfus, N. The EEG and differential hemisphere functions. R. M. Bucke Memorial Society Paper, 1973.

Goldstein, M., Kant, H., Judd, L., Rice, C., and Green, R. Experience with pornography: Rapists, pedophiles, homosexuals, transsexuals, and controls. *Archives of Sexual Behavior,* 1971, 1, pp. 1–15.

Goode, E. Drug use and sexual activity on a college campus. *American Journal of Psychiatry,* 1969, 128, 92–96.

_____. *Drugs in American Society.* New York: Knopf, 1972.

Gordon, L. *Women's Body, Women's Right: A Social History of Birth Control in America.* New York: Grossman Publishers, 1976.

Gordon, S. *The Sexual Adolescent.* Belmont, California: Wadsworth, 1973.

Grant, E. C., and Mears, E. Mental effects of oral contraceptives. *Lancet,* 1967, 11, 945–948.

Green, R. *Sexual Identity Conflict in Children and Adults.* New York: Basic Books, 1974.

Haeberle, E. J. *The Sex Atlas.* New York: Seabury Press, 1978.

Halikas, J. A., Goodwin, D. W., and Guze, S. B. Marihuana effects — a survey of regular users. *Journal of the American Medical Association,* 1971, 217, 692.

Hall, J. E. Sexuality and the mentally retarded. In R. Green (Ed.), *Human Sexuality: A Health Practitioner's Text.* Baltimore: Williams & Wilkins, 1975, pp. 181–196.

Hamburg, D. A., and Lunde, D. T. Sex hormones in the development of sex differences in human behavior. In E. Maccoby (Ed.), *The Development of Sex Differences.* Stanford, Calif.: Stanford University Press, 1966. pp. 1–24.

Harlow, H. F. Love in infant monkeys. *Scientific American,* June 1959, pp. 68–74.

_____, and Harlow, M. K. Social deprivation in monkeys. *Scientific American,* November 1972, pp. 137–146.

Harris, A. What does sex education mean? In R. S. Rogers (Ed.), Sex Education: Rationale and Reaction. London: Cambridge University Press, 1974.

Hartman, W. E., and Fithian, M. A. *Treatment of Sexual Dysfunction.* Center for Marital and Sexual Studies. California, 1972.

Hatcher, R. A., Stewart, G. K., Guest, F., Finkelstein, R., and Godwin, C. *Contraceptive Technology, 1976–1977.* New York: Irvington Publishers, 1976.

Heiman, J.: The physiology of erotica. *Psychology Today,* April 1975.

_____, LoPiccolo, L., and LoPiccolo, J. *Becoming Orgasmic: A sexual growth program for women.* Englewood Cliffs, N.J.: Prentice-Hall, 1976.

Hellerstein, H. K., and Friedman, E. H. Sexual activity and the post-coronary patient. *Archives of Internal Medicine,* 1970, *125,* 987–999.

Henson, D. E., and Rubin, H. B. Voluntary control of eroticism. *Journal of Applied Behavior Analysis,* 1971, *4,* 37–47.

Hertoft, P. Nordic traditions of marriage: The betrothal system. In J. Money and H. Musaph (Eds.), *Handbook of Sexology.* Amsterdam: Elsevier/North Holland Press, 1977, pp. 505–509.

Hill, P., Wynder, E. L., Hilman, P., Hickman, R., Rona, G., and Kuno, K. Plasma hormone levels in different ethnic populations of women. *Cancer Research,* 1976, *36,* 2297–2301.

Hite, S. *The Hite Report.* New York: Macmillan, 1976.

Hoenig, J. Dramatis personae: selected biographical sketches of 19th century pioneers in sexology. In J. Money and H. Musaph (Eds.), *Handbook of Sexology.* Amsterdam: Elsevier/North Holland Press, 1977, pp. 21–43.

Hoffman, M. *The Gay World.* New York: Basic Books, 1968.

_____. The male prostitute. In M. P. Levine (Ed.), *Gay Men: The Sociology of Male Homosexuality.* New York: Harper & Row, 1979, pp. 275–284.

Hook, E. B. Behavioral implications of the human XYY genotype. *Science,* 1973, *179,* 139–150.

Hooker, E. An empirical study of some relations between sexual patterns and gender identity in male homosexuals. In J. Money (Ed.), *Sex Research: New Developments.* New York: Holt, Rinehart and Winston, 1965, pp. 24–52.

Hoon, P., Wincze, J., and Hoon, E. Physiological assessment of sexual arousal in women. *Psychophysiology,* 1976, *13,* 196–204.

Houser, B. B. An investigation of the correlation between hormonal levels in males and mood, behavior, and physical discomfort. *Hormones and Behavior,* 1979, *12,* 185–197.

Huelsman, B. R. An anthropological view of clitoral and other female genital mutilations. In T. R. Lowry and T. S. Lowry (Eds.), *The Clitoris.* St. Louis: Warren H. Green, 1976, pp. 111–161.

Hunt, M. *Sexual Behavior in the 1970's.* New York: Dell, 1974.

_____. *Gay: What You Should Know About Homosexuality.* New York: Farrar, Straus & Giroux, 1977.

Jackson, E. D., and Potkay, C. R. Precollege influences on sexual experiences of coeds. *The Journal of Sex Research,* 1973. Vol. 9, 2, pp. 143–149.

Jensen, G. P. Human sexual behavior in primate perspective. In J. Zubin and J. Money (Eds.), *Contemporary Sexual Behavior: Critical Issues in the 1970's.* Baltimore: Johns Hopkins University Press, 1973, pp. 17–31.

Jessor, S. L., and Jessor, R. Transition from virginity to nonvirginity among youth: a social-psychological study over time. *Developmental Psychology,* 1975, *11,* 4, 473–484.

Johnson, W. R. The handicapped: Recreational sex and procreational responsibility. In J. Money and H. Musaph (Eds.), *Handbook of Sexology.* Amsterdam: Elsevier/North Holland Press, 1977, pp. 933–937.

Jones, E. *The Life and Work of Sigmund Freud.* Volume 1. New York: Basic Books, 1953.

Jourard, S. M. *The Transparent Self.* New York: Van Nostrand, 1964.

Kaats, G. R., and Davis, K. E. The dynamics of sexual behavior of college students. *Journal of Marriage and the Family,* August 1970, 390–399.

Kagan, J. *Change and Continuity in Infancy.* New York: Wiley, 1971.

_____. The emergence of sex differences. In F. Rebelsky (Ed.), *Life, The Continuous Process.* New York: Knopf, 1975, pp. 247–252.

_____. The psychology of sex differences. In F. Beach (Ed.), *Human Sexuality in Four Perspectives.* Baltimore: Johns Hopkins University Press, 1976, pp. 87–114.

Kantner, J. F., and Zelnick, M. Sexual experiences of young unmarried women in the United States. *Family Planning Perspectives,* 1972, *4,* 9–18.

_____. Contraception and pregnancy: Experience of young unmarried women in the U.S. *Family Planning Perspectives,* 1973, *5,* 1, 21–35.

Kaplan, H. S. *The New Sex Therapy.* New York: Brunner/Mazel, 1974.

_____. Hypoactive sexual desire. *Journal of Sex and Marital Therapy,* 1977, *3,* 3–9.

_____. *Disorders of Sexual Desire*. New York: Simon & Schuster, 1979.

_____, Kohl, R. N., Pomperoy, W. B., Offit, A. K., and Hogan, B. Group treatment of premature ejaculation. *Archives of Sexual Behavior*, 1974, *3*, 443–452.

Kegel, A. H. Sexual functions of the pubococcygeus muscle. *Western Journal of Surgery*, 1952, *60*, 521–524.

Kelly, J. The aging male homosexual: Myth and reality. In M. P. Levine (Ed.), *Gay Men: The Sociology of Male Homosexuality*. New York: Harper & Row, 1979, pp. 253–262.

Kennedy, D. M. *Birth Control in America: The Career of Margaret Sanger*. New Haven: Yale University Press, 1970.

Kisekka, M. N. Sexual attitudes and behavior among students in Uganda. *The Journal of Sex Research*, 1976, *12*, 2, 104–116.

King, M., and Sobel, D. Sex on the college campus: Current attitudes and behavior. *Journal of College Student Personnel*, 1975, *16*.

Kinsey, A. C., Pomeroy, W. B., and Martin, C. E. *Sexual Behavior in the Human Male*. Philadelphia: Saunders, 1948.

_____, and Gebhard, P. H. *Sexual Behavior in the Human Female*. Philadelphia: Saunders, 1953.

Knapp, J. J., and Whitehurst, R. N. Sexually open marriage and relationships: Issues and prospects. In R. W. Libby and R. N. Whitehurst (Eds.), *Marriage and Alternatives: Exploring Intimate Relationships*. Glenview, Ill.: Scott, Foresman, 1977, pp. 147–161.

Koff, W. C. Marihuana and sexual activity. *Journal of Sex Research*, 1974, *10*, 194–204.

Kohlberg, L. A cognitive-developmental analysis of children's sex-role concepts and attitudes. In E. Maccoby (Ed.), *The Development of Sex Differences*. Stanford, Calif.: Stanford University Press, 1966, pp. 82–172.

_____. Moral stages and sex education. In M. S. Calderone (Ed.), *Sexuality and Human Values*. New York: Association Press, 1974, pp. 111–121.

_____, and Zigler, E. The impact of cognitive maturity on the development of sex role attitudes in the years four to eight. *Genetic Psychology Monographs*, 1967, *75*.

Kolodny, R. C., Masters, W. H., Hendryx, J., and Toro, G. Plasma testosterone levels and semen analysis in male homosexuals. *New England Journal of Medicine*, 1971, *285*, 1170–1174.

_____, Kolodny, R. M., and Toro, G. Depression of plasma testosterone levels after chronic intensive marihuana use. *New England Journal of Medicine*, 1974, *290*, 872–874.

Korner, A. F. Neonatal startles, smiles, erections, and reflex sucks as related to state, sex, and individuality. *Child Development*, 1969, *40*, 1039–1053.

Kraemer, H. C., Becker, H. B., Brodie, H. K., Doering, C.

H., Moos, R. H., and Hamburg, D. A. Orgasmic frequency and plasma testosterone levels in normal human males. *Archives of Sexual Behavior*, 1976, *5*, 125–132.

Krafft-Ebing, R. V. *Psychopathia Sexualis*. New York: Putnam, 1965. (Originally published in 1886)

Kreuz, L. E., and Rose, R. M. Assessment of aggressive behavior and plasma testosterone in a young criminal population. Paper presented at a meeting of the American Psychosomatic Society, Denver, April 3, 1971.

Kuhn, M. E. Sexual myths surrounding the aging. In W. W. Oaks, G. A. Melchiode, and I. Ficher (Eds.), *Sex and the Life Cycle*. New York: Grune and Stratton, 1976, pp. 117–134.

Lacey, L. *Lunaception*. New York: Coward, McCann & Geoghegan, 1974.

Lamaze, F. *Painless Childbirth: The Lamaze Method*. New York: Simon & Schuster, 1972.

Lao Tsu, *The Way of Life*. New York: Mentor Books, 1955.

Laws, D. R., and Rubin, H. B. Instructional control of an autonomic sexual response. *Journal of Applied Behavior Analysis*, 1969, *2*, 93–99.

Laws, J. L., and Schwartz, P. *Sexual Scripts: The Social Construction of Female Sexuality*. Hinsdale, Ill.: Dryden Press, 1977.

Lazarus, A. A. The treatment of chronic frigidity by systematic desensitization. *Journal of Nervous and Mental Disease*, 1963, *136*, 272–278.

Leboyer, F. *Birth Without Violence*. New York: Knopf, 1975.

Leiblum, S. R., and Ersner-Hershfield, R. Sexual enhancement groups for dysfunctional women: An evaluation. *Journal of Sex and Marital Therapy*, 1977, *2*, 3, 139–152.

_____, and Miller, M. Post-coital responses in males and females. Unpublished study, 1980.

_____, and Pierce, D. Group treatment format: Mixed sexual dysfunctions. *Archives of Sexual Behavior*, 1976, *5*, 313–321.

_____, and Rosen, R. C. The weekend workshop for dysfunctional couples: Assets and limitations. *Journal of Sex and Marital Therapy*, 1979, *5*, 57–69.

Levinson, D. J. *The Seasons of a Man's Life*. New York: Knopf, 1978.

Levitt, E. E., and Duffy, R. E. Objective estimates of the duration of sexual behaviors: A laboratory analog study. Paper presented at the International Academy of Sex Research, Bloomington, Indiana, August 1977.

Libby, R. W. Extramarital and comarital sex: A critique of the literature. In R. W. Libby and R. N. Whitehurst (Eds.), *Marriage and Alternatives: Exploring Intimate Relationships*. Glenview, Ill.: Scott, Foresman, 1977, pp. 80–111.

_____, Gray, L., and White, M. A test and reformulation

of reference group and role correlates of premarital sexual permissiveness theory. *Journal of Marriage and the Family*, February 1978, pp. 79–92.

Lipton, M. A. Fact and myth: The work of the Commission on Obscentiy and Pornography. In J. Zubin and J. Money (Eds.), *Contemporary Sexual Behavior: Critical Issues in the 1970's*. Baltimore: Johns Hopkins University Press, 1973, pp. 231–257.

Lobitz, W. C., and Lobitz, G. K. Clinical assessments in the treatment of sexual dysfunctions. In J. LoPiccolo and L. LoPiccolo (Eds.), *Handbook of Sex Therapy*. New York: Plenum Press, 1978, pp. 85–102.

LoPiccolo, J. Direct treatment of sexual dysfunction in the couple. In J. Money and J. Musaph (Eds.), *Handbook of Sexology*. Amsterdam: Elsevier/North Holland Press, 1977, pp. 1227–1244.

_____. Direct treatment of sexual dysfunction. In J. Lo-Piccolo and L. LoPiccolo (Eds.), *Handbook of Sex Therapy*. New York: Plenum Press, 1978, pp. 1–18.

_____, and Heiman, J. The role of cultural values in the prevention and treatment of sexual problems. In C. B. Qualls, J. P. Wincze, and D. H. Barlow (Eds.), *The Prevention of Sexual Disorders*. New York: Plenum Press, 1978, pp. 43–71.

_____, and Lobitz, W. C. The role of masturbation in the treatment of orgasmic dysfunction. *Archives of Sexual Behavior*, 1973, 2, 153–164.

Maccoby, E., and Jacklin, C. *The Psychology of Sex Differences*. Stanford, Calif.: Stanford University Press, 1974.

Mace, D. R. Marital intimacy and the deadly love-anger cycle. *Journal of Marriage and Family Counselling*, April 1976, pp. 131–137.

Mackey, F. G. Sexuality and heart disease. In A. Comfort (Ed.), *Sexual Consequences of Disability*. Philadelphia: George F. Stickley, 1978, pp. 107–120.

MacLean, P. D. New findings relevant to the evolution of psychosexual functions of the brain. *Journal of Nervous and Mental Disease*, 1962, 135, 289–301.

Manaster, G. J. *Adolescent Development and the Life Tasks*. Boston: Allyn & Bacon, 1977.

Mann, J. Retarded ejaculation and treatment. Paper presented at the International Congress of Sexology, Montreal, 1976.

Marks, C. Positions of intercourse in three cultures. Paper presented at the International Congress of Medical Sexology, Rome, October 1978.

Marshall, D. S. Sexual behavior on Mangaia. In D. S. Marshall and R. C. Suggs (Eds.), *Human Sexual Behavior*. New York: Basic Books, 1971, pp. 103–162.

Maslow, A., and Sakoda, J. M. Volunteer-error in the Kinsey study. *Journal of Abnormal and Social Psychology*, 1952, 47, 259–267.

Masters, R. E. L. *Sexual Self-Stimulation*. Los Angeles: Sherbourne Press, 1967.

Masters, W., and Johnson, V. E. *Human Sexual Response*. Boston: Little, Brown, 1966.

_____. *Human Sexual Inadequacy*. Boston: Little, Brown, 1970.

_____. *The Pleasure Bond*. Boston: Little, Brown, 1970.

_____. *Homosexuality in Perspective*. Boston: Little, Brown, 1979.

Maxwell, J. W., Sack, A. R., Frary, R. B., and Keller, J. F. Factors influencing contraceptive behavior of single college students. *Journal of Sex and Marital Therapy*, 1977, 4, (3), 265–273.

May, R. A. A preface to love. In A. Montagu (Ed.), *The Practice of Love*. Englewood Cliffs, N.J.: Prentice-Hall, 1975, pp. 114–119.

Mayor LaGuardia's Committee on Marihuana. *The Marihuana Problem in the City of New York*. Lancaster, Pa: Catell, 1944.

McCary, J. L. *Human Sexuality*. New York: Van Nostrand, 1973.

_____. *Freedom and Growth in Marriage*. Santa Barbara: Hamilton, 1975.

McCauley, E., and Ehrhardt, A. A. Female sexual response: Hormonal and behavioral interactions. *Primary Care*, 1976, 3, 455–476.

McConaghy, N. Penile volume change to moving pictures of male and female nudes in heterosexual and homosexual roles. *Behavior Research and Therapy*, 1967, 5, 43–48.

McCormick, E. P., Johnson, R. L., Friedman, H. L., and David, H. P. Psychosocial aspects of fertility regulation. In J. Money and H. Musaph (Eds.), *Handbook of Sexology*. Amsterdam: Elsevier/North Holland Biomedical Press, 1977, pp. 621–653.

McFarland, L. Z. Comparative anatomy of the clitoris. In T. R. Lowry and T. S. Lowry (Eds.), *The Clitoris*. St. Louis: Warren H. Green, 1976, pp. 22–34.

McGuire, R. J., Carlisle, J. M., and Young, B. G. Sexual variation as conditioned behavior: A hypothesis. *Behavior Research and Therapy*, 1965, 2, 185–190.

McMullen, S., and Rosen, R. C. The use of self-administered masturbation training in the treatment of primary orgasmic dysfunction. *Journal of Consulting and Clinical Psychology*, 1979, 47, 912–918.

Mead, M. *Sex and Temperament in Three Primitive Socieites*. New York: Morrow, 1939.

_____. *Male and Female*. New York: Morrow, 1949.

_____. Jealousy: primitive and civilized. In A. M. Krich (Ed.), *The Anatomy of Love*. New York: Dell, 1960.

Melville, K. *Marriage and the Family Today*. New York: Random House, 1977.

Mendelson, J. H., Kuehnle, J., Ellingboe, J., and Babor, T. F. Plasma testosterone levels before, during, and after chronic marihuana smoking. *New England Journal of Medicine*, 1974, *290*, 1051–1055.

———, Meyer, R. E., Ellingboe, J., Mirin, S. M., and McDougle, M. Effects of heroin and methadone on plasma cortisol and testosterone. *Problems of Drug Dependence, 1975*. Washington, D.C.: National Academy of Sciences, 1975.

Menninger, K. *Love Against Hate*. New York: Harcourt, Brace & World, 1970.

Mercer, G. W., and Kohn, P. M. Gender differences in the integration of conservatism, sex urge, and sexual behaviors among college students. *The Journal of Sex Research*, 1979, 15, 2, 129–142.

Meyer, T. P. The effects of sexually arousing and violent films on aggressive behavior. *Journal of Sex Research*, 1972, 8, 324–333.

Miller, N. E., and Dollard, J. *Learning and Imitation*. New Haven: Yale University Press, 1941.

Millet, K. *Sexual Politics*. Garden City, N.Y.: Doubleday, 1970.

Mitchell, G. D. Attachment differences in male and female monkeys. *Child Development*, 1968, *39*, 611–620.

Mohr, J. W., Turner, R. E., and Jerry, M. B. *Pedophilia and Exhibitionism*. Toronto: University of Toronto Press, 1964.

Money, J. Use of an androgen-depleting hormone in the treatment of male sex offenders. *Journal of Sex Research*, 1970, *6, 3,* 165–172.

———. The American heritage of three traditions of pair-bonding: Mediterranean, Nordic, and Slav. In J. Money and H. Musaph (Eds.), *Handbook of Sexology*. Amsterdam: Elsevier/North Holland Press, 1977, pp. 497–504.

———. Determinants of human gender identity/role. In J. Money and H. Musaph (Eds.), *Handbook of Sexology*. Amsterdam: Elsevier/North Holland Biomedical Press, 1977, pp. 57–79.

———. Paraphilias. In J. Money and H. Musaph (Eds.), *Handbook of Sexology*. Amsterdam: Elsevier/North Holland Biomedical Press, 1977, 917–928.

———, and Erhardt, A. *Man and Woman, Boy and Girl*. Baltimore: Johns Hopkins University Press, 1972.

———, and Lewis, V. IQ, genetics, and accelerated growth: Adrenogenital syndrome. *Bulletin of the Johns Hopkins Hospital*, 1966, *118*, 365–373.

———, and Tucker, P. *Sexual Signatures: On Being a Man or a Woman*. Boston: Little, Brown, 1975.

Montagu, A. *The Humanization of Man*. New York: Grove Press, 1962.

———. *Touching: The Human Significance of the Skin*. New York: Columbia University Press, 1971.

———, and Matson, F. *The Human Connection*. New York: McGraw-Hill, 1979.

Moore, E. C. Fertility regulation: Friend or foe of the female? In J. Money and H. Musaph (Eds.), *Handbook of Sexology*. Amsterdam: Elsevier/North Holland Biomedical Press, 1977. Pp. 655–674.

Moos, R. H. A typology of menstrual cycle symptoms. *American Journal of Obstetrics and Gynecology*, 1969, *103*, 390–402.

Morgan, R. *Going Too Far*. New York: Random House, 1977.

Morokoff, P. Determinants of female orgasm. In J. LoPiccolo and L. LoPiccolo (Eds.), *Handbook of Sex Therapy*. New York: Plenum Press, 1978, pp. 147–166.

Morris, D. *The Naked Ape*. New York: McGraw-Hill, 1967.

———. *Intimate Behavior*. New York: Bantam Books, 1972.

Morris, H. *The Art of Kissing*. New York: Doubleday, 1977.

Morris, N. M., The frequency of sexual intercourse during pregnancy. *Archives of Sexual Behavior*, 1975, 4, 501–507.

Mosher, D. L., and Cross, H. J. Sex guilt and premarital sexual experiences of college students. *Journal of Consulting and Clinical Psychology*, 1971, 36, 27–32.

Moss, H. A. Early sex differences and mother-infant interaction. In R. C. Friedman, R. M. Richart, and R. L. Vande Wiele (Eds.), *Sex Differences in Behavior*. New York: Wiley, 1974, pp. 149–164.

Musaph, H. Sexology, a multidisciplinary science. In J. Money and H. Musaph (Eds.), *Handbook of Sexology*. Amsterdam: Elsevier/North Holland Press, 1977 , pp. 81–85.

———, and Abraham, G. Frigidity or hypogyneismus. In J. Money and H. Musaph (Eds.), *Handbook of Sexology*. Elsevier/North Holland Press, 1977, pp. 873–878.

Naeye, R. L. Coitus and associated amniotic-fluid infections. *New England Journal of Medicine*, 1979, *22* (30), 1198–1200.

National Commission on the Causes and Prevention of Violence. *Crimes of Violence*. Washington, D.C.: U.S. Government Printing Office, 1969, Vol. 2.

Netter, F. H. *Reproductive System*. The CIBA Collection of Medical Illustrations, Vol. 2. Summit, N.J.: CIBA, 1974.

Neubeck, G. *Extramarital Relations*. Englewood Cliffs: N.J.: Prentice-Hall, 1969.

Neugarten, B. L. Women's attitudes toward the menopause. *Vita Humana*, 1963, *6*, 140.

Newton, N., and Modahl, C. Pregnancy: The closest human relationship. *Human Nature*, March 1978, pp. 40–49.

O'Connor, J. F. Sexual problems, therapy, and prognostic factors. In J. K. Meyer (Ed.), *Clinical Management of Sexual Disorders*. Baltimore: Williams & Wilkins, 1976, pp. 74–98.

Paige, K. E. Women learn to sing the menstrual blues. In J. L. McCary and D. R. Copeland (Eds.), *Modern Views of Human Sexual Behavior*. Chicago: Science Research Associates, 1976, pp. 109–115.

————, and Paige, J. M. The politics of birth practices: A strategic analysis. *American Sociological Review*, 1973, *38*, 663–676.

Parfitt, R. R. *The Birth Primer*. Philadelphia: Running Press, 1977.

Parlee, M. B. The premenstrual syndrome. In S. Cox, (Ed.), *Female Psychology: The Emerging Self*. Chicago: Science Research Associates, 1976.

Peele, S. *Love and Addiction*. New York: New American Library, 1976.

Perlman, D., Josephson, W., Hwang, W. T., Begum, H., and Thomas, T. L. Cross-cultural analysis of students' sexual standards. *Archives of Sexual Behavior*, 1978, *1*, 545–558.

Peterman, D. J., Ridley, C. A., and Anderson, S. M. A comparison of cohabiting and noncohabiting college students. *Journal of Marriage and the Family*, May 1974, 344–354.

Pirke, K. M., Kockott, G. and Dittmen, F. Psychosexual stimulation and plasma testosterone in men. *Archives of Sexual Behavior*, 1974, *3*, 577–584.

Playboy. "What's really happening on campus." *Playboy*, 23, October 1976, 128–169.

Plummer, K. *Sexual Stigma: An Interactionist Account*. London: Routledge & Kegan Paul, 1975.

Pomeroy, W. B. *Boys and Sex*. New York: Delacorte Press, 1968.

Presidential Commission on Obscenity and Pornography. New York: Bantam Books, 1970.

Purvis, K., Landgren, B. M., Cekan, Z., Diczfalusy, E. Endocrine effects of masturbation in men. *Journal of Endocrinology*, 1976, *70*, 439–444.

Raboch, J., Mellan, J., and Starka, L. Plasma testosterone in male patients with sexual dysfunction. *Archives of Sexual Behavior*, 1975, *4*, 541–545.

————, and Starka, L. Reported coital activity of men and levels of plasma testosterone. *Archieves of Sexual Behavior*, 1973, *2*, 309–315.

Rada, R. T., Laws, D. R., and Kellner, R. Plasma testosterone levels in the rapist. *Psychosomatic Medicine*, 1976, *38*, 4, 257–268.

Reinisch, J. M. Effects of prenatal hormone exposure on physical and psychological development in humans and animals. In E. J. Sacher (Ed.), *Hormones, Behavior, and Pseudopathology*. New York: Raven Press, 1976.

Reiss, A. J. The social integration of queers and peers. *Social Problems*, IX, 102–120.

Reiss, I. L. The influence of contraceptive knowledge on premarital sexuality. *Medical Aspects of Human Sexuality*, 1970, *4*, 71.

————. Adolescent sexuality. In W. W. Oakes, G. A. Melchiode, and I. Ficher (Eds.), *Sex and the Life Cycle*. New York: Grune & Stratton, 1976, pp. 45–52.

————. Changing sociosexual mores. In J. Money and H. Musaph (Eds.), *Handbook of Sexology*. Amsterdam: Elsevier/North Holland Press, 1977, pp. 311–324.

————, Banwart, A., and Foreman, H. Premarital contraceptive usage: A study and some theoretical explorations. *Journal of Marriage and the Family*, 1975, pp. 619–630.

Rekers, G. A., and Lovaas, O. I. Behavioral treatment of deviant sex role behaviors in a male child. *Journal of Applied and Behavioral Analysis*, 1974, *7*, 173–190.

Renshaw, D. C. Impotence in diabetics. In J. LoPiccolo and L. LoPiccolo (Eds.), *Handbook of Sex Therapy*. New York: Plenum Press, 1978, pp. 433–440.

————. Impotence in diabetics. *Diseases of the Nervous System*, 1975, *36* (7), 369–371.

Report of the Commission on Obscenity and Pornography. New York: Bantam, 1970.

Report of the Indian Hemp Drugs Commission, 1893–1894. Silver Springs, Md.: Thomas Jefferson Publishing, 1969.

Reynolds, B. S. Psychological treatment models and outcome results for erectile dysfunction: A critical review. *Psychological Bulletin*, 1977, *6* (84), 1218–1238.

Rich, A. *Of Woman Born*. New York: Bantam Books, 1977.

Rindfuss, R., and Westoff, C. F. The initiation of contraception. *Demography*, 1974, *11*, 75–87.

Robbins, M., and Jensen, G. D. Multiple orgasm in males. *Journal of Sex Research*, 1978, *14*, 21–26.

Robinson, P. *The Modernization of Sex*. New York: Harper & Row, 1976.

Rogers, C. R. *Becoming Partners: Marriage and Its Alternatives*. New York: Delta, 1972.

Rogers, R. S. The effects of televised sex education at the primary school level. In R. S. Rogers (Ed.), *Sex Education: Rationale and Reaction*. London: Cambridge University Press, 1974, pp. 251–264.

Rooth, F. G., and Marks, I. M. Persistent exhibitionism: Short-term response to aversion, self-regulation, and relaxation treatment. *Archives of Sexual Behavior*, 1974, *3* (3), 227–248.

Rorvik, D. M., and Shettles, L. B. *Choose Your Baby's Sex*. New York: Dodd, Mead, 1977.

Rose, R. M. Plasma testosterone levels in the male rhesus: Influences of sexual and social stimuli. *Science*, 1972, *178*, 643–645.

———, Bernstein, I. S., and Gordon, T. P. Sexual and social influences of testosterone secretion in the rhesus monkey. Paper presented at a meeting of the American Psychosomatic Society, Boston, April 15, 1972.

Rosen, A. C., Rekers, G. A., and Friar, L. R. Theoretical and diagnostic issues in child gender disturbances. *Journal of Sex Research*, 1977, *13* (2), 89–103.

Rosen, L. J., and Lee, C. Acute and chronic effects of alcohol use on organizational processes in memory. *Journal of Abnormal Psychology*, 1976, *85*, 309–317.

———, and Rosen, R. C. How long should a man last? *Forum*, July 1977.

Rosen, R. C. Suppression of penile tumescence by instrumental conditioning. *Psychosomatic Medicine*, 1973, *35*, 509–514.

———, and Keefe, F. J. The measurement of human penile tumescence. *Psychophysiology*, 1978, *45*, 366–376.

———, and Leiblum, S. Unequal sex drives: Helping mates match up. *Sexology*, 1975, *42*, 11–16.

———, and Kopel, S. The use of penile plethysmography and biofeedback in the treatment of a transvestite-exhibitionist. *Journal of Consulting and Clinical Psychology*, 1977, *45* (5), 908–916.

———, and Leiblum, S. R. Unequal sex drives. *Sexology*, January 1976, pp. 12–14.

———, Shapiro, D., and Schwartz, G. E. Voluntary control of penile tumescence. *Psychosomatic Medicine*, 1975, *37*, 479–483.

Ryder, N. B. Contraceptive failure in the U.S. *Family Planning Perspectives*, 1973, *5*, 133.

Sagarin, E. Power to the peephole. In L. Gross (Ed.), *Sexual Behavior: Current Issues*. Flushing, N.Y.: Spectrum Publications, 1974, pp. 205–214.

Sage, W. Inside the colossal closet. In M. P. Levine (Ed.), *Gay Men: The Sociology of Male Homosexuality*. New York: Harper & Row, 1979, pp. 148–163.

SAR Guide for a Better Sex Life. Multi Media Resource Center, San Francisco, 1977.

Sarnoff, S., and Sarnoff, I. *Sexual Excitement—Sexual Peace*. New York: Evans, 1979.

Sarrel, L. J., and Sarrel, P. M. The college subculture. In M. S. Calderone (Ed.), *Sexuality and Human Values*. New York: Association Press, 1974, pp. 71–84.

Schacter, S. The interaction of cognitive and physiological determinants of emotional state. In L. Berkowitz (Ed.), *Advances in Experimental Social Psychology*. Vol. 1. New York: Academic Press, 1964, pp. 49–80.

Schiavi, R. C., and White, D. Androgens and male sexual function: A Review of human studies. *Journal of Sex and Marital Therapy*, 1976, *2*, 214–228.

Seaman, B. *Free and Female*. Greenwich, Conn.: Fawcett, 1972.

———, and Seaman, G. *Women and the Crisis in Sex Hormones*. New York: Rawson Associates, 1977.

Sears, R. R., Maccoby, E. E., and Levin, H. Toilet training. In P. H. Mussen, J. J. Conger, and J. Kagan (Eds.), *Readings in Child Development and Personality*. New York: Harper & Row, 1965, pp. 195–211.

———. *Patterns of Child-Rearing*. Evanston, Ill.: Row, Peterson, 1957.

Semans, J. H. Premature ejaculation: A new approach. *Southern Medical Journal*, 1956, *49*, 353–358.

Sevely, J. L., and Bennett, J. W. Concerning female ejaculation and the female prostate. *Journal of Sex Research*, 1978, *14* (1), 1–20.

Sheehy, G. *Passages*. New York: Dutton, 1974.

Sherfey, M. J. *The Nature and Evolution of Female Sexuality*. New York: Vintage Books, 1973.

Sherwin, R. V. Law and sex. In J. Money and H. Musaph (Eds.), *Handbook of Sexology*. Amsterdam: Elsevier/North Holland Biomedical Press, 1977, pp. 1121–1133.

Shettles, L. B. Nuclear morphology of human spermatazoa. *Nature*, 1960, *187*, p. 254.

———. Predetermining children's sex. *Medical Aspects of Human Sexuality*, 1972, *6*, 72.

Simon, W., Berger, A. S., and Gagnon, J. H. Beyond anxiety and fantasy: the coital experiences of college youth. *Journal of Youth and Adolescence*, 1972, *1*, *3*, 203–222.

Sintchak, G., and Geer, J. A vaginal plethysmograph system. *Psychophysiology*, 1975, *12*, 113–115.

Sobotka, J. J. An evaluation of Afrodex in the management of male impotency: A double-blind cross-over study. *Current Therapy Research*, 1969, *11*, 87–94.

Socarides, C. W. *Beyond Sexual Freedom*. New York: Quadrangle Books, 1975.

Solberg, D. A., Butler, J., and Wagner, N. A. Sexual behavior in pregnancy. In J. LoPiccolo, and L. LoPiccolo (Eds.), *Handbook of Sex Therapy*. New York: Plenum Press, 1978.

Sorenson, R. C. *Adolescent Sexuality in Contemporary America*. New York: World Books, 1973.

Soyinka, F. Sexual behavior among university students in Nigeria. *Archives of Sexual Behavior*, 1979, *8*, *1*, 15–26.

Spark, R. F., White, R. A., and Connolly, P. B. Impotence is not always psychogenic: Newer insights into hypothalamic-pituitary-gonadal dysfunction. *Journal of the American Medical Association*, 1980, (243), 750–755.

Spitz, C. J., Gold, A. R., and Adams, D. B. Cognitive and hormonal factors affecting coital frequency. *Archives of Sexual Behavior*, 1975, *4*, 249–263.

Spock, B. *Baby and Child Care*. New York: Pocket Kangaroo Books, 1976.

Sprenkle, D. H., and Weiss, D. L. Extramarital sexuality: Implications for marital therapy. *Journal of Sex and Marital Therapy*, 1978, 3, 279–291.

Stein, M. L. Prostitution. In J. Money and H. Musaph (Eds.), *Handbook of Sexology*. Amsterdam: Elsevier/North Holland Biomedical Press, 1977, pp. 1069–1085.

Steiner, C. M. *Scripts People Live*. New York: Bantam, 1974.

Stoller, R. J. *Sex and Gender: On the Development of Masculinity and Femininity*. New York: Science House, 1968.

Story, M. D. A longitudinal study of the effects of a university human sexuality course on sexual attitudes. *Journal of Sex Research*, 1979, 15, 3, 184–204.

Story, N. L. Sexual dysfunction resulting from drug side effects. *Journal of Sex Research*, 1974, 10, 132–149.

Stuart, R. B. Operant-interpersonal treatment for marital discord. *Journal of Consulting and Clinical Psychology*, 1969, 33, 675–682.

Sturup, G. K. Castration: The total treatment. In H. Resnick and M. Wolfgang (Eds.), *Sexual Behaviors: Social, Clinical, and Legal Aspects*. Boston: Little, Brown, 1972, pp. 361–382.

Sulloway, F. J. *Freud: Biologist of the Mind*. New York: Basic Books, 1979.

Szasz, T. S. Legal and moral aspects of homosexuality. In J. Marmor (Ed.), *Sexual Inversion*. New York: Basic Books, 1965, pp. 124–139.

Tanner, J. M. Earlier maturation in man. *Scientific American*, January 1968, pp. 21–27.

_____. Sequence, tempo, and individual variation in the growth and development of boys and girls aged 12 to 16. *Daedalus*, 1971, *100*, 907–930.

_____. Growing up. *Scientific American*, September 1973, p. 40.

Tart, C. T. *On Being Stoned: A Psychological Study of Intoxication*. Palo Alto, Calif.: Science and Behavior Books, 1971.

Tavris, C., and Sadd, S. *The Redbook Report on Female Sexuality*. New York: Delacorte Press, 1977.

Temerlin, M. K. *Lucy: Growing Up Human*. Palo Alto, Calif.: Science and Behavior Books, 1975.

Terkel, S. *Working*. New York: Avon Books, 1976, pp. 91–103.

Tiefer, L. The Kiss. *Human Nature*, July 1978, pp. 28–37.

_____. *Human Sexuality: Feelings and Functions*. New York: Harper & Row, 1979.

Tietze, C. Induced abortion. In J. Money and H. Musaph (Eds.), *Handbook of Sexology*. Amsterdam: Elsevier/North Holland Press, 1977, pp. 605–620.

Tripp, C. A. *The Homosexual Matrix*. New York: McGraw-Hill, 1975.

Udry, J. R. *The Social Context of Marriage*. Philadelphia: Lippincott, 1971.

_____, and Morris, N. Distribution of coitus in the menstrual cycle. *Nature*, 1968, *220*, 593–596.

_____, and Waller, L. Effect of contraceptive pills on sexual activity in the luteal phase of the human menstrual cycle. *Archives of Sexual Behavior*, 1973, *2*, 205–214.

Ueno, M. *Sex and Your Heart*. New York: Award Books, 1968.

Vance, E. B., and Wagner, N. W. Written descriptions of orgasm: A study of sex difference. *Archives of Sexual Behavior*, 1976, *5*, 87–98.

Van de Velde, T. H. *Ideal Marriage*. New York: Ballantine Books, 1975.

Vatsayana, *The Kama Sutra*. New York: Putnam, 1966.

Vener, A. M., and Stewart, C. S. Adolescent sexual behavior in middle America revisited: 1970–1973. *Journal of Marriage and the Family*, November 1974, pp. 728–735.

Vuocolo, A. B. *The Repetitive Sex Offender*. Roselle, N.J.: Quality Printing, 1969.

Wagner, N. M. Sexual activity and the cardiac patient. In R. Green (Ed.), *Human Sexuality: A Health Practitioner's Text*. Baltimore: Williams & Wilkins, 1975, pp. 173–180.

Walster, E., and Walster, G. W. *A New Look at Love*. Reading, Mass.: Addison-Wesley, 1978.

Waxenburg, S. E., Drellich, M. G., and Sutherland, A. M. Changes in female sexuality after adrenalectomy. *Journal of Clinical Endocrinology*, 1959, *19*, 193–202.

Weinberg, G. *Society and the Healthy Homosexual*. New York: Anchor Books, 1973.

Weinberg, M. S., and Williams, C. J. *Male Homosexuals*. New York: Oxford Univ. Press, 1974.

_____. Gay baths and the social organization of impersonal sex. In M. P. Levine (Ed.), *Gay Men: The Sociology of Male Homosexuality*. New York: Harper & Row, 1979, pp. 164–181.

Weiss, H. D. The physiology of human penile erection. *Annals of Internal Medicine*, 1972, *76*, 793–799.

Westoff, C. F. Coital frequency and contraception. *Family Planning Perspectives*, 1974, *6*, 3, 136–141.

_____, and Rindfuss, R. R. Sex preselection in the United States: Some implications. *Science*, 184, May 1974, pp. 633–636.

Whalen, R. E. Cyclic changes in hormones and behavior. *Archives of Sexual Behavior*, 1975, *4*, 313–314.

Wieland, W. F., and Yunger, M. Sexual effects and side effects of heroin and methadone. *Proceedings of the Third National Conference on Methadone Treatment.* Public Health Service Publication No. 2172, 1971, pp. 50–53.

Wilson, G. T. Alcohol and human sexual behavior. *Behavior Research and Therapy*, 1977, *15*, 239–252.

———, and Lawson, D. M. The effects of alcohol on sexual arousal in women. *Journal of Abnormal Psychology*, 1976, *85*, 489–497.

Wilson, R. A. *Feminine Forever.* New York: Evans, 1966.

Windemiller, D. *Sexuality, Pairing, and Family Forms.* Cambridge, Mass.: Winthrop, 1976.

Winkler, R. C. What types of sex-role behavior should behavior modifiers promote? *Journal of Applied Behavior Analysis*, 1977, *10*, 549–552.

Wolpe, J. *Psychotherapy by Reciprocal Inhibition.* Stanford: Stanford University Press, 1958.

Yale Student Committee on Human Sexuality, *The Student Guide to Sex on Campus.* New York: New American Library, 1971.

Yalom, I. D. Aggression and forbiddenness in voyeurism. *Archives of General Psychiatry*, 1960, *3*, 305.

Zelnick, M., and Kantner, J. F. The probability of premarital intercourse. *Social Science Research*, 1972, *1*, 335–341.

———. The resolution of first pregnancies. *Family Planning Perspectives*, 1974, *6*, 74.

———. Sexual and contraceptive experience of young unmarried women in the U.S., 1976 & 1971. *Family Planning Perspectives*, 1977, *9*, 2, 55–71.

Zilbergeld, B. *Male Sexuality: A Guide to Sexual Fulfillment.* Boston: Little, Brown, 1978.

Zuckerman, M. Physiological measures of sexual arousal in the human. *Psychological Bulletin*, 1971, *75*, 347–356.

———. Research on pornography. In W. W. Oaks, G. A. Melchiode, and I. I. Ficher (Eds.), *Sex and the Life Cycle.* New York: Grune & Stratton, 1976, pp. 147–161.

———, Tushup, R., and Finner, S. Sexual attitudes and experience: attitude and personality correlates and changes produced by a course in sexuality. *Journal of Consulting and Clinical Psychology*, 1976, *44* (1), 7–19.

Glossary

Index

Index

Credits and Acknowledgments

133   From Dickinson, R. L., *Atlas of Human Sex Anatomy*, The Williams & Wilkins Co., 1933, fig. 81.

145   From Dickinson, R. L., *Atlas of Human Sex Anatomy*, The Williams & Wilkins Co., 1933, fig. 80.

151   From Dickinson, R. L., *Atlas of Human Sex Anatomy*, The Williams & Wilkins Co., 1933, fig. 103.

176   From Heiman, J. "The physiology of erotica," *Psychology Today*, April, 1975, p. 67.

178   From *Human Sexual Response*, W. Masters and V. Johnson, 1966, Little Brown, and Company, p. 5.

185-186   From Vance and Wagner, "Written Descriptions of orgasm: A study of sex difference," *Archives of Sexual Behavior*, 1976, Volume 5, Number 1, 87-98, pp. 93-94.

383   *New Estimates of Fertility and Population in the United States: A Study of Annual White Births from 1855 to 1960 and of completeness of enumeration in the Censuses from 1880 to 1960*, by Ansley J. Coale and Melvin Zelnik (copyright © 1963 by Princeton University Press): Table 2, p. 36. Reprinted by permission of Princeton University Press.

390   From Zelnik, M., and Kantner, J. F., "Sexual and Contraceptive Experience of Young Unmarried Women in the United States, 1976 and 1971," *Family Planning Perspectives*, Volume 9, Number 2, p. 63.

397   From Westoff, C., "Coital Frequency and Contraception," *Family Planning Perspectives*, Volume 6, Number 3, pp. 136-141.

418   Adapted from Luria, Z., and Rose, M., *Psychology of Human Sexuality*, Wiley, 1979, p. 273.

462-463   From Terkel, S., *Working: People Talk About What They Do All Day and How They Feel About What They Do*, Pantheon, 1974, pp. 57-65.

Specified Excerpts from *Patterns of Sexual Behavior* by Clellan S. Ford and Frank A. Beach. Copyright 1951 by Clellan Stearns Ford and Frank Ambrose Beach. Reprinted by permission of Harper & Row, Publishers, Inc.

Specified excerpts from *The Hite Report* by Shere Hite (Copyright © 1976 by Shere Hite). Reprinted by permission of Macmillan Publishing Co., Inc.

Specified excerpts from *Male Sexuality* by Bernie Zilbergeld. © 1978 by Bernie Zilbergeld. Permission by Little, Brown, and Company.

Specified excerpts from Kinsey, A. C., Pomeroy, W. B., and Martin, C. E. *Sexual Behavior in the Human Male*, W. B. Saunders Co., 1958. Reprinted by permission of the Institute for Sex Research.

Specified excerpts from Kinsey, A. C., and Gebhard, P. H. *Sexual Behavior in the Human Female*, W. B. Saunders Co., 1953. Reprinted by permission of the Institute for Sex Research.

Selected excerpts from Kaplan, H. S. *The New Sex Therapy*, Brunner/Mazel, 1974.

About the Authors

RAYMOND CHARLES ROSEN

Since receiving his Ph.D in clinical psychology from SUNY at Stony Brook in 1972, he has been a member of the faculty at Rutgers Medical School. In addition to his clinical position as co-director of the Sexual Counselling Service at Rutgers, he has taught courses in human sexuality and behavioral sciences to students from various disciplines. Dr. Rosen's major research interest has been in the psychophysiology of sexual response for which he has received a number of research grants; in addition, he has numerous professional publications in this field. In 1976, he was elected a member of the Academy of Sexual Research.

LINDA REICH ROSEN

Upon receiving her Ph.D in experimental psychology from Tufts University in 1974, she was appointed as a research psychologist with the New York State Office of Drug Abuse Services where she worked until 1976. The author of numerous popular and professional articles on alcohol use, drug addiction, and human sexuality, Dr. Rosen is also consultant on a Ford Foundation project to develop gaming-simulation techniques for contraceptive education. Most recently, she has taught classes in human sexuality at Douglass College.